Frank Kleiner

A Semantic Wiki-based Platform
for IT Service Management

A Semantic Wiki-based Platform for IT Service Management

by
Frank Kleiner

KIT Scientific Publishing

Dissertation, Karlsruher Institut für Technologie (KIT)
Fakultät für Wirtschaftswissenschaften, 2015

Tag der mündlichen Prüfung: 22. Januar 2015
Referenten: Prof. Dr. Rudi Studer, Prof. Dr. Ralf Reussner

Impressum

KIT Scientific Publishing

Karlsruher Institut für Technologie (KIT)
KIT Scientific Publishing
Straße am Forum 2
D-76131 Karlsruhe

KIT Scientific Publishing is a registered trademark of Karlsruhe Institute of Technology. Reprint using the book cover is not allowed.

www.ksp.kit.edu

Print on Demand 2015

ISBN 978-3-7315-0333-0
DOI 10.5445/KSP/1000045291

A Semantic Wiki-based Platform for IT Service Management

Retaining and Utilizing Structured and Unstructured Information in a Lightweight Service Knowledge Management System

Zur Erlangung des akademischen Grades eines
Doktors der Ingenieurwissenschaften
(Dr.-Ing.)

von der Fakultät für Wirtschaftswissenschaften
des Karlsruher Instituts für Technologie (KIT)

genehmigte
DISSERTATION

von

Dipl.-Inform. Frank Kleiner

Datum der mündlichen Prüfung:	22.01.2015
Referent:	Prof. Dr. Rudi Studer
Korreferent:	Prof. Dr. Ralf Reussner

Für meine Eltern.

Abstract

IT Service Management (ITSM) as a management discipline is concerned with the structured and efficient delivery of information technology (IT) services. The currently (2014) most commonly used ITSM framework is the IT Infrastructure Library (ITIL).

Wikis are used for collaboratively creating, reading, and editing information by using a Web-based interface. Semantic wikis make use of Semantic Web technologies in order to enable wikis, which are normally designed for storing unstructured text, to additionally store structured content. This makes possible the machine-based processing of information stored in the semantic wiki.

This dissertation researches the use of a semantic wiki in the area of IT Service Management within the IT department of a medium-sized enterprise. A fundamental aspect of this work is the relevancy to practice of the designed and implemented components.

The Configuration Management System (CMS), which is implemented in the semantic wiki, is used to manage all entities, which are used for providing IT services, as well as their relationships. The data model is an ontology that was developed as part of the thesis.

By using Semantic MediaWiki as the underlying platform, complex queries can be used on the whole information base stored in the wiki. This enables the displaying of textual information together with information resulting from dynamic queries in a homogeneous Web-based user interface.

An emphasis of the thesis lies in the design and prototypical implementation of tools for the integration of ITSM-relevant information into the semantic wiki, as well as tools for interactions between the wiki and external programs.

The result of the thesis is a platform for agile, semantic wiki-based IT Service Management for IT administration teams of small and medium-sized enterprises (SME). It builds on functionalities provided by Semantic MediaWiki, but in addition extends these functionalities by the following ITSM-specific ones: (1) automatic gathering of configuration information and their import into the semantic wiki-based Configuration Management System; (2) integration of infrastructure monitoring software; (3) connection to an intrusion detection system; (4) an assistant for detecting the cause of incidents and problems; (5) connection to virtual machines and Infrastructure-as-a-Service (IaaS) instances.

The concluding part of the thesis consists of a validation of the requirements and a user study.

Zusammenfassung

IT Service Management (ITSM) ist als Managementdisziplin für die strukturierte und effiziente Erbringung von Informationstechnologie-Diensten zuständig. Das derzeit (2014) am weitesten verbreitete ITSM-Rahmenwerk ist die IT Infrastructure Library (ITIL).

Wikis erlauben das kollaborative Erstellen, Lesen und Bearbeiten von Informationen mit Hilfe einer webbasierten Oberfläche. Semantische Wikis nutzen aus dem Semantic Web bekannte Ansätze, um die ansonsten nur für Texte ausgelegten Wikis auch für strukturierte Inhalte einsetzbar zu machen, was die maschinenbasierte Verarbeitung von Teilen bzw. Aspekten der gespeicherten Informationen ermöglicht.

In der vorliegenden Dissertation wird die Verwendung eines semantischen Wikis im Bereich des IT Service Managements innerhalb der IT-Abteilung eines mittelgroßen Unternehmens untersucht. Ein grundlegender Aspekt der Arbeit ist die Praxistauglichkeit der entworfenen und implementierten Komponenten.

Das in einem semantischen Wiki implementierte Configuration Management System (CMS) verwaltet alle für die Erbringung von IT-Diensten benötigten Bestandteile inklusive deren Abhängigkeiten voneinander. Als Datenmodell kommt eine im Rahmen der Arbeit entworfene Ontologie zur Anwendung.

Durch die Verwendung von Semantic MediaWiki als Basis können komplexe Abfragen auf die gesamte im Wiki enthaltene Informationsbasis gestellt werden. Dies ermöglicht die Darstellung textueller Informationen zusammen mit dynamisch aus Abfragen gewonnenen Informationen in einer einheitlichen, webbasierten Benutzeroberfläche. Einen Schwerpunkt der Arbeit bilden der Entwurf und die prototypische Implementierung von Werkzeugen für die Integration ITSM-relevanter Informationen in das semantische Wiki, sowie Werkzeuge für die Interaktion des Wikis mit externen Programmen.

Das Ergebnis der Arbeit ist eine erweiterbare Plattform für agiles, Semantic Wiki-basiertes IT Service Management für IT-Administrations-Teams innerhalb von kleinen und mittleren Unternehmen (KMU). Diese baut auf Funktionen von Semantic MediaWiki auf, erweitert diese aber zusätzlich um die folgenden ITSM-spezifischen Funktionalitäten: (1) automatische Erfassung von Konfigurationsinformationen und deren Import in das Semantic Wiki-basierte Configuration Management System; (2) Integration einer Infrastruktur Monitoring-Software; (3) Anbindung einer Intrusion Detection-Lösung; (4) Bereitstellung eines Assistenten für das Finden von Problemursachen; (5) Anbindung von virtuellen Maschinen und Infrastructure-as-a-Service (IaaS)-Instanzen.

Den abschließenden Teil der Arbeit bilden die Validierung der Anforderungen und eine Benutzerstudie.

Danksagung

Ich danke meinem Doktorvater Prof. Dr. Rudi Studer ganz herzlich für die Betreuung dieser Arbeit. Auch danke ich meinem Korreferenten Prof. Dr. Ralf Reussner, meinem Prüfer Prof. Dr. Andreas Oberweis, sowie Prof. Dr. Ute Werner für die Übernahme des Vorsitzes des Prüfungskomitees.

Mein besonderer Dank gilt Dr. Andreas Abecker für die fortwährende Unterstützung während des Erstellens dieser Arbeit, selbst nach seiner Zeit am FZI. Ohne seine Unterstützung und seine Bereitschaft, sich auch nach langen Arbeitstagen noch Zeit für mich zu nehmen, hätte ich diese Arbeit wohl nicht fertiggestellt.

Diese Arbeit entstand während ich am FZI Forschungszentrum Informatik in der Abteilung Rechner- und Datenkommunikationsdienste (RuD) beschäftigt war. Bei meinen Kolleginnen und Kollegen Axel Jerger, Herta Krämer, Jeron Mehl, Florian Sickelmann und Ana Suzana Skrenkovic, sowie allen studentischen Mitarbeiterinnen und Mitarbeitern möchte ich mich ganz herzlich für die immer sehr schöne Zusammenarbeit bedanken.

Auch möchte ich mich bei allen übrigen Mitarbeiterinnen und Mitarbeitern des FZI Forschungszentrum Informatik und der Forschungsgruppe Wissensmanagement des AIFB für die gute Zusammenarbeit bedanken.

Für die Mitarbeit bei der Implementierung der MediaWiki-Erweiterungen bedanke ich mich bei Sven Brinkmann, Marco Mauritczat, Patrick Schmidt und Soner Kalayci.

Bei Lisa Weiß bedanke ich mich dafür, dass sie die Benutzerstudie als neutrale Person begleitet hat. Mein weiterer Dank gilt den Teilnehmerinnen und Teilnehmern der Benutzerstudie.

Für das Korrekturlesen bedanke ich mich bei meiner Schwester Linda Koch.

Zusätzlich bedanke ich mich bei den Entwicklerinnen und Entwicklern der in dieser Arbeit eingesetzten Software, insbesondere den Mitgliedern der MediaWiki- und Semantic MediaWiki-Community.

Bei meiner Familie bedanke ich mich dafür, dass sie mir während der Erstellung der Arbeit stehts unterstützend zur Seite gestanden ist. Mein Dank gilt meinen Eltern Renate und Klaus Kleiner, meinen Schwiegereltern Nadja und Viktor Pulter, sowie ganz herzlich meiner Ehefrau Natalja.

Abschließend gebührt meinem Sohn Juri der Dank, mich durch seine Geburt zur Fertigstellung der Arbeit motiviert zu haben.

Contents

1. Introduction

1.1. Background and Motivation

IT Service Management (ITSM) is the management discipline concerned with delivering information technology (IT) services in a structured and effective way. The most widely used ITSM framework is the IT Infrastructure Library (ITIL), which was first introduced in the 1980s by the British government, and subsequently extended in the 1990s and 2000s. Currently (2014), ITIL is available in version 3 and provides best practices for almost all aspects of IT [Arr13].

Wikis are a Web-based technology that use a Web server, which is running an environment for delivering dynamic Web pages, and a Web browser for accessing content. Classic content management systems impose a fixed structure on users, which cannot be changed dynamically. In contrast, a wiki's structure is created and modified by users while entering content. While traditional Web pages work in a one-to-many way (i.e., the creator of a Web page or a team of Web authors creates content, which is consumed by many), wikis allow modifications by a broader user base, in some cases being open to being edited by everyone [EGHW07].

While classic wikis are text-based and offer only simplistic approaches for structuring information, semantic wikis bring together the flexibility of wikis with the goal of making possible the management of structured data. In order to accomplish this goal, the ability to include structured data is added to wiki platforms. The format of this structured data is most often derived from Semantic Web technologies (i.e., semantic annotations, and ontologies). By using the structured information, which is present in wiki pages, information can be processed and displayed (e.g., as tables, or lists). Furthermore, information that is not explicitly stated can be accessed by making use of reasoning. By using a special query language, which is provided by the semantic wiki engine, users can formulate queries that can be used to generate dynamic information from structured information found within the wiki [KVV+07, BSVW12].

There exist a wide range of specialized tools for the professional planning and execution of IT Service Management. However, there are hardly any integrated ITSM tools available, which address the needs of IT administrators for a flexible, lightweight solution that allows mixing structured and unstructured information. Flexibly documenting IT infrastructures in a lightweight Configuration Management System, as well as maintaining documentation about processes, technical procedures, and best practices in an agile environment promises the potential for improving the performance of IT departments. Furthermore, the integration of various tools for different aspects of IT administration by using a single structured information base promises further potentials for eliminating error-prone and labor-intensive manual maintenance of configurations in different tools. Areas of interest are automated information gathering, infrastructure monitoring, intrusion detection, incident and problem detection, and the management of virtualized and IaaS instances.

The primary focus of the thesis lies in the use and extension of semantic wikis in the context of ITSM in small and medium-sized enterprises. In contrast to large enterprises, which adhere more to structured processes, the processes in SMEs are usually more flexible. In order to address this flexibility, a lightweight tool, such as a semantic wiki, seems promising.

1.2. Approach

The main focus of this thesis is the improvement of practical aspects of IT Service Management in flexible and dynamic IT administration teams. This is accomplished by designing and implementing an ITSM platform based on Semantic MediaWiki [KVV+07], which brings together the capability to store and manage structured, as well as unstructured information within the same environment.

At the time of writing this thesis (2008–2014), the author was working as a member of the IT administration team at FZI Research Center for Information Technology[1] in Karlsruhe. The practical experiences with existing tools for the documentation and management of FZI's IT environment led to an interest in researching potentials for improvement.

After analyzing the strengths and weaknesses of the tools already in use for documenting and managing various aspects of FZI's IT infrastructure, the need for a single platform that brings together the information, which is in some instances stored redundantly,

[1] In German: FZI Forschungszentrum Informatik am Karlsruher Institut für Technologie

became clear. While initial steps aimed at using and extending an existing tool as a platform to store all relevant information, it also became clear that integrating structured and unstructured information was not possible with the tools in use at the time. Further research showed that there were no tools available, which satisfied the requirements of FZI's IT administration team.

Requirements, which were considered for the ITSM platform, were:

- *Storage of structured information:* The platform has to provide efficient mechanisms for storing structured information (e.g., hardware attributes of a computer, and connections between network devices).
- *Storage of unstructured information:* There has to be support for conveniently storing unstructured information, including proper formatting, tables, the possibility to add images, as well as the functionality to create links between individual pages.
- *Web-based collaborative editing:* The platform has to offer features that enable members of the IT administration team to create and edit information collaboratively.
- *Reporting capabilities:* In order to perform organizational tasks, reporting capabilities have to be available (e.g., a mechanism for creating a list of active notebook computers, running the Windows operating system, sorted by organizational units).
- *Customizability and extensibility:* In order to be tailored to the special requirements of individual IT departments in general, and to the requirements of FZI's IT department in particular, the solution has to be highly customizable and extensible.
- *Adaptability to changes:* IT environments change at a fast pace. Because of that, the solution has to be able to adapt to organizational and technical changes in a flexible manner.
- *License:* Customizability and extensibility require a license, which allows access to the source code and permits extensions and possible changes to the code base. Furthermore, the software has to be available free of charge in order to keep low the operational costs of the IT department.

After determining that no single tool was available that fulfilled the requirements, the strengths and weaknesses of the existing tools with regard to their potential as the basis of an integrated ITSM platform were assessed. While a number of existing tools were quickly ruled out as possibilities on which the ITSM platform could be based (e.g., Microsoft Excel, or special-purpose software, such as the firewall management application), there were two options left.

The first option was to add functions as typically provided by wikis (i.e., formatting of text elements within pages, table support, and links between pages) to the OTRS::-ITSM platform, which was used as a Configuration Management Database (CMDB) for managing structured information about IT assets at the time.

The second option was to extend the (non-semantic) wiki, which was used for documenting working procedures and retaining information about IT systems, by adding functionalities for storing structured data.

Questions, which guided the way in determining the path to the integrated ITSM platform, were:

- Is it possible to extend existing Configuration Management software in order to allow the storage of unstructured information and the linking between the information (as available in wikis)?
- Is it possible to extend a wiki in a way that it can be used to manage structured information about IT assets typically stored in a Configuration Management Database (CMDB), such as the one found in OTRS::ITSM?
- What are the benefits and disadvantages of using a wiki as the platform; what are the ones of the CMDB platform?

After performing an analysis of the benefits of the two approaches, it became clear that semantic wikis are the best choice for the intended purpose. Semantic wikis are in essence wikis, which allow the storage and processing of structured data, in addition to storing traditional unstructured text. By retaining information in a structured format, semantic wikis allow users to employ reasoning in order to make use of information that is not explicitly stated. Furthermore, semantic wikis enable users to flexibly create (complex) queries, which display information based on statements stored in the semantic wiki. A comparison of several semantic wiki platforms left Semantic MediaWiki as the most promising one.

Based on Semantic MediaWiki, a framework for using semantic wikis in IT Service Management was created, which included the following activities:

- Analysis of requirements for a semantic wiki-based platform, which supports the aspects of ITIL that are relevant for the work of IT administration teams in SMEs, such as at FZI.
- Creation of a semantic wiki-based solution (ITSM Wiki) for real world IT documentation needs.
- Design of an IT Service Management ontology, which describes all aspects of IT Service Management (hardware, software, services, processes, and people), which are relevant for FZI's IT landscape, and which serves as the data model for the information managed in the wiki.

- Populating the semantic wiki with real world data.
- Extending the platform by designing and implementing ITSM-specific extensions for Semantic MediaWiki, which help IT administration teams to work more efficiently. The extensions address the following areas: (1) automatically gathering information from networked hosts, (2) integrating infrastructure monitoring into the wiki, (3) integrating an intrusion detection system, (4) providing support for tracking down the causes of incidents and problems, and (5) enabling the management of virtualized and IaaS instances from within the wiki.

1.3. Contribution

The contributions of this thesis can be separated into two areas.

The first area of contribution is the *facilitation of a semantic wiki as a central hub for storing information* necessary for managing IT resources in the context of SMEs. By using a semantic wiki, textual information, such as descriptions of best practices and technical instructions, can be combined with structured information, such as information about computer configurations and dependencies between services. In summary, the contributions of the thesis with regard to the first aspect are:

- Analysis of the interactions between the information and the tools, which were used for the management of the information within an SME's IT department.
- Design and implementation of a semantic wiki-based approach for the management of information in the context of FZI's IT department.
- Development of an ITSM ontology, which models the information and the dependencies between information items within the environment. The ontology is used as the data model for the semantic wiki.

The second area of contribution is the *design and implementation of tools*, which support and enable various ITSM activities. With regard to the second area, the contributions are the design and implementation of the following components:

- A component for automatically gathering configuration information from networked hosts for inclusion in the ITSM Wiki.
- Interfaces to an infrastructure monitoring application for monitoring the availability of hosts and services.
- A component for the integration of a network intrusion detection tool.
- Support for finding the source of incidents and problems within IT infrastructures.
- An interface for orchestrating virtualization and IaaS resources.

In summary, when looking at the *aspect of application*, the contribution of the thesis can be divided into two parts:

- *Conceptual contribution:* The thesis' conceptual contribution is the analysis of data and the associated tools, which are used to store information relevant for providing IT services in an SME. Based on these observations, a conceptual approach was envisioned for unifying the relevant information, in order to gain maximum benefits in supporting the IT administration team.
- *Practical contribution:* The thesis' practical contribution consists of a tool for the practical use as an ITSM information system within FZI's IT infrastructure.

1.4. Thesis Outline

The thesis is structured as follows:

1. *Introduction:* First, the background and the motivation for the thesis are given in Section 1.1 (page 1). Second, the approach that is taken in this thesis is outlined in Section 1.2 (page 2). After that, in Section 1.3 (page 5), the contribution is described, followed by the thesis outline in Section 1.4 (page 6). Finally, the list of publications is given in Section 1.5 (page 9).
2. *Fundamentals:* In Chapter 2 (page 11), basic principles and technologies, which are necessary for understanding the remaining parts of the thesis, are outlined. Aspects of IT Service Management (Section 2.1, page 12) and ITIL (Section 2.2, page 16) are described, followed by ontologies (Section 2.3, page 59) and Semantic Web basics (Section 2.4, page 61). Finally, wikis (Section 2.5, page 70) and semantic wikis (Section 2.6, page 77) are introduced.
3. *Analysis:* In Chapter 3 (page 81) an analysis of the current state of IT Service Management in a small and medium-sized enterprise (SME) is given. The environment, for which the toolset presented in this thesis was designed, is introduced in Section 3.1 (page 82). In Section 3.2 (page 98), the requirements for a Configuration Management System in the context of the previously described environment are determined. In Section 3.3 (page 109), an overview of existing Configuration Management tools is given.
4. *Design of the Semantic Wiki-based ITSM Platform:* A description of the design and implementation of the core component of this thesis is given in Chapter 4 (page 115). In Section 4.1 (page 116), the selection of the technical platform is described. In Section 4.2 (page 136), it is shown how a semantic wiki can be used as a platform for supporting IT Service Management. The ontologies, which form the data models for the work presented in this thesis, are described in Section 4.3 (page 161).

5. *Design and Implementation of the System Components:* In Chapter 5 (page 185), an overview of the components developed for this thesis, as well as their interactions, is given. The components are described in more detail in the following sections:

   a) *Information Gathering Component:* In Section 5.1 (page 188) the component developed for populating and updating the semantic wiki-based IT Service Management platform, by reading information from different sources (e.g., Windows hosts, and Active Directory), is described.

   b) *Infrastructure Monitoring Component:* In Section 5.2 (page 234), mechanisms for integrating an infrastructure monitoring application into the wiki are designed. This allows specifying from the wiki, which hosts and services should be monitored, as well as to monitor the status of hosts and services from within the wiki.

   c) *Intrusion Detection Component:* Section 5.3 (page 261), describes how data from an external intrusion detection system can be processed within the wiki by exploiting semantic features.

   d) *Incident and Problem Analyzer Component:* In Section 5.4 (page 284), the Incident and Problem Analyzer Component is described. This component enables members of the IT administration team to quickly track down possible sources of incidents and problems by automatically comparing configuration items for aspects that are likely to be the root cause of the incident or problem.

   e) *Virtualization and IaaS Connector:* In Section 5.5 (page 298), the Virtualization and IaaS Connector is described, which allows IT administrators to manage virtual machines and IaaS instances from within the ITSM Wiki.

6. *Evaluation:* In Chapter 6 (page 317), it is evaluated how the semantic wiki-supported approach to IT Service Management benefits IT administration teams. First, the results of the validation are presented in Section 6.1 (page 318), followed by the presentation of the results of the user study in Section 6.2 (page 384).

7. *Conclusion:* In Chapter 7 (page 425), the conclusion is given. The achievements of this thesis are summarized (Section 7.1, page 425), and an outlook on possible future work is given (Section 7.2, page 427).

Appendix A (page 433) includes installation instructions. Appendix B (page 437) contains selected listings, while in Appendix C.1 (page 451), the evaluation forms of the user study are presented. Appendix C.2 (page 547) presents the raw data of the user study.

A graphical representation of the structure of the thesis can be found in Figure 1.1.

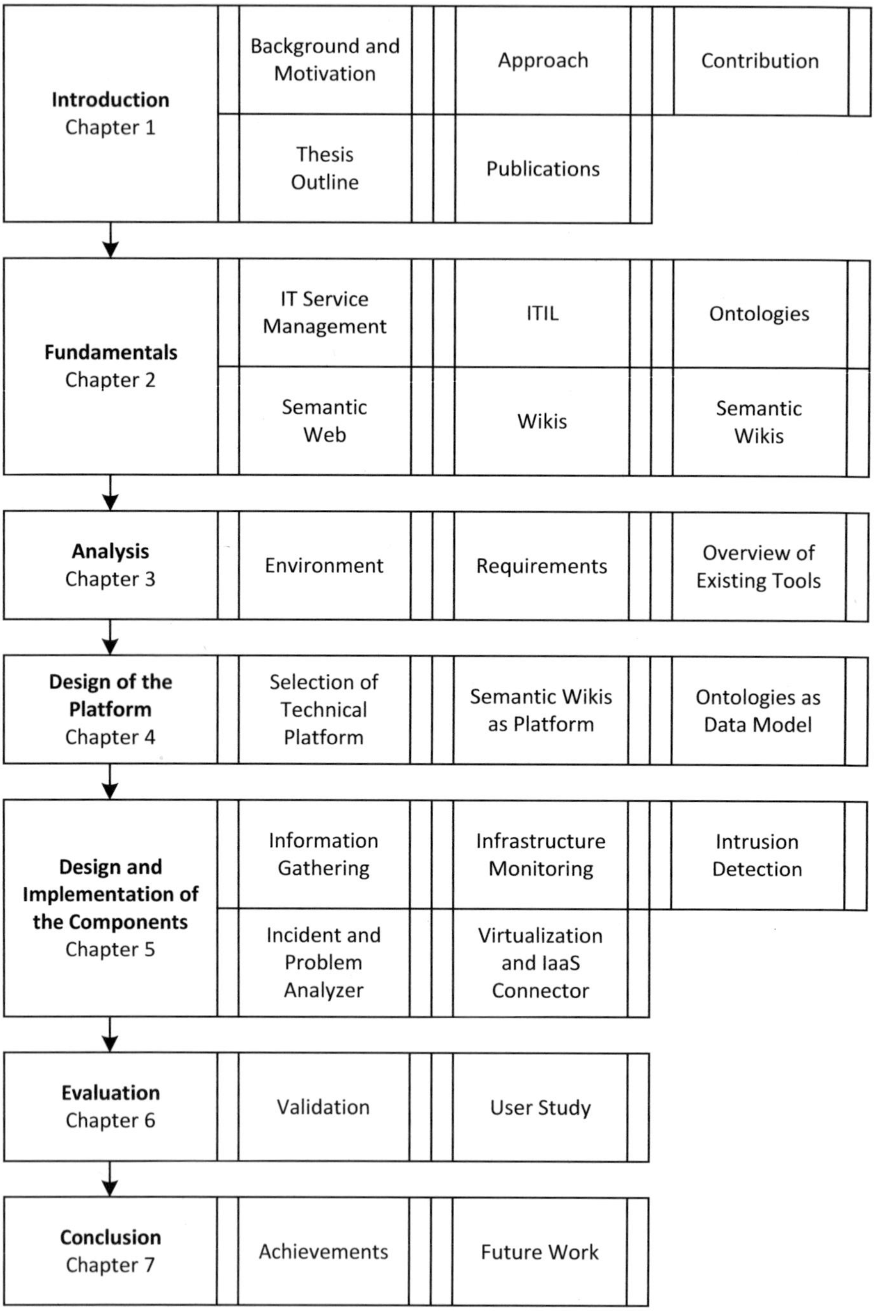

Figure 1.1.: Thesis Outline

1.5. Publications

The work presented in this thesis is partly published in the following publications:

- Frank Kleiner and Andreas Abecker. Towards a Collaborative Semantic Wiki-based Approach to IT Service Management. In Adrian Paschke, Hans Weigand, Wernher Behrendt, Klaus Tochtermann, and Tassilo Pellegrini, editors, *Proceedings of I-SEMANTICS 09, 5th International Conference on Semantic Systems*, pages 424–434, Graz, Austria, September 2009.
- Frank Kleiner, Andreas Abecker, and Sven F. Brinkmann. WiSyMon: Managing Systems Monitoring Information in Semantic Wikis. In Dirk Riehle and Amy Bruckman, editors, *WikiSym 09: Proceedings of the 5th International Symposium on Wikis and Open Collaboration*, Orlando, Florida, USA, October 2009. ACM, New York, NY, USA, 2009. Poster Session.
- Frank Kleiner, Andreas Abecker, and Ning Liu. Automatic Population and Updating of a Semantic Wiki-based Configuration Management Database. In Stefan Fischer, Erik Maehle, and Rüdiger Reischuk, editors, *Informatik 2009 – Im Focus das Leben*, volume P-154 of *Lecture Notes in Informatics (LNI)*, pages 3076–3090, Lübeck, Germany, October 2009. Köllen, Bonn. 4th International Workshop on Applications of Semantic Technologies (AST 2009).
- Frank Kleiner, Andreas Abecker, and Sven F. Brinkmann. WiSyMon – Managing Systems Monitoring Information in Semantic Wikis. In *Proceedings of the Third International Conference on Advances in Semantic Processing 2009 (SEMAPRO 09)*, pages 77–85, Sliema, Malta, October 2009. IEEE Computer Society.
- Frank Kleiner and Andreas Abecker. Semantic MediaWiki as an Integration Platform for IT Service Management. In Klaus-Peter Fähnrich and Bogdan Franczyk, editors, *Informatik 2010 – Service Science – Neue Perspektiven für die Informatik*, volume P-176 of *Lecture Notes in Informatics (LNI)*, pages 73–78, Leipzig, Germany, September 2010. Köllen, Bonn. 5th International Workshop on Applications of Semantic Technologies (AST 2010).
- Frank Kleiner, Andreas Abecker, and Marco Mauritczat. Incident and Problem Management Using a Semantic Wiki-enabled ITSM Platform. In Joaquim Filipe and Ana Fred, editors, *4th International Conference on Agents and Artificial Intelligence (ICAART 2012)*, pages 363–372, Vilamoura, Portugal, February 2012. SciTePress, Setubal.

2. Fundamentals

This chapter introduces the fundamental concepts relevant for the understanding of the thesis. First, an introduction to IT Service Management (ITSM) is given in Section 2.1 (page 12), including a short history of the road from the early computing machines to a service-oriented, customer-focused approach. Following that, an overview of the IT Infrastructure Library (ITIL), which is currently (2014) the most widely used IT Service Management framework, is given in Section 2.2 (page 16). Furthermore, ontologies (Section 2.3, page 59) and Semantic Web technologies (Section 2.4, page 61) are presented, which are used to model, store and automatically process information in the context of this thesis. After that, wikis (Section 2.5, page 70) and semantic wikis (Section 2.6, page 77), the platforms, on which the tools presented in this thesis are based, are introduced.

2.1. IT Service Management

This section gives an introduction into the IT Service Management discipline. First, definitions for core concepts are given, followed by a historical overview from early approaches of IT provisioning and delivery to modern service-oriented approaches.

2.1.1. Definitions

In order to gain a better understanding of the IT Infrastructure Library (ITIL) framework that forms the theoretical basis of this thesis, and which is described in Section 2.2 (page 16), the following definitions form a helpful foundation. First, services are defined, followed by definitions of Service Management and IT Service Management.

The basic term in IT Service Management is the term *service*. In [IN07], a service is defined as

> “a means of delivering value to customers by facilitating outcomes customers want to achieve without the ownership of specific costs and risks” [IN07, page 16].

In order to provide a structured portfolio of services, services have to be managed. Reference [CW07, page 12] defines Service Management as

> “a set of specialized organizational capabilities for providing value to customers in the form of services.” [CW07, page 12]

The definition given in [Add07, page 46] describes IT Service Management as

> “the planned and controlled utilization of IT assets (including systems, infrastructure and tools), people and processes to support the operational needs of the business as efficiently as possible whilst ensuring that the organization has the ability to quickly and effectively react to unplanned events, changing circumstances and new business requirements as well as continuously evaluating its processes and performance in order to identify and implement opportunities for improvement” [Add07, page 46].

In [CJ07], IT Service Management is defined as

> "a process-oriented approach for managing large-scale IT systems that focuses on the delivery and support of quality IT services rather than on technology per se" [CJ07].

Figure 2.1 shows the relationships between services, processes, and systems. On the logical layer, IT services support business processes and are implemented by IT systems. On the physical layer, IT components form IT systems [CS07, page 98].

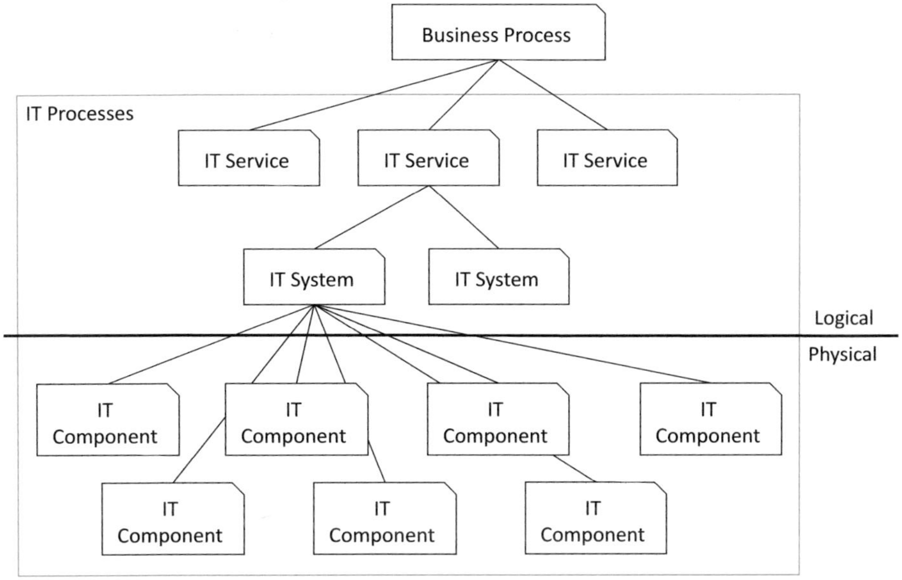

Figure 2.1.: Services, Processes and Systems (cf. [CS07, page 98])

2.1.2. History

The following paragraphs give an introduction into the epochs of computing technology, starting from mechanical tabulating machines, over centralization, computing centers, minicomputers, personal computers, client-server computing to the Internet and distributed systems. Each approach worked on fixing some of the problems of the older ones, while almost always also introducing new problems.

Although technologies were most prevalent in a particular epoch, computer landscapes almost always consist of a mixture of approaches (e.g., an organization using client-server computers, which are connected to the Internet while retaining a mainframe for special purposes) [Mas06, page 2].

1950–1960: Mechanical Tabulating Machines

The years between 1950 and 1960 were dominated by mechanical tabulating machines, which were used for basic arithmetic operations (i.e., additions, or subtractions) and sorting. Tabulating machines were used mainly for processing financial data, and generating reports [Mas06, page 3].

1960–1970: Electronic Computers

In the 1960s, electronic computers were introduced for the use in companies. While they were too expensive to be used company-wide, they were initially used in accounting. This gave power to the accounting departments, because other departments within a company had to come to the accounting department for having calculations executed on the computer systems [Mas06, page 3].

This made accounting departments the first providers of computing services, preceding dedicated IT departments. Nevertheless, the main use for computers were in operational areas (for example, order processing, payroll accounting, invoice processing, costing, and financial accounting) [Mas06, page 3].

1970–1980: Computing Centers

Computing centers were built as a reaction to the increase in use of computers by departments other than accounting. Multitasking and multi-user systems were introduced. Dedicated IT departments were founded, following the rising demand for information processing by all kinds of departments within companies. First adopters of computers for processing information where financial institutions, insurance companies, and travel agencies [Mas06, pages 3–4].

While the use of computers in the 1970s was still in the operational area (e.g., accounting, control, and account management), some applications for the use in planning emerged (for example, marketing strategy, process planning, manpower planning, and financial modeling) [Mas06, pages 3–4].

1975–1985: Minicomputers

The declining prices of computing hardware enabled departments to gain independence from central computing centers. Minicomputers could be purchased and operated on the department level, which led to departments no longer using the services of computing centers. This resulted in rising prices for computing for the remaining customers of the computing centers due to the distribution of costs on a smaller number of customers, resulting in an even more declining number of customers [Mas06, page 4].

1985–1995: Personal Computers

Beginning in the mid-1980s, personal computers began to complement and replace minicomputers and centrally offered services. The rise of personal computers led to the loss of market share for traditional computing hardware vendors and to the rise of companies focusing on personal computing hardware and software [Mas06, pages 4–5].

The use of personal computers, while helpful for ensuring the employment of office workers (who were doing their jobs with new technology on their desks, instead of having their work processed in data centers by computers), did lead to chaotic IT infrastructures. This chaos was caused by the lack of communication between isolated personal computers. The organizational effect of the IT confusion was the creation of the CIO function [Mas06, pages 4–5].

1990–2000: Client-Server Computing

Due to the chaotic situation generated by the introduction of personal computers, client-server systems were introduced. This allowed users to access central database systems, store files on file servers for access by co-workers, and use central user management functions [Mas06, page 5].

1995–2000: Internet

The rise of the Internet outside of the traditional academic cycles (mainly due to the emergence of the World Wide Web) led to a giant increase in potential customers for hardware and software. Furthermore, new business models emerged (e.g., online shopping, and online auctions) [Mas06, pages 5–6].

Since 2002: Services in Distributed Systems, Virtualization, Cloud

The use of distributed systems, starting in the early 2000s has led to a decreasing role of hardware in the provisioning of IT services. Furthermore, cheap, fast, and reliable network connectivity decreased the importance of location. This led to a situation where services are offered without the constraints of hardware or location (e.g., a Web site can be located in a place halfway around the world) [Mas06, page 6].

Virtualization offers additional flexibility and a higher utilization of resources when compared to physical computers. It offers to run multiple operating systems at a given hardware at the same time by multiplexing resources (i.e., CPU, hard disk, memory, and network interfaces). Virtual machines can be copied, and templates for the creation of new virtual machines can be configured. Given certain prerequisites (e.g., shared storage for the virtual machines' disk images), virtual machines can be moved from one physical server to another while running [BKNT09, pages 7–15].

Cloud computing offers flexible services via the Internet, mostly with dynamic payment models (for example, per time units, or per consumed resources). The basic idea behind cloud computing [BKNT09] is to exploit scalability effects in order to offer cheaper and more efficient services. In [Car08], the situation of using computing resources is compared to a similar situation at the beginning of industrialization where every company, which used electricity for manufacturing, had to produce its own electricity. By making electricity a commodity (i.e., outsourcing the production of electricity to companies specialized in electricity generation), the prices could be lowered for everyone [Car08]. While a good mental model, this analogy is only partly true when applied to data. In contrast to electricity, data is personal and not interchangeable, which makes it harder to switch providers. Furthermore, data can contain sensitive information, which the owner does not want to, or is not allowed to share with providers.

2.2. IT Infrastructure Library (ITIL)

The IT Infrastructure Library (ITIL) framework aims at providing a "good practice" [IN07, page 7] baseline for Service Management. It is used by organizations all over the world in order to establish and improve Service Management capabilities. While the ISO/IEC 20000 standard [Dis09] can be used by organizations for having Service Management capabilities audited and certified, ITIL provides the knowledge to achieve the standard [LR07, page 6].

ITIL was developed in the 1980s by the British government in order to improve IT service quality for government agencies and has since then been developed into a framework, which addresses the needs of organizations from both, the governmental, as well as the private sectors. The current version V3 was published in 2007. In this thesis, ITIL V3 is used as the basis when referring to IT Service Management and ITIL.

The work presented in this thesis uses ITIL as its theoretical foundation. The reasons for using ITIL in the context of this work are as follows:

- ITIL is the currently most widely used and most mature ITSM framework.
- ITIL is the most general framework, compared to other frameworks.
- With its widespread use, building on ITIL promises the broadest adaptability of the approach presented in this thesis to other organizations.

ITIL consists of two main parts: ITIL Core and the ITIL Complementary Guidance. While ITIL Core deals with providing fundamental best practices, which fit all application fields, the Complementary Guidance is more specific, providing "guidance specific to industry sectors, organization types, operating models, and technology architectures" [IN07, page 7].

The ITIL Core consists of the following five publications: Service Strategy, Service Design, Service Transition, Service Operation, and Continual Service Improvement [IN07, pages 7–8]. The topics described in the five publications form an iterative, multidimensional lifecycle. The reason for having chosen a lifecycle is to make sure "that organizations are set up to leverage capabilities in one area for learning and improvements in others" [IN07, page 8].

Figure 2.2 provides a detailed view of the ITIL lifecycle. It can be seen that Service Strategy forms the center, with Service Design, Service Transition, and Service Operation forming a lifecycle, which is subject to improvements from Continual Service Improvement [IN07, page 8].

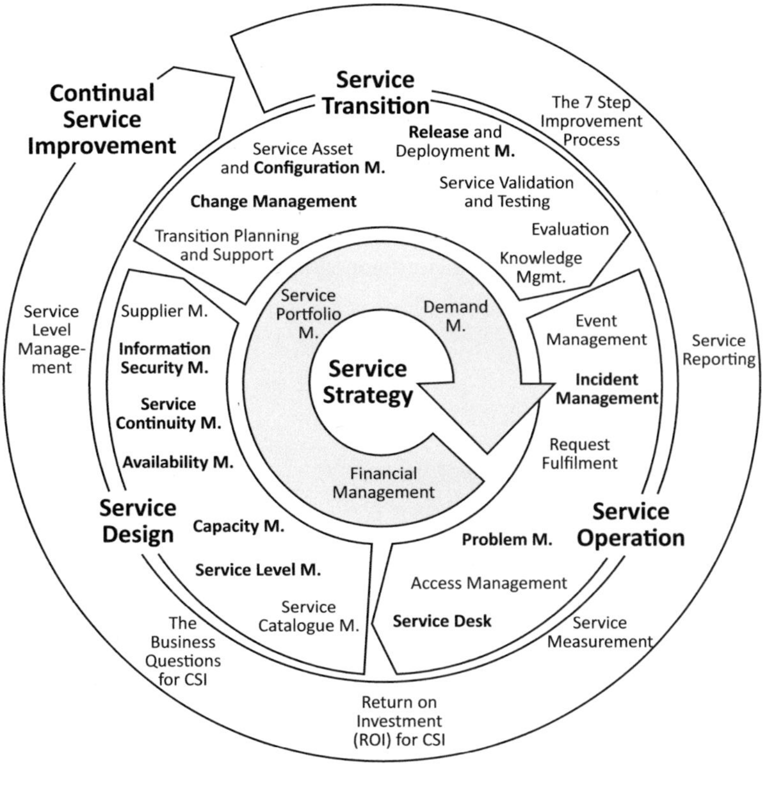

Figure 2.2.: ITIL Lifecycle including Processes (cf. [BVGM08, page 58])

The Service Strategy publication forms the basis for all other activities in the lifecycle. Services start their life in the processes described in the Service Design publication. The Service Transition publication outlines how services are transitioned from planning and designing into productive use. After completion of the Service Transition phase, services enter the operation phase. The processes used in running the IT services in the operation phase are described in the Service Operation publication. Continual Service Improvement provides guidelines on adapting IT services to changing business needs.

Functions and processes are central concepts in ITIL, which are used in all ITIL publications. Functions are defined to have the following characteristics [IN07, page 26]:

> "Functions are units of organizations specialized to perform certain types of work and be responsible for specific outcomes. They are self-contained with capabilities and resources necessary for their performance and outcomes. Capabilities include work methods internal to the functions. Functions have their own body of knowledge, which accumulates from experience. They provide structure and stability to organizations.
>
> "Functions are a way of structuring organizations to implement the specialization principle. Functions typically define roles and the associated authority and responsibility for a specific performance and outcomes. Coordination between functions through shared processes is a common pattern in organization design. Functions tend to optimize their work methods locally to focus on assigned outcomes. Poor coordination between functions combined with an inward focus lead to functional silos that hinder alignment and feedback critical to the success of the organization as a whole. Process models help avoid this problem with functional hierarchies by improving cross-functional coordination and control. Well-defined processes can improve productivity within and across functions." [IN07, page 26]

Also according to [IN07, page 26], "Process definitions describe actions, dependencies and sequence." Processes are characterized as having the following properties:

- *Measurable:* "[W]e are able to measure the process in a relevant manner. It is performance driven. Managers want to measure cost, quality and other variables while practitioners are concerned with duration and productivity." [IN07, page 26]
- *Specific results:* "[T]he reason a process exists is to deliver a specific result. This result must be individually identifiable and countable." [IN07, page 26]
- *Customers:* "[E]very process delivers its primary results to a customer or stakeholder. They may be internal or external to the organization but the process must meet their expectations." [IN07, page 26]
- *Response to specific events:* "[W]hile a process may be ongoing or iterative, it should be traceable to a specific trigger." [IN07, page 26]

An activity is defined as "[a] set of actions designed to achieve a particular result. Activities are usually defined as part of Processes or Plans, and are documented in Procedures." [IN07, page 233].

There are numerous books and articles, which deal with various aspects of ITIL. The official ITIL publications are Service Strategy [IN07], Service Design [LR07], Service Transition [LM07], Service Operation [CW07], and Continual Service Improvement [CS07]. An introduction to ITIL is given in [CHR$^+$08] and [Nis08]. While [KÖ7] describes aspects of ITIL V2, [Add07] is based on ITIL, but extended with additional materials and best practices. In [BT05], practice-oriented aspects of ITIL, as well as surveys of organizations about ITIL, are described. In [Gre07], a brief comparison between ITIL V2 and V3 is given. Reference [KT06] presents work on determining the contribution of ITIL to business/IT alignment.

In the following subsections, an introduction into the five ITIL publications Service Strategy, Service Design, Service Transition, Service Operation, and Continual Service Improvement is given. The introduction is based on the official ITIL V3 publications and aims at giving a general overview of ITIL. While Service Strategy (Section 2.2.1, page 19), Service Design (Section 2.2.2, page 25), and Continual Service Improvement (Section 2.2.5, page 53) are only of secondary importance in the context of this thesis, they are included for reasons of comprehensiveness.

Aspects of ITIL, which are at the center of this thesis' study—mostly parts of the Service Transition (Section 2.2.3, page 33) and Service Operation (Section 2.2.4, page 43) publications—are described in more detail in Chapter 3 (page 81).

2.2.1. Service Strategy

In the Service Strategy publication [IN07] of the ITIL series, it is described, how Service Management is implemented as a strategic asset in contrast to merely an organizational capability. Guidance on principles "for developing service management policies, guidelines and processes across the ITIL Service Lifecycle" [IN07, page 8] are provided.

Service Strategy provides the processes described in the other ITIL publications with vital information about economic viewpoints. Aspects are the "development of markets, internal and external, service assets, Service Catalogue, and implementation of strategy through the Service Lifecycle" as well as "Financial Management, Service Portfolio Management, Organizational Development, and Strategic Risks" [IN07, page 8].

The guidance from the Service Strategy publication is used as follows [IN07, page 8]:

> "[T]o set objectives and expectations of performance towards serving customers and market spaces, and to identify, select, and prioritize opportunities. Service Strategy is about ensuring that organizations are in a position to handle the costs and risks associated with their Service Portfolios, and are

> set up not just for operational effectiveness but also for distinctive performance. Decisions made with respect to Service Strategy have far-reaching consequences including those with delayed effect." [IN07, page 8]

The Service Strategy publication puts a strong emphasis on the rationale of doing something *("why")* rather than the way of achieving something *("how")* [IN07, page 9, emphasis in original]. Service Strategy employs knowledge from various domains not related to the classic aspects of information technology (e.g., "operations management, marketing, finance, information systems, organizational development, systems dynamics, and industrial engineering" [IN07, page 10]). By providing a wide focus, the good practices in the Service Strategy publication are applicable to a wide range of organizations.

When looking at the economic value of a service, there are various dimensions to consider. First, there is the financial perspective, which is concerned with the business results of the customer. In addition, there is the perceived view of the service by the customer, however. This view is influenced by more subjective parameters (e.g., prior experiences with this or other service providers, and value indicators, which are not quantifiable monetarily). In addition, the customer's actual or perceived place in the market plays an important role on his decision when choosing a service or service provider [IN07, page 31].

Because of this tendency to select services on non-objective parameters, it is the service provider's obligation to "demonstrate value, influence perceptions, and respond to preferences" [IN07, page 31]. By realizing the importance of a customer's expectations on the benefits gained from utilizing a service (either hard facts or perceived value gains are the basis of the customer's view of a service), a service provider can tailor a service to fit the customer's needs. IT organizations have to provide services, which satisfy the customer's actual needs, and not the IT department's perceived needs (i.e., "Customers do not buy services; they buy the fulfilment of particular needs.") [IN07, page 31].

When looking at the results, the customer's view has to be taken into account (i.e., the view from outside the IT organization) rather than the technical view (i.e., the view from inside the IT organization). Questions which are the starting point for a view from the customer's perspective are, as described in [IN07, page 32]:

- "What is our business?
- "Who is our customer?
- "What does the customer value?
- "Who depends on our services?
- "How do they use our services?
- "Why are they valuable to them?" [IN07, page 32]

Value, from the perspective of the customer, is made up of two elements: "*utility* or fitness for purpose and *warranty* or fitness for use" [IN07, page 17, emphasis in original].

Figure 2.3 shows how value is created through services. Only when the customer receives utility *and* warranty, value is created. Utility means that either performance is supported, or constraints removed, i.e., the customer is able to achieve something he would not be able to achieve without the service, or he does not have to do something he does not want to do. Warranty means that the service has certain attributes, e.g., an Internet connection, which breaks down every hour, is of not much use for a customer who bases his business on being reachable via the Internet [IN07, page 17].

Attributes associated with warranty are availability, capacity, continuity, and security. *Availability* means that the service is available under terms agreed on by both, the customer and the service provider [IN07, page 35]. *Capacity* means that it is assured that the service supports "a specified level of business activity or demand at a specified level of quality" [IN07, page 36]. *Continuity* assures that the service does not fail even when there are failures or events, which cause disruptions. *Security* guarantees that the service provider ensures that users have to authorize and are accountable when using a service and that assets are protected "from unauthorized or malicious access" [IN07, page 36].

In summary, "Utility is *what* the customer gets, and warranty is *how* it is delivered." [IN07, page 17, emphasis in original]. In order for a customer to fully capitalize on a service, utility and warranty have to be balanced with a combination of high utility and high warranty [IN07, page 37].

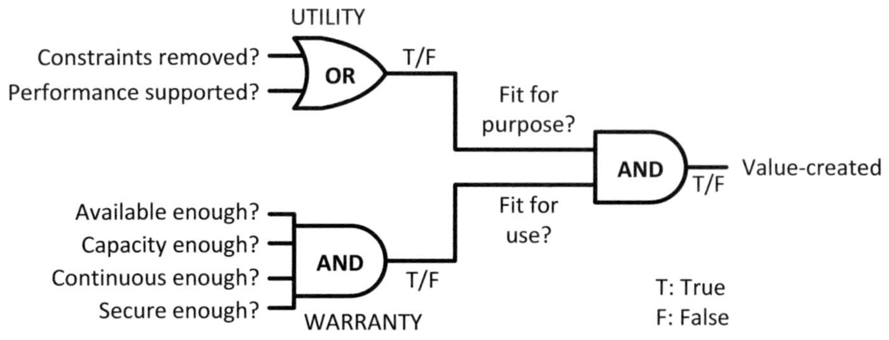

Figure 2.3.: Logic of Value Creation through Services (cf. [IN07, page 17])

Service Provider Types

ITIL distinguishes between three types of service providers: internal, or type I providers, shared service units, or type II providers, and external, or type III providers. While the three kinds of providers have many similarities, they differ on "customers, contracts, competition, market spaces, revenue and strategy take on different meanings" [IN07, page 41]. The following paragraphs list the characteristics of the three service provider types.

Type I Providers Type I, or internal service providers are "typically business functions embedded within the business units they serve" [IN07, page 41]. As such, they are a part of an organization and provide services to other parts of the organization. Typical examples of type I providers are "functions such as finance, administration, logistics, human resources, and IT" [IN07, page 41].

Type I providers "are funded by overheads and are required to operate strictly within the mandates of the business" [IN07, page 41]. They "have the benefit of tight coupling with their owner-customers, avoiding certain costs and risks associated with conducting business with external parties" [IN07, page 41]. Furthermore, achieving "functional excellence and cost-effectiveness for their business units" is their primary goal [IN07, page 41].

Type II Providers In contrast to type I providers, which are managed at the chief executive level, Type II providers, also referred to as shared service units, are managed autonomously. Type II providers are used for functions that "are not [...] at the core of an organization's competitive advantage" [IN07, page 42], such as "finance, IT, human resources, and logistics" [IN07, page 42]. While type I providers are closely tied to the organization, type II providers operate as entities, which provide services to other organizational units, but do so in competition to external service providers. By using market-based pricing, "complex discussions and negotiations over specific requirements, technologies, resource allocations, architectures, and designs" are minimized [IN07, page 42].

While type II providers have advantages stemming from using "internal agreements and accounting policies" [IN07, page 42] when compared to external providers, they can lose customers to external competition when performing poorly. On the other hand, excellently performing type II providers in some cases are able to accept external customers and generate additional revenue for its parent organization [IN07, pages 42–43].

Type III Providers Type III providers, or external service providers, are separate entities, which provide services to other organizations. In contrast to type I and type II providers, type III providers offer more flexibility and provide "access to knowledge, experience, scale, scope, capabilities, and resources that are either beyond the reach of the organization or outside the scope of a carefully considered investment portfolio" [IN07, pages 43–44].

Because type III providers compete in the free market, they also offer services to other organizations, including the organization's competitors. While this levels competitive advantages between competitors, security is an even bigger issue. Type III providers have to make sure that resources, which are shared between different organizations, are kept strictly separate [IN07, pages 43–44].

Selection of a Provider Type The decision, which type of provider to use in an organization, depends on several factors. In addition to the costs of purchasing a service,

> "they include but are not limited to the cost of finding and selecting qualified providers, defining requirements, negotiating agreements, measuring performance, managing the relationship with suppliers, cost of resolving disputes, and making changes or amends to agreements" [IN07, page 45].

Processes

The following paragraphs describe the processes Financial Management, Service Portfolio Management, and Demand Management.

Financial Management Financial Management is a process within ITIL's Service Strategy publication that aims at enabling an organization's "[o]perational visibility, insight and superior decision making" [IN07, page 97], which applies to all three kinds of service providers that were described in the previous paragraph.

One of Financial Managements paramount functions is to financially quantify the value of services, as described in [IN07, page 97]:

> "Financial Management provides the business and IT with the quantification, in financial terms, of the value of IT Services, the value of the assets underlying the provisioning of those services, and the qualification of operational forecasting. Talking about IT in terms of services is the crux of changing the perception of IT and its value to the business. Therefore, a significant portion of Financial Management is working in tandem with IT and the business to help identify, document and agree on the value of the services being received, and the enablement of service demand modelling and management." [IN07, page 97]

Service Portfolio Management Service Portfolio Management is another process within Service Strategy. Its objective is to describe "a provider's services in terms of business value" and to state "business needs and the provider's response to those needs" [IN07, page 119].

Service portfolios help customers to compare offerings from different service providers. Questions answered by looking at service portfolios are whether a customer should buy a service and from which provider the service should be bought [IN07, page 119].

Furthermore, service portfolios help to clarify pricing models and help to define a service provider's strengths and weaknesses, as well as their risk and priorities. Also, its helps in allocating capabilities and resources [IN07, page 119].

Reference [IN07, page 120] defines Service Portfolio Management as follows:

> "Service Portfolio Management is a dynamic method for governing investments in service management across the enterprise and managing them for value." [IN07, page 120]

The work method of Service Portfolio Management comprises four steps: Define, analyze, approve, and charter. In the *define* step, information about existing services as well as proposed services is gathered, followed by the *analyze* step, in which the "long-term goals of the service organization" [IN07, page 126] are determined. Furthermore, it is analyzed, which services are necessary for accomplishing these goals, as well as which resources and capabilities are needed. In the *approve* step, it is decided, which new services are offered and whether existing services continue to be part of the organization's service offering. Finally, in the *charter* step, the service portfolio is communicated to the customers [IN07, pages 123–128].

Demand Management Demand Management is concerned with making sure that there are always enough resources available for providing services to customers, while at the same time making sure that resources are not wasted in the form of over-capacities. While managing techniques, "such as off-peak pricing, volume discounts and differentiated service levels" [IN07, page 129] can help to channel demand into beneficial patterns, they are effective only up to a certain degree [IN07, page 129].

Further Reading

The content of this subsection is based on [IN07]. In [BT05, pages 90–91] and [ZHB05, pages 123–140], Financial Management is outlined, while in [TC09], decision support techniques for the selection of IT investments in the context of IT Portfolio Management are described.

2.2.2. Service Design

After the previous subsection gave an overview of Service Strategy, this subsection describes the foundations outlined in the ITIL framework on how the design of new services can be accomplished methodologically.

The Service Design volume is the second ITIL V3 publication [LR07]. Its primary objective, as described in [LR07, page 3],

> "is to design IT services, together with the governing IT practices, processes and policies, to realize the strategy and to facilitate the introduction of these services into the live environment ensuring quality service delivery, customer satisfaction and cost-effective service provision" [LR07, page 3].

In [LR07, page 7], the goal of the Service Design publication is summarized as follows:

> "The Service Design publication provides guidance for the design and development of services and Service Management processes. It covers design principles and methods for converting strategic objectives into portfolios of services and service assets. The scope of Service Design is not limited to new services. It includes the changes and improvements necessary to increase or maintain value to customers over the lifecycle of services, the continuity of services, achievement of service levels and conformance to standards and regulations. It guides organizations on how to develop design capabilities for Service Management." [LR07, page 7]

Figure 2.4 gives an overview of Service Design. The Service Design processes described in the following paragraphs (Service Catalogue Management, Service Level Management, Capacity Management, Availability Management, IT Service Continuity Management, Information Security, and Supplier Management) can be seen in the lower part of the figure. Furthermore, interactions between Service Design and other ITIL processes can be seen in the figure. The central storage facility in the context of Service Design is the Service Portfolio, which includes the Service Catalogue [LR07, page 60].

Processes

ITIL V3 defines seven processes in the Service Design publication. The processes are Service Catalogue Management, Service Level Management, Capacity Management, Availability Management, IT Service Continuity Management, Information Security Management, and Supplier Management. The following paragraphs give an introduction into these processes.

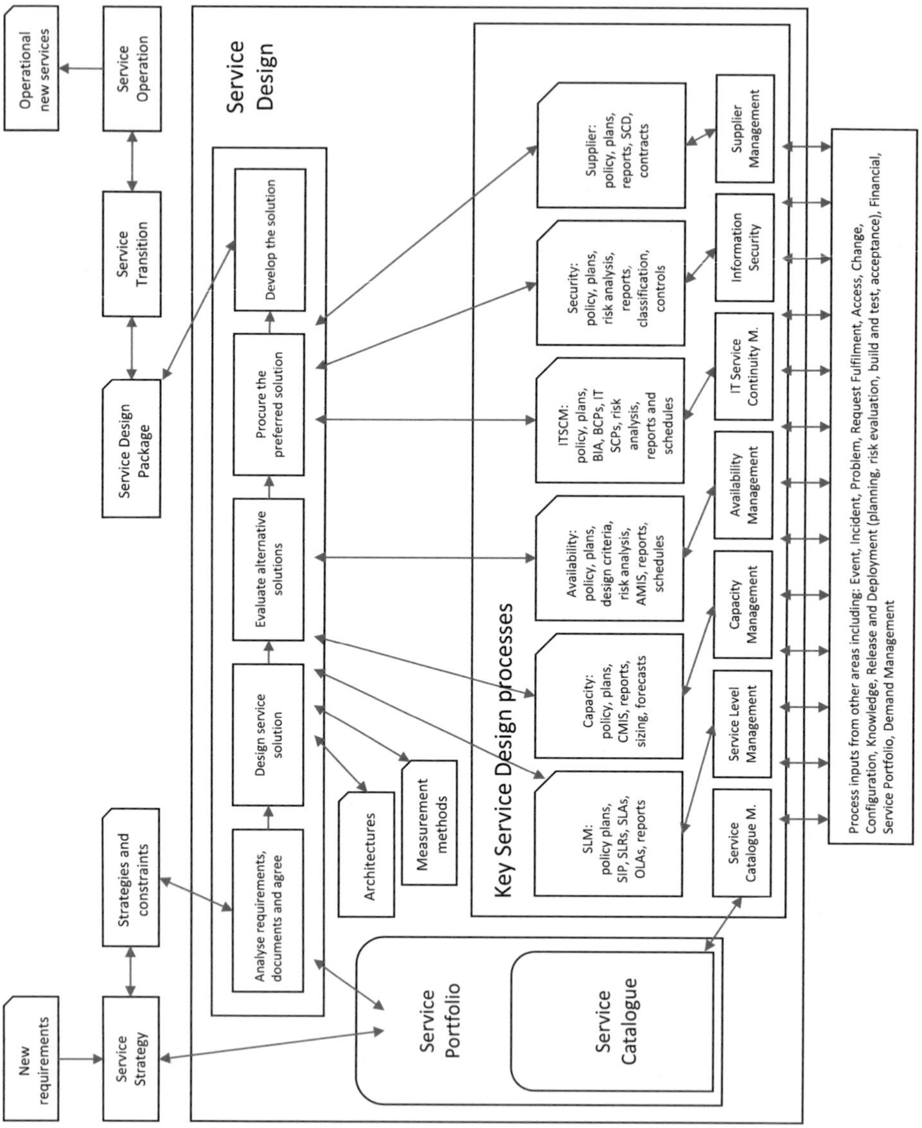

Figure 2.4.: Service Design Overview (cf. [LR07, page 60])

Service Catalogue Management The Service Catalogue Management process ensures that a service catalogue is composed and regularly updated. An organization's service catalogue includes "accurate information on all operational services and those being prepared to run operationally" [LR07, page 19]. It is important that the information in the service catalogue is consistent and that the service catalogue is the "single source" [LR07, page 60] for information about services. Furthermore, it has to be made sure that the service catalogue is accessible for authorized persons [LR07, page 60].

The service catalogue is part of the service portfolio, which was described in Section 2.2.1 (page 23). While the service portfolio also includes services, which are proposed or being developed, as well as retired services, the service catalogue only contains services that are currently available [IN07, page 251].

Activities within Service Catalogue Management are the "[d]efinition of the service" [LR07, page 61], producing and maintaining "an accurate Service Catalogue" [LR07, page 61], the definition of interfaces and dependencies, as well as ensuring "consistency between the Service Catalogue and Service Portfolio" [LR07, page 61]. Furthermore, "[i]nterfaces and dependencies between all services and supporting services within the Service Catalogue and the [Configuration Management System]" should be part of Service Catalogue Management [LR07, page 61]. Additional parts should be "[i]nterfaces and dependencies between all services, and supporting components and Configuration Items (CIs) within the Service Catalogue and the [Configuration Management System]" [LR07, page 61].

The business value of Service Catalogue Management is that it improves transparency by enabling customers to "view an accurate, consistent picture of the IT services, their details and their status". Enabling customers to find information about how services "are intended to be used, the business processes they enable, and the levels and quality of service the customer can expect for each service" are further business values [LR07, page 61].

Service Level Management Service Level Management (SLM), as a process within Service Design, makes sure that targets of IT services are negotiated, agreed upon, and documented in cooperation with business representatives. These targets are then monitored in order to make sure that services perform according to previously agreed on service levels. Within the Service Level Management process, targets for services are agreed upon and documented [LR07, page 19].

A Service Level Requirement (SLR) describes the customer's requirements for a service. Furthermore, a Service Level Agreement (SLA) is an agreement between a service provider and the customer which "describes the IT Service, documents Service Level Targets, and specifies the responsibilities of the IT Service Provider and the Customer" [LR07, page 310].

The Service Level Management process builds on the Service Portfolio and Service Catalogue and relies on accurate information in order to manage services. Service Level Management's objectives are described in [LR07, page 65] as follows:

- "Define, document, agree, monitor, measure, report and review the level of IT services provided
- "Provide and improve the relationship and communication with the business and customers
- "Ensure that specific and measurable targets are developed for all IT services
- "Monitor and improve customer satisfaction with the quality of service delivered
- "Ensure that IT and the customers have a clear and unambiguous expectation of the level of service to be delivered
- "Ensure that proactive measures to improve the levels of service delivered are implemented wherever it is cost-justifiable to do so." [LR07, page 65]

In summary, Service Level Management improves transparency and helps to make sure that agreed services are provided according to their underlying agreement. It is the binding element between IT service providers and the business side. The business value of Service Level Management lies in providing "a reliable communication channel and a trusted relationship with the appropriate customers and business representatives" by providing "a consistent interface to the business for all service-related issues", and by providing "business with the agreed service targets and the required management information to ensure that those targets have been met" [LR07, page 66].

Capacity Management Capacity Management, as a process within Service Design, helps to ensure that there is always enough capacity available to ensure the fulfillment of the customer's needs, while making sure that there exist no expensive, unneeded capacities [LR07, pages 79–80]. Capacity Management's task is to make sure

> "that cost-justifiable IT capacity in all areas of IT always exists and is matched to the current and future agreed needs of the business, in a timely manner" [LR07, page 19].

As can be seen in this statement, two requirements have to be banded together. On the one hand, the needs in IT capacity have to be predicted as accurately as possible, in order to always be able to fulfill customer's needs. On the other hand, wasting of money by having excess capacity in store, which will not be needed in the near future, has to be avoided.

Capacity Management produces and maintains a "Capacity Plan, which reflects the current and future needs of the business" [LR07, page 79]. Furthermore, another job of Capacity Management is to advise "all other areas of the business and IT on all capacity- and performance-related issues" [LR07, page 79]. To "[e]nsure that service performance achievements meet or exceed all of their agreed performance targets, by managing the performance and capacity of both services and resources" is another one of Capacity Management's objectives [LR07, page 79].

In addition, changes are analyzed for their impact on capacity and performance. While Capacity Management works on preventing shortages by acting proactively, it helps in tracking down and resolving "performance- and capacity-related incidents and problems" [LR07, page 79]. The business value of Capacity Management is to provide consistent levels of service, "matched to the current and future needs of the business, as agreed and documented within [Service Level Agreements] and [Operational Level Agreements]" [LR07, page 81].

Availability Management Availability Management, as a process within Service Design, makes sure "that the level of service availability delivered in all services is matched to, or exceeds, the current and future agreed needs of the business, in a cost-effective manner" [LR07, page 19].

Figure 2.5 provides an overview of the Availability Management process. It can be seen that Availability Management consists of proactive and reactive activities, as well as an Availability Management Information System (AMIS).

Reference [LR07, page 97] lists as objectives of Availability Management, the production and maintenance of an "up-to-date Availability Plan that reflects the current and future needs of the business", and providing "advice and guidance to all other areas of the business and IT on all availability-related issues". In addition, making sure "that service availability achievements meet or exceed all their agreed targets", and assisting "with the diagnosis and resolution of availability-related incidents and problems" are additional objectives. Furthermore, assessing "the impact of all changes on the Availability Plan and the performance and capacity of all services and resources", and ensuring "that proactive measures to improve the availability of services are implemented wherever it is cost-justifiable to do so" are objectives of Availability Management [LR07, page 97].

The *Infrastructure Monitoring Component*, which is described in Section 5.2 (page 234), is used for availability monitoring.

IT Service Continuity Management Business processes, which are supported by IT, are dependent on the correct working of the underlying components. According to [LR07, page 125], IT Service Continuity Management (ITSCM) is responsible for supporting

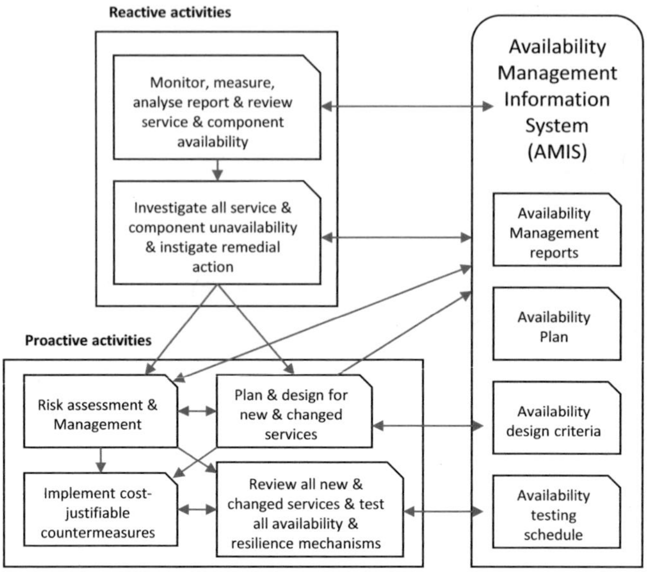

Figure 2.5.: Availability Management Process (cf. [LR07, page 99])

> "the overall Business Continuity Management process by ensuring that the required IT technical and service facilities (including computer systems, networks, applications, data repositories, telecommunications, environment, technical support and Service Desk) can be resumed within required, and agreed, business timescales" [LR07, page 125].

The goals of IT Service Continuity Management are to "[m]aintain a set of IT Service Continuity Plans and IT recovery plans that support the overall Business Continuity Plans (BCPs) of the organization", and to regularly perform a Business Impact Analysis (BIA) in order to make sure that continuity plans are aligned "with changing business impacts and requirements" [LR07, page 126].

Furthermore, "regular Risk Analysis and Management exercises", are conducted, together with Availability Management, Security Management, and the business [LR07, page 126].

In addition, other business and IT areas are advised "on all continuity- and recovery-related issues" [LR07, page 126] by the ITSCM process. It has to be made sure "that appropriate continuity and recovery mechanisms are put in place to meet or exceed the agreed business continuity targets", and that "all changes on the IT Service Continuity Plans and IT recovery plans" are assessed with regard to their impact [LR07, page 126].

Moreover, availability is increased by implementing "proactive measures to improve the availability of services", if it is economical to do so [LR07, page 126]. In addition, contracts for recovery capabilities with suppliers are negotiated within the ITSCM process [LR07, page 126].

Information Security Management The purpose of Information Security Management (ISM) is to align "IT security with business security, and [to] ensure that information security is effectively managed in all service and Service Management activities" [LR07, page 19]. According to [LR07, page 141], Information Security Management plays a role in *corporate governance*, which

> "is the set of responsibilities and practices exercised by the board and executive management with the goal of providing strategic direction, ensuring the objectives are achieved, ascertaining the risks are being managed appropriately and verifying that the enterprise's resources are used effectively" [LR07, page 141].

Information security is defined as being "a management activity within the corporate governance framework, which provides the strategic direction for security activities and ensures [that] objectives are achieved" [LR07, page 141]. Furthermore, Information Security Management "ensures that the information security risks are appropriately managed and that enterprise information resources are used responsibly", with "a focus for all aspects of IT security" [LR07, page 141].

Security in most contexts means that the following five demands have to be met: availability, confidentiality, integrity, authenticity, and non-repudiation. *Availability* means that "[i]nformation is available and usable when required", even in the case of failures or attacks [LR07, page 141]. *Confidentiality* ensures that information can only be accessed by authorized persons. *Integrity* means that information cannot be tampered with, without being noticed. Finally, *authenticity and non-repudiation* mean that "transactions, as well as information exchanges between enterprises, or with partners, can be trusted" [LR07, page 141]. For a more in-depth discussion of the principles, please cf. [Bis04, pages 1–4].

Figure 2.6 shows the IT Security Management Framework, which consists of five elements, namely Control, Plan, Implement, Evaluate, and Maintain, which form a lifecycle for IT Security Management [LR07, page 143].

Supplier Management When providing IT services, an entity is dependent on suppliers and partners, from which products or services are purchased. The Supplier Management process ensures the management of "suppliers and the services they supply, to provide seamless quality of IT service to the business, ensuring value for money is obtained" [LR07, page 19].

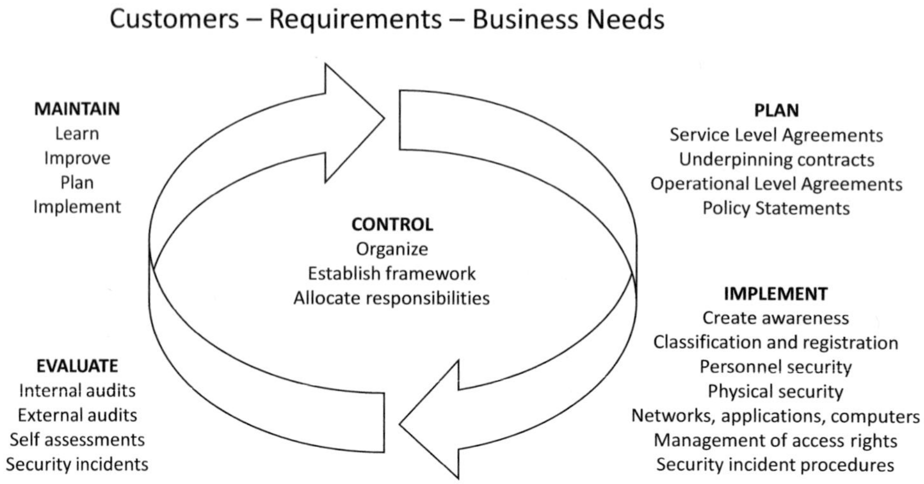

Figure 2.6.: IT Security Management Framework (cf. [LR07, page 143])

According to [LR07, page 149], the goal of the Supplier Management process is to "[o]btain value for money from supplier and contracts" [LR07, page 149]. Additional goals are to make sure "that underpinning contracts and agreements with suppliers are aligned to business needs, and support and align with agreed targets in [Service Level Requirements] and [Service Level Agreements], in conjunction with [Service Level Management]" [LR07, pages 149–150]. Furthermore, managing "relationships with suppliers" and the suppliers' performances are part of the Supplier Management process, as well as negotiating, agreeing and managing contracts [LR07, page 150]. In addition, maintaining "a supplier policy and a supporting Supplier and Contract Database (SCD)" is part of the Supplier Management process [LR07, page 150].

Further Reading

The official ITIL Service Design publication [LR07], on which this subsection is based, provides a detailed description of Service Design. In [Add07, pages 81–85], more information about Service Catalogue Management can be found, while Service Level Management is described in [Add07, pages 275–296] and [ZHB05, pages 25–47]. Capacity Management and Availability Management are outlined in [Add07, pages 313–315] and [ZHB05, pages 49–102]. More information about Service Continuity Management can be found in [ZHB05, pages 103–122]. In [Bru06], the Security Management process is described in detail, while [KRS07] described IT Security Management according to ISO 27001.

2.2.3. Service Transition

Service Transition, described in detail in the third ITIL volume [LM07], is concerned with ensuring "that the transition processes are streamlined, effective and efficient so that the risk of delay is minimized" [LM07, page 3]. Reference [LM07, page 6] summarizes Service Translation as follows:

> "The Service Transition publication provides guidance for the development and improvement of capabilities for transitioning new and changed services into operations. This publication provides guidance on how the requirements of Service Strategy encoded in Service Design are effectively realized in Service Operations while controlling the risks of failure and disruption. The publication combines practices in release management, programme management and risk management and places them in the practical context of Service Management. It provides guidance on managing the complexity related to changes to services and Service Management processes, preventing undesired consequences while allowing for innovation. Guidance is provided on transferring the control of services between customers and service providers." [LM07, page 6]

Processes and Activities

There are five processes and two sets of activities described in the Service Transition publication. The processes are Change Management, Service Asset and Configuration Management, Service Validation and Testing, Evaluation, and Knowledge Management. The sets of activities are Transition Planning and Support, and Release and Deployment Management [LM07, pages 35–154]. An overview of these processes and sets of activities is given in the following paragraphs.

Transition Planning and Support Transition Planning and Support is the first number of activities described in the Service Transition publication. Their aim is described as follows [LM07, page 35]:

- "Plan appropriate capacity and resources to package a release, build, release, test, deploy and establish the new or changed service into production
- "Provide support for the Service Transition teams and people
- "Plan the changes required in a manner that ensures the integrity of all identified customer assets, service assets and configurations can be maintained as they evolve through Service Transition

- "Ensure that Service Transition issues, risks and deviations are reported to the appropriate stakeholders and decision makers
- "Coordinate activities across projects, suppliers and service teams where required." [LM07, page 35]

Translation Planning and Support's goals are described as planning and coordinating "the resources to ensure that the requirements of Service Strategy encoded in Service Design are effectively realized in Service Operations". Additionally, identifying, managing and controlling "the risks of failure and disruption across transition activities" are further goals [LM07, page 35].

The objectives are to "[p]lan and coordinate the resources to establish successfully a new or changed service into production within the predicted cost, quality and time estimates". Furthermore, to "[e]nsure that all parties adopt the common framework of standard re-usable processes and supporting systems in order to improve the effectiveness and efficiency of the integrated planning and coordination activities", and to "[p]rovide clear and comprehensive plans that enable the customer and business change projects to align their activities with the Service Transition plans" are additional objectives [LM07, page 35].

Change Management IT systems and services are not static entities but are subject to changes. These changes can be either proactive or reactive. Proactive changes, on the one hand, are initiated to provide benefits to customers and providers, e.g., by lowering costs, or by increasing the quality of services. Reactive changes, on the other hand, are initiated to correct errors or adapt to a changing environment. In an organization, there should be processes and mechanisms present, which help to make sure that risk exposure is optimized, the "severity of any impact and disruption" is minimized, and that changes are "successful at the first attempt" [LM07, page 42].

Change Management as a process within Service Transition provides recommendations for achieving these goals. Reference [LM07, page 43] describes the Change Management process' purpose as follows: Make sure the use of "[s]tandardized methods and procedures [...] for efficient and prompt handling of all changes", record "[a]ll changes to service assets and configuration items [...] in the Configuration Management System, and to optimize "[o]verall business risk" [LM07, page 43].

The goals of Change Management lie in responding "to the customer's changing business requirements while maximizing value and reducing incidents, disruption and re-work", as well as in "[r]espond[ing] to the business and IT requests for change that will align the services with the business needs" [LM07, page 43].

Change Management's objective "is to ensure that changes are recorded and then evaluated, authorized, prioritized, planned, tested, implemented, documented and reviewed in a controlled manner" [LM07, page 43].

A *Service Change* in ITIL is defined as [LM07, page 43]

> "[t]he addition, modification or removal of authorized, planned or supported service or service component and its associated documentation." [LM07, page 43]

According to [LM07, page 43], organizations should define the borders of their Service Change process by excluding changes with a wide impact on the one hand (e.g., "departmental organization, policies and business operations", and day-to-day maintenance changes on the other hand (e.g., printer repairs) [LM07, page 43].

Change Management distinguishes between the following types of changes: Standard Operational Changes, Standard Changes, and Normal Changes [LM07, pages 46–50].

Standard Operational Changes are the simplest form of a change, which include resetting forgotten user passwords, or rebooting computers in order to fix a problem [LM07, page 61]. An example of a Standard Operational Change process flow can be seen in Figure 2.7.

Standard Changes, which are more complex than Standard Operational Changes, are pre-authorized and are applied in order to execute routine changes, for which proven work procedures exist, e.g., adding new computers to a network, or installing standard software. Standard Changes are defined by the following criteria [LM07, page 48]:

- "There is a defined trigger to initiate the RFC
- "The tasks are well known, documented and proven
- "Authority is effectively given in advance
- "Budgetary approval will typically be preordained or within the control of the change requester
- "The risk is usually low and always well understood" [LM07, page 48]

Figure 2.8 shows the process flow of a Standard Change. It can be seen that it is more complex than the Standard Operational Change shown in Figure 2.7.

The process flow displayed in Figure 2.9 shows an example of a *Normal Change*, which is applied if there exist no predefined procedures for handling the change. It can be seen that a Request for Change (RFC) is created to initiate a change. Following that, the RFC is recorded and reviewed. After assessing and evaluating the change, it is either authorized or alternative changes are proposed. After authorization, updates are planned, followed by the implementation of the change. After that, the change record is reviewed. Finally, the change record is closed. During the whole change process, information about the change and configuration information is updated in the Configuration Management System (CMS) [LM07, page 49].

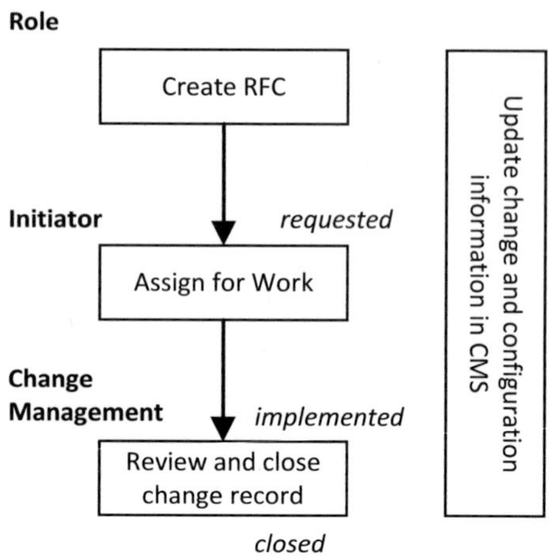

Figure 2.7.: Standard Operational Change (cf. [LM07, page 50])

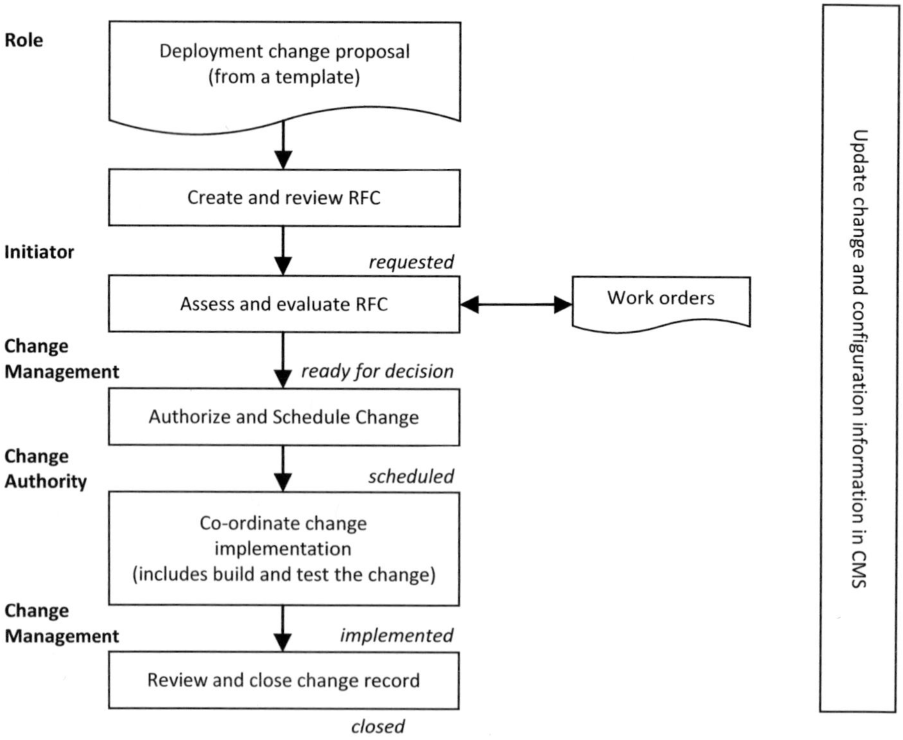

Figure 2.8.: Standard Change (cf. [LM07, page 50])

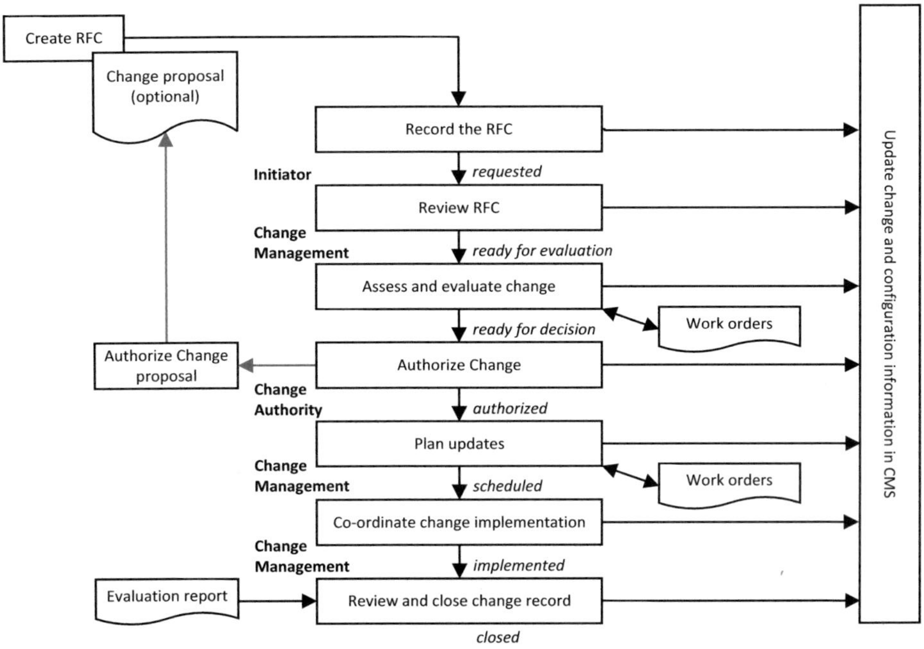

Figure 2.9.: Normal Change (cf. [LM07, page 49])

There is certain information, which has to be present before a change can be initiated. Reference [LM07, page 53] list seven questions, which must be answered when performing changes. The questions are:

- "Who *raised* the change?
- "What is the *reason* for the change?
- "What is the *return* required from the change?
- "What are the *risks* involved in the change?
- "What *resources* are required to deliver the change?
- "Who is *responsible* for the build, test and implementation of the change?
- "What is the *relationship* between this change and other changes?" [LM07, page 53, all capitalized emphasis in original, italic emphasis added]

There is always the possibility that changes go wrong, i.e., every change has a risk associated with it. In order to minimize change-related risks, risks should be categorized, e.g., by using a change impact/probability matrix, which categorizes risk by their impact (high or low), and their probability (high or low) [LM07, page 54].

The Change Advisory Board (CAB) brings together stakeholders of the Change Management process. Members include persons who are able to evaluate changes from a business or technical perspective. CABs can have permanent members, as well as persons who only attend CAB meetings, which deal with changes within their domain. CAB meetings are chaired by the change manager. In the case of time-critical problems, which have to be fixed by initiating a prompt change, there often is not the time to gather the full CAB. In this case, the *Emergency Change Advisory Board (ECAB)* makes the decision to initiate an emergency change [LM07, pages 58–61].

More information about Change Management can be found in Section 4.2.3 (page 153), which describes how changes are handled in the ITSM Wiki.

Service Asset and Configuration Management Well-managed assets are important for an organization's success. It is the task of the Service Asset and Configuration Management (SACM) process to support other ITSM processes by managing assets. SACM's purpose lies in performing the following tasks [LM07, page 65]:

- "Identify, control, record, report, audit and verify service assets and configuration items, including versions, baselines, constituent components, their attributes, and relationships
- "Account for, manage and protect the integrity of service assets and configuration items (and, where appropriate, those of its customers) through the service lifecycle by ensuring that only authorized components are used and only authorized changes are made
- "Protect the integrity of service assets and configuration items (and, where appropriate, those of its customers) through the service lifecycle
- "Ensure the integrity of the assets and configurations required to control the services and IT infrastructure by establishing and maintaining an accurate and complete Configuration Management System." [LM07, page 65]

SACM's goals are the supporting of "the business and customer's control objectives and requirements", as well as supporting "efficient and effective Service Management processes by providing accurate configuration information to enable people to make decisions at the right time, e.g., to authorize change and releases, resolve incidents and problems faster". Minimizing "the number of quality and compliance issues caused by improper configuration of services and assets" and optimizing "the service assets, IT configurations, capabilities and resources" are further goals [LM07, page 65].

The objectives of the Service Asset and Configuration Management process lie in defining and controlling "the components of services and infrastructure and maintain[ing] accurate configuration information on the historical, planned and current state of the services and infrastructure" [LM07, page 65]. Assets are covered by Asset Management throughout their lifecycle, starting from purchase to retirement. Furthermore, information about persons, responsible for controlling assets, are retained within Asset Management. Besides IT assets, non-IT assets can be covered by SACM. Configuration Management makes sure the identification, baselining, maintaining, and controlling of changes to components of services, systems, and products. Furthermore, "a configuration model of the services, assets and infrastructure" is provided "by recording the relationships between service assets and configuration items" [LM07, page 65].

In Figure 2.10, an example of a "logical configuration model" is shown. It is a model of assets and services as well as their relations towards each other. It helps to "assess the impact and cause of incidents and problems" and helps in planning changes, new services, or with optimizing costs and utilization [LM07, pages 66–67]

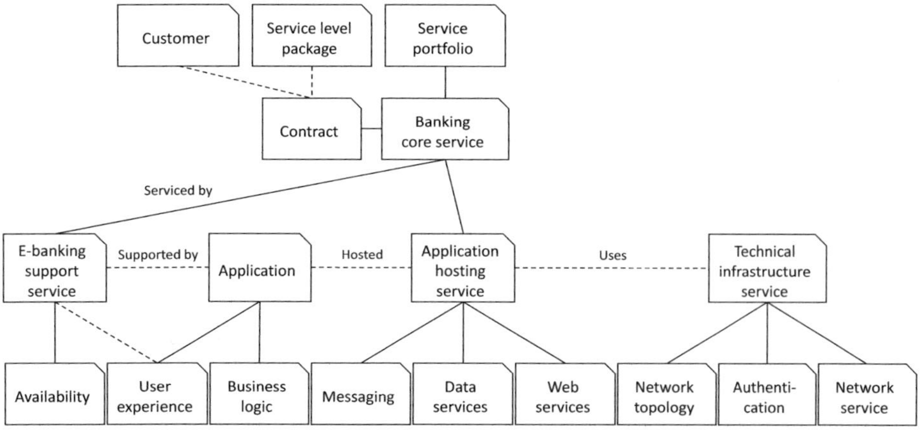

Figure 2.10.: Logical Configuration Model (cf. [LM07, page 67])

Service Asset and Configuration Management is one of the processes, which plays an extended role in this thesis' context. It is described in more detail in Section 3.2 (page 98).

Release and Deployment Management Release and Deployment Management is an activity described in the Service Transition publication. Reference [LM07, page 84] defines the *goals* of Release and Deployment Management as follows:

> "Release and Deployment Management aims to build, test and deliver the capability to provide the services specified by Service Design and that will accomplish the stakeholders' requirements and deliver the intended objectives." [LM07, page 84]

According to [LM07, page 84], Release and Deployment Management's *purpose* lies in defining and agreeing "release and deployment plans with customers and stakeholders", ensuring "that each release package consists of a set of related assets and service components that are compatible with each other" and "that integrity of a release package and its constituent components is maintained throughout the transition activities and recorded accurately in the CMS". Furthermore, it makes sure "that all release and deployment packages can be tracked, installed, tested, verified, and/or uninstalled or backed out if appropriate" and "that organization and stakeholder change is managed during the release and deployment activities" [LM07, page 84].

Other purposes are "[r]ecord[ing] and manag[ing] deviations, risks, issues related to the new or changed service and tak[ing] necessary corrective action", "[e]nsur[ing] that there is knowledge transfer to enable the customers and users to optimize their use of the service to support their business activities" and to "[e]nsure that skills and knowledge are transferred to operations and support staff to enable them to effectively and efficiently deliver, support and maintain the service according to required warranties and service levels" [LM07, page 84].

Release and Deployment Management aims at "deploy[ing] releases into production and establish[ing] effective use of the service in order to deliver value to the customer and be able to handover to service operations". Its *objectives* are to make sure that "clear and comprehensive release and deployment plans" exist, which "enable the customer and business change projects to align their activities with these plans" and to ensure that release packages "can be built, installed, tested and deployed efficiently to a deployment group or target environment successfully and on schedule" [LM07, page 84].

Further objectives are making sure that "[a] new or changed service and its enabling systems, technology and organization are capable of delivering the agreed service requirements, i.e. utilities, warranties and service levels" with a "minimal unpredicted impact on the production services, operations and support organization". Moreover, making sure that "[c]ustomers, users and Service Management staff are satisfied with the Service Transition practices and outputs, e.g. user documentation and training" is another objective [LM07, page 84].

An organization *benefits* from a well-working Release and Deployment Management due to being more cost-effective, faster and minimizing risk. Furthermore, customers have a higher degree of actually being able to use new services due to diligently implemented Release and Deployment Management activities. Consistency, as well as the contribution "to meeting auditable requirements for traceability through Service Transition" are further benefits [LM07, pages 84–85].

Service Validation and Testing Assuring the quality of newly installed or modified services by testing is the task of the Service Validation and Testing process. It makes sure that negative impact on business processes due to faulty IT services, as well as calls to the service desk due to malfunctioning services, are minimized. Furthermore, by testing early, problems can be tracked down more easily in a more manageable test environment than in the live environment, which saves time and money. Moreover, services which do not "deliver the desired value" can be avoided [LM07, page 115].

Service Validation and Testing's *purpose* is the planning and implementation of "a structured validation and test process that provides objective evidence that the new or changed service will support the customer's business and stakeholder requirements, including the agreed service levels", as well as assuring a release's quality, "its constituent service components, the resultant service and service capability delivered by a release". Furthermore, the identification, assessing, and addressing of "issues, errors and risks throughout Service Transition" is another purpose of Service Validation and Testing [LM07, page 115].

The *goal* of the process is to make sure that value is provided for customers by a service. Service Validation and Testing's *objectives* are to "[p]rovide confidence that a release will create a new or changed service or service offerings that deliver the expected outcomes and value for the customers within the projected costs, capacity and constraints", making sure a service's fitness for purpose as well as its fitness for use (cp. Figure 2.3, page 21). Furthermore, another objective is to "[c]onfirm that the customer and stakeholder requirements for the new or changed service are correctly defined and remedy any errors or variances early in the service lifecycle as this is considerably cheaper than fixing errors in production" [LM07, page 115].

Evaluation Evaluation is a "generic process" in Service Transition, which "considers whether the performance of something is acceptable, value for money etc. – and whether it will be proceeded with, accepted into use, paid for, etc." [LM07, page 138].

Evaluation's *purpose* "is to provide a consistent and standardized means of determining the performance of a service change in the context of existing and proposed services and IT infrastructure". The measured performance of a change is compared to its prediction, which allows to understand and manage the deviations [LM07, page 138]. Evaluation's *goal* "is to set stakeholder expectations correctly and provide effective and accurate information to Change Management to make sure changes that adversely affect service capability and introduce risk are not transitioned unchecked" [LM07, page 139].

Evaluation's *objectives* are as follows [LM07, page 139]:

- "Evaluate the intended effects of a service change and as much of the unintended effects as is reasonably practical given capacity, resource and organizational constraints

- "Provide good quality outputs from the evaluation process so that Change Management can expedite an effective decision about whether a service change is to be approved or not." [LM07, page 139]

Knowledge Management Knowledge Management is a process within the Service Transition publication. It accommodates the fact that the quality of services and processes largely depends on persons and their knowledge. Elements of knowledge in the context of Service Transition can be the "[i]dentity of stakeholders", "[a]cceptable risk levels and performance expectations", as well as "[a]vailable resource[s] and timescales" [LM07, page 145]. The knowledge's "quality and relevance" depends on the "accessibility, quality and continued relevance of the underpinning data and information available to service staff" [LM07, page 145].

The *purpose* of Knowledge Management is to make sure "that the right information is delivered to the appropriate place or competent person at the right time to enable informed decision". Its *goal* is "to improve the quality of management decision making by ensuring that reliable and secure information and data is available throughout the service lifecycle" [LM07, page 145].

The *objectives* of Knowledge Management in the context of ITIL are to enable service providers to increase their efficiency, service quality, and customer satisfaction as well as help in reducing costs. Furthermore, making sure that employees share a "common understanding of the value that their services provide to customers and the ways in which benefits are realized from the use of those services" is another objective. Still, another aim is to make sure that employees of service providers "have adequate information" on who uses the provider's services, what are "[t]he current states of consumption", what are the constraints to service delivery, and what are the "[d]ifficulties faced by the customer in fully realizing the benefits expected from the service" [LM07, page 145].

More information about Knowledge Management in the context of this thesis can be found in Section 4.2.2 (page 142), which describes how a semantic wiki is used to store both, structured and unstructured information about IT systems.

Further Reading

While this section presented the information found in the Service Transition publication [LM07], there are other sources, which also describe aspects of Service Transition. Change Management is described in [Add07, pages 185–224]. More about Knowledge Management in general can be found in [NT95,Nor02,PRR03]. Reference [Add07, pages 155–161] describes Knowledge Management in the context of IT Service Management.

2.2.4. Service Operation

The Service Operation publication [CW07] is the fourth volume of the ITIL series. Its focus is on how to establish and maintain processes and functions, which help in operating the IT infrastructures needed for delivering IT services. Reference [CW07, page 6] summarizes its content as follows:

> "[The Service Operation] volume embodies practices in the management of Service Operations. It includes guidance on achieving effectiveness and efficiency in the delivery and support of services so as to ensure value for the customer and the service provider. Strategic objectives are ultimately realized through Service Operations, therefore making it a critical capability. Guidance is provided on how to maintain stability in Service Operations, allowing for changes in design, scale, scope and service levels. Organizations are provided with detailed process guidelines, methods and tools for use in two major control perspectives: reactive and proactive. Managers and practitioners are provided with knowledge allowing them to make better decisions in areas such as managing the availability of services, controlling demand, optimizing capacity utilization, scheduling of operations and fixing problems. Guidance is provided on supporting operations through new models and architectures such as shared services, utility computing, web services and mobile commerce." [CW07, page 6]

In this subsection, a description of the processes and functions, which are defined in the Service Operation publication, is given.

Processes

Service Operation consists of five processes, which are described in this subsection. The processes are Event Management, Incident Management, Request Fulfilment, Problem Management, and Access Management.

Event Management Event Management, as a process within Service Operation, is tasked with monitoring events occurring in an IT infrastructure, in order to ensure the proper functioning of the infrastructure, and to detect errors. An event is defined "[a]s any detectable or discernible occurrence that has significance for the management of the IT Infrastructure or the delivery of IT service and evaluation of the impact a deviation might cause to the Service Operation processes services" [CW07, pages 35–36].

Monitoring tools, which are used to detect events, can be divided into two classes: First, there are tools, which *actively* monitor configuration items (CIs) and which report misbehaving (e.g., not responding) CIs. Second, there are tools which *passively* monitor

CIs by detecting and correlating "operational alerts or communications generated by CIs" [CW07, page 36]. By detecting critical conditions, Event Management can help to mitigate problems before customers are affected. Furthermore, Event Management supports other processes, such as Availability Management and Capacity Management, as well as the automation of operations triggered by events [CW07, pages 36–37].

In the context of this thesis, the Infrastructure Monitoring Component, which is presented in Section 5.2 (page 234), implements a tool for supporting the Event Management process from within the ITSM Wiki. In addition, the Intrusion Detection Component, which is introduced in Section 5.3 (page 261), implements a tool for integrating security-relevant events into the ITSM Wiki.

Incident Management When offering IT services to customers, issues can occur, where a service does not perform as expected or intended. Incident Management, as a process, deals with finding and providing fixes for these issues [CW07, page 46].

The term *incident* is defined in ITIL as follows [CW07, page 46]:

> "[An incident is a]n unplanned interruption to an IT service or reduction in the quality of an IT service. Failure of a configuration item that has not yet impacted service is also an incident, for example failure of one disk from a mirror set." [CW07, page 46]

As can be seen in the definition, issues can either be noticed by customers, or only by the IT provider's employees. A broken network connection, for example is noticed by the customer if there is no redundancy. If there is redundancy, it is only noticed by the provider, who can start fixing the issue without the customer knowing that there was an issue at all.

Incident Management as a process within the Service Operation publication is defined as follows [CW07, page 46]:

> "Incident Management is the process for dealing with all incidents; this can include failures, questions or queries reported by the users (usually via a telephone call to the Service Desk), by technical staff, or automatically detected and reported by event monitoring tools." [CW07, page 46]

The *goal* of Incident Management is to restore the functionality of malfunctioning services to an acceptable level (i.e., to limits defined by Service Level Agreements), in order to reduce the impact on affected business processes [CW07, page 46]. As can be seen in the definition, there are various ways in which incidents can be reported. On the one hand, monitoring tools can alert personnel, which leaves time to fix issues before they impact customers, given redundancy is present. On the other hand, incidents can be reported through the Service Desk by customers or the provider's technical personnel [CW07, pages 46–47].

The process flow of the Incident Management process is shown in Figure 2.11. There are several ways, in which an incident can be reported (e.g., Event Management, Web interface, phone call, or e-mail). After being reported, the incident is identified, logged, and categorized. If it is determined that a reported incident is in fact a service request, it is handed off to Request Fulfilment. If it is an incident, it is assigned a priority. If the incident is a major incident, it is handed off to a specialized procedure, which handles major incidents. If considered a regular incident, it is determined if there is need for either a functional escalation to a higher level, or need for a hierarchic escalation to a higher management level. If none of these is the case, or after the feedback from the higher levels, the steps investigation and diagnosis, as well as resolution and recovery are performed. After that, the incident is closed and the Incident Management process is terminated [CW07, page 48].

There are many aspects that speak for implementing and maintaining an organization's Incident Management process, for example, being able "to detect and resolve incidents, which results in lower downtime to the business, which in turn means higher availability of the service", which "means that the business is able to exploit the functionality of the service as designed". Other reasons are "[t]he ability to align IT activity to real-time business priorities", identifying potential service improvements, as well as being able to "identify additional service or training requirements found in IT or the business" [CW07, page 47].

Related to Incident Management is the *Problem Management* process, which is described in the next paragraph but one. While Incident Management is concerned with fixing issues as fast as possible with the focus on recovering a broken service, Problem Management has its focus on tracking down and permanently resolving an issue's underlying problems.

More information about Incident Management and Problem Management in the context of this thesis can be found in Section 4.2.4 (page 156), which uses semantic wiki functionalities in order to manage incidents and problems. In Section 5.4 (page 284), a component is presented, which implements functionalities for tracking down and suggesting possible causes of incidents and problems to IT administrators.

Request Fulfilment To avoid the overhead created by channeling routine changes and small issues through the Change Management and Incident Management processes, which are designed for handling more complex entities, the Request Fulfilment process is defined. The *objectives* of Request Fulfilment are defined as follows [CW07, page 56]:

- "To provide a channel for users to request and receive standard services for which a pre-defined approval and qualification process exists
- "To provide information to users and customers about the availability of services and the procedure for obtaining them

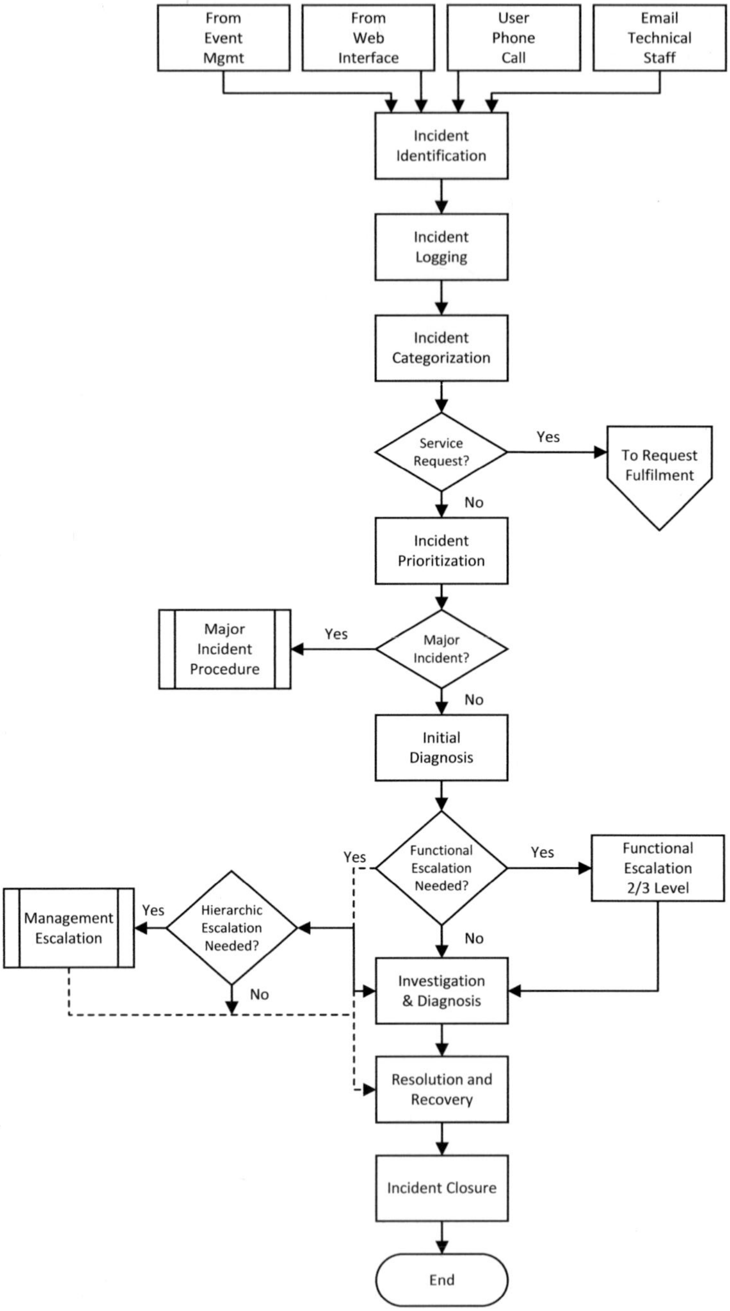

Figure 2.11.: Incident Management Process Flow (cf. [CW07, page 48])

- "To source and deliver the components of requested standard services (e.g. licences and software media)
- "To assist with general information, complaints or comments." [CW07, page 56]

Examples of requests handled by Request Fulfilment are password change requests, minor changes to the configurations of single computers (e.g., installing an instance of a software application, which was installed before on identical hardware), or the relocation of hardware items, e.g., a computer or a printer. Depending on an organization's size and requirements, requests can either be handled in parallel to incidents, or separate from incidents [CW07, pages 55–56].

In comparison to Change Management, Request Fulfilment is less formal, which means it can perform in a faster and more flexible way, provided that requests are easy and standardized. More complex changes are the domain of the Change Management process [CW07, pages 55–56]. The Change Management Process was described in Section 2.2.3 (page 34).

Problem Management A *problem*, according to the definition given in ITIL, is "the unknown cause of one or more incidents". The *Problem Management* process "is [...] responsible for managing the lifecycle of all problems" [CW07, page 58]. Problem Management's main *objectives* "are to prevent problems and resulting incidents from happening, to eliminate recurring incidents and to minimize the impact of incidents that cannot be prevented" [CW07, pages 58–59].

The main purpose of the Problem Management process includes diagnosing the cause of incidents, as well as determining the problem's resolution. Furthermore, making sure that "appropriate control procedures" are used when implementing the problem resolution, namely following Change Management and Release Management procedures is part of the Problem Management process. The documentation of problems, as well as their resolutions is another aspect of Problem Management. This helps to reduce "the number and impact of incidents over time" [CW07, page 59].

While being separate processes, Incident Management and Problem Management "are closely related and will typically use the same tools, and may use similar categorization, impact and priority coding systems", which "ensure[s] effective communication when dealing with related incidents and problems" [CW07, page 59].

The process flow of Problem Management is shown in Figure 2.12. The process starts with input from the service desk, event management, incident management, proactive problem management, or from a supplier or contractor. After that, the problem is detected, logged, categorized, and prioritized. Following that, an investigation and diagnosis is performed. Investigation and diagnosis interact with the Configuration Management System (CMS), where information about configuration items and their interrelationships is stored. The following steps are potentially repeated multiple times until the problem is resolved: After the investigation and diagnosis, it is checked whether a workaround for the problem exists. After that, a known error record is created. This step interacts with the known error database. If a change is needed, the Change Management process is invoked. If this is not the case, or after the completion of the Change Management process invocation, the problem resolution is reached. If the problem was rated a major problem, after closure, a major problem review is performed, otherwise the process ends [CW07, page 60].

When comparing the process flows of Incident Management, which is shown in Figure 2.11, and Problem Management, which is shown in Figure 2.12, it can be seen that the process flows are similar to each other. It can also be seen that Incident Management is one of the inputs of the Problem Management process. The Incident Management process flow checks, if an issue reported as an incident is in fact an incident, and not a request. In contrast to the Incident Management process flow, which does not involve changes, the Problem Management process flow can involve Change Management, if changes are necessary for accomplishing the solution of a problem.

Problem Management's *value* for an organization lies in increasing "service availability and quality" by documenting encountered problems and being able "to speed up the resolution time and identify permanent solutions, reducing the number and resolution time of incidents", which leads to "less downtime and less disruption to business critical systems". Further benefits are gained through a "[h]igher availability of IT services", "[h]igher productivity of business and IT staff", "[r]educed expenditure on workarounds or fixes that do not work", and a "[r]eduction in cost of effort in fire-fighting or resolving repeat incidents" [CW07, page 59].

As is the case with Incident Management, which was presented in the last paragraph but one, aspects of Problem Management are described in more detail in Section 4.2.4 (page 156), as well as in Section 5.4 (page 284).

Access Management Access Management is defined in [CW07, page 68] as "the process of granting authorized users the right to use a service, while preventing access to non-authorized users". The process referred to as Access Management in ITIL is also known as "Rights Management", or "Identity Management" in other publications. Access Management is "the execution of policies and actions defined in Security and Availability Management" [CW07, page 68].

The *value* for an organization provided by Access Management lies in being "able to maintain more effectively the confidentiality of [...] information" within an organization by controlling "access to services", as well as providing employees with "the right level of access to execute their jobs effectively". Furthermore, Access Management prevents unskilled users from causing widespread damage, gives "[t]he ability to audit use of services and to trace the abuse of services", and makes possible the revocation of access

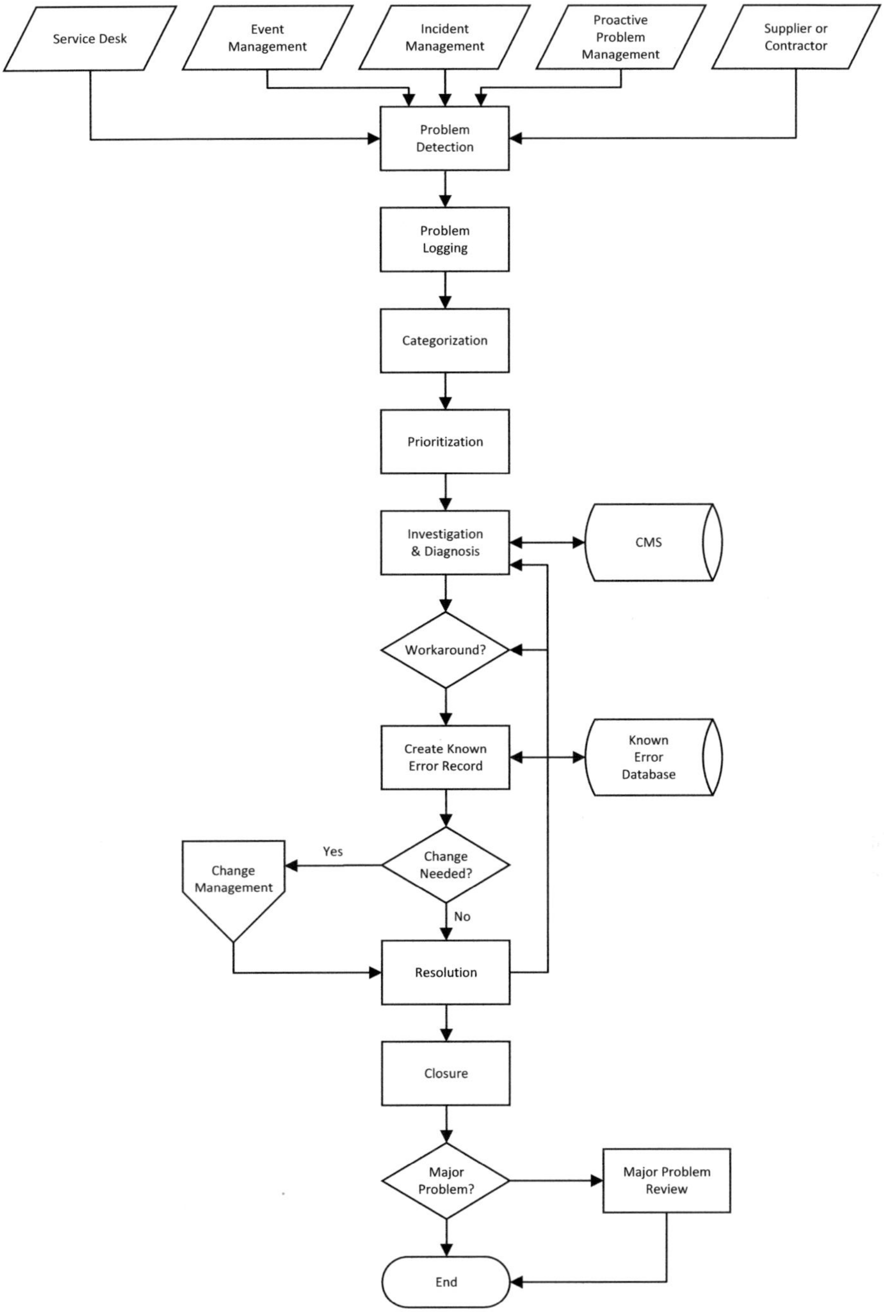

Figure 2.12.: Problem Management Process Flow (cf. [CW07, page 60])

rights. Another factor which speaks for implementing Access Management is that it is in some cases "needed for regulatory compliance (e.g. SOX, HIPAA, COBIT)" [CW07, page 68].

Functions

In addition to the processes described above, there are four functions described in the Service Operation volume [CW07], namely Service Desk, Technical Management, IT Operations Management, and Application Management, which are outlined in the following paragraphs.

Service Desk Service Desk is a function described in the Service Operation publication. It is defined as "a functional unit made up of a dedicated number of staff responsible for dealing with a variety of service events, often made via telephone calls, web interface, or automatically reported infrastructure events" [CW07, page 109].

The Service Desk function serves as "the single point of contact for IT users on a day-by-day basis" and handles "all incidents and service requests, usually using specialist software tools to log and manage all such events". Reasons for the implementation of the Service Desk function include "[i]mproved customer service, perception and satisfaction", "[i]ncreased accessibility through a single point of contact, communication and information", as well as "[b]etter-quality and faster turnaround of customer or user requests". Furthermore, it improves "teamwork and communication" and leads to an "[e]nhanced focus and a proactive approach to service provision". Moreover, "[b]etter-managed infrastructure and control", "[i]mproved usage of IT Support resources and increased productivity of business personnel", as well as "[m]ore meaningful management information for decision support" often result from the implementation of the Service Desk function [CW07, page 110].

The *goal* of the Service Desk function "is to restore the 'normal service' to the users as quickly as possible". Restoring "normal service" in this context can range from "fixing technical faults" to "fulfilling a service request or answering a query", in short: "anything that is needed to allow the users to return to working satisfactorily" [CW07, page 110].

There are different approaches with regard to the structure and location of the Service Desk. First, the *Local Service Desk* is "a desk [that] is co-located within or physically close to the user community it serves", which can lead to better communication between customers and the Service Desk, but can be expensive compared to other alternatives. The *Centralized Service Desk* merges the Service Desk of several locations into a single location, which can help in reducing costs. In the *Virtual Service Desk*, making use of the Internet, as well as using "corporate support tools", makes the Service Desk location-independent [CW07, pages 111–113].

Technical Management Technical Management, as defined in [CW07, page 121] "refers to the groups, departments or teams that provide technical expertise and overall management of the IT Infrastructure". The two roles of Technical Management are the following [CW07, page 121]:

- First, Technical Management "is the custodian of technical knowledge and expertise related to managing the IT Infrastructure", which means it makes sure "that the knowledge required to design, test, manage and improve IT services is identified, developed and refined" [CW07, page 121].
- Second, by providing "the actual resources to support the ITSM Lifecycle", Technical Management makes sure "that resources are effectively trained and deployed to design, build, transition, operate and improve the technology required to deliver and support IT services" [CW07, page 121].

Technical Management makes sure that organizations have "access to the right type and level of human resources to manage technology", which enables them to "meet business objectives". By making decisions about needed skill levels and whether to hire long-term employees or short-term contractors, Technical Management has the potential to save money. Another approach is to form a company-wide pool of specialists, who are assigned to tasks, which require their specific skill-sets [CW07, page 121].

Technical Management's *objectives* are to assist in planning, implementing, and maintaining "a stable technical infrastructure to support the organization's business processes". This is accomplished by providing a "[w]ell designed and highly resilient, cost-effective technical topology", by using "adequate technical skills to maintain the technical infrastructure in optimum condition", and by making "use of technical skills to speedily diagnose and resolve any technical failures that do occur" [CW07, pages 121–122].

IT Operations Management Reference [CW07, page 125] defines IT Operations Management "as the function responsible for the ongoing management and maintenance of an organization's IT Infrastructure to ensure delivery of the agreed level of IT services to the business". *IT Operations* are "defined as the set of activities involved in the day-to-day running of the IT Infrastructure for the purpose of delivering IT services at agreed levels to meet stated business objectives" [CW07, page 126].

IT Operations Management's *role* "is to execute the ongoing activities and procedures required to manage and maintain the IT Infrastructure so as to deliver and support IT Services at the agreed levels". This includes "Operations Control" (i.e., "Console Management", "Job Scheduling", "Backup and Restore", "Print and Output management", and "maintenance activities"), as well as "Facilities Management" (i.e., the management of the physical data center, including power and air conditioning) [CW07, page 126].

On the one hand, IT Operations Management is concerned with keeping systems running and optimally performing within the parameters defined during the Service Design and Service Transition phases. On the other hand, it in itself has to be innovative and adaptive when it comes to keeping up with "business requirements and demand" [CW07, page 126]. IT Operation Management's *objectives* comprise maintaining "the status quo to achieve stability of the organization's day-to-day processes and activities", improving "service at reduced costs, while maintaining stability", as well as the "application of operational skills to diagnose and resolve any IT operations failures that occur" [CW07, page 126].

Application Management Application Management, as a function within Service Operation, "is responsible for managing applications throughout their lifecycle". It "is performed by any department, group or team involved in managing and supporting operational applications". Furthermore, it "plays an important role in the design, testing and improvement of applications that form part of IT services". Application Management applies to applications, which were "developed in-house", as well as purchased applications [CW07, page 128].

The *role* of Application Management is, on the one hand, to make sure "that the knowledge required to design, test, manage and improve IT services is identified, developed and refined". On the other hand, it has to ensure "that resources are effectively trained and deployed to design, build, transition, operate and improve the technology required to deliver and support IT services" [CW07, pages 128–129].

Application Management's *objectives* "are to support the organization's business processes by helping to identify functional and manageability requirements for application software, and then to assist in the design and deployment of those applications and the ongoing support and improvement of those applications" by making sure that applications "are well designed, resilient and cost-effective" as well as to ensure "that the required functionality is available to achieve the required business outcome". Moreover, organizing and making use of "technical skills" are further ways through which Application Management's objectives are reached [CW07, page 129].

Further Reading

The work presented in this section is primarily based on [CW07].

Further information about Incident Management can be found in [Add07, pages 111–154] and [ZHB05, pages 143–157], while more information about Request Fulfilment can be found in [Add07, pages 103–110]. Problem Management is described in more detail in [Add07, pages 163–183] and [ZHB05, pages 159–177]. More information about Application Management can be found in [ZHB05, pages 241–249].

2.2.5. Continual Service Improvement

Continual Service Improvement (CSI) is the fifth ITIL publication [CS07]. As can be seen in Figure 2.2 (page 17), it is different from the previously described publications in so far as its objective is to facilitate improvements in all other processes.

Reference [CS07, pages 6–7] summarizes Continual Service Improvement as follows:

> "[The Continual Service Improvement] volume provides instrumental guidance in creating and maintaining value for customers through better design, introduction and operation of services. It combines principles, practices and methods from quality management, Change Management and capability improvement. Organizations learn to realize incremental and large-scale improvements in service quality, operational efficiency and business continuity. Guidance is provided for linking improvement efforts and outcomes with service strategy, design and transition. A closed-loop feedback system, based on the Plan-Do-Check-Act (PDCA) model specified in ISO/IEC 20000, is established and capable of receiving inputs for change from any planning perspective." [CS07, pages 6–7]

The *objectives* of Continual Service Improvement are to "[r]eview, analyse and make recommendations on improvement opportunities in each lifecycle phase", and to "[r]eview and analyse Service Level Achievement results". Additional objectives are to "[i]dentify and implement individual activities to improve IT service quality and improve the efficiency and effectiveness of enabling ITSM processes". Further objectives are improving "cost effectiveness of delivering IT services without sacrificing customer satisfaction", and ensuring that "applicable quality management methods are used to support continual improvement activities" [CS07, page 14].

Continual Service Improvement's *scope* lies in ensuring "[t]he overall health of ITSM as a discipline", continually aligning "the portfolio of IT services with the current and future business needs", and to ensure "[t]he maturity of the enabling IT processes for each service in a continual service lifecycle model" [CS07, page 14].

The Continual Service Improvement process is supported by the following *activities*: Checking the compliance with service levels, as well as checking if "desired results" are achieved, is done by "[r]eviewing management information and trends". The periodic conduction of "maturity assessments" helps in finding potentials for improvement, while "internal audits" verify "employee and process compliance". Further activities are "[r]eviewing existing deliverables for relevance", "[m]aking ad-hoc recommendations for approval", "[c]onducting periodic customer satisfaction surveys", and "[c]onducting external and internal service reviews to identify CSI opportunities" [CS07, page 14].

Reference [CS07, page 15] describes a six-step approach for Continual Service Improvement, which includes the following steps:

- “Embrace the vision by understanding the high-level business objectives. The vision should align the business and IT strategies.
- “Assess the current situation to obtain an accurate, unbiased snapshot of where the organization is right now. This baseline assessment is an analysis of the current position in terms of the business, organization, people, process and technology.
- “Understand and agree on the priorities for improvement based on a deeper development of the principles defined in the vision. The full vision may be years away but this step provides specific goals and a manageable timeframe.
- “Detail the CSI plan to achieve higher quality service provision by implementing ITSM processes
- “Verify that measurements and metrics are in place to ensure that milestones were achieved, processes compliance is high, and business objectives and priorities were met by the level of service.
- “Finally, the process should ensure that the momentum for quality improvement is maintained by assuring that changes become embedded in the organization.” [CS07, page 15]

Details on how these high-level goals can be achieved are shown in the description of the Continual Service Improvement processes.

Processes

Continual Service Improvement is made up of six processes, which are described in the following paragraphs. First, the 7-Step Improvement Process is presented, followed by Service Reporting and Service Measurement. After that, Return on Investment for CSI, the Business Questions for CSI, and Service Level Management are introduced.

The 7-Step Improvement Process Continual Service Improvement defines a 7-Step Improvement Process, which can be seen in Figure 2.13. The seven steps, which form a lifecycle, are described in this paragraph.

The first step is concerned with defining what *should be measured*. The Service Catalogue and Service Level Requirements are candidates from where to start. Keeping low the complexity of what should be measured is important [CS07, page 44].

The second step rules out data, which *cannot be measured*. These data items should not be included in Service Level Agreements. What can and cannot be measured is largely dependent on the available tools, which means that appropriate tools have to be purchased if the measuring requirements exceed the capabilities of the currently available tools [CS07, pages 44–45].

Gathering data is the function of the third step. Data in most cases is gathered by the use of monitoring tools. In some cases, where automatic gathering is not feasible, manual processes can be used. Monitoring in the context of Continual Service Improvement "focus[es] on the effectiveness of a service, process, tool, organization or Configuration Item (CI)", in order to identify "where improvements can be made to the existing level of service, or IT performance". Continual Service Improvement usually focuses on a limited number of monitored items in order to reduce the information load, which has to be processed. The items that are monitored in the context of Continual Service Improvement change over time, in conjunction with the areas, which are the current focus of CSI processes. There exist "three types of metrics that an organization will need to collect to support CSI activities as well as other process activities", namely technology metrics, process metrics, and service metrics [CS07, page 45].

The fourth step is concerned with the *processing* of the gathered data, i.e., converting gathered data into a format, which can be processed in the following data analysis step. Points that have to be addressed in the data processing step are at which frequency (i.e., hourly, daily, weekly, or monthly) data has to be processed, what are the desired output formats, which tools are used for data processing, and how the accuracy of data is evaluated [CS07, pages 48–49].

The *analysis* of data is the focus of the fifth step. Reference [CS07, page 50] describes the data analysis step as follows:

> "Data analysis transforms the information into knowledge of the events that are affecting the organization. More skill and experience is required to perform data analysis than data gathering and processing. Verification against goals and objectives is expected during this activity. This verification validates that objectives are being supported and value is being added. It is not sufficient to simply produce graphs of various types but to document the observations and conclusions." [CS07, page 50]

The analysis of data includes checking for "clear trends", checking whether they are positive or negative, and determining whether changes or "corrective actions" are required. When analyzing data, it has to be put into the right context, and it has to be made clear what the meaning of the data is. Only properly analyzed data can act as the foundation for making "strategic, tactical and operational decisions about whether there is a need for service improvement" [CS07, page 51].

In the sixth step, data is *presented and used*. The key aspect of this step is to have data presented in the right format and abstraction to the respective audience. Audiences are divided into three groups: the business, senior (IT) management, and internal IT, each with their own requirements for the presentation of information [CS07, pages 52–53].

The seventh step is concerned with the *implementation of corrective action*. In this step, building on the results obtained in the previous six steps, issues are identified, and solutions are presented. Because not all solutions can be implemented, prioritization has to be made [CS07, pages 54–55].

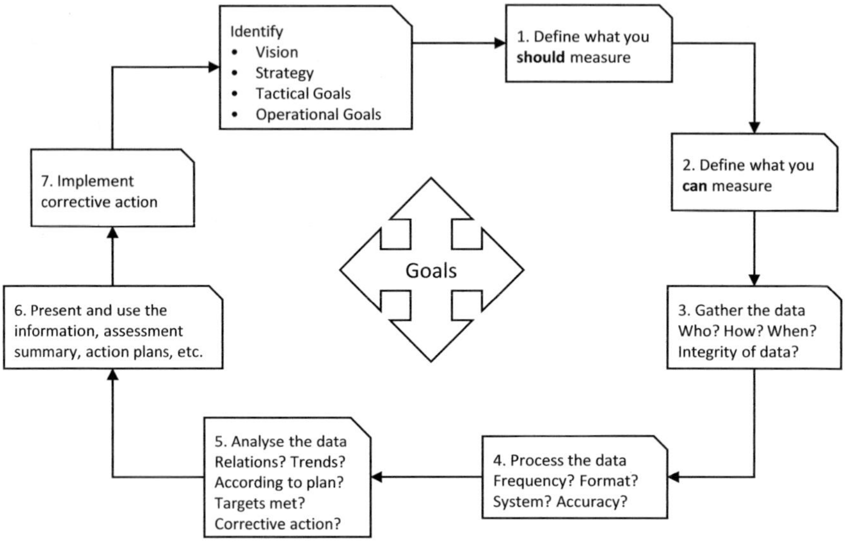

Figure 2.13.: 7-Step Improvement Process (cf. [CS07, page 43])

Service Reporting Service Reporting's goal is to prepare and deliver reports in a format suitable for a particular audience. While there is a multitude of data items gathered within IT, only a small amount of that data is of interest on the varying levels of the organization. For example, the business part of an organization is only interested in future threats and their mitigations rather than a list of past events [CS07, page 65].

According to [CS07, page 65], "IT needs to build an actionable approach to reporting. [I].e. this is what happened, this is what we did, this is how we will ensure it doesn't impact you again, and this is how we are working to improve the delivery of IT services generally" [CS07, page 65].

Service Measurement The dependence of organizations on IT services has led to a change about which parts of IT to measure, in order to get qualified results. While it was sufficient in the past "to measure and report against the performance of an individual component such as a server or application", this is no longer the case. In today's IT landscape, measuring and reporting is made "against an end-to-end service" [CS07, page 66].

Parameters, which are measured, are the availability, reliability, and performance of services. Figure 2.14 shows the measurement of availability on different levels by example of an e-mail service. While the top level is the one that users perceive (i.e., e-mail is working or not working), the underlying levels become more and more technical. They include different mail services on the service level, a logical view on the components of the mail server infrastructure, and the view on the physical infrastructure on the component level at the bottom [CS07, page 67].

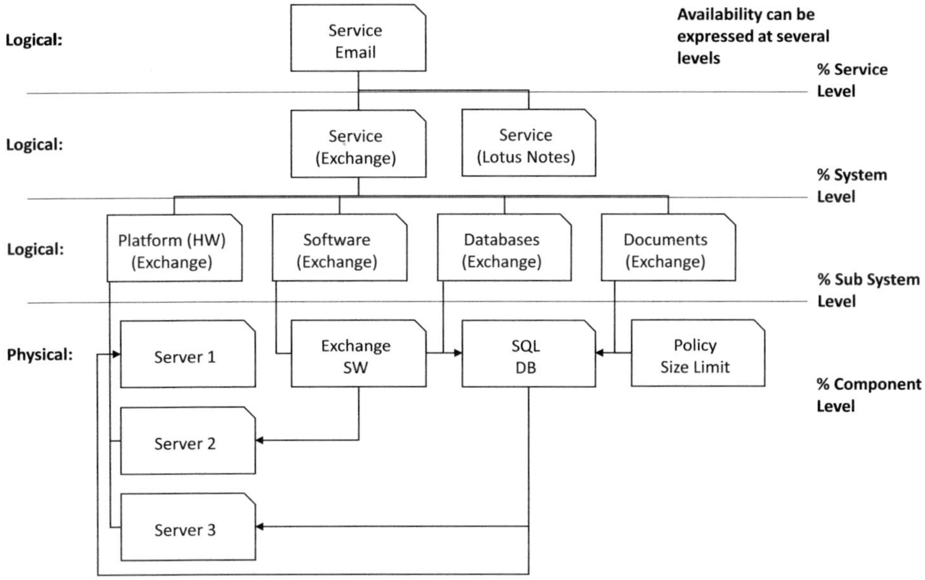

Figure 2.14.: Availability Reporting (cf. [CS07, page 67])

Return on Investment for CSI Before investing into processes and measures, which help to improve Continual Service Improvement, the benefits for the organization have to be quantified. This requires the knowledge of several parameters that determine from which measures the organization benefits most. Parameters include the costs associated with service downtimes and the costs of incidents and their escalation [CS07, page 84].

In order to calculate the Return on Investment for Continual Service Improvement measures, the cost of downtimes of services can be calculated based on the number of users of the service and the infrastructure, which provides the service. Metrics can be, for example, downtime costs, costs for having to redo lost work due to an IT error, and the costs of duplicate work due to insufficient IT systems [CS07, page 84].

Business Questions for CSI In order to derive gains from Continual Service Improvement, the business side of an organization has to be involved in order to determine the maximum positive effect for the organization [CS07, page 89]. Questions which help in determining the business side's requirements for CSI are [CS07, page 89]:

- "Where are we now?"
- "What do we want?"
- "What do we actually need?"
- "What can we afford?"
- "What will we get?"
- "What did we get?" [CS07, page 89]

The question "Where are we now?" helps in determining a baseline for planned improvements. Additionally, the question "What do we want?" is used to collect items for a wish list, which does not yet take into account feasibility and cost aspects (e.g., 100 percent uptime, or no limits with respect to capacity). Furthermore, the reasons for the articulated needs should be identified. In the next step, helped by the question "What do we actually need?", the requirements are reviewed and fine-tuned. The question "What can we afford?" checks if the articulated improvements are within the budget. By asking "What will we get?", business and IT can come to a clear understanding of the requirements and the improvement project's desired output. Finally, by asking "What did we get?", it is determined if the improvements had the desired effects and which further improvements might be needed [CS07, pages 89–91].

Service Level Management Improving the Service Level Management process that is part of Service Design, and which was described in Section 2.2.2 (page 27), is the task of the Service Level Management process within Continual Service Improvement. Service Level Management, as described in [CS07, page 91], can be summarized as follows:

> "Service Level Management can be described in two words: building relationships. That is building relations with IT customers, building relationships between functional groups within IT, and building relationships with the vendor community who provide services to IT. Service Level Management is so much more than simply a SLA." [CS07, page 91]

Based on this characterization of Service Level Management, there is a number of potential points of improvement within Continual Service Improvement. This is even the case if there do not exist formal SLAs, but rather informal SLAs that base customer expectations on the service quality experienced in the past [CS07, pages 91–92].

Further Reading

Reference [CS07], on which this subsection is based, describes how to implement Continual Service Improvement. References [Nis08, pages 103–112] and [Add07, pages 275–296] give additional insights into the topic.

2.3. Ontologies

The data model developed as the foundation of this thesis is an ontology. This section provides an overview of the most prominent definitions and standards, while the ontology developed as the data model of the ITSM Wiki, together with formal methods for its development, are discussed in detail in Section 4.3 (page 161).

Historically, the word *ontology* has its origins in philosophy, and there deals "with the study of being or existence" [Gru09]. In computer science, it "is a technical term denoting an artifact that is *designed* for a purpose, which is to enable the modeling of knowledge about *some* domain, real or imagined" [Gru09, emphasis in original].

There are multiple definitions of the term ontology in the context of computer science, which emphasize different aspects and in most parts complement each other. This section provides an overview of the most prominent ones in chronological order.

According to Gruber's widely known definition formulated in 1993 [Gru93] and published in an updated paper in 1995 [Gru95],

> "[a]n ontology is an explicit specification of a conceptualization." [Gru93]

A later work from 1998 by Guarino [Gua98] defines an ontology as

> "a logical theory accounting for the *intended meaning* of a formal vocabulary, i.e. its *ontological commitment* to a particular *conceptualization* of the world. The intended models of a logical language using such a vocabulary are constrained by its ontological commitment. An ontology indirectly reflects this commitment (and the underlying conceptualization) by approximating these intended models." [Gua98, emphasis in original]

Another work, also from 1998, by Studer, Benjamins, and Fensel [SBF98] states that an ontology is

> "*a formal, explicit specification of a shared conceptualisation*" [SBF98, emphasis in original]

By giving further explanations of the terms used in the definition given in [SBF98], a better understanding is achieved:

- *Conceptualisation:* "A 'conceptualisation' refers to an abstract model of some phenomenon in the world by having identified the relevant concepts of that phenomenon." [SBF98]
- *Explicit:* "'Explicit' means that the type of concepts used, and the constraints on their use are explicitly defined. For example, in medical domains, the concepts are diseases and symptoms, the relations between them are causal and a constraint is that a disease cannot cause itself." [SBF98]
- *Formal:* "'Formal' refers to the fact that the ontology should be machine readable, which excludes natural language." [SBF98]
- *Shared:* "'Shared' reflects the notion that an ontology captures consensual knowledge, that is, it is not private to some individual, but accepted by a group." [SBF98]

A later definition by Gruber [Gru09] defines an ontology as follows:

> "In the context of computer and information sciences, an ontology *defines a set of representational primitives with which to model a domain of knowledge or discourse.*" [Gru09, emphasis mine]

Continuing in his definition, Gruber defines classes, attributes and relations, and differentiates between ontologies and databases [Gru09]:

> "The representational primitives are typically classes (or sets), attributes (or properties), and relationships (or relations among class members). The definitions of the representational primitives include information about their meaning and constraints on their logically consistent application. In the context of database systems, ontology can be viewed as a level of abstraction of data models, analogous to hierarchical and relational models, but intended for modeling knowledge about individuals, their attributes, and their relationships to other individuals. Ontologies are typically specified in languages that allow abstraction away from data structures and implementation strategies; in practice, the languages of ontologies are closer in expressive power to first-order logic than languages used to model databases. For this reason, ontologies are said to be at the 'semantic' level, whereas database schemata are models of data at the 'logical' or 'physical' level. Due to their independence from lower level data models, ontologies are used for integrating heterogeneous databases, enabling interoperability among disparate systems, and specifying interfaces to independent, knowledge-based services. In the technology stack of the Semantic Web standards, ontologies are called out as an explicit layer. There are now standard languages and a variety of commercial and open source tools for creating and working with ontologies." [Gru09]

In this thesis, with regard to the description of ontologies, the following terms are used:

- *Classes:* also known as *concepts*, or in the context of Semantic MediaWiki, *categories*.
- *Object properties:* also known as *relations*.
- *Data properties:* also known as *attributes*.
- *Individuals:* also known as *instances*, or in the context of Semantic MediaWiki, *articles*, or *pages*.

More information about ontologies in general and their applications can be found in [SS03] and [SS09]. An in-depth analysis of what constitutes an ontology can be found in [GOS09]. Reference [Hor11] describes how to model ontologies with the Protégé ontology editor.

The following section first gives an introduction into the Semantic Web, which makes use of ontologies in order to explicitly state information, and then discusses the Semantic Web standards relevant for this thesis. Its purpose is not to provide a comprehensive study of Semantic Web topics, but rather to provide a basic background information necessary for understanding the thesis. In addition to a short introduction, links for further reading are given, which can be consulted if additional and more in-depth information is required by the reader.

2.4. Semantic Web

The World Wide Web is a set of protocols and implementations, which enable users to view rich-media content and allows browsing between different pages via the use of hyperlinks. The World Wide Web was invented at the European Organization for Nuclear Research (CERN)[1] by Tim Berners-Lee and presented to the public in the early 1990s [Con00]. Since then, it has grown in the most significant way into the ubiquitous network it is today.

When taking a closer look at the World Wide Web and its protocols, it can be seen that it is designed for presenting content to, and to allow the navigation by human users. Computer programs, however, have difficulties understanding and processing the text on Web pages and the meaning of hyperlinks between Web pages. In order to solve these shortcomings, the Semantic Web vision was presented in [BHL01] and revisited later in [SBH06].

The Semantic Web's goal is to make information on the World Wide Web explicit and understandable to computers, which allows automatic processing. There exist several languages, which provide different levels of expressiveness, which allow the explicit statement of information. These languages are presented in the following subsections.

[1] `http://www.cern.ch/`

Figure 2.15 shows the Semantic Web Layer Cake, a model of the hierarchy of the languages, which make up the World Wide Web Consortium's (W3C)[2] ongoing Semantic Web effort. While the layer cake is not intended as an implementation guideline, which has to be followed exactly when implementing applications for the Semantic Web, and while it is not an accurate model with regard to rules [HPPSH05], it helps to understand the relations between different Semantic Web languages.

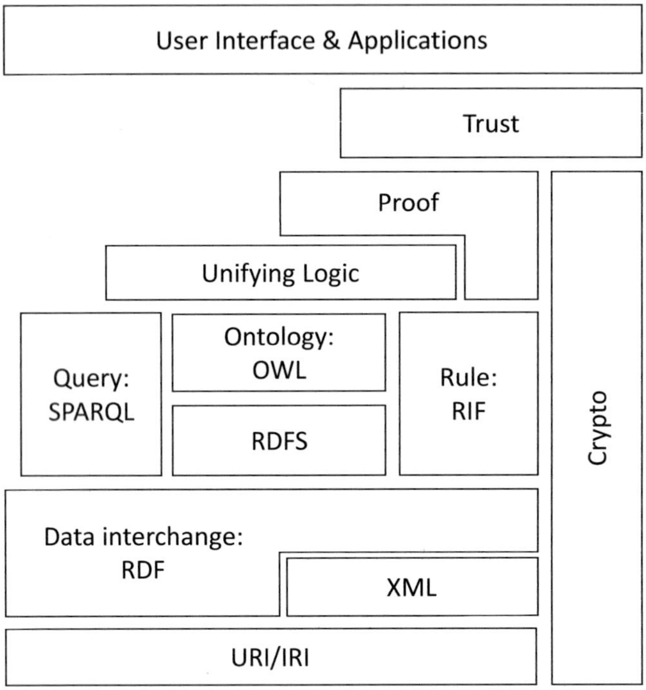

Figure 2.15.: Semantic Web Layer Cake (cf. [W3C07])

More information about the Semantic Web efforts and standards by the World Wide Web Consortium (W3C) can be found in [W3C10b]. In [AvH04] and [HKRS08], a comprehensive introduction into Semantic Web technologies and the underlying principles is given, while [AH08] focuses on giving practical guidelines for users of Semantic Web technologies. The next subsections present three of the Semantic Web languages (namely RDF, RDFS, and OWL), which are relevant in the context of this thesis.

[2] `http://www.w3.org/`

2.4.1. Resource Description Framework (RDF)

The Resource Description Framework (RDF) is a W3C Recommendation[3], which provides a mechanism for stating explicit facts in the Semantic Web. Because of the distributed and global nature of the Semantic Web, various design criteria had to be considered when designing RDF—the fact that there is no single truth on the Web, as well as scalability issues. Concerning the single truth, because of the Web's global reach and numerous participants, there are always disputes about facts, which have to be able to be represented in RDF. Furthermore, the Semantic Web consists of a large number of nodes, in contrast to a single database that contains all information. Because of this, there have to be mechanisms for aggregating facts from different sources, which can be distributed across multiple servers around the world [AH08, pages 31–36].

Triples

In RDF, statements about facts are represented as triples. The first element of the triple is the *subject*, which "is the thing that a statement is about". The second element, the *predicate* describes the kind of relationship to the third element, the *object* [AH08, page 35].

Table 2.1 shows an example of RDF triples. There are three computers, with different operating systems, which is expressed in the first three lines. Lines four and five state that the company Microsoft is the manufacturer of the operating systems Windows 7 and Windows XP. Finally, line six states that Microsoft is located in Redmond.

Subject	**Predicate**	**Object**
Computer A	Operating System	Windows 7
Computer B	Operating System	Windows XP
Computer C	Operating System	Linux
Windows 7	Manufacturer	Microsoft
Windows XP	Manufacturer	Microsoft
Microsoft	Location	Redmond

Table 2.1.: RDF Triples about Computers

A second data source, located on another server, contains geographical information, which are in part shown in Table 2.2.

[3]Although not officially named standards, W3C Recommendations are standards for the Web [W3C05]. Other W3C Recommendations are the well-known markup languages HTML and XML. A list of W3C Recommendations can be found at `http://www.w3.org/TR/`.

The facts contained in this table give information about the city of Redmond, its relation towards the city of Seattle and in which state the two cities are located. Finally, it is said that the state of Washington is located in the USA.

Subject	Predicate	Object
Redmond	Near	Seattle
Seattle	PartOf	Washington
Redmond	PartOf	Washington
Washington	PartOf	USA

Table 2.2.: RDF Triples about Geographics

RDF Graphs

RDF triples can be represented as graphs. While in general the visualization can be helpful for humans to grasp the information shown in a graph, in most cases it is practical only for a relatively low number of items. A graphical representation of all items of a larger data set in a single graph is in most cases not possible due to space constraints and the tendency of graphs to become cluttered.

URIs

In order to generate a more extensive graph from multiple smaller graphs, graphs can be merged. A prerequisite for merging graphs is the existence of a mechanism for expressing that two entities are, in fact, the same. This is accomplished by using Uniform Resource Identifiers (URIs). URIs identify entities unambiguously, which means that when two entities have the same URI, they are, in fact, the same [AH08, pages 37–40].

In Table 2.2, there could be confusion, whether the state of Washington, or the capital Washington D.C., or even George Washington is referred to. By using URIs, these ambiguities are cleared. Blank nodes are used when the identity of an entity is not known, but there are known facts about the entity [AH08, pages 54–55].

Reification

Reification is the process of making statements about other statements, e.g., formulating the expression *the Microsoft license agreement states that Windows XP is manufactured by Microsoft*, or the expression that *it is said on my map of the USA that Redmond is located near Seattle*. RDF supports reification, which means that statements about statements can be expressed in RDF [AH08, pages 49–51].

Notations

There are different notations for serializing RDF as text, namely N-Triples, N3, as well as RDF/XML. While N-Triples is the most basic notation, N3 allows for a more compact representation in books and better readability by humans. When representing RDF information for the use on the Web, RDF/XML is most often used [AH08, pages 51–54].

RDF/XML is a serialization of RDF data in the XML format, which is widely used on the Web. RDF/XML serialization is described in detail in [Bec04].

Triple Store

A triple store, or RDF store "is a database that is tuned for storing and retrieving data in the form of triples. In addition to the familiar functions of any database, an RDF store has the additional ability to merge information from multiple data sources, as defined by the RDF standard" [AH08, pages 59–60].

Examples of triple stores are Sesame[4] [BKvH02], Jena[5] [WSKR03], 3store[6] [HG03], and RDFBroker[7] [SK06]. Further information about triple stores can be found in [HBS09].

Query Engines

RDF query engines are used to access the information in a triple store, similar to the SQL engines, which allow access to data stored in database systems. RDF stores are usually accessed by query languages [AH08, pages 66–73].

There exist several query languages for RDF— [HBEV04] provides an overview and compares the features of the languages. The SPARQL[8] language, which is described in detail in [PS08], has emerged as the W3C Recommendation.

Architecture

Figure 2.16 shows a typical Semantic Web architecture consisting of a triple store, which contains the data. Data can be imported into the triple store by converting existing data. Likewise, data can be exported, i.e., serialized, from the store into RDF files. The inference and query engine implements an interface, via which the triple store is

[4] `http://www.openrdf.org/`
[5] `http://jena.sourceforge.net/`
[6] `http://sourceforge.net/projects/threestore/`
[7] `http://rdfbroker.opendfki.de/`
[8] **S**PARQL **P**rotocol **a**nd **R**DF **Q**uery **L**anguage

accessed. By using inferencing, queries also return results, which are not contained in the store explicitly, but which are generated from other explicit statements in the store [AH08, pages 79–90].

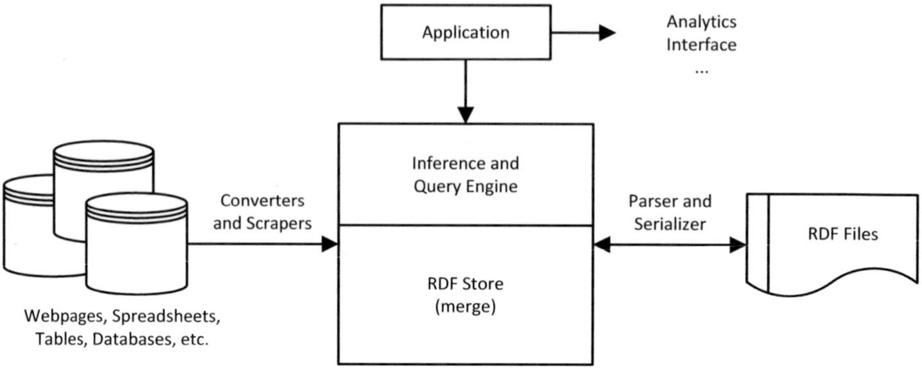

Figure 2.16.: Semantic Web Architecture (cf. [AH08, page 84])

More information about RDF can be found in the following works: In [Wei09], an overview is given. The RDF Primer [MM04] gives an introduction into RDF and provides examples on its use. In [Hay04], RDF's semantics and inference rules are specified, while [KC04] defines RDF's abstract syntax and [Bec04] specifies how to serialize RDF in XML. In [AH08], RDF is described, among other Semantic Web technologies, and examples of its use are given. Another introduction can be found in [DOS03].

2.4.2. RDF Schema (RDFS)

While the expressive power of RDF allows making statements about instances and their types and allows defining relations between instances, it is not possible to make statements about class hierarchies or about the relations between instances themselves. RDF Schema (RDFS) is the language, which addresses these shortcomings and "defines classes and properties that may be used to describe classes, properties and other resources" [BG10].

The most important constructs defined by RDFS are [AH08, pages 91–102]:

- `rdfs:Class`
- `rdfs:subClassOf`
- `rdfs:subPropertyOf`
- `rdfs:domain`
- `rdfs:range`

Classes are defined by stating that an entity is of type `rdfs:Class` [AH08, page 93]. An example[9], which defines that `Computer` and `NotebookComputer` are classes, is shown in Listing 2.1.

Listing 2.1: RDFS Class Definition

```
Computer rdf:type rdfs:Class
NotebookComputer rdf:type rdfs:Class
```

Class hierarchies are defined by using the `rdfs:subClassOf` construct. This allows to define complex hierarchies where the membership in a superclass can be inferred from an instance's membership in a specific class [AH08, pages 94–95]. For example, a notebook computer will be considered a computer, even if it is not directly a member of the class `Computer`, as long as the class `NotebookComputer` is defined as a subclass of `Computer`. The relationship between `Computer` and `NotebookComputer`, as well as the fact that `ComputerA` is a notebook computer is defined as shown in Listing 2.2.

Listing 2.2: RDFS Class Hierarchy

```
NotebookComputer rdfs:subClassOf Computer
ComputerA rdf:type NotebookComputer
```

By using inferencing, i.e., a mechanism for deriving facts that are implicitly stated from explicitly stated ones, it can be determined that `ComputerA` is, in fact, a computer, although it is only explicitly stated that it is a notebook computer [AH08, page 95].

Hierarchies between properties are defined by using the `rdfs:subPropertyOf` construct, which can be used to state that one property is more specific than another [AH08, pages 95–96]. Furthermore, a property's domain and range can be defined by using `rdfs:domain` and `rdfs:range` [AH08, pages 98–99].

Examples of the use of RDF Schema as well as more constructs defined in RDFS can be found in [MM04] and [AH08]. A general overview is given in [Chr09]. For a more formal description, please refer to the work presented in [BG10].

2.4.3. Web Ontology Language (OWL)

The Web Ontology Language (OWL) extends the expressiveness for encoding machine interpretable content provided by RDF and RDF Schema "by providing additional vocabulary along with a formal semantics" [MvHe04].

[9] The following examples are adaptions of the ones presented in [AH08, pages 93–95].

OWL is published as a W3C Recommendation. In addition to the older OWL standard, a newer OWL 2 standard, which is compatible to OWL, but adds additional features, is available. Because the work presented in this thesis builds on a platform, which does not yet support OWL 2 language features, this section limits itself to features of the original OWL language, which was specified in 2004 [MvHe04].

Compared to RDF and RDFS, "OWL adds more vocabulary for describing properties and classes: among others, relations between classes (e.g. disjointness), cardinality (e.g. 'exactly one'), equality, richer typing of properties, characteristics of properties (e.g. symmetry), and enumerated classes" [MvHe04].

OWL is subdivided into three sublanguages (OWL Lite, OWL DL[10], and OWL Full), which differ in their expressiveness and extend each other. The decision to define three languages was made in order to address the different needs of users.

The intended use scenarios for the different sublanguages are summarized as follows [MvHe04]:

- "*OWL Lite* supports those users primarily needing a classification hierarchy and simple constraints. For example, while it supports cardinality constraints, it only permits cardinality values of 0 or 1. It should be simpler to provide tool support for OWL Lite than its more expressive relatives, and OWL Lite provides a quick migration path for thesauri and other taxonomies. OWL Lite also has a lower formal complexity than OWL DL" [MvHe04, emphasis in original].
- "*OWL DL* supports those users who want the maximum expressiveness while retaining computational completeness (all conclusions are guaranteed to be computable) and decidability (all computations will finish in finite time). OWL DL includes all OWL language constructs, but they can be used only under certain restrictions (for example, while a class may be a subclass of many classes, a class cannot be an instance of another class). OWL DL is so named due to its correspondence with *description logics*, a field of research that has studied the logics that form the formal foundation of OWL." [MvHe04, emphasis in original]
- "*OWL Full* is meant for users who want maximum expressiveness and the syntactic freedom of RDF with no computational guarantees. For example, in OWL Full a class can be treated simultaneously as a collection of individuals and as an individual in its own right. OWL Full allows an ontology to augment the meaning of the pre-defined (RDF or OWL) vocabulary. It is unlikely that any reasoning software will be able to support complete reasoning for every feature of OWL Full." [MvHe04, emphasis in original]

The relationships between ontologies specified in OWL Lite, OWL DL, and OWL Full are [MvHe04]:

[10] **D**escription **L**ogics

- "Every legal OWL Lite ontology is a legal OWL DL ontology.
- "Every legal OWL DL ontology is a legal OWL Full ontology.
- "Every valid OWL Lite conclusion is a valid OWL DL conclusion.
- "Every valid OWL DL conclusion is a valid OWL Full conclusion." [MvHe04]

The price one pays for the additional expressiveness of OWL Full in contrast to OWL DL, as well as between OWL DL and OWL Lite is the less powerful support for automatic reasoning. Because there are no tools, which fully cover reasoning in OWL Full, the developer of an ontology has to carefully consider which one of the OWL sublanguages makes the best sense in the intended scenario. While every valid OWL document is a valid RDF document, the opposite is only true in the case that every valid RDF document is a valid OWL Full document [MvHe04].

There are several tools, which allow to deal with certain aspects of OWL ontologies. Examples of integrated ontology engineering environments are the freely available Protégé[11] [RNM07] and the NeOn Toolkit[12] [HLS$^+$08]. An analysis of the state of ontology engineering environments can be found in [MK09].

An introduction into ontologies in general, as well as OWL in particular, is given in [HKRS08] and [AH08]. Information about the OWL language, as well as its successor, the OWL 2 language can be found on the Web site of the World Wide Web Consortium (W3C) [W3C10a].

In [MvHe04], an overview of the OWL language is given, while an overview of the documents, which describe OWL 2, can be found at [W3C09]. In [SWM04], the OWL language is described and examples, as well as a glossary for the terms used in the context of OWL, are given. Reference [Hef04] presents OWL use cases. While [DS04] provides an informal description of OWL's modeling primitives, [PSHH04] gives the formal definition.

While this section provided the reader with the necessary basics about ontologies and Semantic Web standards, in Section 4.3 (page 161), the ontology, which forms the data model used in this thesis, is described in detail. The following Section 2.5 (page 70) introduces wikis, followed by semantic wikis, which have ontologies as the underlying data model, in Section 2.6 (page 77).

[11] `http://protege.stanford.edu/`
[12] `http://neon-toolkit.org/`

2.5. Wikis

Wikis are a special form of Web pages, which facilitate collaboration. This section gives an introduction into wikis and describes key aspects and characteristics of wikis. While this section serves as a basic introduction into wikis and their underlying principles, Section 4.1.1 (page 117) returns to the subject with a focus on selecting the most suitable wiki—by comparing five popular wiki engines—as the platform for the work presented in this thesis. This section is dedicated to describing non-semantic wikis. Semantic wikis are discussed in the following Section 2.6 (page 77).

The first wiki was introduced by Ward Cunningham in 1995 for discussing and documenting Design Patterns in the Portland Pattern Repository[13]. The original characterization of a wiki, according to Cunningham, is "[t]he simplest online database that could possibly work" [Cun02]. A more verbose characterization is given in the same work. It characterizes a wiki as [Cun02]

> "a piece of server software that allows users to freely create and edit Web page content using any Web browser. Wiki supports hyperlinks and has a simple text syntax for creating new pages and crosslinks between internal pages on the fly.
>
> "Wiki is unusual among group communication mechanisms in that it allows the organization of contributions to be edited in addition to the content itself.
>
> "Like many simple concepts, 'open editing' has some profound and subtle effects on Wiki usage. Allowing everyday users to create and edit any page in a Web site is exciting in that it encourages democratic use of the Web and promotes content composition by nontechnical users." [Cun02]

As can be seen in the quote, there are three kinds of aspects when looking at wikis. The aspects are:

- *Technical aspects*: Wikis are a Web-based technology, which uses a server running an environment for delivering dynamic Web pages and a Web browser for accessing content.
- *Editing of structure*: Normal content management systems impose a fixed structure on users, which cannot be changed dynamically. Within wikis, on the other hand, structure is created by users while entering content. Wiki words are transformed into links for navigating by clicking on highlighted key words.

[13] `http://c2.com/cgi/wiki?WelcomeVisitors`

- *Social aspects*: While traditional Web pages work in a one-to-many way (i.e., the creator of a Web page or a team of Web authors creates content, which is consumed by many), wikis allow modifications by everyone (restrictions may apply for certain pages in some cases).

While the technological aspects of wikis are not groundbreaking, the social implications are far more interesting. While usually, there is a general assumption that content needs protection from changes, the widespread success of wikis contradicts this mindset. In [Cun09b], multiple reasons for why wikis do, in fact, work can be found. Ward Cunningham's reasoning is that wikis, as a pool of a collective collection of ideas, evolve over time and with changing users, who contribute as volunteers. In [Cun09b], the idea is expressed as follows:

> "A wiki is a body of ideas that a community is willing to know and maintain. That community has every right to be cautiously selective in what it will groom. This particular wiki has been blessed with thoughtful, diligent, diverse and open-minded volunteers, who have invested years learning what works here and what doesn't. When volunteers tire and depart, others take their place. I remain amazed that this works without mechanically enforced authority." [Cun09b]

Another reason that wikis work is that wikis are essentially self-policing because it is made easy to delete unwanted content. This point is described in [Cun09b] as follows:

> "Any information can be altered or deleted by anyone. Wiki pages represent consensus because it's much easier to [delete insults] and remove [wiki spam] than indulge them. What remains generates new ideas by the interactive integration of multiple points of view." [Cun09b]

2.5.1. Principles

The social aspects of wikis are influenced by the Open Source[14] movement. Reference [SEG+09] lists the following wiki principles:

- *Everybody is allowed to edit wiki pages*: Wiki pages are not protected from modification. In fact, changing pages is made easy for users.
- *Ease of use*: Wikis are designed in a way, which allows average computer users with knowledge in basic word processing, to create pages and change the content of existing pages.
- *Linkable content*: Content in wikis can be put in relation to each other by linking from one page to another.

[14] `http://www.opensource.org/docs/osd/`

- *Versioning*: Content in a wiki is never deleted, which enables authors to be bold when it comes to making editing decisions, because the wiki page before the change can always be returned to. Another point for retaining all versions of a page is to protect a wiki from badly behaving users.
- *Support for all media*: Almost all kinds of content can be added to wikis, e.g., text, images, audio, and video [SEG$^+$09].

2.5.2. Syntax

Wikis are in most cases edited by using a special syntax that abstracts from the more complicated HTML[15] syntax, which is the markup language interpreted by Web browsers. While most wikis aim at providing an intuitive, easy to learn and efficient way to format and structure wiki pages, different wiki implementations have different syntax. In addition to the text-based wiki syntax, some wikis provide a WYSIWYG[16], or near-WYSIWYG interface, which allows to edit wiki pages in a way that is more familiar to users of mainstream office suites. In [SSB07], a common wiki syntax named *WikiCreole* is described, which aims at providing an interchange syntax for transferring text from one wiki implementation to another. Table 2.3 compares the syntax of WikiCreole[17] with that of MediaWiki, a widely used wiki, which is the technical platform behind Wikipedia. It can be seen that both use simple characters and strings for expressing formatting, but differ in their syntax.

Although different wiki implementations differ in their detailed architecture, they follow a common pattern. Figure 2.17 shows a high-level generalized architecture of a wiki. The content of the wiki is stored in a way, which allows to track changes, compare the differences between pages, and to revert changes. There are wiki implementations, which use databases (e.g., MySQL[18], or PostgreSQL[19]) to store their content, while others use a simpler file system-based approach. The wiki software is a component, which implements the concrete functionality of the respective wiki. It is here where the wiki pages are transformed from the raw data, which are read from the storage, into the HTML format, which can be interpreted by Web browsers. When a user loads a wiki page, at first, it is like a regular Web page, but with the exception that a button for editing the page can be found on the Web page. When the button is pressed, the content of the page is displayed in wikitext [Med10e], which can be edited from within the browser. Some wikis offer features, which support authors when editing pages, e.g., by checking for correct syntax. When saving the page, the changed wikitext is sent back to the wiki software running on the Web server and is being processed.

[15] `http://www.w3.org/html/`
[16] **W**hat **Y**ou **S**ee **I**s **W**hat **Y**ou **G**et
[17] `http://www.wikicreole.org/`
[18] `http://www.mysql.com/`
[19] `http://www.postgresql.org/`

<table>
<tr><th>Format</th><th>WikiCreole Syntax</th><th>MediaWiki Syntax</th></tr>
<tr><td>italics</td><td>//italics//</td><td>''italics''</td></tr>
<tr><td>bold</td><td>**bold**</td><td>'''bold'''</td></tr>
<tr><td>Itemization</td><td>* First item
* Second item
** Subitem</td><td>* First item
* Second item
** Subitem</td></tr>
<tr><td>Numbered list</td><td># First item
Second item
Subitem</td><td># First item
Second item
Subitem</td></tr>
<tr><td>Link to wiki page</td><td>[[Wiki_page]]</td><td>[[Wiki_page]]</td></tr>
<tr><td>Link to URL</td><td>[[URL|link_name]]</td><td>[URL link_name]</td></tr>
<tr><td>Image</td><td>{{file_name|title}}</td><td>[[File:file_name|title]]</td></tr>
<tr><td>Headings</td><td>== large heading
=== medium heading
==== small heading</td><td>= large heading =
== medium heading ==
=== small heading ===</td></tr>
<tr><td>Table</td><td>|=|=table|=header|
|a|table|row|
|b|table|row|</td><td>{|
!table
!header
|-
|table
|row
|-
|table
|row
|}</td></tr>
</table>

Table 2.3.: Wiki Syntax (adapted from [SSB07, Med10a, Med10b, Med10c, Med10d])

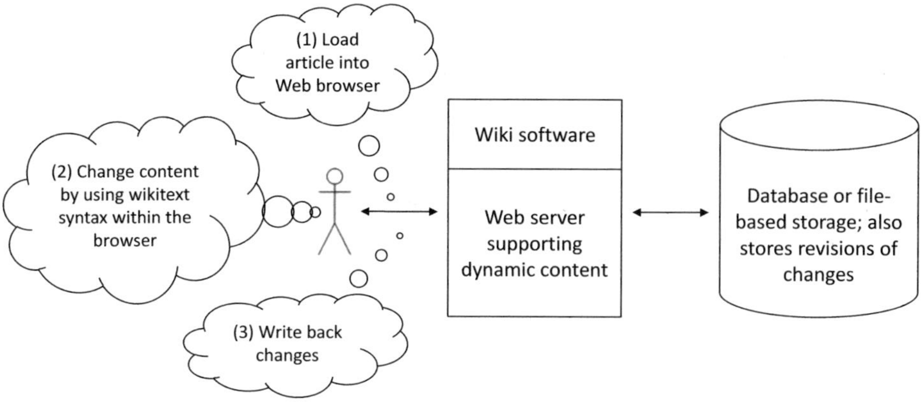

Figure 2.17.: Generalized Wiki Architecture

2.5.3. Use Cases

Wikis, on the one hand, as a technical platform, and, on the other hand, as an idea on how to work collaboratively, have found many uses in today's global Internet and within corporate intranets. Wikis are used for collective information gathering within communities (e.g., software developers, movie fans, or people sharing cooking recipes), encyclopedias (e.g., Wikipedia), and for the use in organizations (so-called Enterprise Wikis).

Communities

The original use case for wikis was to allow a community of software engineers to document common knowledge collaboratively and without the need to create and maintain complex rights management systems and structures. Ward Cunningham's original wiki was used for providing a collaborative environment for programmers and designers within the Design Patterns community [EGHW07].

In today's Internet (2014), the use of wikis is a widespread phenomenon. There are wikis for almost every area of interest, e.g., computer-related communities (e.g., Linux, and Linux distributions), cooking, law, regional communities, and many more. While wikis still have a dominant user base in computer-related and technical communities (e.g., programming, and operating systems), they are used more and more in non-technical ones.

Encyclopedias

Wikipedia[20] is a wiki-based encyclopedia, which is open to being edited over the Internet by everybody. Launched in the beginning of 2001 by Jimmy Wales and Larry Sanger, it was first thought of as an addition to Nupedia, an expert-written encyclopedia, also founded by, among others, Jimmy Wales. While Nupedia was relatively slow in growing, Wikipedia's size exceeded 1000 pages after one month, and 20,000 pages after its first year [Wik10b]. Wikipedia contains a huge amount of pages, written by individuals all over the world. By August of 2014, the number of Wikipedia pages in all languages combined has grown to more than 33.1 million, with the English version being the largest one, containing more than 4.7 million pages [Wik14c].

Figure 2.18 shows an example of a Wikipedia page when being viewed in the browser. As can be seen, the wikitext is hidden from the user of the Web page. In Figure 2.19, the same page as displayed when being edited from within the user's Web browser is shown. In the bottom half of the screenshot, the wikitext of the page is displayed. By editing and saving the page, changes can be applied to the wiki page.

[20] `http://www.wikipedia.org/`

Figure 2.18.: Wikipedia Page when Viewed in the Browser (Screenshot of [Wik10c])

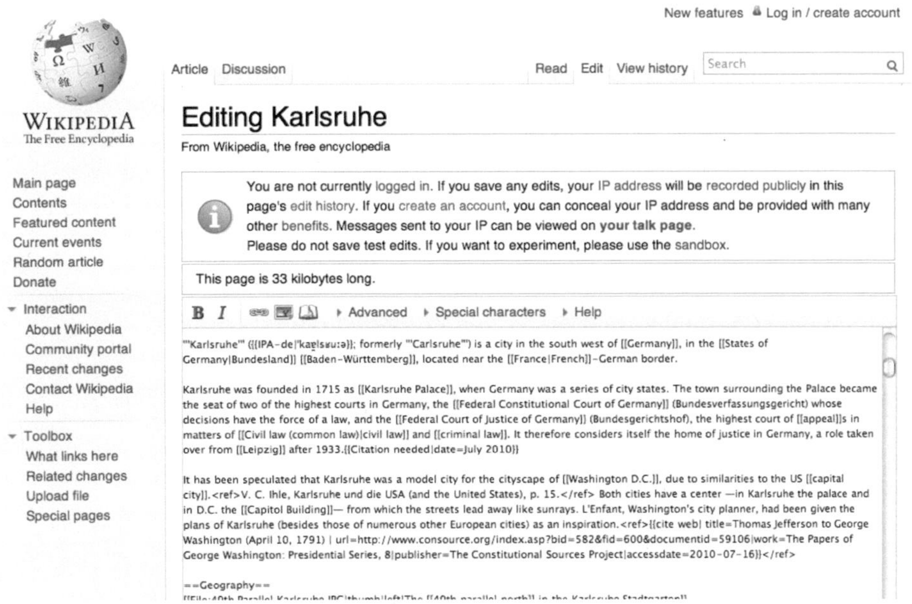

Figure 2.19.: Wikipedia Page when Being Edited (Screenshot of [Wik10c])

The work presented in [FB05] and [RA08] analyzes the motivation of individuals who contribute to Wikipedia. More general thoughts of collaboration, including within the context of Wikipedia and wikis in general, can be found in [TW07] and [Shi08].

While there are some high-profile cases of Wikipedia articles, which contained intentionally wrong information, a study published in Nature found that the quality of Wikipedia articles does not differ much from articles found in the renowned Encyclopedia Britannica[21]. The study, which was conducted in 2005, had experts in various fields compare 50 articles covering scientific topics. While an average Wikipedia article contained four inaccuracies, the average Britannica article contained three [Gil05].

Enterprise Wikis

Wikis are used within organizations for managing internal knowledge. While traditionally, wikis are considered too anarchical for the use in companies, specialized Enterprise Wikis aim at unifying wiki aspects with more controlled mechanisms suitable for companies. Mechanisms include more sophisticated access control, and support for accessing directory services (e.g., LDAP, or Microsoft Active Directory)[22].

Moreover, functions traditionally found in Content Management Systems[23] are implemented in Enterprise Wikis (e.g., embedding and managing Microsoft Office documents). In order to simplify the use for non-technical people, Enterprise Wikis implement WYSIWYG editing of pages. Support for WebDAV, a mechanism for uploading and changing files on a Web server, e-mail integration, and export mechanisms (e.g., for PDF or Microsoft Office documents) is a feature often found in Enterprise Wikis. Even project management and spreadsheet features, as well as instant messengers, can be found in some products. Sophisticated search mechanisms (full text, as well as search within documents), as well as classification and tagging mechanisms, are another feature typically found in Enterprise Wikis [Som07].

Examples of Enterprise Wikis are Atlassian Confluence, Socialtext, Near-time, and Traction Software Teampage, which are available commercially [Som07]. An example of an open source Enterprise Wiki is TWiki[24].

[21] `http://www.britannica.com/`

[22] Some wikis not explicitly developed for the use in enterprises also support directory services access, sometimes through the use of extensions or plugins (e.g., MediaWiki).

[23] Due to possible confusion with the term Configuration Management System, which is also abbreviated CMS, the term Content Management System is used in its unabbreviated form throughout this thesis.

[24] `http://twiki.org/`

2.5.4. Further Reading

Ward Cunningham's description of a wiki can be read in [Cun02] while a more recent summary on wikis can be found in [O'L08]. References [EGHW07] and [Cho08] give a comprehensive discussion of wikis, while [Mad07] presents successful patterns for the introduction of wikis. References [AGJP09] and [Due08] look into the use of wikis in the corporate context at IBM. A detailed description of MediaWiki is given in [Bar08].

In this thesis, a closer look at wikis and a comparison between wikis as candidates for the technical foundation for this thesis are given in Section 4.1.1 (page 117). A detailed description of MediaWiki, the wiki chosen as the basis of this thesis, can be found in Section 4.1.3 (page 121).

2.6. Semantic Wikis

As discussed in Section 2.5 (page 70), wikis are great tools for collaboratively building and maintaining knowledge bases. When it comes to structured knowledge, however, wikis are limited because they are primarily designed for representing text for use by humans. These limitations are addressed by semantic wikis, which are discussed in this section. Semantic wikis are based on the concept of ontologies and the Semantic Web, which were described in Section 2.3 (page 59) and Section 2.4 (page 61). While this section provides a short introduction into semantic wikis, different approaches and implementations are compared, and one implementation is selected as the technical foundation for this thesis in Section 4.1.2 (page 117). In Section 4.1.4 (page 124), the selected semantic wiki is discussed in more detail.

Non-semantic wikis, which were described in the previous section, allow for easy editing and linking of pages, which greatly supports collaboration between wiki users. However, non-semantic wikis lack the ability to input structured data and information into the wiki. Furthermore, information is hard to extract due to the lack of structure. Semantic wikis, which make use of Semantic Web technologies, e.g., ontologies and reasoning, extend traditional wikis in order to better support structured data and information [SBBK08].

Semantic wikis are an approach for bringing the flexibility of wikis from unstructured texts to structured data. In order to accomplish this goal, the ability to include metadata is added to wiki platforms. The format of this metadata is most often derived from Semantic Web technologies (i.e., semantic annotations, and ontologies). While the general principle of semantic wikis is to allow the input and retrieval of structured data, there are many different implementations with different approaches and goals (e.g., for improving collaboration and navigation, or for providing a platform for collaborative ontology engineering) [SBBK09].

Semantic wikis usually implement the following functionalities: semantic annotations can be used to give meaning to links between wiki pages, for queries, and the generation of dynamic lists from queries. Standard-based annotations (e.g., RDF, or OWL) facilitate the exchange of data with external applications (e.g., an external search tool). Deductive approaches can be used for generating conclusions [SBBK09].

The following subsections describe annotations and use cases in more detail.

2.6.1. Annotations

Annotations are the basic building block of semantic wiki functionality. The ontology of a semantic wiki is the sum of all annotations on single wiki pages. There are two approaches for using annotations in semantic wikis: First, there exists an *extended wiki syntax*, which allows annotations in wikitext; second, *separate forms* are used for annotations. Almost all wikis use the page, in which the annotation is expressed, as the subject of the statement. The object generally is another wiki page (e.g., the location of a country) or an attribute (i.e., a numeric value; for example the population number). A page about countries, for example, states the location as `located in::Europe`. In order to find all countries located in Europe, a query can be used. There are three main uses for annotations: Semantic Navigation, Semantic Search, and Display Adaption [SBBK09].

Semantic Navigation

Semantic Navigation exploits the semantic annotations contained in the wiki for simplifying navigation. Each wiki page contains a separate section where navigation data derived from semantic annotations is displayed. Semantic MediaWiki (as described in more detail in Section 4.1.4, page 124) displays all outgoing relations found in the page's text in a *Factbox* beneath the text. By clicking on a relation or an object, more information can be obtained [SBBK09].

Semantic Search

Semantic Search enables queries based on semantic annotations. For example, all pages describing countries located in Europe can be listed based on a semantic statement (`located in::Europe`). Semantic Search can be used in two different ways: First, a semantic query can be entered into a search form comparable to the search form found in most wiki platforms. Second, inline queries can be used to generate dynamic lists within wiki pages [SBBK09].

Display Adaption

Display Adaption is the third field, where wikis benefit from semantic technologies. In order to provide an enhanced user experience, relevant information can be added to wiki pages based on semantic characteristics of a page and using semantic relationships. For example, a box containing information about a country can be displayed that contains more information, about which continent a country belongs to, as well as its neighbor countries [SBBK09].

2.6.2. Use Cases

Semantic wikis can be used in all areas where non-semantic wikis are used. In addition, the ability to represent structured data opens new areas of use for semantic wikis, e.g., in the Knowledge Management and ontology engineering disciplines. The following paragraphs describe these two use cases.

Knowledge Management

Non-semantic wikis were used for managing knowledge within companies for some time, because of their collaborative nature and ability to allow quick editing of information. Especially in the area of software development, there is a large wiki use base. There are problems associated with using wikis in corporate environments, however: information is hard to find, and there are often multiple wikis, which are not interlinked with each other. Structures provided by semantic wikis are a welcome addition to wikis for solving these problems. For example, visualizations can be generated from semantic annotations, search can be made more efficient and information can be shared between multiple wiki platforms through exchanging and sharing annotations and ontologies [SBBK09].

Ontology Engineering

Ontology engineering is the discipline of formalizing the knowledge of a domain. While domain experts have the knowledge of their domain, it is often hard for them to employ the mechanisms for formalizing the knowledge. Semantic wikis can help to ease ontology engineering by providing a platform, which is more usable for domain experts. In a semantic wiki, knowledge can be put in textual form first and later be transferred into a more formal representation by adding semantic annotations [SBBK09].

2.6.3. Further Reading

More information about semantic wikis can be found in Section 4.1.2 (page 117), which describes semantic wikis in detail and selects one semantic wiki implementation as the technical platform of this thesis. In Section 4.1.4 (page 124), Semantic MediaWiki, a widely-used semantic wiki implementation is presented.

Reference [SBBK08] provides a brief introduction into semantic wikis and presents an overview of the most popular implementations. In [KVV^{+}07], Semantic MediaWiki, as well as general semantic wiki concepts, are described. Reference [Sem09] provides an overview of a number of semantic wiki implementations. The use of semantic wikis in a corporate context using the example of Semantic MediaWiki+ is outlined in [HSP09]. In [SSFH08], among others, semantic wiki and Semantic MediaWiki+ components are outlined, while [Str09] provides an overview of Semantic MediaWiki and Semantic Forms.

2.7. Summary

In this chapter, the basic principles and technologies necessary for understanding the remaining parts of the thesis were outlined. In Section 2.1 (page 12), foundations of IT Service Management were presented, followed by an overview of the IT Infrastructure Library (ITIL) in Section 2.2 (page 16). In Section 2.3 (page 59) an introduction to ontologies was given. Moreover, in Section 2.4 (page 61), Semantic Web basics were presented. Furthermore, wikis (Section 2.5, page 70) and semantic wikis (Section 2.6, page 77) were introduced.

In the following Chapter 3, an analysis of the IT management tool landscape of the environment in which the thesis was written, is presented, followed by a look at the theoretical foundations of Configuration Management and a presentation of three open source ITSM tools.

3. Analysis

IT Service Management comprises, like other knowledge-intensive disciplines, interactions between people, processes, and technological aspects (tools). ITIL, a popular ITSM framework, as described in Section 2.2 (page 16), contains a multitude of good practices, especially in the organizational and people domains. Moreover, there are suggestions for ITSM tools, which support IT administrators in different aspects of their work. None of the suggestions, however, describe concrete tools, which leave a number of commercial and open source software providers to offer various solutions.

In the area of Configuration Management, specialized software for managing configuration items (CIs) and their interactions in a database is available. This software, described as a Configuration Management Database (CMDB), is available from various vendors. Together with other features, CMDBs form a Configuration Management System (CMS).

This chapter is structured as follows: Section 3.1 (page 82) describes the environment, in which the analysis was performed. Configuration Management as a practice, as well as characteristics of Configuration Management Systems in general, are described in Section 3.2 (page 98). In Section 3.3 (page 109), some examples of Configuration Management tools are presented. Finally, Section 3.4 (page 113) gives a summary of the chapter.

3.1. Environment

The thesis was written while the author was working as an IT administrator at FZI Research Center for Information Technology in Karlsruhe[1]. With 171 employees (2014), FZI is an SME organization tightly connected to the Karlsruhe Institute of Technology (KIT) [FZI14]. Because the organization's core business is mainly IT-centric, the IT proficiency of the majority of its employees can be rated high or very high.

The IT department, named *Rechner- und Datenkommunikationsdienste (RuD)*[2], which consists of five full-time employees and eight student assistants, provides IT services mostly for in-house customers, and to some extend to associated entities. Services include the design and maintenance of the network infrastructure (i.e., Ethernet, wireless networks, telephone, and VoIP), e-mail services, Web services, and database services. Furthermore, it includes the coverage of IT equipment through its lifecycle, e.g., the acquisition, testing, commissioning, maintenance and decommissioning of servers, desktop computers, and notebooks. While key infrastructure components and services are maintained by the IT department, employees are allowed to install software required for their work on their workstations, as well as to set up services for testing purposes within the internal network after checking with the IT department. Other than providing services, RuD handles all IT Service Management tasks, including running a service desk for all IT matters, as well as counseling FZI employees in the area of Information Technology.

When looking at the classification of provider types as described in Section 2.2.1 (page 21), the IT department at FZI meets the criteria of some aspects of a type I provider, and some aspects of a type II provider. While the funding from overheads and the operation within the business' mandate define the department as a type I provider, an aspect, which defines it as a type II provider, is its autonomous management at the operational level. In contrast to the definition given for type II providers, there is generally no external competition to services provided to other departments. While there is no external competition, some aspects of IT administration can be performed by departments themselves, if they choose not to make use of the services provided by the IT department.

[1] `http://www.fzi.de/`

[2] Computer and data communication services

With regard to the type of the service desk function, as described in Section 2.2.4 (page 50), it can be said that the function, as performed by RuD, is a local service desk. This type of service desk is characterized by its close proximity to its customers. Due to the non-standard nature of some research-oriented IT demands, a number of tasks would not be able to be accomplished by a centralized service desk.

The following subsections describe the tools, which were used for documenting and managing the IT infrastructure at FZI before the migration to Semantic MediaWiki and the development of the ITSM-specific tools presented in Chapter 5 (page 185). In addition, the shortcomings of the old tools are outlined, which led to the migration to Semantic MediaWiki and the design and development of the Semantic MediaWiki-based ITSM platform (ITSM Wiki).

3.1.1. PmWiki Used as a Documentation Platform

Before the introduction of Semantic MediaWiki for the documentation of IT-internal processes and best practices, PmWiki[3] was used for this purpose. PmWiki is a wiki written in the PHP programming language and uses files for storing wiki pages. It is released under the GPL license, has a relatively small code base, and is extensible by plugins. Access control is implemented in PmWiki and can make use of existing password databases (e.g., the Apache .htaccess mechanism, LDAP, or password stored in an SQL database) [Lan06, pages 394–400]. More information about PmWiki can be found in [Lan06, pages 393–455].

In Figure 3.1, a screenshot of the main page of the PmWiki-based documentation platform is given. It shows a list of wiki pages sorted by topics. Wiki pages in PmWiki included a list of suppliers and internal cost units, a list of contact persons for IT-related matters within other departments, documentation for new IT administrators, and subject-oriented documentation, as well as information about IT infrastructure (for example, e-mail service-related documentation, and information about the network infrastructure). In addition to the information shown in the screenshot, the PmWiki instance was used to maintain a list of selected infrastructure servers, which were documented in more detail due to their importance in providing essential services.

Figure 3.2 shows the representation of one of the servers, which is part of the core infrastructure (it serves as a Windows Domain Controller, and provides DNS and DHCP services). Information shown in the screenshot includes the operating system of the server, information about the services it provides, and the alias, under which it is available on the internal network. The number of computers documented in this way in the PmWiki was relatively low with only 19 documented servers. Workstation computers

[3] `http://www.pmwiki.org/`

and notebooks were not documented in PmWiki at all. This was mostly due to the work-intensive process of manually maintaining information about servers and the limited ability to re-use server-specific information in other parts of the PmWiki installation.

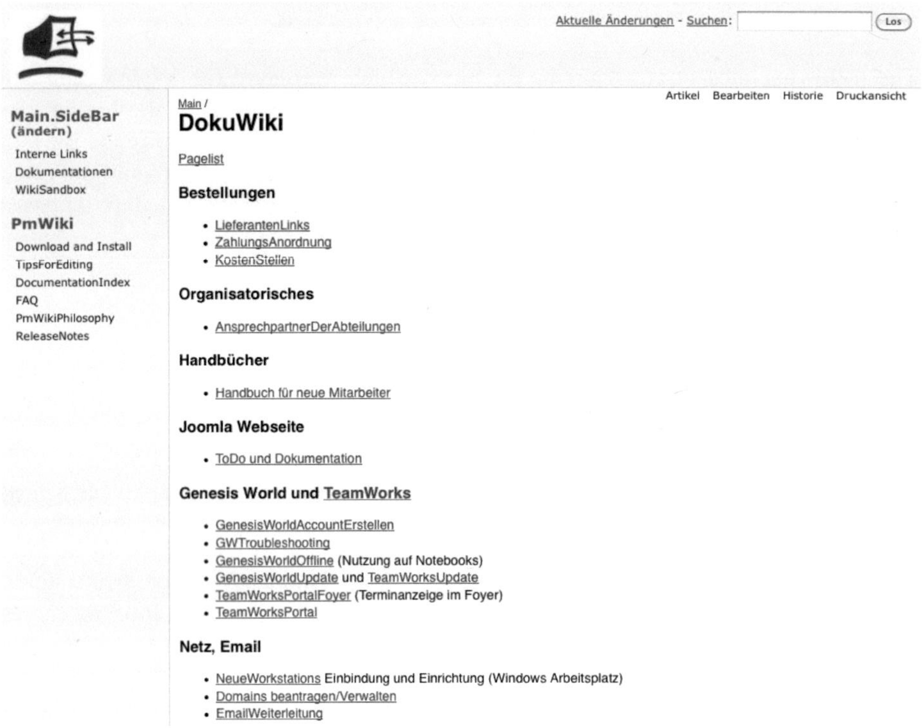

Figure 3.1.: Main Page of PmWiki Used for Documentation

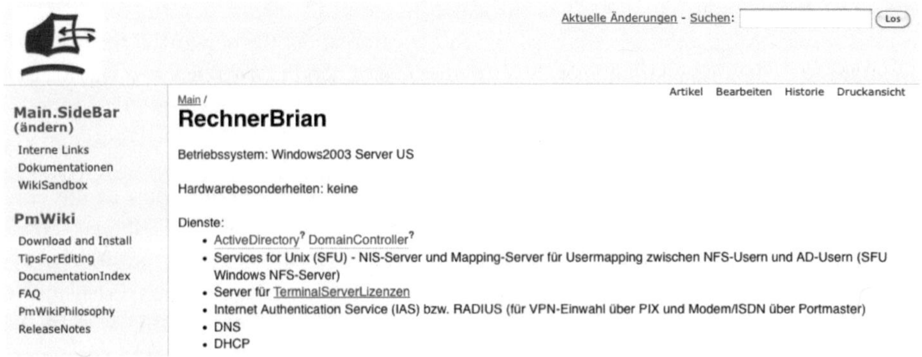

Figure 3.2.: Representation of a Computer in PmWiki

Shortcomings

The shortcomings of the PmWiki installation, which led to the use of Semantic MediaWiki and the development of extensions customized to the needs of the ITSM environment, were as follows:

- *Unstructured representation of information:* In PmWiki, the representation of information was limited to unstructured text-based information. This put limits to the automatic processing of information, and to the modification of information by customized tools.
- *Low number of documented hosts:* The number of documented hosts was limited to a small number of servers, which provided infrastructure services (e.g., Windows Active Directory Domain Services, DNS, DHCP, and e-mail). Documenting and keeping up to date more hosts proved to be too labor-intensive to be of use for all computers.
- *Limited use of information about servers and services:* The information about the few documented servers in the PmWiki was a text-only representation, and as such only useful for looking up information about a particular server by members of the IT administration team. Information was not machine-understandable, which led to the inability to derive information stored in the individual server's wiki pages. For example, it was not possible to automatically create a table, which listed the operating systems and services used by the individual servers.
- *Limited use of information about persons, their roles, and their dependencies:* The PmWiki instance contained a small number of persons, in the form of contact persons of departments and suppliers. Their use was limited, however, because specifying relations between persons and items proved to be difficult without a formal means to state the relations.
- *Information scattered over different tools:* Although not a problem of the PmWiki instance per se, information regarding computers and services was distributed over several specialized tools, which hampered the ease of use of managing information.

3.1.2. OTRS::ITSM Used as a CMDB

OTRS[4] as a service desk tool was introduced in the RuD department in 2006 in order to provide a unified point of contact for service requests from in-house customers. OTRS is a web-based service desk solution, which allows accepting service requests from customers via e-mail and via a Web interface. While the customer benefits from the availability of a single point of contact, the IT department benefits from a structured

[4] http://otrs.org/

workflow, which allows monitoring the status of service requests. Because of the growing need of documenting configuration items in a more formal way, combined with the good experiences gathered by the use of OTRS, the then newly released IT Service Management component OTRS::ITSM[5] was added to the existing OTRS instance[6].

In Figure 3.3, a screenshot of a configuration item represented in OTRS::ITSM is shown. In the left part of the screenshot, information about the CI, which was manually entered, can be seen. The information includes the hardware manufacturer, the model type, the serial number, the supplier, and the date the computer was brought into service. Further information includes the services provided by the CI, a link to the representation of the CI in the Nagios infrastructure monitoring Web interface, the type of computer, the computer's owner, various information about the computer's hardware and network configuration, and information about which services should be monitored by Nagios. In addition, free-text notes are present, which protocol changes to the CI. The bottom part of the screenshot shows relations to other entities (e.g., service contracts for hardware repairs, and internal service contracts). On the right side of the screenshot, meta-information about the CI is shown.

Shortcomings

The shortcomings of the OTRS::ITSM installation, which led to the use of Semantic MediaWiki and the development of extensions customized to the needs of the ITSM environment, were the following:

- *Separation of text-centric documentation and CMDB:* While structured information about configuration items was managed in OTRS::ITSM, text-centric documentation, for example, instructions on how to perform maintenance tasks, were stored in PmWiki. This led to the separation of relevant information for certain tasks, which slowed down looking up relevant information when performing these tasks. Examples of such tasks are the maintenance of server hardware, where factual information such as the quantity of installed RAM was stored in OTRS::ITSM, whereas the text-centric procedure for the upgrade process was stored in PmWiki.

- *No automatic information gathering:* All information about configuration items stored in OTRS::ITSM had to be updated manually, because no mechanisms for automatically gathering configuration information from devices over the network were available.

[5] `http://www.otrs.com/products/itsm/`

[6] Another solution evaluated at the time was i-doit open (`http://www.i-doit.org/`). The decision fell in favor of OTRS::ITSM because of its tight integration with the already used OTRS service desk system.

[Inhalt Config Item: 1029000002]

Zurück - Versionen einblenden - Bearbeiten - Verknüpfen - Duplizieren

I-->>> 19. brian (Produktiv) kleiner (Frank Kleiner) - 27.09.2007 09:51:28

Name:	brian
Status:	Produktiv
Inventarnummer:	
Anbieter:	Dell
Model:	PowerEdge 2850
Modell-Nummer:	
Seriennummer:	
Lieferant:	Dell
Rechnungs-Nr:	
Rechnungs-Datum:	09/27/2007
Lieferschein-Nr:	
Lieferschein-Datum:	09/27/2007
Bestellungs-Nr:	
Bestellungs-Datum:	09/27/2007
Bestellt von:	
Dienste:	AD, DNS, DHCP, IAS, TS-Lizenzserver, Enterprise-CA
Nagios:	http://pedahel.fzi.de/nagios/cgi-bin/extinfo.cgi?type=1&host=brian
Beschreibung:	
Typ:	Server
Privatrechner:	No
Besitzer:	Frank Kleiner
Akku 1 S/N:	
Akku 2 S/N:	
CPU:	Xeon 3.0GHz
Arbeitsspeicher:	DIMM1_A 1024MB
Arbeitsspeicher:	DIMM1_B 1024MB
Festplatte:	SCSI-Festplatte
Kapazität:	68.24GB
Festplatte:	SCSI-Festplatte
Kapazität:	68.24GB
FQDN:	brian.fzi.de
Netzwerk Adapter:	
IP über DHCP:	No
IP Addresse:	141.21
Netzwerk Adapter:	deaktiviert
IP über DHCP:	No
Grafik Adapter:	RADEON 7000 SERIES
Abrechung Beginn:	09/27/2007
Abrechung Ende:	09/27/2007
Abrechung Gewichtung:	
Garantie Ablaufdatum:	09/05/2009
Installiert durch:	Frank Kleiner
Backup:	Yes
Nagios Ping:	Yes
Nagios HTTP:	No
Nagios SSH:	No
Notiz:	2007-07-25: Fehlermeldung IB110 SBE Log Disabled; Speicherbank DIMM1_B meldet Fehler 2007-07-26: Gespräch mit Dell Gold-Support; Techniker kommt um 18 Uhr vorbei und tauscht den Speicher aus 2007-07-26: Austausch beider Speichermodule durch Servicetechniker; Server meldet keine Probleme mehr
Beobachtung:	No

Klasse:	Computer
Name:	brian
Aktueller Status:	Produktiv
Erstellt:	06.07.2007 10:04:47
Erstellt von:	kleiner (Frank Kleiner)
Zuletzt geändert:	27.09.2007 09:51:28
Zuletzt geändert von:	kleiner (Frank Kleiner)

Abhängige Objekte: Config Item Network

Nummer	Name	Status	Letzte Änderung	Verknüpfungstyp
1031000007	intern	Production	09/14/2007 14:25:39	Connected to

Abhängige Objekte: Config Item Software

Nummer	Name	Status	Letzte Änderung	Verknüpfungstyp
1032000004	Microsoft Windows Server 2003 Standard	Production	10/12/2007 21:13:10	Depends on

Abhängige Objekte: Lokation

Name	Typ	Phone 1	E-Mail	Letzte Änderung	Verknüpfungstyp
FZI::UG::Serverraum::Dell-Rack 2	Rack			07/06/2007 09:54:34	Depends on

Abhängige Objekte: Service

Name	Typ	Kritikalität	Letzte Änderung	Verknüpfungstyp
Dell GOLD Support 4h 365/24/4 069-50070424	IT Operational	3 normal	10/01/2007 12:26:09	Depends on
FZI-Rechner::FZI-Server::RuD-Server	IT Management	3 normal	09/17/2007 10:25:29	Depends on
RuD Komplett-Wartung	End User Service	3 normal	09/14/2007 13:22:05	Depends on
FZI-Rechner::RuD-Rechner	IT Management	3 normal	09/17/2007 10:25:46	Depends on

Figure 3.3.: View of a Configuration Item in OTRS::ITSM

- *Only explicitly stated information was accessible:* As a system, which relied on a classic SQL database system, only explicitly stated information could be retrieved, without the benefits available from systems, which allow access to implicit information, e.g., semantic information systems.

- *Lack of flexibility in reporting mechanisms:* While OTRS::ITSM offered some reporting mechanisms, in practice they turned out to lack the required flexibility to be of use in the FZI environment.

- *No connection to Nagios infrastructure monitoring:* When looking at the information, which was stored in the OTRS::ITSM-based CMDB, it can be seen that a significant amount of information overlapped with the information necessary for infrastructure monitoring. Because there was no mechanism available for synchronizing the information stored in the OTRS::ITSM-based CMDB with the text-based Nagios configuration files, redundant information had to be maintained at two locations, which led to excessive and error-prone additional manual work.

- *Information scattered over different tools:* As was the case with PmWiki, the distribution of relevant information over multiple tools hampered the IT administrators in their work with OTRS::ITSM. This was especially the case when it came to the task of combining structured information, stored in OTRS::ITSM, and free-text information, which was stored in PmWiki (e.g., documentation of a process related to a CI described in OTRS::ITSM).

3.1.3. Spreadsheet Used for Accounting

Information relevant for the internal accounting between the IT department and the different departments was stored in a Microsoft Excel[7] spreadsheet. As can be seen in Figure 3.4, information stored in the spreadsheet was separated according to departments.

The spreadsheet contained one row per computer, which consisted of the computer's name, the type of computer (notebook, workstation, server, or others), the start and end date of the service, and a weight factor, which allowed to give discounts to less frequently used computers or embedded devices.

Resulting from this information, the costs for network access were calculated. In addition to network access fees, additional contracts could be subscribed to, which included additional benefits, e.g., software installation and free help with solving problems from the IT department for the respective computer.

[7] `http://office.microsoft.com/en-us/excel/`

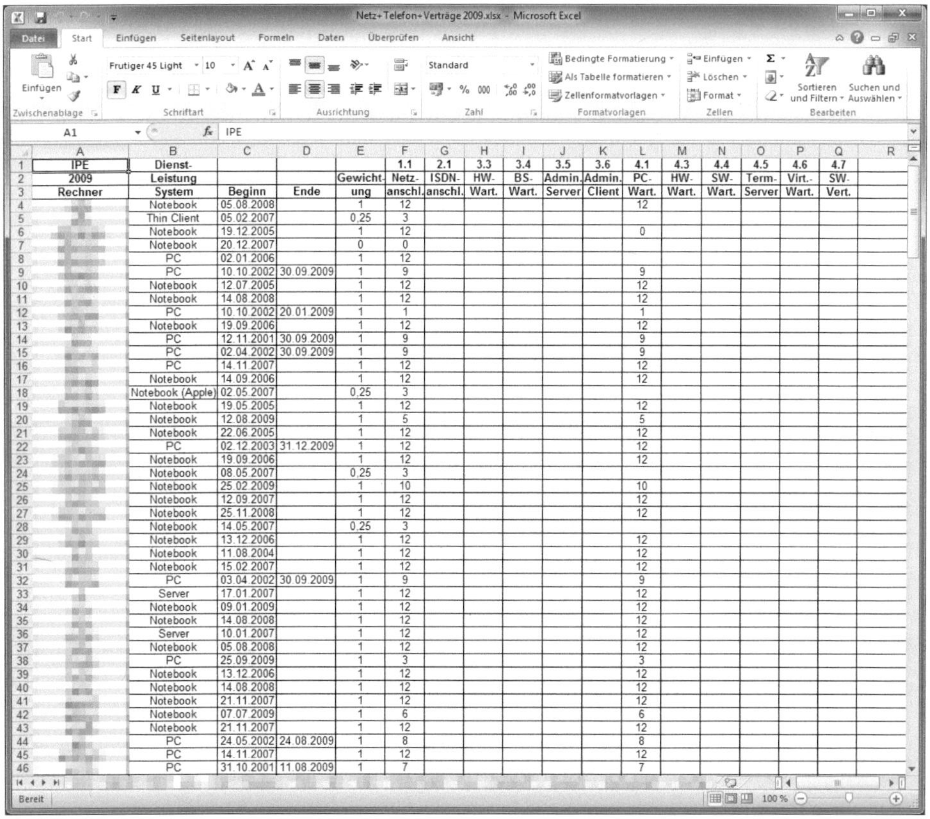

	A	B	C	D	E	F	G	H	I	J	K	L	M	N	O	P	Q
1	IPE	Dienst-				1.1	2.1	3.3	3.4	3.5	3.6	4.1	4.3	4.4	4.5	4.6	4.7
2	2009	Leistung			Gewicht-	Netz-	ISDN-	HW-	BS-	Admin.	Admin.	PC-	HW-	SW-	Term-	Virt.-	SW-
3	Rechner	System	Beginn	Ende	ung	anschl.	anschl.	Wart.	Wart.	Server	Client	Wart.	Wart.	Wart.	Server	Wart.	Vert.
4		Notebook	05.08.2008		1	12						12					
5		Thin Client	05.02.2007		0,25	3											
6		Notebook	19.12.2005		1	12						0					
7		Notebook	20.12.2007		0	0											
8		PC	02.01.2006		1	12											
9		PC	10.10.2002	30.09.2009	1	9						9					
10		Notebook	12.07.2005		1	12						12					
11		Notebook	14.08.2008		1	12						12					
12		PC	10.10.2002	20.01.2009	1	1						1					
13		Notebook	19.09.2006		1	12						12					
14		PC	12.11.2001	30.09.2009	1	9						9					
15		PC	02.04.2002	30.09.2009	1	9						9					
16		PC	14.11.2007		1	12						12					
17		Notebook	14.09.2006		1	12						12					
18		Notebook (Apple)	02.05.2007		0,25	3											
19		Notebook	19.05.2005		1	12						12					
20		Notebook	12.08.2009		1	5						5					
21		Notebook	22.06.2005		1	12						12					
22		PC	02.12.2003	31.12.2009	1	12						12					
23		Notebook	19.09.2006		1	12						12					
24		Notebook	08.05.2007		0,25	3											
25		Notebook	25.02.2009		1	10						10					
26		Notebook	12.09.2007		1	12						12					
27		Notebook	25.11.2008		1	12						12					
28		Notebook	14.05.2007		0,25	3											
29		Notebook	13.12.2006		1	12						12					
30		Notebook	11.08.2004		1	12						12					
31		Notebook	15.02.2007		1	12						12					
32		PC	03.04.2002	30.09.2009	1	9						9					
33		Server	17.01.2007		1	12						12					
34		Notebook	09.01.2009		1	12						12					
35		Notebook	14.08.2008		1	12						12					
36		Server	10.01.2007		1	12						12					
37		Notebook	05.08.2008		1	12						12					
38		PC	25.09.2009		1	3						3					
39		Notebook	13.12.2006		1	12						12					
40		Notebook	14.08.2008		1	12						12					
41		Notebook	21.11.2007		1	12						12					
42		Notebook	07.07.2009		1	6						6					
43		Notebook	21.11.2007		1	12						12					
44		PC	24.05.2002	24.08.2009	1	8						8					
45		PC	14.11.2007		1	12						12					
46		PC	31.10.2001	11.08.2009	1	7						7					

Figure 3.4.: Excel Spreadsheet Used for Accounting

Furthermore, additional service contracts were available for servers, e.g., for the maintenance of virtual servers. Not shown in the screenshot is information about the accounting of phone services, which was stored in a spreadsheet in almost the same manner.

In order to produce invoices for the departments, the information about the computers stored in the spreadsheet was added by using Excel functions and then sent to the departments for review. After review, internal cost centers were billed for the services provided by the IT department.

Shortcomings

The shortcomings of managing accounting information in a Microsoft Excel spreadsheet, which led to the use of Semantic MediaWiki, and the development of extensions customized to the needs of the ITSM environment, were the following:

- *Separate storage of information:* While information about accounting and service contracts was stored in the Excel spreadsheet, additional other information was stored in the OTRS::ITSM-based CMDB. In addition to that, text-based information about computers was stored in PmWiki. Tests, which aimed at replacing the spreadsheet with an OTRS::ITSM-based solution failed due to the following reasons: First, OTRS::ITSM did not include mechanisms for the automatic creation of invoices, which were comparable to the ones needed by RuD and provided by the spreadsheet. Second, building a customized tool, which would have accessed OTRS::ITSM's database and created invoices would not have solved the problems with regard to the separation of information stored in PmWiki and OTRS::ITSM, and was thus discarded.
- *Limited to explicitly stated information:* Only explicitly stated information could be retrieved from the spreadsheet (for example, who owns a computer), without the benefits available from systems, which allow access to implicit information (e.g., create a list of all computers owned by a person).

3.1.4. Management of Virtual Machines

In addition to the Excel spreadsheet used for managing accounting information, an Excel spreadsheet was used for keeping track of provisioned virtual machines. At FZI, physical servers could be bought by individual departments and then maintained within service contracts by the IT department. Virtual machines were then provisioned on demand by requests sent to the service desk. In contrast to cloud services, which have benefits when dynamic scaling is an issue, virtual servers provisioned by RuD were aimed at longer-running tasks, e.g., project Web servers, or wikis.

The following information was stored in the virtual machines spreadsheet: the name of the virtual machine, the installed operating system and version, the owner of the virtual machine, as well as the start and end date of the virtual machine's lifecycle. Furthermore, the purpose of the virtual machine as well as information about the virtual machine's hardware configuration (e.g., the number of virtual processors, the quantity of RAM, and the amount of hard disk space allocated to the virtual machine) were stored in the spreadsheet.

Besides the information stored in the virtual machines spreadsheet, information about virtual machines was stored directly in the XenCenter configuration. While the information found in the Excel spreadsheet were more organizational in nature, the information stored in XenCenter was more technical. Technical information includes the amounts of RAM and hard disk used by a virtual machine, its CPU configuration and its network connections. Furthermore, the physical machine, on which the virtual machine was running, could be viewed in XenCenter[8]. At the time, documenting technical configuration

[8]XenCenter is the user interface provided by Citrix for its XenServer product.

information found in XenCenter in the Excel spreadsheet was not deemed necessary because updating configuration information each time would have had to result in a manual update of the spreadsheet.

While the OTRS::ITSM-based CMDB would seem like a perfect location for storing information about virtual machines, instead of storing this information in the Excel spreadsheet, in practice, the lacking export functions, respectively the lack of generating structured, customized reports, hampered this approach. Export and report generation functions were required, because information about virtual machines was from time to time shared with the stakeholders in the departments, in order to determine potential for optimization, and in order to track down virtual machines, which were no longer in active use by the departments.

Shortcomings

The shortcomings of managing information about virtual machines in a Microsoft Excel spreadsheet, which led to the use of Semantic MediaWiki and the development of extensions customized to the needs of the ITSM environment, were the following:

- *Duplicate information:* Information about virtual machines was stored in various locations. For example, the start and stop date of a virtual machine's lifecycle was stored in both, the accounting spreadsheet, as well as the virtual machines management spreadsheet. Information about the hardware was stored in the virtual machines spreadsheet for planning and reporting purposes and as configuration data in the XenCenter management interface.
- *No possibility to store structured information in XenCenter:* While it would seem attractive to store the configuration information in XenCenter, this approach was not feasible because of the lacking possibilities to store structured information in XenCenter.
- *Limitation to explicitly stated information:* Only explicitly stated information could be retrieved from the spreadsheet, without the benefits available from systems, which allow access to implicit information.

3.1.5. Nagios Used for Infrastructure Monitoring

Nagios[9] is used at FZI for monitoring the availability of the network infrastructure, services, infrastructure servers, as well as project servers. The configuration of Nagios was accomplished by editing text-based configuration files. Nagios is described in more detail in Section 5.2.5 (page 243).

[9]`http://www.nagios.org/`

In Figure 3.5, a screenshot of a text editor showing one of the Nagios configuration files can be seen. Each host is defined with the properties relevant to infrastructure monitoring. The definition of a host includes the template it uses, its host name and an alias, its IP address, and the name of the parent host. The relationships between hosts and their parent hosts are used to create a map of the infrastructure, which takes into account the dependencies between the hosts, if network outages are encountered. Furthermore, a host can have an action URL, which is shown as a link in the Nagios Web front-end.

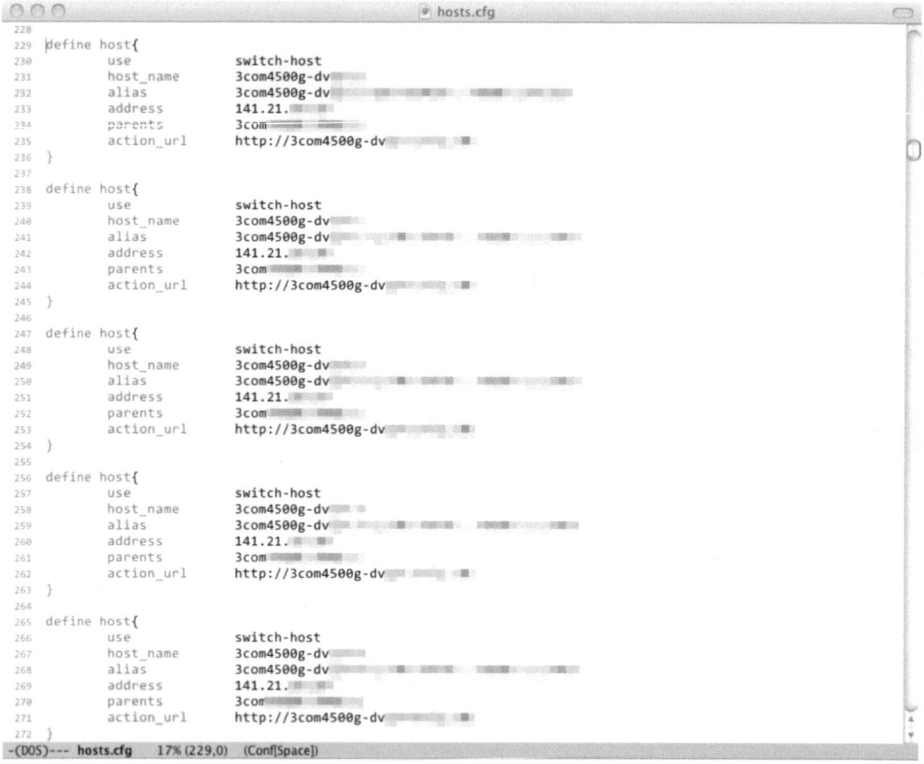

Figure 3.5.: Manual Editing of Nagios Configuration Files

Shortcomings

The shortcomings of managing information relevant to infrastructure monitoring in Nagios configuration files, which led to the use of Semantic MediaWiki and the development of the Infrastructure Monitoring Component (Section 5.2, page 234), were the following:

- *Duplicate information:* Information relevant to infrastructure monitoring was stored in manually maintained Nagios configuration files. These files contained information, which was to a large amount also found in the OTRS::ITSM-based CMDB (e.g., the IP addresses, host names, and locations of configuration items). Furthermore, information was duplicated in XenCenter and the Nagios configuration files, for example, information about which virtual machines ran on which physical hardware. While this information is contained in XenCenter for the purpose of configuring the XenServer instance, it is contained in Nagios for the purpose of specifying the dependencies between hosts, which helps in tracking down outages in the IT infrastructure.

- *One-dimensional dependencies:* Dependencies between hosts in Nagios help to locate the cause of a network outage and prevent Nagios from generating excess error messages (if, for example, a network router fails; only a single notification is created, in contrast to a notification for each host behind the router). While working with Nagios in the FZI environment, it was realized that there is a number of dependencies in different dimensions. For example, dependencies can be about physical network connections, logical network connections, and power circuits. Manually editing this information in the Nagios configuration files would have increased the amount of time spent on editing the configuration files even further, while the information would have been already present in most cases in the Configuration Management Database.

- *Manual notification of VM owner:* The monitoring of virtual machines and its associated services was done via a centralized Nagios instance, which reported failures of VMs and services to the RuD administrators. In the case of issues that required contacting the owner of a VM, the owner was looked up in the spreadsheet, which contained information about the virtual machines' owners. Due to the manual steps, the process was only available during business hours.

3.1.6. Management of Firewall Rules

Firewall rules specify, which connections between hosts are allowed to pass the borders of network segments. Connections are filtered, among others, based on the IP addresses of the source and destination, the TCP or UDP ports of the source and destination, and, for some protocols, protocol-specific details of other layers within the TCP/IP network stack. Figure 3.6 shows a screenshot of the Microsoft Forefront Threat Management Gateway[10] (TMG) 2010 firewall management console[11].

[10] `http://technet.microsoft.com/library/ff355324.aspx`

[11] Before the migration to Microsoft Forefront Threat Management Gateway (TMG) 2010, Microsoft Internet Security and Acceleration (ISA) Server 2004 was used, which was managed via a similar management console.

Each row in the management console represents a firewall rule, which represents an allowed or denied type of connection (e.g., allow connections from the Internet to a certain Web server on TCP port 80).

The window in front shows parts of the configuration of one of the rules. As can be seen, besides technical information, which defines the rule (by specifying the IP addresses and TCP or UDP ports), there is a name, which identifies the rule to the administrators of the firewall. In addition, an optional description exists, where information about the reason for the rule, or the person who requested the creation of the rule, can be entered.

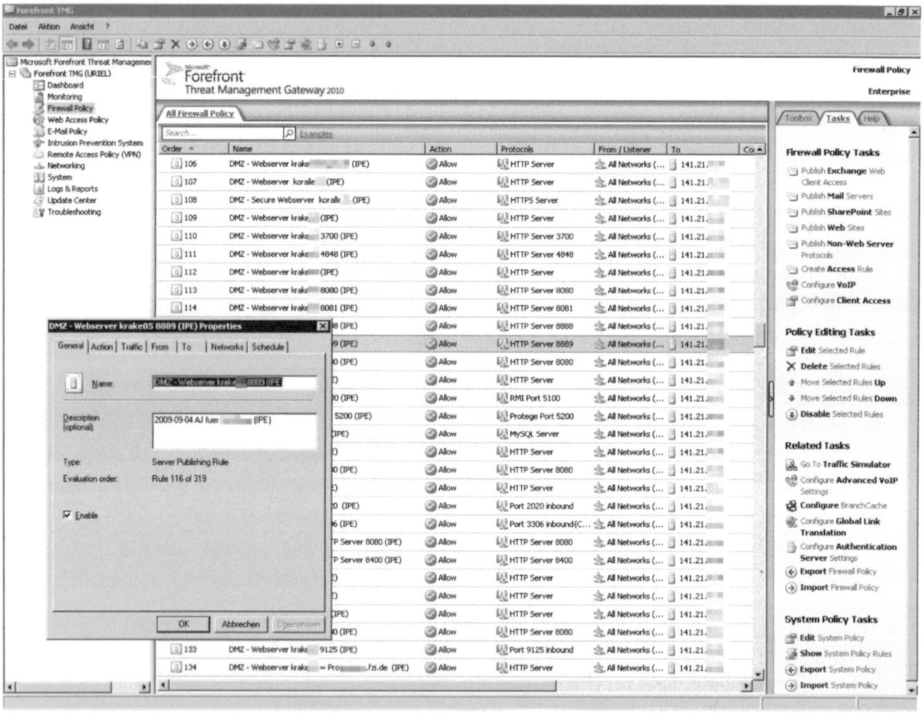

Figure 3.6.: Firewall Rules Management

More information about firewalls in general can be found in [FG05], while TMG-specific information can be found in [DDS10].

Shortcomings

The shortcomings of managing firewall rules directly in the TMG management console were as follows:

- *Not possible to store structured meta-data:* In the TMG management console, it is only possible to enter additional information, which exceeds the technical information required for the definition of a firewall rule (i.e., network addresses, and ports) in free text format. It is not possible to store structured information about firewall rules. Information, which is needed to be stored in the FZI scenario, is the purpose of the rule, its owner (the person who requested the creation of the rule), the date of creation, the RuD administrator who created the rule, and the project for which the rule was created.
- *No linking of information:* Meta-information about firewall rules could not be linked to other information. For example, it was not possible to link firewall rules in the wiki with responsible persons within the departments, or information about whether a computer is still in active duty with the corresponding firewall rules.
- *Lack of reporting mechanisms for meta-data:* While the TMG management console provides mechanisms for displaying information, which directly influence the firewall rule (e.g., network addresses, and ports), it is not possible to create reports based on the description of firewall rules. This is mostly due to the lack of mechanisms for storing structured information in the description. A scenario for reporting would be to list all rules that were requested by a certain user, or which are used for a certain project.
- *No mechanisms for advanced queries:* Queries, which make use of information not directly found in the firewall rule database, are not possible with the means provided by TMG. Scenarios, in which this would be of relevance, include the querying for rules, which open network ports with vulnerable software (e.g., due to a recently discovered vulnerability, for which no patch is available yet) to the Internet. By finding these ports, mitigation measures could be deployed (e.g., by temporarily disabling the affected rules until a patch becomes available).

3.1.7. License Management

Managing licenses is important for making sure that, on the one hand, there exist licenses for all software instances used within an organization, and, on the other hand, ensuring that no money is spent on unnecessary licenses. Within FZI's IT department, the management of licenses was done in a Filemaker Pro[12] database, which is shown in Figure 3.7. As can be seen, information that is stored in the license database includes the name and version of the product, the number of licenses per purchase, and the language in which the license was purchased. Furthermore, the computer for which the license was bought, the department, distributor, and order number, as well as the license serial number, notes, and the person for whom the license was purchased is included.

[12] `http://www.filemaker.com/products/filemaker-pro/`

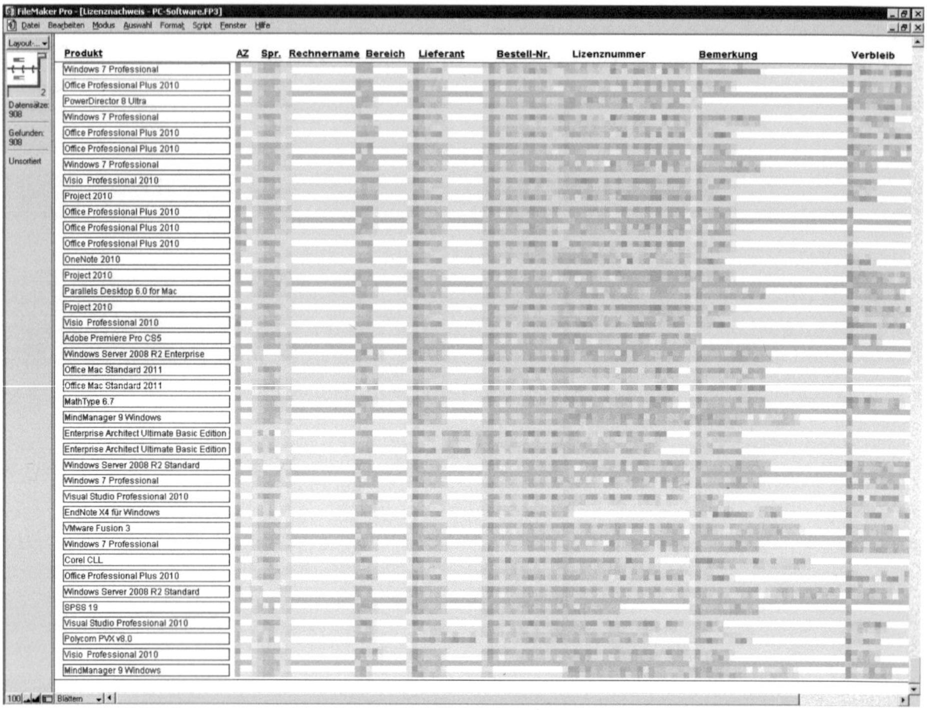

Figure 3.7.: License Management

Shortcomings

The shortcomings of managing license information in a dedicated database, which led to the use of Semantic MediaWiki, and the development of extensions customized to the needs of the ITSM environment, were the following:

- *Stand-alone database:* The database, which contained the license information, was separate from all other information about computers. No links between the OTRS::ITSM-based CMDB, the Microsoft Excel-based accounting spreadsheet, and the Filemaker Pro-based license database existed. For this reason, information about licenses, which were not in use anymore, due to decommissioned computers, was not available, because the information existed in two separate parts, first in the accounting spreadsheet, and second in the license database.

- *Only limited reporting:* Reporting of information about licenses was limited to the mechanisms provided by the Filemaker Pro database. While the application allowed to search and sort the database in several ways, information from outside the database could not be used, which in some cases would have been convenient.

3.1.8. Analysis of Duplicate Information

Table 3.1 and Table 3.2 show a summary of the information, which is stored in the different tools used by RuD for storing information about FZI's IT infrastructure. The columns of the tables show the different tools that are used, while the rows show which information is stored in which tool. If information is stored in a tool, it is distinguished between whether structured (abbreviated as *"s"*) or unstructured (abbreviated as *"u"*) information is stored. Structured information refers to information that is stored in a database according to a defined schema, while unstructured information refers to information, which is stored as plain text without a defined schema.

	PmWiki	OTRS::ITSM	Spreadsheet	XenCenter
Owner of a CI	no	s	s	u
Location of a CI	no	s	no	u
Monitoring	no	s	s	no
Documentation	u	no	no	no
Best practices	u	no	no	no
Open firewall ports	no	no	no	no
License information	no	no	no	no

Table 3.1.: Duplicate Information (Part 1)

	Nagios	Firewall	License DB
Owner of a CI	no	no	no
Location of a CI	u	no	no
Monitoring	s	no	no
Documentation	no	no	no
Best practices	no	no	no
Open firewall ports	no	s	no
License information	no	no	s

Table 3.2.: Duplicate Information (Part 2)

As can be seen in Table 3.1 and Table 3.2, a number of information is stored multiple times in different tools. This leads to the following problems:

- Information is stored redundantly, which leads to inconsistencies when not updating all instances. Furthermore, manually keeping up to date redundant information is time-consuming.

- Structured information is stored in different formats in different tools. This leads to the problem that information cannot be linked seamlessly between the different tools.
- In some cases, the same information is stored in both, structured, as well as unstructured form in different tools. Linking between structured and unstructured information across tool borders is not supported.

3.2. Configuration Management

After the environment of FZI's IT department was analyzed in Section 3.1 (page 82), approaches for managing Configuration Management information were looked into, in order to find potential points for improvement. As shown in Section 3.1.8 (page 97), at the time of the analysis, the landscape for storing information relevant to IT Service Management was not consolidated and contained multiple tools, which were not able to access each other's data. Furthermore, information in some cases was stored more than once, which contributed to inconsistent information and an increased amount of necessary additional work in order to keep the information consistent.

Configuration Management as a discipline within IT Service Management serves as the foundation on which other processes are built. While Configuration Management is not a discipline, which helps in solving ITSM problems by itself, knowledge about existing entities relevant to Service Management and the relationships between these entities are of the essence for other disciplines [BT05, page 20].

Service Asset and Configuration Management (SACM), which was introduced in Section 2.2.3 (page 38), is the ITIL process, which manages information about the entities used to fulfill services, as well as their interrelationships. This section gives a more comprehensive overview of SACM. Additional information about Configuration Management can be found in [Add07, pages 244–245].

In the following subsections, configuration items are described in Section 3.2.1, followed by Configuration Management Databases in Section 3.2.2 (page 101). In Section 3.2.3 (page 103) the Federated Configuration Management Database approach, which provides mechanisms for accessing multiple databases is presented, followed by Configuration Management Systems in Section 3.2.4 (page 103).

3.2.1. Configuration Items

Configuration items are the entities, which are used to fulfill services. A configuration item (CI) is defined as

> "an asset, service component or other item that is, or will be, under the control of Configuration Management." [LM07, page 67]

There can be a large variety of configuration items with regard to "complexity, size and type, ranging from an entire service or system including all hardware, software, documentation and support staff to a single software module or a minor hardware component" [LM07, page 67]. Configuration items are allowed to "be grouped into a release" in order to simplify their management [LM07, page 67]. Furthermore, "[c]onfiguration items should be selected using established selection criteria, grouped, classified and identified in such a way that they are manageable and traceable throughout the service lifecycle" [LM07, page 67].

Configuration items can be classified as follows [LM07, pages 67–68]:

- "**Service lifecycle CIs** such as the Business Case, Service Management Plans, service lifecycle plans, Service Design Package, release and change plans, and test plans. They provide a picture of the service provider's services, how these services will be delivered, what benefits are expected, at what cost, and when they will be realized.
- "**Service CIs** such as:
  - "Service capability assets: management, organization, processes, knowledge, people
  - "Service resource assets: financial capital, systems, applications, information, data, infrastructure and facilities, financial capital, people
  - "Service model
  - "Service package
  - "Release package
  - "Service acceptance criteria.
- "**Organization CIs** – Some documentation will define the characteristics of a CI whereas other documentation will be a CI in its own right and need to be controlled, e.g. the organization's business strategy or other policies that are internal to the organization but independent of the service provider. Regulatory or statutory requirements also form external products that need to be tracked, as do products shared between more than one group.
- "**Internal CIs** comprising those delivered by individual projects, including tangible (data centre) and intangible assets such as software that are required to deliver and maintain the service and infrastructure.

- "**External CIs** such as external customer requirements and agreements, releases from suppliers or sub-contractors and external services.
- "**Interface CIs** that are required to deliver the end-to-end service across a service provider interface (SPI)." [LM07, pages 67–68, emphasis in original]

The following subsections describe the attributes and relationships of configuration items. Additional information about configuration items in general, and attributes of CIs and relationships between CIs in particular can be found in [Add07, pages 229–235] and [Add07, pages 240–244].

Attributes

The following attributes of configuration items are suggested to be stored in the Configuration Management Database [LM07, page 75]:

- "Unique identifier
- "CI type
- "Name/description
- "Version (e.g. file, build, baseline, release)
- "Location
- "Supply date
- "Licence details, e.g. expiry date
- "Owner/custodian
- "Status
- "Supplier/source
- "Related document masters
- "Related software masters
- "Historical data, e.g. audit trail
- "Relationship type
- "Applicable SLA" [LM07, page 75]

The ontology, which was created as the data model for this thesis, and which is presented in Section 4.3 (page 161), uses most of the just outlined attributes as a foundation for describing configuration items in the ITSM Wiki.

Relationships

Besides defining the attributes of configuration items, the specification of the relationships between configuration items further adds to the usefulness of Configuration Management.

Examples of relationships between configuration items are [LM07, page 77]:

- "A CI is a part of another CI, e.g. a software module is part of a program; a server is part of a site infrastructure – this is a 'parent-child' relationship.
- "A CI is connected to another CI, e.g. a desktop computer is connected to a LAN.
- "A CI uses another CI, e.g. a program uses a module from another program; a business service uses an infrastructure server.
- "A CI is installed on another [one], e.g. MS Project is installed on a desktop PC." [LM07, page 77]

Relationships between configuration items can be classified as "one-to-one, one-to-many and many-to-one" [LM07, page 77]. Figure 3.8 shows an example of a service (an online order management service) and the relations between the configuration items, which work together to make the service function. As can be seen, the configuration items are a mix of other services, network equipment, servers, people, and databases. There exist different types of relationships between the configuration items. For example, the online management service utilizes an IT system, which consists of multiple configuration items, including firewalls and Web servers. The Web servers depend on other configuration items in order to provide their services, e.g., single sign-on services and application servers. These again depend on underlying databases [Add07, pages 241–242].

The modeling of relationships between configuration items also played a role in developing the ITSM ontology, which is described in detail in Section 4.3 (page 161).

3.2.2. Configuration Management Database

Information about entities relevant for IT Service Management, which are referred to as configuration items, is stored in a structured format in one or more databases. These databases are referred to as Configuration Management Databases.

Reference [LM07, page 230] defines a Configuration Management Database (CMDB) as follows:

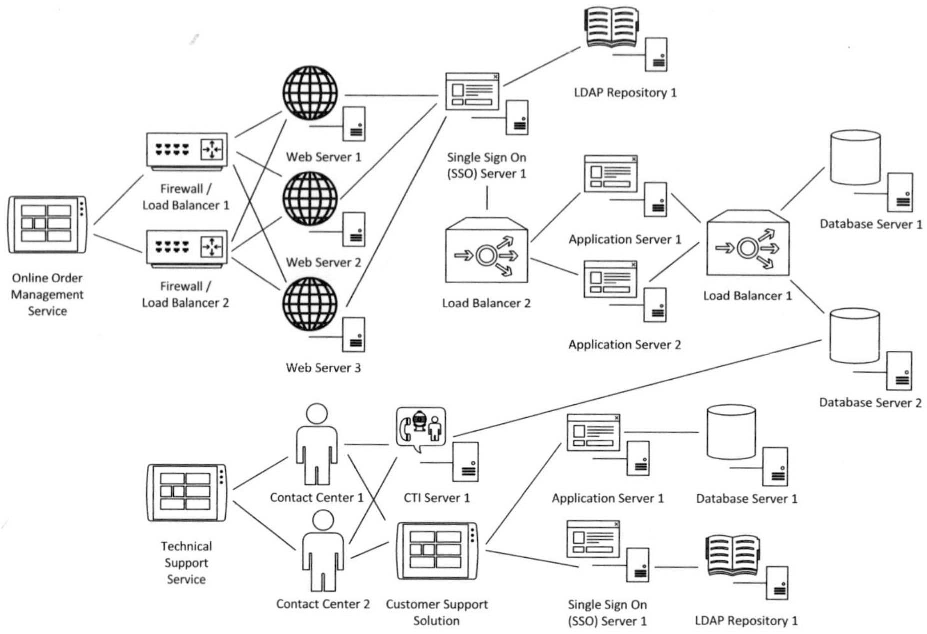

Figure 3.8.: Relationships between CIs (cf. [Add07, page 241])

> "A database used to store Configuration Records throughout their Lifecycle. The Configuration Management System maintains one or more CMDBs, and each CMDB stores Attributes of CIs, and Relationships with other CIs." [LM07, page 230]

Configuration Management Databases can be viewed either from a physical perspective, or from the logical perspective. While the physical perspective is concerned with the actual database, which holds the data (e.g., a MySQL database server instance running on a particular server), the logical perspective abstracts from the physical one.

The use of multiple Configuration Management Databases, which are combined into a single Federated Configuration Management Database (FCMDB), is described in the following Section 3.2.3 (page 103). Following that, the use of logical and physical CMDBs in the more encompassing context of a Configuration Management System is described in Section 3.2.4 (page 103).

More information about CMDBs and FCMDBs can be found in [Add07, pages 236–240].

3.2.3. Federated Configuration Management Database

Federated Configuration Management Databases form an access layer for accessing information, which is distributed across multiple databases, via a centralized mechanism. While there often exist multiple databases, which contain information relevant for ITSM functions, the federation layer presents a uniform layer for accessing the otherwise heterogeneous information [JDBN+10].

In [Ris09], a *distributed database* is defined as "a database where data management is distributed over several nodes (computers) in a computer network". Federated databases, as a special form of distributed databases, are defined as follows [Ris09]:

> "In a *federated database* the database administrator defines a single *global integration schema* describing how data in underlying databases are mapped to the integration schema view. This provides distribution transparency for integrated data." [Ris09, emphasis in original]

The work presented in [JDBN+10] compares several commercial CMDB products with the needs of Siemens IT Solutions and Services, an international IT service and outsourcing provider. Products compared in the article are from the vendors BMC, CA, HP, and IBM. While the main focus of these CMDB solutions lies on data visualization and monitoring, global write access is not supported [JDBN+10].

3.2.4. Configuration Management System

While the capturing of information and the modeling as configuration items, followed by the subsequent storage in a Configuration Management Database serve as the first steps when introducing Service Asset and Configuration Management (SACM), value is derived from SACM only if the information can be accessed satisfactorily. The Configuration Management System (CMS) serves as a collection of tools and databases, which offer an encompassing view and reporting mechanisms with regard to Service Asset and Configuration Management [LM07, pages 68–69].

Reference [LM07, page 230] defines a Configuration Management System as follows:

> "A set of tools and databases that are used to manage an IT Service Provider's Configuration data. The CMS also includes information about Incidents, Problems, Known Errors, Changes and Releases; and may contain data about employees, Suppliers, locations, Business Units, Customers and Users. The CMS includes tools for collecting, storing, managing, updating, and presenting data about all Configuration Items and their Relationships. The CMS is maintained by Configuration Management and is used by all IT Service Management Processes." [LM07, page 230]

Architecture

The architecture of a Configuration Management System, as it is described in [LM07, page 68], is shown in Figure 3.9. It gives an overview of the components of a Configuration Management System, as suggested by ITIL, by presenting a layered architecture. The architecture includes starting from bottom to top, the Data Information Sources and Tools, the Information Integration Layer, the Knowledge Processing Layer, and the Presentation Layer. The following paragraphs give an overview of these layers.

Data Information Sources and Tools The bottom-most layer of the Configuration Management Systems includes the data information sources and tools, which are required for the storage and acquisition of the SACM information. Parts of this layer are the following components [LM07, page 68]:

- Project documents and project software
- Definitive Media Library: Copies of all installation versions and related data of used software is archived at a safe location [LM07, page 69]
- Physical CMDBs: Databases, which store information about configuration items and together form the Federated Configuration Management Database
- Tools
- Software Configuration Management
- Tools for discovery, asset management and audits
- Connections to enterprise applications [LM07, page 68]

Information Integration Layer The information integration layer, which is located above the data information sources and tools layer, contains the following components [LM07, page 68]:

- Integrated CMDB
  - Service portfolio
  - Service catalogue
  - Service model
  - Service release
  - Service change
  - Mapping between business/customer/supplier/user, service, application, infrastructure

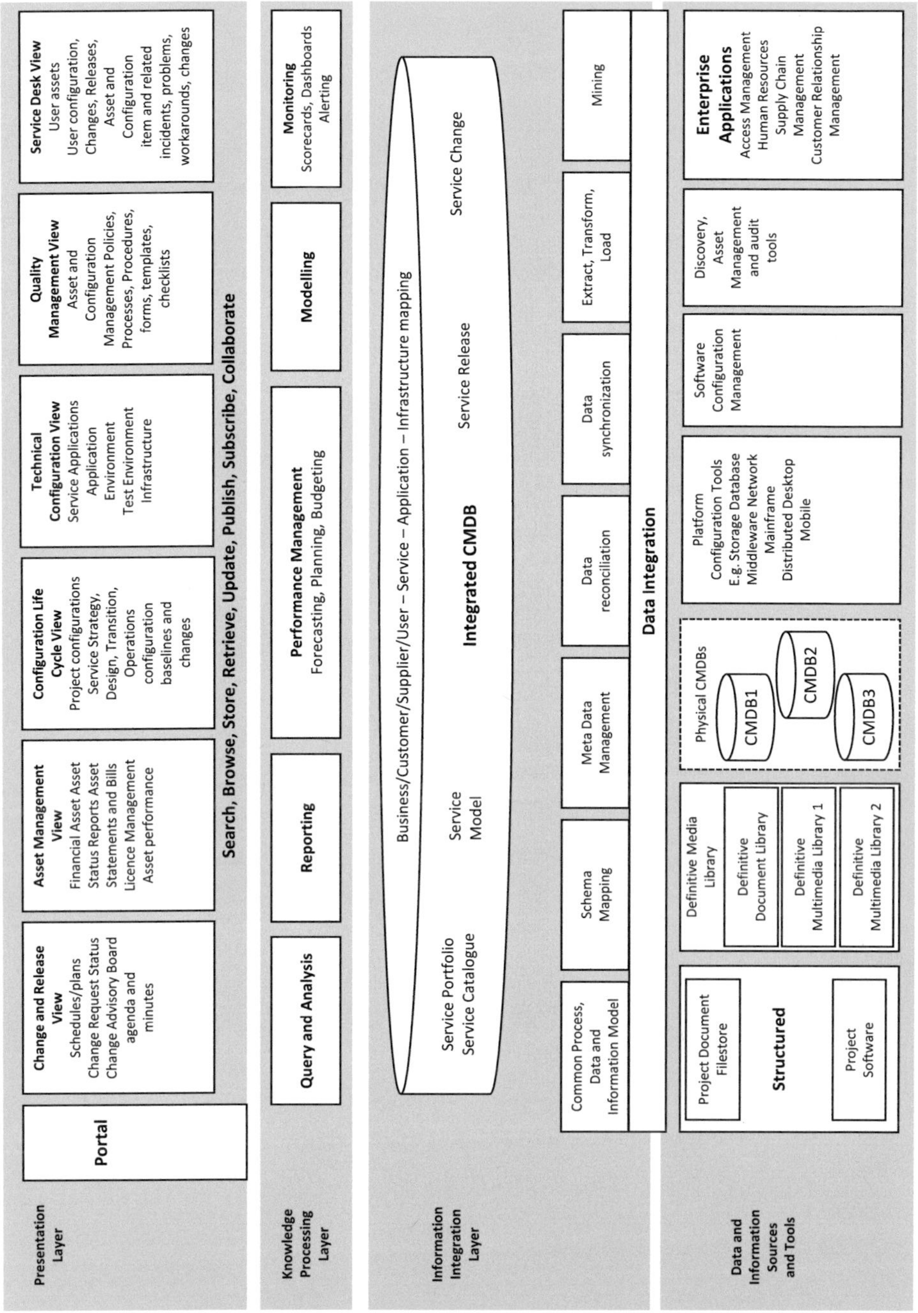

Figure 3.9.: Configuration Management System (cf. [LM07, page 68])

- Common process, data and information model
- Schema mapping
- Meta data management
- Data reconciliation
- Data synchronization
- Extract, transform, load
- Mining [LM07, page 68]

Knowledge Processing Layer The knowledge processing layer, which is located above the information integration layer, consists of the following components [LM07, page 68]:

- Query and analysis
- Reporting
- Performance management
- Modeling
- Monitoring [LM07, page 68]

Presentation Layer The presentation layer, which is the topmost layer of the Configuration Management System, as presented in [LM07, page 68], consists of the following components:

- Portal
- Change and release view
- Asset management view
- Configuration lifecycle view
- Technical configuration view
- Quality management view
- Service desk view [LM07, page 68]

Technical Requirements

From a technical perspective, Configuration Management Systems should have the following properties [LM07, pages 194–195]:

- "CMDB should be linked to the [Definitive Media Library]" [LM07, page 194]
- "The Configuration Management System should prevent changes from being made to the IT infrastructure or service configuration baseline without valid authorization via Change Management." [LM07, page 195]
- "As far as possible, all changes should be recorded on the CMS at least by the time that the change is implemented." [LM07, page 195]
- "The status (e.g. 'live', 'archive', etc.) of each CI affected by a change should be updated automatically if possible. Example ways in which this automatic recording of changes could be implemented include automatic updating of the CMS when software is moved between libraries (e.g. from 'acceptance test' to 'live', or from 'live' to an 'archive' library), when the service catalogue is changed, and when a release is distributed." [LM07, page 195]

Further technical requirements for a Configuration Management System are [LM07, page 195]:

- "Sufficient security controls to limit access on a need-to-know basis
- "Support for CIs of varying complexity, e.g. entire systems, releases, single hardware items, software modules
- "Hierarchic and networked relationships between CIs; by holding information on the relationships between CIs, Configuration Management tools facilitate the impact assessment of RFCs
- "Easy addition of new CIs and deletion of old CIs
- "Automatic validation of input data (e.g. are all CI names unique?)
- "Automatic determination of all relationships that can be automatically established, when new CIs are added
- "Support for CIs with different model numbers, version numbers, and copy numbers
- "Automatic identification of other affected CIs when any CI is the subject of an incident report/record, problem record, known error record or RFC

- “Integration of problem management data within the CMS, or at least an interface from the Configuration Management System to any separate problem management databases that may exist
- “Automatic updating and recording of the version number of a CI if the version number of any component CI is changed
- “Maintenance of a history of all CIs (both a historical record of the current version – such as installation date, records of Changes, previous locations, etc. – and of previous versions)
- “Support for the management and use of configuration baselines (corresponding to definitive copies, versions etc.), including support for reversion to trusted versions
- “Ease of interrogation of the CMS and good reporting facilities, including trend analysis (e.g. the ability to identify the number of RFCs affecting particular CIs)
- “Ease of reporting of the CI inventory so as to facilitate configuration audits
- “Flexible reporting tools to facilitate impact analyses
- “The ability to show graphically the configuration models and maps of interconnected CIs, and to input information about new CIs via such maps
- “The ability to show the hierarchy of relationships between ‘parent’ CIs and ‘child’ CIs.” [LM07, page 195]

With regard to automatic discovery, ITIL recommends an automatic tool for reading configuration information into the CMS [LM07, page 195]:

> “Automating the initial discovery and configuration audits significantly increases the efficiency and effectiveness of Configuration Management. These tools can determine what hardware and software is installed and how applications are mapped to the infrastructure.” [LM07, page 195]

The technical requirements listed in this subsection are the basis for the development of the Semantic MediaWiki-based ITSM platform (ITSM Wiki), which is presented in Section 4.2 (page 136). They also form the basis for the validation of the ITSM Wiki platform in Section 6.1 (page 318).

3.3. Open Source Configuration Management Tools

In this section, based on the analysis of the approaches to Configuration Management, as outlined in Section 3.2 (page 98), open source tools which support organizations in the area of Configuration Management are analyzed.

Commercially available integrated tools, which support organizations with regard to IT Service Management in general, and Configuration Management in particular are mostly complex systems. These systems rarely work out of the box, but need customization, which takes into account the differing demands, requirements, and technical circumstances of different organizations. While there clearly existed demand for a Configuration Management solution within the IT department at FZI, it was quickly established that purchasing a commercial solution was not feasible. This was due to the following facts:

- *Customizability:* The non-standard demands at FZI lead to the need for being able to customize nearly all aspects of the system, which is only possible if the source code is available and the permission for modifications is given.
- *Costs:* Large investments into Configuration Management tools were not possible due to FZI's status as a government-backed organization and the associated requirements for saving money.

The focus of the analysis of existing tools in the context of this thesis is thus limited to freely available open source tools. The reasons for this restriction are as follows:

- Open source tools are freely available for testing and evaluation.
- Changes can be performed in order to customize and extend the tools for different environments and changing needs.
- Open source tools are provided free of charge, which makes it attractive for SMEs, which are not able to spend large amounts of money on ITSM tools.

Commercial tools in the area of Configuration Management, which are not further discussed in this thesis, are IBM Tivoli CMDB [IBM10, JBD+08a, ACC+10, JBD+08b], BMC Atrium CMDB [BMC06], CA CMDB [CA07a, CA07b], and HP Universal CMDB [Hew11].

The following subsection provides an overview of three open source Configuration Management tools, namely OTRS::ITSM, i-doit open, and OneCMDB, which were evaluated in the context of this thesis. While the evaluation of OTRS::ITSM took place within the production environment and took about one year, the evaluation of i-doit open and OneCMDB is based on a shorter testing period.

3.3.1. OTRS::ITSM

OTRS::ITSM[13] is an extension for the OTRS service desk system, which is available as open source software. OTRS::ITSM is described as follows [OTR11c]:

> "OTRS ITSM is an integrated IT Service Management Solution, combining the good practices of the IT Infrastructure Library ITIL with the proven power of OTRS, the leading Open Source Service Management Solution. This freely licensed open source IT Service Management solution provides superior support to service desks by aiding in implementing ITIL good practices. OTRS ITSM bridges the gap between the business processes of your company, your IT service management and your IT infrastructure, and supports you in meeting today's IT challenges. OTRS ITSM fulfills Enterprises' need for a scalable, high performance and integrated solution, capable of easily administering complex processes and IT infrastructures. It is a platform-independent, flexible, quick to install and yet an extremely powerful solution, ideal for small, medium and large businesses, as well as for 'global players'." [OTR11c]

Due to the fact that OTRS had already been in use at FZI's IT department for the management of service desk requests since 2006, it was evaluated whether OTRS-::ITSM fulfilled the requirements for an integrated Configuration Management and documentation solution. At the time an initial evaluation of possible technical platforms was performed (2007), OTRS::ITSM was available as version 1.0. Since 2011, it has been available in version 3.0. OTRS::ITSM was intensively tested at FZI's IT department for about one year, as described in Section 3.1.2 (page 85). Figure 3.3 (page 87) shows a screenshot of OTRS::ITSM.

OTRS::ITSM (version 3.0) covers the following functionalities [OTR11b]:

- "Incident Management
- "Problem Management
- "Change Management
- "Request Fulfillment Management
- "Service Asset & Configuration Management (CMDB/CMS)
- "Knowledge Management
- "Service Catalog Management
- "Event Management
- "Service Level Management" [OTR11b]

[13] `http://www.otrs.com/en/products/itsm/`

Reference [OTR11a] describes the administration of the OTRS ticketing system, which forms the basis for the OTRS::ITSM component, while [OTR10] shows how OTRS can be extended. In [OTR09], the basics of the OTRS::ITSM tool (version 2) are outlined. Reference [Kni10] describes the implementation of an OTRS::ITSM-based CMDB at TU München.

3.3.2. i-doit open

i-doit open[14] is a Web-based tool for managing a Configuration Management Database and other aspects of ITIL. It is available in two different versions, a functionally limited open source version, and a commercial version with additional functionalities [i-d11a]. Reference [i-d08a] describes i-doit open as follows:

> "i-doit is an IT documentation system based on ITIL guidelines. It documents IT systems and their changes, defines emergency plans, displays vital information, and helps to ensure a stable and effcient [*sic*] operation of IT networks. i-doit allows a rich amount of technical information to be filed for each element from a wall outlet to a mainframe in a structured way. Every employee can access this information easily (and in a selective way) through a Web browser. Due to its modular architecture, it is possible to deploy functionality add-ons or even develop extensions." [i-d08a]

Figure 3.10 shows a screenshot of i-doit open. On the left side of the screenshot, a hierarchical overview of the different aspects of the selected configuration item can be seen. On the right side, more information about the configuration item with regard to the selected aspect is shown.

With regard to the functionalities of a Configuration Management Database, i-doit open provides all necessary standard functionalities. In the open source version however, the reporting functionalities are restricted to pre-defined reports. When looking at the functionalities that were needed at FZI, and which extend the realm of CMDB systems (e.g., the close coupling between documentation and CMDB), i-doit open does not provide those out-of-the-box.

By providing a large number of pre-defined categories and object properties, configuration efforts are minimized. For environments where an approach, which requires more flexibility is needed, the static framework is limiting. i-doit open is extensible by using modules. Files can be attached to configuration items. While plain-text comments can be attached to configuration items, no formatting can be provided, and there is no mechanism for using hyperlinks between text fragments. Information can be imported via XML files, but no mechanism for the automatic gathering of information about computers is implemented.

[14] `http://www.i-doit.org/`

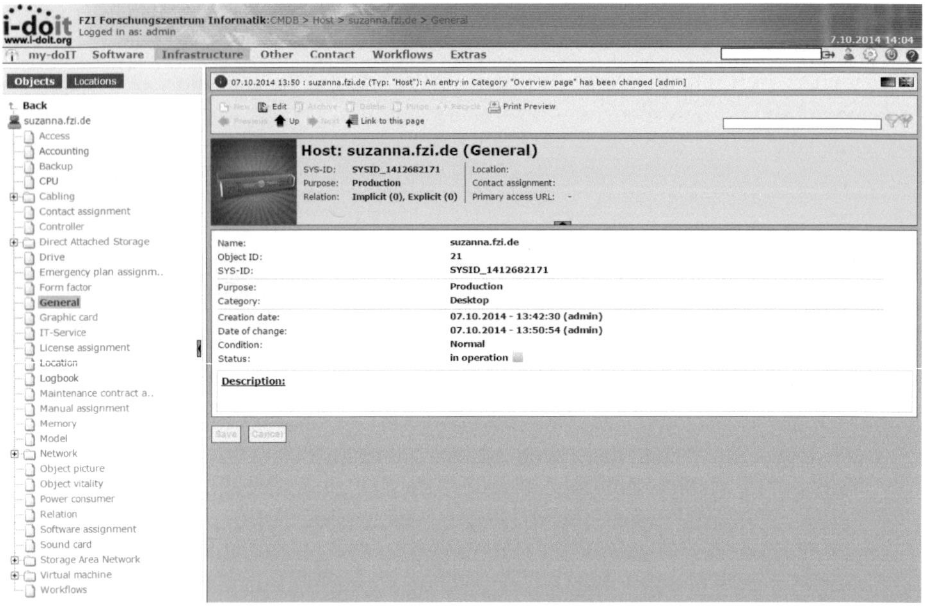

Figure 3.10.: i-doit open Screenshot

In i-doit open, functionalities for Change Management and Problem Management are not implemented. Information about configuration items is stored in a database. This enables to retain and query structured information, but does not provide more advanced query and reporting mechanisms, as made possible by ontology-based systems. Moreover, it is not possible to add new categories for configuration items from the user interface without performing changes in the source code. The i-doit open manual [i-d10a] describes all features of the tool, while [i-d11e] provides a summary of its most important features.

3.3.3. OneCMDB

OneCMDB[15] is an open source CMDB management tool. Reference [One09] describes OneCMDB as follows:

> "OneCMDB is a CMDB aimed at small and medium sized businesses. One-CMDB can be used as a stand-alone CMDB to keep track of software and hardware assets and their relations. Thanks to its open API:s [*sic*] it can also be a flexible and powerful Configuration Management engine for other Service Management software." [One09]

[15] `http://www.onecmdb.org/`

Figure 3.11 shows a screenshot of the OneCMDB user interface. The left part of the screenshot shows a tree, which lists a hierarchy of configuration item classes. In the right part of the screenshot, a table of server CIs is shown.

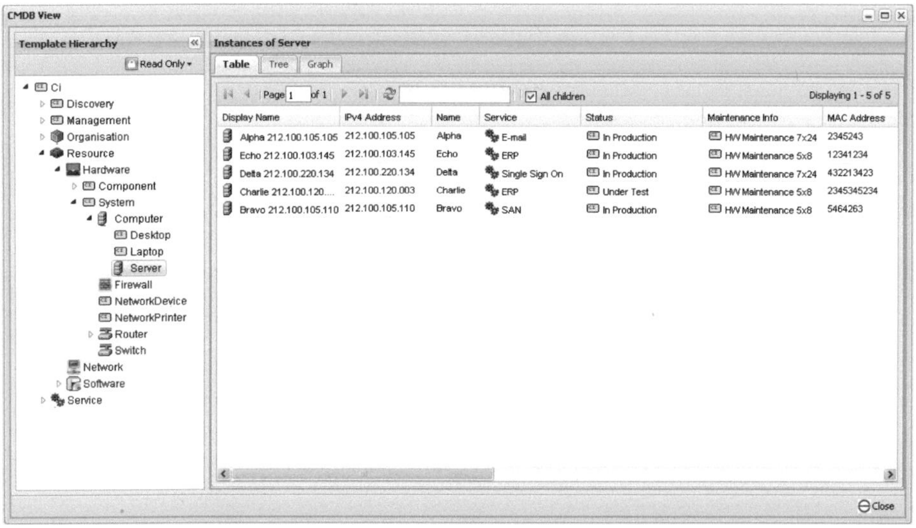

Figure 3.11.: OneCMDB Screenshot (Source: [One09])

3.4. Summary

In this chapter, an analysis of the current state of IT Service Management at FZI, a medium-sized enterprise, was given. In Section 3.1 (page 82), the environment, for which the toolset presented in this thesis was designed, was introduced. In Section 3.2 (page 98), the requirements for a Configuration Management System in the context of the previously described environment were determined. Finally, in Section 3.3 (page 109), an overview of existing open source Configuration Management tools was given.

In the following Chapter 4, the technical foundation for the ITSM Wiki is selected, and approaches for integrating methods of ITIL with the ITSM Wiki are presented. Furthermore, the design of the ontologies, which serve as the data models for the ITSM Wiki, is described.

4. Design of the Semantic Wiki-based ITSM Platform

In Chapter 3 (page 81) an analysis was performed of the environment, in which this thesis was written, and the relevant approaches from the literature were analyzed for their usefulness in the FZI environment.

This chapter describes the design and implementation of an improved tool, which addresses the shortcomings of the previously used tools. The work presented in this chapter builds on the work previously published in [KA09] and [KA10].

In Section 4.1 (page 116), wikis and semantic wikis are introduced as a possible technical platform, followed by the selection of one semantic wiki, namely Semantic MediaWiki, as the technical platform for the IT administration information management tool. In Section 4.2 (page 136), it is described, how the deficient situation with regard to the sharing and integration of information described in Chapter 3 can be improved by the use of a semantic wiki as an integration platform. Various aspects of IT Service Management, for example, Configuration Management, and Service Knowledge Management, are addressed. In Section 4.3 (page 161), an ontology is developed, which serves as the data model for the semantic wiki-based ITSM platform. Finally, Section 4.4 (page 184) gives a summary.

4.1. Selection of the Technical Platform

The mixture of different tools and the associated distribution of structured, as well as unstructured information, slowed down daily work processes. Starting from the idea of extending existing tools, different scenarios were considered in order to mitigate these issues. An early attempt was to tightly couple the OTRS::ITSM-based CMDB with the existing PmWiki, which would have resulted in a dual system, storing structured data in OTRS::ITSM, while storing unstructured data in the wiki. There were two options considered, each with a different degree of integration between the platforms and a different amount of needed work for the realization:

- The first approach would have resulted in a system, which used Web links to connect information between the two platforms. If, for example, a computer, whose information was stored in a structured format in the OTRS::ITSM CMDB, had additional text associated with it (e.g., a work procedure), there would have been a link generated in OTRS::ITSM, which would have pointed to the corresponding wiki page. The creation and maintenance of the links would have been manual work done by the IT administrators.
- The second plan consisted of extending OTRS::ITSM and PmWiki's source codes, which are both available as open source, in order to accomplish a tighter integration of the two platforms. This approach would have resulted in a highly customized system, which would have complicated further updates.

While the first approach was tried in practice for a short time, it soon became frustrating to manually create and update the links between the platforms. Furthermore, the integration was not tight enough to be of much use, because queries for information distributed over the two platforms were not possible.

Storing accounting information in the OTRS::ITSM-based CMDB was tried but would have needed the creation of a customized program for the creation of the annual accounting statements. Using the open source business intelligence tool Pentaho[1] for the generation of the accounting statements was considered, but not pursued further because it would not have solved the above-mentioned problems of integrating information between the CMDB and PmWiki.

Based on the author's previous encounters with a semantic wiki, first as an academic interest, and second, as a productively used Knowledge Management platform for a research group, the next approach was to look into adapting a semantic wiki for the use within the IT department. After some initial testing of Semantic MediaWiki, the approach seemed to be worth pursuing and resulted in the Semantic MediaWiki-based ITSM Wiki platform, which is described in detail in the following sections.

In the following subsections, first, an overview of different wiki platforms is given in Section 4.1.1 (page 117), followed by an overview of semantic wiki platforms in Section 4.1.2 (page 117). Based on a comparison of the platforms, MediaWiki with the Semantic MediaWiki extension is selected as the technical platform for the ITSM Wiki. MediaWiki and Semantic MediaWiki are described in detail in Section 4.1.3 (page 121) and Section 4.1.4 (page 124), followed by a short introduction of additionally used MediaWiki extensions in Section 4.1.5 (page 132).

4.1.1. Wiki Platforms

There exists a number of different wiki engine implementations. Reference [Cos09a] currently lists 121 different wiki engines, which differ in various aspects. In the area of programming languages, PHP is dominating (31 %), followed by Java (18 %) and Perl (11 %) [Cos09c]. Concerning software licenses, the majority (85 %) is free or open source, while only 15 % is commercially licensed [Cos09b]. Regarding comparisons with other wiki engines on the WikiMatrix Web site, MediaWiki, DokuWiki, PmWiki, TWiki, and PhpWiki are the most popular ones [Cos09a]. A list, which names the top ten wiki engines can be found in [Cun09a], while [CEL$^+$08] gives an introduction into five different wiki platforms.

4.1.2. Semantic Wiki Platforms

There exist several different semantic wiki platforms, mostly as extensions to existing wiki software and with different focuses and approaches on using semantics and on usability. Reference [SBBK08] gives an overview of five semantic wikis. Semantic MediaWiki, which is the platform used for the extensions presented in this thesis, is described in more detail in Section 4.1.3 (page 121).

[1] `http://www.pentaho.com/`

Reference [Sem09] provides a comprehensive overview of the semantic wikis available, as well as detailed information about the wikis (e.g., programming language, license, status, and activity), which is shown in Table 4.1. Information about the status and activity was checked on the wiki's project Web page, if it was available. Active wikis are wikis, which were updated less than a year ago (the semantic wiki platform was selected in 2009). The last reported activity was derived from the project site of the respective wiki by the author of the thesis. A table that compares several different semantic wikis can be found in [BGE+08, page 87]. Furthermore, an overview of the state-of-the-art, as well as applications and use cases, with regard to semantic wikis, can be found in [BSVW12].

Analysis of Different Approaches

Semantic wikis offer a highly flexible environment for managing structured as well as unstructured data. They allow information re-use (e.g., the generation of tables from semantically annotated information stored in wiki pages), as well as the interpretation of information by computers. Furthermore, browsing can be improved by taking into account the explicitly specified relations between information stored in the wiki. With regard to finding information in the wiki, semantic wikis offer better results by taking into account the semantic relations (i.e., information that is only implicitly stated through other explicit relations can also be found in the wiki).

There are several approaches for implementing semantic functionality in the context of wikis. With regard to the underlying platform, semantic wikis can be either based on existing non-semantic wikis, or be built from scratch. Building on top of an established platform eases development because base functionalities do not have to be re-implemented. Furthermore, there is an already existing ecosystem of extensions and developers, from which one can benefit. On the other hand, developing from scratch can benefit the design of the semantic wiki because the whole platform can be tailored around the semantic functionality of the wiki.

When looking at different semantic wikis, it can be seen that there are different approaches to whether to enrich wikitext with semantic annotations or whether to design a platform for managing ontologies from within a Web-based collaborative environment. While Semantic MediaWiki is an example of a text-centric semantic wiki, OntoWiki [ADR06] is an example of a data-centric semantic wiki. In the area of semantic wiki-based IT Service Management, there exist needs for both, data-centric as well as text-centric wikis, because on the one hand, highly structured information (e.g., configuration items) has to be managed, while on the other hand, documentation of ITSM processes and best practices are more text-centric. After taking into account the benefits of both approaches, it can be seen that the text-centric approach offers more flexibility and that there exist tools, which help in implementing a structured approach (e.g., Semantic Forms, as described in Section 4.1.5, page 132).

Wiki Name	Language	License	Status	Active
AceWiki	Java	LGPL	alpha	yes (2009-05-28)
BOWiki		GPL	stable	no (2008-06-23)
Braindump	PHP	MIT		no (2008-08-13)
COW	Java			no
IkeWiki [Sch06, GWS06]	Java	GPL	superseded	no (2008-03-05)
Kaukolu [Kie06]	Java			no
KendraBase	Python			no
KiWi [SEG+09]	Java EE	BSD	beta	yes (2009-07-01)
KnowWE [BRP10]	Java	LGPL	beta	yes (2009-05-29)
Makna	Java		unknown	no
OntoWiki [ADR06]	PHP		unknown	yes (2009-11-08)
Paux	Java			no
PlatypusWiki [TCC04]	Java		unknown	no (2006)
Rhizome	Python			no
Semantic MediaWiki [VKV+06]	PHP	GPL	stable	yes
SemperWiki	Ruby			no
SMW+ [HSP09]	PHP	GPL	stable	yes
SweetWiki [BGE+08]	Java			no (2008-02-29)
SWiM	Java XSLT	GPL	alpha	no (2008-06)
SWOOKI	Java	GPL		no
TaOPis	FLORA-2 Python PostgreSQL PHP	GPL	prototype	yes
WikSAR	Perl	GPL		no
Wikidsmart	Java	AGPL	stable	yes

Table 4.1.: List of Semantic Wikis (adapted from [Sem09])

Selection Based on Requirements

For building the ITSM Wiki, one semantic wiki had to be selected as the underlying platform. The following requirements had to be taken into account in order to have a solid, adaptable, and legally clean foundation:

1. The *functionality* of the semantic wiki platform: It has to provide support for editing both, structured, as well as unstructured information.
2. The *status* of the semantic wiki platform: For providing a solid basis for building the ITSM platform, the semantic wiki has to have reached a *stable* status.
3. The semantic wiki has to have a *license*, which allows free use (e.g., GPL, LGPL, or BSD license) and source code that is freely available for download.
4. The *activity* of the platform: In order to be able to react to changing external factors (e.g., new or updated standards), the semantic wiki has to be under active development.
5. The platform has to be *free from dependencies*, which limit or prevent its use in the ITSM platform (e.g., dependencies on commercial software, or software that has not reached a stable status).
6. The semantic wiki has to be *extensible* (i.e., the platform has to provide mechanisms for adding new features).
7. The semantic wiki has to be written in a *mainstream programming language* and has to have a *clean code basis* in order to simplify changes and additions.

After checking the first four requirements and eliminating all platforms with non-free or unknown licenses, which were not in a stable state, or were not modified for more than a year, there were three platforms left, which are shown in Table 4.2.

Wiki Name	Language	License	Status	Active
Semantic MediaWiki	PHP	GPL	stable	yes
SMW+	PHP	GPL	stable	yes
Wikidsmart	Java	AGPL	stable	yes

Table 4.2.: Narrowed-down Selection of Semantic Wiki Platforms

After checking the three semantic wikis, which fulfill the first four requirements (Semantic MediaWiki [VKV+06, KVV+07], SMW+ [HSP09], and Wikidsmart [zAg09]), for the remaining requirements, it became clear that Wikidsmart had to be discarded because it builds on top of the commercial Atlassian Confluence platform.

The two remaining platforms Semantic MediaWiki and SMW+ are related to each other: SMW+ builds on top of Semantic MediaWiki and provides additional features and usability improvements. Both platforms are extensible (there already exist extensions using Semantic Media features, e.g., Semantic Drilldown [Med09b], Semantic Forms [Med09c], and Semantic Maps [Med09d]). The programming language for both semantic wikis is PHP, a popular language mainly used in the area of Web development. Both code bases are clearly structured and well documented.

4.1.3. MediaWiki in Detail

MediaWiki is one of the most widely used wiki platforms. It is actively developed and used in the Wikipedia encyclopedia. MediaWiki is written in the PHP programming language and uses an SQL database (e.g., the open source MySQL database software). It is highly scalable and can be extended by using several mechanisms. This subsection gives an introduction into basic principles of MediaWiki and how MediaWiki is used, as well as into how MediaWiki can be extended and customized.

Using MediaWiki

MediaWiki is designed to provide a user interface, which is user-friendly and easy to learn. When looking at how a wiki is used, it can be seen that although wiki pages are editable, a large amount of users only read wiki pages. A statistic from September 2009 that includes all languages available in Wikipedia lists 11.4 billion page views, compared to 12.6 million edits in the same time span [Wik09b]). Because there is no fundamental difference between wiki pages and normal Web pages when reading, the following section only addresses aspects relevant for using MediaWiki to edit pages.

Pages in MediaWiki are written in a special syntax, called *wikitext*. The reason for using wikitext is to provide a relatively easy to learn syntax (compared to, for example, HTML), which is sufficiently powerful to allow formatting, linking and categorizing. Table 4.3 gives an overview of MediaWiki wikitext types.

Categories in MediaWiki allow to group wiki pages, which belong to a common topic, or are otherwise related. Each page can belong to none, one, or multiple categories. The membership in categories is expressed as `[[Category:CategoryName]]`, where the expression `Category` is a reserved keyword and `CategoryName` is the name of the category. Categories can belong to other categories, and form a directed graph (there is no mechanism for disallowing loops) [Bar08]. Categories are used for representing ontology classes in the Semantic MediaWiki extension (see Section 4.1.4, page 124).

<table>
<tr><th>Special Symbols</th><th>Examples</th><th>Purpose</th></tr>
<tr><td>Single quotes, two or more</td><td>'''bold words''', ''italic phrase''</td><td>Bold, italics, and other typestyles</td></tr>
<tr><td>Square brackets</td><td>[[link]], [http://www.example.com]</td><td>Create link</td></tr>
<tr><td>Equals sign</td><td>== Hello World ==</td><td>Headings and subheadings</td></tr>
<tr><td>Symbols at the beginning of a line</td><td>*, ***, #, {|, |, !</td><td>Lists and tables</td></tr>
<tr><td>Angled brackets</td><td><tagname>Text here</tagname> <hello/></td><td>XML-like tags with many purposes; similar to HTML, but full HTML is not supported</td></tr>
<tr><td>Curly braces</td><td>{{expression}}</td><td>Many purposes, including variables, templates, and parser functions</td></tr>
<tr><td>Double underscores</td><td>__TOC__</td><td>Many purposes, usually an overall effect on one Wiki page</td></tr>
</table>

Table 4.3.: Types of MediaWiki Wikitext (Source: [Bar08])

Extending MediaWiki

There exist more than 1400 extensions for MediaWiki (2009), which can be browsed and downloaded [Med09a]. All these plugins build on MediaWiki's extension architecture, which provides mechanisms for implementing additional functionality. Because some components developed for this thesis are implemented as MediaWiki extensions, the mechanisms are described here. The goal of this subsection is to give a high-level view of extension development. More details of implementation aspects will be given in Chapter 5 (page 185), where the components, which were developed as part of this thesis, are presented.

Extensions generally use *hooks* and *callbacks* for connecting to MediaWiki. A hook is a code location in MediaWiki, to which code from an extension can connect. When doing so, the functionality of the original function is replaced by the one in the extension, which allows changing the behavior of MediaWiki operations (e.g., a custom function can be executed on saving a page) [Bar08] (cf. [Med09e] for more details and a list of available hooks). A callback function is a PHP function, which contains the logic for passing information to and getting information from hooks. An entry in a global array registers a callback function with the desired hook. Callback functions can either keep the functionality of the original MediaWiki function and just add some functionality, or replace the MediaWiki function. An extension can implement hooks on its own so it can be accessed from other extensions [Bar08].

MediaWiki is extensible in the following ways [Bar08]:

- *Magic words* usable in the wikitext can display the content of variables or perform computations.
- MediaWiki's *behavior* can be changed.
- Creation of Web applications, so called *special pages* [Bar08].

The extensibility mechanisms are described in more detail in the following paragraphs.

Magic Words Magic words are a mechanism for displaying the content of variables or outputting the result of a computation. The output of a value stored in a *variable* is the simplest way of generating output, but also the most limited. Variables are accessed from wikitext by putting the variable name in double curly braces (e.g., `{{VARIABLE_NAME}}`). *Parser functions* are the second way of implementing magic words. They are more powerful than variables, because they are able to process parameters, perform complex tasks, and are able to display wikitext. Parser functions are accessed from wikitext by using the syntax `{{#functionName:parameter}}`. There can be multiple parameters, which are separated by the pipe symbol. *Tag extensions* are similar to parser functions, but output HTML text instead of wikitext. They are accessed by custom tags, e.g., `<customtag/>` for a parameterless call. A single parameter can be passed to the tag extension by putting it into the tag, e.g., `<customtag>parameter</customtag>`. More than one parameter is passed by using attributes, e.g., `<customtag param1=value param2=value/>` [Bar08].

Change of Behavior While magic words are used within wiki pages, behavior changes affect more than single pages. For example, additional functionality can be implemented, which is available from every page within the wiki. Furthermore, global aspects can be changed, e.g., the sort order of lists [Bar08].

Special Pages Special pages are Web applications, which are running within MediaWiki. They are grouped within the `Special` namespace and accessed by viewing the respective wiki page. Special page names follow the name scheme `Special:SpecialPageName` [Bar08]. Special pages in MediaWiki are mainly used for the following purposes [Wik09a]:

- List all pages, categories, protected pages, or images
- Show record pages (e.g., list of redirects, pages with most categories, short pages, and long pages)
- List problems (e.g., disambiguation pages, broken and double redirects, orphaned and dead-end pages)

- Pages without categories
- Unused files, categories, and templates
- Provisioning of tools (e.g., uploading files, page export)
- Provide search functionality
- Show user actions (e.g., recent changes, related changes, and new pages)
- User management functions (e.g., create user accounts, list user accounts, block users) [Wik09a]

Special pages can be added as extensions, e.g., as a way to configure parameters of the extension or to add functionality [Med13]. More implementation-specific details are given in later chapters, where the implementation of the ITSM Wiki components is described.

MediaWiki API

While magic words, change of behavior, and special pages allow the implementation of ways for accessing data from within MediaWiki, the MediaWiki API[2] provides a way for external programs to access data stored in the wiki. The API can be used by performing HTTP operations and allows retrieving of, for example, wikitext, images, and categories, as well as to create, modify, and delete pages [Bar08]. The MediaWiki API is described in more detail in [Med09f].

4.1.4. Semantic MediaWiki in Detail

Semantic MediaWiki[3] is an extension to MediaWiki, the software used in the popular user-editable Wikipedia encyclopedia. It extends MediaWiki in order to enable users to describe structural information in a machine-readable manner, which enables the dynamic generation of information from information contained in other pages. Wikipedia in its current form consists of a multitude of pages, which are linked among each other. Each of these (unannotated) links enables users to get more information by clicking on a link. While this navigation between pages works fine for human beings, it is not possible to have the information contained in pages and links interpreted by machines. Structural information contained in pages cannot be interpreted because it is not formally described in a machine-interpretable notation. This prevents the automatic processing of information contained in pages. Furthermore, numerical information is only available in textual form, which means that their meaning cannot be understood by computers and the information cannot be processes for further use [VKV$^+$06].

[2]**A**pplication **P**rogramming **I**nterface

[3]`http://semantic-mediawiki.org/wiki/Semantic_MediaWiki`

The structure of Wikipedia pages is optimized for human users, i.e., persons have to read a page in order to use the information contained in the page. If the information is distributed among several pages, a person has to read or at least skim through a page in order to gather the desired information. Although there are tables within Wikipedia that aggregate information found in pages, these are user-generated tables, which depend on dedicated Wikipedia users to be created and updated. While it is easy to find volunteers to create tables with popular and relatively static information, e.g., the size of countries, it is hard or impossible to find volunteers for more obscure or dynamic information, e.g., a table naming all movies by Italian directors from the 1960s. In addition, the manual editing of tables with information gathered from several pages introduces a potential for errors and inconsistencies due to changing facts in pages. The Semantic MediaWiki extension allows the typing of links between pages in order to give machine-interpretable meaning to these links. Furthermore, the extension allows the typification of data within a page in order to make this data machine-interpretable. By doing so, the extension improves searching and browsing in pages. In order to implement these functionalities, the Semantic MediaWiki extension uses RDF, XSD, RDFS and OWL, which are Semantic Web standards created by the W3C. The focus of the extension is on enabling users to use semantic technologies while adhering to the principles of the Wikipedia community. In addition, vital design choices were usability, expressiveness, flexibility, scalability as well as interchange and compatibility [VKV+06].

Key Elements

The key elements of the Semantic MediaWiki extension are categories, typed links, and attributes [VKV+06]. In the following paragraphs, a detailed description of the elements is given.

Categories Categories are used to classify pages based on the page's content. While categories already exist in Wikipedia in order to assist browsing, the Semantic MediaWiki extension uses categories in the sense of classes or concepts in ontologies [VKV+06].

Typed Links Typed links are an extension to normal links commonly used in Wikipedia pages for linking other pages. While normal links do not have any meaning except that there is some kind of connection between two pages, typed links are used to explicitly express the kind of connection between the pages. New typed links can be created by any user by adding a link for the first time. While normal Wikipedia links are created by using the name of the page in double brackets, e.g., `[[England]]`, typed links express the meaning of the link by explicitly stating the relation, e.g., `[[is capital of::England]]`. While a single relation is usually sufficient for linking pages, it is possible to use multiple links by using the syntax `[[type-1::type-2::...::type-n::target page]]`. By using previously stated information (e.g., the relation "is capital of" is a special case of "is located in"), information that is not explicitly stated, can be inferred. For example, it can be inferred that London is located in England. Additionally, aggregated queries can be used to combine several search criteria, e.g., it can be inferred that London should be included in the list of European countries because London is a member of the category "City" and England is located in Europe [VKV+06].

Attributes Attributes are used in Semantic MediaWiki in order to give meaning to data values by explicitly stating an attribute, the data and a unit of measurement. Attributes in Semantic MediaWiki are expressed with a := between the attribute and the value in the form `[[population:=7,421,328]]` [VKV+06].

Semantic MediaWiki Syntax

When comparing the syntax of standard MediaWiki with that of Semantic MediaWiki, it can be seen that the additional semantic information is integrated into the page in a way, which keeps the overall structure and syntax of the page intact [VKV+06]. An excerpt from the page about London looks as following in the standard MediaWiki syntax [VKV+06]:

```
''London'' is the capital city of [[England]] and of
the [[United Kingdom]]. As of [[2005]], the total
resident population of London was estimated 7,421,328.
Greater London covers an area of 609 square miles.
[[Category:City]]
```

The same passage from the page looks like that when enriched by the possibilities provided by the Semantic MediaWiki extension [VKV+06]:

```
''London'' is the capital city of
[[capital of::England]] and of the
[[is capital of::United Kingdom]]. As of [[2005]],
the total resident population of London was estimated
[[population:=7,421,328]]. Greater London covers an
area of [[area:=609 square miles]].
[[Category:City]]
```

The upper part of Figure 4.1 shows how pages and links interact with each other in MediaWiki. As can be seen in the lower part, Semantic MediaWiki adds concepts, data and relations, in order to express statements in an explicit form. While in standard MediaWiki syntax, the link to the page about England does have no explicit meaning, the link does have explicit meaning in the Semantic MediaWiki syntax [VKV+06].

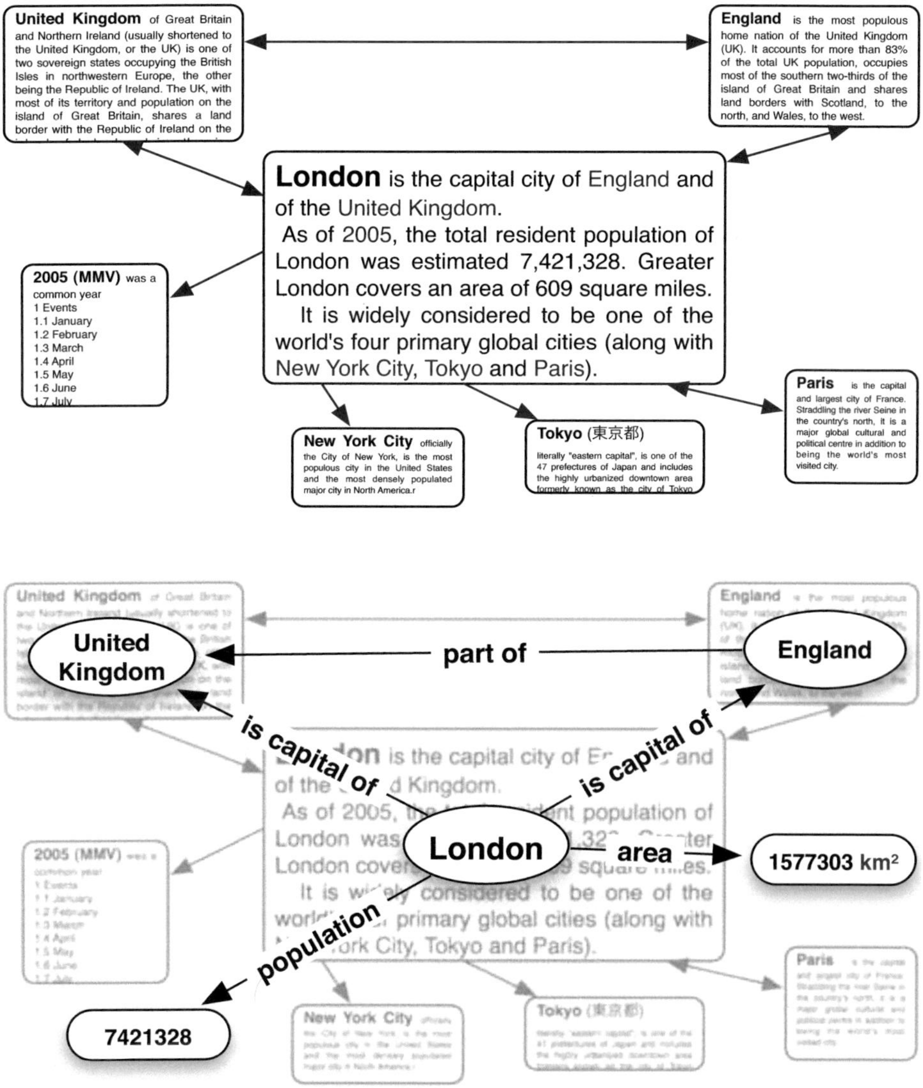

Figure 4.1.: Concepts, Data, and Relations in SMW (Source: [VKV+06])

Semantic MediaWiki provides a specialized text-based syntax, which extends the syntax used in MediaWiki by mechanisms for describing semantic properties. By embedding Semantic MediaWiki statements into MediaWiki wikitext, relations and attributes can be generated and used. MediaWiki category hierarchies are used as mechanisms for describing class hierarchies in an ontology [VKV+06]. Figure 4.2 and Figure 4.3 give a summary of the Semantic MediaWiki syntax and the syntax of extensions (e.g., Semantic Forms), which work together with Semantic MediaWiki.

Semantic MediaWiki Datatypes

Semantic MediaWiki provides a number of built-in datatypes, which are used to represent structured data [Sem13]. Table 4.4 shows an overview of the datatypes.

Datatype	**Description**
Annotation URI	Holds URIs, but has some technical differences during export compared to the "URL" type
Boolean	Holds boolean (true/false) values
Code	Holds technical, pre-formatted texts (similar to type Text)
Date	Holds particular points in time
Email	Holds e-mail addresses
Geographic coordinate	Holds coordinates describing geographic locations
Number	Holds integer and decimal numbers, with an optional exponent
Page	Holds names of wiki pages, and displays them as a link
Quantity	Holds values that describe quantities, containing both a number and a unit
Record	Allows saving compound property values that consist of a short list of values with fixed type and order
Telephone number	Holds international telephone numbers based on the RFC 3966 standard
Temperature	Holds temperature values (similar to type Quantity)
Text	Holds text of arbitrary length
URL	Holds URIs, URNs and URLs

Table 4.4.: Semantic MediaWiki Datatypes (Excerpt from Source: [Sem13])

Semantic MediaWiki+

Semantic MediaWiki+ (SMW+) is a semantic wiki based on Semantic MediaWiki with focus on the enterprise market. The main features of SMW+ are [Ont09]:

Semantic MediaWiki quick reference (1 of 2)

Covers MediaWiki extensions Semantic MediaWiki 1.5, Semantic Result Formats 1.5, Semantic Maps 0.6, Semantic Internal Objects 0.6, Semantic Compound Queries 0.2 and Semantic Forms 2.0

Properties

Special pages: Types, CreateProperty, Properties, UnusedProperties, Browse, SearchByProperty

Defining a triple:
[[*property-name*::*value*]]
{{#set:*property-name*=*value*}} (silent definition)

Defining a property:
[[Has type::*type-name*]]
[[Allows value::*enum-value*]] (for enumerations)

Property types: Page (default), String, Text, Code, Number, Date, Boolean, URL, Email, Telephone number, Temperature; *from Semantic Maps:* Geographical coordinate

Defining an internal object:
{{#set_internal:*object-to-page-property*|*prop1*=*val1*|*prop2#list*=*val2*|...}}

Example (on a page called "United States"):

```
{{#set_internal:Is president of|Has name=James Madison|Has start year=1801|Has end year=1809|Has vice president#list=George Clinton, Elbridge Gerry}}
```

Defining a recurring event:
{{#set_recurring_event:property=*date property*|start=*start date*|end=*end date*|period=*number*|unit=*{day|week|month|year}*|week number=*number*|include=*additional dates*|exclude=*excluded dates*}}

Notable settings for LocalSettings.php

$smwgLinksInValues - set to true to allow wiki-links within property values
$smwgNamespacesWithSemanticLinks - all namespaces that can hold semantic values
$smwgShowFactbox - set to SMW_FACTBOX_NONEMPTY to display factbox at bottom of pages
$smwgInlineErrors - set to false to hide SMW error messages

Semantic templates

Special pages: CreateTemplate, Templates

Simple semantic template definition:

```
Field-label: [[property-name::{{{field-name|}}}]]
[[Category:category-name]]
```

Alternate declaration of property in template:
{{#declare:*property-name*=*field-name*}}

Setting a field to represent multiple property values:
{{#arraymap:*value*|*delimiter*|*var*|*formula*|*new_delimiter*}}
{{#arraymaptemplate:*value*|*template-name*|*delimiter*|*new_delimiter*}})

Inline queries

Special pages: Ask

Syntax: {{#ask:*parameter1*|*parameter2*|...}}

Standard parameters:

query conditions	sort=	default=
?*property-name*=*label* |+*property-param*=*value*	order={asc|desc|random} headers={show|hide|plain}	intro= outro=
limit=	mainlabel=	searchlabel=
offset=	link={none|subject|all}	format=

Query conditions: [[Category:*category-name*]]... [[Concept:*concept-name*]]... [[*property-name*::*value*]]...

Subquery: [[*prop1.prop2.prop3*::*value*]]

Inverse query: [[-*property-name*::*page-name*]]

Comparators: :: (equals), ::< (less than), ::> (greater), ::~ (like), ::! (not), ::!~ (not like)

Property parameter types: limit, order, align, index

Format types: list, ol, ul, table, broadtable, category, rss, csv, json, embedded, template, count, debug; *from Semantic Result Formats:* timeline, eventline, calendar, graph, process, googlebar, googlepie, jqplotbar, jqplotpie, exhibit, outline, gallery, sum, average, min, max, bibtex, vcard, icalendar; *from Semantic Maps:* map, googlemaps, yahoomaps, openlayers

Notes on formats:
- list, ol, ul, category, template and calendar formats allow the 'template' parameter
- sum, average, min and max require 'limit' to be greater than number of queried pages
- for calendar, use #calendarstartdate and #calendarenddate to limit query to current month

Sample query: To create a table of all cities in Europe and their populations, sorted by population:

```
{{#ask:mainlabel=City|[[Category:Cities]][[Has country.Has continent::Europe]]|
  ?Has population=Pop.|sort=Has population}}
```

Running a compound query:
{{#compound_query:*query1*|*query2*|...|*joint parameters*}}
Each query's parameters should be separated by semicolons, instead of pipes.

Sample compound query: to show a map with one icon for clothing stores and another for fast food restaurants:

```
{{#compound_query:[[Category:Clothing stores]];?Has coordinates;icon=Shirt.png|
  [[Category:Restaurants]][[Has cuisine::Fast food]];?Has coordinates;
  icon=Hamburger.png|format=googlemaps|height=400|width=600}}
```

Notable settings for LocalSettings.php

$smwgQDefaultLimit - default number of results displayed on a page; default is 50
$smwgQMaxInlineLimit - maximum results displayed on a page; default is 500
$smwgQMaxLimit - maximum results retrieved for a query; default is 10000

Concepts

Defining a concept: In the 'Concept' namespace:
{{#concept:*query-conditions*|*description*}}

Last updated August 25, 2010. Created by Yaron Koren; inspired by the "cheat sheets" at addedbytes.com.
Distributed under the Creative Commons by-3.0 license.

Figure 4.2.: Semantic MediaWiki Syntax Overview (Part 1, Source: [Kor10])

Semantic MediaWiki quick reference (2 of 2)

Covers MediaWiki extensions Semantic MediaWiki 1.5, Semantic Forms 2.0, Semantic Drilldown 0.8, External Data 1.0 and others

Forms

Special pages: CreateForm, Forms, CreateCategory, CreateClass, RunQuery

Simple form definition:

```
{{{for template|template-name}}}
field-label: {{{field|field-name}}}
{{{end template}}}
Free text:
{{{standard input|free text}}}
{{{standard input|save}}}
```

Form tags:
info, field, for template, standard input, end template

'info' parameters:
add title=, partial form, edit title=, page name=, includeonly free text

'for template' parameters:
label=, strict, multiple

'field' parameters:
input type=, hidden, size=, mandatory, rows=, restricted, cols=, uploadable, class=, values=, maxlength=, default=, list, preload=, delimiter=, property=, autogrow, default filename=, values from {category|concept}=, autocomplete, no autocomplete, autocomplete on {property| category|concept|namespace}=, autocomplete from url=, remote autocompletion, show on select=

'standard input' types:
free text, preview, minor edit, changes, watch, cancel, summary, run query, save

'standard input' parameters:
label=, class=

Input types

Field type	Default input type	Other allowed input types
Page, String, Number, URL, Email, etc.	text	textarea, combobox, category
Text, Code	textarea	text
Date	date	
Enumeration	dropdown	radiobutton
Boolean	checkbox	
List of Page, String, etc.	text	textarea, categories
List of enumerations	checkboxes	listbox

More input types: *from Semantic Maps:* googlemaps, yahoomaps, openlayers; *from Semantic Forms Inputs:* datepicker, simpledatepicker, regexp

Form input:
{{#forminput:form=|size=|default value=|button text=|query string=|autocomplete on category=|autocomplete on namespace=}}

Form input query string options:
template_name[field_name]=
namespace= super_page=

Setting the 'edit with form' tab:
(in a namespace page (*project-namespace: namespace-name*) or category page)
[[Has default form::*form-name*]]
(in a regular or template page)
[[Page has default form::*form-name*]]

Pointing red links to forms:
(in a property page)
[[Has default form::*form-name*]]
[[Has alternate form::*form-name*]]
(in a namespace page)
[[Has default form::*form-name*]]

Making red links create pages automatically:
(in a property page)
[[Creates pages with form::*form-name*]]

Forms that set an automatic page name

In form definition:
{{{info|page name=...<*template-name[field-name]*> ... <unique number>}}}

Linking to the form:
{{#formlink:form=|link text=|link type=|query string=}}

Notable settings for LocalSettings.php

$sfgRenameEditTabs - set true to change 'edit with form' to 'edit', 'edit' to 'edit source'
$sfgRenameMainEditTab - set to true to change 'edit' to 'edit source'
$wgAmericanDates - set to true to show month first in date input
$sfg24HourTime - set to true to display time input in 24-hour notation

Drilldown

Special pages: CreateFilter, Filters, BrowseData

Defining a filter:
[[Covers property::*property-name*]]
[[Has value::*value*]]
[[Use time period::{Year|Month}]]
[[Gets values from category::*category-name*]]
[[Has input type::{combo box|date range}]]
[[Requires filter::Filter:*filter-name*]]
[[Has label::*label*]]

In a category page:
[[Has filter::Filter:*filter-name*]]
[[Has display parameters::*parameters*]]
'parameters' should have same structure as #ask query parameters, but separated by semicolons
__HIDEFROMDRILLDOWN__
__SHOWINDRILLDOWN__

Notable settings for LocalSettings.php

$sdgFiltersSmallestFontSize, $sdgFiltersLargestFontSize - font sizes for "tag cloud" display of filter values

External data

Getting data from a URL:
{{#get_external_data:*URL*|*format*|*external-variable-name==filter-value*|...|*local-variable-name=external-variable-name*|...}}

Getting data from a database, LDAP server:
{{#get_db_data:server=*server_id*|from=*from-clause*|where=*where-clause*|data=*data-mappings*}}

{{#get_ldap_data:domain=*domain-id*|filter=*ldap-filter*|data=*data-mappings*}}

For #get_db_data and #get_ldap_data, data mappings should be separated by commas.

Displaying external data:
{{#external_value:*variable_name*}}
{{#for_external_table:*expression*}}
The expression value in #for_external_table should contain variables in the form {{{variable_name}}}.

Storing external data - examples:
Storing an external value with SMW:
The capital of {{PAGENAME}} is [[Has capital::{{#external_value:capital}}]].

Storing a table of external values (requires Semantic Internal Objects extension):
{{#store_external_table:Is leader of|Has name={{{name}}}|Has start year={{{start year}}}|Has end year={{{end year}}} }}

Notable settings for LocalSettings.php

$edgStringReplacements - array for hiding API keys
$edgAllowExternalDataFrom - array for an API "whitelist" - necessary if API keys are being hidden
$edgCacheTable - database table for caching data
DB and LDAP access have other required settings.

Last updated August 25, 2010. Created by Yaron Koren; inspired by the "cheat sheets" at addedbytes.com.
Distributed under the Creative Commons by-3.0 license.

Figure 4.3.: Semantic MediaWiki Syntax Overview (Part 2, Source: [Kor10])

- Improved import of data from external applications
- Built-in WYSIWYG editor
- Graphical ontology browser in the wiki, which allows browsing and editing
- Gardening tool, which supports users in finding inconsistencies in the wiki
- Improved access control [Ont09]

In [PNJB08], a case study is presented, which shows how Semantic MediaWiki benefits from user interface improvements in SMW+. Because semantic wikis add complexity to wikis by introducing annotations, which "are both syntactically and conceptually more complex than the hyperlinks found in a normal wiki", mechanisms have to be developed to simplify annotations in order to gain acceptance from users [PNJB08].

In order to improve the handling of queries, which can be quite complex in Semantic MediaWiki (a user has to learn the syntax of the query language), a graphical front-end is implemented, which enables users to create queries without having to input text-mode queries. An auto-complete feature further improves the usability by offering possible completions. Because users normally do not have more than a basic understanding of the underlying ontology, queries can be refined in order to allow the gradual finding of results [PNJB08].

The introduction of the *Semantic Toolbar* enables wiki users to add and edit annotations without having to edit wikitext. When clicking on a text fragment in edit mode, the text fragment is automatically put into the properties section of the toolbar. After that, the user can select the according property, supported by auto completion, where the system suggests properties already in the wiki, based on user input. An additional *Annotation Mode* allows adding and editing of annotations without having to edit wikitext [PNJB08].

Further usability improvement is provided by the *Ontology Browser*, shown in Figure 4.4. It provides users with information about instances and properties of a class, as well as the class hierarchy. By using filters, search results can be narrowed down [PNJB08].

While SMW+ improves usability, reference [PNJB08] is realistic about how migrating Wikipedia from MediaWiki to SMW+ would affect Wikipedia editors: Most Wikipedia users would not start to instantly add annotations and queries, but instead would continue contributing article texts. A small group, however, would start adding and editing annotations [PNJB08].

Wiki *gardeners* are wiki users, who contribute to the wiki by getting rid of inconsistencies and redundancies in the wiki (e.g., multiple relations with the same meaning). Tool support for gardeners is provided in the form of *gardening tools* [PNJB08].

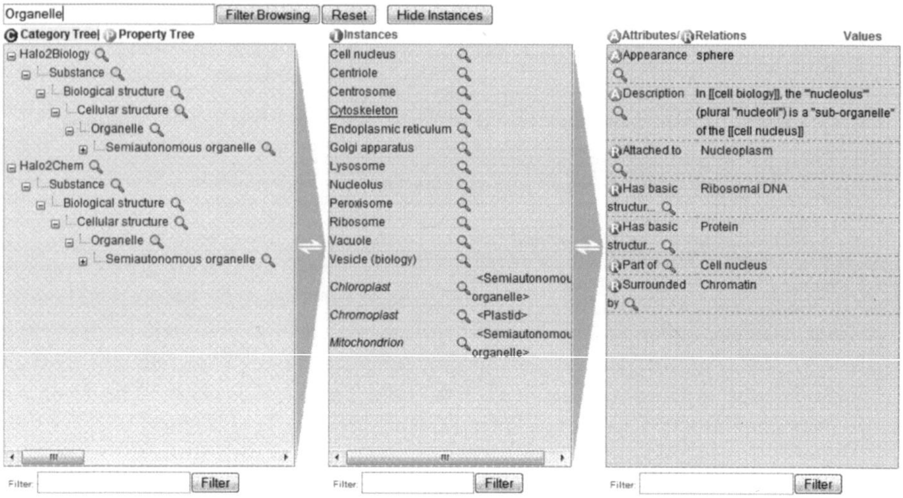

Figure 4.4.: SMW+ Ontology Browser (Source: [PNJB08])

4.1.5. Extensions Used with Semantic MediaWiki

While Semantic MediaWiki is by itself an extension for the MediaWiki platform, there are other extensions, which are designed for extending Semantic MediaWiki. Two of these extensions are used in the ITSM Wiki and are described in this subsection.

Semantic Forms

Semantic Forms is a MediaWiki extension for the use together with Semantic MediaWiki. It allows defining and using forms in order to simplify the input of data. Furthermore, the use of queries can be simplified by the Semantic Forms extension. The part of Semantic Forms, which is visible to users of the wiki, are forms, which consist of fields. Semantic Forms makes use of templates. Although the creation and editing of forms require some understanding of SMW and Semantic Forms, it does not require programming skills [Med09c]. Compared to plain SMW, the use of Semantic Forms provides the following benefits [Med09c]:

- The structure of a wiki page is enforced by the forms used for editing the page; in addition, plain text can be added, which provides flexibility for adding information that does not fit the fields implemented in the form.

- Semantic features are usable by persons not familiar with the underlying concepts (i.e., users are not shown the semantic relations, but only forms, which are less confusing to the average user).
- Auto completion improves usability by suggesting matching field entries based on semantic information (i.e., only pages in the range of the defined property are suggested) [Med09c].

In this thesis, the Semantic Forms extension is used to simplify the input of structured data in the ITSM Wiki. This enables users who are not experienced with semantic wikis to use the system and improves usability for users already familiar with semantic wikis (cp. Section 4.2.6, page 159). Semantic Forms consists of the components properties, templates, and forms, which are discussed in the following paragraphs. More information about Semantic Forms and its usage can be found in [Kor12, pages 139–167].

Properties Properties define how data stored in the semantic wiki is related to each other. Properties can store a value (e.g., a text string, a number, or a date), or a link to a wiki page. While this is a standard mechanism of Semantic MediaWiki, the Semantic Forms extension makes use of the mechanism for managing information added and edited in forms. For each property, a page within the `Property:` namespace should be created, which specifies the characteristics of the property (e.g., its domain and range) [Med09c].

Templates Semantic Forms makes use of MediaWiki templates [Wik10a] in order to display information [Med09c]. A simple template looks as shown in Listing 4.1[4].

Forms Forms contain markup code for specifying the content of the form used when adding or editing information. Because form definition pages are edited in the same way as regular wiki pages, forms can be defined by every user of the wiki. Forms are grouped in the `Form:` namespace. After the Semantic Forms extension is installed, pages which are associated with a form can be edited in two ways: First, in the regular way (i.e., by editing wikitext), and second, by using the form to edit structured information (an *edit with form* button is added next to the regular *edit* button) [Med09c]. A simple form looks as shown in Listing 4.2.

Categories Categories, which are used for grouping pages in MediaWiki, are used for assigning templates to pages in Semantic Forms. In the definition page of a category, the default form can be specified. Each page belonging to a certain category uses the category's default form [Med09c].

[4]The template and form shown in the example are excerpts from the templates and forms shown in Appendix B (page 437).

Listing 4.1: Semantic Forms Template

```
<noinclude>This is the 'Person' template.<br>It is used to
    display persons and their attributes<br></noinclude><
    includeonly>
= General =
{| class="wikitable"
! Name
| [[Name::{{{Name|}}}]]
|-
! Description
| [[Description::{{{Description|}}}]]
|-
! FamilyName
| [[FamilyName::{{{FamilyName|}}}]]
|-
! GivenName
| [[GivenName::{{{GivenName|}}}]]
|-
! IsMemberOfOrganizationalUnit
| {{#arraymap:{{{IsMemberOfOrganizationalUnit|}}}|,|@@@|[[
    IsMemberOfOrganizationalUnit::OrganizationalUnit-@@@|@@@]]}}
|-
! PhoneNumber
| {{#arraymap:{{{PhoneNumber|}}}|,|@@@|[[PhoneNumber::@@@]]}}
|-
! EmailAddress
| {{#arraymap:{{{EmailAddress|}}}|,|@@@|[[EmailAddress::@@@]]}}
|-
! HasOffice
| [[HasOffice::{{{HasOffice|}}}]]
|-
|}
<headertabs/>
{{#set:Page has default form=Person}}
[[Category:Person]]</includeonly>
```

Listing 4.2: Semantic Forms Form

```
<noinclude>This is the 'Person' form.<br>To add a page with this
    form, enter the page name below;<br> If a page with that
    name already exists, you will be sent to a form to edit that
    page.<br> {{#forminput:Person}}</noinclude><includeonly>
{{{info|page name=Person-<Person[Name]><unique number>|create
    title=Create new person}}}
{{{for template|Person}}}
= General =
{| class="wikitable"
! Name:
| {{{field|Name|input type=text}}}
|-
! Description:
| {{{field|Description|input type=textarea}}}
|-
! FamilyName:
| {{{field|FamilyName|input type=text}}}
|-
! GivenName:
| {{{field|GivenName|input type=text}}}
|-
! IsMemberOfOrganizationalUnit:
| {{{field|IsMemberOfOrganizationalUnit|input type=text with
    autocomplete|values from category=OrganizationalUnit}}}
|-
! PhoneNumber:
| {{{field|PhoneNumber|input type=text}}}
|-
! EmailAddress:
| {{{field|EmailAddress|input type=text}}}
|-
! HasOffice:
| {{{field|HasOffice|input type=text with autocomplete|values
    from category=Room}}}
|-
|}
<headertabs/>
{{{end template}}}
{{{standard input|save|label=Save}}} {{{standard input|preview|
    label=Preview}}} {{{standard input|changes|label=Changes}}}
    {{{standard input|cancel|label=Cancel}}}</includeonly>
```

Semantic Drilldown

Another extension used together with Semantic MediaWiki is Semantic Drilldown. It allows drilling down (i.e., to zoom in from a summarized view to a more detailed view) by using categories. Furthermore, "filters on semantic properties" [Med09b] can be used to drill down. The *Browse data page* is the starting point for a semantic drill down. It contains all top-level categories (i.e., all categories, which do not have supercategories). Users can further limit the returned results by applying constraints. There are two types of constraints: subcategories, and filters. Subcategories of the listed categories are shown below the categories and can be selected in order to make the category more specific. This way, the category tree can be navigated. By using filters based on semantic properties, the selection can be further narrowed down. Multiple formatting styles allow to output filtered data in the most appropriate way, either as a list of results, tables with additional properties, or as a tag cloud [Med09b].

4.2. Requirements for ITSM within a Semantic Wiki

The previous Section 4.1 (page 116) compared different wiki and semantic wiki platforms and provided a selection of an appropriate platform for implementing a semantic wiki-based IT Service Management system at FZI.

In Section 4.2.1 (page 137), features required for Configuration Management as described in ITIL are mapped to functions of Semantic MediaWiki. Following that, in Section 4.2.2 (page 142), Service Knowledge Management, which extends Configuration Management, is introduced. In addition, requirements from Service Knowledge Management are mapped to mechanisms of Semantic MediaWiki, which can be used to implement a semantic wiki-based Service Knowledge Management System. In Section 4.2.3 (page 153), Change Management, as implemented with Semantic MediaWiki mechanisms, is discussed, followed by a description of SMW-based Incident and Problem Management in Section 4.2.4 (page 156). A discussion of the use of a semantic wiki in the context of Continual Service Improvement follows in Section 4.2.5 (page 158). In Section 4.2.6 (page 159), usability aspects of semantic wiki-based ITSM are discussed, followed by an outline of prior and related work in Section 4.2.7 (page 160).

While in this section, classes and properties for the use in the ITSM Wiki are identified from ITIL and informally described, Section 4.3 (page 161) describes the classes and properties more formally in the context of the ITSM Ontology.

In order to improve usability, the Semantic Forms extension is used in order to provide a convenient mechanism for inputting structured information.

The results of the requirements validation are presented in Section 6.1 (page 318).

4.2.1. Configuration Management

Configuration Management, as described in Section 3.2 (page 98), describes the entities of an IT infrastructure, as well as the relations between the entities. A description of the entities, which are referred to as configuration items (CI) are stored in a Configuration Management Database (CMDB). A collection of multiple CMDBs forms a Federated Configuration Management Database (FCMDB). A more encompassing system, which uses CMDBs as the data storage, is referred to as Configuration Management System (CMS).

In this subsection, the requirements for a technical platform for supporting Configuration Management, as described in Section 3.2.4 (page 103), are mapped to existing features of Semantic MediaWiki. Furthermore, requirements that cannot be satisfied by Semantic MediaWiki, are outlined as candidates for customized implementations, which are described in Chapter 5 (page 185).

Table 4.5 shows the mapping between the requirements for a Configuration Management System, as described in [LM07, pages 194–195], and corresponding candidates of Semantic MediaWiki features, which can be used for implementing the requirements. The *ID* column contains the identifier of the respective requirement, which is used to uniquely identify requirements throughout the thesis.

Table 4.5.: Mapping between CMS Requirements and SMW Features

ID	CMS Requirement	MediaWiki/SMW Feature
R-A01	"CMDB should be linked to the [Definitive Media Library]" [LM07, page 194]	Links in the wiki point to files on a central storage server. Description of physical location of media, which is not stored on a central storage server (e.g., a DVD in shelf space).
R-A02	"The Configuration Management System should prevent changes from being made to the IT infrastructure or service configuration baseline without valid authorization via Change Management." [LM07, page 195]	Changes cannot be prevented by MediaWiki or Semantic MediaWiki because changes are performed in administration tools, which are not linked to the wiki. The documentation of changes has to be solved via a policy, which states that changes have to be authorized before execution.
R-A03	"As far as possible, all changes should be recorded on the CMS at least by the time that the change is implemented." [LM07, page 195]	The recording of changes in the wiki has to be solved via a policy, which states that changes have to be entered into the wiki before performing the change.

(table continues)

Table 4.5.: Mapping between CMS Requirements and SMW Features (continued)

ID	CMS Requirement	MediaWiki/SMW Feature
R-A04	"The status (e.g. 'live', 'archive', etc.) of each CI affected by a change should be updated automatically if possible. Example ways in which this automatic recording of changes could be implemented include automatic updating of the CMS when software is moved between libraries (e.g. from 'acceptance test' to 'live', or from 'live' to an 'archive' library), when the service catalogue is changed, and when a release is distributed." [LM07, page 195]	Each CI has an associated status, which can be queried by CIs depending on it.
R-A05	"Sufficient security controls to limit access on a need-to-know basis" [LM07, page 195]	While MediaWiki provide basic mechanisms for restricting access to pages, this mechanism cannot be used as a mechanism for implementing access controls for a strict need-to-know basis. While this is problematic for large-scale IT landscapes with a strict separation of privileges and fields of responsibilities between various administrators and teams, this is less a problem in small IT teams found in SMEs.
R-A06	"Support for CIs of varying complexity" [LM07, page 195]	The representation of CIs as Semantic MediaWiki pages provides a high degree of flexibility in defining the CIs properties. The complexity of CIs stored in the wiki can range from named items without any properties, up to items with hundreds of properties.
R-A07	"Hierarchic and networked relationships between CI" [LM07, page 195]	Hierarchies and relationships are modeled in Semantic MediaWiki using relations, e.g., *is connected to*.
R-A08	"Easy addition of new CIs and deletion of old CIs" [LM07, page 195]	New CIs are added using mechanisms from the Semantic Forms extension. CIs which are no longer needed are deleted by using the MediaWiki delete mechanism.
R-A09	"Automatic validation of input data" [LM07, page 195]	Input is checked for syntax using Semantic Forms mechanisms (including auto complete and selection from lists).
R-A10	"Automatic determination of all relationships that can be automatically established, when new CIs are added" [LM07, page 195]	Relationships are derived from transitive connections and hierarchies of CIs.

(*table continues*)

Table 4.5.: Mapping between CMS Requirements and SMW Features (continued)

ID	CMS Requirement	MediaWiki/SMW Feature
R-A11	"Support for CIs with different model numbers, version numbers, and copy numbers" [LM07, page 195]	CIs with different attributes are supported. Individual CIs can be grouped into CI families. For example, instance of Microsoft Windows 7 Professional x64 and Microsoft Windows 8 Professional x64 are part of the Windows CI family.
R-A12	"Automatic identification of other affected CIs when any CI is the subject of an incident report/record, problem record, known error record or RFC" [LM07, page 195]	Affected CIs are highlighted by using a custom-created MediaWiki extension. More information about the component can be found in Section 5.4 (page 284).
R-A13	"Integration of problem management data within the CMS, or at least an interface from the Configuration Management System to any separate problem management databases that may exist" [LM07, page 195]	Problem management is integrated into the wiki.
R-A14	"Automatic updating and recording of the version number of a CI if the version number of any component CI is changed" [LM07, page 195]	Possibly implementable through an extension, which updates associated CIs by exploiting semantic relations between the CIs.
R-A15	"Maintenance of a history of all CIs (both a historical record of the current version – such as installation date, records of Changes, previous locations, etc. – and of previous versions)" [LM07, page 195]	MediaWiki stores a history of changes to pages, which can be used to fulfill this requirement.
R-A16	"Support for the management and use of configuration baselines (corresponding to definitive copies, versions etc.), including support for reversion to trusted versions" [LM07, page 195]	Configuration baselines can be managed as wiki pages and make use of mechanisms provided by Semantic MediaWiki.
R-A17	"Ease of interrogation of the CMS and good reporting facilities, including trend analysis (e.g. the ability to identify the number of RFCs affecting particular CIs)" [LM07, page 195]	Queries are formulated using Semantic MediaWiki. Results are displayed in dynamically generated tables.
R-A18	"Ease of reporting of the CI inventory so as to facilitate configuration audits" [LM07, page 195]	The Semantic MediaWiki query mechanisms is used to generate dynamically updated tables, which contain information about CIs.
R-A19	"Flexible reporting tools to facilitate impact analyses" [LM07, page 195]	Semantic MediaWiki ask queries can be used to create tables for the purpose of impact analyses.

(*table continues*)

Table 4.5.: Mapping between CMS Requirements and SMW Features (continued)

ID	CMS Requirement	MediaWiki/SMW Feature
R-A20	"The ability to show graphically the configuration models and maps of interconnected CIs, and to input information about new CIs via such maps" [LM07, page 195]	A graphical representation of CI interconnections is generated using a custom-developed tool, which is described in detail in Section 5.4 (page 284).
R-A21	"The ability to show the hierarchy of relationships between 'parent' CIs and 'child' CIs" [LM07, page 195]	A custom-developed tool, which is described in detail in Section 5.4 (page 284), is used to show the hierarchy of parent-child relationships.
R-A22	"Automating the initial discovery and configuration audits significantly increases the efficiency and effectiveness of Configuration Management. These tools can determine what hardware and software is installed and how applications are mapped to the infrastructure." [LM07, page 195]	A tool for automatically gathering information about hardware and software is presented in Section 5.1 (page 188).

In Table 4.6, the properties of configuration items, as given in [LM07, page 75] are mapped to Semantic MediaWiki mechanisms, which can be used to implement the desired functionality. Table 4.7 describes the mapping between CI relationships, as given in [LM07, page 77], and Semantic MediaWiki features.

The management of configuration items in the ITSM Wiki can be summarized as follows:

- Each configuration item is represented as a wiki page.
- Attributes of configuration items are stored as SMW attributes.
- Relations between configuration items are modeled as SMW relations.

The ability to retain and access structured information and unstructured information side-by-side is one of the central requirements in the context of Configuration Management as implemented at FZI. Examples of structured information are relations between configuration items, or properties of configuration items. An example of unstructured information is the text-based description of a service and possible steps required for solving problems with the service. Semantic MediaWiki as a technical platform provides mechanisms for managing both, structured and unstructured information in a single user interface. For that reason, it is an environment, which makes unnecessary the maintenance of two dedicated systems, one for storing structured information, and one for storing unstructured information.

CI Property	SMW Feature
"Unique identifier" [LM07, page 75]	Wiki page name
"CI type" [LM07, page 75]	Wiki category
Name [LM07, page 75]	In most cases the wiki page name.
Description [LM07, page 75]	SMW attribute
"Version (e.g. file, build, baseline, release)" [LM07, page 75]	SMW attribute
"Location" [LM07, page 75]	SMW relation
"Supply date" [LM07, page 75]	SMW attribute
"Licence details, e.g. expiry date" [LM07, page 75]	SMW attribute for expiry date, SMW relation to a page if more information is necessary.
"Owner/custodian" [LM07, page 75]	SMW relation
"Status" [LM07, page 75]	SMW relation
"Supplier/source" [LM07, page 75]	SMW relation
"Related document masters" [LM07, page 75]	SMW relation
"Related software masters" [LM07, page 75]	SMW relation
"Historical data, e.g. audit trail" [LM07, page 75]	Wiki history
"Relationship type" [LM07, page 75]	Information in the page of the property.
"Applicable SLA" [LM07, page 75]	SMW relation

Table 4.6.: Mapping between CI Properties and SMW Features

CI Relationships	SMW Feature
CI is parent of other CI relationship [LM07, page 77]	SMW relation or category hierarchy
CI is connected to other CI relationship [LM07, page 77]	SMW relation
CI makes use of other CI relationship [LM07, page 77]	SMW relation
CI is installed on other CI relationship [LM07, page 77]	SMW relation

Table 4.7.: Mapping between CI Relationships and SMW Features

4.2.2. Service Knowledge Management

Knowledge Management as a tool to support IT Service Management is described in [LM07, pages 145–154]. The *purpose* of Knowledge Management, as defined in [LM07, page 145] is

> "to ensure that the right information is delivered to the appropriate place or competent person at the right time to enable informed decision." [LM07, page 145]

Knowledge Management's *goal*, as defined in [LM07, page 145], is

> "to enable organizations to improve the quality of management decision making by ensuring that reliable and secure information and data is available throughout the service lifecycle." [LM07, page 145]

Knowledge Management's *objectives* are [LM07, page 145]:

- "Enabling the service provider to be more efficient and improve quality of service, increase satisfaction and reduce the cost of service
- "Ensuring staff have a clear and common understanding of the value that their services provide to customers and the ways in which benefits are realized from the use of those services
- "Ensuring that, at a given time and location, service provider staff have adequate information on:
  - "Who is currently using their services
  - "The current states of consumption
  - "Service delivery constraints
  - "Difficulties faced by the customer in fully realizing the benefits expected from the service." [LM07, page 145]

Examples of knowledge in the context of ITSM are [LM07, page 145]:

- "Identity of stakeholders
- "Acceptable risk levels and performance expectations
- "Available resource and timescales." [LM07, page 145]

As described in [CS07, page 125], Knowledge Management helps organizations to adapt to an increased change rate with regard to industry and markets, increased employee turnover rates, increased information access, and an increased competition. Knowledge Management helps organizations to perform the following improvements:

- "Enhancing the **organization's effectiveness** through better decision making enabled by having the right information at the right time, and facilitating enterprise learning through the exchange and development of ideas and individuals
- "Enhancing **customer-supplier relationships** through sharing information and services to expand capabilities through collaborative efforts
- "Improving **business processes** through sharing lessons learned, results and best practices across the organization." [CS07, page 125, emphasis in original]

While the customer-supplier relationships play a less significant role in the context of small IT teams, the organizational effectiveness of the IT department and the improvement of IT-internal business processes are areas where a semantic wiki-based Knowledge Management platform is of interest. Before describing the ITSM Wiki platform, definitions of the terms data, information, knowledge, and wisdom are given.

Data, Information, Knowledge, and Wisdom

Figure 4.5 gives an overview of the progress from data to wisdom. As can be seen in the figure, data is the starting point. With more context and understanding, it can be transformed into information, knowledge, and wisdom [LM07, page 147].

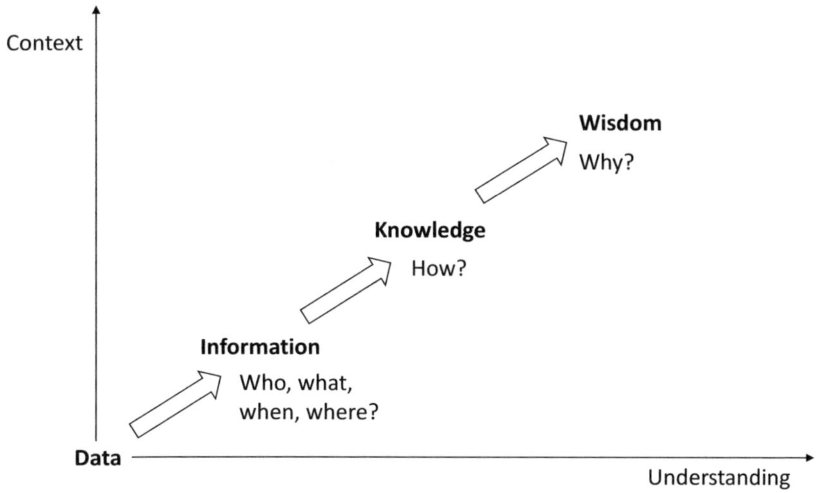

Figure 4.5.: Data, Information, Knowledge, and Wisdom (cf. [LM07, page 147])

Reference [LM07, page 146] defines data as follows:

> "**Data** is a set of discrete facts about events. Most organizations capture significant amounts of data in highly structured databases such as Service Management and Configuration Management tools/systems and databases." [LM07, page 146, emphasis in original]

Activities within Knowledge Management with regard to data are [LM07, page 146]:

- "Capture accurate data
- "Analyse, synthesize, and then transform the data into information
- "Identify relevant data and concentrate resources on its capture." [LM07, page 146]

Information is described as follows [LM07, page 146]:

> "**Information** comes from providing context to data. Information is typically stored in semi-structured content such as documents, e-mail, and multimedia. The key Knowledge Management activity around information is managing the content in a way that makes it easy to capture, query, find, re-use and learn from experiences so that mistakes are not repeated and work is not duplicated." [LM07, page 146, emphasis in original]

Reference [LM07, page 146] defines knowledge as follows:

> "**Knowledge** is composed of the tacit experiences, ideas, insights, values and judgements of individuals. People gain knowledge both from their own and from their peers' expertise, as well as from the analysis of information (and data). Through the synthesis of these elements, new knowledge is created. Knowledge is dynamic and context based. Knowledge puts information into an 'ease of use' form, which can facilitate decision making. In Service Transition this knowledge is not solely based on the transition in progress, but is gathered from experience of previous transitions, awareness of recent and anticipated changes and other areas that experienced staff will have been unconsciously collecting for some time." [LM07, page 146, emphasis in original]

Finally, wisdom is described as follows [LM07, page 146]:

> "**Wisdom** gives the ultimate discernment of the material and having the application and contextual awareness to provide a strong common sense judgement." [LM07, page 146, emphasis in original]

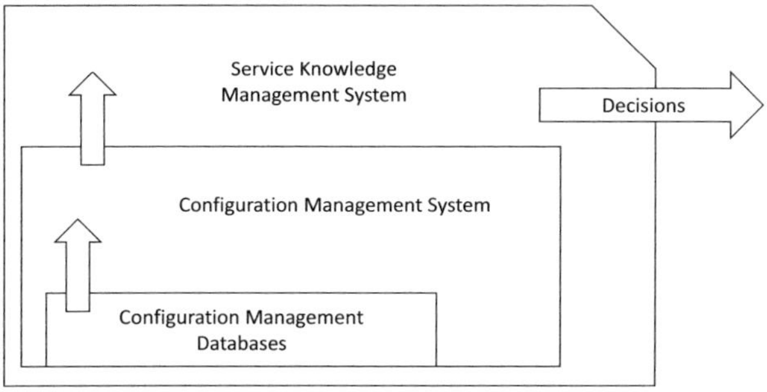

Figure 4.6.: CMDB, CMS, and SKMS (cf. [LM07, page 147])

While the description of Knowledge Management in [LM07, pages 145–154] only gives a basic overview of the aspects of Knowledge Management that are relevant for ITSM, a more comprehensive description of Knowledge Management in general can be found in [NT95, Dav00, Nor02, PRR03, Dav05].

The Service Knowledge Management System

The Service Knowledge Management System (SKMS) extends the Configuration Management System, as shown in Figure 4.6. The Configuration Management System, which is described in Section 3.2.4 (page 103), is an extension of the Configuration Management Database, which is described in Section 3.2.2 (page 101). Data that is gathered and stored in the CMDB is fed through the CMS and the SKMS, and finally supports decision making [LM07, page 147].

A schematic overview of the SKMS as proposed by ITIL [LM07, page 151] is given in Figure 4.7. As is the case with the Configuration Management System, which is shown in Figure 3.9 (page 105), the Service Knowledge Management System consists of four layers.

The layers are (from bottom to top) [LM07, page 151]:

- Data and information sources and tools
  - Structured data
  - Unstructured data
  - One or more Configuration Management Databases
  - The definite media library
  - Application, system and infrastructure management

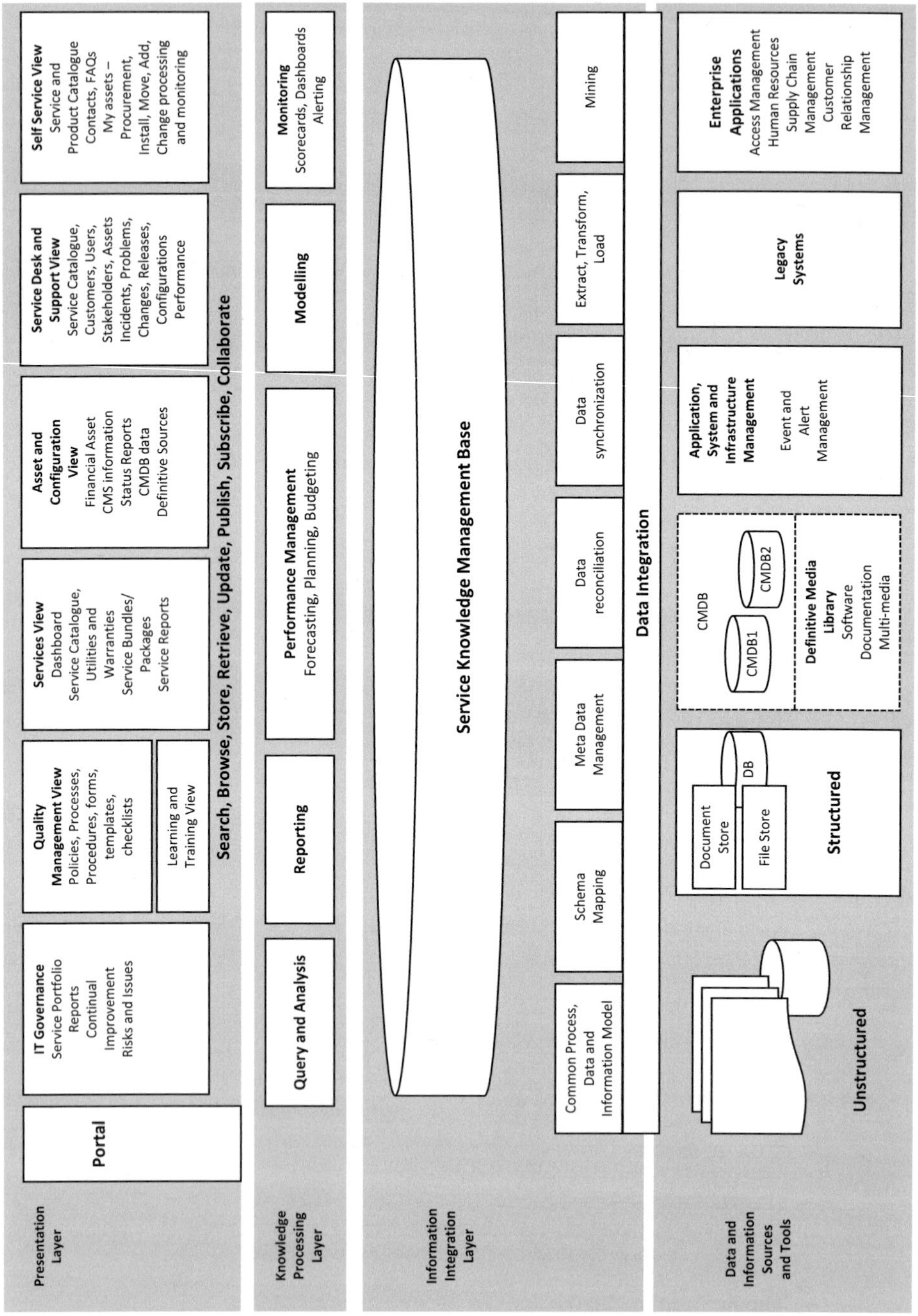

Figure 4.7.: Service Knowledge Management System (cf. [LM07, page 151])

  - Legacy systems
  - Enterprise applications
- Information integration layer
  - Service Knowledge Management base
  - Common process, data and information model
  - Schema mapping
  - Meta data management
  - Data reconciliation
  - Data synchronization
  - Extract, transform, load
  - Mining
  - Data integration
- Knowledge processing layer
  - Query and analysis
  - Reporting
  - Performance management
  - Modeling
  - Monitoring
- Presentation layer
  - "Search, Browse, Store, Retrieve, Update, Publish, Subscribe, Collaborate" [LM07, page 151]
  - Portal
  - IT governance
  - Quality management view
  - Services view
  - Asset and configuration view
  - Service desk and support view
  - Self service view [LM07, page 151]

As can be seen in the items which make up the Service Knowledge Management System, the SKMS exceeds the capabilities and the information stored in the Configuration Management System. Examples of knowledge that can be stored in the SKMS are [LM07, page 147]:

- "The experience of staff
- "Records of peripheral matters, e.g. weather, user numbers and behaviour, organization's performance figures
- "Suppliers' and partners' requirements, abilities and expectations
- "Typical and anticipated user skill levels." [LM07, page 147]

Reference [CS07, page 125] gives two factors that are the basis for a successful implementation of Knowledge Management, namely an open culture, and infrastructure. With regard to the open culture, it is important to encourage the sharing of knowledge, best practices, and lessons learned [CS07, page 125]:

> "An **open culture** where knowledge, both best practices and lessons learned is shared across the organization and individuals are rewarded for it. Many cultures foster an environment where 'knowledge is power' (the more you know that others do not, the more valuable you are to the company). This type of knowledge hoarding is a dangerous behaviour for a company to reward since that knowledge may leave the company at any time. Another tenet of an open culture is a willingness to learn. This is an environment where growing an individual's knowledge base is rewarded and facilitated through open support and opportunities." [CS07, page 125, emphasis in original]

Besides an open culture, it is important to provide an appropriate technical infrastructure, which enables employees to store and share knowledge, in order to facilitate Knowledge Management [CS07, page 125]:

> "The **infrastructure** – a culture may be open to knowledge sharing, but without the means or infrastructure to support it, even the best intentions can be impaired, and over time this serves as a demotivator, quelling the behaviour. This infrastructure can be defined in various ways, it may be a technical application or system which allows individuals to conduct online, self-paced training, or it may be a process such as post-mortems or knowledge sharing activities designed to bring people together to discuss best practices or lessons learned." [CS07, page 125, emphasis in original]

The ITSM Wiki platform provides the potential to serve as a technical infrastructure for facilitating Knowledge Management in SME IT administration teams. While classic CMDB software solutions have their strengths in storing and retrieving structured information (e.g., technical information about a server, including the processor, amount of memory, serial number, and operating system), storing CMDB information in a semantic wiki benefits from the ability to additionally store unstructured information. An example of unstructured information is the description of best practices in handling hardware, which is linked to a configuration item, e.g., a server.

By combining the ability to store structured and unstructured information as made possible by Semantic MediaWiki, the ITSM Wiki can serve as a unified resource for storing structured Configuration Management data, as well as unstructured information. Examples of knowledge that can be stored in the Semantic MediaWiki-based Service Knowledge Management System are described in the following paragraphs.

While in this section, the classes and properties of the ITSM Ontology are identified and described informally, a formal data model is presented in Section 4.3 (page 161).

Best Practices Best practices consist of the components shown in Table 4.8, which are stored in the SMW-based Service Knowledge Management Database. The properties that are shown in the table belong to the BestPractice class, which is part of the ITSM Ontology.

Information	Property	Description
Application to CIs	appliesTo	Link to configuration items to which the best practice applies.
Caption	–	Stored in the wiki as the page name.
Context	ContextDescription	Free text description of the context, in which the best practice should be applied.
Description	Description	Free text description of the best practice.
Reverse links	–	Reverse links from the affected configuration items, so the best practice can be reached from the affected configuration item (realized as SMW queries).
Relations to best practices	isRelatedToBestPractice	Links to other best practices, which are related to the described best practice.
Specialists	hasSpecialist	Links to persons who are specialists in the area that is described by the best practice.
Type	hasBestPracticeType	The type of the best practice.

Table 4.8.: Best Practices

Lessons Learned Table 4.9 shows elements, which comprise a description of a learned lesson. The properties that are shown in the table belong to the LessonLearned class.

Information	Property	Description
Additional information	AdditionalInformation	Contains additional information in free text.
Application to CIs	appliesTo	Links to configuration items, to which the lesson applies.
Caption	–	Stored in the wiki as the page name.
Description	Description	Description of the learned lesson in free text (e.g., what should be done different the next time).
Problem statement	ProblemStatement	Free text description of the problem.
Related learned lesson	isRelatedTo	Link to a related learned lesson.
Reverse links	–	Reverse links from affected configuration items (realized as SMW queries).
Specialist	hasSpecialist	Links to persons who can contribute additional information.
Type of the learned lesson	hasLessonLearnedType	Type to which the learned lesson belongs.

Table 4.9.: Lessons Learned

Operating Procedures When, for example, installing hardware and software, or customizing a service, there is a number of operating procedures, which have to be followed. The procedures consist of the components that are shown in Table 4.10. The properties that are shown in the table belong to the OperatingProcedure class.

Key Persons and Stakeholders Information about the domains of knowledge of individual stakeholders is stored in the wiki[5]. Stored information types are shown in Table 4.11. The properties that are shown in the table belong to the Person class.

Recommended Literature and Web Sites Information about literature or Web sites is stored in the wiki. Stored information includes the items listed in Table 4.12. The properties that are shown in the table belong to the Literature class.

[5]Managing information about key persons is more beneficial for larger organizations, but can also benefit smaller teams in SMEs.

Information	Property	Description
Additional information	AdditionalInformation	Additional information in free text.
Application to CIs	appliesTo	Links to configuration items, to which the operating procedure applies.
Caption	–	Stored in the wiki as the page name.
Description	Description	Description of the procedure in free text.
Purpose	Purpose	Purpose of the procedure in free text.
Reverse links	–	Reverse links from configuration items, to which the operating procedures have to be applied (realized as SMW queries).
Specialist	hasSpecialist	Links to persons who can contribute additional information.
Type of the operating procedure	hasOperatingProcedureType	Type to which the operating procedure belongs.
Working steps	WorkingStepDescription	Free text description of the steps that have to be followed in order to reach the desired goal.

Table 4.10.: Operating Procedures

Summary of Requirements

A tool, which supports Service Knowledge Management, has to be able to support the management of the following information in a combination of structured and unstructured formats:

- Best Practices (R-B01)
- Lessons Learned (R-B02)
- Operating Procedures (R-B03)
- Key Persons and Stakeholders (R-B04)
- Recommended Literature and Web Sites (R-B05)

The categories, which are used to group the pages in the wiki, form an ontology, which is used as the ITSM Wiki's data model. The ontology is described in detail in Section 4.3 (page 161). Change Management, as well as Incident and Problem Management, are

Information	Property	Description
Caption	–	Stored in the wiki as the page name.
Description	Description	Additional free text description of the person.
E-Mail address	EMailAddress	The person's e-mail address.
Family name	FamilyName	Family name of the person.
Fax number	FaxNumber	The person's fax number.
Given name	GivenName	Given name of the person.
Knowledge domains	hasKnowledgeDomain	Links to knowledge domains.
Organization	isMemberOfOrganization	A link to the organization, to which the person belongs.
Organizational Unit	isMemberOfOrganizationalUnit	The person's organizational unit.
Phone number	PhoneNumber	The person's phone number.
Reverse links	–	Reverse links from knowledge domains to key persons (realized as SMW queries).
Role	hasRole	The role of the person.
Room number	hasOffice	The office, in which the person resides.

Table 4.11.: Key Persons and Stakeholders

Information	Property	Description
Author	Author	The author of the literature.
Caption	–	Stored in the wiki as the page name.
Description	Description	Additional free text description.
Information about CIs	containsInformationAbout	A link to configuration items, which are described by the literature.
Link	Link	Link to information (e.g., a Web site, a white paper, an e-book, or an online shop, where a book can be acquired).
Type of literature	hasLiteratureType	Type to which the literature or Web site belongs.

Table 4.12.: Literature and Web Sites

other ITIL disciplines, in which the management of knowledge in a platform that supports storing structured and unstructured information side by side, is of value. The following Section 4.2.3 describes the use of the ITSM Wiki in Change Management, while the storage and management of information required for Incident and Problem Management are described in Section 4.2.4 (page 156).

4.2.3. Change Management

Change Management, which was described in Section 2.2.3 (page 34), is the ITIL discipline responsible for the structured planning, documentation, and execution of changes [LM07, page 43].

Retained Information

When maintaining information about changes in a semantic wiki, the possibility to tightly integrate structured and unstructured information again is beneficial. Information that is stored about changes follows the seven questions, which were previously described in Section 2.2.3 (page 34). The questions, as presented in [LM07, page 53] are:

- "Who *raised* the change?
- "What is the *reason* for the change?
- "What is the *return* required from the change?
- "What are the *risks* involved in the change?
- "What *resources* are required to deliver the change?
- "Who is *responsible* for the build, test and implementation of the change?
- "What is the *relationship* between this change and other changes?" [LM07, page 53, all capitalized emphasis in original, italic emphasis added]

By using the seven questions as a guideline, a schema for the storage of information in the ITSM Wiki with regard to performing a change was designed. The information about changes, which is stored in the ITSM Wiki, is found in Table 4.13. The properties that are shown in the table belong to the Change class, which is part of the ITSM Ontology.

Table 4.13.: Change Management

Information	Property	Description
Affected configuration items	affects	Affected configuration items are expressed by using Semantic MediaWiki relations.
Change identifier	–	The change identifier is stored in the wiki as the page name.
Date and time of the change authorization	DateOfChangeAuthorization	The date and time of the change authorization is stored in a structured format.
Date and time of the change execution	DateOfChangeExecution	The date and time of the change execution is stored in a structured format.
Date and time of the change initiation	DateOfChangeInitiation	The date and time of the change initiation is stored in a structured format.
Description	Description	Additional free text description.
Link to service desk ticket	ServiceDeskTicketURL	Most changes are a reaction to a requirement, which is in most cases received via the service desk tool.
Person who authorizes the change	isAuthorizedByPerson	A change is linked to the wiki page of the person who authorizes the change. The corresponding person's page links back to the changes authorized by that person by using semantic wiki queries.
Person who checks if the change was performed right	isCheckedByPerson	Changes are linked to person pages. The corresponding person pages are linked back to the changes checked by that person by using semantic wiki queries.
Person who executes the change	isExecutedByPerson	Changes are linked to person pages. The corresponding person pages are linked back to the changes executed by that person by using semantic wiki queries.
Person who wants the change performed	isInitiatedByPerson	Every person is represented by a separate wiki page. This way, changes can be linked to person pages and the corresponding person pages can be linked back to the changes initiated by that person by using semantic wiki queries.
Reason for change	Reason	The reason for the change is stated in free text.

(*table continues*)

Table 4.13.: Change Management (continued)

Information	Property	Description
Relationships to other changes	isRelatedToChange	Relationships to other changes are expressed by the use of Semantic MediaWiki relations.
Required resources (structured)	hasRequiredResource	Resources, which are represented as configuration items or otherwise stored in the wiki in a structured format, are linked by making use of relations. Examples of this type of resources are physical hardware servers, or services.
Required resources (unstructured)	AdditionalRequiredResource	Resources, which are not represented in a structured format in the wiki, are added in an unstructured format as free text (e.g., an elevator that is used to transport hardware, and which is not considered a configuration item).
Risks	Risk	Risks associated with the change are stated in free text.
Type of the change	hasChangeType	Expresses the type of a change.

Change Types

Changes can be categorized into three categories, with regard to their complexity and the amount of needed prior planning and preparation [LM07, pages 46–50]. Change types that are stored in the ITSM Wiki, are shown in Table 4.14. The properties given in the table belong to the ChangeType class, which is part of the ITSM Ontology.

In the context of the IT department at FZI, standard operational changes (e.g., resetting forgotten passwords, unlocking locked out user accounts) are not explicitly documented in the ITSM Wiki. With regard to standard changes (e.g., setting up a new computer, or reinstalling the operating system of an existing computer), the changes are documented in the wiki. Normal changes (e.g., setting up a new mail service) are documented as a mixture of structured information in a form, as well as in complementary plain text, in the ITSM Wiki.

Summary of Requirements

When looking at the information, which is stored about a change, it can be seen that the following requirements have to be fulfilled by the Change Management tool:

Information	Description
Normal Change	This type of change is applied when non-standard changes have to be performed. Individual changes have to go through a formal change process. An example of a normal change is the introduction of a new mail service.
Standard Change	A pre-authorized type of change that has a set of established procedures. Examples are hardware upgrades to workstations, or the installation of standard software.
Standard Operational Change	This is the simplest form of a change, which is performed routinely and does not require planning for individual changes. Examples of standard operational changes are resetting forgotten user passwords and restarting services or computers.

Table 4.14.: Change Types

- Management of changes in *structured* format (R-C01).
- Management of changes in *unstructured* format (R-C02).
- Management of changes in a combination of structured *and* unstructured format (R-C03).

The Information Gathering Component, which is described in Section 5.1 (page 188), supports the ITSM Wiki-based Change Management process by automatically populating and updating information stored in the wiki. This is accomplished by retrieving information over the network by making use of standardized mechanisms.

4.2.4. Incident and Problem Management

Keeping information about known errors and their associated retaining of solutions or workarounds [CW07, page 64] in a *Known Error Database* [CW07, page 66] is another aspect of ITSM that can be managed in the ITSM Wiki. Information about incidents and problems can be stored in Semantic MediaWiki in plain text, and enriched by semantic properties and attributes. In the context of this thesis, the incident class and the problem class are subclasses of the issue class. This is due to the fact that incidents and problems share common characteristics. Information stored about issues (i.e., incidents, and problems) is as presented in Table 4.15. The properties that are shown in the table belong to the Issue class, which is part of the ITSM Ontology.

While storing and retrieving incident and problem management information is possible this way, in order to fully benefit from the information stored about incidents and problems, an ITSM-specific custom extension is required. A component, which

Information	Property	Description
Affected hardware	affects	SMW relations to the affected hardware configuration items.
Affected hosts	affects	SMW relations to the affected hosts.
Affected services	affects	SMW relations to the affected services.
Affected software	affects	SMW relations to the affected software configuration items.
Description	Description	Additional free text description.
Incident/problem identifier	–	The identifier is stored in the wiki as the page name.
Other affected persons	affects	Besides the person who reported the incident/problem, other persons can be affected by the incident/problem. Besides the possibility to add a list of users, groups of users (e.g., departments), or all users can be added.
Person who reported the incident/problem	isReportedBy	Every person is represented by a separate wiki page. Incidents/problems are linked to the person who reported the incident/problem.
Priority	hasPriorityType	Priority of the issue.
Relations to other incidents/problems	isRelatedTo	Incidents can be related to other incidents or be an indication of an underlying problem. By using different types of SMW relations, it is possible to link incidents and problems to each other.
Relations to solutions	hasSolution	Solutions to incidents and problems are stored as pages in the ITSM Wiki. SMW relations are used to link incidents and problems to solutions.
Relations to workarounds	hasWorkaround	Workarounds for incidents and problems are stored as pages in the ITSM Wiki. SMW relations are used to link incidents and problems to workarounds.
Severity	hasSeverityType	Severity of the issue.
Type of the issue	hasIssueType	Type, which helps to classify if the entry is an incident or a problem. Furthermore, more fine-grained distinctions are possible (e.g., normal incident, or major incident).

Table 4.15.: Incident and Problem Management

extends Semantic MediaWiki's capabilities with regard to supporting the user in tracking down the cause of incidents and problems, namely the Incident and Problem Analyzer Component, is described in Section 5.4 (page 284).

Summary of Requirements

A tool for the management of incidents and problems has to provide the following capabilities:

- Management of incidents and problems in *structured* format (R-D01).
- Management of incidents and problems in *unstructured* format (R-D02).
- Management of incidents and problems in a combination of structured *and* unstructured format (R-D03).

4.2.5. Continual Service Improvement

Continual Service Improvement (CSI) [CS07] is the fifth publication in the ITIL V3 series and was introduced in Section 2.2.5 (page 53). Its focus is on the ongoing improvement of ITSM processes within an organization. Continual Service Improvement, in order to realize the potential for improvements, needs to have access to various kinds of information about ITSM activities.

Semantic MediaWiki, with its ability to query for structured information and the ability to present information from queries as tables helps to realize the requirements of *Service Reporting* [CS07, page 65] and *Service Measurement* [CS07, pages 66–67] in the context of the requirements of the IT department at FZI. Data that is needed for the generation of reports is aggregated by two components, namely the Information Gathering Component (Section 5.1, page 188), and the Infrastructure Monitoring Component (Section 5.2, page 234).

Summary of Requirements

In order to support Continual Service Improvement, a tool has to provide the following capabilities:

- Provide mechanisms for service reporting and service measurement (G-E01).
- Processing of queries for structured information (R-E01).
- Presentation of results in tables (R-E02).
- Access information from across all ITSM disciplines (R-E03).

4.2.6. Usability Aspects

Usability aspects play a critical role in the acceptance of software systems (cp. [SP04]). In the case of the ITSM Wiki, the points that had to be addressed are as follows:

- The input and formatting of unstructured data (i.e., text) have to be easy and efficient.
- The input of structured data has to be easy and efficient.

When looking at (non-semantic) wikis, it can be seen that most of the implementations use wikitext (see Section 4.1.3, page 121), an easy to use abstraction of the most often used elements of HTML, for formatting page content. Most wiki implementations also provide help in the form of toolbars, which contain buttons for adding formatting to the wikitext. While this further eases the task of editing, it still requires a certain amount of imagination on the user's part, to mentally transfer the text-based markup used in edit mode, to the formatted output found in view mode. This aspect is especially hard for users accustomed to WYSIWYG mode text processors. While there are extensions for editing content in MediaWiki in WYSIWYG mode [Med11d], these extensions only cover basic editing functionalities.

With regard to editing semantic information, there exist two mechanisms: The first mechanism is built into the Semantic MediaWiki extension and consists of a special text-based syntax in which properties are described (see Section 4.1.4, page 126). While this mechanism makes it possible to describe relations on the fly while editing text, in the context of editing CMDB information, it is far from intuitive for users accustomed to form-based user interfaces, as found in most CMDB tools (e.g., OTRS::ITSM). The second mechanism uses a form-based editing approach, as provided by the Semantic Forms extension (see Section 4.1.5, page 132). While this mechanism is not as flexible with regard to editing properties on the fly, it makes editing of structured information easier in contexts where the same kind of information is edited repeatedly, as is the case in the ITSM Wiki-based Configuration Management Database.

When presenting information to the user of the ITSM Wiki, it has to be made sure that the user is not overwhelmed with information, which is not needed at a particular moment. For example, when viewing or editing information about the hardware of a computer, the information about installed software or accounting information is of no importance and should not be displayed. On the other hand, additional information should be accessible quickly if needed. In the ITSM Wiki, these two requirements were solved by using the Header Tabs extension [Med11b], which allows to separate information within a wiki page, but allows fast access to all information provided by a page via tabs.

SMW+, which was described in Section 4.1.4 (page 128), provides additional mechanisms for editing structured information. During the ontology engineering phase, the ontology browser proved to be a valuable tool for visualizing and graphically editing class hierarchies and properties. When enriching text by adding semantic relations, SMW+ helps by providing a graphical tool. While this can be helpful in some instances in the context of the ITSM Wiki, the most common case is the editing of structured information in Semantic Forms.

Summary of Requirements

With regard to usability, the following requirements have to be satisfied:

- Ability to easily edit structured data (R-F01).
- Ability to easily edit unstructured data (R-F02).
- Ability to selectively present relevant data (R-F03).

4.2.7. Prior and Related Work

While in the area of CMDB and CMS software, there exist numerous solutions, both commercially available and available as open source (see Section 3.3, page 109), only a limited amount of related work in the area of semantic wiki-supported CMS tools can be found.

Reference [AMJ09] describes a Semantic MediaWiki-based system, which, in its core aspects is comparable to the solution presented in this chapter. The presented solution, knowIT, although located in a different environment (IT department of a large organization, in contrast to the SME environment for which the ITSM Wiki was developed), also came to the conclusion that providing a Semantic Forms-based mechanism for editing structured information in the wiki is beneficial. The ITSM Wiki as a project was motivated by the benefits of creating a single information base for all aspects of the IT department's information, for which a semantic wiki provided a solution to the requirements. knowIT started from an existing relational database, in which the relevant information was stored prior to the migration to the semantic wiki. When comparing the functionality of knowIT to the ITSM Wiki presented in this thesis, the following observations can be made: Both tools use the same underlying platform in order to collaboratively manage information about IT environments. In the ITSM Wiki, additional functionality is included by the components presented in Chapter 5 (page 185), however. These components distinguish the ITSM Wiki from a pure information management system by providing mechanisms for interacting with external tools. This provides a number of additional benefits, such as enabling the automatic import of information, as well as the re-use of information (e.g., for infrastructure monitoring and intrusion detection).

In [GBS09], “a knowledge-based collaboration environment for ITIL” is described, which aims at being used by IT consultants. The focus of the environment lies on “planning, designing and implementing ITIL processes”. The paper describes a domain wiki for IT Service Management, which models “[c]ommon ITSM knowledge” in a Semantic MediaWiki [GBS09]. When compared to the ITSM Wiki, the focus of the tool is on retaining and collaboratively working on ITIL processes rather than on providing a lightweight tool for information and Knowledge Management in IT environments.

The work presented in [Lan10b, Lan10a] uses Semantic MediaWiki, as well as Semantic Forms for implementing a ticketing system, as well as a prototypical “datacenter inventory” tool. Compared to the ITSM Wiki, the datacenter inventory tool only retains basic information about hardware and settings (such as IP addresses). Functionality for the management of more encompassing ITSM-relevant information, as provided by the ITSM Wiki, is not implemented. Furthermore, no mechanisms for interactions with external tools are implemented.

In summary, the presented prior and related work uses the same underlying technology as the ITSM Wiki, namely Semantic MediaWiki, in order to provide tool support for the management of information with regard to IT Service Management. None of the presented implementations provides advanced functionality as provided by the ITSM Wiki's components, such as automatic import of information, or the integration of infrastructure monitoring, or intrusion detection, however.

4.3. Data Model: The Ontologies

The central data model of the ITSM Wiki is an ontology. For an introduction of ontologies, please refer to Section 2.3 (page 59). The following Section 4.3.1 gives a motivation for using ontologies as the data model. In Section 4.3.2 (page 163), the design of the ontologies is described, while Section 4.3.3 (page 166) goes into the partitioning of the ontologies. Section 4.3.4 (page 167), presents the ITSM Ontology. Finally, an overview of prior and related work about ontologies in the context of IT Service Management is given in Section 4.3.5 (page 181).

4.3.1. Motivation

Due to its use of Semantic MediaWiki as a technical platform, the ITSM Wiki's underlying data model is an ontology. While it is the intention to not have users of the ITSM Wiki interact directly with the ontology and thus avoid the need for in-depth understanding of the more formal aspects of ontologies, there are various benefits gained from the use of ontologies in the ITSM Wiki. Because of the use of ontologies in Semantic MediaWiki, it would be hard, if not impossible, to implement the ITSM Wiki without using the underlying ontology. In fact, not using ontologies would defy the whole purpose of using Semantic MediaWiki in the first place and would result in, most likely, a database-based system without some of the advanced features required in the context of its use in FZI's IT department.

In order to present the benefits of using an ontology as the data model of the ITSM Wiki, first, the general benefits of making use of ontologies and Semantic Web technologies are presented. Following that, a look at the concrete benefits of using ontologies and Semantic Web technologies in the context of the ITSM Wiki is given.

With regard to managing information in Semantic MediaWiki, the general benefits are as follows [KVV$^+$07]:

- "*Consistency of content:* The same information often occurs on many pages. How can one ensure that information in different parts of the system is consistent, especially as it can be changed in a distributed way?
- "*Accessing knowledge:* Large wikis have thousands of pages. Finding and comparing information from different pages is challenging and time-consuming.
- "*Reusing knowledge:* Many wikis are driven by the wish to make information accessible to many people. But the rigid, text-based content of classical wikis can only be used by reading pages in a browser or similar application." [KVV$^+$07, emphasis in original]

When looking at definitions of ontologies (see Section 2.3, page 59), the definition by Studer et al., which states that "[a]n ontology is a formal, explicit specification of a shared conceptualisation" [SBF98] summarizes the most important aspects of an ontology.

With regard to the concrete benefits of using an ontology as the data model for the ITSM Wiki, the following can be said:

- With regard to the "consistency of content" [KVV$^+$07], information about configuration items and other structured information has only to be stored once, which avoids duplication of work as well as faulty information due to not updated information (see Section 3.1, page 82).
- The ITSM Wiki is used for managing thousands of pages. A large amount of these pages contains structured information about configuration items, which benefits from Semantic MediaWiki's mechanisms for "accessing knowledge" [KVV$^+$07].
- By "[r]eusing knowledge" [KVV$^+$07], duplication of information with regard to configuration items can be avoided. By using a structured data format, together with the flexible query mechanism provided by Semantic MediaWiki, information about configuration items can be processed automatically.

- Due to the "formal, explicit specification" [SBF98] of the information in the ontology, automatic reasoning can be performed on the structured information, which enables capabilities that exceed the ones found in classic database-based systems.

- With regard to the "shared conceptualization" [SBF98], by using an ontology, information in the ITSM Wiki can be used between different users and tools without the risk of misinterpretation of information due to a different understanding.

4.3.2. Design of the Ontologies

Engineering an ontology requires a structured and planned approach in order to lead to consistent and usable results. In this subsection, the foundations for engineering ontologies are presented, with the goal of choosing an appropriate approach or extracting usable patterns for the design of the ontologies. There are several approaches, which differ in various aspects (for example, the scope and size of the ontology, the direction taken when engineering the ontology, e.g., top-down, or bottom-up, and the intended use of the ontology, e.g., upper ontology, or domain ontology).

The perspective of viewing the creation of an ontology as an engineering discipline (ontology *engineering*) stems from adapting principles of software engineering into the domain of ontology creation. Reference [FL99] gives an early overview of ontology development methodologies motivated by software engineering principles. Furthermore, the NeOn Methodology describes a number of approaches for different ontology engineering scenarios. The scenarios include the development of an ontology from scratch, and the re-use and re-engineering of ontological and non-ontological resources [SFGPFL12].

There are several publications, which deal with developing methodologies as well as giving account of applications of methodologies. Examples of methodologies are the Uschold and King methodology [UK95], the Grüninger and Fox methodology [GF95], the KACTUS approach [BnLC96], METHONDOLOGY [FLGPJ97, FLGPSS99], the Sensus method [SPKR97], and the On-To-Knowledge methodology [SSSS01, SS02].

More information about the creation of ontologies can be found in [Gru95, NM01, WVV+01, CFLGPLC03, CFLGP06, BCC06, DNMN09, Gal09].

There exist tools that enable the collaborative creation, editing, and annotation of ontologies. Collaborative Protégé supports "discussions integrated with [the] ontology-editing process, chats, and annotations of changes and ontology components" [TNTM08]. A second tool is Web Protégé, which is characterized as "a lightweight ontology editor and knowledge acquisition tool for the Web" [TNNM13]. Both tools use Protégé [RNM07] as the underlying infrastructure.

The methodological approach with regard to the basic design of the ontologies in the context of this thesis is mainly based on some aspects of the On-To-Knowledge methodology [SSSS01, SS02], as well as the guidelines presented in [NM01]. With regard to the actual creation of the individual ontologies, a middle-out approach was selected, because it harmonized best with the collaborative, ad-hoc way of editing pages in Semantic MediaWiki.

Ontology Requirements Specification

According to the On-To-Knowledge methodology [SSSS01], the requirements of an ontology should be specified. The ITSM Ontology's requirements are as follows:

- *Domain:* IT Service Management and IT administration (with a special focus on IT administration in the context of SME organizations).
- *Goal of the ontology:* Data model for the use in a semantic wiki-based tool for documenting and managing the IT infrastructure at FZI.
- *Domain and Scope:* IT Service Management, IT administration, managing hardware, software and services in SME environments, infrastructure monitoring, intrusion detection, incident and problem management, management of virtualized servers and IaaS resources.
- *Supported applications:* Semantic MediaWiki-based platform for managing and documenting an SME's IT infrastructure.
- *Knowledge sources:* Knowledge can be extracted from the following knowledge sources:
  - IT administrators (domain experts)
  - Configurations of existing tools (Nagios, Snort)
  - Existing data (Excel spreadsheets)
- *Users:* IT administrators
- *Use cases:* There are five major use cases for the ITSM ontology. The partitioning of the ontologies, which are used as the data models for the use cases, is shown in Figure 4.8 (page 166). The use cases are as follows:
  - Use Case 1: Documentation of the IT infrastructure (ITSM Ontology, Information Gathering Ontology)
  - Use Case 2: Management of infrastructure monitoring (Infrastructure Monitoring Ontology)

- Use Case 3: Management of intrusion detection (Intrusion Detection Ontology)
- Use Case 4: Tracking down the cause of incidents and problems in IT environments (Information Gathering Ontology)
- Use Case 5: Management of virtualization and IaaS resources (Virtualization and IaaS Ontology)

- *Competency questions:* The competency questions can be found in the following *Competency Questionnaire* subsection.
- *Potentially re-usable ontologies:* There are no known ontologies, which exactly match the intended field of application. Ontologies that cover some aspects of the field of application are presented in Section 4.3.5.

Competency Questionnaire

The On-To-Knowledge methodology suggests building a competency questionnaire, which includes "possible queries to the system that can indicate the scope and content of the domain ontology" [SSSS01]. An exemplary part of a competency questionnaire for the ontologies presented in this thesis is shown in Table 4.16.

Competency Question	Concepts	Relations
What is the solution to a given problem?	Problem, Solution	Problem has Solution
Generate a list of computers of a certain department.	Computer, Organizational Unit	Computer is part of Organizational Unit
What operating system is running on a certain computer?	Computer, Software	Computer uses Software
List the hardware configuration of a computer.	Computer, Hardware, Mainboard, Graphics Adapter, Sound Adapter, Hard Disk, Memory Module, Network Adapter	Hardware is part of Computer
Which changes to computers were performed during the last month?	Change, Computer, Date	Computer is affected by Change; Change is performed at date
When was a certain computer installed the last time?	Computer, Change, Date	Change is performed on Computer; Change is performed at date

Table 4.16.: Exemplary Part of the Ontology Competency Questionnaire

4.3.3. Partitioning of the Ontologies

The ontology that is used as the data model of the ITSM Wiki consists of multiple different areas of interest. In order to make the presentation of the data model more accessible to the reader, the classes and properties of the ontology are divided into multiple smaller ontologies, which are aligned to the separations between the different components that are described in the following Chapter 5 (page 185). The relationships between the ontologies can be seen in Figure 4.8.

The partitioning of the ontologies is motivated by the use cases, which were presented in Section 4.3.2 (page 164).

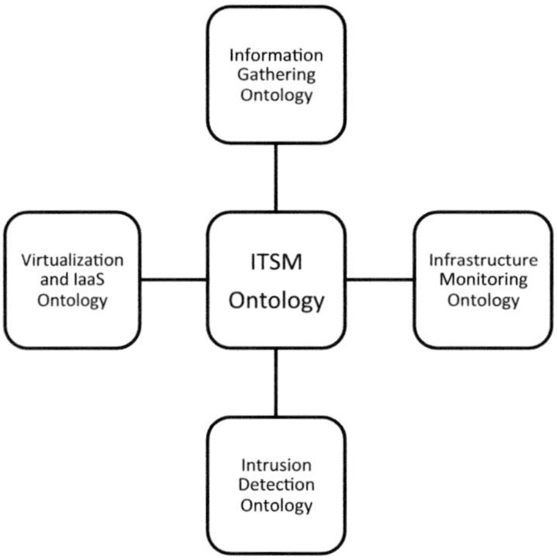

Figure 4.8.: Ontology Partitioning

The ITSM Ontology, which is presented in Section 4.3.4 (page 167), contains the core ITSM parts. Domain-specific ontologies are the Information Gathering Ontology, the Infrastructure Monitoring Ontology, the Intrusion Detection Ontology, and the Virtualization and IaaS Ontology. While there exists a separation between ontologies with regard to the different tasks as a mechanism for providing a clearer picture to the reader of the thesis, in the context of the ITSM Wiki implementation, all concepts and properties are within the same ontology.

Using only a single ontology instead of modularization is motivated by the following facts: First, Semantic MediaWiki does not include mechanisms for modularized ontologies. Second, the intended user base of the ITSM Wiki are IT administrators, who extend the ontology on demand without prior consultation of ontology engineering experts. In this regard, adding classes and properties quickly without having to consider module structures is more important than the benefits gained by modularization.

Component Ontologies

The component ontologies contain the classes and properties, which are relevant to the respective component. While the ITSM Ontology is described in the following subsection, the component ontologies are described in their respective component sections:

- Information Gathering Ontology: Section 5.1.7 (page 219)
- Infrastructure Monitoring Ontology: Section 5.2.7 (page 251)
- Intrusion Detection Ontology: Section 5.3.7 (page 276)
- Virtualization and IaaS Ontology: Section 5.5.6 (page 309)

4.3.4. ITSM Ontology

The ITSM Ontology contains the classes and properties that are central to the ITSM activities within the IT department at FZI. Parts of the ITSM Ontology are used by the more specialized components described in Chapter 5 (page 185).

Class Hierarchy

Figure 4.9 shows the class hierarchy of the ITSM Ontology. All classes are subclasses of the *Thing* class. Class hierarchies are expressed with the *is-a* property.

Classes, Object Properties, and Data Properties

Table 4.17 shows the classes, object properties, and data properties of the ITSM Ontology. The property column either represents a data property, or an object property. While data properties start with uppercase letters, object properties start with lowercase letters. The cardinality of the properties is shown after the property name in the property column. In most cases, the cardinality is specified as $\{0..1\}$, or as $\{0..n\}$. The first case allows zero or one instances, while the second case allows any number of instances (including zero). By refraining from strictly defining the cardinality, the ITSM Wiki that makes use of the ontology can be flexibly used even in scenarios in which not all relevant information is present. The range either is one of the Semantic MediaWiki datatypes (as presented in Section 4.1.4, page 128, and expressed in angle brackets), or one of the classes of the ITSM Ontology. Class properties are inherited from superclasses. In the table, classes and properties that are relevant in the context of the core ITSM Ontology are shown in boldface type. Classes and properties, which are only of secondary interest in this context are displayed in regular type.

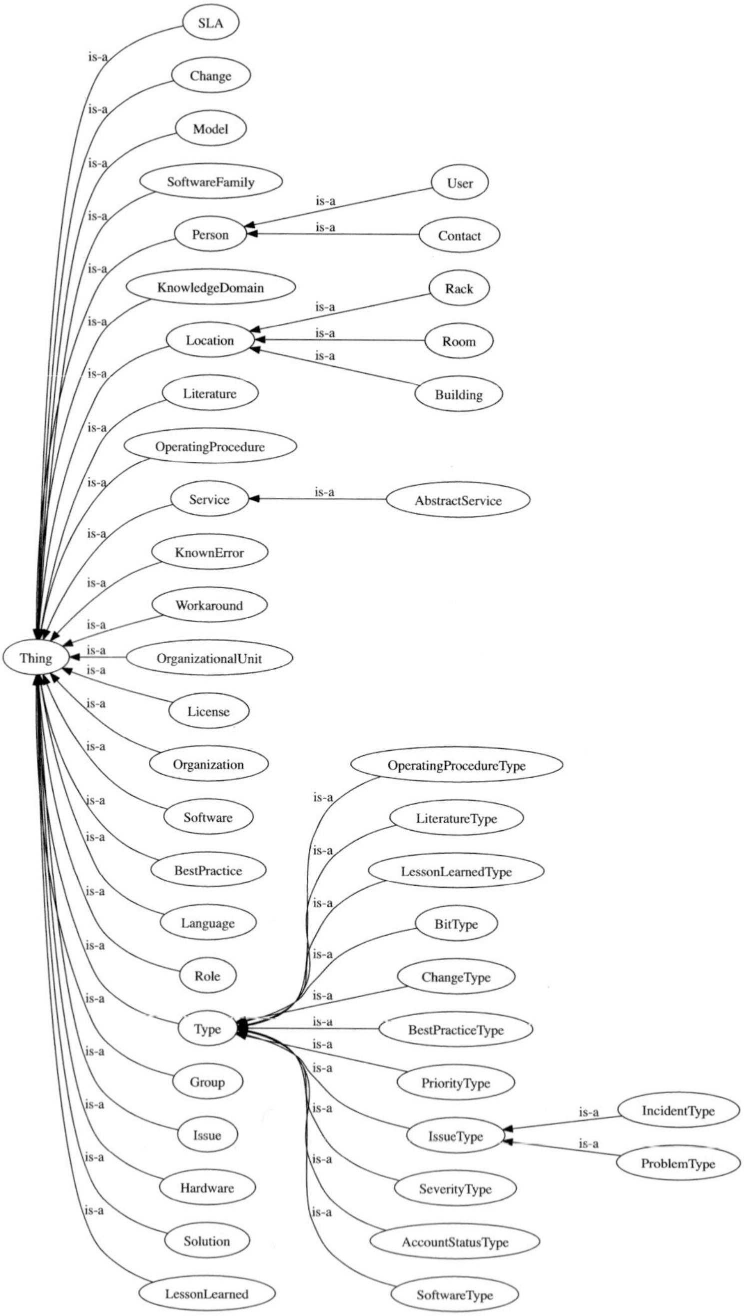

Figure 4.9.: Class Hierarchy of the ITSM Ontology

Table 4.17.: ITSM Ontology

Domain Class	Property	Range
AbstractService	*inherited from Service class*	
	consistsOfService {0..n}	Service
BestPractice	*inherited from Thing class*	
	ContextDescription {0..1}	<Text>
	appliesTo {0..n}	Thing
	hasBestPracticeType {0..1}	BestPracticeType
	hasSpecialist {0..n}	Person
	isRelatedToBestPractice {0..n}	BestPractice
BestPracticeType	*inherited from Type class*	*no additional properties*
BitType	*inherited from Type class*	*no additional properties*
Building	*inherited from Location class*	
	City {0..1}	<String>
	Street {0..1}	<String>
	ZipCode {0..1}	<String>
Change	*inherited from Thing class*	
	AdditionalRequiredResource {0..1}	<Text>
	DateOfChangeAuthorization {0..1}	<Date>
	DateOfChangeInitiation {0..1}	<Date>
	DateOfChangeExecution {0..1}	<Date>
	Reason {0..1}	<Text>
	Risk {0..1}	<Text>
	ServiceDeskTicketURL {0..n}	<URL>
	affects {0..n}	Thing
	hasChangeType {1}	ChangeType
	hasRequiredResource {0..n}	Thing
	isAuthorizedByPerson {0..n}	Person
	isCheckedByPerson {0..n}	Person
	isExecutedByPerson {0..n}	Person
	isInitiatedByPerson {0..n}	Person
	isRelatedToChange {0..n}	Change
ChangeType	*inherited from Type class*	*no additional properties*
Contact	*inherited from Person class*	*no additional properties*
Group	*inherited from Thing class*	
	isMemberOfGroup {0..n}	Group
Hardware	*inherited from Thing class*	
	ProductNumber {0..1}	<String>
	SerialNumber {0..1}	<String>
	hasManufacturer {0..1}	Organization
	hasModel {0..1}	Model
	hasVendor {0..1}	Organization
	isCompatibleWith {0..n}	Thing
	isIncompatibleWith {0..n}	Thing
IncidentType	*inherited from IssueType class*	*no additional properties*

(*table continues*)

Table 4.17.: ITSM Ontology (continued)

Domain Class	**Property**	**Range**
Issue	*inherited from Thing class*	
	affects {0..n}	Thing
	hasIssueType {0..1}	IssueType
	hasPriorityType {0..1}	PriorityType
	hasSeverityType {0..1}	SeverityType
	hasSolution {0..n}	Solution
	hasWorkaround {0..n}	Workaround
	isRelatedTo {0..n}	Issue
	isReportedBy {0..n}	Person
IssueType	*inherited from Type class*	*no additional properties*
KnowledgeDomain	*inherited from Thing class*	*no additional properties*
KnownError	*inherited from Thing class*	
	DateOfResolution {0..1}	<Date>
	affects {0..n}	Thing
Language	*inherited from Thing class*	*no additional properties*
LessonLearned	*inherited from Thing class*	
	AdditionalInformation {0..1}	<Text>
	ProblemStatement {0..1}	<Text>
	appliesTo {0..n}	Thing
	hasAdditionalInformation {0..n}	Person
	hasLessonLearnedType {0..1}	LessonLearnedType
	hasSpecialist {0..n}	Person
LessonLearnedType	*inherited from Type class*	*no additional properties*
License	*inherited from Thing class*	
	LicenseCount {0..1}	<Number>
	OrderPurchaseNumber {0..1}	<String>
	SerialNumber {0..n}	<String>
	hasVendor {0..1}	Organization
	isInstalledOnHost {0..n}	Host
	isLicenseForSoftware {0..n}	Software
	isOrderedByPerson {0..n}	Person
	isOrderedForOrganizationalUnit {0..n}	OrganizationalUnit
Literature	*inherited from Thing class*	
	Author {0..n}	<String>
	Link {0..1}	<URL>
	containsInformationAbout {0..n}	Thing
	hasLiteratureType {0..1}	LiteratureType
LiteratureType	*inherited from Type class*	*no additional properties*
Location	*inherited from Thing class*	*no additional properties*

(*table continues*)

Table 4.17.: ITSM Ontology (continued)

Domain Class	**Property**	**Range**
OperatingProcedure	*inherited from Thing class*	
	AdditionalInformation {0..1}	<Text>
	Purpose {0..1}	<Text>
	WorkingStepDescription {0..1}	<Text>
	appliesTo {0..n}	Thing
	hasOperatingProcedureType {0..1}	OperatingProcedureType
	hasSpecialist {0..n}	Person
OperatingProcedureType	*inherited from Type class*	*no additional properties*
Model	*inherited from Thing class*	*no additional properties*
Organization	*inherited from Thing class*	
	City {0..1}	<String>
	Country {0..1}	<String>
	EMailAddress {0..1}	<String>
	FaxNumber {0..1}	<String>
	PhoneNumber {0..1}	<String>
	Street {0..1}	<String>
	WebPage {0..1}	<String>
	ZipCode {0..1}	<String>
OrganizationalUnit	*inherited from Thing class*	
	hasDeputyManager {0..n}	<Person>
	hasITContact {0..n}	<Person>
	hasManager {0..n}	<Person>
	isPartOfOrganization {0..1}	Organization
	isPartOfOrganizationalUnit {0..1}	OrganizationalUnit
Person	*inherited from Thing class*	
	EMailAddress {0..n}	<Email>
	FamilyName {0..1}	<String>
	FaxNumber {0..n}	<Telephone number>
	GivenName {0..1}	<String>
	JobTitle {0..1}	<String>
	PhoneNumber {0..n}	<Telephone number>
	hasKnowledgeDomain {0..n}	KnowledgeDomain
	hasManager {0..1}	Person
	hasOffice {0..1}	Room
	hasRole {0..n}	Role
	isMemberOfGroup {0..n}	Group
	isMemberOfOrganization {0..n}	Organization
	isMemberOfOrganizationalUnit {0..n}	OrganizationalUnit
PriorityType	*inherited from Type class*	*no additional properties*
ProblemType	*inherited from IssueType class*	*no additional properties*
Rack	*inherited from Location class*	
	Height {0..1}	<Quantity>
	isLocatedInRoom {0..1}	Room
Role	*inherited from Thing class*	*no additional properties*

(*table continues*)

Table 4.17.: ITSM Ontology (continued)

Domain Class	**Property**	**Range**
Room	*inherited from Location class* isLocatedInBuilding {0..1}	 Building
Service	*inherited from Thing class* hasOwner {0..1}	 Person
SeverityType	*inherited from Type class*	*no additional properties*
SLA	*inherited from Thing class*	*no additional properties*
Software	*inherited from Thing class* SoftwareVersion {0..1} hasBitType {0..1} hasLanguage {0..n} hasManufacturer {0..1} hasSoftwareType {0..1} hasVendor {0..1} isCompatibleWith {0..n} isIncompatibleWith {0..n} isPartOfSoftwareFamily {0..1}	 <String> BitType Language Organization SoftwareType Organization Thing Thing SoftwareFamily
SoftwareFamily	*inherited from Thing class* isPartOfSoftwareFamily {0..1}	 SoftwareFamily
SoftwareType	*inherited from Type class*	*no additional properties*
Solution	*inherited from Thing class*	*no additional properties*
Thing	Description {0..1} Name {1} Version {0..1} hasDependency {0..n} hasParent {0..n} isConnectedTo {0..n} isRelatedTo {0..n}	<Text> <String> <Number> Thing Thing Thing Thing
Type	*inherited from Thing class*	*no additional properties*
User	*inherited from Person class* CreationDate {0..1} DeletionDate {0..1} LastLoginDate {0..1} LoginName {0..1} UniqueIdentifier {0..1} hasAccountStatusType {0..1}	 <Date> <Date> <Date> <String> <String> AccountStatusType
Workaround	*inherited from Thing class*	*no additional properties*

Descriptions and Exemplary Instances

Table 4.18 shows a short description, as well as exemplary instances, for each class of the ITSM Ontology. Furthermore, the descriptions and instances of the ontologies that are presented in Chapter 5 (page 185) are also contained in the table. This is done in order to avoid unnecessary duplication of information.

The class hierarchies, classes, and properties of the component ontologies are described in Section 5.1.7 (page 219), Section 5.2.7 (page 251), Section 5.3.7 (page 276), and Section 5.5.6 (page 309).

Table 4.18.: Ontology Descriptions and Instances

Domain Class	Description	Exemplary Instances
AbstractService	An abstract service is a service in the non-technical sense, e.g., the mail service. An abstract service is provided by one or more technical services (e.g., an SMTP service).	Mail service
AccountStatusType	The status of an account indicates, if an account can be used. For example, an enabled account can be used to log into a computer, while a deleted one cannot. Accounts, which no longer exist in the directory service, are marked as deleted in the ITSM Wiki.	Enabled, disabled, deleted
AvailabilityTime	A time period, in which a service is checked for availability.	24x7
BestPractice	A best practice describes an approach, which is known to work, and provide known good results. ITIL definition: "Proven Activities or Processes that have been successfully used by multiple Organizations. ITIL is an example of Best Practice." [LM07, page 227]	Definition when to change passwords.
BestPracticeType	Defines the type of a best practice.	Operational best practice, strategic best practice
BitType	Computer architectures, operating systems, and applications use different address widths for addressing memory. This class contains instances for representing this address width.	16 bit, 32 bit, 64 bit
Building	Buildings comprise a number of rooms.	FZI Building 1

(*table continues*)

Table 4.18.: Ontology Descriptions and Instances (continued)

Domain Class	Description	Exemplary Instances
Change	Contains different types of changes, which are further specified by its change type. ITIL definition: "The addition, modification or removal of anything that could have an effect on IT Services. The Scope should include all IT Services, Configuration Items, Processes, Documentation, etc." [LM07, page 228]	Installation of a new operating system on a computer.
ChangeType	Specifies the type of a change.	Standard Change, Standard Operational Change, Normal Change
CheckTimeInterval	The check time interval specifies, how often a host or service is checked for availability.	Every minute
CommissioningStatusType	The commissioning status indicates the phase, in which a host is in its lifecycle.	Productive, testing, in repair, decommissioned
Computer	A computer is defined as a host, which can be directly used by a user or an administrator. This means, that desktop computers, servers, tablet computers are all categorized as computer. In contrast, network switches are not categorized as computers.	*See subclasses for instance examples*
ComputerFormFactorType	Computers exist in different sizes and shapes. The form factor type represents these different types of sizes and shapes.	*See subclasses for instance examples*
ComputerModel	This class contains computer models.	*See subclasses for instance examples*
ComputerUsageType	The computer usage type specifies, how a computer is used.	Workstation, server
ConcreteService	A concrete service is a service in the technical sense, in contrast to an abstract service.	SMTP service
ConnectionType	Different networks use different mechanisms (cable, wireless), speeds, and connection types.	LAN Connection
Contact	Represents a person. Members of the contact class do not have accounts in the user management system of the managed organization.	A printer support company representative.

(*table continues*)

Table 4.18.: Ontology Descriptions and Instances (continued)

Domain Class	**Description**	**Exemplary Instances**
GraphicsAdapter	Graphics adapters are hardware devices, built into a computer, which enable the display of content on screens.	Graphics adapter in computer suzanna.fzi.de
GraphicsAdapterModel	This class contains graphics adapter models.	NVIDIA GeForce 9400M
Group	Groups in the Directory Service, which contain objects (e.g., users, computers, or groups).	IT-Department-Users
Hardware	The hardware class is the superclass for all hardware components that are represented in the ITSM Wiki (e.g., graphics adapters, and network cards).	*See subclasses for instance examples*
HardwareModel	This class is a superclass for all hardware model classes.	*See subclasses for instance examples*
Host	Hosts can be of different types (e.g., computers, and network equipment), and consist of different hardware components.	*See subclasses for instance examples*
HostModel	This class is a superclass for all host model classes.	*See subclasses for instance examples*
HostTemplate	A template, which describes how the host is monitored by the Infrastructure Monitoring Component.	Windows host template
IaasInstance	An instance of a virtual computer that is hosted in an Infrastructure as a Service environment.	OpenStack or EC2 instance
IaasInstanceType	The type of an IaaS instance.	Large OpenStack instance with 8 CPU cores and 16 GB of RAM
IncidentType	Defines the type of an incident. ITIL definition (incident): "An unplanned interruption to an IT Service or reduction in the Quality of an IT Service. Failure of a Configuration Item that has not yet affected Service is also an Incident. For example Failure of one disk from a mirror set." [LM07, page 235]	Normal Incident, major incident
IntrusionDetectionEvent	An intrusion detection event is an event that is generated when the intrusion detection system detects a suspicious packet.	IntrusionDetection-Event-1821373

(*table continues*)

Table 4.18.: Ontology Descriptions and Instances (continued)

Domain Class	**Description**	**Exemplary Instances**
IntrusionDetectionSignature	An intrusion detection signature contains the characteristics of an attack. The intrusion detection system scans network traffic for occurrences of signatures.	IntrusionDetection-Signature-1926
Issue	An issue is something that describes the malfunctioning of a CI, namely an incident, or a problem.	Failed hard disk, incompatible software
IssueType	Defines the type of an issue.	*See subclasses for instance examples*
KnowledgeDomain	A knowledge domain describes an area, in which a person has knowledge.	Network protocols, Windows operating system
KnownError	ITIL definition: "A Problem that has a documented Root Cause and a Workaround. Known Errors are created and managed throughout their Lifecycle by Problem Management. Known Errors may also be identified by Development or Suppliers." [LM07, page 237]	A program has to be started manually after a computer reboots, instead of starting automatically, as intended.
Language	A spoken or written language.	English, German
LessonLearned	A lesson, which has been learned and documented.	Program A has to be started before program B in order to avoid inconsistent data.
LessonLearnedType	The type of a learned lesson.	IT, organizational
License	A license, which allows the use of a computer software.	Microsoft Windows 8 License
Literature	Literature, which gives more information about a topic, e.g., the Windows operating system.	Book 'Windows 7 – The Definite Guide'
LiteratureType	The type of literature.	Book, Web page
Location	Describes a location.	*See subclasses for instance examples*
Mainboard	The mainboard is the hardware component of a host, to which the other hardware components connect.	Mainboard in computer suzanna.fzi.de
MainboardModel	This class contains mainboard models.	ASUS M5A78L-M/USB3
Model	The superclass of all model classes. Models are an abstraction for concrete entities that are represented in the CMDB.	*See subclasses for instance examples*

(table continues)

Table 4.18.: Ontology Descriptions and Instances (continued)

Domain Class	**Description**	**Exemplary Instances**
MonitoringTemplate	The superclass of all infrastructure monitoring template classes.	*See subclasses for instance examples*
NetworkAdapter	A network adapter provides the physical interface and the logic for connecting a host to a network.	Network adapter in computer suzanna.fzi.de
NetworkAdapterModel	This class contains all network adapter models.	Intel Ethernet Server Adapter I210-T1
NetworkAdapterType	The type of a network adapter.	Ethernet 802.3
NetworkEquipment	A network equipment instance is an instance of a host, which is specialized for providing network services.	*See subclasses for instance examples*
NetworkEquipmentModel	This class contains all network equipment models.	*See subclasses for instance examples*
NetworkSegment	Network segments are separate parts of a company's network. Segmentation is used to separate different types of hosts, e.g., create a separation between internal hosts and hosts that are accessible from the Internet. Hosts in different segments cannot communicate directly, but have to connect over a router.	Internal network, DMZ
NetworkSwitch	A network switch is used to physically connect hosts on the data link layer of the OSI model.	3com4500g-12-b.fzi.de
NetworkSwitchModel	This class contains all network switch models.	3com 4500-48G-PoE
NetworkWAP	Wireless access points are the part of the network infrastructure, which allows wireless clients to connect to the network.	fzi-ap-4-3.fzi.de
NetworkWAPModel	This class contains all wireless access point models.	LANCOM L-321agn
OperatingProcedure	A procedure, which has been documented and which has to be followed when performing a certain task.	Steps that have to be performed when installing the monthly operating system updates.
OperatingProcedureType	Specifies the type of an operating procedure.	IT, organizational

(*table continues*)

Table 4.18.: Ontology Descriptions and Instances (continued)

Domain Class	Description	Exemplary Instances
Organization	ITIL definition: "A company, legal entity or other institution. Examples of Organizations that are not companies include International Standards Organization or itSMF. The term Organization is sometimes used to refer to any entity that has People, Resources and Budgets. For example, a Project or Business Unit." [LM07, page 239]	FZI, KIT
OrganizationalUnit	Organizational units are entities, which are part of an organization. In most cases, they form hierarchical structures, e.g., divisions, departments, and teams.	IPE, RuD
PersistentStorage	Persistent storage allows to retain data between reboots of a host. It stores the operating system, applications, and user data.	Hard disk in computer suzanna.fzi.de
PersistentStorageIfType	The interface type specifies the connection (e.g., physical cables, and transport protocol) of the persistent storage device.	SATA, IDE, SAS
PersistentStorageModel	This class contains all persistent storage models.	WD3200BEKT-00PVMT0
PersistentStoragePartition	Most operating systems allow the creation of logical partitions on persistent storage devices in order to, for example, separate user files from files of the operating system.	C:, D:
PersistentStorageType	There exist different types of persistent storage devices that have different parameters. For example, there are solid state disks based on flash memory, as well as hard disk drives that contain spinning platters.	SSD, HDD
Person	The person class is the superclass, which provides common properties for the contact and user classes.	*See subclasses for instance examples*
PhysicalComputer	A physical computer is a computer with an enclosure that consists of hardware.	suzanna.fzi.de
PhysicalComputerModel	This class contains all physical computer models.	Lenovo ThinkPad T430s
Port	A port is a mechanism for multiplexing connections on the transport layer.	Port 80/tcp

(table continues)

Table 4.18.: Ontology Descriptions and Instances (continued)

Domain Class	**Description**	**Exemplary Instances**
PortableFormFactorType	A form factor, which allows a host to be portable.	Notebook computer, tablet computer, smartphone
Printer	A device to transfer ink or toner to paper.	fzi-printer-2-14.fzi.de
PriorityType	Defines the priority of an issue.	low, normal, high
ProblemType	The problem type gives more insight into the nature of a stated problem. ITIL definition (problem): "A cause of one or more Incidents. The cause is not usually known at the time a Problem Record is created, and the Problem Management Process is responsible for further investigation." [LM07, page 240]	Normal problem, major problem, unspecified problem, network problem
Processor	The central processing unit of a host.	Processor in computer suzanna.fzi.de
ProcessorModel	This class contains all processor models.	Intel Core 2 Duo 2.53 GHz
Rack	An enclosure, in which servers and network equipment is operated.	Rack DV 0.7
RAM	Working memory that is used for storing temporary data, which is not retained between reboots.	RAM module in computer suzanna.fzi.de
RAMModel	This class contains all RAM models.	2 GB RAM module
Role	A role is a function, which a person of an organization can hold.	Department Manager, IT Manager
Room	Part of a building, in which other entities (e.g., persons, server racks, computers) can be located.	Room 1.0.02
Service	The service class is the superclass that provides common properties for the abstract service and concrete service classes.	*See subclasses for instance examples*
ServiceTemplate	A template that describes how the service is monitored by the Infrastructure Monitoring Component.	HTTP service template
SeverityType	Defines the severity of an issue.	low, normal, high
Software	This class contains instances of concrete software, e.g., operating systems, or application software. Software is grouped into families by making use of the Software Family class.	Microsoft Windows 8 Professional German 64 bit

(*table continues*)

Table 4.18.: Ontology Descriptions and Instances (continued)

Domain Class	Description	Exemplary Instances
SLA	A Service Level Agreement.	24x7 4h reaction time, 99.95 % uptime
SoftwareFamily	A software family is a related group of software, which shares common characteristics.	Microsoft Windows
SoftwareType	This class specifies the type of software.	Operating System, Application Software
Solution	This class contains solutions, which solve issues.	Updating a software application, in order to resolve incompatibilities.
SoundAdapter	A sound adapter is a hardware device that enables a computer to be connected to loudspeakers in order to output sound.	Sound adapter in computer suzanna.fzi.de
SoundAdapterModel	This class contains all sound adapter models.	SoundMAX Integrated Digital HD Audio
StationaryFormFactorType	A form factor that is too heavy or large in order to be portable.	Desktop computer, 19" rack computer
Template	The superclass of all template classes.	*See subclasses for instance examples*
Thing	The Thing class is the superclass for all other classes of the ontology.	*See subclasses for instance examples*
Time	The superclass of all time-related classes.	*See subclasses for instance examples*
TimeInterval	The superclass of all time interval-related classes.	*See subclasses for instance examples*
Type	The type class is the superclass, which is used to group all kinds of types.	*See subclasses for instance examples*
UnknownHost	An unknown host is a host, which is not part of the organizational network that is represented in the ITSM Wiki.	46.xx.yy.234
User	Members of the user class have an account in the user management system of the managed organization.	Frank Kleiner
VirtualComputer	A virtual computer, in contrast to a physical computer, only exists virtually within another computer.	*See subclasses for instance examples*
VirtualComputerModel	This class contains all virtual computer models.	XenServer-based virtual machine

(*table continues*)

Table 4.18.: Ontology Descriptions and Instances (continued)

Domain Class	Description	Exemplary Instances
VirtualizedInstance	A virtualized instance that is hosted in a virtualization environment.	Virtual instance fzi-323-53-1.fzi.de
VirtualNetworkAdapter	A virtualized network adapter.	Network adapter of virtual instance fzi-323-53-1.fzi.de
VirtualPersistentStorage	Virtualized persistent storage.	Hard disk of virtual instance fzi-323-53-1.fzi.de
VirtualResource	The virtual resource class is the superclass for all virtualized resources that are represented in the ITSM Wiki.	*See subclasses for instance examples*
Workaround	ITIL definition: "Reducing or eliminating the Impact of an Incident or Problem for which a full Resolution is not yet available. For example by restarting a failed Configuration Item. Workarounds for Problems are documented in Known Error Records. Workarounds for Incidents that do not have associated Problem Records are documented in the Incident Record." [CW07, page 250]	Restart computer when a certain application keeps on crashing.

4.3.5. Prior and Related Work

This subsection gives an overview of previous work in the area of ontologies that deal with IT Service Management or ITSM-related topics. There are various approaches, which cover aspects of IT Service Management, ranging from ontologies that describe IT Service Management's strategic aspects and processes, down to ontologies describing more technical aspects of IT Service Management.

General ITSM Ontologies

The ONION ("ONtologies In ONtology") project describes the idea of a "Community of Practice" ontology for the following domains: "IT Service Management Best Practice e.g. ISO 20000, ITIL", "IT Control Frameworks e.g. ISACA COBIT", "Information Security e.g. ISO / IEC 27001, ISO 17799", "IT Auditor Control Objectives e.g. COSO", and "SOA (Service Oriented Architecture) e.g. OASIS BCM (Business Centric Methodology)". The project's goal was the publication of an open source "Business Of Information Technology Ontology" [MY06]. The information found in [MY06] dates from the end of 2006 and contains a brief project description as well as the notes from a single conference call between the members of the working group. It seems that, since the end of 2006, no further process has been made in the project. The initial version of the ONION ontology can be found in [ONI06].

In [FCeA08], a "formal ontology for IT services" is proposed, which aims "at supporting services at different abstraction levels such as infrastructure management services, software outsourcing or even web services", as well as "generic services concepts such as SLAs, QoS or business processes" [FCeA08]. When compared to the ontologies developed in this thesis, it can be seen that the Ontology for IT Services does not describe the technical aspects of IT Service Management. Furthermore, aspects such as Configuration Management, as well as Incident and Problem Management are not addressed.

The ITSMO IT Service Management Ontology is outlined in [Fag11]. It is described as "a powerful vocabulary for describing all of the detail of IT Services in a way friendly to search engines, inventory applications, and browser extensions" [Fag11]. In [Fag12], the language specification of the ITSMO IT Service Management Ontology is given. While the focus of the ontologies that were developed in this thesis lies in supporting IT administrators, the focus of the ITSMO IT Service Management Ontology lies in providing a mechanism for "publish[ing] an IT Service Catalog" in a machine-processable way [Fag11]. Due to this fact, the ontology does not model aspects of ITIL such as Incident and Problem Management or Service Knowledge Management.

Reference [VGBS12] describes the integration of ontologies from the software engineering domain with ontologies from the ITSM domain. This enables organizations to better integrate ITSM with the software components that are used to provide services. While there exist a number of benefits from this approach for organizations that use software that is developed in-house in order to provide IT services, this is not the case in the scenario described in this thesis.

Configuration Management Ontologies

An introduction into Configuration Management was given in Section 2.2.3 (page 38). Reference [XX06] proposes the use of ontologies in the context of intelligent Configuration Management for IP networks. While an approach is introduced, that uses Semantic Web technologies for Configuration Management, only a single exemplary use case is described, without presenting an ontology that could be used in the scenario of this thesis.

In [BCCG09], a domain ontology for "IT Service Configuration Management (ITSCM)" is presented. The work describes ontologies, which build on top of the Unified Foundation Ontology (UFO) [GW05]. Based on this foundation, an "IT Service and Components Ontology" and a "Configuration Items Ontology" [BCCG09] are presented. The IT Service and Components Ontology models the interactions between service providers and customers (i.e., classes such as IT services, and Service Level Agreements). The Configuration Items Ontology provides a more fine-grained model by describing classes such as configuration items, hardware, and software. When compared to the ontologies developed in this thesis, it can be seen, that the work presented in [BCCG09] is more formal, which contrasts with the more lightweight approach of collaborative ontology development as used in semantic wikis. Moreover, not all classes that are needed to represent configurations in the environment of the thesis are modeled (e.g., a more fine-grained model of hardware components, such as network adapters, which is needed by IT administrators, is not described).

Reference [SSZ11] describes challenges that are encountered when integrating ITSM with ontologies and semantics. It proposes the use of ontologies and semantics in order to manage "complex relations within ITSM service trees", especially with regard to requests for changes and Service Level Agreements [SSZ11]. Compared to the requirements of the ontology that was developed in this thesis, the work presented in [SSZ11] is limited to a smaller area of IT Service Management and because of that not suitable for modeling in detail the IT environment described in this thesis.

Incident and Problem Management Ontologies

In [ZCGZ10], the use of ontologies in the area of ITSM Knowledge Management, with regard to Incident Management and Problem Management is described. The work presented in the paper outlines an ontology that models the interactions between problems and solutions. With regard to the aspects of the ITSM Ontology that is developed in this thesis, the notion of having a problem, which is solved by a solution is quite similar, as both are motivated by the Incident and Problem Management processes as described in ITIL. By also integrating other aspects of ITSM and their relations to Incident and Problem Management, the ITSM Ontology presented in this thesis covers the described aspects in more detail.

In [VRVC10], the "ITIL-based Service Management Model" is described, which "aim[s] at capturing ITSM best practices by means of a formal ontology-based business DSL (Domain-Specific Language)" [VRVC10, emphasis omitted]. The work proposes building the Onto-ITIL ontology based on OWL, and using the Semantic Web Rule Language (SWRL) for the definition of rules. The approach is further described and extended in [VB11] and [VVCR11]. The work described in [VVCR11] "presents a modeling approach, formalized in ontological terms, for defining high-level requirements models of software systems that provide support for the implementation of Information Technology Service Management Systems (ITSMSs)". Furthermore, a case study, which describes the approach in the area of Incident Management, is presented. While the focus of [VRVC10] and [VVCR11] is on modeling an ontology for the Incident Management

System domain, the work presented in [VB11] is more encompassing. However, technical domains that are relevant for IT departments in order to provide IT services are not addressed.

Observations and Remarks

When comparing the different ontologies to the ontologies presented in this thesis, the following observations can be made: First, the ontologies that are described as related work each describe certain parts of the ITSM domain. Second, none of the ontologies describes all parts of the ITSM domain that are relevant in the context of this thesis. Based on the realization, that re-using parts of multiple ontologies would require a large amount of work comparable to creating an ontology from scratch, a custom ontology was created for the ITSM Wiki. This ontology serves as a starting point, which covers all aspects of ITSM that are relevant at this time. By using Semantic MediaWiki as the underlying platform, the ontology can be extended collaboratively if needed.

Additional prior and related work with regard to ontologies is described for the system components that were developed in this thesis. In Section 5.1.10 (page 232), network and system management ontologies are described, while in Section 5.3.10 (page 283), the use of ontologies in the intrusion detection domain is outlined. Finally, related work with regard to the use of ontologies in the virtualization and IaaS domain is presented in Section 5.5.7 (page 314).

4.4. Summary

In this chapter, a description of the design and implementation of the core component of this thesis was given. In Section 4.1 (page 116), the selection of the technical platform was described. Section 4.2 (page 136) showed, how a semantic wiki can be used as a platform for the delivery of IT Service Management. In Section 4.3 (page 161), the ITSM Ontology, which forms the data model for the work presented in this thesis, was described.

The following Chapter 5 describes the system components that were developed as part of the thesis in order to extend the functionalities of Semantic MediaWiki in the area of IT Service Management.

5. Design and Implementation of the System Components

Semantic MediaWiki as a platform, as described in Chapter 4 (page 115), provides a solid foundation for storing unstructured information, e.g., documenting IT Service Management processes within IT administration teams, as well as storing structured information, for example, logical or physical relations between services and hardware components. In order to be of true value for the IT Service Management domain, however, it lacks several functionalities, which prevents it from tapping its full potential. This chapter describes a number of custom components developed within this thesis. These components add ITSM-specific functionalities to Semantic MediaWiki by making use of MediaWiki's ability to include extensions, as well as its API, which allows the creation and modification of content.

The work presented in this thesis consists of a Semantic MediaWiki-based core, as well as several components, which implement IT Service Management-specific functionalities. Figure 5.1 gives an overview of the components developed as part of this thesis. The rationales behind using a semantic wiki as the technical foundation of the platform were outlined in Section 4.2 (page 136). The following paragraphs give a short overview of the components, which are described in more detail in the following sections. The general idea of the ITSM Wiki was published in [KA09] and later refined in [KA10].

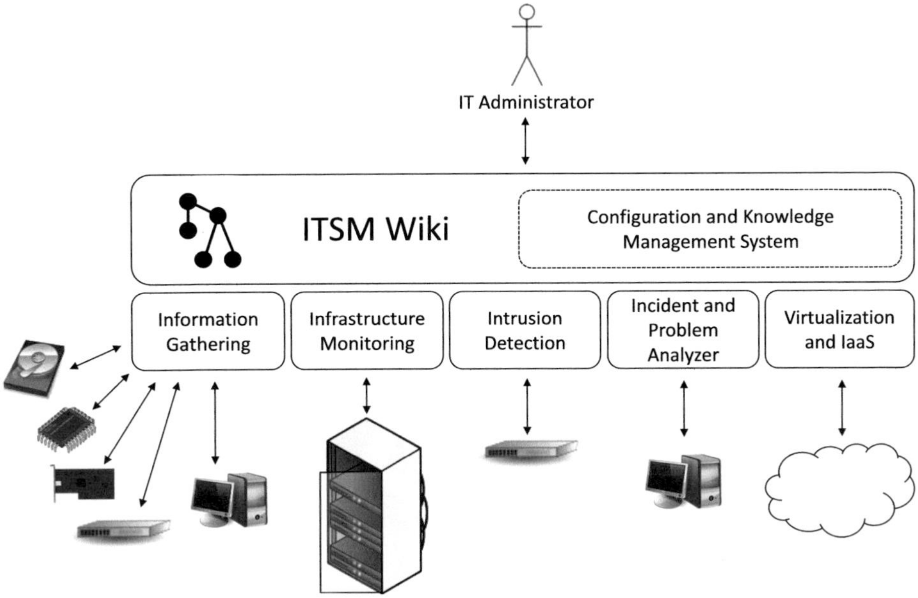

Figure 5.1.: Overview of the System Components

The *Information Gathering Component*, which is described in more detail in Section 5.1 (page 188) is used for reading information from directory services and devices. Information from the directory service is read by using the LDAP [TEG+04] protocol. From devices (e.g., computers, network equipment, and printers) information is gathered over the network via standardized mechanisms (i.e., Windows Management Instrumentation (WMI) [Mic09], or the Simple Network Management Protocol (SNMP) [CFSD90]) and stored as properties in the semantic wiki. This frees IT administrators from the otherwise cumbersome and error-prone task of manually gathering and inputting information about configuration items into the wiki. An example is reading the hardware configuration of a computer over the network and writing the results to the wiki page representing the computer, or automatically updating the list of a computer's installed software in the wiki.

The *Infrastructure Monitoring Component*, described in detail in Section 5.2 (page 234), implements an interface between Semantic MediaWiki and the open source infrastructure monitoring application Nagios [Bar05]. Infrastructure monitoring applications are used for monitoring the availability of computers, network equipment and services, in order to alert IT administrators in the case of a failure. While Nagios provides a Web-based user interface, it is shown that there are several benefits from combining Nagios with a Semantic MediaWiki by implementing a MediaWiki extension. One of the main benefits is the possibility to derive Nagios configuration files from the information about configuration items and their relationships, which is retained in the semantic wiki. Furthermore, by making use of Semantic MediaWiki's dynamic query mechanism, custom queries can be used in order to satisfy the need for statistical information, e.g., display all Windows servers, running the Apache Web server in a certain server rack, which are not answering to network requests.

In Section 5.3 (page 261), the *Intrusion Detection Component* is presented. This component serves as a connection between the external open source intrusion detection tool Snort [Roe99] and the semantic wiki. Snort, which is a signature-based network intrusion detection system, monitors organizational networks for possible security-related incidents. The Intrusion Detection Component implements a mechanism for integrating data about possible intrusions into the knowledge base of the ITSM Wiki. By doing so, background knowledge about the characteristics of systems and services (e.g., the operating system a computer is running, or the version of a Web server) can be included in the process that determines if an attack is significant enough to alert IT administrators. Furthermore, custom statistics can be generated, which also benefit from the background knowledge stored in the semantic wiki.

The *Incident and Problem Analyzer Component*, which is described in detail in Section 5.4 (page 284), helps IT administrators in tracking down problems in complex IT landscapes. The Incident and Problem Analyzer Component supports two classes of problems. First, problems that involve multiple entities (e.g., hardware, software, or services) and have a single common cause, can be tracked down by comparing the configurations of the affected entities and looking for similarities. Furthermore, problems that involve a single entity, but developed over time, can be tracked down by looking for changes in the history of the affected or related entities.

In Section 5.5 (page 298), the *Virtualization and IaaS Connector* is presented. This component is used to manage virtual machines and IaaS resources from within the ITSM Wiki.

5.1. Information Gathering Component

The Information Gathering Component presented in this section is an extensible framework for gathering information from IT landscapes and importing this information into the ITSM Wiki. Extensions for the most common ways of importing information from a Microsoft Windows landscape—namely Active Directory, and Windows Management Instrumentation (WMI)—and from generic hardware via the Simple Network Management Protocol (SNMP) are described. The work presented in this section builds on the work previously published in [KAL09].

Computers, network equipment and other IT components contain information relevant for providing IT services. This information can be divided into static and dynamic information. Static information, on the one hand, rarely or never changes (e.g., the mainboard or CPU of a computer, or its serial and type number). Dynamic information, on the other hand, is subject to, in some case frequent, changes (e.g., the list of installed applications, the names of running programs, or the amount of available memory). Manually gathering and keeping this information up to date can be cumbersome at best for static information and next to impossible for the dynamic kind.

Figure 5.2 gives a high-level overview of the Information Gathering Component described in this section. As shown in the right part of the illustration, the Information Gathering Component uses information from two classes of sources. The first source are directory services, such as Microsoft Active Directory, from where information about users and computers is read. Second, the Information Gathering Component accesses hosts directly via standardized protocols (e.g., WMI, and SNMP). Information gathered by the component is stored in the semantic wiki and can be accessed by IT administrators.

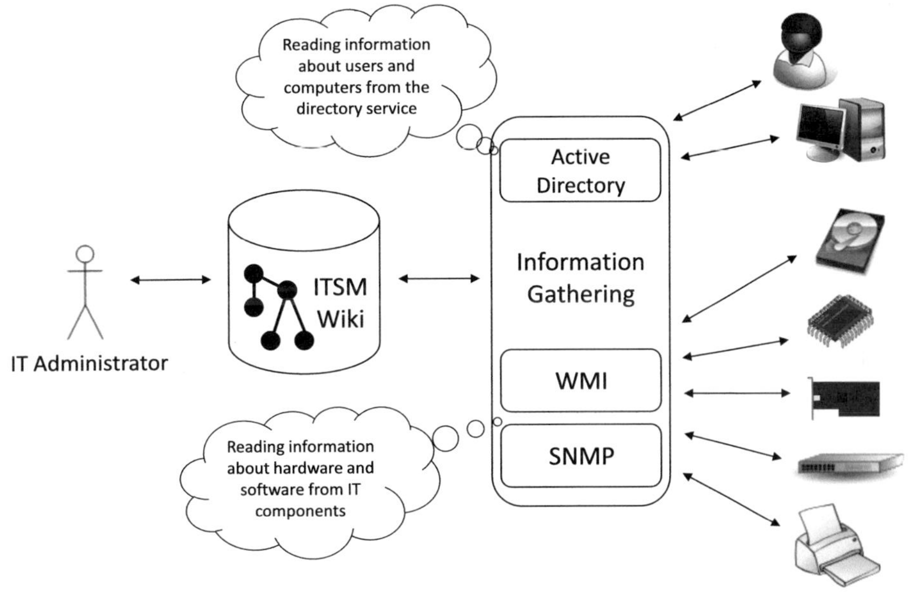

Figure 5.2.: Information Gathering

This section is structured as follows: In Section 5.1.1 (page 190), the motivation for the Information Gathering Component is outlined. Section 5.1.2 (page 191) describes the requirements analysis, followed by a description of the use cases in Section 5.1.3 (page 197). Relevant information of the component is shown in Section 5.1.4 (page 200). Technologies and protocols used in the component are explained in Section 5.1.5 (page 211). Following that, Section 5.1.6 (page 217) describes the design of the Information Gathering Component. In Section 5.1.7 (page 219), the Information Gathering Ontology is presented. Section 5.1.8 (page 227) provides a description of the implementation, while Section 5.1.9 (page 228) shows how information is presented in the ITSM Wiki. Finally, Section 5.1.10 (page 230) provides an overview of prior and related work.

5.1.1. Motivation

The Configuration Management Database (CMDB), which stores information about configuration items (CIs) has to be populated with all relevant information and has to be updated when changes to the IT landscape are performed. While it would theoretically be possible to perform these tasks through the application of manual labor, it is best avoided because of the associated labor costs and the amount of mistakes due to human errors. While some information needs manual updating because no mechanisms can reliably determine the information automatically, this can be avoided for a large amount of information when applying mechanisms for the automatic gathering of information. In ITIL, the need for the automatic gathering of Configuration Management information is expressed as follows [LM07, page 69]:

> "Automated processes to load and update the Configuration Management database should be developed where possible so as to reduce errors and optimize costs. Discovery tools, inventory and audit tools, enterprise systems and network management tools can be interfaced to the CMS. These tools can be used initially to populate a CMDB, and subsequently to compare the actual 'live' configuration with the information and records stored in the CMS." [LM07, page 69]

In addition, [LM07, page 195] states:

> "Automating the initial discovery and configuration audits significantly increases the efficiency and effectiveness of Configuration Management. These tools can determine what hardware and software is installed and how applications are mapped to the infrastructure." [LM07, page 195]

In [Add07, page 245], auto discovery tools for the automatic population of a Configuration Management Database are motivated as follows:

> "Automated discovery tools work in a variety of ways to discover and identify IT devices (either by passively monitoring network traffic and extracting machine details from the packet headers or by proactively broadcasting messages across the network and waiting for devices to respond). Having discovered and identified a target device, the discovery tool then attempts to collect data about the system. This auditing activity can be achieved using

> remote commands such as MSI, SNMP etc or via a dedicated client agent application that is installed upon the discovered machine to interrogate the system configuration before transmitting the results back to a centralised server." [Add07, page 245]

According to [Add07, page 245], automatic discovery tools can be classified into the following three categories:

- "Configuration discovery
- "Topology discovery
- "Security discovery (Systems administration/Vulnerability testing)" [Add07, page 245]

Configuration discovery, which is the aspect of automated discovery of most relevance within the context of FZI's IT department, is described as follows [Add07, page 246]:

> "Configuration discovery tools perform periodic audits of the hardware configuration and the installed software on a target machine. The level of detail and accuracy of information gathered will vary from vendor to vendor and will often depend upon the operating system running on the target machine. For this reason it may be appropriate to use multiple discovery tools within an environment to ensure that all of the required data is captured accurately." [Add07, page 246]

Topology discovery, which is used, for example, to discover the topology of networks (e.g., discover which network switches are connected to each other), is not considered further in this thesis. This is mostly due to the relatively static layout of FZI's network environment, which leads to the fact that changes are more efficiently performed through manual labor in this context than they could be performed through automatic discovery tools. Another aspect not included into the ITSM Wiki is security discovery, which at FZI at the moment is handled through a commercial solution. Figure 5.3 shows a graphical representation of the three auto discovery categories and their points of intersection.

5.1.2. Requirements Analysis

After the need for a component for the automated discovery of information was motivated in the previous subsection, this subsection outlines the requirements for the Information Gathering Component. Before starting work on the design and implementation, a requirements analysis was performed, which included the explicit formulation of the Information Gathering Component's vision and goals, its constraints and system boundaries, as well as its requirements.

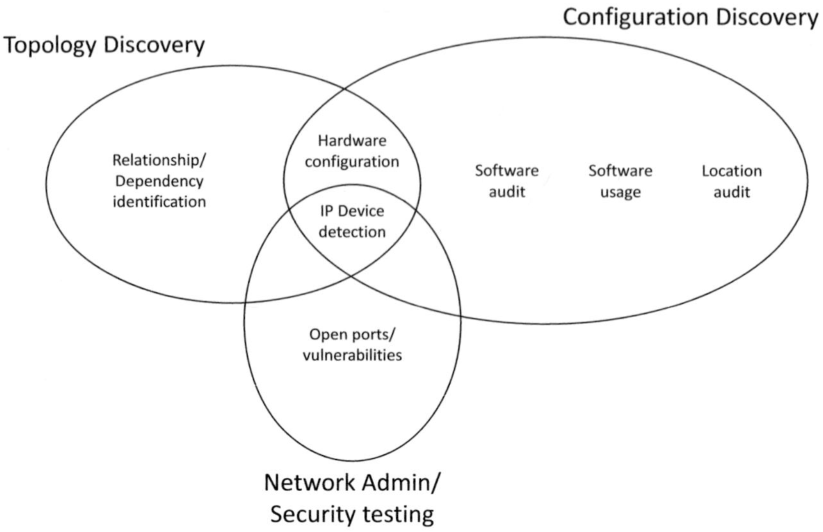

Figure 5.3.: Automated Discovery (cf. [Add07, page 246])

A comprehensive description of the requirements analysis phase can be found in [Bal09, pages 433–513].

The results of the requirements validation are presented in Section 6.1 (page 318).

Vision and Goals

Before beginning the work on the Information Gathering Component, the vision and goals were defined. This helps in keeping focus on the goals when defining requirements. The vision defines *what* the software should accomplish, *without* defining *how*, while the goals help in refining the vision [Bal09, pages 456–459]. The Information Gathering Component's vision and goals are motivated mostly by the amount of work required for manually populating and updating the Configuration Management Database. The use case is the IT infrastructure environment at FZI Research Center for Information Technology, which was described in Section 3.1 (page 82).

Vision The vision for the Information Gathering Component is as follows:

To design and implement a tool that automatically reads data from the directory service, as well as from networked devices, and automatically writes the information into the ITSM Wiki (V-G01).

Goals The goals, which refine the vision of the Information Gathering Component, can be summarized as follows:

- Reduce the amount of work necessary for keeping up-to-date the information about configuration items in the ITSM Wiki (G-G01).
- Reduce the number of human errors by automating the process of maintaining information about configuration items (G-G02).
- Store information about configuration items in the ITSM Wiki, which can be used by IT administrators as well as the other components presented in this thesis (G-G03).
- Enable the 'intelligent' use of information stored in the ITSM Wiki by using an ontology as the data model (G-G04).

After determining the vision and goals for the component, the constraints were collected.

Constraints

Constraints define restrictions for a software system or the software development process. Constraints can be organizational or technical. Organizational constraints are the area of application, the intended user group, and the operating conditions. The technical constraints are the technical application environment and the requirements on the development environment [Bal09, pages 459–461].

Organizational Constraints The organizational constraints for the Information Gathering Component are as follows:

- The ITSM Wiki is used by the members of the IT department, who are responsible for running systems and services.

Technical Constraints (Server) The technical constraints for the server are as follows:

- The Information Gathering Component is a part of the ITSM Wiki, which is realized by using the MediaWiki software. MediaWiki is extensible by programming against an API (for more information about extending MediaWiki, please see Section 4.1.3, page 122).
- Semantic MediaWiki is used by the Information Gathering Component in order to store explicit information gathered from devices.

- MediaWiki and Semantic MediaWiki are programmed in the PHP language [Med11a], which imposes the technical constraints of also using this language on the Information Gathering Component.
- MediaWiki runs on Web servers, which allow the execution of PHP scripts. Most often, the LAMP[1] platform is used for running MediaWiki.
- The Information Gathering Component accesses MediaWiki by using documented API calls. With regard to the database system, all databases that are supported by MediaWiki are also supported by the Infrastructure Monitoring Component.
- Information is read through standardized mechanisms and APIs, namely the LDAP protocol, Windows Management Instrumentation (WMI), and the SNMP protocol.

Technical Constraints (Client) The ITSM Wiki in general and the Information Gathering Component in particular are accessed by using a Web browser. As long as a browser that complies with current Web standards is available, any device and operating system can be used.

Development Environment Constraints With regard to development environment constraints, it can be said that the use of a simple text editor is sufficient, although ease of use can be gained by reverting to specialized PHP programming environments, e.g., the commercially available Zend Studio[2].

System Boundaries

System boundaries separate the respective system from its environment and other systems. Parts, which fall outside of the system boundaries cannot be manipulated by the system. There are three contexts that can be distinguished[3]: the system, the relevant environment, and the irrelevant environment [Bal09, page 462]. In Figure 5.4, the systems boundaries of the Information Gathering Component, as well as the components that make up the system, are visualized. The graph is inspired by the graph found in [Bal09, page 462].

[1]The term LAMP refers to the combination of the **L**inux operating system, the **A**pache Web server, the **M**ySQL database, and the **P**HP programming language (although the combination of using Linux, Apache, and MySQL in conjunction with the **P**ython and **P**erl programming languages is also referred to as LAMP) [Dou01]. For more information about LAMP, please cf. [WL02].

[2]`http://www.zend.com/en/products/studio/`

[3]Reference [Bal09, page 462], in fact, distinguishes between two more contexts, which represent the borderland between the three contexts. In this thesis, these borderland contexts are not relevant, and thus omitted.

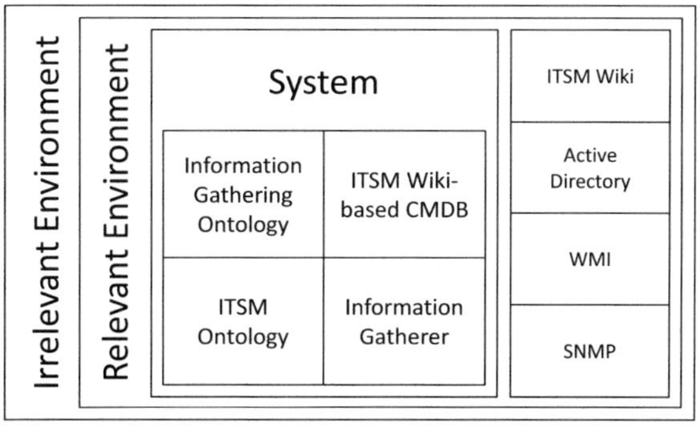

Figure 5.4.: System Boundaries of the Information Gathering Component

System The following elements are part of the system:

- *Information Gathering Ontology:* Classes and properties that represent information that is gathered by the component described in this section, are retained in the Information Gathering Ontology.
- *ITSM Ontology:* Classes and properties of the core ITSM parts are modeled in the ITSM Ontology, as described in Section 4.3.4 (page 167).
- *ITSM Wiki-based CMDB:* The ITSM Wiki-based Configuration Management Database contains information about the CIs and their dependencies.
- *Information Gatherer:* This part interacts with the various sources of information that are accessible via defined protocols (e.g., LDAP, WMI, and SNMP).

Relevant Environment The relevant environment consists of elements, which are not by themselves considered parts of the Information Gathering Component, but which interact with it on a regular basis. Parts of the relevant environment are:

- *ITSM Wiki:* The ITSM Wiki, which contains all the information that is relevant for providing IT services, is accessed by the Information Gathering Component in order to write information about configuration items.
- *Active Directory:* Information stored in Microsoft Active Directory (e.g., information about users, group memberships, and computers) is read and copied to the ITSM Wiki.
- *WMI:* The Windows Management Instrumentation infrastructure is used as a mechanism for reading information from Windows computers.
- *SNMP:* The Simple Network Management Protocol is used to read information from various networked devices (e.g., printers, or network switches).

Requirements

Requirements are subdivided into functional and non-functional requirements. While functional requirements define the functions the software performs, non-functional requirements are concerned with the software's quality [Bal09, page 456]. The next two paragraphs outline the functional and non-functional requirements for the Information Gathering Component.

Functional Requirements The functional requirements for the Information Gathering Component are defined in the following list. The requirements are as follows:

- New information has to be integrated into the ITSM Wiki automatically and without user intervention (R-G01).
- Changed information has to be detected and updated in the ITSM Wiki (R-G02).
- When upgrading changed information, a history of changes has to be kept and made available to the user of the ITSM Wiki (R-G03).
- Information should be gathered without the need for installing a dedicated agent on computers from which information is gathered (R-G04).
- Information relevant to users, computers, software, and hardware has to be gathered (R-G05).
- Information about computers that are not available when gathering information has to be kept at the state of the last information gathering. The date of the last information gathering has to be shown to the user when accessing a page representing a configuration item (R-G06).
- The mechanism for gathering information has to be smart (e.g., take into account the operating system installed on a computer when trying to gather information) (R-G07).
- Information gathered from components has to be retained in a structured format that is processable by Semantic MediaWiki in order to be used in queries and dynamically created tables (R-G08).
- A notification mechanism has to be present for changes to static information (e.g., users of the ITSM Wiki interested in a hardware component have to be notified when the mainboard is changed) (R-G09).

The requirements for the Information Gathering Component show that a way has to be found to integrate gathered information into the semantic wiki by making use of existing technologies and protocols. Suitable mechanisms for gathering information were identified to be:

- Microsoft Active Directory for reading information about users, computers, and group memberships.
- The Windows Management Instrumentation (WMI) infrastructure for gathering information from clients running Microsoft Windows (the Common Information Model (CIM), and Web-Based Enterprise Management (WBEM) form the foundation of WMI).
- The Simple Network Management Protocol (SNMP) for gathering information from networked hardware devices (e.g., printers, and network switches), non-Windows computers, as well as managed infrastructure components (e.g., uninterruptible power supply systems, and temperature sensors within the data center).
- DNS queries for getting information about the mapping between host names and IP addresses.

Non-functional Requirements The non-functional requirements for the Information Gathering Component are:

- The component has to be integrated into the ITSM Wiki.
- It has to be made sure that only valid data is written to the wiki.
- It has to be made sure that gathering information does not negatively impact the performance of the devices or the network.
- Data from devices has to be read in a timely manner (i.e., gathering information from a client should not take longer than 30 s).
- Information should be gathered in parallel from multiple hosts at the same time.
- No changes should be necessary in the code base of MediaWiki or Semantic MediaWiki.

5.1.3. Use Cases

This subsection shows a selected number of use cases in order to present the purpose and the benefits of the Information Gathering Component. First, the use case for importing information about users and computers is presented, followed by the use case for gathering information from newly acquired computers. Furthermore, the use case for monitoring computers for changes is presented, followed by the use case of checking computers for needed updates. License management is another use case.

Importing Users and Computers from a Directory Service

In corporate environments, user accounts are used to represent employees. User accounts, including attributes, such as a user's phone number, mail address, and group memberships are stored in a central directory (e.g., Microsoft Active Directory). In order to use these attributes from the ITSM Wiki, account information has to be imported into the wiki.

Analogously to user accounts, computers, which are part of the Windows domain, are also represented in Microsoft Active Directory. Information about these computers is also imported from Active Directory into the wiki.

Gathering Information from a Newly Acquired Computer

Computers in the FZI environment are replaced every three to four years on average. Depending on the company's policy, new employees get new workstations or notebooks when starting their job, which means that there is a constant flux of new computers replacing old ones. Also depending on the policy, employees or departments are able to pick, within defined limits, the computer model that best fits their requirements. One of the challenges for IT administration in these heterogeneous environments with regard to computer hardware is that there exists a large number of different configurations.

Dealing with these different configurations requires efficient tools and a high degree of flexibility from IT administrators, because each configuration differs in varying degree from all other configurations. Each different configuration has its own set of drivers and potential problems. Documenting all characteristics of a computer when it is integrated into the corporate environment helps in supporting IT administrators. Manually acquiring and entering the information is cumbersome and error-prone. Due to this facts, the need for an automatic information gathering mechanism exists.

When a new computer is integrated into the corporate environment, all relevant information has to be automatically read via the network and put into the ITSM Wiki. In Section 5.1.4 (page 200), an overview of relevant information is given. By assigning semantic relations to all gathered information items, all benefits of the semantic wiki can be utilized. This allows to generate tables containing information about the computers' hardware and software (e.g., its processor, graphics adapter, network addresses, as well as the model and serial number).

Monitoring Computers for Changes

Computers in use are subject to changes, which means that the information stored in the ITSM Wiki has to be updated regularly to reflect these changes. Examples of changing information are additionally installed applications, as well as changed hardware components (e.g., due to a memory upgrade).

Upgrading information has to be done regularly over the network without being noticed by the user. While stationary workstations can be expected to be always accessible, this is not the case with portable notebooks. The Information Gathering Component has to take into account temporarily inaccessible computers and keep previously gathered information until new information can be read. In order to provide a history of changes, information about past configurations has to be retained in the ITSM Wiki.

Checking Computers for Needed Updates

Keeping computer systems up to date requires to regularly install patches and updates for the operating system, applications, and drivers. Keeping track of updates that are installed on computers is important, because failed or ignored updates can lead to security-related incidents. Which updates are needed on a computer depends on the installed operating system, the installed applications and the hardware. Information about operating system updates that are needed can be managed via Windows Server Update Services (WSUS)[4]. With regard to Windows updates, the central management infrastructure provided by WSUS keeps track of needed updates, which means that manual interventions are necessary only in the case of unexpected problems. Information about updates for applications, however, has to be managed by using a third party tool. By aggregating information about installed applications and comparing to a list of known current versions, out-of-date versions can be detected.

License Management

By managing the use of software licenses, corporations can make sure that they stay in compliance with software licenses, on the one hand, and avoid overspending by buying unnecessary licenses on the other hand. In [Add07, page 263], software license management is defined as

> "the combination of a set of IT Service Management tools and disciplines/ processes to ensure that an organization is in complete control of the usage (including the re-use (recycling) and re-deployment), distribution and disposal of its valuable software assets." [Add07, page 263]

While the license management discipline exceeds the domains that can be solved by using technical tools [Add07, page 263], in the context of this work, only the tool aspects are considered.

There are many reasons for introducing license management [Add07, page 264]. In the context of this thesis, the focus is on making sure that the right amount of licenses is purchased (i.e., make sure that no violations of software licenses are performed, while, on

[4] `http://technet.microsoft.com/en-us/wsus/bb332157`

the other hand, making sure that no money is wasted by purchasing unnecessary licenses). The use case for the Information Gathering Component is to provide a mechanism, which reads information that is relevant to license management from networked computers and puts it into a structured format, which can be processed by SMW queries.

5.1.4. Relevant Information

Computer systems, as well as other IT components, comprise a multitude of fixed and dynamic properties. The following subsections give an overview of some relevant properties, which lead to benefits when made available from within the ITSM Wiki.

When looking at how information is gathered, it can be seen that there exist six different ways, which can be expressed in two dimensions. The first dimension describes, whether information is gathered actively from a directory service, actively from a host, or passively. Active information gathering means that a program actively contacts another component (e.g., a hardware device, a software API, a service, or a database) in order to get information. In contrast to active information gathering, passive information gathering only listens to information transmitted between other parties (e.g., a tool listens to network broadcasts). The second dimension describes whether information is gathered directly or indirectly. Direct gathering means that the hardware or software component, which is represented in the wiki, is queried directly (e.g., the serial number of a computer is read over the network). Indirect gathering, on the other hand, means that information is gathered via a third party (e.g., a service or a database, which contains information about a component). An example of indirect gathering is information about IP addresses and host names, which are read from the DNS server. Table 5.1 shows examples of technologies and protocols for information gathering and their position within the two dimensions. Section 5.1.5 (page 211) gives an overview of the technologies and protocols in the table.

	active (directory service)	**active (host)**	**passive**
direct	LDAP	WMI, SNMP	–
indirect	DNS, DHCP	–	ARP

Table 5.1.: Information Gathering Methods

Information that is gathered from directory services and hosts can be of one of the following types: The first type of information represents an individual entity (e.g., hardware, or software), which is uniquely identified and whose uniqueness plays a role in the larger context of the IT organization. An example of the first type is a network adapter, which is uniquely identified by its MAC address. This MAC address can be used to assign a fixed IP address by using a DHCP server. In the case of a replacement of the network adapter, the mapping between MAC and IP addresses would also need to change.

The second type of information represents entities that are generic and which are not uniquely identified. An example is a graphics adapter, which is replaceable by another instance of the same model without causing effects in other parts of the organization.

Microsoft Windows Active Directory

Microsoft Active Directory [RKM+08] is a central directory in which all relevant information for the use in Microsoft Windows environments is stored. Examples of information stored in Active Directory are user accounts, computer accounts, contacts, and groups. A user account in Active Directory contains all information concerning this user. Examples of information stored in a user account are the account name and password, the user's family name and given name, his address, phone number, e-mail address, as well as further information relevant to certain aspects of using Windows (e.g., dial-in privileges). Computer accounts represent computers running Microsoft Windows in Active Directory. All computers that are members of a Windows domain must have accounts in Active Directory. Users and computers can be members of groups. Groups can contain other groups, which makes it possible to form group hierarchies.

Static Information Information about users is read from Active Directory. Relevant static information is as follows:

- Name
  - Family name
  - Given name
- Contact information
  - Phone number
  - E-mail address
  - Fax number
- Organizational information
  - Membership in organizational units
  - Office room number
- Account-specific information
  - Account name
  - Unique identifier of the account
  - Account creation date

Dynamic Information Examples of dynamic information stored in Active Directory are:

- Date of a user's last logon
- Account lockout status

A user's last logon date is of interest when looking for user accounts that are not active anymore and are possible candidates for deletion. Analogous to user accounts, the last logon date for computers can be read from computer accounts in Active Directory, which can be used for finding computers that are no longer in use. In most environments, user accounts are locked out for a certain amount of time when the wrong password is entered repeatedly. The account lockout status shows whether an account is currently locked out.

Computer Hardware

Computer hardware comprises a number of components, which have a number of properties on their own. The author's experience has shown that in day-to-day work, the following properties described in the following paragraphs are most often considered when finding and solving problems related to computer hardware.

Computer System The system manufacturer and the system model are the main characteristics of a computer system. They are of importance when looking for possible hardware extensions (e.g., a memory upgrade). They are also the most obvious system characteristics to end users because they are in most cases printed on a user-visible spot (e.g., "Lenovo Thinkpad T60p" on the TFT lid of a notebook). The type number defines the hardware even closer for technical personnel, such as IT administrators, but is not as memorable to end users as the model (e.g., 2737-GHG). Type numbers help in distinguishing between several variations of the model. For example, there can be models with slightly different processors, a different amount of memory and different keyboard layouts, each represented by a different type number but sold as the same model. The serial number (e.g., L3-12AB99A), together with the type number identifies a system unambiguously.

Relevant information of computer systems is:

- Manufacturer (e.g., Dell, or IBM)
- Model
- Type number
- Serial number

Mainboard The mainboard is the central circuit board of a computer, which contains a number of core components (e.g., memory controller, and storage controller), as well as sockets and slots for the CPU and extension cards (e.g., the graphics adapter). The mainboard manufacturer and mainboard type are important when looking for the right chipset drivers. The number of processor slots and extension card slots is important when looking at possibilities for extending existing hardware in order to meet performance needs or when additional hardware has to be added.

Relevant information of a mainboard is:

- Manufacturer
- Type
- Chipset
- Number of available processor sockets
- Number of used processor sockets
- Number of available extension card slots
- Number of used extension card slots

CPU The central processing unit is another main component of a computer system. It has several characteristics, including a manufacturer, an architecture, and a processor type. The processor type together with its clock rate, number of cores, and the cache size is an indicator for the processor's overall speed.

Relevant information of a CPU is:

- Manufacturer (e.g., Intel, or AMD)
- Architecture (e.g., x86, x64, or Itanium)
- Type (e.g., Core Duo, or Xeon)
- Clock rate
- Number of cores
- Amount of cache

RAM Random access memory stores the applications currently running on a computer including their data. Physical memory is packaged in modules and connected to the mainboard by plugging into memory slots. Each module has a manufacturer and is of a certain type. The type (e.g., SD-RAM, DDR, DDR2, or DDR3) specifies how a memory module is connected to the mainboard. The speed of the memory module is primarily determined by its type, but there are variations within a type family. Because the overall speed of the system's memory is in most cases determined by the speed of the slowest memory module, it is wise to use modules of matching speeds when extending the system's memory. The amount of installed memory and the amount of installable memory are of interest when upgrading a system's memory is considered. Furthermore, the configuration of memory slots is of interest when extending the system's memory. In some system types, for example, memory can be grouped only in certain combinations, which has to be considered when upgrading memory.

Relevant information of RAM is:

- Manufacturer
- Type
- Speed
- Amount of installed memory
- Amount of installable memory
- Configuration of memory slots (used slots vs. unused slots)

Persistent Storage Hard disks drives and solid state drives provide a persistent location for storing a computer's applications and data. Persistent storage drives have a manufacturer and are of a certain model. Furthermore, each drive has a serial number by which it can be identified. The type is an indicator for the drive's characteristics. Types currently found in computers are classic drives with rotating disks, as well as the more advanced solid state drives using flash memory. The interface between the drive and the mainboard determines how fast data can be transferred (ATA, SATA, SCSI, and SAS are the most common interfaces). The main characteristic of a persistent storage drive is its capacity (i.e., the amount of data that can be stored on it). The speed of the drive is expressed by how fast data can be read and written, as well as how fast random blocks on the disk can be accessed. For hard disks with rotating disks, another measure is the number of rotations per minute. Each drive stores information about read and write failures, which in some cases can predict failing drives and avoid data loss or the need of data restoration from backups.

Relevant information of persistent storage is:

- Manufacturer

- Model
- Serial number
- Type
- Interface
- Capacity
- Speed (rotations per minute)
- Failure information

Graphics Hardware Graphics hardware is responsible for converting digital data into images, which are displayed on the user's screen. In addition to displaying two-dimensional images, modern graphics hardware is mainly optimized for rendering three-dimensional animations in games. In most cases, graphics hardware is implemented as extension cards and connected to dedicated slots on the mainboard. In cases where there is need for only a limited amount of graphics power (e.g., word processing), graphics hardware can be found directly on the mainboard. Graphics hardware has a manufacturer and is of a certain model. Hardware chipsets are manufactured by a small number of companies (e.g., Nvidia, and AMD). Driver software for graphics hardware is tailored to chipsets and models, which means that for the best results, a driver matching the exact manufacturer and model has to be found. If that option is unavailable, generic drivers provided by the operating system can be used. In addition to the chipset, the amount of memory determines the quality of the output (i.e., more memory is used to store graphics textures in a better resolution).

Relevant information of graphics hardware is:

- Manufacturer
- Model
- Chipset
- Amount of graphics memory

Networking Hardware Networking hardware is used to connect computers to local networks and the Internet. The most prevalent standards in today's networks are Ethernet and Wireless Ethernet (Wi-Fi) for local networks and 2G and 3G networks (GPRS, EDGE, UMTS) in cellular networks. In most cases, networking hardware is located on the mainboard, but in some cases can be found in extension slots. The manufacturer of the chipset or networking card is the primary contact for driver software if not included with the operating system. The type indicates which protocols are supported (e.g., Ethernet, or Wireless Ethernet). The connector specifies the physical connection between the network card and its uplink (e.g., Twisted Pair cables). The speed of the hardware, together with the speed of the overall network infrastructure determines how fast data can be transmitted (the current standard is Gigabit for copper-based cables). Each networking hardware has an address, which identifies the hardware and is used by others to address data transmitted over the network to a certain location (e.g., the MAC address in Ethernet and Wireless Ethernet).

Relevant information of networking hardware is:

- Manufacturer
- Chipset
- Model
- Type
- Connector
- Speed
- MAC address

Peripherals Peripherals are devices that are connected to the computer system (e.g., a keyboard, and a mouse). There are additional peripherals, which are mostly connected via USB[5]. Further information about computer hardware, which exceeds the scope of this thesis, is provided in [HPGA02].

Microsoft Windows Operating System

The Microsoft Windows operating system family is the most widely used desktop operating system, both by consumers and businesses. There exists a large amount of information relevant to managing the services provided by Windows computers. This information is accessible remotely through the Windows Management Instrumentation (WMI) interface, which is described in Section 5.1.5 (page 215).

While hardware contains mostly static information (the failure information in hard disks is an example of an exception from that rule), information provided by the operating system can be divided into static and dynamic information. Static information is defined as information that rarely changes. While some static information never changes during the lifetime of the operating system (from installation to re-installation), some information changes from time to time (e.g., service packs, which are distributed about once per year, or security updates, which are distributed monthly). Dynamic information, on the other hand, changes more frequently.

[5] **U**niversal **S**erial **B**us

Static Information Static information is characterized by changing rarely, if at all. Examples of static information in the Microsoft Windows operating system are:

- Operating system version
- Operating system type
- Operating system edition
- Installed features
- Patch level (installed service packs, and updates)
- List of installed applications
  - Manufacturer of each installed application
  - Version of each installed application

New major versions of Microsoft Windows are released about once every three years. Windows is divided into two product types, server and workstation. While the server operating system is optimized for providing services (e.g., file server, Web server, or database server), the workstation operating system is optimized for using services provided by servers. Each version and type of Microsoft Windows can be further distinguished by its edition. The edition is a mechanism for distributing versions with different functionalities for different prices (e.g., Windows 7 Home Premium, Professional, and Ultimate) [Mic10]. After installation, depending on the system version, type and edition, a number of popular features are installed, some others can be added when needed. In order to add functionality and to fix security-related bugs, service packs and updates are released. While updates are in most cases targeted at fixing time-critical bugs and vulnerabilities (e.g., a security issue in a Windows service, or in Internet Explorer), service packs are most often a collection of all previously released updates and some new minor features. While security updates are released monthly, service packs are released about once a year. A list of installed applications is kept on each Windows instance and can be read remotely. Furthermore, each application has a manufacturer and version number. Version numbers of applications are of significance when there are security issues with a certain version, which are fixed in subsequent versions.

Dynamic Information Dynamic information changes more often than static information (i.e., more than once every hour). Examples of dynamic information in Microsoft Windows are:

- Amount of available random access memory (RAM)
- Amount of free persistent storage space

The amount of available random access memory is an indication of a system's performance. The amount of free persistent storage space is of importance when deciding whether additional applications can be installed on a computer.

Printers

Printers are, despite all efforts to introduce the paperless office, one of the most often used devices in corporate environments. When servicing printers, the following parameters are of significance.

Static Information Examples of static information relevant for supporting printers are:

- Manufacturer
- Model
- Type number
- Serial number
- Capabilities (e.g., duplex capability, and supported paper formats)

When supporting printer hardware, knowing the manufacturer and model of the printer is essential. The type number and serial number are needed when a warranty claim has to be submitted. Capabilities of a printer include whether it can provide duplex functionality, provide color printing, and the supported paper formats.

Dynamic Information Dynamic information with regard to printers is:

- Printed pages count
- Status information (e.g., errors)
- Status of consumables (e.g., toner, and paper)

The page count of a printer can be relevant in situations where costs are billed by the number of printed pages (either by the internal IT department, or by third-party contractors). Status information is relevant for providing preventive support, or when contacting the manufacturer in case of a problem. The status of consumables helps in determining if toner, paper, or other consumables are needed.

Network Equipment

Network equipment provides connectivity to local networks and the Internet. Network equipment is a general term for devices, which are used for transferring network traffic (e.g., network switches, or routers).

Static Information Static information with regard to network equipment is:

- Manufacturer
- Model
- Type number
- Serial number
- Capabilities (e.g., speed, number of network ports, and supported protocols)
- Connections between networked components
- Virtual LANs (VLANs)

As with other hardware components, the manufacturer, model, type number, and serial number are used for finding software tools and when submitting warranty claims. Capabilities of networking components include the speed and number of network ports, and supported protocols. Connections between different networked components are of interest when looking for dependencies, e.g., in order to predict the consequences of failing networking components.

Dynamic Information Examples of dynamic information found in network equipment are:

- Current network load
- Number of transmitted network packets
- Number of erroneous network packets

The current load on network equipment, parts of network equipment (e.g., switch ports), and network connections is of significance when looking for stressed components. By storing network load, the average can be calculated. The ratio between the number of transmitted network packets and the number of erroneous network packets can be used to calculate the percentage of errors per network connection in order to find faulty hardware.

Infrastructure Equipment

Infrastructure equipment plays a supporting role when providing IT services. Examples of infrastructure equipment are uninterruptible power supplies (UPS) and power generators, which are used to mitigate power losses. Computer racks are sometimes equipped with sensors, which collect the temperature and humidity. These sensors can be read over the network (e.g., by using the SNMP protocol, or proprietary protocols).

Static Information Examples of static information in the context of infrastructure equipment are:

- Location of a component
- Person or group responsible for maintaining the component
- Type and serial number
- Technical specifications (e.g., a device's maximum capacity)

Dynamic Information Information gathered from infrastructure equipment is mostly dynamic, because static information rarely changes. Examples are:

- Current power usage of the data center
- Current temperature in computer racks
- Error log of infrastructure components (e.g., uninterruptible power supplies (UPS), or the cooling system)

The current power usage of the data center, as well as the average power consumption, can help in looking for potentials for power saving and for planning future extensions. Measuring and tracking the temperature in server racks helps in finding the perfect balance between cooling and power saving. Gathering notifications about errors in infrastructure components (e.g., uninterruptible power supplies, and cooling systems) helps to track patterns that help in anticipating failing components.

Linux Operating System

The Linux operating system (cp. [GA07]) is the most-used system in the UNIX operating system family. There is numerous information provided by the system that can be gathered remotely via the network. The available information is roughly the same as in Microsoft Windows; the methods of connecting and reading the information are different, however. While the Information Gathering Component presented in this thesis mainly implements a mechanism for gathering information from Microsoft Windows, it is possible to target the Linux platform by implementing a custom extension which is specialized in gathering data from Linux.

5.1.5. Technologies and Protocols

This subsection gives an introduction into the mechanisms used for importing information into the ITSM Wiki. First, the Lightweight Directory Access Protocol (LDAP) is described, which is used to read information about users and domain-joined Windows computers from Active Directory. After that, the Windows Management Instrumentation (WMI) platform is described, which is used to read information from individual Windows computers. Finally, the Simple Network Management Protocol (SNMP) is outlined, which provides mechanisms for reading information from several types of networked devices (e.g., network switches, and network printers).

Lightweight Directory Access Protocol (LDAP)

The Lightweight Directory Access Protocol (LDAP) is a protocol, which allows clients to communicate with a directory service [TEG+04, page 7]. In the context of the Information Gathering Component, LDAP is used to access Active Directory in order to gather information about users and computers.

Directories are defined as follows [TEG+04, page 5]:

> "In computer terms, a directory is a specialized database, also called a data repository, that stores typed and ordered information about objects. A particular directory might list information about printers (the objects) consisting of typed information such as location (a formatted character string), speed in pages per minute (numeric), print streams supported (for example PostScript or ASCII), and so on." [TEG+04, page 5]

The use of directories is motivated as follows [TEG+04, page 5]:

> "Directories allow users or applications to find resources that have the characteristics needed for a particular task. For example, a directory of users can be used to look up a person's e-mail address or fax number. A directory could be searched to find a nearby PostScript color printer. Or a directory of application servers could be searched to find a server that can access customer billing information." [TEG+04, page 5]

Reference [TEG+04, pages 7–8] describes LDAP as follows:

> "LDAP is an open industry standard that defines a standard method for accessing and updating information in a directory. LDAP has gained wide acceptance as the directory access method of the Internet and is therefore also becoming strategic within corporate intranets. It is being supported by a growing number of software vendors and is being incorporated into a growing number of applications.
>
> "LDAP defines a communication protocol. That is, it defines the transport and format of messages used by a client to access data in an X.500-like directory. LDAP does not define the directory service itself. When people talk about the LDAP directory, that is the information that is stored and can be retrieved by the LDAP protocol." [TEG+04, pages 7–8]

Figure 5.5 shows the architecture of a distributed network that uses LDAP. Clients use LDAP in order to formulate queries. Servers use information stored in LDAP databases in order to answer the queries.

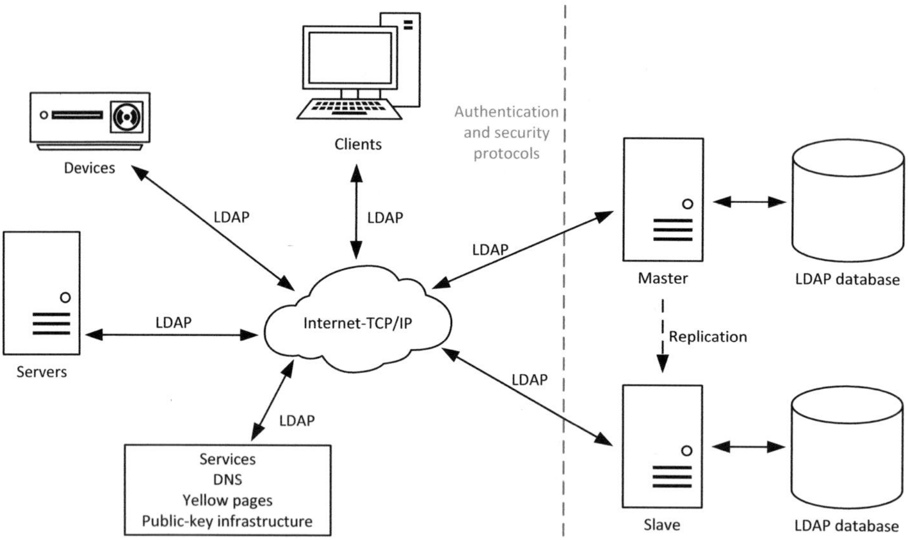

Figure 5.5.: LDAP Architecture (cf. [KV04])

In Figure 5.6, an example of an LDAP directory information tree can be seen. In this tree, objects can be accessed by walking the tree from the top node towards the bottom.

Searches can be expressed as LDAP queries. In the context of the Information Gathering Component, LDAP is used to access information stored in Active Directory. Reference [Mic12a] describes the Active Directory classes, while [Mic12b] gives a description of the Computer class, from which relevant information is read.

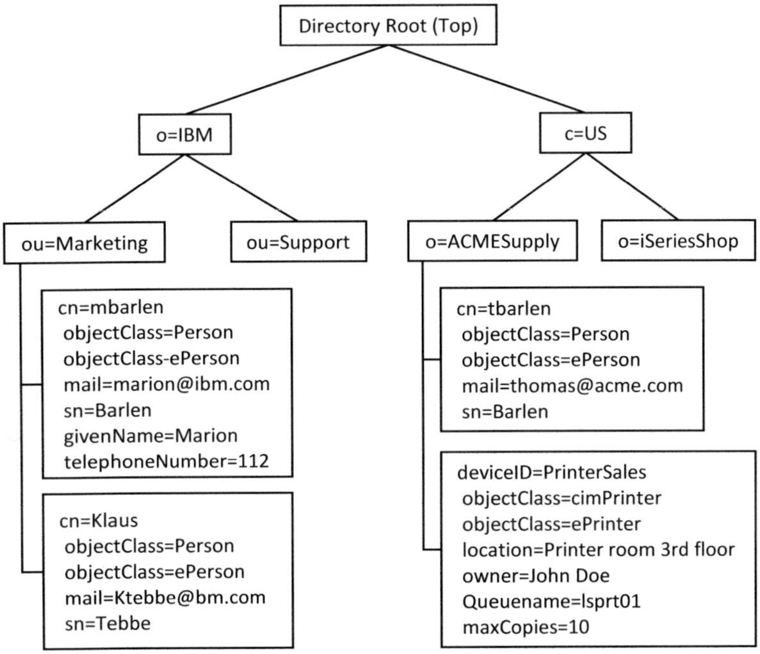

Figure 5.6.: LDAP Directory Information Tree (cf. [TEG+04, page 17])

Reference [PBD+06, pages 459–481] gives an introduction to LDAP, while [TEG+04] gives more detail. In [AH06], information about LDAP in the context of Microsoft Active Directory can be found. More information about LDAP is available in [Zei06b, Zei06a, Ser06]. Reference [The12a] describes how LDAP can be accessed from the PHP programming language.

The Common Information Model (CIM)

The Common Information Model (CIM) is a standard for the management of IT components, developed by the Distributed Management Task Force (DMTF). Its purpose is stated as follows [DMT13b]:

> "CIM provides a common definition of management information for systems, networks, applications and services, and allows for vendor extensions. CIM's common definitions enable vendors to exchange semantically rich management information between systems throughout the network." [DMT13b]

CIM is an object-oriented model, which allows to describe environments by using capabilities such as abstraction, classification, inheritance, dependencies, and associations [DMT03]. CIM consists of two parts, namely the CIM Specification, and the CIM Schema [DMT13a].

CIM consists of three layers, which have the following purposes [DMT12a, pages 8–9]:

- *Core model:* "The core model is an information model that applies to all areas of management. The core model is a small set of classes, associations, and properties for analyzing and describing managed systems. It is a starting point for analyzing how to extend the common schema. While classes can be added to the core model over time, major reinterpretations of the core model classes are not anticipated." [DMT12a, page 8]

- *Common model:* "The common model is a basic set of classes that define various technology-independent areas, such as systems, applications, networks, and devices. The classes, properties, associations, and methods in the common model are detailed enough to use as a basis for program design and, in some cases, implementation. Extensions are added below the common model in platform-specific additions that supply concrete classes and implementations of the common model classes. As the common model is extended, it offers a broader range of information." [DMT12a, pages 8–9] "The common model is an information model common to particular management areas but independent of a particular technology or implementation. The common areas are systems, applications, networks, and devices. The information model is specific enough to provide a basis for developing management applications. This schema provides a set of base classes for extension into the area of technology-specific schemas. The core and common models together are referred to in this document as the CIM schema." [DMT12a, page 9]

- *Extension schemas:* "The extension schemas are technology-specific extensions to the common model. Operating systems (such as Microsoft Windows® or UNIX®) are examples of extension schemas. The common model is expected to evolve as objects are promoted and properties are defined in the extension schemas." [DMT12a, page 9]

An overview of CIM can be found in [DMT03], the CIM Infrastructure is described in [DMT12a], while a description of the CIM Metamodel can be found in [DMT12b]. Furthermore, reference [DMT12c] describes the CIM Managed Object Format (MOF).

Windows Management Instrumentation (WMI)

Windows Management Instrumentation (WMI) is a mechanism that can be used to gather information from computers, which are running Microsoft Windows. Reference [Mic11a] describes WMI as follows:

> "Windows Management Instrumentation (WMI) is the Microsoft implementation of Web-based Enterprise Management (WBEM), which is an industry initiative to develop a standard technology for accessing management information in an enterprise environment. WMI uses the Common Information Model (CIM) industry standard to represent systems, applications, networks, devices, and other managed components. CIM is developed and maintained by the Distributed Management Task Force (DMTF)." [Mic11a]

Figure 5.7 shows the architecture of WMI. The Information Gathering Component, which was developed within this thesis runs as a WMI consumer on the third layer. More information about WMI can be found in [Jon07, Mic09, Mic00].

Simple Network Management Protocol (SNMP)

The Simple Network Management Protocol (SNMP) is used to read information from devices, in order to integrate the information into the ITSM Wiki-based Configuration Management System.

Reference [PBD+06, page 624] defines the purpose of SNMP as follows:

> "The fundamental use of the Simple Network Management Protocol [...] is to manage all aspects of a network, as well as applications related to that network." [PBD+06, page 624]

Figure 5.8 shows the components of the SNMP architecture. The management application, which is part of the management station, uses the SNMP manager in order to send messages to the SNMP agent over an IP network. The agent accesses managed objects on the clients in order to read or write information.

The relevant aspects of SNMP for the Information Gathering Component are monitoring and managing. Reference [PBD+06, page 624] describes monitoring as follows:

> "Monitor: SNMP implementations allow network administrators to monitor their networks in order to–among other things–ensure the health of the network, forecast usage and capacity, and in problem determination. Aspects which can be monitored vary in granularity, and can be something as global as the total amount of IP traffic experienced on a single host, or can be as minute as the current status of a single TCP connection." [PBD+06, page 624]

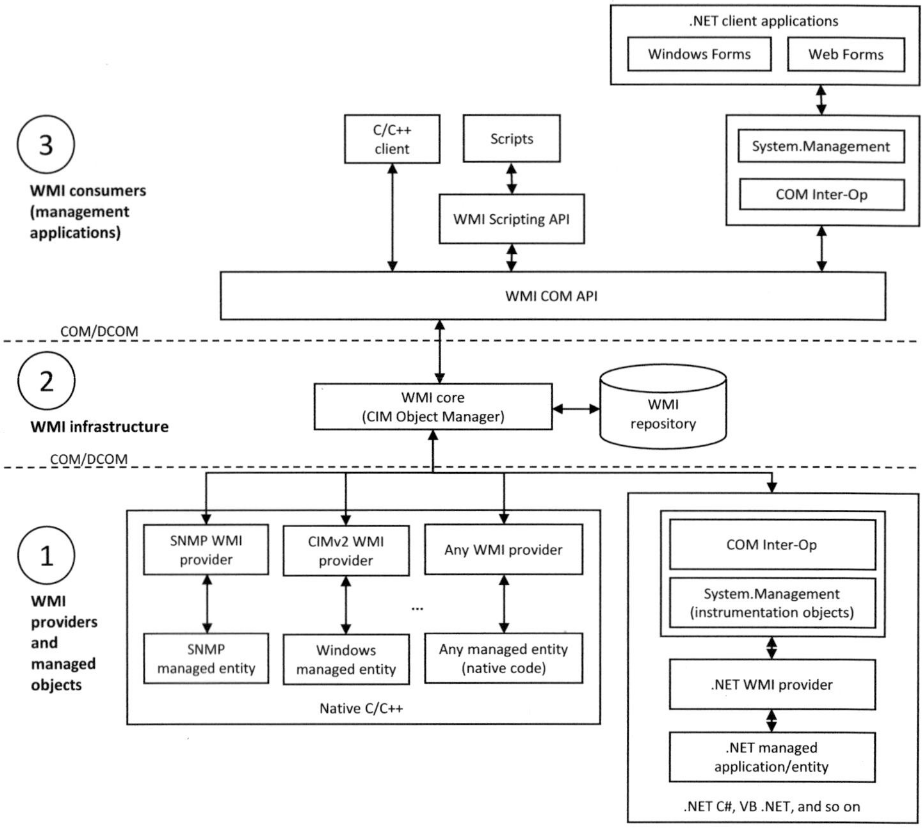

Figure 5.7.: WMI Architecture (cf. [Mic11c])

The aspects of SNMP with regard to the management of devices are as follows [PBD+06, page 624]:

> "Manage: In addition to monitoring a network, SNMP provides the capability for network administrators to affect aspects with the network. Values which regulate network operation can be altered, allowing administrators to quickly respond to network problems, dynamically implement new network changes, and to perform real-time testing on how changes may affect their network." [PBD+06, page 624]

One of the central parts of SNMP is the Management Information Base (MIB). The MIB "defines a set of objects which can be monitored or managed using an SNMP implementation" [PBD+06, page 625].

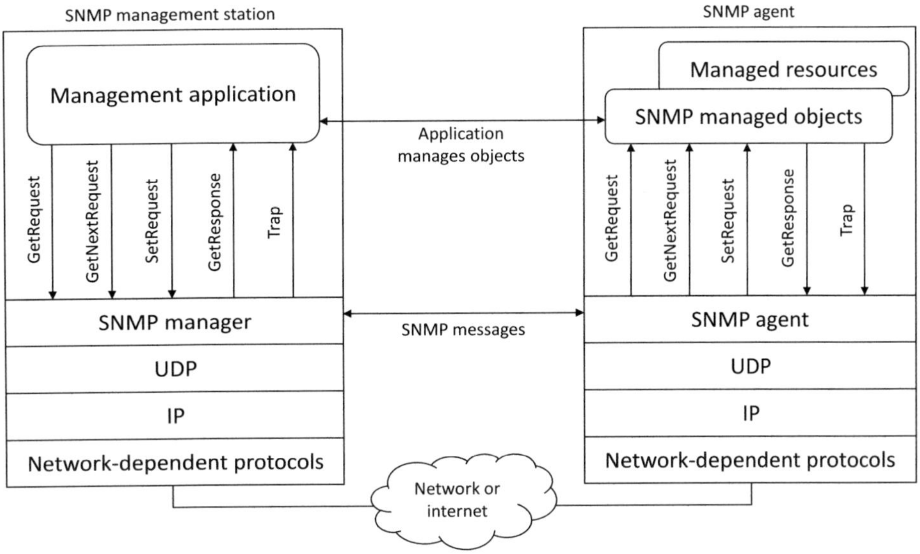

Figure 5.8.: SNMP Architecture (cf. [Sta98])

Additional information about SNMP can be found in [Ste93, pages 359–388], [Sta98], [PBD$^+$06, pages 623–648], [Com00, pages 553–574], and [Sch05, pages 69–150]. In [The12b], the PHP SNMP extension, which is used by the Information Gathering Component, is described.

5.1.6. Design of the Information Gathering Component

Figure 5.9 shows the architecture of the Information Gathering Component. As can be seen in the figure, Semantic MediaWiki forms the basis of the component. On top of Semantic MediaWiki, the Information Gathering Component is located. The component uses three different protocols for accessing different information sources. First, the LDAP protocol is used to access information stored in Active Directory. The second protocol is WMI, which is used to access information on Windows hosts. Third, the SNMP protocol is used to access information found on network devices (e.g., network switches, and networked printers).

Access to Information Stored in the Directory Service

Information about users and computers is stored in a central directory service (Microsoft Active Directory). In order to avoid manual input of information that already exists in

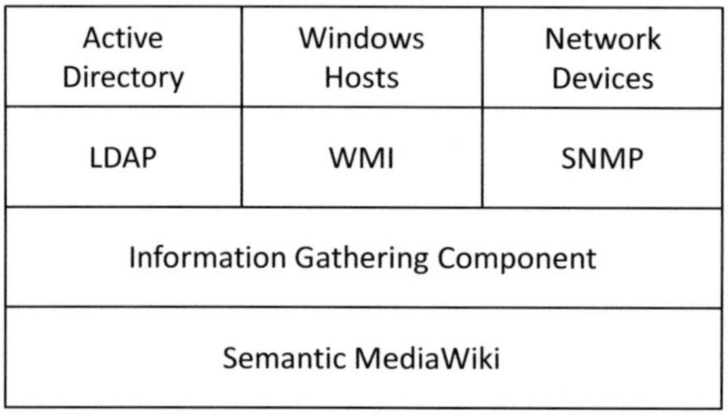

Figure 5.9.: Architecture of the Information Gathering Component

the directory service, the information is automatically imported by a recurring task (e.g., once an hour, or once a day, depending on the requirements of the IT environment).

Algorithm 5.1 describes the high-level steps for importing information about users and computers from the directory into the ITSM Wiki. About users, information includes the following elements: given name, family name, group memberships, and contact information. Information about computers includes group membership, as well as information about the first and most recent connection of a computer to the directory service.

Algorithm 5.1: Gathering Information from the Directory Service

---

Data: Active Directory instance, ITSM Wiki instance, login credentials
Result: Updated information about users and computers in the ITSM Wiki
user[] = Get list of users from Active Directory;
for *(int i=1; i <= count(user[]); i++)* **do**
  Read information about user[i] from the directory;
  Write information about user[i] to the ITSM Wiki;
end
computer[] = Get list of computers from Active Directory;
for *(int i=1; i <= count(computer[]); i++)* **do**
  Read information about computer[i] from the directory;
  Write information about computer[i] to the ITSM Wiki;
end

Access to Windows Hosts via the WMI Mechanism

In order to gather information from Windows hosts, the WMI protocol is used. Algorithm 5.2 describes the steps that are performed in order to read information from Windows hosts, and to store the information in the ITSM Wiki.

First, a list of computers is read from Active Directory via the LDAP protocol. After that, each computer in the list is contacted. An ICMP echo request is sent, in order to check if the computer is reachable via the network. If this is the case, a connection via the WMI mechanism is established. Over this connection, information about hardware and software is read from the computer. After being read, the information is written to the ITSM Wiki in a structured format (i.e., as instances, and properties).

Algorithm 5.2: Gathering Information from Windows Hosts

Data: Active Directory instance, ITSM Wiki instance, login credentials
Result: Updated information about Windows computers in the ITSM Wiki
computer[] = Get list of Windows computers from Active Directory;
for *(int i=1; i <= count(computer[]); i++)* **do**
    if *(Computer is reachable via the network)* **then**
        Connect to client computer[i] via WMI;
        Read information from computer[i];
        Write information about computer[i] to the ITSM Wiki;
    end
end

Access to Devices via the SNMP Protocol

Accessing information from devices other than Windows computers is accomplished via the SNMP protocol, which is supported by most network-enabled devices (e.g., network switches, and printers). Algorithm 5.3 shows how information is read from devices and stored in the wiki.

The algorithm works as follows: First, a list of SNMP-enabled devices is created. This list contains the IP addresses of devices that are reachable via the network and reply to packets sent to the SNMP port. Next, the DNS names of the devices are resolved via reverse lookups. This is done because the DNS names are used as the title for the wiki page. If an IP address cannot be resolved to a DNS name, the IP address is added to the error log and is not processed further. For each device, a connection is established via the SNMP protocol. Then information is read, and written to the wiki in a structured format.

5.1.7. Information Gathering Ontology

The data model of the Information Gathering Component is an ontology. An introduction to ontologies is given in Section 2.3 (page 59), while the partitioning of the ontologies is described in Section 4.3.3 (page 166). The ITSM Ontology, which is the data model

Algorithm 5.3: Gathering Information from SNMP-enabled Devices

```
Data: Address range of devices, ITSM Wiki instance, login credentials
Result: Updated information about SNMP-enabled devices in the ITSM Wiki
ip[] = Get list of IPs of SNMP-enabled devices by scanning for open SNMP
ports;
for (int i=1; i <= count(ip[]); i++) do
    device = Resolve DNS name of ip[i] via reverse lookup;
    if (name != null) then
        Connect to device via the SNMP protocol;
        Read information from device;
        Write information about device to the ITSM Wiki;
    else
        Add unresolvable IP address to error list;
    end
end
```

for the core ITSM classes and properties, is described in Section 4.3.4 (page 167). The Information Gathering Component uses a subset of these classes and properties and introduces the parts of the ontology that are relevant to the component[6].

Class Hierarchy

Figure 5.10 shows the class hierarchy of the Information Gathering Ontology. All classes are subclasses of the *Thing* class. Class hierarchies are expressed with the *is-a* property.

Classes, Object Properties, and Data Properties

Table 5.2 shows the classes, object properties, and data properties of the Information Gathering Ontology. There are two types of information present in the ontology. First, there is information that can be gathered automatically by the Information Gathering Component. This information is characterized by being stored in directories or on devices (e.g., the manufacturer and the serial number of a device). Second, there is information that cannot be gathered automatically because it is not available in the directory or on devices, but is still relevant when describing configuration items (e.g., the vendor, from which hardware was purchased).

[6]The ontologies presented in this chapter partly contain redundant classes. This is due to the fact that each ontology was designed to contain all classes that are relevant in the context of the modeled domain. For example, the Person class is part of each single ontology, because the class is used in each component.

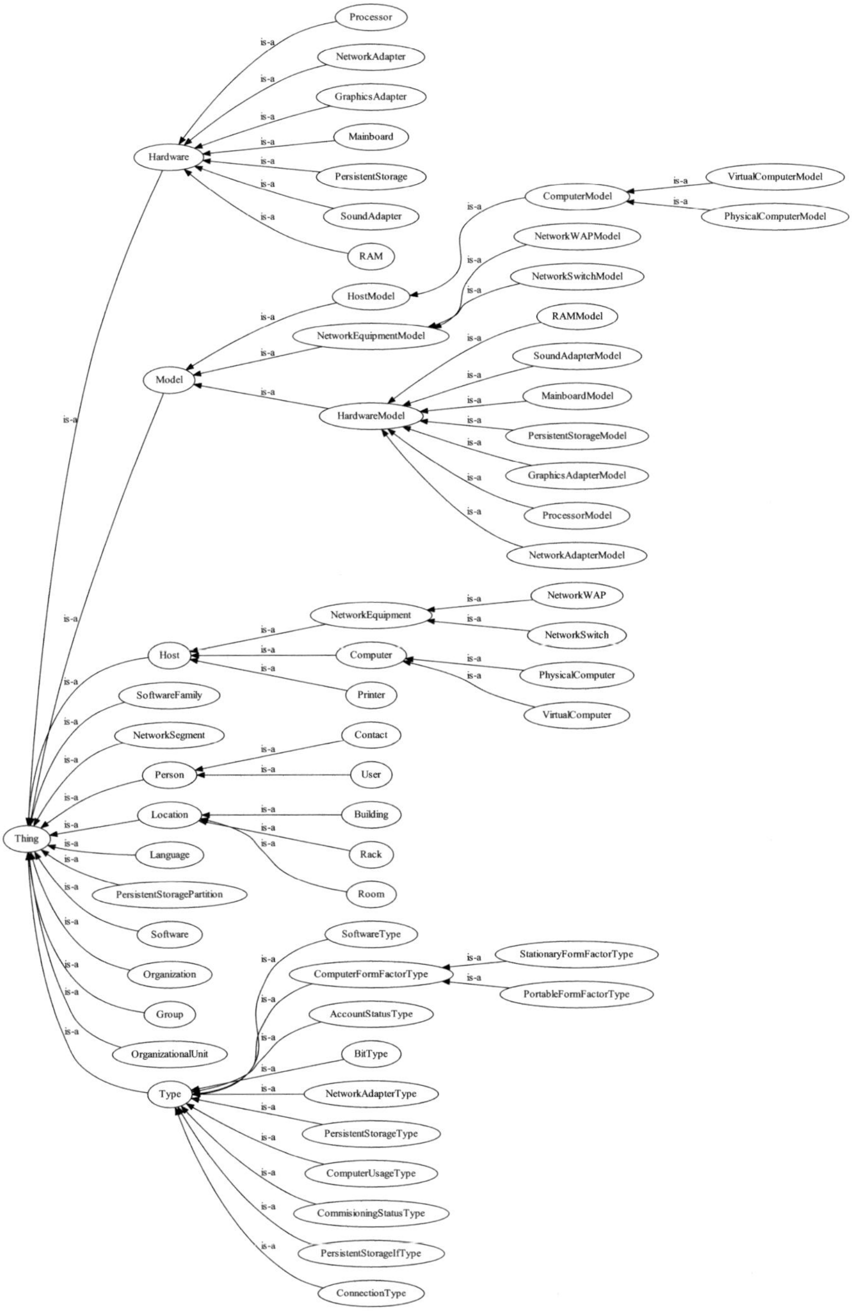

Figure 5.10.: Class Hierarchy of the Information Gathering Ontology

In Table 5.2, classes and properties that are printed in boldface type are read automatically by the Information Gathering Component, while classes in regular type have to be stored and updated manually.

Table 5.2.: Information Gathering Ontology

Domain Class	**Property**	**Range**
AccountStatusType	*inherited from Type class*	*no additional properties*
BitType	*inherited from Type class*	*no additional properties*
Building	*inherited from Location class* City {0..1} Street {0..1} ZipCode {0..1}	 <String> <String> <String>
CommissioningStatusType	*inherited from Type class*	*no additional properties*
Computer	*inherited from Host class* **LastDomainConnectDate** {0..1} **MemberOfWindowsDomain** {0..1} **OperatingSystemInstallationDate** {0..1} hasComputerUsageType {0..1} **hasLocalAdministrator** {0..n}	 <Date> <Boolean> <Date> ComputerUsageType Contact, User
ComputerFormFactorType	*inherited from Type class*	*no additional properties*
ComputerModel	*inherited from Model class*	*no additional properties*
ComputerUsageType	*inherited from Type class*	*no additional properties*
ConnectionType	*inherited from Type class*	*no additional properties*
Contact	*inherited from Person class*	*no additional properties*
GraphicsAdapter	*inherited from Hardware class* **ColorDepth** {0..1} **Driver** {0..1} **GraphicsMemory** {0..1} **XResolution** {0..1} **YResolution** {0..1}	 <Number> <String> <Quantity> <Quantity> <Quantity>
GraphicsAdapterModel	*inherited from Model class*	*no additional properties*
Group	*inherited from Thing class* **isMemberOfGroup** {0..n}	 Group
Hardware	*inherited from Thing class* **ProductNumber** {0..1} **SerialNumber** {0..1} **hasManufacturer** {0..1} **hasModel** {0..1} hasVendor {0..1} isCompatibleWith {0..n} isIncompatibleWith {0..n}	 <String> <String> Organization Model Organization Thing Thing
HardwareModel	*inherited from Model class*	*no additional properties*

(*table continues*)

Table 5.2.: Information Gathering Ontology (continued)

Domain Class	Property	Range
Host	*inherited from Thing class*	
	ProductNumber {0..1}	<String>
	SerialNumber {0..1}	<String>
	hasCommissioningStatusType {0..1}	CommissioningStatusType
	hasContactPerson {0..n}	Person
	hasInstalledHardware {0..n}	Hardware
	hasInstalledSoftware {0..n}	Software
	hasManufacturer {0..1}	Organization
	hasModel {0..1}	Model
	hasOwner {0..1}	Person
	hasVendor {0..1}	Organization
	isLocatedIn {0..1}	Location
HostModel	*inherited from Model class*	*no additional properties*
Language	*inherited from Thing class*	*no additional properties*
Location	*inherited from Thing class*	*no additional properties*
Mainboard	*inherited from Hardware class*	
	BiosDescription {0..1}	<String>
	BiosVersion {0..1}	<String>
MainboardModel	*inherited from Model class*	*no additional properties*
Model	*inherited from Thing class*	*no additional properties*
NetworkAdapter	*inherited from Hardware class*	
	ConnectionSpeed {0..1}	<Quantity>
	IPv4Address {0..1}	<String>
	IPv4DefaultGateway {0..1}	<String>
	IPv4DHCPEnabled {0..1}	<Boolean>
	IPv4DHCPServer {0..1}	<String>
	IPv4DNSServer {0..n}	<String>
	IPv4SubnetMask {0..1}	<String>
	IPv6Address {0..1}	<String>
	IPv6DefaultGateway {0..1}	<String>
	IPv6DNSServer {0..n}	<String>
	MACAddress {0..1}	<String>
	hasConnectionType {0..1}	ConnectionType
	hasNetworkAdapterType {0..1}	NetworkAdapterType
	hasNetworkConnectionTo {0..1}	NetworkAdapter
	isPartOfNetworkSegment {0..1}	NetworkSegment
NetworkAdapterModel	*inherited from Model class*	*no additional properties*
NetworkAdapterType	*inherited from Type class*	*no additional properties*
NetworkEquipment	*inherited from Host class*	
	supportsNetworkAdapterType {0..1}	NetworkAdapterType
NetworkEquipmentModel	*inherited from Model class*	*no additional properties*

(*table continues*)

Table 5.2.: Information Gathering Ontology (continued)

Domain Class	**Property**	**Range**
NetworkSegment	*inherited from Thing class* DefaultIPv4Gateway {0..1} DefaultIPv6Gateway {0..1} EndIPv4Address {0..1} EndIPv6Address {0..1} StartIPv4Address {0..1} StartIPv6Address {0..1} IPv4SubnetMask {0..1} IPv6SubnetMask {0..1} VirtualLANIdentifier {0..1}	 <String> <String> <String> <String> <String> <String> <String> <String> <Number>
NetworkSwitch	*inherited from NetworkEquipment class*	*no additional properties*
NetworkSwitchModel	*inherited from Model class*	*no additional properties*
NetworkWAP	*inherited from NetworkEquipment class*	*no additional properties*
NetworkWAPModel	*inherited from Model class*	*no additional properties*
Organization	*inherited from Thing class* City {0..1} Country {0..1} EMailAddress {0..1} FaxNumber {0..1} PhoneNumber {0..1} Street {0..1} WebPage {0..1} ZipCode {0..1}	 <String> <String> <String> <String> <String> <String> <String> <String>
OrganizationalUnit	*inherited from Thing class* hasDeputyManager {0..n} hasITContact {0..n} hasManager {0..n} isPartOfOrganization {0..1} isPartOfOrganizationalUnit {0..1}	 <Person> <Person> <Person> Organization OrganizationalUnit
PersistentStorage	*inherited from Hardware class* **TotalCapacity** {0..1} **UnallocatedCapacity** {0..1} **containsPartition** {0..n} **hasInterfaceType** {0..1}	 <Quantity> <Quantity> PersistentStoragePartition PersistentStorageIfType
PersistentStorageIfType	*inherited from Type class*	*no additional properties*
PersistentStorageModel	*inherited from Model class*	*no additional properties*
PersistentStoragePartition	*inherited from Thing class* **DriveLetter** {0..1} **FileSystem** {0..1} **Size** {0..1}	 <String> <String> <Quantity>
PersistentStorageType	*inherited from Type class*	*no additional properties*

(*table continues*)

Table 5.2.: Information Gathering Ontology (continued)

Domain Class	Property	Range
Person	*inherited from Thing class*	
	EMailAddress {0..n}	<Email>
	FamilyName {0..1}	<String>
	FaxNumber {0..n}	<Telephone number>
	GivenName {0..1}	<String>
	JobTitle {0..1}	<String>
	PhoneNumber {0..n}	<Telephone number>
	hasKnowledgeDomain {0..n}	KnowledgeDomain
	hasOffice {0..1}	Room
	hasManager {0..1}	Person
	hasRole {0..n}	Role
	isMemberOfGroup {0..n}	Group
	isMemberOfOrganization {0..n}	Organization
	isMemberOfOrganizationalUnit {0..n}	OrganizationalUnit
PhysicalComputer	*inherited from Computer class*	
	hasComputerFormFactorType {0..1}	ComputerFormFactorType
PhysicalComputerModel	*inherited from Model class*	*no additional properties*
PortableFormFactorType	*inherited from FormFactorType class*	*no additional properties*
Printer	*inherited from Host class*	*no additional properties*
Processor	*inherited from Hardware class*	
	AddressWidth {0..1}	<Quantity>
	DataWidth {0..1}	<Quantity>
	Family {0..1}	<String>
	ID {0..1}	<String>
	Level2Cache {0..1}	<Quantity>
	Level3Cache {0..1}	<Quantity>
	NumberOfCores {0..1}	<Number>
	ProcessorVersion {0..1}	<String>
ProcessorModel	*inherited from Model class*	*no additional properties*
Rack	*inherited from Location class*	
	Height {0..1}	<Quantity>
	isLocatedInRoom {0..1}	Room
RAM	*inherited from Hardware class*	
	ModuleSize {0..n}	<Quantity>
RAMModel	*inherited from Model class*	*no additional properties*
Room	*inherited from Location class*	
	isLocatedInBuilding {0..1}	Building

(*table continues*)

Table 5.2.: Information Gathering Ontology (continued)

Domain Class	Property	Range
Software	*inherited from Thing class* **SoftwareVersion** {0..1} hasBitType {0..1} hasLanguage {0..n} **hasManufacturer** {0..1} hasSoftwareType {0..1} hasVendor {0..1} isCompatibleWith {0..n} isIncompatibleWith {0..n} isPartOfSoftwareFamily {0..1}	 <String> BitType Language Organization SoftwareType Organization Thing Thing SoftwareFamily
SoftwareFamily	*inherited from Thing class* isPartOfSoftwareFamily {0..1}	 SoftwareFamily
SoftwareType	*inherited from Type class*	*no additional properties*
SoundAdapter	*inherited from Hardware class*	*no additional properties*
SoundAdapterModel	*inherited from Model class*	*no additional properties*
StationaryFormFactorType	*inherited from FormFactorType class*	*no additional properties*
Thing	**ConfigurationGatheringDate** {0..1} Description {0..1} Name {1} Version {0..1} hasDependency {0..n} hasParent {0..n} isConnectedTo {0..n} isRelatedTo {0..n}	<Date> <Text> <String> <Number> Thing Thing Thing Thing
Type	*inherited from Thing class*	*no additional properties*
User	*inherited from Person class* **CreationDate** {0..1} DeletionDate {0..1} **LastLoginDate** {0..1} **LoginName** {0..1} **UniqueIdentifier** {0..1} **hasAccountStatusType** {0..1}	 <Date> <Date> <Date> <String> <String> AccountStatusType
VirtualComputer	*inherited from Computer class*	*no additional properties*
VirtualComputerModel	*inherited from Model class*	*no additional properties*

Descriptions and Exemplary Instances

In Section 4.3.4 (page 173), a short description, as well as exemplary instances, are shown for each class of the Information Gathering Ontology. The presentation in a single table is done in order to avoid unnecessary duplication of information.

5.1.8. Implementation

The Information Gathering Component is implemented using the PHP programming language. The following functionality is implemented in the component described in this section: First, importing of user and computer information from an Active Directory instance into the ITSM Wiki is supported. Second, gathering information from computers that are running the Microsoft Windows operating system is supported.

The import of information from hosts that support the SNMP protocol was implemented as a proof-of-concept prototype. Because the implementation is to a large extent analogous to the implementation of the WMI part, it is not discussed further in this thesis.

Configuring devices by writing information from the ITSM Wiki to devices over the network by using the SNMP protocol was also tested by implementing a proof-of-concept prototype. Writing information enables IT administrators to update, for example, virtual networks (VLANs) directly from the wiki, without having to log into the specific management interface of a network switch. This simplifies changes by providing a single point of administration for different classes of devices from different vendors.

The functionality of the Information Gathering Component is implemented in several PHP files as follows:

- `WMIToMW.php`: This is the main file of the Windows part of the Information Gathering Component. The file is either started manually from the command line for an on-demand scan, or automatically on a regular basis via the cron [Red08b, pages 559–561] mechanism. `WMIToSMW.php` implements the functions for getting the list of users, groups, and Windows computers from Active Directory, and the subsequent reading of information from the individual hosts. Readable information includes all information that is accessible through WMI. At the current state, information about a computer's CPU, mainboard, RAM, graphics adapter, networking, hard disks operating system, and installed applications is read. While it would be possible to read information sequentially host after host, it was realized that this approach would lengthen the time it takes for a gathering run. Because of that, `WMIToMW.php` reads information from multiple hosts in parallel. The files, which are described in the following list items, contain implementations of functions that are used by `WMIToMW.php`.
- `config.inc.php`: This file contains configuration information, which is used in order to access Active Directory, client computers, and the Semantic MediaWiki instance (e.g., user names, passwords, and paths).
- `CurlWrapper.php`: This file implements a wrapper mechanism for the cURL[7] tool, which is used to access the Semantic MediaWiki instance.

[7] `http://curl.haxx.se/`

- LDAP.php: Functions that are used to access Active Directory via the LDAP protocol are contained in this file.
- Logger.php: This file is a helper class, which provides logging capabilities to other classes. It is mostly used for debugging purposes.
- SWList.php: In order to protect the privacy of users, only a subset of information about software, which is installed on client computers, is gathered. In SWList.php, functions for the management of lists are implemented. Information about applications that are in the whitelist are imported into the wiki, while information about applications, which are on the blacklist are not imported. Applications, which are found on clients, for which there exists neither a blacklist nor a whitelist entry, are shown in the greylist, without revealing on which client computer the application is installed.
- WebApi.php: This file implements functions that are used to access a MediaWiki instance.
- WMIException.php: In this file, code for exception handling is provided. Handled exceptions are errors in the configuration file, errors about host connections, and errors with regard to WMI queries.
- WMIHost.php: This file provides functions for reading information from client computers via the WMI interface.
- WMI.php: This file implements functions that simplify the use of the wmic[8] tool, which is used to get information from hosts via the WMI mechanism.
- wmitest.php: This file is used for testing purposes. The script sends WMI queries to hosts and displays the results on the console.

5.1.9. Representation of Information in the Wiki

This subsection shows how information about users and computers is represented.

Users

Information about users is read from Active Directory and stored in Semantic Forms syntax. Listing 5.1 shows a user as represented in the ITSM Wiki. The listing shows organizational information, which is gathered from the directory. In addition, information about the account status, such as whether the account is active is gathered. Further information is the date of the account creation, as well as the date of the last login.

[8] http://dev.zenoss.org/svn/trunk/inst/externallibs/wmi-1.3.13.tar.bz2

Listing 5.1: Semantic Forms Wikitext Representing a User

```
{{User
|Name=Lina Hartmann (lhartm@fzi.de)
|Description=RuD-Mitarbeiter
|FamilyName=Hartmann
|GivenName=Lina
|IsMemberOfOrganization=FZI Forschungszentrum Informatik
|IsMemberOfOrganizationalUnit=RuD
|PhoneNumber=+49 721 9654-XXX
|EmailAddress=lhartm@fzi.de
|FaxNumber=+49 721 9654-XXX
|HasOffice=Room 1.1.03
|HasManager=Max Jung (jung@fzi.de)
|JobTitle=IT Administrator
|IsMemberOfGroup=IT-Mitarbeiter
}}
```

In Figure 5.11, a screenshot of the exemplary user page is shown. As can be seen in the screenshot, the wiki page that represents the user contains links, which can be used in order to navigate to the linked pages. For example, if the manager of the user is of interest, one can click on the link in order to access information about the user's manager.

Computers

Information, which is extracted from computers by the Information Gathering Component, is stored in the wiki. The following Listing 5.2 shows an example of parts of a computer page, as represented in the ITSM Wiki. The information shown in the listing is limited to the information shown in the corresponding screenshot. In addition, information about software, as well as other aspects of the computer is gathered.

Listing 5.2: Semantic Forms Wikitext Representing a Computer's Hardware

```
{{Computer
|Mainboard=SABERTOOTH 990FX R2.0
|Processor=AMD FX(tm)-8350 Eight-Core Processor
|RAM=8192MB-1, 8192MB-2, 8192MB-3, 8192MB-4
|NetworkAdapter=60:A4:4C:60:XX:XX, 08:00:27:00:XX:XX, 00:FF
    :36:40:XX:XX
|GraphicsAdapter=AMD Radeon HD 6700 Series 1024 MB
|SoundAdapter=AMD High Definition Audio Device
|PersistentStorage=Generic STORAGE DEVICE USB Device 0, Samsung
    SSD 840 PRO Seri SATA Disk Device 0, [...]
}}
```

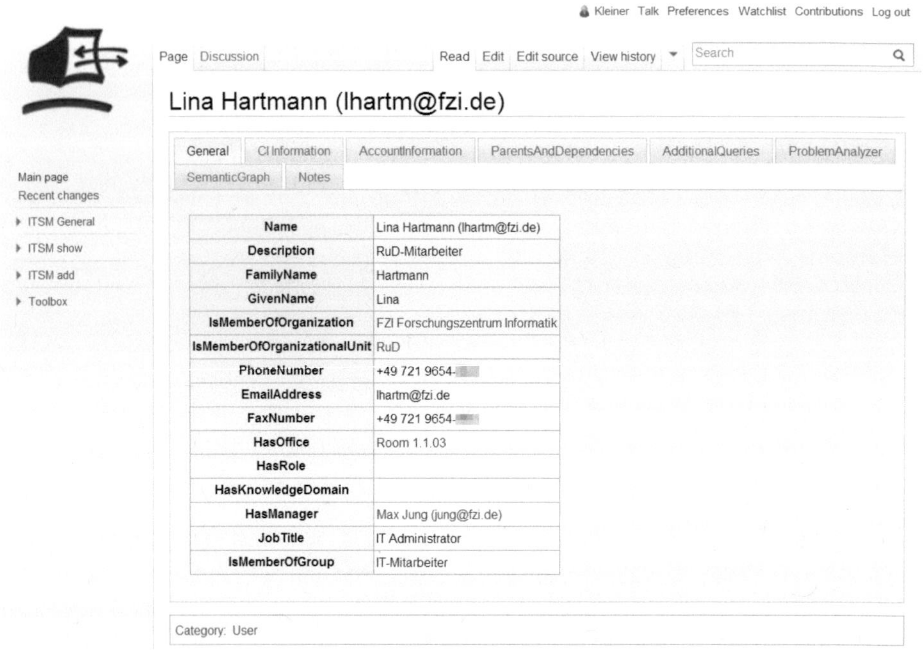

Figure 5.11.: Information about a User in the ITSM Wiki

Figure 5.12 shows a screenshot of a wiki page, which gives information about a computer's hardware. The information is presented using the Semantic Forms extension. As can be seen in the screenshot, hardware components are listed, which are part of the computer. By clicking on each of the component representations, the wiki page that represents this component is loaded. For example, in order to get more information about the processor, one can click on the corresponding link.

5.1.10. Prior and Related Work

This subsection describes prior work about automatic information gathering, as well as about network and system management ontologies.

Automatic Information Gathering

There are several tools for the automatic discovery of networked devices, both available commercially and as open source software. While the management capabilities, as well as the capabilities with regard to discovery of the described tools, exceed the capabilities

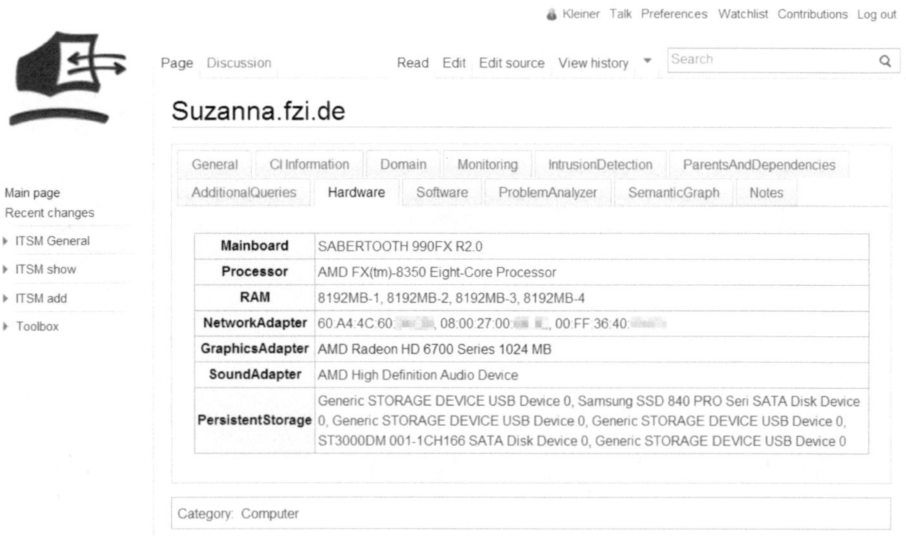

Figure 5.12.: Information about a Computer's Hardware in the ITSM Wiki

provided by the Information Gathering Component, they lack in flexibility and do not implement some of the features provided by the ITSM Wiki. Furthermore, they do not provide an environment for retaining and editing formatted text and structured information within a common environment. While initial thoughts existed for re-using an existing automatic discovery tool for the ITSM Wiki, the flexibility of directly accessing LDAP, WMI, and SNMP was considered more promising. In contrast to the Information Gathering Component, which uses an ontology as the data model, the following tools use relational databases.

Spiceworks[9] is a freely available, advertisement-financed software, which includes functionalities for "Network Inventory, Help Desk, Mapping, Reporting, Monitoring and Troubleshooting" [Spi11]. With regard to automated discovery, Spiceworks offers the following capabilities:

- Discovery of "Windows, Mac, and Linux PCs and servers, routers, printers and any other IP-based devices" without the need of installing a client [Spi11].
- Management of information about hardware and software (including licenses), as well as the capabilities to add additional information about devices, which is not being able to be automatically discovered [Spi11].
- Importing information from Active Directory [Spi11].

[9] `http://www.spiceworks.com/free-pc-network-inventory-software/`

Open-AudIT[10] is an open source solution, which provides mechanisms for discovering hardware and software information over the network, and a user interface for managing the information [Ope11]. OCS Inventory NG[11] is an agent-based [OCS11b] inventory tool that can discover and network devices, as well as read information about hardware and software from computers, on which an agent is installed [OCS11a].

From Microsoft, there are several tools available, both freely and as commercial solutions [Mic11b]. Further examples of automated discovery tools, which provide functionalities for discovering information about hardware and software via the network are DEKSI Network Inventory[12], Lansweeper[13], and LOGINventory[14].

Network and System Management Ontologies

There exist various network management models, which allow the definition of a managed domain through a management definition language. Examples of management models are the Simple Network Management Protocol (SNMP), the Common Management Information Protocol (CMIP), the Desktop Management Interface (DMI), and Web-Based Enterprise Management (WBEM) [dVVAB03].

The management models make use of the following management information definition languages [dVVAB03]:

- SNMP: Structure of Management Information (SMI)
- CMIP: Guidelines for the Definition of Managed Objects (GDMO)
- DMI: Managed Information Format (MIF)
- WBEM: Managed Object Format/Common Information Model (MOF/CIM)

Reference [dVVAB03] proposes the use of Ontologies in order to manage environments, which make use of multiple management models. The goal is to "reach semantic interoperability of different management models and languages" [dVVAB03]. After analyzing the characteristics of the different models, the authors came to the conclusion that MOF/CIM provides the best semantic expressiveness of the analyzed models [dVVAB03].

The work presented in [dVVB04] describes an "approach that uses an XML-based ontology language to define network and system management information" [dVVB04]. Motivated from the observation that XML provides benefits when applied to network and system management, namely a large number of available libraries and tools, as well

[10] `http://www.open-audit.org/`
[11] `http://www.ocsinventory-ng.org/en/`
[12] `http://www.deksoftware.com/dni/index.html`
[13] `http://www.lansweeper.com/`
[14] `http://www.loginventory.de/loginventory/`

as the ability to use style sheets for information representation, it is observed that plain XML lacks some desired capabilities. By making use of OWL, these limitations, namely lack of semantics, are overcome. An approach is described, which allows the mapping of network and system management models to OWL [dVVB04].

There are various publications, which describe benefits and outline methods for converting CIM to formal ontologies. In [LDR03], a conceptual framework for converting CIM schemas from the network and systems management domain to frame-based ontologies, is presented. In [QAW+04], an approach is presented, which provides a framework for constructing a formal ontology based on CIM, in order to facilitate self-managing distributed systems.

An approach for the formalization of the CIM metaschema is presented in [dVVB05]. The Object Constraint Language (OCL)[15], which is part of the Unified Modeling Language (UML), is used for the formal definition of rules. This is done, because in standard CIM, these rules are otherwise expressed in natural language, which impedes the automatic processing and checking by computers [dVVB05].

In [MKK07], an approach for translating CIM to OWL is presented. In addition, the tool CIM2OWL, which supports the automatic conversion of CIM to OWL, is introduced.

Reference [TSK10] describes the automatic conversion of the Common Information Model (CIM) into an OWL ontology, in order to enable "knowledge interoperability and aggregation, as well as reasoning" [TSK10]. In [TSK11], "a complete OWL representation of the Common Information Model (CIM) and management rules defined in the Semantic Web Rule Language (SWRL)" are described [TSK11].

In [Maj10], the i2mapCore ontology is introduced, which allows the semantic description of aspects of service-oriented environments [Maj10, page 6]. The i2mapCore uses the CIM2OWL tool [QAW+04, MKK07] for generating an OWL ontology from CIM. In addition, the ontology was extended in order to include additional aspects such as Service Level Agreements and roles. The i2mapCore ontology is used to provide a common data model for aggregating information from various organizational units, which retain heterogeneous data about IT systems. While the model is suitable for implementing the functionality of a Federated Configuration Management Database in larger organizations, it requires a heavyweight approach when adding additional classes to the ontology [Maj10, pages 61–102]. This observation conflicts with the requirements of the approach developed in this thesis, which aims at providing a lightweight tool for SMEs, which allow the ad-hoc modification of the data model.

The scope and goals of the approaches presented in this subsection differ from the ones presented in this thesis in the following aspects:

[15] `http://www.omg.org/spec/OCL/`

- The outlined approaches adhere far more strictly to the formal aspects of transforming CIM into an ontology. In contrast, the work presented in this thesis follows a more lightweight approach. This approach does not aim at creating an ontology that encompasses all aspects of CIM, or any other network and system management model, but rather provides an extensible model that can be tailored to individual environments.

- The technical platform is a semantic wiki, which provides mechanisms for retaining, as well as displaying and processing the information, while the approaches described in related work only define models. By building on a semantic wiki, information can be managed more flexibly and in a lightweight manner, as compared to formal ontologies based on CIM.

With regard to re-using CIM as the underlying data model, the following observations were made: First, CIM as a data model is limited to describing instances of hosts, without describing the connections or dependencies between hosts. Second, re-using CIM as a whole would have introduced a large number of classes, which are not relevant in the ITSM Wiki. This would have led to a large and heavyweight data model, which would have been hard do maintain. Third, re-using parts of CIM would have been possible, but would have introduced a number of characteristics of CIM, which are not desirable in the lightweight approach of the ITSM Wiki (e.g., dependencies in the data model). Fourth, by starting with a small set of attributes that are read from hosts, the lightweight approach of using a platform that allows to dynamically extend the data model was validated.

5.2. Infrastructure Monitoring Component

Monitoring computer infrastructures (i.e., hosts, and services) for availability and correct functioning is imperative when providing IT services. Monitoring applications, which periodically send requests to, and process answers from services and systems help IT administrators to ensure the correct functioning of services and systems by generating alerts if errors are encountered.

The Infrastructure Monitoring Component described in this section is an extension for MediaWiki, which allows to manage an external monitoring application from within the ITSM Wiki. This frees IT administrators from having to maintain a separate infrastructure monitoring configuration apart from the information stored in the ITSM Wiki's CMDB. Furthermore, the availability of hosts and services can be tracked from within the ITSM Wiki, without the need of consulting a dedicated monitoring front-end. The work presented in this section builds on the work previously published in [KAB09a] and [KAB09b].

A high-level overview of the Infrastructure Monitoring Component described in this section is given in Figure 5.13. As can be seen in the figure, IT administrators access infrastructure monitoring information by accessing the ITSM Wiki. Within the ITSM Wiki, the Infrastructure Monitoring Component generates configuration files for the external infrastructure monitoring application. This application checks hosts and services. Upon status changes of monitored hosts and services the ITSM Wiki is updated by the Infrastructure Monitoring Component.

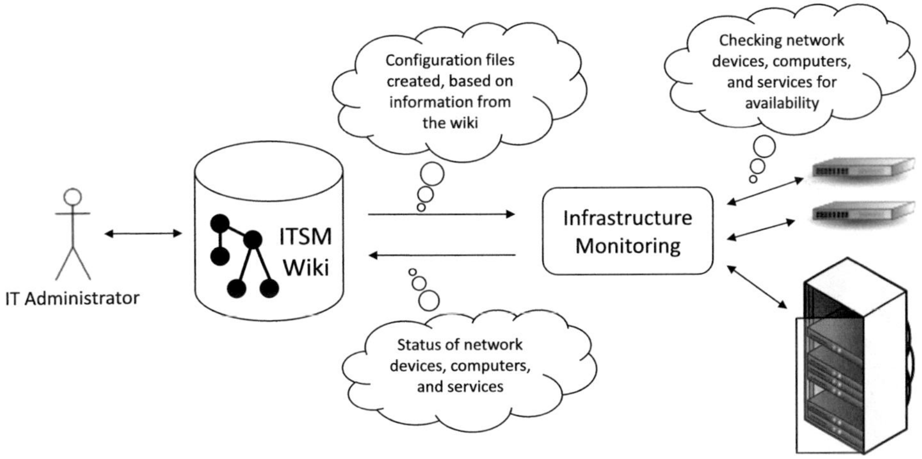

Figure 5.13.: Infrastructure Monitoring

In this section, first, the motivation for the development of the Infrastructure Monitoring Component is outlined in Section 5.2.1 (page 236). Second, the requirements for monitoring IT infrastructures from the ITSM Wiki are collected in Section 5.2.2 (page 237), followed by a description of use cases in Section 5.2.3 (page 242). Following that, relevant information for infrastructure monitoring is listed in Section 5.2.4 (page 243). After that, the Nagios infrastructure monitoring application, which is used as an external monitoring application, is described in Section 5.2.5 (page 243). Following that, the design of the Infrastructure Monitoring Component is described in Section 5.2.6 (page 249), followed by a description of the Infrastructure Monitoring Ontology in Section 5.2.7 (page 251). After that, the implementation of the Infrastructure Monitoring Component is presented in Section 5.2.8 (page 256), followed by a presentation of how infrastructure monitoring information is represented in the ITSM Wiki in Section 5.2.9 (page 259). Section 5.2.10 (page 261) concludes with an overview of prior work.

5.2.1. Motivation

Before the introduction of the semantic wiki-based Infrastructure Monitoring Component, the Nagios infrastructure monitoring application [Bar05,Nag11a] was in productive use at FZI for more than four years. Grown from the necessity of monitoring essential infrastructure services (e.g., mail servers, and Web servers) for availability, it has since then transformed into a setup that monitors more than two hundred hosts and more than nine hundred services. Monitored hosts are mainly servers and virtual servers, network equipment (e.g., network switches, and wireless access points), as well as networking-enabled printers and other devices. Nagios is described in detail in Section 5.2.5 (page 243).

Before introducing the Infrastructure Monitoring Component, the configuration of hosts, host groups, services, service groups, as well as the dependencies between different hosts and services was configured by editing text-based configuration files. At the time of designing the semantic wiki-based Infrastructure Monitoring Component, the manually maintained Nagios configuration files exhibited the following properties:

- 225 individual hosts
- 31 types of hosts
- 913 services
- 20 types of services

The manual maintenance of the text-based configuration files brought with it the following disadvantages:

- The maintenance of the configuration files by the use of a text editor was cumbersome and required the understanding of the configuration file syntax. Learning the basic syntax and being able to apply the knowledge in order to perform changes to existing configuration files required about one day for a person new to the Nagios software. Extending the Nagios configuration or creating a Nagios configuration from scratch required a deeper understanding, which required more extensive study of the Nagios documentation.

- Information about hosts, services and their dependencies was documented mainly in a (non-semantic) wiki, partly in a specialized CMDB software, and partly in a Microsoft Excel spreadsheet. This led to duplicate information, which had to be kept in sync manually.

- The manual editing of the configuration files was error-prone, due to manual labor. This potentially leads to wrong configurations of the infrastructure monitoring application.

Based on these observed shortcomings, a requirements analysis was performed in order to gather the requirements for an integrated management solution for infrastructure monitoring. The finding of this analysis is presented in the following subsection.

From the ITIL perspective, the Infrastructure Monitoring Component integrates the Event Management process into the ITSM Wiki (see the ITIL Service Operation processes described in Section 2.2.4, page 43). Further processes that are covered by the Infrastructure Monitoring Component are Service Reporting, and Service Measurement (see the Continual Service Improvement processes described in Section 2.2.5, page 54).

5.2.2. Requirements Analysis

After the shortcomings of the situation before the introduction of the Infrastructure Monitoring Component, as well as the resulting motivation for its development were described in the previous subsection, this subsection outlines the requirements. First, the methodological approach for the development of the component is given, followed by a presentation of the vision and goals, as well as a discussion of the constraints of the component. After that, the system boundaries and the requirements are described.

The results of the requirements validation are presented in Section 6.1 (page 318).

Methodological Approach

Starting from the realization that manual editing of configuration files has the previously outlined disadvantages, the requirements for a tool for improving the management of infrastructure monitoring were collected. The procedures for analyzing the requirements for the Infrastructure Monitoring Component follow the method described in [Bal09].

Before starting work on the design and implementation, a requirements analysis was performed, which included the explicit formulation of the Infrastructure Monitoring Component's vision and goals, its constraints and system boundaries, as well as its requirements.

Vision and Goals

The vision and goals for the Infrastructure Monitoring Component are motivated mostly by the shortcomings experienced when manually keeping up to date the text-based configuration files of the Nagios infrastructure monitoring application. The use case is the IT infrastructure environment at FZI Research Center for Information Technology, which is described in Section 3.1 (page 82).

Vision The vision for the Infrastructure Monitoring Component can be described as follows:

To design and implement a tool, which simplifies the management of infrastructure monitoring information by enabling the re-use of existing information (V-H01).

Goals The goals, which refine the vision of the Infrastructure Monitoring Component, can be summarized as follows:

- Reduce the need for keeping and maintaining duplicate information in the context of infrastructure monitoring (G-H01).
- Lower the learning curve for users who are new to applying changes to infrastructure monitoring (G-H02).
- Avoid the error-prone manual editing of infrastructure monitoring configuration files (G-H03).
- Integrate infrastructure monitoring with Configuration Management, Change Management, and documentation into a unified user interface (G-H04).
- Make use of existing information about hardware, software, and services, as well as their dependencies (G-H05).
- Make 'intelligent' use of existing information for the purposes of infrastructure monitoring. Information that is implicitly known to the system should not have to be entered again if it can be derived from other information stored in the ITSM Wiki (G-H06).

After determining the vision and goals for the Infrastructure Monitoring Component, the constraints were collected.

Constraints

The following paragraphs describe the organizational, technical and development environment constraints for the Infrastructure Monitoring Component.

Organizational Constraints The organizational constraints for the Infrastructure Monitoring Component are as follows:

- The Infrastructure Monitoring Component is used by the members of the IT department, who are responsible for running systems and services.

Technical Constraints (Server) The technical constraints for the server are as follows:

- The Infrastructure Monitoring Component is a part of the ITSM Wiki, which is realized by using the MediaWiki software. MediaWiki is extensible by programming against an API (for more information about extending MediaWiki, please see Section 4.1.3, page 122).
- Semantic MediaWiki is used by the Infrastructure Monitoring Component in order to store explicit information about monitored systems and services.
- MediaWiki and Semantic MediaWiki are programmed in the PHP language [Med11a], which imposes the technical constraints of also using this language on the Infrastructure Monitoring Component.
- MediaWiki runs on Web servers, which allow the execution of PHP scripts. Most often, the LAMP platform is used for running MediaWiki.
- The Infrastructure Monitoring Component accesses MediaWiki by using documented API calls. With respect to the database system, all databases that are supported by MediaWiki are also supported by the Infrastructure Monitoring Component.
- The monitoring of systems and services is accomplished by using the Nagios infrastructure monitoring application, which is available for UNIX-based operating systems[16]. Because the Infrastructure Monitoring Component writes configuration files for the use by Nagios, it has to have access to the Nagios configuration directory. More information about Nagios can be found in Section 5.2.5 (page 243).

Technical Constraints (Client) The ITSM Wiki in general and the Infrastructure Monitoring Component in particular are accessed by using a Web browser. As long as a browser that complies with current Web standards is available, any device and operating system can be used.

Development Environment Constraints About the development environment constraints, it can be said that the use of a simple text editor is sufficient, although ease of use can be gained by reverting to specialized PHP programming environments.

[16]Nagios system requirements: `http://nagios.sourceforge.net/docs/3_0/about.html`

System Boundaries

In Figure 5.14, the systems boundaries of the Infrastructure Monitoring Component, as well as the components that make up the system, are visualized. The graph is inspired by the graph found in [Bal09, page 462].

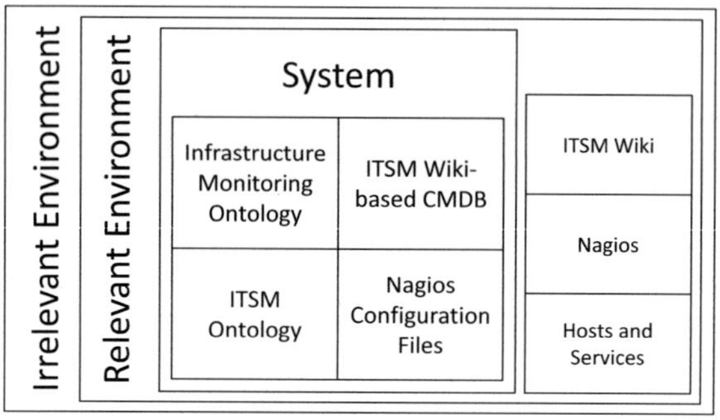

Figure 5.14.: System Boundaries of the Infrastructure Monitoring Component

System The following parts belong to the system of the Infrastructure Monitoring Component:

- *Infrastructure Monitoring Ontology:* The Infrastructure Monitoring Ontology models all classes and properties, which are relevant to infrastructure monitoring.
- *ITSM Ontology:* Classes and properties of the core ITSM parts are modeled in the ITSM Ontology, as described in Section 4.3.4 (page 167).
- *ITSM Wiki-based CMDB:* The ITSM Wiki-based CMDB contains the configuration items and their dependencies. This information forms the foundation, from which Nagios configuration files are created.
- *Nagios configuration files:* The Nagios configuration files are generated from explicit and implicit information stored in the ITSM Wiki.

Relevant Environment The relevant environment consists of elements that are not by themselves considered parts of the Infrastructure Monitoring Component, but which interact with it on a regular basis. Parts of the relevant environment are:

- *ITSM Wiki:* The ITSM Wiki, which includes all the information that is relevant for providing IT services, is accessed by the Infrastructure Monitoring Component in order to get information about configuration items and their dependencies.

- *Nagios infrastructure monitoring application:* The Nagios infrastructure monitoring application is used by the Infrastructure Monitoring Component in order to achieve the actual task of checking hosts and services. It uses the configuration files created by the Infrastructure Monitoring Component.

- *Monitored hosts and services:* The hosts and services, which are monitored by the Infrastructure Monitoring Component, are also part of the relevant environment.

Requirements

The next two paragraphs outline the functional and non-functional requirements for the Infrastructure Monitoring Component.

Functional Requirements The functional requirements for the Infrastructure Monitoring Component are defined in the following list. The component should provide mechanisms for executing the following actions:

- Add new hosts and services to infrastructure monitoring from within the ITSM Wiki (R-H01).

- Apply changes to existing host and service monitoring settings from within the ITSM Wiki (R-H02).

- Allow the specification of which services are run on which hosts (R-H03).

- Define who is responsible for which hosts and services and how the responsible person can be contacted (R-H04).

- Model the dependencies between various hosts and services (e.g., the mail service depends on a functioning mail server) (R-H05).

- Define which protocols and ports are used for which service (e.g., port 80 and protocol HTTP for a Web server) (R-H06).

- Specify how often a host or service has to be checked (e.g., once a minute, or once every 10 min) (R-H07).

- Define the time periods in which the service has to be checked (e.g., business hours, weekdays, or 24x7) (R-H08).

Non-functional Requirements The non-functional requirements of the Infrastructure Monitoring Component are:

- The component has to be integrated into the ITSM Wiki.
- Consistency checks within the Infrastructure Monitoring Component have to make sure that only valid changes can be applied (e.g., it has to be made sure that hosts, on which services depend, have been modeled in the ITSM Wiki, before writing the information to Nagios configuration files).
- Changes, including the necessary consistency checks, have to be performed in a time span that is acceptable to the user of the component (i.e., in less than 10 s).
- The component should not make necessary changes to the code base of Nagios, MediaWiki, or Semantic MediaWiki.

5.2.3. Use Cases

This subsection shows a number of use cases in order to present the purpose and the benefits of the Infrastructure Monitoring Component.

Integration of Monitoring into the ITSM Platform

Information about the availability of hosts and services is integrated into the ITSM Wiki. This allows IT administrators to use the ITSM Wiki as a unified interface for accessing infrastructure monitoring information together with both structured, as well as unstructured information (e.g., the software running on a computer, as well as a free-text description of a computer's purpose).

Reporting and Ad-hoc Queries

The Nagios infrastructure monitoring application provides a Web-based interface, in which the status of hosts and services can be displayed. The configuration of hosts and services, however is done in text-based configuration files, which is relatively static. By using Semantic MediaWiki's query mechanism, generating reports is simplified, and ad-hoc queries are possible (e.g., display all Linux hosts that do not reply to ping requests and which belong to a particular department).

Providing Monitoring Information to Other Components

Other components, which integrate into the ITSM Wiki, can make use of information that is provided by the Infrastructure Monitoring Component. For example, the Incident and Problem Analyzer Component, which is presented in Section 5.4 (page 284), can use information about a host's downtime for tracking down the cause of incidents and problems.

5.2.4. Relevant Information

Relevant information with respect to infrastructure monitoring is as follows:

- Host names and IP addresses
- Information about network connections
- Services running on hosts
- Dependencies between hosts and network equipment
- Dependencies between services
- User groups
- Time and time periods

5.2.5. The Nagios Infrastructure Monitoring Application

IT infrastructures consist of different components, which interact with each other in order to provide services to customers. Making sure that all components function correctly is imperative for providing reliable services.

IT infrastructure monitoring is the discipline that deals with automatically checking the correct functioning of hosts and services, the functioning of connections between hosts, and the compliance with Service Level Agreements (SLAs). There exist several different software products, which realize infrastructure monitoring. A comparison of IT infrastructure monitoring applications can be found in [Wik11].

One of the most widely used infrastructure monitoring applications is the open source software Nagios[17] [Bar05]. Nagios helps IT administrators to provide reliable services by implementing mechanisms for automatically checking hosts and services against given requirements (e.g., availability, response time, or free memory). Nagios allows to notify IT administrators about failed hosts and services via e-mail and other notification methods (e.g., SMS, or pager). This allows IT administrators to initiate mitigation

[17] `http://www.nagios.org/`

measures if a host or service enters a status, which endangers meeting SLAs or stops responding at all.

In Nagios, the availability of monitored hosts is checked by sending periodical ICMP *ping* requests (cp. [Pos81]) over the network and checking if a reply is received. Services are checked by sending service-specific requests to the respective service (e.g., HTTP requests to a Web server application) and checking the reply for status codes (cp. [FGM$^+$99, pages 57–71] and [Ste93, pages 69–96]).

While Nagios is configured by using text-based configuration files, it provides a Web-based front-end for viewing the status of monitored hosts and services. Moreover, hosts and services can be listed based on several different criteria. Furthermore, an availability history of hosts and services can be displayed.

In Figure 5.15, it is shown how Nagios represents a map of the network. The purpose of this map is to give IT administrators a quick overview about the status of hosts and services in a corporate network. In the center of the diagram, the Nagios process is shown, which monitors the availability of all the other hosts and services shown in the diagram. Dependencies between hosts are represented by lines between the hosts. Hosts can form hierarchies, e.g., a host can be connected to a network switch. Each host contains an icon, which gives more information about its type (e.g., whether it is a network router, or a Linux host). In addition, the name of each host is listed. The background of each host is colored depending on its availability status (available hosts are represented with a green (bright) background, while unavailable hosts are represented with a red (dark) background).

Figure 5.16 shows an overview of monitored hosts. Hosts without problems are displayed in green (bright), while hosts that experience problems are displayed in red (dark). The status of the host list is determined using the ICMP ping request mechanism. A similar status report is available for monitored services.

Technical Background There exist three methods supported by Nagios that differ in which aspects of an IT infrastructure can be monitored. The methods are as follows:

- *ICMP Echo-Request:* The simplest form of monitoring is checking a host for availability by sending an ICMP Echo-Request packet and waiting for an ICMP Echo-Reply packet (generally known as sending a *ping* to a host) [Pos81]. While this is usually sufficient for checking if a host is reachable via the network, the monitoring of services requires further checks. Furthermore, responses to ICMP requests contain only little information about the status of a host (e.g., no information about the amount of free RAM, or the host's CPU load is provided). Only in extreme conditions, slow ICMP response times can indicate resource problems on a host.

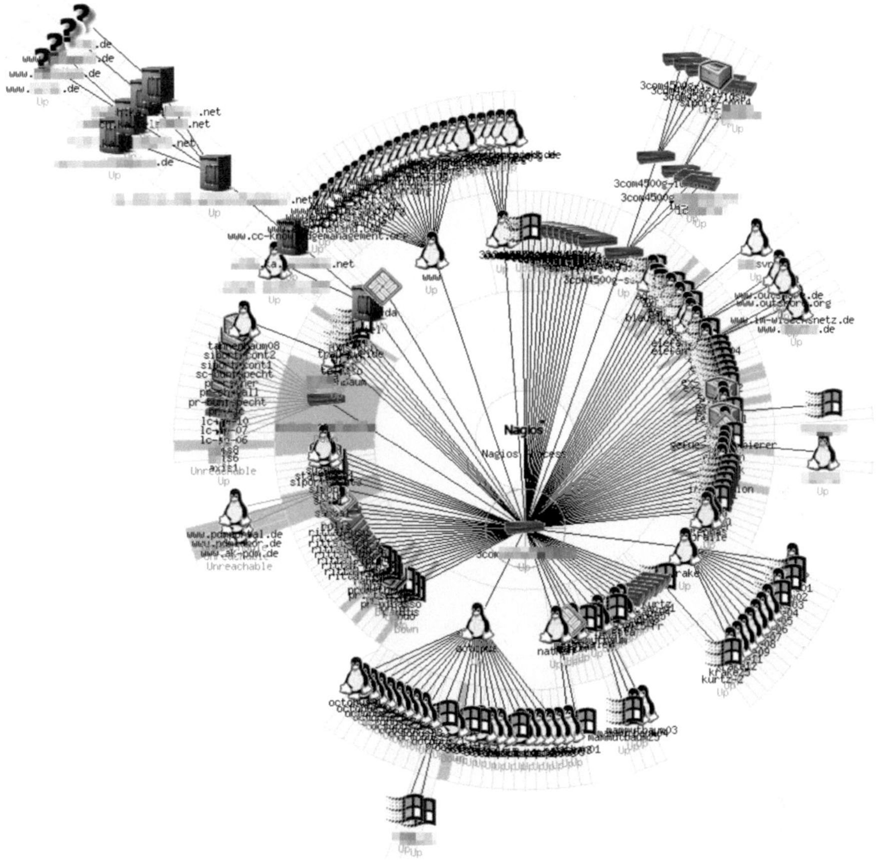

Figure 5.15.: Nagios Status Map

- *Check a service for the correct answer:* In order to monitor a service, an infrastructure monitoring application has to understand the protocol, which is used for providing a service. For example, in order to monitor a Web server, the monitoring application connects to the server and downloads a Web page by using the hypertext transfer protocol (HTTP) [FGM+99]. While this exceeds the possibilities of the ICMP requests, the limitations concerning the abilities to read a host's internal resource situation remain.

- *Read information from an agent:* If the inner status of the host has to be monitored, an agent must be installed on the host. This agent constitutes a software application, which is able to access the relevant information (e.g., free memory, free hard disk space, or CPU load) and makes the information available to the monitoring

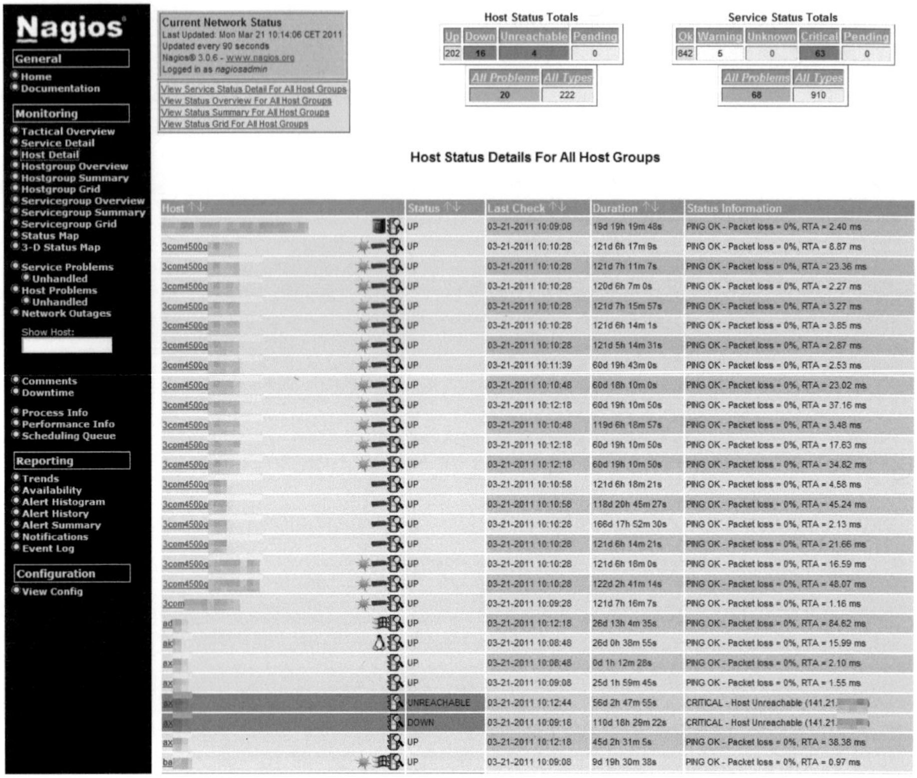

Figure 5.16.: Overview of Hosts in the Nagios Web Interface

application. While this approach offers the most in-depth view of the host's status, it is limited by the availability of agent software for the monitored operating system and hardware (for example, it is generally not possible to run monitoring agent software on network switches). Moreover, deploying and keeping agents up to date can be cumbersome.

While the Infrastructure Monitoring Component is restricted to the first two methods, this is not a limitation of the component, but rather founded in the requirements of the environment for which the component was developed.

Structure of Nagios Configuration Files

The Nagios infrastructure monitoring application is configured through the use of text files. Listing 5.3 shows an excerpt from a configuration file in order to give an impression of the Nagios configuration file syntax.

Listing 5.3: Nagios Service Definition

```
define service {
  use basic-service
  display_name HTTP
  service_description http-service
  notification_interval 0
  contact_groups system-admins, web-admins
  notification_options c,r
  notification_period 24x7
  check_command check_http
  register 1
}
```

The configuration file excerpt shows the definition of a service, namely the HTTP service. In the excerpt, the following information is provided:

- The name of the service template that is used by the service.
- The display name and the description of the service.
- How often additional notifications should be sent for services that are unavailable (in this case, no additional notifications are sent after the first unavailability notification).
- The Nagios groups that should be contacted if a change in the state of the service is detected.
- Which types of notifications should be sent (in this case, critical messages and recovery messages).
- At which times messages should be send (in this case, 24x7).
- Which command is used to check the service. The command is a link to a program that can use a certain protocol (in this case HTTP) in order to communicate with the service.

In addition to the definition of services, as shown in the configuration file excerpt, there are mechanisms for defining other aspects of Nagios (e.g., defining contacts, groups of contacts, hosts, and groups of hosts). Figure 5.17 shows the dependencies between the different Nagios configuration files. More information about the configuration of the Nagios monitoring application can be found in [Bar05] and [Gal08].

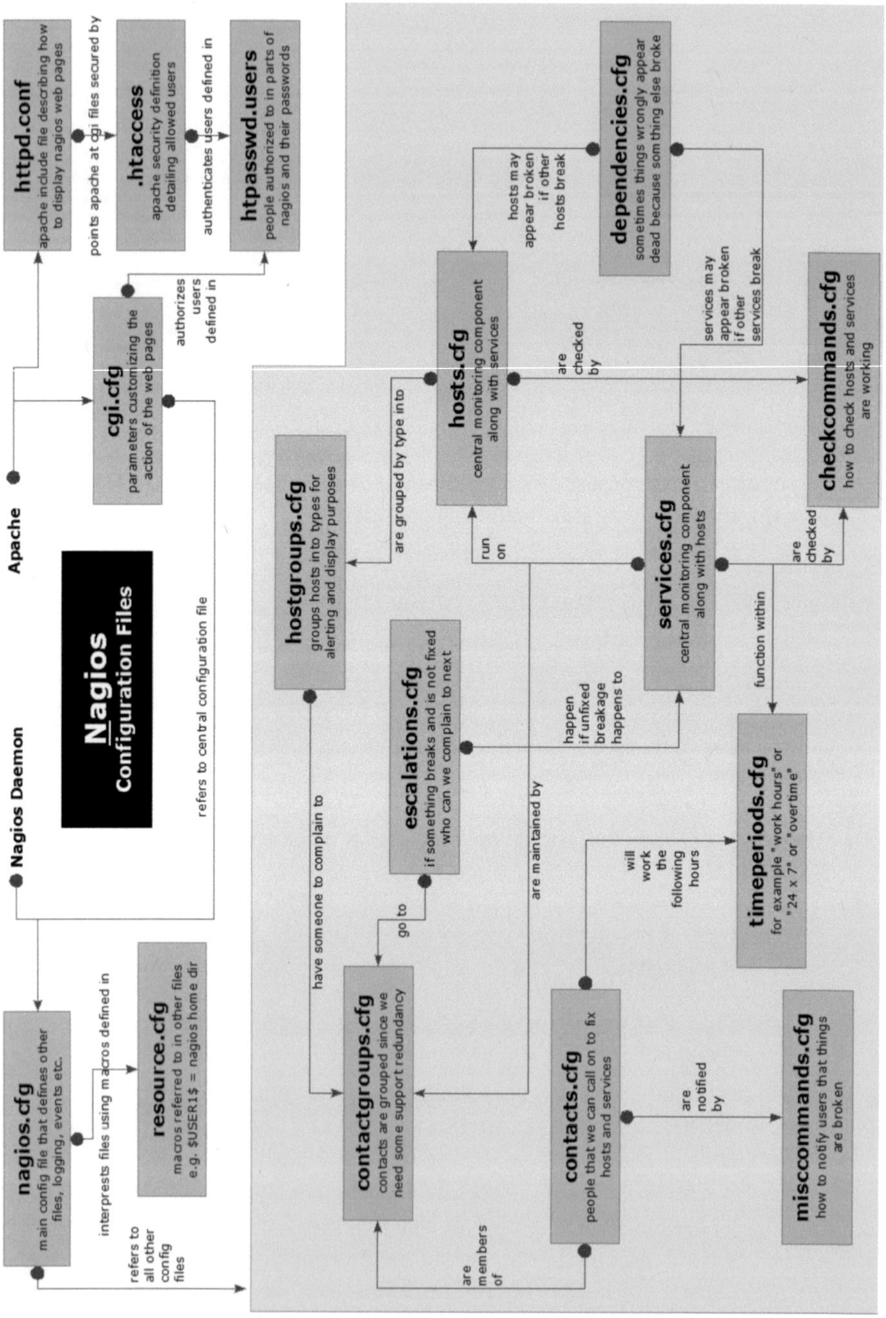

Figure 5.17.: Dependencies between Nagios Configuration Files (Source: [Nag10])

5.2.6. Design of the Infrastructure Monitoring Component

Based on the findings of the requirements analysis that was described in Section 5.2.2 (page 237), and the interface provided by the Nagios infrastructure monitoring application (see Section 5.2.5, page 243), an extension was designed. This extension enables the management of infrastructure monitoring information from within the ITSM Wiki.

One of the design requirements was to avoid changes to the code of the underlying Nagios application in order to simplify future updates of Nagios. Due to Nagios' high amount of configurability through text files, this goal was achieved. Another requirement was to avoid changes to the Semantic MediaWiki and MediaWiki source code. This was made possible due to MediaWiki's architecture, which allows the integration of extensions (see Section 4.1.3, page 122 and Section 4.1.3, page 124).

In Figure 5.18, the different layers of infrastructure monitoring are shown. The layers are as follows:

- *Real world (bottom):* The bottom layer represents the real world, i.e., the physical and logical computers, network equipment, as well as connections between physical and logical entities (e.g., cables, or virtual network connections).
- *Nagios (middle):* The middle layer is a representation of the monitored infrastructure as viewed by the Nagios infrastructure monitoring application. Hosts, services, and dependencies are configured in textual configuration files. Information about the current state of the infrastructure can be accessed via a Web-based interface. Furthermore, changes in the state of the infrastructure are send via e-mail to addresses, which are defined in the configuration files.
- *Semantic wiki (top):* The semantic wiki layer is shown on top of the Nagios layer. The layer contains a standard MediaWiki setup, with a Web server and a database server, on which MediaWiki and Semantic MediaWiki are run. In addition, Semantic Forms and the Infrastructure Monitoring Component are installed as extensions. All infrastructure monitoring tasks are left to the Nagios tool, which monitors the correct working of computers, services and network equipment. Because the Infrastructure Monitoring Component is realized as a MediaWiki extension, MediaWiki's underlying mechanisms for storing and accessing data can be used. Furthermore, information about configuration items, which is already present in the ITSM Wiki (e.g., computers, their IP addresses, and their owners) can be re-used by the Infrastructure Monitoring Component.

Four requirements for the semantic wiki layer were identified. The requirements are:

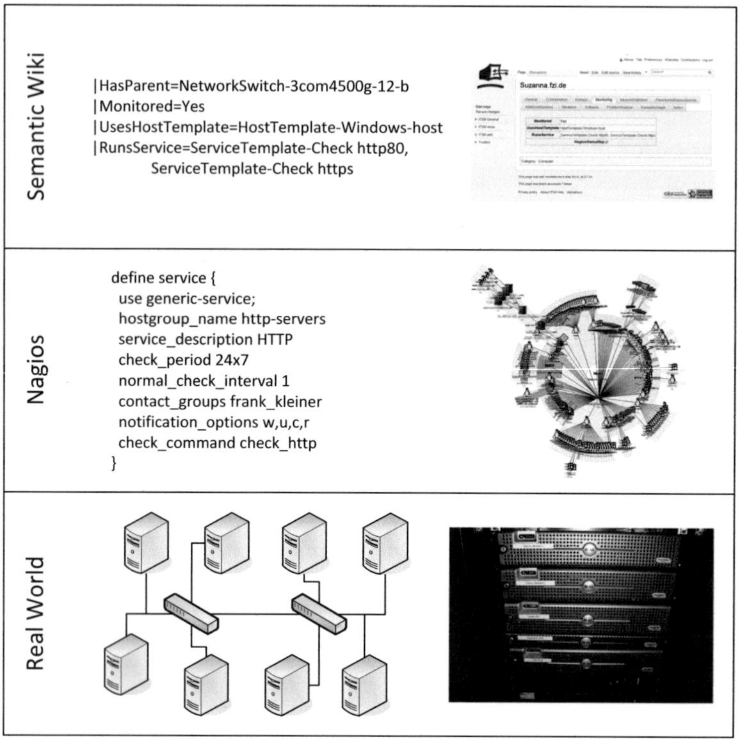

Figure 5.18.: Layers of Infrastructure Monitoring

- By providing a more convenient mechanism for editing Nagios configurations, the maintenance of the infrastructure monitoring configuration is simplified.
- Information that is expressed in the semantic wiki layer has to be in a format that can be automatically processed.
- Information has to be editable collaboratively in order to allow the configuration of Nagios by a team of IT administrators.
- The language, which is used for describing the infrastructure, has to be able to describe complex scenarios. An example of a complex scenario is a computer network with various networking components, servers, and services, which have dependencies between each other.

The analysis of the four requirements showed that they can be fulfilled by the mechanisms provided by a semantic wiki. In order to access the Nagios infrastructure monitoring application, an extension for MediaWiki had to be implemented. The implementation is described in detail in Section 5.2.8 (page 256).

While initial approaches of managing infrastructure monitoring information in Semantic MediaWiki were performed by directly editing wikitext [KAB09b, KAB09a], this approach proved to be too cumbersome in most cases. Due to these observations, configurations for the Semantic Forms extension were created, which allow the editing of the monitoring information in a more convenient environment. Features of Semantic Forms, which are used in the Infrastructure Monitoring Component are auto-completion, drop-down lists populated from class hierarchies, and checkboxes. For an analysis of usability aspects with regard to the manual editing of wikitext on the one hand, and of using Semantic Forms on the other hand, please see Section 4.2.6 (page 159).

5.2.7. Infrastructure Monitoring Ontology

The data model that is used in the Infrastructure Monitoring Component is an ontology. While the ITSM Ontology, which is the data model for the core ITSM classes and properties, is described in Section 4.3.4 (page 167), this subsection describes the parts of the ontology that are relevant to the Infrastructure Monitoring Component.

First, a graphical representation of the class hierarchy of the Infrastructure Monitoring Ontology is shown. Second, the classes, object properties, and data properties are described. Third, exemplary instances and a short description are given for each class.

Class Hierarchy

Figure 5.19 shows the class hierarchy of the Infrastructure Monitoring Ontology. All classes are subclasses of the *Thing* class. Class hierarchies are expressed with the *is-a* property.

Classes, Object Properties, and Data Properties

Table 5.3 shows the classes, object properties, and data properties of the Infrastructure Monitoring Ontology. Classes and properties that are printed in boldface type are the ones that are used actively by the Infrastructure Monitoring Component.

Descriptions and Exemplary Instances

Section 4.3.4 (page 173) presents descriptions for the classes of the Infrastructure Monitoring Ontology, as well as exemplary instances for each class. The presentation in a single table is done in order to avoid unnecessary duplication of information.

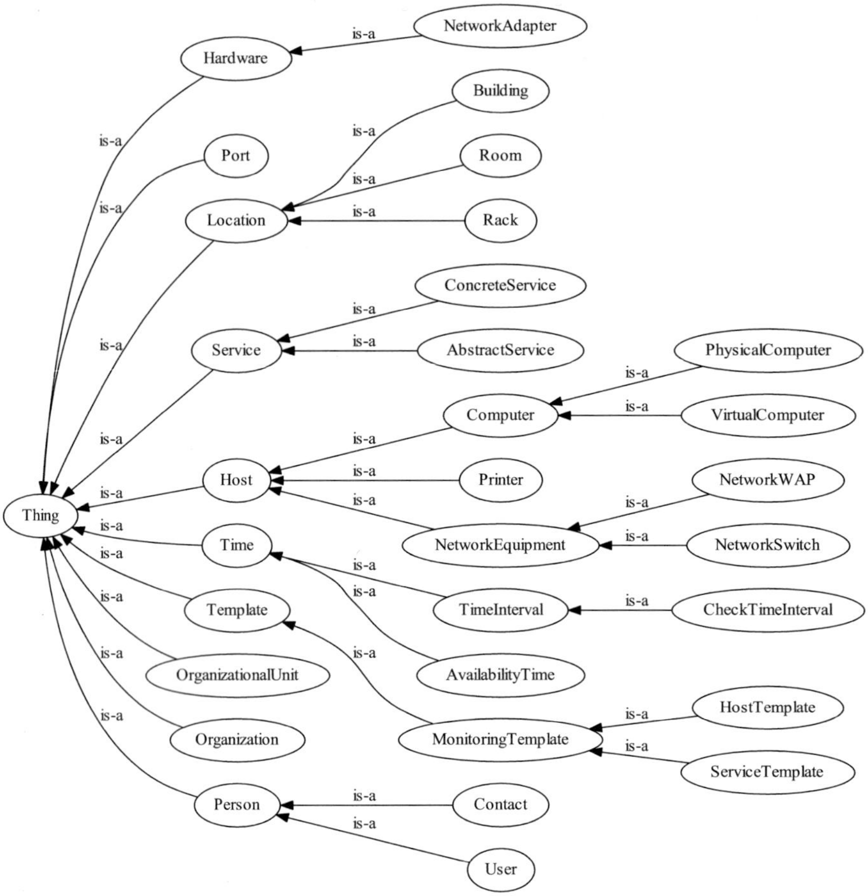

Figure 5.19.: Class Hierarchy of the Infrastructure Monitoring Ontology

Table 5.3.: Infrastructure Monitoring Ontology

Domain Class	Property	Range
AbstractService	*inherited from Service class* **consistsOfService** {0..n}	 Service
AccountStatusType	*inherited from Type class*	*no additional properties*
AvailabilityTime	*inherited from Time class* **MonitoringStatement** {0..1}	 <Text>

(*table continues*)

Table 5.3.: Infrastructure Monitoring Ontology (continued)

Domain Class	**Property**	**Range**
Building	*inherited from Location class*	
	City {0..1}	<String>
	Street {0..1}	<String>
	ZipCode {0..1}	<String>
CheckTimeInterval	*inherited from TimeInterval class*	
	MonitoringStatement {0..1}	<Text>
Computer	*inherited from Host class*	
	LastDomainConnectDate {0..1}	<Date>
	MemberOfWindowsDomain {0..1}	<Boolean>
	OperatingSystemInstallationDate {0..1}	<Date>
	hasComputerUsageType {0..1}	ComputerUsageType
	hasLocalAdministrator {0..n}	Contact, User
ConcreteService	*inherited from Service class*	
	usesServiceTemplate {0..1}	ServiceTemplate
Contact	*inherited from Person class*	*no additional properties*
Hardware	*inherited from Thing class*	
	Model {0..1}	<String>
	ProductNumber {0..1}	<String>
	SerialNumber {0..1}	<String>
	hasManufacturer {0..1}	Organization
	hasVendor {0..1}	Organization
	isCompatibleWith {0..n}	Thing
	isIncompatibleWith {0..n}	Thing
Host	*inherited from Thing class*	
	Model {0..1}	<String>
	Monitored {0..1}	<Boolean>
	MonitoringIssue {0..1}	<Boolean>
	ProductNumber {0..1}	<String>
	SerialNumber {0..1}	<String>
	hasCommissioningStatusType {0..1}	CommissioningStatusType
	hasContactPerson {0..n}	Person
	hasInstalledHardware {0..n}	Hardware
	hasInstalledSoftware {0..n}	Software
	hasManufacturer {0..1}	Organization
	hasOwner {0..1}	Person
	hasParent {0..1}	Host
	hasVendor {0..1}	Organization
	isLocatedIn {0..1}	Location
	runsService {0..n}	ConcreteService
	usesHostTemplate {0..1}	HostTemplate
HostTemplate	*inherited from MonitoringTemplate class*	*no additional properties*
Location	*inherited from Thing class*	*no additional properties*
MonitoringTemplate	*inherited from Template class*	
	MonitoringStatement {0..1}	<Text>

(table continues)

Table 5.3.: Infrastructure Monitoring Ontology (continued)

Domain Class	**Property**	**Range**
NetworkAdapter	*inherited from Hardware class*	
	ConnectionSpeed {0..1}	<Quantity>
	IPv4Address {0..1}	<String>
	IPv4DefaultGateway {0..1}	<String>
	IPv4DHCPEnabled {0..1}	<Boolean>
	IPv4DHCPServer {0..1}	<String>
	IPv4DNSServer {0..n}	<String>
	IPv4SubnetMask {0..1}	<String>
	IPv6Address {0..1}	<String>
	IPv6DefaultGateway {0..1}	<String>
	IPv6DNSServer {0..n}	<String>
	MACAddress {0..1}	<String>
	hasConnectionType {0..1}	ConnectionType
	hasNetworkAdapterType {0..1}	NetworkAdapterType
	hasNetworkConnectionTo {0..1}	NetworkAdapter
	isPartOfNetworkSegment {0..1}	NetworkSegment
NetworkEquipment	*inherited from Host class*	
	supportsNetworkAdapterType {0..1}	NetworkAdapterType
NetworkSwitch	*inherited from NetworkEquipment class*	*no additional properties*
NetworkWAP	*inherited from NetworkEquipment class*	*no additional properties*
Organization	*inherited from Thing class*	
	City {0..1}	<String>
	Country {0..1}	<String>
	EMailAddress {0..1}	<String>
	FaxNumber {0..1}	<String>
	PhoneNumber {0..1}	<String>
	Street {0..1}	<String>
	WebPage {0..1}	<String>
	ZipCode {0..1}	<String>
OrganizationalUnit	*inherited from Thing class*	
	hasDeputyManager {0..n}	<Person>
	hasITContact {0..n}	<Person>
	hasManager {0..n}	<Person>
	isPartOfOrganization {0..1}	Organization
	isPartOfOrganizationalUnit {0..1}	OrganizationalUnit

(*table continues*)

Table 5.3.: Infrastructure Monitoring Ontology (continued)

Domain Class	**Property**	**Range**
Person	*inherited from Thing class*	
	EMailAddress {0..n}	<Email>
	FamilyName {0..1}	<String>
	FaxNumber {0..n}	<Telephone number>
	GivenName {0..1}	<String>
	JobTitle {0..1}	<String>
	PhoneNumber {0..n}	<Telephone number>
	hasKnowledgeDomain {0..n}	KnowledgeDomain
	hasManager {0..1}	Person
	hasOffice {0..1}	Room
	hasRole {0..n}	Role
	isMemberOfOrganization {0..n}	Organization
	isMemberOfOrganizationalUnit {0..n}	OrganizationalUnit
PhysicalComputer	*inherited from Computer class*	
	hasComputerFormFactorType {0..1}	ComputerFormFactorType
Port	*inherited from Thing class*	
	Port {0..1}	<Number>
	Protocol {0..1}	<String>
Printer	*inherited from Host class*	*no additional properties*
Rack	*inherited from Location class*	
	Height {0..1}	<Quantity>
	isLocatedInRoom {0..1}	Room
Room	*inherited from Location class*	
	isLocatedInBuilding {0..1}	Building
Service	*inherited from Thing class*	
	hasOwner {0..1}	Person
ServiceTemplate	*inherited from MonitoringTemplate class*	
	runsOnPort {0..1}	Port
Template	*inherited from Thing class*	*no additional properties*
Thing	Description {0..1}	<Text>
	Name {1}	<String>
	Version {0..1}	<Number>
	hasDependency {0..n}	Thing
	hasParent {0..n}	Thing
	isConnectedTo {0..n}	Thing
	isRelatedTo {0..n}	Thing
Time	*inherited from Thing class*	*no additional properties*
TimeInterval	*inherited from Time class*	*no additional properties*

(*table continues*)

Table 5.3.: Infrastructure Monitoring Ontology (continued)

Domain Class	Property	Range
User	*inherited from Person class*	
	CreationDate {0..1}	<Date>
	DeletionDate {0..1}	<Date>
	LastLoginDate {0..1}	<Date>
	LoginName {0..1}	<String>
	UniqueIdentifier {0..1}	<String>
	hasAccountStatusType {0..1}	AccountStatusType
VirtualComputer	*inherited from Computer class*	*no additional properties*

5.2.8. Implementation

Figure 5.20 shows the interactions between different parts of the Infrastructure Monitoring Component. As can be seen in the figure, the Infrastructure Monitoring Component is located above a stack of the components MediaWiki, Semantic MediaWiki, and Semantic Forms. Within the Infrastructure Monitoring Component, the export subcomponent is responsible for transforming information about infrastructure monitoring into valid Nagios configuration files. The external Nagios infrastructure monitoring application monitors hosts and services and notifies the contacts, which are defined in the wiki, via e-mail. The notification subcomponent gets information from the external Nagios application and writes information back into the ITSM Wiki in Semantic MediaWiki syntax.

Subcomponents

The Infrastructure Monitoring Component consists of two subcomponents, which are described in the following paragraphs. First, the export subcomponent is described, followed by a description of the notification subcomponent.

Export Subcomponent The export subcomponent is responsible for transforming the information, which is relevant to infrastructure monitoring, from the internal Semantic MediaWiki and Semantic Forms format to the Nagios configuration file format. Dependencies between hosts and services, which are expressed as semantic relations within the ITSM Wiki, are exported to Nagios configuration file syntax. The export process has to make sure that the Nagios configuration files stay in a valid state in order to prevent Nagios from not being able to start after applying the new configuration.

The translation process from SMW syntax to Nagios syntax works as shown in Algorithm 5.4. When a page is saved, it is checked if information about infrastructure

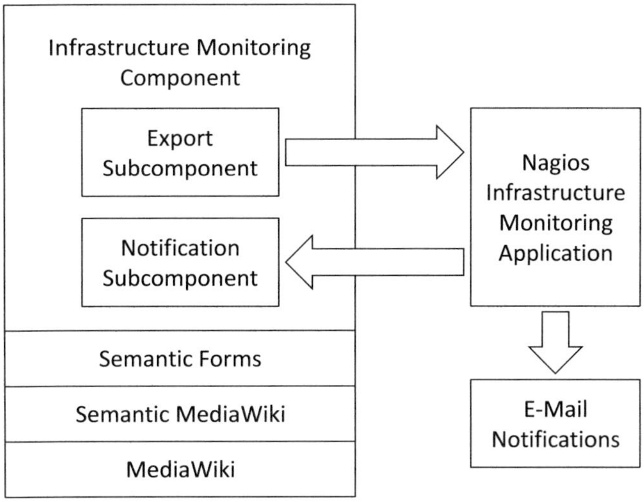

Figure 5.20.: Interactions between Parts of the Infrastructure Monitoring Component

monitoring is included in the page. If this is the case, a check is performed whether adding the information from the page would result in a valid Nagios configuration. If this is also the case, a Nagios configuration file entry is generated and Nagios is restarted.

After restarting Nagios, a list of previously unsatisfied dependencies is checked. If any of the list entries is now in a state that allows it to be added to the Nagios configuration, this is done, and Nagios is restarted. This is done as long as new dependencies can be added to the Nagios configuration.

If adding the edited page would result in an invalid Nagios configuration, there can be two reasons: The first reason is that the edited page is valid but that dependencies exist, which cannot be satisfied. In this case, a warning is added to the page, and the page is added to the list of unsatisfied dependencies. This list is then processed by the save action of other pages in order to check if the editing resolved the unsatisfied dependency. The second reason is that the page in itself has an error. If this is the case, a warning is shown, and the error has to be resolved before the page can be saved.

Notification Subcomponent The notification subcomponent is responsible for writing information about status changes of monitored infrastructure components to the ITSM Wiki. For example, a server that stops replying to network packets will have its wiki page updated accordingly. Furthermore, because status messages are written into the wiki in Semantic MediaWiki format, they can be further processed by Semantic MediaWiki queries. Notifications are written to the wiki by making use of API:Edit [Med12a].

Algorithm 5.4: Export from Semantic Wiki to Nagios When a Page is Saved

---

Data: Relations in Semantic MediaWiki
Result: Nagios configuration file entries
Check if wiki page contains information relevant to infrastructure monitoring;
if *(Wiki page contains information relevant to infrastructure monitoring)* **then**
  Check if adding information results in valid Nagios configuration;
  if *(Adding of information results in valid Nagios configuration)* **then**
    Add entry to Nagios;
    Restart Nagios;
    while *(Items with previously unsatisfied dependencies result in valid configuration)* **do**
      Add missing dependencies;
      Restart Nagios;
    end
  else // Adding of information does *not* result in valid Nagios configuration
    if *(Edited page is valid)* **then**
      Add warning to wiki page;
      Add to list of unsatisfied dependencies;
    else // Errors in page
      Show warning that wiki syntax in page has errors;
    end
  end
end

Source Files

The functionality of the Infrastructure Monitoring Component is implemented in several PHP files. The component is implemented as a MediaWiki extension. The following list shows the functionalities of the individual source files:

- `ApiWrapper.php`: Implements interactions with MediaWiki instances.
- `config.inc.php`: This file stores configuration data, e.g., language settings, the user name and password used to access the wiki, the MediaWiki API URL, and Nagios settings.
- `ConfigWriter.php`: Writing of Nagios configuration files.
- `CurlWrapper.php`: This file implements a wrapper mechanism for the cURL tool, which is used to access the Semantic MediaWiki instance.
- `LanguageStrings.php`: Definition of strings for the use in forms, templates and wikitext.

- `NagiosConfig.alias.php`: Defines aliases for special pages.
- `NagiosConfig.i18n.php`: Internationalization files of the Infrastructure Monitoring Component.
- `NagiosConfig.php`: The main file of the Infrastructure Monitoring Component. This file defines, which MediaWiki mechanisms are used by the extension, and registers with the MediaWiki instance.
- `NagiosConfigGen.php`: Implements mechanisms for interacting with the MediaWiki instance (e.g., hooks for the ArticleSave and ArticleDelete functions, as well as a mechanism to initially setup the wiki for the use with the extension). Furthermore, consistency checks are performed in this file, which prevent the extension from writing invalid Nagios configurations.
- `SpecialNCAdmin.php`: Contains functions related to special pages, which are used for initially setting up the extension, as well as performing maintenance tasks (e.g., rewriting the whole Nagios configuration).
- `userconfig.inc.php`: File for placing user-specified configurations, which override default settings.
- `WebApi.php`: Functions for the manipulation of MediaWiki pages.
- `WikiFeedback.php`: This file provides functions for adding Nagios-related information to MediaWiki pages.
- `defaults/baseconf.php`: Default configuration of various Nagios settings.
- `defaults/cgi.php`: Nagios configuration file.
- `defaults/nagios.php`: Nagios configuration file.

5.2.9. Representation of Information in the Wiki

Figure 5.21 shows a screenshot of the Web-based graphical user interface of the Infrastructure Monitoring Component. As can be seen in the screenshot, Semantic Forms is used for enabling the input of structured data. Settings about infrastructure monitoring are located in the tab named *Monitoring*. A checkbox is used to specify, if the host should be monitored by Nagios. Furthermore, contact groups can be defined, which receive notifications of state changes. Services that should be monitored can be selected from a list.

In Figure 5.22, a screenshot of the host agda.fzi.de is shown. Beneath the name of the computer, a warning message that is inserted by the Infrastructure Monitoring Component, is shown. This message states that there is a problem with the host.

In this instance, it shows that the HTTPS service provided by the host is in the critical state (i.e., not available). As soon as the HTTPS service becomes available again, the message is deleted automatically by the component.

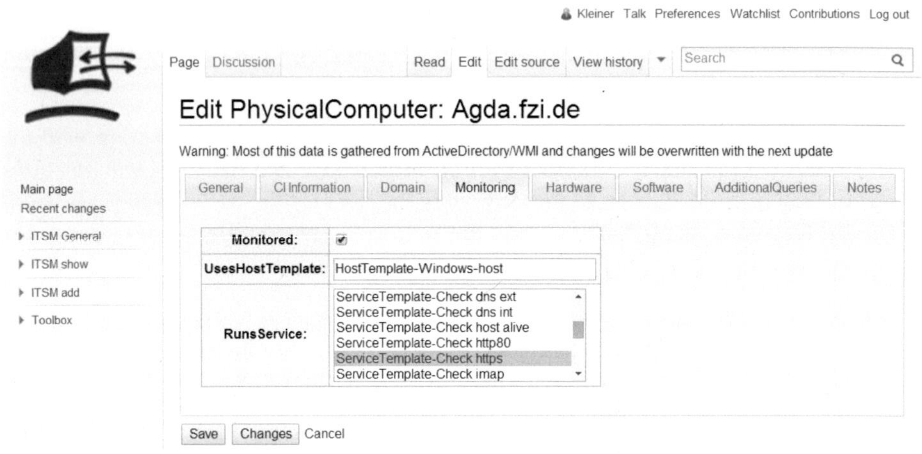

Figure 5.21.: Editing of Infrastructure Monitoring Information

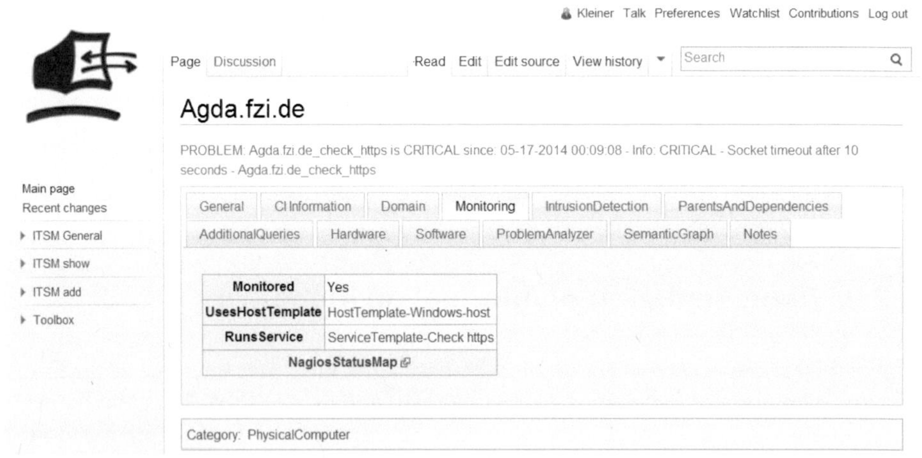

Figure 5.22.: Notification Message Indicating an Unreachable Server

Infrastructure monitoring information can be integrated into wiki pages (e.g., the main page of the wiki). This enables the ITSM Wiki to display information about wiki pages with faulty infrastructure monitoring configurations. Furthermore, hosts that have messages (for example due to not being reachable), can be shown in the Nagios status message box.

Several maintenance tasks with regard to the Infrastructure Monitoring Component can be performed from within the wiki by making use of a MediaWiki special page. Functions provided by the special page are to repair Nagios information in wiki pages and to newly generate all Nagios configuration files from information stored in the ITSM Wiki.

5.2.10. Prior and Related Work

There exist several (non-semantic) Web-based configuration front-ends for the configuration of the Nagios infrastructure monitoring application. Reference [Nag11b] presents a comprehensive list of tools.

NConf[18] is a Web-based front-end implemented in PHP, which allows the management of Nagios configurations. The ability to graphically display dependencies and the integration of templates simplifies the configuration. NConf allows the management of multiple Nagios instances [NCo09]. OneCMDB[19] is a CMDB software, which provides a mechanism for integrating Nagios [One09]. CMon[20] is a tool that works together with IBM Tivoli CCMDB and Nagios Core [Pin12]. Ignoramus[21] is another example of a Web-based Nagios configuration front-end. Monarch[22] is another example, which is part of the GroundWork Monitor project. Finally, Nagios Web Config[23] is another Web-based Nagios configuration utility.

5.3. Intrusion Detection Component

This section describes the Intrusion Detection Component, which implements an interface between the ITSM Wiki and an intrusion detection application.

Figure 5.23 gives an overview of the Intrusion Detection Component. Attacks from the Internet and suspicious activity from hosts within the organizational network are read by hosts running the Snort intrusion detection system. Snort writes events that are classified as attacks to an SQL database. The criteria that define, which patterns are classified as attacks, are stored as rules in configuration files. As can be seen in the figure, the filtering component is the central part of the Intrusion Detection Component. It serves as a link between the ITSM Wiki and the Snort database, in which intrusion detection events are stored. The filtering component uses background information about hosts, which is

[18] http://www.nconf.org/
[19] http://www.onecmdb.org/
[20] http://www.8p8web.it/cmon/
[21] http://developer.berlios.de/projects/ignoramus-anagi/
[22] http://sourceforge.net/projects/monarch/
[23] http://sourceforge.net/projects/nagiosweb/

stored in the ITSM Wiki (e.g., the operating system, or the applications and services running on a host) in order to filter relevant intrusion detection information. Based on the background information, events are read from the Snort database. IT administrators access intrusion detection events via the ITSM Wiki's Web-based user interface. On demand, more information about individual events, which is stored in the Snort database, can be displayed in the ITSM Wiki.

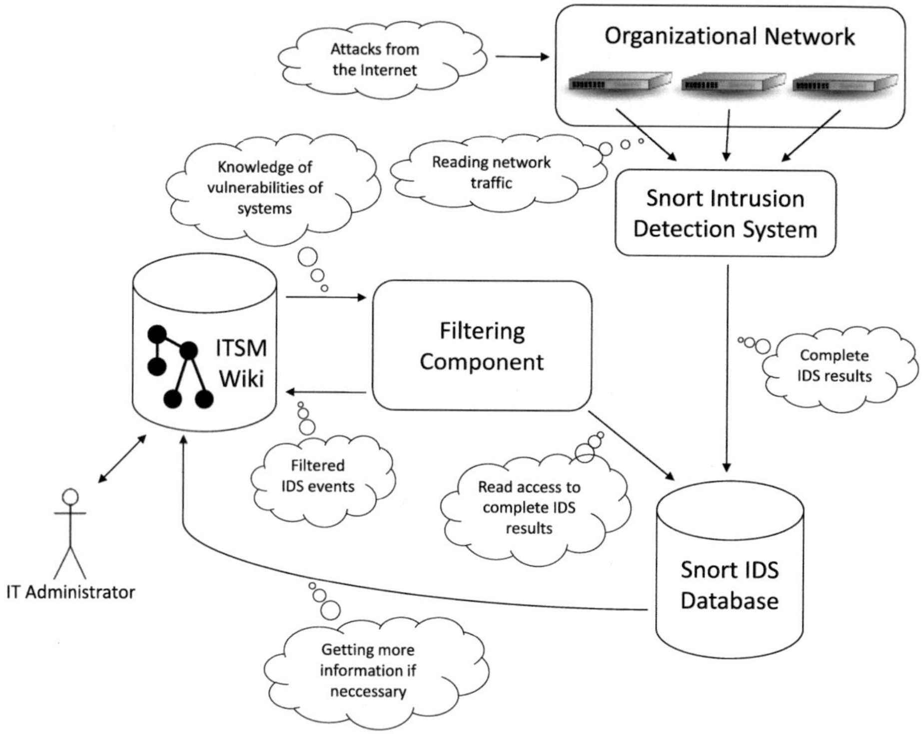

Figure 5.23.: Intrusion Detection

This section is organized as follows: First, the creation of the Intrusion Detection Component is motivated in Section 5.3.1 (page 263). Following that, in Section 5.3.2 (page 264), the results of the requirements analysis are presented, followed by the use cases in Section 5.3.3 (page 268). In Section 5.3.4 (page 270), the relevant information used by the Intrusion Detection Component is shown. Section 5.3.5 (page 270) outlines the tools used by the component. In Section 5.3.6 (page 272), the design of the component is presented, followed by a description of the Intrusion Detection Ontology in Section 5.3.7 (page 276). The implementation of the component is described in Section 5.3.8 (page 280). After that, Section 5.3.9 (page 281) shows the information representation. Finally, Section 5.3.10 (page 282) outlines prior and related work.

5.3.1. Motivation

Detecting suspicious activity that targets hosts and services from the outside, as well as the detection of suspicious activity from hosts within the network is the focus of intrusion detection systems. Experiences at FZI showed that while open source solutions exist for detecting suspicious activity (e.g., Snort), the systems generate a high rate of false positives, which have to be reviewed by IT administrators. While graphical, Web-based tools help in aggregating, sorting, and visualizing intrusion detection events, the results in tests still showed a large number of false positives. The basic motivation of the Intrusion Detection Component is to use background information, available in the ITSM Wiki, in order to reduce the number of false positives in intrusion detection events.

From the ITIL perspective, the use of an intrusion detection system is motivated as follows:

- The *Information Security Management* process, which has the goal of ensuring the effective management of information security from the Service Design perspective, is described in [LR07, pages 141–149]. In this thesis, Information Security Management is introduced in Section 2.2.2 (page 31).
- In the *Event Management* process, the use of tools for passively monitoring CIs in order to detect critical conditions, is described [CW07, pages 35–46]. In this thesis, a description of Event Management can be found in Section 2.2.4 (page 43).
- The *Access Management* process motivates the use of an intrusion detection system in order to detect unauthorized access [CW07, pages 68–72]. In this thesis, Access Management is outlined in Section 2.2.4 (page 48).

References [Axe99] and [Axe00] discuss the effectiveness of intrusion detection systems. It is explored, how the effect known as the base-rate fallacy affects the systems. With regard to intrusion detection systems, the base-rate fallacy has the following implication: In most cases, there is a large number of network packets, which are scanned for suspicious content, while the number of packets that actually contains malicious content is quite small. In combination with intrusion detection signatures, which have a certain percentage of probability of correctly identifying an intrusion attempt, this leads to a number of false positives (i.e., false alarms). The motivation for the creation of the Intrusion Detection Component is to reduce the number of false positives.

With respect to ease of use and information representation, the following aspect motivates the development of an ITSM Wiki-integrated solution: Web-based front-ends for displaying intrusion detection events show only a limited amount of information, mainly about core aspects of intrusion detection (e.g., the source and destination IP addresses and ports, as well as the signature that triggered the event). While in some cases, this information is sufficient for IT administrators in order to understand the implications of an intrusion attempt, in most cases, it is not. Especially background information, such as the applications deployed on the destination host, its operating system, running services, and the owner of the host is not easily accessible to the IT administrators.

5.3.2. Requirements Analysis

Before starting work on the design and implementation, a requirements analysis was performed, which included the explicit formulation of the Intrusion Detection Component's vision and goals, its constraints and system boundaries, as well as its requirements (cp. [Bal09, pages 433–513]).

The results of the requirements validation are presented in Section 6.1 (page 318).

Vision and Goals

The vision and goals for the Intrusion Detection Component are motivated mostly by the shortcomings experienced by using existing open source tools for displaying intrusion detection data. The use case is the IT environment at FZI Research Center for Information Technology, which was described in Section 3.1 (page 82).

Vision The vision for the Intrusion Detection Component can be described as follows:

To design and implement a tool that simplifies and extends the management of intrusion detection information by employing Semantic Web technology, in combination with structured background knowledge stored in a semantic wiki (V-I01).

Goals The goals, which refine the vision of the Intrusion Detection Component, can be summarized as follows:

- Provide a mechanism that enables the displaying of intrusion detection events within the ITSM Wiki (G-I01).
- Integrate intrusion detection with Configuration Management, Change Management, and documentation into a unified user interface (G-I02).
- Make use of Semantic Web technologies in order to enable advanced query mechanisms (G-I03).
- Use Semantic Web technologies in order to reduce the number of false positives (G-I04).

After determining the vision and goals for the component, its constraints were collected.

Constraints

The following paragraphs outline the organizational, technical, and development environment constraints of the component.

Organizational Constraints The Intrusion Detection Component's organizational constraints are as follows:

The Intrusion Detection Component is used by the members of the security administration group who are responsible for maintaining the security of networks and hosts. In small environments (e.g., at FZI), the task is done by one or more members of the IT department.

Technical Constraints (Server) The technical constraints for the server are as follows:

- The Intrusion Detection Component is a part of the ITSM Wiki, which is realized by using the MediaWiki software.
- Semantic MediaWiki is used by the Intrusion Detection Component in order to store explicit information about intrusion detection events.
- MediaWiki and Semantic MediaWiki are programmed in the PHP language [Med11a], which imposes the technical constraints of also using this language on the Intrusion Detection Component.
- MediaWiki runs on Web servers, which allow the execution of PHP scripts. Most often, the LAMP platform is used for running MediaWiki.
- The Intrusion Detection Component accesses MediaWiki by using documented API calls. With regard to the database systems used with MediaWiki, all databases that are supported by MediaWiki are also supported by the Intrusion Detection Component.
- The actual task of gathering intrusion detection events is accomplished by using the Snort intrusion detection system.
- Information is stored in a database by the Snort tool. Access to this database has to be supported by the Intrusion Detection Component.

Technical Constraints (Client) The ITSM Wiki in general and the Intrusion Detection Component in particular are accessed by using a Web browser. As long as a browser that complies with current Web standards is available, any device and operating system can be used.

Development Environment Constraints With respect to development environment constraints, it can be said that the use of a simple text editor is sufficient, although ease of use can be gained by reverting to specialized PHP programming environments.

System Boundaries

In Figure 5.24, the Intrusion Detection Component's systems boundaries, as well as the components that make up the system, are visualized. The graph is inspired by the graph found in [Bal09, page 462].

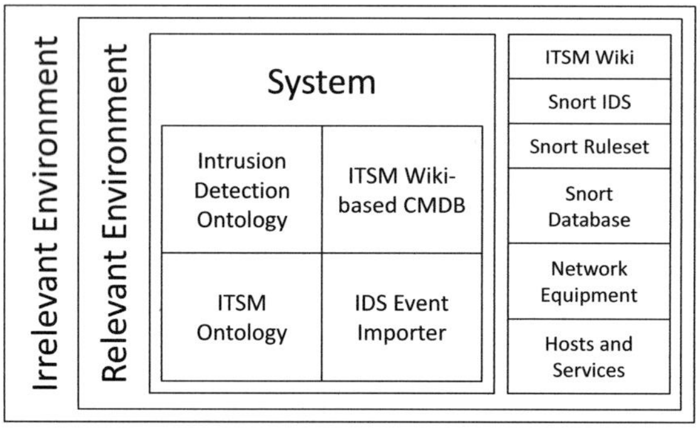

Figure 5.24.: System Boundaries of the Intrusion Detection Component

System With regard to the Intrusion Detection Component, the following parts belong to the system:

- *Intrusion Detection Ontology:* The Intrusion Detection Ontology models classes and properties with relevance to the intrusion detection domain.
- *ITSM Ontology:* Classes and properties of the core ITSM parts are modeled in the ITSM Ontology, as described in Section 4.3.4 (page 167).
- *ITSM Wiki-based CMDB:* The ITSM Wiki-based CMDB contains the configuration items and their dependencies. Information found in the CMDB, which is stored in a structured format, is used to process intrusion detection events.

- *IDS Event Importer:* The Intrusion Detection System Event Importer reads relevant parts of the information from the IDS database and writes it into the ITSM Wiki in a structured format.

Relevant Environment The relevant environment consists of elements, which are not by themselves considered part of the Intrusion Detection Component, but which interact with it on a regular basis. Parts of the relevant environment are:

- *ITSM Wiki:* The ITSM Wiki, which includes all the information that is relevant for providing IT services, is accessed by the Intrusion Detection Component in order to get information about configuration items and their dependencies.
- *Snort Intrusion Detection System:* The Snort intrusion detection system is the tool that is used to perform the actual detection of possible intrusions. More information about Snort can be found in Section 5.3.5 (page 271).
- *Snort Ruleset:* The Snort ruleset contains rules that are evaluated in order to detect suspicious patterns within the monitored network traffic.
- *Snort Database:* Events, which are detected by Snort, are stored in a database. The Intrusion Detection Component imports the parts that are used frequently into the ITSM Wiki and accesses less frequently used parts on demand.
- *Network Equipment:* Network intrusion detection systems work by listening to traffic passed over network equipment.
- *Hosts and Services:* Hosts and services with which traffic is exchanged, are the subject of focus of the intrusion detection system.

Requirements

Requirements are subdivided into functional and non-functional requirements. While functional requirements define the functions the software performs, non-functional requirements are concerned with the software's quality [Bal09, page 456]. The next two paragraphs outline the functional and non-functional requirements for the Intrusion Detection Component.

Functional Requirements The functional requirements for the Intrusion Detection Component are:

- New intrusion detection data has to be integrated into the ITSM Wiki automatically and without user intervention (R-I01).

- The reporting mechanisms about intrusion detection have to be smart and avoid reporting false positives (R-I02).
- Intrusion detection data has to be annotated semantically in order to be used in queries and dynamically created tables (R-I03).

Non-functional Requirements The non-functional requirements for the Intrusion Detection Component are as follows:

- The component has to be integrated into the ITSM Wiki.
- When importing intrusion detection data from the Snort tool, it has to be made sure that the import is fast and does not impact the performance of the wiki.
- Due to the possible large amount of data gathered by the Snort tool, intelligent ways of storing the intrusion detection data have to be found.
- No changes to the code base of Snort, MediaWiki, or Semantic MediaWiki should be necessary.

5.3.3. Use Cases

This subsection shows a number of use cases in order to present the purpose and the benefits of the Intrusion Detection Component.

Lowering False Positives in Detections of Attacks from the Internet

Hosts and applications, which provide services via the Internet (e.g., Web servers, and mail servers) are exposed to various threats. A major class of threats stem from individuals who try to exploit errors in software in order to gain access to hosts, or in order to retrieve or modify information stored on a host. Attacks against software include the exploitation of known vulnerabilities, as well as the exploitation of generic classes of vulnerabilities.

Rule-based intrusion detection systems evaluate rules, which encode patterns that are likely to represent an attack (e.g., network traffic on a certain network port containing a particular string of characters in the network packet).

A use case for the integration of intrusion detection into the Semantic MediaWiki-based ITSM Wiki is the exploitation of knowledge about hosts, applications, and services, which is stored in a structured format, in order to lower the false positive rate of intrusion detections. An example of a possible situation, where knowledge about the IT infrastructure can be used, is to rate the impact of exploits with a lower severity if the targeted hosts or services are not affected by the exploit. An example is an attack that targets a vulnerability in a specific product (such as the Microsoft IIS Web server). If in fact, the attacked service is running another product (such as the Apache Web server), the vulnerability cannot be exploited and does not have to trigger an alert.

Lowering False Positives in Suspicious Activity from Internal Hosts

The identification of hosts in a company's network that are infected by malicious software is another area in which rule-based intrusion detection systems are used. As is the case with the detection of attacks from the Internet, characteristics of network traffic are used to detect suspicious activity (e.g., outgoing network traffic that contains certain strings in network packets).

By using information that is stored in a structured format in the ITSM Wiki, a reduction of false positives in outbound network traffic is expected. The reason for this is the observation that traffic from internal hosts shows patterns that in some cases can be an indication of malicious activities, but can be harmless in other contexts (e.g., sending ICMP packages can be a sign of an attempted unauthorized network mapping attempt, but can also be part of an authorized application that tries to connect to a server[24]). By documenting this information in a machine-processable format instead of in plain text, false positives can be suppressed.

Integrate Intrusion Detection Information into a Unified Interface

Intrusion detection events, which are generated by the Snort application, are stored in a database. In order to present the stored information to IT administrators for review, there is a number of Web-based applications.

The integration of intrusion detection information into the ITSM Wiki promises to increase usability by providing additional information, which is not present in regular Web-based intrusion detection system front-ends. Examples of information that is helpful for IT administrators is the name of the owner of the host, as well as the host's operating system.

Statistics Generation and Interactive Data Analysis

Generating statistics that exceed the information stored in the database of the intrusion detection system is an area, in which structured information about the IT infrastructure as found in the ITSM Wiki, might be useful. An example is to report the number of attacks against different operating systems, applications, or departments.

[24] A real-world example is an application that sends ICMP packages to its licensing server.

In addition, by using Semantic MediaWiki's query mechanism, ad-hoc queries can be run on intrusion detection data (e.g., list all attacks on Web servers running a particular software and belonging to a certain department).

5.3.4. Relevant Information

Relevant information, with regard to the Intrusion Detection Component, is as follows:

- Which host and service were attacked?
- From which host was the attack originating?
- What kind of attack was performed?
- When was the attack taking place?

A more in-depth, technical view or the relevant information can be found in Section 5.3.6 (page 272).

5.3.5. Background and Used Tools

This subsection gives a short introduction into the background of the Intrusion Detection Component, as well as the tool that is used, namely the open source network intrusion detection system Snort.

Network and Host Security

Hosts, which provide services (e.g., a Web server) are exposed to malicious input from other hosts with which it communicates. Most security issues on servers are caused by programming errors in services, which can be exploited remotely (e.g., by causing buffer overflows). While it is the primary focus to update vulnerable software as soon as possible, detecting attacks can help to track down and eliminate security issues (e.g., infections with malicious software). Intrusion detection systems fulfill this task of monitoring and reporting issues.

Snort Intrusion Detection System

Snort is a network intrusion detection system, which is presented in [Roe99]. In [Sou10], Snort is summarized as follows:

> "Snort is an open source network intrusion prevention system, capable of performing real-time traffic analysis and packet logging on IP networks. It can perform protocol analysis, content searching/matching, and can be used to detect a variety of attacks and probes, such as buffer overflows, stealth port scans, CGI attacks, SMB probes, OS fingerprinting attempts, and much more." [Sou10]

Snort uses rules are defined in text-based configuration files and describe patterns of possible attacks on networks and hosts. Rules consist of two parts, which have the following purposes [The12c, page 173]:

- *Rule header:* "The rule header contains the rule's action, protocol, source and destination IP addresses and netmasks, and the source and destination ports information." [The12c, page 173]
- *Rule options:* "The rule option section contains alert messages and information on which parts of the packet should be inspected to determine if the rule action should be taken." [The12c, page 173]

An example of a rule is as follows [The12c, page 173]:

```
alert tcp any any -> 192.168.1.0/24 111 \
    (content:"|00 01 86 a5|"; msg:"mountd access";)
```

In this example, TCP connections are inspected for the content 00 01 86 a5. If this content is found in a packet, the IP addresses and port numbers are analyzed. While any source IP address and source port fits the rule, an alert is triggered only if the destination IP is located in the network 192.168.1.0/24 and if the destination port is 111.

Snort offers multiple destinations, to which intrusion detection events can be logged (e.g., console output, or various databases). In this thesis, Snort events are logged to a MySQL database.

In addition to network intrusion detection systems, there exist other approaches to detecting security-related events, namely host-based intrusion detection systems (e.g., OSSEC [BC08, Tre09a, Tre09b]). At the current state of implementation of the Intrusion Detection Component, the focus is on network intrusion detection systems, while the integration of other classes of IDS is considered future work.

5.3.6. Design of the Intrusion Detection Component

Based on the findings of the requirements analysis, an extension was designed, which enables viewing intrusion detection events within the ITSM Wiki. This subsection first describes the setup of the network, in which Snort was set up. Following that, the Snort database schema is analyzed. After that, the process for importing information from the IDS database is described.

Network Setup

Before designing and developing the component, a reference set of intrusion detection data was captured from the network. Figure 5.25 shows the simplified structure of the network used for capturing the test data. A firewall is positioned between the internal network, the perimeter network[25], and the Internet. The Snort intrusion detection sensor is attached to a switch port, which is configured in monitor mode[26], so it receives all packets entering and leaving the perimeter network. A network adapter, set to promiscuous mode[27] captures all packets from the network (i.e., all traffic entering and leaving the perimeter network). Snort was configured to scan the network traffic for suspicious behavior (e.g., port scans, error messages, and patterns that indicate the attempted exploitation of a known security issue in a particular software). For each detected suspicious behavior, Snort created an entry into its log (that can be either stored in a file or a database).

The data captured from the network was stored in a MySQL database. In the time of capturing the data (from 2009-07-20 to 2009-08-31), 217,192 Snort events were logged. The size of the MySQL Snort database, in which the events are stored, is 280 MB, from which 240 MB are used for storing the content of suspiciously captured packets in a binary format. Each Snort event includes, in addition to the binary content of the offending traffic, its metadata (timestamp, network addresses, network ports, and information about the Snort signature that triggered the logging).

The Snort Database Schema

Figure 5.26 shows the database schema of the Snort intrusion detection system. The Intrusion Detection Component imports parts of the information, which is stored in the Snort database, into the ITSM Wiki. Parts, which are too large or cannot be used by the

[25]The perimeter network is a network separate from the internal network, where servers are positioned, which are accessible from the public Internet. By restricting traffic between the perimeter network and the internal network, malicious behavior of compromised hosts can be contained.

[26]Ports in monitor mode receive a copy of each network packet sent and received over the port being monitored.

[27]Normally, network adapters only process data with their own network address (MAC) as the destination. When set to promiscuous mode, the adapter processes all data received over the network.

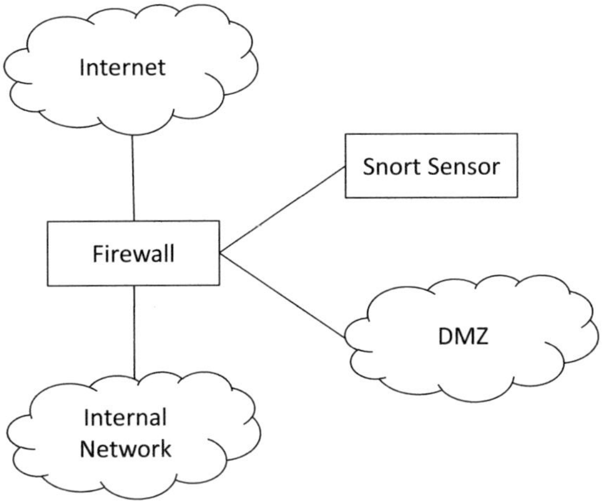

Figure 5.25.: Positioning of the Snort Sensor

ITSM Wiki, are not imported (e.g., the binary content of offending network packets). Instead, this information is accessed in an ad-hoc manner.

The following information is imported into the ITSM Wiki as a representation that is usable by Semantic MediaWiki (i.e., pages, object properties, and data properties):

- *event:* An occurrence of potentially malicious activity.
- *signature:* A signature, which detects potentially malicious activity.
- *sig_class:* The class of the signature.
- *sensor:* The sensor, which detected the activity.
- *iphdr:* Source and destination IP addresses.
- *icmphdr:* ICMP type and code.
- *udphdr, tcphdr:* Source and destination ports (UDP, TCP).

Based on the information, which is necessary in order to describe the domain of intrusion detection for the use in the ITSM Wiki, an ontology was created. The ontology is described in Section 5.3.7 (page 276).

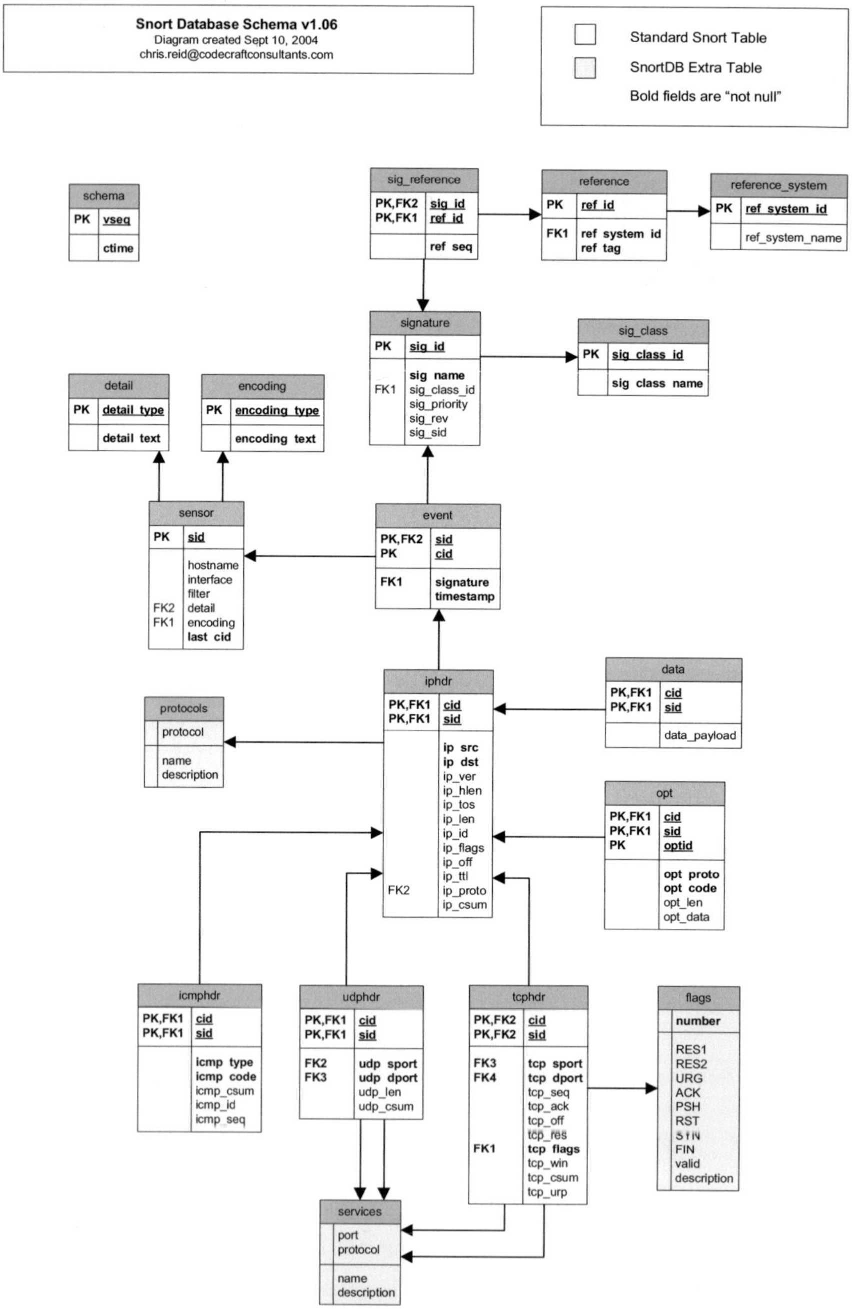

Figure 5.26.: Snort Database Schema (Source: [Rei04])

Importing Information from the IDS Database

Algorithm 5.5 describes the steps for importing information from the IDS database into the ITSM Wiki. In order to import information about events, the Intrusion Detection Component requires the following information:

- IDS database server: Server name, database name, login credentials
- ITSM Wiki: Server name, login credentials

When importing information, a wiki page is created for each intrusion event. Each page contains the relevant information for the event in a structured format (i.e., as information that can be processed by Semantic MediaWiki). For each event, the following information is stored in the ITSM Wiki:

- Source IP
- Destination IP
- Source port
- Destination port
- Timestamp
- Intrusion detection signature

For known hosts (i.e., hosts, which are part of the organization's network), a link to the respective host is created in the event page. Moreover, a new intrusion detection signature page is generated for each signature that was not encountered before. The content for the intrusion detection signature page is read from the Snort Web page[28] and stored in the ITSM Wiki in a structured format. Because the source, from which the meta-information about signatures is downloaded, only provides a semi-structured format[29] the automatically gathered information in the ITSM Wiki is not fully machine-processable. In order to improve the ability to automatically process information, structured information is generated based on predefined keywords. For example, text strings are parsed for common keywords, such as "Linux". This information is then stored as a semantic statement in addition to the downloaded information about the signature. Moreover, explicit statements can be created by the user in addition to the automatically generated ones.

Each page, which represents a host in the ITSM Wiki, includes a tab that lists intrusions that involve the particular host. This tab is implemented as Semantic MediaWiki *ask* statements, which dynamically generate tables from information stored in a structured format in the intrusion detection event pages.

[28] `http://www.snort.org/search/sid/<SID>`, with <SID> equals the signature's identifier.

[29] Information is structured with regard to captions, e.g., summary, impact, and affected systems.

Algorithm 5.5: Importing Information from the IDS Database

Data: IDS database information, wiki instance information
Result: Updated intrusion detection information in the ITSM Wiki
event[] = Get list of new events from IDS database;
for *(int i=1; i<= count(event[]); i++)* **do**
    Read information about event[i] from IDS database;
    Write information about event[i] to ITSM Wiki;
end

5.3.7. Intrusion Detection Ontology

The Intrusion Detection Component's data model is an ontology. While the ITSM Ontology, which is the data model for the core ITSM classes and properties, is described in Section 4.3.4 (page 167), this subsection describes the parts of the ontology that are relevant to the Intrusion Detection Component.

In this subsection, the presentation of the Intrusion Detection Ontology is divided into the following three parts: First, a graphical representation of the class hierarchy is presented. Second, the classes, object properties, and data properties are described. Third, exemplary instances and a short description are given for each class.

Class Hierarchy

Figure 5.27 shows the class hierarchy of the Intrusion Detection Ontology. All classes are subclasses of the *Thing* class. Class hierarchies are expressed with the *is-a* property.

Classes, Object Properties, and Data Properties

In Table 5.4, the classes, object properties, and data properties of the Intrusion Detection Ontology are shown. In the table, classes and properties that are relevant in the context of the Intrusion Detection Ontology are shown in boldface type. Classes and properties, which are only of secondary interest in this context are displayed in regular type.

Descriptions and Exemplary Instances

Section 4.3.4 (page 173) shows a short description, as well as exemplary instances, for each class of the Intrusion Detection Ontology. The presentation in a single table is done in order to avoid unnecessary duplication of information.

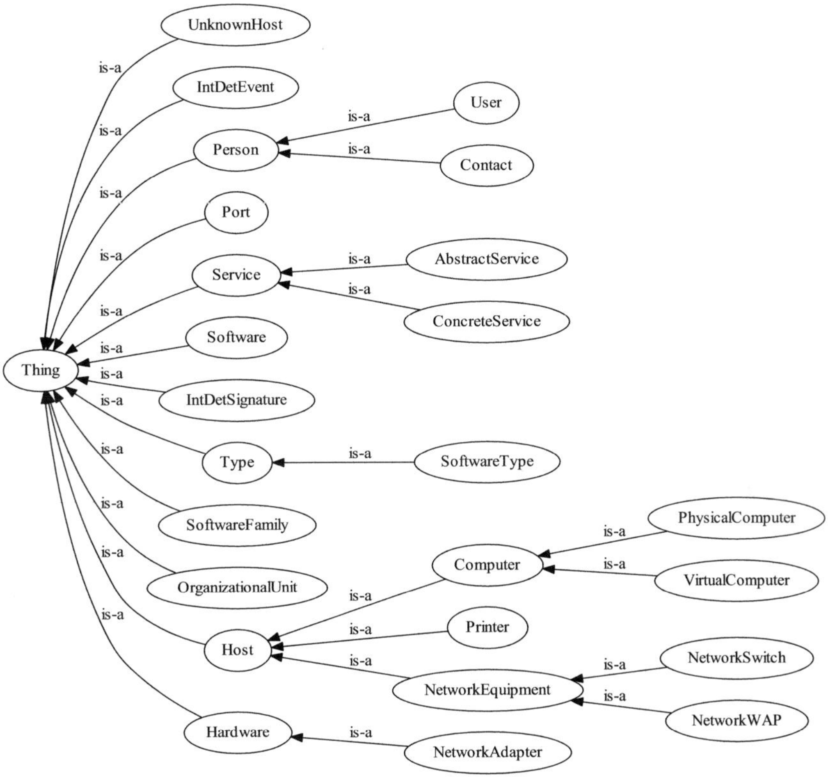

Figure 5.27.: Class Hierarchy of the Intrusion Detection Ontology

Table 5.4.: Intrusion Detection Ontology

Domain Class	**Property**	**Range**
AbstractService	*inherited from Service class* consistsOfService {0..n}	 Service
AccountStatusType	*inherited from Type class*	*no additional properties*
Computer	*inherited from Host class* LastDomainConnectDate {0..1} MemberOfWindowsDomain {0..1} OperatingSystemInstallationDate {0..1} hasComputerUsageType {0..1} hasLocalAdministrator {0..n}	 <Date> <Boolean> <Date> ComputerUsageType Contact, User
ConcreteService	*inherited from Service class* runsOnPort {0..1}	 Port
Contact	*inherited from Person class*	*no additional properties*

(*table continues*)

Table 5.4.: Intrusion Detection Ontology (continued)

Domain Class	Property	Range
Hardware	*inherited from Thing class*	
	Model {0..1}	<String>
	ProductNumber {0..1}	<String>
	SerialNumber {0..1}	<String>
	hasManufacturer {0..1}	Organization
	hasVendor {0..1}	Organization
	isCompatibleWith {0..n}	Thing
	isIncompatibleWith {0..n}	Thing
Host	*inherited from Thing class*	
	Model {0..1}	<String>
	ProductNumber {0..1}	<String>
	SerialNumber {0..1}	<String>
	hasCommissioningStatusType {0..1}	CommissioningStatusType
	hasContactPerson {0..n}	Person
	hasInstalledHardware {0..n}	Hardware
	hasInstalledSoftware {0..n}	Software
	hasManufacturer {0..1}	Organization
	hasOwner {0..1}	Person
	hasVendor {0..1}	Organization
	isLocatedIn {0..1}	Location
	runsService {0..n}	ConcreteService
IntDetEvent	*inherited from Thing class*	
	IntDetEventDate {0..1}	<Date>
	hasDestinationHost {0..1}	Host, UnknownHost
	hasDestinationPort {0..1}	Port
	hasIntDetSignature {0..1}	IntDetSignature
	hasSourceHost {0..1}	Host, UnknownHost
	hasSourcePort {0..1}	Port
IntDetSignature	*inherited from Thing class*	
	targetsSoftware {0..n}	Software
NetworkAdapter	*inherited from Hardware class*	
	ConnectionSpeed {0..1}	<Quantity>
	IPv4Address {0..1}	<String>
	IPv4DefaultGateway {0..1}	<String>
	IPv4DHCPEnabled {0..1}	<Boolean>
	IPv4DHCPServer {0..1}	<String>
	IPv4DNSServer {0..n}	<String>
	IPv4SubnetMask {0..1}	<String>
	IPv6Address {0..1}	<String>
	IPv6DefaultGateway {0..1}	<String>
	IPv6DNSServer {0..n}	<String>
	MACAddress {0..1}	<String>
	hasConnectionType {0..1}	ConnectionType
	hasNetworkAdapterType {0..1}	NetworkAdapterType
	hasNetworkConnectionTo {0..1}	NetworkAdapter
	isPartOfNetworkSegment {0..1}	NetworkSegment

(*table continues*)

Table 5.4.: Intrusion Detection Ontology (continued)

Domain Class	**Property**	**Range**
NetworkEquipment	*inherited from Host class*	*no additional properties*
NetworkSwitch	*inherited from NetworkEquipment class*	*no additional properties*
NetworkWAP	*inherited from NetworkEquipment class*	*no additional properties*
OrganizationalUnit	*inherited from Thing class*	
	hasDeputyManager {0..n}	<Person>
	hasITContact {0..n}	<Person>
	hasManager {0..n}	<Person>
	isPartOfOrganization {0..1}	Organization
	isPartOfOrganizationalUnit {0..1}	OrganizationalUnit
Person	*inherited from Thing class*	
	EMailAddress {0..n}	<Email>
	FamilyName {0..1}	<String>
	FaxNumber {0..n}	<Telephone number>
	GivenName {0..1}	<String>
	JobTitle {0..1}	<String>
	PhoneNumber {0..n}	<Telephone number>
	hasKnowledgeDomain {0..n}	KnowledgeDomain
	hasManager {0..1}	Person
	hasOffice {0..1}	Room
	hasRole {0..n}	Role
	isMemberOfOrganization {0..n}	Organization
	isMemberOfOrganizationalUnit {0..n}	OrganizationalUnit
PhysicalComputer	*inherited from Computer class*	
	hasComputerFormFactorType {0..1}	ComputerFormFactorType
Port	*inherited from Thing class*	
	Port {0..1}	<Number>
	Protocol {0..1}	<String>
Printer	*inherited from Host class*	*no additional properties*
Service	*inherited from Thing class*	
	hasOwner {0..1}	Person
Software	*inherited from Thing class*	
	hasBitType {0..1}	BitType
	hasLanguage {0..n}	Language
	hasManufacturer {0..1}	Organization
	hasSoftwareType {0..1}	SoftwareType
	hasVendor {0..1}	Organization
	isCompatibleWith {0..n}	Thing
	isIncompatibleWith {0..n}	Thing
	isPartOfSoftwareFamily {0..1}	SoftwareFamily
SoftwareFamily	*inherited from Thing class*	
	isPartOfSoftwareFamily {0..1}	SoftwareFamily
SoftwareType	*inherited from Type class*	*no additional properties*

(*table continues*)

Table 5.4.: Intrusion Detection Ontology (continued)

Domain Class	Property	Range
Thing	Description {0..1}	<Text>
	Name {1}	<String>
	Version {0..1}	<Number>
	hasDependency {0..n}	Thing
	hasParent {0..n}	Thing
	isConnectedTo {0..n}	Thing
	isRelatedTo {0..n}	Thing
Type	*inherited from Thing class*	*no additional properties*
UnknownHost	*inherited from Thing class*	
	IPv4Address {0..1}	<String>
	IPv6Address {0..1}	<String>
User	*inherited from Person class*	
	CreationDate {0..1}	<Date>
	DeletionDate {0..1}	<Date>
	LastLoginDate {0..1}	<Date>
	LoginName {0..1}	<String>
	UniqueIdentifier {0..1}	<String>
	hasAccountStatusType {0..1}	AccountStatusType
VirtualComputer	*inherited from Computer class*	*no additional properties*

5.3.8. Implementation

The Intrusion Detection Component is realized as an external application, which performs the import of the intrusion detection data into the ITSM Wiki. By running the external application periodically (e.g., once every 5 min), information about intrusion detection events is kept up-to-date in the wiki. When importing information about events, the information is written to the wiki in Semantic MediaWiki format.

Because importing all information about events from the intrusion detection system would produce too much unnecessary information in the wiki, only a limited selection is imported and stored in a structured format. The separation of the imported information is as follows:

- Information, which benefits from being available via the Semantic MediaWiki query mechanism is read from the Snort database and written to the ITSM Wiki database as pages and properties.
- Information, which does not benefit from being available via queries, is not imported into the ITSM Wiki, which helps to increase the performance of the wiki.

Source Files

The functionality of the Intrusion Detection Component is implemented in the following source files:

- `config.php.inc`: Contains configuration information, such as the login data for the Snort database, as well as the ITSM Wiki.
- `controller.php`: This file implements the functionality of the component.
- `CurlWrapper.php`: Implements a wrapper mechanism for the cURL tool that is used to access the Semantic MediaWiki instance.
- `importSnort.php`: Main file, which is called periodically in order to import information.
- `runSql.php`: Implements SQL-related helper functions.
- `WebApi.php`: Contains functions for manipulating MediaWiki pages.

5.3.9. Representation of Information in the Wiki

There are two types of information representation with respect to intrusion detection events. First, intrusion detection events and information about signatures are stored in a structured format and displayed as pages in ITSM Wiki. Second, information that is stored in a structured format is used within other pages (e.g., a query within a computer page results in a table, which uses the structured information stored in the event pages).

In Figure 5.28, the representation of an event as presented to the ITSM Wiki user is shown.

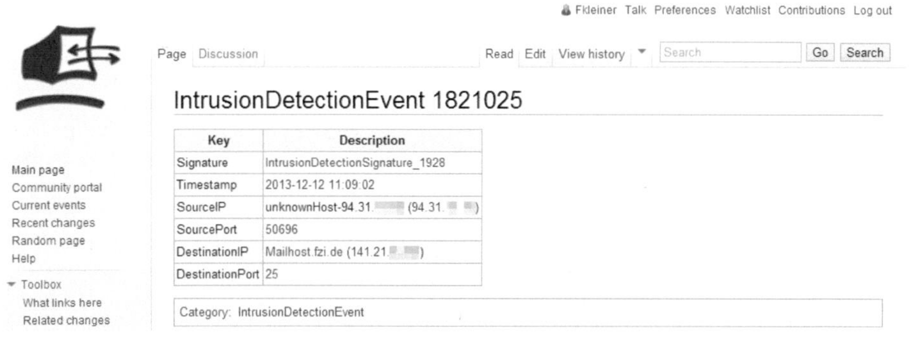

Figure 5.28.: Single Intrusion Detection Event

Listing 5.4 shows the wikitext representation of an intrusion detection event. Information about intrusion detection signatures is also stored in a structured format in the Wiki. Each intrusion detection signature contains Semantic MediaWiki queries, which display the events that were generated by the signature. Each host page also includes queries that generate a dynamic list of relevant events.

Listing 5.4: Semantic Forms Wikitext Representing an Intrusion Event

```
[[Category:IntrusionDetectionEvent]]
{| class="wikitable"
|-
! Key !! Description
|-
| Signature || [[hasIntrusionDetectionSignature::
    IntrusionDetectionSignature_1928]]
|-
| Timestamp || [[IntrusionDetectionEventDate::2013-12-12
    11:09:02]]
|-
| SourceIP || {{#ask: [[Category:Hardware]] [[NetworkAdapter::<q
    >[[Category:NetworkAdapter]][[IPv4Address::94.31.XX.XX]]</q
    >]] |default=unknownHost-94.31.XX.XX}}  ([[hasSourceHost
    ::94.31.XX.XX]])
|-
| SourcePort || [[hasSourcePort::50696]]
|-
| DestinationIP || {{#ask: [[Category:Hardware]] [[
    NetworkAdapter::<q>[[Category:NetworkAdapter]][[IPv4Address
    ::141.21.XX.XX]]</q>]] |default=unknownHost-141.21.XX.XX}}
    ([[hasDestinationHost::141.21.XX.XX]])
|-
| DestinationPort || [[hasDestinationPort::25]]
|}
```

5.3.10. Prior and Related Work

This subsection describes prior work about intrusion detection system front-ends, as well as intrusion detection ontologies.

Intrusion Detection System Front-ends

Reference [Sno11] provides an overview of graphical user interfaces for the management of intrusion detection events, which are able to process events generated by Snort.

Examples of Web-based user interfaces for open source intrusion detection systems (e.g., Snort) are BASE[30], OSSIM[31], and Snorby[32]. Squil[33] is a cross-platform GUI for monitoring events generated by an intrusion detection system.

Common to these front-ends is the fact that they are solely concerned with displaying intrusion detection information. When comparing the approaches with the ITSM Wiki-integrated front-end, it can be seen that the use of a semantic wiki makes possible a wider range of queries, which are not restricted to intrusion detection events. By combining background information about hosts, as well as organizational information, the context of intrusion attempts can be better put into perspective by the IT administrators that are using the system.

Intrusion Detection Ontologies

In [RHTN01], the use of ontologies in the information security domain is motivated. While the paper outlines the general benefits of using ontologies in information security, it does not present a concrete ontology.

References [UJP03] and [UPJF04] describe the use of DAML+OIL[34] ontologies in the context of intrusion detection. The purpose of using an ontology for intrusion detection is in the area of distributed intrusion detection systems. By using an ontology as a data model, different instances of (heterogeneous) intrusion detection systems can contribute to a unified view of an attack that involves multiple hosts. This enables to detect and classify complex attacks, which would not have been possible when only using data from single intrusion detection system instances [UPJF04].

In [AK09], the use of an ontology for reducing false positives and false negatives in distributed intrusion detection systems is described. The approach uses an architecture, which uses a master agent, on which all intrusion detection events are retained, as well as multiple detection agents. An ontology is presented, which is derived from the taxonomy described in [HH05]. The ontology allows to classify attacks into technical categories, such as buffer overflows, worms, or viruses [AK09].

With regard to re-use of the ontologies, the following observations can be made: First, the purpose of the described ontologies lies in the area of modeling attacks that involve multiple detection instances. Second, the information from multiple intrusion detection instances is used in order to improve the detection rate of the system. These two aspects of the ontologies aim at larger-scale deployments, which are typically found in larger organizations. In contrast, the Intrusion Detection Ontology that was developed in this

[30] `http://base.secureideas.net/`
[31] `http://code.google.com/p/ossiem/`
[32] `http://snorby.org/`
[33] `http://sguil.sourceforge.net/`
[34] DAML+OIL is the predecessor of the OWL ontology language.

thesis aims at supporting SMEs by adding intrusion detection support to a semantic wiki. Due to this fact, the scope of the ontologies presented as related work differs from the ontology developed in this thesis. For example, information about the organizational structure, persons, software, and background information about targeted hosts is of greater relevance for the ITSM Wiki than providing a detailed taxonomy of intrusion types.

5.4. Incident and Problem Analyzer Component

The Incident and Problem Analyzer Component is a tool, which supports IT administrators in finding the underlying cause of incidents and problems in IT landscapes. In ITIL, incident management deals with finding solutions for malfunctioning hosts and services in order to quickly recover the affected configuration items into a working state. Problem management, on the other hand, deals with finding the underlying cause, and is concerned with fixing problems in order to prevent their re-occurrence. The Incident and Problem Analyzer Component, which makes use of the semantic wiki-based Configuration Management Database, covers the following two use cases:

- First, two system configurations can be analyzed for similarities that are candidates for possible common causes of incidents or problems. The idea behind this use case is as follows: There exist (partly complex) dependencies in IT environments (e.g., there exist multiple network switches, to which hosts are connected), which are modeled in the ITSM Wiki. When an issue is reported that affects multiple configuration items, finding properties that are common between these CIs is the first use case of the Incident and Problem Analyzer. By showing these properties, IT administrators are pointed to the configuration item that is a candidate for being the cause of the issue.

- Second, changes to system configurations can be analyzed over time in order to find differences. This functionality can be used to track down possible sources of problems when comparing a working state to a non-working one. The idea behind this functionality is as follows: Computers are subject to continual changes over time (e.g., updates for applications are automatically installed). These changes can cause issues (e.g., an application is unable to perform a certain function), which are not necessarily caused by the affected application, which makes finding the cause of the issue difficult. By retaining snapshots of information about host configurations in the ITSM Wiki, a snapshot of the affected host in a working state can be compared to a snapshot in the non-working state. The results of the comparison are the changes that are possible causes of the issue.

The component presented in this section builds on the work that was previously published in [KAM12].

In this section, first, the motivation for the development of the Incident and Problem Analyzer Component is outlined in Section 5.4.1 (page 285). After that, in Section 5.4.2 (page 285), the requirements for the Incident and Problem Analyzer Component are collected. Section 5.4.3 (page 292) outlines use cases, while Section 5.4.4 (page 293) lists information, which is relevant for the component. After that, the design is presented in Section 5.4.5 (page 294), followed by the presentation of the Incident and Problem Analyzer Ontology in Section 5.4.6 (page 295). Following that, the implementation is presented in Section 5.4.7 (page 295). Section 5.4.8 (page 296) gives an overview of how information is represented in the wiki, followed by a description of prior and related work in Section 5.4.9 (page 297).

5.4.1. Motivation

IT landscapes, depending on their size and purpose, consist of a multitude of configuration items, which form complex interactions. Services, which are presented to the user as single entities (e.g., e-mail access, and Web pages), are formed from a number of interacting configuration items (e.g., computer hardware, operating system, mail server software, Web server software, and network equipment). Tracking down problems in these complex IT landscapes is hard and time-consuming, especially for IT administrators who are not familiar with all relevant aspects of the IT landscape (e.g., part time employees, or new hires). Even when assuming a perfect documentation of all components and their interactions, finding the causes for seemingly unrelated problems, which have a common cause, however, can be a challenging endeavor.

In the Incident and Problem Management process flow, as outlined in ITIL (see Figure 2.11, page 46, and Figure 2.12, page 49), the Incident and Problem Analyzer Component supports IT administrators in the diagnosis phases of the processes.

The analyzer uses structured information, which is stored in the semantic wiki-based CMDB. Information describes, among others, hardware components, software, and services, as well as their dependencies. Structured information originates either from other components (e.g., the Information Gathering Component), or from manual input. IT administrators access the Incident and Problem Analyzer Component via a Web-based interface, which is integrated into the ITSM Wiki.

5.4.2. Requirements Analysis

Before starting work on the design and implementation, a requirements analysis was performed, which included the explicit formulation of the Incident and Problem Analyzer Component's vision and goals, its constraints and system boundaries, as well as its requirements (cp. [Bal09, pages 433–513]).

The results of the requirements validation are presented in Section 6.1 (page 318).

Vision and Goals

The following paragraphs list the vision and the goals for the Incident and Problem Analyzer Component.

Vision The vision for the Incident and Problem Analyzer Component is as follows:

To design and implement a tool, which helps IT administrators to track down the cause of incidents and problems (V-J01).

Goals The goals, which refine the vision of the Incident and Problem Analyzer Component, can be summarized as follows:

- Provide a mechanism for finding the cause of an incident or problem, given a number of affected configuration items (G-J01).
- Provide a mechanism for finding the cause of an incident or problem, given the history of the affected configuration item (G-J02).
- Implement the capability to visualize the configuration items involved in causing the incident or problem (G-J03).

After determining the vision and goals for the Incident and Problem Analyzer Component, its constraints were collected.

Constraints

The following paragraphs list the constraints for the component.

Organizational Constraints The Incident and Problem Analyzer Component's organizational constraints are as follows:

- The Incident and Problem Analyzer Component is used by members of the IT department in order to track down problems in the IT landscape.

Technical Constraints (Server) The technical constraints for the server are as follows:

- The Incident and Problem Analyzer Component is part of the ITSM Wiki, which is realized by using the MediaWiki software. MediaWiki is extensible by programming against the MediaWiki API.
- The Incident and Problem Analyzer Component uses information, which is stored in a structured format in the ITSM Wiki, as the basis for tracking down incidents and problems.
- MediaWiki and Semantic MediaWiki are programmed in the PHP language [Med11a], which imposes the technical constraints of also using this language on the Incident and Problem Analyzer Component.
- MediaWiki runs on Web servers, which allow the execution of PHP scripts.
- The Incident and Problem Analyzer Component accesses MediaWiki by using documented API calls. With regard to the database system, all databases that are supported by MediaWiki are also supported by the Incident and Problem Analyzer Component.

Technical Constraints (Client) The ITSM Wiki in general and the Incident and Problem Analyzer Component in particular, are accessed by using a Web browser. As long as a browser that complies with current Web standards is available, any device and operating system can be used.

Development Environment Constraints With respect to development environment constraints, it can be said that the use of a simple text editor is sufficient, although ease of use can be gained by reverting to specialized PHP programming environments.

System Boundaries

Figure 5.29 shows the systems boundaries of the Incident and Problem Analyzer Component. The graph is inspired by the graph found in [Bal09, page 462].

System The following items are part of the Incident and Problem Analyzer Component's system:

- *ITSM Ontology:* Classes and properties of the core ITSM parts are modeled in the ITSM Ontology, as described in Section 4.3.4 (page 167).

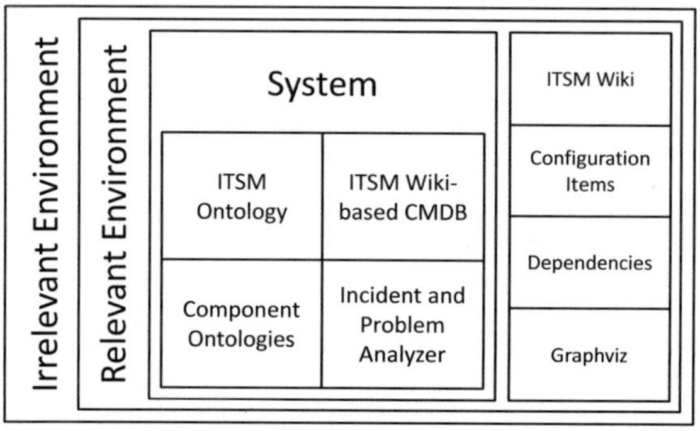

Figure 5.29.: System Boundaries of the Incident and Problem Analyzer

- *Component Ontologies:* The ontologies of the other components presented in this chapter contain all classes and properties, which are relevant to the Incident and Problem Analyzer Component.

- *ITSM Wiki-based CMDB:* The ITSM Wiki-based CMDB contains the configuration items and their dependencies.

- *Incident and Problem Analyzer:* The Incident and Problem Analyzer is the component, which compares configurations and shows possible sources of incidents and problems.

Relevant Environment The relevant environment consists of elements, which are not by themselves considered parts of the Incident and Problem Analyzer Component, but which interact with it on a regular basis. Parts of the relevant environment are:

- *ITSM Wiki:* The Incident and Problem Analyzer Component uses information, which is stored in a structured format in the ITSM Wiki.

- *Configuration Items:* Configuration items, which are represented in the CMDB, are part of the relevant environment.

- *Dependencies:* Dependencies between configuration items are part of the Incident and Problem Analyzer Component's relevant environment.

- *Graphviz:* The MediaWiki extension GraphViz [Med12b], as well as the underlying open source graph visualization software Graphviz [Gra12], are used for visualization.

Requirements

The next two paragraphs give a description of incident classes and the manual finding of incidents and problems. After that, the Incident and Problem Analyzer Component's functional and non-functional requirements are presented.

Incident Classes After analyzing the incidents reported to FZI's IT department's help desk system and their underlying causes, it was observed that there are four main classes of incidents. The incident classes are as follows:

- *Class 1: Stand-alone incident:* An incident occurs on a single system without a previous change to any component. Examples are mostly found when looking at hardware failures (e.g., a failed hard disk, or mainboard).
- *Class 2: Multiple incidents with a common cause:* Two or more incidents occur, which are related to each other by a common cause. An example of this kind of incident is the failure or malfunction of a network switch that leads to a number of users having network problems.
- *Class 3: Single incident evolved over time:* An incident occurs, where a single computer evolves an issue that can be traced back to a change, which was applied to the computer by the user or the IT department. An example is an upgrade to a Web browser that crashes when visiting a certain Web page, which loaded perfectly fine before the upgrade.
- *Class 4: Multiple incidents with a common cause evolved over time:* Two or more incidents occur that have a common cause, as well as a common change, which is tracked in the ITSM Wiki's history. This kind of incidents can be caused by a mechanism that centrally applies settings on a set of computers (e.g., distribute new software, which causes issues not caught during testing). Class 4 incidents are a combination of class 2 and class 3 incidents.

Figure 5.30 illustrates the dimensions of the incident classes. Stand-alone incidents occur separated from each other in space and time, i.e., they are unrelated to each other in the dependency tree and do not share a common or comparable history. Multiple incidents with a common cause share one or more common configuration items in the space dimension, while they do not share a common or comparable history in the ITSM Wiki. Single incidents that evolve over time can be tracked down by comparing their list of changes in the history. Multiple incidents, which evolved over time, are active in both dimensions.

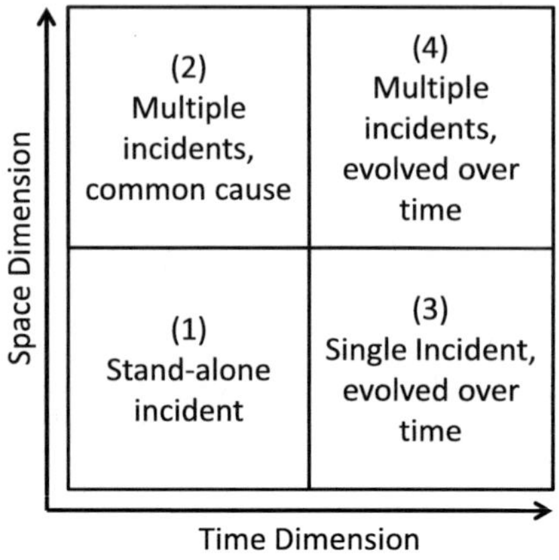

Figure 5.30.: Incident Classes

Finding Incidents and Problems Manually Because incidents generally have an underlying problem, which has to be found and fixed in order to prevent an error from re-occurring, tracking down the cause of the incident means finding the incident's underlying problem. Depending on the class of the incident, different techniques have to be applied, and different knowledge of the IT administrator is required.

When looking at class 1 incidents, it can be seen that they are independent of other problems and do not have a history that can be used for tracking down the problem, which causes the incident. This type of incident is best resolved by searching the knowledge base for similar problems, which occurred in the past. For the remainder of this section, class 1 incidents will be ignored, because they cannot be tracked down by looking for common items within the Configuration Management Database or changes in the history of configuration items.

In order to find the cause of a class 2 incident, detailed knowledge of similarities between IT components has to be possessed by the person assigned to find the problem. If this is not the case, information has to be gathered from the CMDB, which can be cumbersome if done manually.

For class 3 incidents, in some cases the user of a system can give valuable hints by narrowing down the time interval, in which the undesired behavior occurred for the first time. Class 4 incidents, being a mixture of class 2 and class 3 incidents, would be detected without tools support by comparing affected items, their possible connection, and their changes over time, in order to find the common cause of the incidents.

In addition to the different classes, incidents with the same class of an underlying problem can occur on different hosts independently from each other and distributed over time. This means that in order to speed up locating problems, it is necessary to document fixed problems and make them searchable for further use.

Functional Requirements The Incident and Problem Analyzer Component presented in this section offers a solution for helping to track down the causes of issues within complex IT landscapes. By making use of explicitly stated facts that are stored in the ITSM Wiki-based Configuration Management Database (see Section 4.2.1, page 137), it builds a tree representation of the relations between configuration items. In this tree, possible areas of interest are flagged for a closer examination by IT administrators.

There are three separate modes of operation of the Incident and Problem Analyzer Component:

- First, incidents and problems that occur within a specific time interval on multiple configuration items (e.g., hosts, hardware, software, or services) can be tracked down by searching for common or similar configuration items within the dependency set of both configuration items.
- Second, incidents and problems that develop over time and are encountered on a single configuration item, can be tracked down by looking at their history in the semantic wiki-based Configuration Management Database.
- Third, incidents and problems witnessed both, on multiple configuration items, as well as within a specific time interval, can be tracked down by building dependency trees, which consider both, common dependencies between configuration items, as well as their histories.

After studying the different classes of incidents, the requirements for a tool that helps in tracking down the underlying problems were formulated. Because class 1 incidents are on the one hand restricted to a single system, which makes locating them relatively easy, and on the other hand not detectable via comparing CIs, class 1 incidents are not pursued further and partly left to mechanisms used for detecting failing equipment (e.g., S.M.A.R.T. for hard disks).

The requirements for the Incident and Problem Analyzer Component are as follows:

- Ability to find the cause of class 2 incidents by comparing a given list of IT components for similarities, e.g., to identify a failing network switch from incidents reported by independent users indicating a problem (R-J01).
- Ability to find the cause of class 3 incidents by comparing configurations in time. For example, to detect the cause of an incident report, which states that a program was running fine two days ago, was not used yesterday and does not start today (R-J02).

- Ability to find class 4 incidents, which are a combination of class 2 and class 3 incidents. Class 4 incidents are most often caused by centrally applied configuration changes, e.g., the automatic distribution of a software package, or a setting to a set of computers. If there is an issue with the configuration change, a subset of the computers, or all computers of the set can be affected (R-J03).
- Ability to find problems, which were fixed on the same or other computers in the past, e.g., a browser update caused problems with a browser plugin, which happened again on another computer, with another browser version and another plugin (R-J04).

Non-functional Requirements The non-functional requirements for the Incident and Problem Analyzer Component are:

- The component has to be integrated into the ITSM Wiki.
- The amount of time for finding the result has to be kept down to acceptable limits.
- No changes should be needed in the code base of MediaWiki or Semantic MediaWiki.

5.4.3. Use Cases

The following subsections show a number of use cases in order to present the purpose and the benefits of the Incident and Problem Analyzer Component.

Finding the Cause of Incidents Based on a Given Set of CIs

IT administrators are supported by the Incident and Problem Analyzer Component in finding the underlying causes of incidents and problems. This functionality makes use of structured information that is stored in the ITSM Wiki, and which is in part written to the wiki by the Information Gathering Component.

Finding the Cause of Incidents Based on a Timeline

The timeline of changes of a configuration item is used to identify possible causes for incidents and problems. This functionality uses structured information stored in the ITSM Wiki, as well as the different versions of configurations that are stored in MediaWiki's page history.

5.4.4. Relevant Information

Relevant information in the context of the Incident and Problem Analyzer Component comprises information about incidents and problems, as outlined by ITIL, as well as information used in addition by the Incident and Problem Analyzer Component.

According to ITIL, information relevant for describing an incident is as follows [CW07, page 49]:

- "Unique reference number
- "Incident categorization (often broken down into between two and four levels of sub-categories)
- "Incident urgency
- "Incident impact
- "Incident prioritization
- "Date/time recorded
- "Name/ID of the person and/or group recording the incident
- "Method of notification (telephone, automatic, e-mail, in person, etc.)
- "Name/department/phone/location of user
- "Call-back method (telephone, mail, etc.)
- "Description of symptoms
- "Incident status (active, waiting, closed, etc.)
- "Related CI
- "Support group/person to which the incident is allocated
- "Related problem/Known Error
- "Activities undertaken to resolve the incident
- "Resolution date and time
- "Closure category
- "Closure date and time." [CW07, page 49]

Information relevant for describing a problem, is, as described in ITIL, as follows [CW07, page 61]:

- "User details
- "Service details

- “Equipment details
- “Date/time initially logged
- “Priority and categorization details
- “Incident description
- “Details of all diagnostic or attempted recovery actions taken.” [CW07, page 61]

Relevant information with respect to incident and problem detection is as follows:

- Information about configuration items
- Configuration item changes
- Dependencies between configuration items
- Similarities between configuration items

5.4.5. Design of the Incident and Problem Analyzer

Based on the requirements analysis’ findings, which were described in Section 5.4.2 (page 285), an extension was designed, which supports IT administrators in tracking down the root causes of incidents and problems from within the ITSM Wiki.

When the component is started, the user is prompted, which mode of operation should be performed. Depending on the user’s input, one of the two following variants is executed:

- *Analyze a single configuration item for changes in time:* This mode of operation allows to compare one state of a configuration item’s wiki page to another state of the wiki page of the same configuration item. This mode helps in tracking down the cause of problems that are caused by changes to attributes of the configuration item. For example, an updated application on the affected host could cause the problem.
- *Analyze two configuration items for shared properties:* This operation mode allows to find the cause of problems that affect both compared configuration items. This is accomplished by building a tree structure, which allows to identify configuration items that are used by both configuration items.

After either comparing a single configuration item to a previous version or comparing two configuration items, the visualization is performed. First, it is decided, which nodes need to be printed. Then, these nodes are visualized by making use of GraphViz and displayed in the ITSM Wiki.

5.4.6. Incident and Problem Analyzer Ontology

The Incident and Problem Analyzer Component makes use of numerous classes of the ITSM Ontology, as well as the Information Gathering Ontology, which were previously described in Section 4.3.4 (page 167) and Section 5.1.7 (page 219).

5.4.7. Implementation

The Incident and Problem Analyzer Component is implemented using the PHP programming language and builds on top of MediaWiki and Semantic MediaWiki. The user interface of the component is realized as a MediaWiki Special Page. The visualization of the trees is implemented using Graphviz [Gra12].

After the general design of the Incident and Problem Analyzer Component was presented in Section 5.4.5 (page 294), this subsection gives an overview of its implementation.

Analysis of a Single Configuration Item

When using the Incident and Problem Analyzer Component in order to analyze the history of a configuration item, the following steps are performed:

1. *Get available revisions:* For each modification of a wiki page, the changes are stored as a revision. In this step, the time stamps of all available revisions are read and displayed. The user then selects the two revisions that should be compared to each other.
2. *Find differing properties:* After two revisions are selected by the user, the revisions are compared. In order to perform the comparison, for each revision of the page a separate tree is created. These trees contain all dependent configuration items (e.g., if a certain graphics adapter is part of a computer, the wiki page of the graphics adapter is added to the tree). In order to build full trees of the initial revisions of the configuration item, the trees are built recursively until no more dependent configuration items can be added. After that, a compare tree is created, which contains the merged information of both trees. This compare tree is generated by comparing the two trees of the revisions and increasing an internal counter per node, if the node is already present in the tree. If a node is not yet present, it is added. Following that, relevant nodes are marked in the compare tree. In the case of the analysis of a single configuration item, relevant properties are the ones that occur in different form in the two compared trees.
3. *Display results:* The results of the comparison are visualized by using Graphviz and displayed.

Comparison of Two Configuration Items

When using the component in order to find a possible common cause for a problem that affects two configuration items, the following steps are performed by the Incident and Problem Analyzer Component:

1. *Selection of configuration items:* In the first step, the user inputs the names of the two configuration items that should be compared to each other.
2. *Find common properties:* For each one of the two given configuration items, a separate tree is generated, which contains all configuration items that are used by each of the two compared configuration items. In order to accomplish this, the trees are built recursively starting at each of the selected configuration items and ending when no more configuration items are left to be added. Following that, a compare tree is created, which contains the merged information of both trees. This compare tree is generated by comparing the two trees of the two selected configuration items and increasing an internal counter per node, if the node is already present in the tree. If a node is not yet present, it is added. Following that, relevant nodes are marked in the compare tree. In the case of comparing two configuration item with each other, relevant properties are the ones that occur in both compared trees.
3. *Display results:* The results are visualized by using Graphviz and displayed.

5.4.8. Representation of Information in the Wiki

Figure 5.31 shows an excerpt of a screenshot of a comparison tree, as generated by the Incident and Problem Analyzer Component. In the example, two desktop computers were compared, in order to find potential sources of a common problem.

As can be seen in the screenshot, there exist green, as well as red nodes. Green nodes indicate that the two compared configurations differ in that aspect (e.g., the two compared computers are different instances). Nodes, which are shown in red, indicate that the represented property are present in both compared systems. Tree nodes are shown as rectangles, which are divided into three parts: The top part shows the category, respectively, the class of the node. The middle part shows the description of the instance, while the bottom part shows, how many matches were found.

In Figure 5.31, the two compared configurations both run the same versions of Microsoft Windows, Adobe Shockwave Player, Java, and the McAfee Agent. Furthermore, both computers share the user Administrator and the group Domain Admins as local administrators. In addition, both computers are manufactured by Dell. Provided with this narrowed-down view of possible sources for a common cause of the problem, an IT administrator analyzes the red nodes for the cause of the problem.

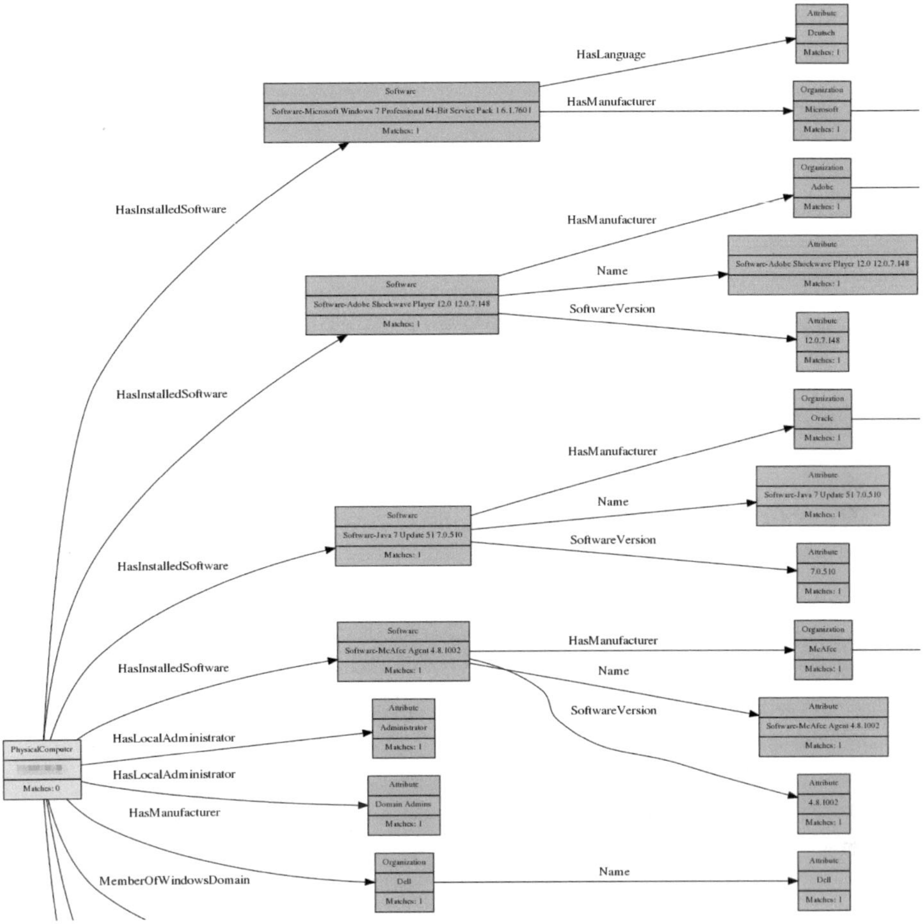

Figure 5.31.: Incident and Problem Analyzer Screenshot

5.4.9. Prior and Related Work

The Incident and Problem Analyzer Component was in parts described in [KAM12].

Systems for the diagnosis of problems in complex technical systems were investigated in the area of knowledge-based systems (KBS) for many years. Reference [Dar99] gives an introduction into these systems. An example of a commercially available KBS "for [the] use in knowledge-intensive technical customer service" is SemanticGuide [Sem12].

The Incident and Problem Analyzer Component, in contrast to more traditional KBS, can be classified as a lightweight, intelligent advisory and assistant system. By re-using information already present in ITSM Wiki's knowledge base (e.g., information gathered by the Information Gathering Component), the Incident and Problem Analyzer Component avoids the necessity for manual knowledge engineering.

Reference [KZKB09] describes an approach, which uses semantic similarity measurement for matching incident cases in order to improve the Incident Management process.

5.5. Virtualization and IaaS Connector

This section describes the Virtualization and IaaS Connector, which is used for creating and managing virtualized computing instances from within the ITSM Wiki. By making use of information stored in the ITSM Wiki, computing instances can be managed in ways that exceed the capabilities of classical management environments. The Virtualization and IaaS Connector was implemented as a proof of concept.

Figure 5.32 shows an overview of the Virtualization and IaaS Connector. The ITSM Wiki serves as a repository, in which the states of managed resources are retained and managed. IT administrators manage virtualized instances and IaaS resources via the Web-based wiki interface. Configuration parameters are stored in the wiki in a structured format as Semantic MediaWiki properties. When changes are performed by IT administrators, the Virtualization and IaaS Connector interacts with the respective management solution (e.g., XenServer, EC2, or OpenStack) in order to perform the change in the virtualized environment.

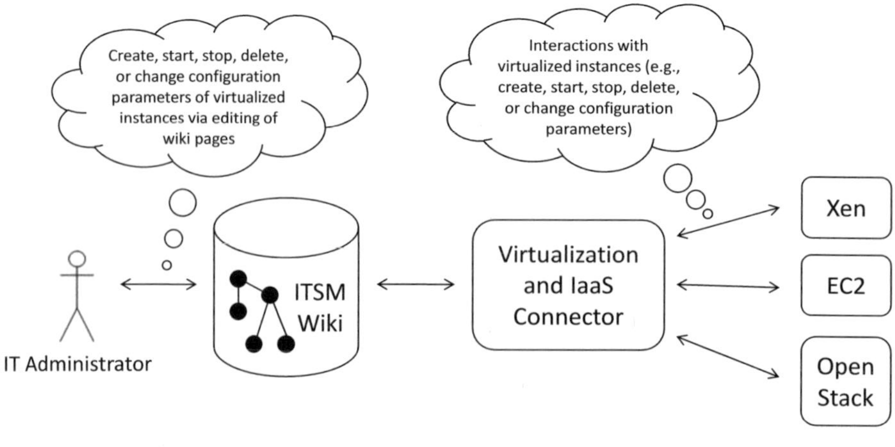

Figure 5.32.: Virtualization and IaaS Connector

This section is structured as follows: First, the motivation for the Virtualization and IaaS Connector is given in Section 5.5.1 (page 299), followed by a description of the connector's requirements in Section 5.5.2 (page 300). After that, use cases are described in Section 5.5.3 (page 304), followed by an outline of relevant information in Section 5.5.4 (page 305). Following that, a description of the underlying technologies is given in Section 5.5.5 (page 306), including virtualization and the IaaS aspects of cloud computing. After that, a description of the ontology, which models the domain-specific aspects of the Virtualization and IaaS Connector, is presented in Section 5.5.6 (page 309). Finally, an overview of prior work is given in Section 5.5.7 (page 314).

5.5.1. Motivation

While it was common for x86/x64-based servers to run only a single operating system till the mid-2000s, hardware support for virtualization in processors manufactured by Intel and AMD enabled the use of virtualization in order to run multiple operating systems on a single server[35]. While initial evaluations of a hardware-supported virtualization environment, namely the Xen [BDF$^+$03] platform, were performed at FZI in 2006, continuing improvements in hardware and software technology provided a foundation for a widespread adaption of virtualization during the following years. Currently (2012), FZI's IT department manages 18 virtualization servers with 214 virtual machines, running a freely available edition of the Citrix XenServer virtualization platform[36].

Recent trends in the area of cloud computing [BKNT09], namely Infrastructure as a Service (IaaS) use virtualization in combination with improved management capabilities and the promise of more flexibility in order to enable new business models (i.e., renting virtual computers for a short period instead of buying hardware).

When looking at solutions for the management of virtualized computer instances, freely available tools (e.g., Citrix XenCenter) provide basic functions, but lack more advanced ones. Commercially available solutions (e.g., from Citrix, and VMware) offer more advanced management capabilities but require the purchase of licenses. Freely available platforms for building private clouds, e.g., OpenStack[37], are improving rapidly, but are currently (2012) not mature enough to fully replace the XenServer-based infrastructure.

At FZI, an integration of a system, which allows the management of virtualized instances in combination with retaining structured, as well as unstructured, information, with regard to infrastructure monitoring, intrusion detection, incident and problem management, documentation, and Change Management, would be helpful for IT administrators.

[35]Software-based approaches existed on the x86 platform prior to the introduction of hardware support but brought with them various performance penalties.

[36]`http://www.citrix.com/products/xenserver/overview.html`

[37]`http://www.openstack.org/`

5.5.2. Requirements Analysis

The requirements analysis for the Virtualization and IaaS Connector encompasses the vision and goals, the constraints, a discussion of the system boundaries, as well as a list of the requirements for the component.

The results of the requirements validation are presented in Section 6.1 (page 318).

Vision and Goals

The vision and goals for the Virtualization and IaaS Connector are motivated mostly by the shortcomings experienced with software tools for the management of virtual machines at FZI Research Center for Information Technology (see Section 3.1, page 82). Aspects that provide potential for improvement are creating and deleting virtual machines, applying changes to virtual machines, as well as managing dependencies between virtual machines and its owners.

Vision The vision for the Virtualization and IaaS Connector can be described as follows:

To implement a tool that simplifies the management of virtual machines, as well as of IaaS resources, by enabling the re-use of existing explicitly stored, and implicitly derived information (V-K01).

Goals The goals of the Virtualization and IaaS Connector can be summarized as follows:

- Integrate the management of virtual machines and IaaS resources into a unified interface for Configuration Management, Change Management, infrastructure monitoring, intrusion detection, Incident and Problem Management, as well as documentation (G-K01).
- Reduce the need for keeping and maintaining duplicate information, e.g., as configuration in the virtualization management console, and as separate information in the Configuration Management System (G-K02).
- Make possible the re-use of existing information about hardware, software, virtual machines, IaaS resources, services, as well as their dependencies (G-K03).
- Allow structured linking between technical information and organizational information (e.g., between a virtual machine, the project in which the virtual machine is used, as well as the owner of the virtual machine) (G-K04).

- Allow the structured linking between service dependencies (e.g., between a Web server in a virtual machine, and a database server, which is run in another virtual machine) (G-K05).
- Make 'intelligent' use of existing information for the purposes of virtual machine management and IaaS resources management (G-K06).

After determining the vision and goals for the Virtualization and IaaS Connector, the constraints were collected.

Constraints

The following paragraphs list the organizational and technical constraints of the Virtualization and IaaS Connector.

Organizational Constraints Organizational constraints are the area of application, the intended user group and the operating conditions [Bal09, pages 459–460]. The Virtualization and IaaS Connector's organizational constraints are as follows:

- The Virtualization and IaaS Connector is primarily used by the members of the IT department, who create and maintain virtual machines and IaaS resources.
- Additionally, the Virtualization and IaaS Connector can be used by persons who are not members of the IT administration department, in order to manage IaaS resources (i.e., creating, starting, stopping, changing, and deleting IaaS instances).
- The Virtualization and IaaS Connector can manage virtualization platforms (e.g., Xen), as well as private and public IaaS platforms (e.g., OpenStack, and EC2).

Technical Constraints (Server) The technical constraints for the server side of the Virtualization and IaaS Connector are as follows:

- The Virtualization and IaaS Connector is a part of the ITSM Wiki, which is realized by using the MediaWiki software. MediaWiki is extensible by programming against an API (for more information about extending MediaWiki, please see Section 4.1.3, page 122).
- MediaWiki is programmed in the PHP language [Med11a], which imposes the technical constraint of also using this language for the Virtualization and IaaS Connector.
- MediaWiki runs on Web servers, which allow the execution of PHP scripts. Most often, the LAMP platform is used for running MediaWiki.

- The Virtualization and IaaS Connector accesses MediaWiki by using documented API calls. With respect to the database system, all databases that are supported by MediaWiki are also supported by the Virtualization and IaaS Connector.
- XenServer is accessed via the XenServer Management API[38].
- IaaS resources are accessed via an abstraction layer.

Technical Constraints (Client) The ITSM Wiki in general and the Virtualization and IaaS Connector in particular are accessed by using a Web browser. As long as a browser that complies with current Web standards is available, any device and operating system can be used.

System Boundaries

Figure 5.33 shows the systems boundaries of the Virtualization and IaaS Connector, as well as the components that make up the system. The graph is inspired by the graph found in [Bal09, page 462].

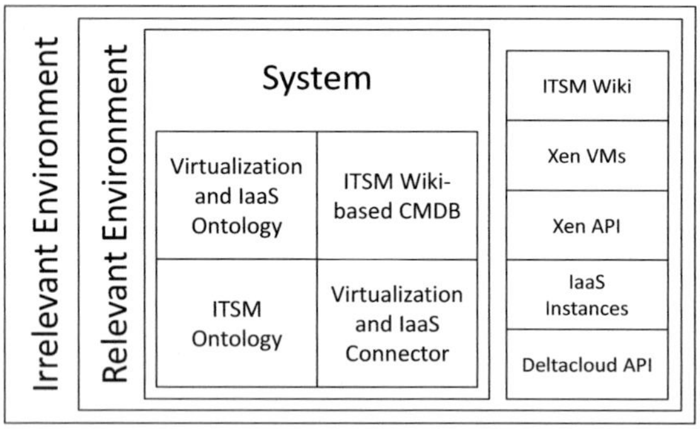

Figure 5.33.: System Boundaries of the Virtualization and IaaS Connector

System With respect to the Virtualization and IaaS Connector, the following items are part of the system:

- *Virtualization and IaaS Ontology:* The Virtualization and IaaS Ontology models all classes and properties that are relevant to the management of virtualized and IaaS resources.

[38] `http://docs.vmd.citrix.com/XenServer/6.0.0/1.0/en_gb/api/`

- *ITSM Ontology:* Classes and properties of the core ITSM parts are modeled in the ITSM Ontology, as described in Section 4.3.4 (page 167).
- *ITSM Wiki-based CMDB:* The ITSM Wiki-based CMDB retains configuration items and their dependencies.
- *Virtualization and IaaS Connector:* The Virtualization and IaaS Connector implements the functionalities for executing changes made to ITSM Wiki pages in the corresponding virtualization infrastructure (e.g., a virtual machine is created after the corresponding wiki page is generated).

Relevant Environment The relevant environment consists of elements that are not by themselves considered parts of the Virtualization and IaaS Connector but which interact with it on a regular basis. Parts of the relevant environment are:

- *ITSM Wiki:* The ITSM Wiki contains all the information that is relevant for providing IT services. It is accessed by the Virtualization and IaaS Connector in order to get information about configuration items and their dependencies.
- *Xen Virtual Machines:* Virtual machines managed by the Xen virtualization platform.
- *Xen API:* The Xen API is used in order to manage (e.g., create, start, stop, delete, and modify) virtual machines.
- *IaaS Instances:* IaaS instances are virtualized computers that run in IaaS environments (e.g., OpenStack, or EC2). The instances can be run either in private clouds or public clouds.
- *Deltacloud API:* Deltacloud is an API, which abstracts from the APIs used by different IaaS providers.

Requirements

The following two paragraphs outline the functional and non-functional requirements for the Virtualization and IaaS Connector.

Functional Requirements The functional requirements for the Virtualization and IaaS Connector can be summarized as follows:

- The creation and maintenance of virtualized instances, as well as IaaS resources, has to be made possible from within the ITSM Wiki (R-K01).

- When creating and changing parameters of virtualized instances, and IaaS resources, consistency checks based on the information contained in the ITSM Wiki have to be performed in order to avoid misconfigurations (R-K02).
- Virtualized instances and IaaS resources can be checked for availability by the Infrastructure Monitoring Component (Section 5.2, page 234), based on information stored in the ITSM Wiki (R-K03).
- When encountering problems with virtualized instances and IaaS resources (e.g., due to failing hardware), the remaining resources have to be assigned according to information stored in the ITSM Wiki. This information can include dependencies between services and instances, as well as the priority of services and instances (e.g., depending on SLAs, projects, and people who make use of the services and instances) (R-K04).
- By providing information to the Incident and Problem Analyzer Component (Section 5.4, page 284), the diagnosis of the cause of incidents and problems should be simplified (R-K05).
- The Intrusion Detection Component (Section 5.3, page 261) has to be able to use information about virtualized instances and IaaS resources stored in the ITSM Wiki (R-K06).

Non-functional Requirements The non-functional requirements for the Virtualization and IaaS Connector are:

- The component has to be integrated into the ITSM Wiki.
- It has to be made sure that only valid data is written to the wiki.
- No changes should be necessary in the code base of MediaWiki, Semantic MediaWiki, or the used virtualization and IaaS platforms.

5.5.3. Use Cases

This subsection shows a number of use cases in order to present the purpose and the benefits of the Virtualization and IaaS Connector.

Creating Virtual Machines

Virtual machines are instantiated by creating a wiki page in the ITSM Wiki. The wiki page uses Semantic Forms in order to provide a form-based mechanism for entering structured information.

Modifying Virtual Machines

Modifying virtual machines is accomplished by changing information within the form-based interface of the ITSM Wiki.

Deleting Virtual Machines

Virtual machines are deleted by changing the category of the instance's wiki page. Before a virtual machine can be moved to this category, checks are performed that prevent IT administrators from deleting virtual machines, which are still needed (e.g., because a Web server from another virtual machine uses the database server that is running on the machine).

Listing the Owners of Virtual Machines

When managing virtual machines for internal customers, the owners of the machines have to be able to be contacted. An example is the announcement of a maintenance shutdown of a virtualization server. In this case, a list of all affected users has to be created in order to send a notification.

Statistics and Data Analysis

Statistics can be generated from information retained in the ITSM Wiki. Simple examples of statistics are the number of virtual machines per entity (e.g., per department, per user, or per project). More complex examples are statistics that make use of information provided by other components (e.g., the intrusion detection component). In addition, Semantic MediaWiki's query mechanism provides a tool for flexible ad-hoc queries over the whole information stored in the ITSM Wiki.

5.5.4. Relevant Information

Relevant information with regard to virtualization and IaaS management is as follows:

- Virtual machine identifier
- Virtualization host or IaaS service
- Location of the host or service
- Owner of the VM
- Instance size (e.g., number of CPUs)

- RAM size
- Hard disk configuration
- Network segment and IP address
- Status of the host (e.g., stopped, or running)
- Operating system and template
- Dependencies between VMs

5.5.5. Used Technologies

This subsection provides a short introduction into the technologies that are used in the Virtualization and IaaS Connector. First, virtualization is described, followed by an overview of relevant IaaS platforms. Finally, APIs for the management of IaaS instances are presented.

Virtualization

There exist various virtualization platforms (e.g., VMware vSphere Hypervisor[39], and Citrix XenServer[40]). Because of FZI's already existing XenServer-based virtualization infrastructure, this platform is used in the context of this work. In general, every virtualization infrastructure that provides an API should be able to be accessed by the Virtualization and IaaS Connector. Reference [BDF^{+}03] describes the Xen platform, while the Citrix XenServer Management SDK and API are described in [Cit10a, Cit10b].

Infrastructure as a Service Platforms

Reference [FE10, page 5] defines the term Infrastructure as a Service as follows:

> "Infrastructure-as-a-service (IaaS) refers to computing resources as a service. This includes virtualized computers with guaranteed processing power and reserved bandwidth for storage and Internet access." [FE10, page 5]

The definition in [KBNT11, page 18] is as follows:

[39] `http://www.vmware.com/products/vsphere-hypervisor/overview.html`
[40] `http://www.citrix.com/products/xenserver/overview.html`

> "The IaaS layer gives the users an abstracted view on the hardware, i.e., computers, mass storage systems, networks, etc. This is achieved by providing a user interface for the management of a number of resources in the resource set sub-layer (RS). It enables the users to allocate a subset of the resources for their own use. Typical functions available from the user interface include creating or removing operating system images, scaling required capacities, or defining network topologies. Moreover, the interface provides the required functionality for operations, such as starting and stopping operating system instances." [KBNT11, page 18]

In the context of the Virtualization and IaaS Connector, IaaS is limited to computing resources, including local storage and network connectivity. Larger mass storage systems or complex networks are not included and considered future work.

IaaS resources can be classified as being part of a public cloud, a private cloud, or a hybrid cloud. Hybrid clouds, which are a mixture of public and private cloud, are not addressed further in the context of this work.

Public Cloud Reference [FE10, page 7] defines the term public cloud as follows:

> "In the public cloud (or external cloud) computing resources are dynamically provisioned over the Internet via Web applications or Web services from an off-site third-party provider. Public clouds are run by third parties, and applications from different customers are likely to be mixed together on the cloud's servers, storage systems, and networks." [FE10, page 7]

Reference [KBNT11, page 15] defines a public cloud as follows:

> "A public cloud (also called 'external cloud') comprises all cloud offerings where the providers and the potential users do not belong to the same organizational unit. The providers make their cloud accessible to the public and usually offer a self-service Web portal where the users can specify their desired scope of services. For this purpose, no overall framework agreement is necessary, but the contractual obligations are entered within the scope of the performance specifications. The services are billed on the basis of the resources actually used in the corresponding period." [KBNT11, page 15]

Infrastructure as a Service is provided by several companies, e.g., Amazon Elastic Compute Cloud (Amazon EC2)[41]. More information about EC2 can be found in [Mur08, pages 161–237]. A table of public IaaS offerings is given in [KBNT11, page 19].

[41] `http://aws.amazon.com/ec2/`

Private Cloud In [FE10, page 7], the term private cloud is defined as follows:

> "Private cloud (or internal cloud) refers to cloud computing on private networks. Private clouds are built for the exclusive use of one client, providing full control over data, security, and quality of service. Private clouds can be built and managed by a company's own IT organization or by a cloud provider." [FE10, page 7]

In [KBNT11, page 15], private cloud is defined as follows:

> "[T]he providers and users of a so-called private cloud (also referred to as 'internal cloud' or 'IntraCloud') belong to the same organizational unit. The main reason why a private cloud would be preferred over a public cloud is usually security: In the private cloud, control over the data remains with the users or their organization." [KBNT11, page 15]

There is a number of platforms for the deployment of private clouds, e.g., OpenStack[42], Eucalyptus [NWG+09], and CloudStack[43]. An overview of platforms can be found in [KBNT11, page 55].

APIs for the Management of IaaS Instances

There exist various providers of cloud virtualization instances, each with its own mechanisms and sets of APIs for managing instances. While the different APIs are not a problem as long as all instances are run at a single cloud provider, it becomes a problem as soon as the need for interacting with multiple providers arises. In order to address the problem of the different APIs, abstraction layers, which provide a single API, and which can be used to manage various instances hosted at different providers, were created. There are several projects that provide free APIs, among them Apache Libcloud[44] and Apache Deltacloud[45].

Deltacloud, which is used as the abstraction API in the Virtualization and IaaS Connector, is a cloud API that is based on the REpresentational State Transfer (REST) concept [FT02, RR07] and as such, in contrast to Libcloud, is not dependent on a single language, which has to be used with the API.

[42] http://www.openstack.org/
[43] http://cloudstack.apache.org/
[44] http://libcloud.apache.org/
[45] http://deltacloud.apache.org/

5.5.6. Virtualization and IaaS Ontology

The Virtualization and IaaS Connector's data model is an ontology. While the ITSM Ontology, which is the data model for the core ITSM classes and properties, is described in Section 4.3.4 (page 167), this subsection describes the parts of the ontology that are relevant to the Virtualization and IaaS Connector.

Class Hierarchy

Figure 5.34 shows the class hierarchy of the Virtualization and IaaS Ontology. All classes are subclasses of the *Thing* class. Class hierarchies are expressed with the *is-a* property.

Figure 5.34.: Class Hierarchy of the Virtualization and IaaS Ontology

Classes, Object Properties, and Data Properties

Table 5.5 shows the classes, object properties, and data properties of the Virtualization and IaaS Ontology. In the table, classes and properties that are relevant in the context of the Virtualization and IaaS Ontology are shown in boldface type. Classes and properties, which are only of secondary interest in this context are displayed in regular type.

Table 5.5.: Virtualization and IaaS Ontology

Domain Class	Property	Range
BitType	*inherited from Type class*	*no additional properties*
Building	*inherited from Location class*	
	City {0..1}	<String>
	Street {0..1}	<String>
	ZipCode {0..1}	<String>
Computer	*inherited from Host class*	
	LastDomainConnectDate {0..1}	<Date>
	MemberOfWindowsDomain {0..1}	<Boolean>
	OperatingSystemInstallationDate {0..1}	<Date>
	hasComputerUsageType {0..1}	ComputerUsageType
	hasLocalAdministrator {0..n}	Contact, User
ComputerUsageType	*inherited from Type class*	*no additional properties*
ConnectionType	*inherited from Type class*	*no additional properties*
Contact	*inherited from Person class*	*no additional properties*
Hardware	*inherited from Thing class*	
	Model {0..1}	<String>
	ProductNumber {0..1}	<String>
	SerialNumber {0..1}	<String>
	hasManufacturer {0..1}	Organization
	hasVendor {0..1}	Organization
	isCompatibleWith {0..n}	Thing
	isIncompatibleWith {0..n}	Thing
Host	*inherited from Thing class*	
	Model {0..1}	<String>
	ProductNumber {0..1}	<String>
	SerialNumber {0..1}	<String>
	hasCommissioningStatusType {0..1}	CommissioningStatusType
	hasContactPerson {0..n}	Person
	hasInstalledHardware {0..n}	Hardware
	hasInstalledSoftware {0..n}	Software
	hasManufacturer {0..1}	Organization
	hasOwner {0..1}	Person
	hasVendor {0..1}	Organization
	isLocatedIn {0..1}	Location

(*table continues*)

Table 5.5.: Virtualization and IaaS Ontology (continued)

Domain Class	Property	Range
IaasInstance	*inherited from VirtualComputer class*	
	hasIaasInstanceType {0..1}	IaasInstanceType
	runsInLocation {0..1}	Location
IaasInstanceType	*inherited from Type class*	
	NumberOfCores {0..1}	<Number>
	RamSize {0..1}	<Quantity>
	hasVirtualNetworkAdapter {0..n}	VirtualNetworkAdapter
	hasVirtualPersistentStorage {0..n}	VirtualPersistentStorage
Location	*inherited from Thing class*	*no additional properties*
NetworkAdapter	*inherited from Hardware class*	
	ConnectionSpeed {0..1}	<Quantity>
	IPv4Address {0..1}	<String>
	IPv4DefaultGateway {0..1}	<String>
	IPv4DHCPEnabled {0..1}	<Boolean>
	IPv4DHCPServer {0..1}	<String>
	IPv4DNSServer {0..n}	<String>
	IPv4SubnetMask {0..1}	<String>
	IPv6Address {0..1}	<String>
	IPv6DefaultGateway {0..1}	<String>
	IPv6DNSServer {0..n}	<String>
	MACAddress {0..1}	<String>
	hasConnectionType {0..1}	ConnectionType
	hasNetworkAdapterType {0..1}	NetworkAdapterType
	hasNetworkConnectionTo {0..1}	NetworkAdapter
	isPartOfNetworkSegment {0..1}	NetworkSegment
NetworkAdapterType	*inherited from Type class*	*no additional properties*
NetworkSegment	*inherited from Thing class*	
	DefaultIPv4Gateway {0..1}	<String>
	DefaultIPv6Gateway {0..1}	<String>
	EndIPv4Address {0..1}	<String>
	EndIPv6Address {0..1}	<String>
	StartIPv4Address {0..1}	<String>
	StartIPv6Address {0..1}	<String>
	IPv4SubnetMask {0..1}	<String>
	IPv6SubnetMask {0..1}	<String>
	VirtualLanIdentifier {0..1}	<Number>
Organization	*inherited from Thing class*	
	City {0..1}	<String>
	Country {0..1}	<String>
	EMailAddress {0..1}	<String>
	FaxNumber {0..1}	<String>
	PhoneNumber {0..1}	<String>
	Street {0..1}	<String>
	WebPage {0..1}	<String>
	ZipCode {0..1}	<String>

(*table continues*)

Table 5.5.: Virtualization and IaaS Ontology (continued)

Domain Class	**Property**	**Range**
OrganizationalUnit	*inherited from Thing class*	
	hasDeputyManager {0..n}	<Person>
	hasITContact {0..n}	<Person>
	hasManager {0..n}	<Person>
	isPartOfOrganization {0..1}	Organization
	isPartOfOrganizationalUnit {0..1}	OrganizationalUnit
PersistentStorage	*inherited from Hardware class*	
	TotalCapacity {0..1}	<Quantity>
	UnallocatedCapacity {0..1}	<Quantity>
	containsPartition {0..n}	PersistentStoragePartition
	hasInterfaceType {0..1}	PersistentStorageIfType
PersistentStorageIfType	*inherited from Type class*	*no additional properties*
PersistentStoragePartition	*inherited from Thing class*	
	DriveLetter {0..1}	<String>
	FileSystem {0..1}	<String>
	Size {0..1}	<Quantity>
PersistentStorageType	*inherited from Type class*	*no additional properties*
Person	*inherited from Thing class*	
	EMailAddress {0..n}	<Email>
	FamilyName {0..1}	<String>
	FaxNumber {0..n}	<Telephone number>
	GivenName {0..1}	<String>
	JobTitle {0..1}	<String>
	PhoneNumber {0..n}	<Telephone number>
	hasKnowledgeDomain {0..n}	KnowledgeDomain
	hasManager {0..1}	Person
	hasOffice {0..1}	Room
	hasRole {0..n}	Role
	isMemberOfOrganization {0..n}	Organization
	isMemberOfOrganizationalUnit {0..n}	OrganizationalUnit
PhysicalComputer	*inherited from Computer class*	
	hasComputerFormFactorType {0..1}	ComputerFormFactorType
Rack	*inherited from Location class*	
	Height {0..1}	<Quantity>
	isLocatedInRoom {0..1}	Room
Room	*inherited from Location class*	
	isLocatedInBuilding {0..1}	Building

(*table continues*)

Table 5.5.: Virtualization and IaaS Ontology (continued)

Domain Class	Property	Range
Software	*inherited from Thing class*	
	SoftwareVersion {0..1}	<String>
	hasBitType {0..1}	BitType
	hasLanguage {0..n}	Language
	hasManufacturer {0..1}	Organization
	hasSoftwareType {0..1}	SoftwareType
	hasVendor {0..1}	Organization
	isCompatibleWith {0..n}	Thing
	isIncompatibleWith {0..n}	Thing
	isPartOfSoftwareFamily {0..1}	SoftwareFamily
SoftwareFamily	*inherited from Thing class*	
	isPartOfSoftwareFamily {0..1}	SoftwareFamily
SoftwareType	*inherited from Type class*	*no additional properties*
Thing	Description {0..1}	<Text>
	Name {1}	<String>
	Version {0..1}	<Number>
	hasDependency {0..n}	Thing
	hasParent {0..n}	Thing
	isConnectedTo {0..n}	Thing
	isRelatedTo {0..n}	Thing
Type	*inherited from Thing class*	*no additional properties*
User	*inherited from Person class*	
	CreationDate {0..1}	<Date>
	DeletionDate {0..1}	<Date>
	LastLoginDate {0..1}	<Date>
	LoginName {0..1}	<String>
	UniqueIdentifier {0..1}	<String>
	hasAccountStatusType {0..1}	AccountStatusType
VirtualComputer	*inherited from Computer class*	
	State {0..1}	<String>
	hasVirtualNetworkAdapter {0..n}	VirtualNetworkAdapter
	hasVirtualPersistentStorage {0..n}	VirtualPersistentStorage
VirtualizedInstance	*inherited from VirtualComputer class*	
	NumberOfCores {0..1}	<Number>
	RamSize {0..1}	<Quantity>
	runsOnPhysicalComputer {0..1}	PhysicalComputer
VirtualNetworkAdapter	*inherited from VirtualResource class*	
	Active {0..1}	<Boolean>
	MACAddress {0..1}	<String>
	isPartOfNetworkSegment {0..1}	NetworkSegment
VirtualPersistentStorage	*inherited from VirtualResource class*	
	PersistentStorageCapacity {0..1}	<String>
VirtualResource	*inherited from Thing class*	*no additional properties*

Descriptions and Exemplary Instances

Section 4.3.4 (page 173) shows a short description, as well as exemplary instances, for each class of the Virtualization and IaaS Ontology. The presentation in a single table is done in order to avoid unnecessary duplication of information.

5.5.7. Prior and Related Work

There exist several non-semantic management interfaces for managing virtual instances and IaaS environments.

Citrix XenServer provides a GUI-based interface for managing virtualization servers [Cit12]. Amazon provides a Web-based GUI interface for managing instances in its EC2 offering [Ama12]. Platforms for running private IaaS environments come with Web-based management interfaces, e.g., OpenStack [Ope12b, 274–281], and CloudStack [Apa12].

An overview of cloud management services and tools is given in [KBNT11, pages 41–46]. The interfaces of these management interfaces are designed to provide an efficient way to manage the underlying virtualization platforms. However, they do not provide mechanisms for seamlessly integrating additional information, as implemented in the ITSM Wiki. As most tools provide the possibility to add a textual description to resources, these descriptions cannot be linked to each other or formatted. Furthermore, while properties can be stored in a structured format, this information cannot be used in ad-hoc queries. Finally, integrating information with regard to virtualization and IaaS with information such as infrastructure monitoring and intrusion detection is not possible in the management interfaces.

In the area of ontologies and semantic approaches in the context of cloud computing, [HR10] describes the use of ontologies for modeling cloud infrastructures. However, no concrete ontology is described that could be re-used. Reference [KC12] describes an ontology in the cloud computing domain. In [MJL11], an ontology-supported approach for cloud resource management is presented, which focuses on allocating jobs to cloud resources based on information retained in an ontology. In [MADM+11], an ontology that supports user in discovering services in clouds, which span multiple providers, is described.

Reference [HMS+10] addresses the use of semantic technologies in the area of enterprise cloud management. Addressed topics are "data integration, collaborative documentation and annotation and intelligent information access and analytics" [HMS+10]. The approach builds on top of an existing commercial cloud management suite, eCloudManager[46], makes use of a Semantic Wiki, and presents an ontology for enterprise cloud management.

When compared to the work presented in this thesis, the following observations can be made: The cloud ontologies described as related work are focused on modeling certain aspects of the cloud domain, without modeling the virtualization domain that is relevant in this component. With regard to the integration of the other components, such as monitoring or intrusion detection, no classes are present in the ontologies. With regard to providing an integrated environment for managing and documenting cloud infrastructures, the eCloudManager Intelligence Edition [HMS+10] uses a similar approach. However, in contrast to the work presented in this thesis, it aims at larger-scale installations. In this domain, as a dedicated cloud management solution, it exceeds the capabilities of the ITSM Wiki with regard to cloud management.

5.6. Summary

In this chapter, an overview of the components developed for this thesis was given. In Section 5.1 (page 188) the Information Gathering Component, which automatically populates and updates the ITSM Wiki by reading information directly from hosts over the network, was introduced. In Section 5.2 (page 234) the Infrastructure Monitoring Component, which implements an interface to the infrastructure monitoring application Nagios, was presented. Following that, in Section 5.3 (page 261), the Intrusion Detection Component, which processes data from the intrusion detection system Snort, was described. In Section 5.4 (page 284), the Incident and Problem Analyzer Component, which helps IT administrators to track down the causes of incidents and problems, was presented. Finally, in Section 5.5 (page 298), the Virtualization and IaaS Connector, which enables IT administrators to manage virtual machines and IaaS instances from within the ITSM Wiki, was introduced.

In the following Chapter 6, the evaluation of the ITSM Wiki and its components is presented.

[46] `http://www.fluidops.com/ecloudmanager/`

6. Evaluation

In this chapter, the results of the evaluation of the ITSM Wiki are presented. The scope of the evaluation are the aspects of the tool, which were described in Chapter 4 (page 115) and Chapter 5 (page 185). The references for the evaluation are the environment, as well as the tools, which were described in Chapter 3 (page 81), Chapter 4 (page 115), and Chapter 5 (page 185).

The evaluation consists of three parts that are presented in the following sections.

First, in Section 6.1 (page 318), the ITSM Wiki is validated against the requirements, which were outlined in previous chapters of the dissertation. Second, in Section 6.2 (page 384), the results of the user study are presented. Third, in Section 6.3 (page 424), a summary of the evaluation results is given.

6.1. Validation

The first part of the evaluation is the validation of the requirements, which were defined in Chapter 4 (page 115) and Chapter 5 (page 185). In addition, the previously used legacy tools, as well as two open source ITSM tools, are validated against the same requirements.

In the following subsections, first, the approach for the requirements validation is described in Section 6.1.1 (page 318), followed by a description of the resources, which were used to perform the validation, in Section 6.1.2 (page 319). After that, Section 6.1.3 (page 321) presents the results of the validation. Finally, in Section 6.1.4 (page 375), the results of the validation are interpreted.

6.1.1. Approach

In this subsection, first, the foundation of the approach that was used for validating the criteria, is outlined. Following that, the scoring system, which is used to rate individual requirements, is defined. After that, the types of validation criteria are described.

The validation of the requirements follows the approach described in [Bal09, pages 513–514]. According to [Bal09, pages 514][1], validation means to check if the product meets the requirements. This is considered hard, because there is no document that fully describes against what the checks can be performed. There are two approaches listed, which can be used, and which complement each other. The first approach is to check all specified requirements against the visions and goals, while the second approach is to have stakeholders check the requirements specification [Bal09, pages 514].

Scores

In order to describe the degree, to which the criterion is satisfied by one of the evaluated tools, a scale is defined. The scale is oriented on the four-point system, with four being the best score and zero being the worst. Table 6.1 shows the scores, as well as a textual description of the meaning of the individual scores.

[1] In German: "Validieren bedeutet, die Anforderungsspezifikation daraufhin zu überprüfen, ob sie das gewünschte Produkt richtig beschreibt. Das ist schwierig, da es kein Dokument gibt, gegen das die Prüfung durchgeführt werden kann. Es bieten sich zwei ergänzende Prüfverfahren an:

- Alle spezifizierten Anforderungen werden nochmals gegen die beschriebenen Visionen und Ziele geprüft. Trägt jede Anforderung dazu bei, die Visionen und Ziele zu verwirklichen? Wenn nein, dann ist sie zu entfernen.
- Alle Stakeholder bekommen die Anforderungsspezifikation zur Überprüfung – entweder jeder für sich oder im Rahmen eines gemeinsamen Reviews. Nach Durchführung dieser Aktivitäten sollten die Anforderungen konsolidiert sein." [Bal09, page 514]

Score	Description
4	All criteria fully satisfied.
3	All criteria fairly satisfied.
2	Most criteria satisfied.
1	Some criteria satisfied.
0	No criteria satisfied.

Table 6.1.: Scores Used in Validation

Validation Criteria Types

In order to uniquely identify the criteria of the validation, such as goals, visions, and requirements, each criterion is assigned an identifier. The identifier (e.g., 'R-C02') is structured as follows: The first character describes the type of the criterion (e.g., 'R' for requirement). The character after the dash (e.g., 'C') describes the block, in which the criterion was described (throughout the thesis, blocks are named sequentially, starting with 'A'). The next two characters form a sequentially increasing number, which identifies the criterion within the block.

Table 6.2 shows the types of validation criteria, which are used in this chapter.

Criterion Type	Description
G	Goal
I	Improvement
O	Objective
R	Requirement
V	Vision

Table 6.2.: Validation Criteria Types

6.1.2. Used Resources

In order to perform the validation, the reference tools were installed, and a hands-on validation was performed. In addition, information from the Web sites of the tools, as well as documentation, was used.

For the purpose of the validation, the following tools and references were used:

- BASE
  - Software version 1.4.5 [Sou14a]

- i-doit open
  - Software version 0.9.9-7 [Sou14b]
  - Manual: The German version of the manual [i-d11c], including its subpages was used, which was more exhaustive than the English version.
  - Description of features [i-d14]
- MediaWiki and extensions
  - MediaWiki software version 1.22.0 [Wik14a]
  - Semantic MediaWiki software version 1.9.0.1 [Sou14c]
  - Semantic Forms software downloaded on 2014-01-13 [Wik14b]
- Microsoft Excel 2013
- OTRS::ITSM
  - OTRS software version 3.3.3 [OTR14b]. For the evaluation, the OTRS Appliance [OTR14a] was used.
  - OTRS::ITSM Bundle version 3.3.3 [OTR14f]. The bundle consists of the following subcomponents:
    * GeneralCatalog version 3.3.3
    * ITSMCore version 3.3.3
    * ITSMIncidentProblemManagement version 3.3.3
    * ITSMConfigurationManagement version 3.3.3
    * ITSMChangeManagement version 3.3.3
    * ITSMServiceLevelManagement version 3.3.3
    * ImportExport version 3.3.3
  - OTRS FAQ Module version 2.3.1 [OTR14c]
  - OTRS SystemMonitoring Module version 2.5.2 [OTR14e]
  - OTRS admin manual version 3.3 [OTR13a]
  - OTRS::ITSM manual version 3.3 [OTR13d]
  - OTRS developer manual version 3.3 [OTR13b]
  - OTRS FAQ manual version 2.3.1 [OTR13c]
  - OTRS SystemMonitoring manual version 2.5.2 [OTR13e]
  - Description of features [OTR14d]

- Snorby
  - Software version 2.6.2 [Sno14a]
  - Manual: E-book [Sno14b] and its subpages

The items in the list were the most up-to-date versions of the tools when starting the evaluation in January 2014.

There are two versions of i-doit, namely the open source software *i-doit open*, and the commercially available software *i-doit pro*. The commercial version offers a number of features that are not available in the open source version [i-d14]. In the validation, the open source version i-doit open is used as a reference.

All tools that were used as references, namely Microsoft Excel, PmWiki, OTRS::ITSM, i-doit open, BASE, and Snorby are mature tools that are ready for enterprise use and which have dedicated developers and companies behind them. In contrast, the tools developed in the context of this thesis are in a far less refined state and do not intent to directly compete with the reference tools at the current stage of implementation. The validation of the criteria aims at comparing the criteria, in which ITSM Wiki adds new and improved features.

6.1.3. Results of the Validation of Criteria

In this subsection, the visions, goals, improvements, objectives, and functional requirements of the ITSM Wiki and its subcomponents are validated.

The structure of the subsection follows the order, in which the requirements were presented in the dissertation. First, the requirements, which cover the relevant parts of the ITIL framework, as described in Section 4.2 (page 136), are validated, followed by the validation of the requirements of the components presented in Chapter 5 (page 185).

The ITSM Wiki, which is the platform that is developed in this thesis, is compared to five other solutions. The first is the one that was used for the respective task before designing the ITSM Wiki. These legacy tools were a combination of Microsoft Excel for managing structured information, and the non-semantic PmWiki, which was used for managing unstructured information. The second and third solutions are two established open source ITSM tools, namely OTRS::ITSM and i-doit open. Additionally, in Table 6.12, the Intrusion Detection Component is evaluated against two additional open source tools, namely BASE and Snorby.

Validation of the ITSM Platform

In this subsection, the various criteria of the core component of the ITSM Wiki, which were described in Section 4.2 (page 136), are validated.

The reference tools that are shown in columns four and five of the following tables are the open source ITSM and CMDB platforms OTRS::ITSM and i-doit open, which were presented in Section 3.3.1 (page 110) and Section 3.3.2 (page 111).

Configuration Management Requirements for the Configuration Management Systems, as specified in [LM07] are described in Section 4.2.1 (page 137). Table 6.3 shows the validation criteria, as well as the scores for the evaluated tools. The value in the ID column of the table is a reference to the associated criterion as given in Table 4.5 (page 137).

Table 6.3.: Validation of Configuration Management Criteria

ID	Criterion	Legacy	OTRS::ITSM	i-doit open	ITSM Wiki
R-A01	"CMDB should be linked to the [Definitive Media Library]" [LM07, page 194]	1	2	2	3
R-A02	"The Configuration Management System should prevent changes from being made to the IT infrastructure or service configuration baseline without valid authorization via Change Management." [LM07, page 195]	0	1	1	1
R-A03	"As far as possible, all changes should be recorded on the CMS at least by the time that the change is implemented." [LM07, page 195]	0	1	1	1

(*table continues*)

Table 6.3.: Validation of Configuration Management Criteria (continued)

ID	Criterion	Legacy	OTRS::ITSM	i-doit open	ITSM Wiki
R-A04	"The status (e.g. 'live', 'archive', etc.) of each CI affected by a change should be updated automatically if possible. Example ways in which this automatic recording of changes could be implemented include automatic updating of the CMS when software is moved between libraries (e.g. from 'acceptance test' to 'live', or from 'live' to an 'archive' library), when the service catalogue is changed, and when a release is distributed." [LM07, page 195]	0	2	1	3
R-A05	"Sufficient security controls to limit access on a need-to-know basis" [LM07, page 195]	0	2	1	2
R-A06	"Support for CIs of varying complexity" [LM07, page 195]	1	3	3	4
R-A07	"Hierarchic and networked relationships between CI" [LM07, page 195]	0	3	3	4
R-A08	"Easy addition of new CIs and deletion of old CIs" [LM07, page 195]	2	4	4	4
R-A09	"Automatic validation of input data" [LM07, page 195]	0	2	2	2
R-A10	"Automatic determination of all relationships that can be automatically established, when new CIs are added" [LM07, page 195]	0	2	2	3
R-A11	"Support for CIs with different model numbers, version numbers, and copy numbers" [LM07, page 195]	1	4	4	4
R-A12	"Automatic identification of other affected CIs when any CI is the subject of an incident report/record, problem record, known error record or RFC" [LM07, page 195]	0	4	2	4

(table continues)

Table 6.3.: Validation of Configuration Management Criteria (continued)

ID	Criterion	Legacy	OTRS::ITSM	i-doit open	ITSM Wiki
R-A13	"Integration of problem management data within the CMS, or at least an interface from the Configuration Management System to any separate problem management databases that may exist" [LM07, page 195]	1	4	2	3
R-A14	"Automatic updating and recording of the version number of a CI if the version number of any component CI is changed" [LM07, page 195]	0	3	1	1
R-A15	"Maintenance of a history of all CIs (both a historical record of the current version – such as installation date, records of Changes, previous locations, etc. – and of previous versions)" [LM07, page 195]	2	4	4	4
R-A16	"Support for the management and use of configuration baselines (corresponding to definitive copies, versions etc.), including support for reversion to trusted versions" [LM07, page 195]	0	1	1	1
R-A17	"Ease of interrogation of the CMS and good reporting facilities, including trend analysis (e.g. the ability to identify the number of RFCs affecting particular CIs)" [LM07, page 195]	0	4	2	4
R-A18	"Ease of reporting of the CI inventory so as to facilitate configuration audits" [LM07, page 195]	1	4	4	4
R-A19	"Flexible reporting tools to facilitate impact analyses" [LM07, page 195]	0	4	4	4
R-A20	"The ability to show graphically the configuration models and maps of interconnected CIs, and to input information about new CIs via such maps" [LM07, page 195]	0	1	1	1

(*table continues*)

Table 6.3.: Validation of Configuration Management Criteria (continued)

ID	Criterion	Legacy	OTRS::ITSM	i-doit open	ITSM Wiki
R-A21	"The ability to show the hierarchy of relationships between 'parent' CIs and 'child' CIs" [LM07, page 195]	0	4	4	4
R-A22	"Automating the initial discovery and configuration audits significantly increases the efficiency and effectiveness of Configuration Management. These tools can determine what hardware and software is installed and how applications are mapped to the infrastructure." [LM07, page 195]	0	1	2	3
	Mean score	0.4	2.7	2.3	2.9
	Standard deviation	0.7	1.2	1.2	1.2

While Table 6.3 contains the numerical results of the validation, the following list gives a more detailed textual explanation of the scores for each item:

- Requirement **R-A01**
  - *Legacy tools:* In the legacy tools, which were a combination of an Excel spreadsheet and a non-semantic wiki (PmWiki) no links to the Definitive Media Library were stored. While it is theoretically feasible to store links in Excel spreadsheets, the results are limited with regard to flexibility and the ability to use queries. In a non-semantic wiki, links can be stored to the DML, but cannot be further processed intelligently (e.g., by using queries).
  - *OTRS::ITSM:* Files can be attached directly to CIs. In addition, a link to the directory or file path can be stored as a structured link.
  - *i-doit open:* In i-doit open, files can be attached in two ways: The first way is to directly attach the file to a CI within i-doit open. The second way is to store a link to the directory path of the software in a structured format.
  - *ITSM Wiki:* In the ITSM Wiki, links to the DML can be stored in a structured format, and processed automatically (e.g., by queries). This allows to formulate more complex queries, such as 'get all locations of Windows media', from information items that store the links for each software CI (e.g., 'Windows 8 Professional'), as well as the information of the membership to software families (e.g., 'Windows'). The installation media for software has to be stored externally in a separate file share. In the ITSM Wiki, links are added to the file share in a structured format.

- Requirement **R-A02**
  - *All tools:* Changes as documented in the Configuration Management Systems are only representations of actual changes performed in the real world. Because of this fact, the Configuration Management System cannot prevent performing changes to the IT infrastructure. The fact that certain procedures have to be followed when performing changes has to be part of the policy, which has to be followed by IT administrators. Excel as a spreadsheet application does not allow to store automatic timestamps when information is modified, which prevents the checking of conformity with the policy.
- Requirement **R-A03**
  - *All tools:* Because the actual implementation of a change is done in other tools than the CMS, recording changes can only be mandated by policy. This means that none of the systems can actively force IT administrators to record changes to the CMS. Excel does not allow to store automatic timestamps when information is modified. This prevents the checking of conformity with the policy.
- Requirement **R-A04**
  - *Legacy tools:* In the legacy tools, the status of affected CIs could not be automatically updated due to the lack of structured information that represented the status.
  - *OTRS::ITSM:* Changes can be modeled. Automatic status updates are not implemented.
  - *i-doit open:* Changes are not modeled directly in i-doit open. Due to its extensibility, the ability to describe changes could be implemented as an add-on, which makes use of the structured information stored in the i-doit open database.
  - *ITSM Wiki:* In the ITSM Wiki, Semantic MediaWiki queries can be used in order to dynamically update information on wiki pages that are affected by information about changes in other pages.
- Requirement **R-A05**
  - *Legacy tools:* As part of the legacy tools, Excel provided only very limited security controls for restricting access to IT administrators (permissions were granted on the file level, which allowed to either access the whole file, or prevented users from doing so). In PmWiki, user accounts existed.
  - *OTRS::ITSM:* There exists a role-based access system. Users can be assigned to a number of roles (e.g., “itsm-change”, “itsm-change-builder”, and “itsm-change-manager”) [OTR13d].

- *i-doit open:* In i-doit open, users can be granted one of five different access levels, which specifies that the user is allowed to read, change, create, archive, or delete configuration items. The access level is the same for all CIs, which is enough for smaller IT teams in SME environments, but might be a problem for large teams.
- *ITSM Wiki:* While MediaWiki as the platform on which the ITSM Wiki is based, allows the restriction of pages, it is hard or impossible in practice, to lock down the wiki in order to provide minimal access, on the one hand, and allow IT administrators to work unhampered on the other hand. In SME scenarios, with a low number of IT administrators, fine-grained access is not so much of an issue as in very large IT environments.

- Requirement **R-A06**
  - *Legacy tools:* Microsoft Excel, as the first legacy tool did allow to add columns for each additional property. In PmWiki, adding more information equaled the editing of text. When looking at mechanisms that allowed to use the additional information, it can be seen that the information is unstructured and not usable flexibly, however.
  - *OTRS::ITSM:* Configuration items are defined by using classes. Each CI is part of one class. New classes can be created. Furthermore, the schema of each class can be defined. It is not possible, to create ad-hoc definitions of additional properties for single CIs that extend the properties of its class.
  - *i-doit open:* Information is structured in the form of object types and categories. Object types define a family of objects that have the same properties (e.g., servers, racks, and software). Object types consist of categories. Categories define forms, functions, and attributes. While object types can be modified, categories cannot be modified [i-d09a]. User-defined categories can be created and assigned to object types. The ad-hoc definition and structured storage of additional attributes are not possible.
  - *ITSM Wiki:* In the ITSM Wiki, additional properties and information can be added by users of the wiki in order to accommodate more complex configuration items.

- Requirement **R-A07**
  - *Legacy tools:* In the Excel spreadsheet, no hierarchic and networked relationships between configuration items could be stored and queried in an acceptable way. PmWiki allowed the textual representation of hierarchies and relationships, but didn't provide a way to store the information in a structured format. Due to this fact, the stored information was not understandable by PmWiki in order to gain benefits from the stored information.

  - *OTRS::ITSM:* Relationships between CIs can be expressed. Hierarchic information can be stored in CIs (e.g., CPUs or network adapters are modeled as parts of a computer).
  - *i-doit open:* In i-doit open, hierarchic relationships can be defined for some CI types (e.g., CPUs that are part of a server, or network adapters that contain ports) [i-d11b]. Special networked relationships can be defined to express connections between CIs (e.g., power connections, or data connections) [i-d08e]. Moreover, custom structured relations between CIs can be defined.
  - *ITSM Wiki:* In the ITSM Wiki, hierarchies and networks can be created by using object properties between wiki pages that represent configuration items. By using the query mechanism of Semantic MediaWiki, the hierarchies and relations can be processed in order to get additional insights.

- Requirement **R-A08**
  - *Legacy tools:* In the legacy tools, configuration items had to be created and deleted in both environments (Excel and PmWiki), if a textual description of the CI was necessary. This brought with it additional overhead, as well as potential for inconsistencies due to CIs that were deleted only in one of the two tools.
  - *OTRS::ITSM:* Configuration items can be easily added and retired.
  - *i-doit open:* CIs can be easily added and archived. The deletion of configuration items requires the highest level of access.
  - *ITSM Wiki:* The ITSM Wiki allows the easy addition and deletion of configuration items. Furthermore, a history is retained for deleted CIs.

- Requirement **R-A09**
  - *Legacy tools:* The legacy tools provided no method for automatic input validation.
  - *OTRS::ITSM:* Input fields can be specified as required. The syntax of fields is not checked for correct syntax by default. Regular expressions can be defined for checking the syntax of CI attributes [OTR13d, page 2].
  - *i-doit open:* Error messages are displayed, if the type of input data and the type of the field do not match (e.g., if letters are typed into a field that is used to represent the weight of a computer).
  - *ITSM Wiki:* By providing data types, the ITSM Wiki checks the syntax of certain properties before saving.

- Requirement **R-A10**
  - *Legacy tools:* In the legacy tools, no relationships could be automatically determined.
  - *OTRS::ITSM* and *i-doit open:* Automatic relationships can be added based on the information in the CMDB and limited by the used database.
  - *ITSM Wiki:* In the ITSM Wiki, some relationships are expressed as the result of Semantic MediaWiki queries. These relationships can be automatically established based on existing information. Furthermore, the Information Gathering Component reads information from the directory and Windows hosts.
- Requirement **R-A11**
  - *Legacy tools:* In the legacy tools, information about different model numbers, version numbers, and copy numbers could be stored in an additional column of the Excel spreadsheet, or in textual format in PmWiki. This information was not usable by mechanisms that exceeded the capabilities of sorting or full-text search.
  - *OTRS::ITSM* and *i-doit open:* Support exists for storing CIs with different model numbers, version numbers, and copy numbers.
  - *ITSM Wiki:* In the ITSM Wiki, model numbers, version numbers, and copy numbers can be stored in a structured format. This information can be made usable with Semantic MediaWiki mechanisms (e.g., queries).
- Requirement **R-A12**
  - *Legacy tools:* The legacy tools did not provide any mechanisms for automatically identifying affected CIs.
  - *OTRS::ITSM:* The status of CIs that have modeled dependencies in the CMDB is changed when CIs are marked as having issues.
  - *i-doit open:* SQL queries can be used in order to determine other affected CIs. A structured description of incidents, problems, or RFCs is not possible.
  - *ITSM Wiki:* In the ITSM Wiki, affected CIs can be found by using queries.
- Requirement **R-A13**
  - *Legacy tools:* In PmWiki, problems could be documented in plain text. While this allowed to store information and search for it by full-text search, no structured links between Problem Management and the CMS existed.
  - *OTRS::ITSM:* Incidents and problems are managed as tickets in OTRS::-ITSM. Incident and Problem Management is fully integrated.

  - *i-doit open:* Problems are not directly represented in i-doit open. A separate problem management database can be connected by using links.
  - *ITSM Wiki:* The ITSM Wiki provides a unified platform for managing problems and performing Configuration Management. Problems can be linked to configuration items by using object properties.

- Requirement **R-A14**
  - *Legacy tools:* In the legacy tools, no version numbers were used. Furthermore, implementing the functionality to automatically update CI versions would only have been possible in the Excel spreadsheet, because information in PmWiki could not be stored in a structured format.
  - *OTRS::ITSM:* Components can be modeled in two different ways. First, the definition of a CI class includes all possible subcomponents. In this mode, changes to component CIs trigger an update of the version number of the main CI. Second, CIs can be linked to other CIs. In this mode, version numbers are not updated.
  - *i-doit open:* Version numbers are not kept explicitly in the CMDB. Changes to CIs are documented, however.
  - *ITSM Wiki:* In the ITSM Wiki, version numbers are stored as Semantic MediaWiki data properties. The relations between configuration items are stored as object properties. While not supported at the current state of implementation, a tool could be implemented, which updates the version numbers in wiki pages based on the version numbers and the page history of its component CIs.

- Requirement **R-A15**
  - *Legacy tools:* In the Excel spreadsheet, no historical information was stored. In PmWiki, however, the wiki provided a mechanism for storing the history of all changes.
  - *OTRS::ITSM* and *i-doit open:* A history is kept of changes to the CMDB.
  - *ITSM Wiki:* The ITSM Wiki stores a history of all revisions of wiki pages.

- Requirement **R-A16**
  - *Legacy tools:* Configuration baselines and reversion to trusted versions were not supported in the legacy tools.
  - *OTRS::ITSM* and *i-doit open:* Support for configuration baselines is not directly implemented. Templates for CIs, which are duplicated, could be created, however. Reverting to trusted versions is possible by undoing documented changes to the CI.

- *ITSM Wiki:* In the ITSM Wiki, at the current state of implementation, configuration baselines are not supported. Baselines could be represented as a special category. Reverting to trusted versions is possible by reverting to a snapshot in the MediaWiki page history.

- Requirement **R-A17**
  - *Legacy tools:* In the legacy tools, reporting facilities were not present.
  - *OTRS::ITSM:* A number of existing statistics can be used. Furthermore, customized statistics can be created via the Web-based user interface.
  - *i-doit open:* Reports can be generated from information found in the CMDB by using SQL queries. RFCs are not stored explicitly in i-doit open.
  - *ITSM Wiki:* In the ITSM Wiki, queries can be used to create tables from all structured information found in the wiki.
- Requirement **R-A18**
  - *Legacy tools:* Basic reports could be created from the information found in the Excel spreadsheets.
  - *OTRS::ITSM:* Reports can be generated via the Web-based user interface.
  - *i-doit open:* Reports can be created by using SQL statements.
  - *ITSM Wiki:* In the ITSM Wiki, queries can be used to generate reports of CI inventories.
- Requirement **R-A19**
  - *Legacy tools:* In the legacy tools, no flexible reporting mechanisms existed, which allowed the performance of impact analysis. This is due to the fact that Excel is a spreadsheet application, which is not designed for performing queries in order to generate flexible reports. Furthermore, the unstructured format that was used to store information in PmWiki does not allow the generation of reports.
  - *OTRS::ITSM:* Impact analyses can be created based on structured information stored in the CMDB.
  - *i-doit open:* Impact analyses can be generated by using SQL statements.
  - *ITSM Wiki:* The ITSM Wiki, with its foundation on Semantic MediaWiki allows both, flexibility, as well as advanced query mechanisms.

- Requirement **R-A20**
  - *Legacy tools:* Viewing graphical information about CI interconnections was not possible with the legacy tools.
  - *OTRS::ITSM* and *i-doit open:* A graphical representation of CI interconnections is not implemented. The generation of a graphical representation could be implemented as an add-on based on the structured information found in the database.
  - *ITSM Wiki:* At the current state of implementation, the ITSM Wiki does not offer mechanisms for showing graphical representations of configuration models or interconnections between configuration items. Based on the Semantic MediaWiki properties, mechanisms for a graphical representation could be implemented as future work, however.
- Requirement **R-A21**
  - *Legacy tools:* The legacy tools did not provide mechanisms for showing hierarchy relationships between parent and child configuration items. This is because no structured information could be stored that expressed hierarchies in an acceptable and machine-understandable way.
  - *OTRS::ITSM* and *i-doit open:* The hierarchy of relationships between parent and child CIs can be shown.
  - *ITSM Wiki:* In the ITSM Wiki, hierarchic relationships are stored in a structured format and can be further processed.
- Requirement **R-A22**
  - *Legacy tools:* In the legacy tools, no mechanisms for the automatic discovery of configuration items were present.
  - *OTRS::ITSM:* Information about configuration items can be imported as CSV files. In order to generate these CSV files, an external discovery software has to be configured to store the information in the format that is required by OTRS::ITSM.
  - *i-doit open:* Information about configuration items can be imported from an external discovery software. This software requires the installation of a client on the hosts, from which information is gathered, however.
  - *ITSM Wiki:* The Information Gathering Component described in Section 5.1 (page 188) implements mechanisms for the automatic discovery of configuration items from Active Directory and Windows hosts without the installation of a client. Linux hosts are not supported at the current stage of implementation.

Service Knowledge Management The requirements for a Service Knowledge Management System, which are given in [LM07], are described in this thesis in Section 4.2.2 (page 142). In Table 6.4 the requirements, as well as the scores of the evaluated tools, are shown.

Table 6.4.: Validation of Service Knowledge Management Criteria

ID	Criterion	Legacy	OTRS::ITSM	i-doit open	ITSM Wiki
G-B01	"[E]nable organizations to improve the quality of management decision making by ensuring that reliable and secure information and data is available throughout the service lifecycle." [LM07, page 145]	1	3	2	4
O-B01	"Enabling the service provider to be more efficient and improve quality of service, increase satisfaction and reduce the cost of service" [LM07, page 145]	0	3	2	3
O-B02	"Ensuring staff have a clear and common understanding of the value that their services provide to customers and the ways in which benefits are realized from the use of those services" [LM07, page 145]	1	3	2	3
O-B03	"Ensuring that, at a given time and location, service provider staff have adequate information on:" "Who is currently using their services", "The current states of consumption", "Service delivery constraints", and "Difficulties faced by the customer in fully realizing the benefits expected from the service." [LM07, page 145]	1	2	2	2
I-B01	"Enhancing the **organization's effectiveness** through better decision making enabled by having the right information at the right time, and facilitating enterprise learning through the exchange and development of ideas and individuals" [CS07, page 125, emphasis in original]	1	3	2	4

(*table continues*)

Table 6.4.: Validation of Service Knowledge Management Criteria (continued)

ID	Criterion	Legacy	OTRS::ITSM	i-doit open	ITSM Wiki
I-B02	"Enhancing **customer-supplier relationships** through sharing information and services to expand capabilities through collaborative efforts" [CS07, page 125, emphasis in original]	1	2	0	2
I-B03	"Improving **business processes** through sharing lessons learned, results and best practices across the organization." [CS07, page 125, emphasis in original]	1	2	0	3
R-B01	Management of best practices in structured and unstructured formats.	2	2	2	4
R-B02	Management of lessons learned in structured and unstructured formats.	2	2	0	4
R-B03	Management of operating procedures in structured and unstructured formats.	2	3	2	4
R-B04	Management of key persons and stakeholders in structured and unstructured formats.	1	3	3	4
R-B05	Management of recommended literature and Web sites in structured and unstructured formats.	1	2	1	4
	Mean score	1.3	2.5	1.5	3.4
	Standard deviation	0.5	0.5	1.0	0.8

The following list gives an explanation of the scores given in Table 6.4:

- Goal **G-B01**
  - *Legacy tools:* The legacy tools, namely Microsoft Excel and PmWiki provided an information base, which satisfied the goal partially. In PmWiki, information was stored in free-text format, which allowed the documentation of knowledge. In order to be truly useful, mechanisms for storing information in a structured format were missing.
  - *OTRS::ITSM:* Structured information with respect to Incident and Problem Management, Service Level Management, Configuration Management, and

Change Management can be stored [OTR13d, page 17]. Moreover, rich-media text can be stored in predefined fields.

- *i-doit open:* Structured information about Configuration Management can be retained in i-doit open. With regard to unstructured information, as well as information about other ITIL disciplines, i-doit open does not offer all technical means to represent information that is required in order to fully support organizations in improving the quality of their decisions.
- *ITSM Wiki:* The ITSM Wiki provides means to store information in both, structured and unstructured format, which fully satisfies the technical aspects of the goal.

- Objective **O-B01**
  - *Legacy tools:* The legacy tools did not support Knowledge Management with regard to the mentioned objective.
  - *OTRS::ITSM:* Structured information that supports people and processes with respect to the objective can be retained. Furthermore, unstructured rich-media text can be stored alongside structured information.
  - *i-doit open:* In i-doit open, structured information that supports people and processes with regard to the objective can be retained. With respect to formatted, rich-media, unstructured information (e.g., formatted text with embedded graphics), i-doit open does not provide the necessary functionality.
  - *ITSM Wiki:* The ITSM Wiki provides a technical platform for supporting the people and process aspects of the objective.
- Objective **O-B02**
  - *Legacy tools:* The value of services could be documented in an unstructured format in PmWiki.
  - *OTRS::ITSM:* Structured information about Incident and Problem Management, Service Level Management, Configuration Management, and Change Management can be stored [OTR13d, page 17]. In addition, rich-media text can be stored alongside structured information.
  - *i-doit open:* Information about services and their dependencies can be retained in a structured format. Annotating services in a free-text, rich-media, unstructured format is not possible, however.
  - *ITSM Wiki:* In the ITSM Wiki, the value of services can be documented in a combination of structured and unstructured format. This allows the usage of the information in order to create new views on the information (e.g., a ranking of the importance of services, and the consequences of failing services).

- Objective **O-B03**
  - *Legacy tools:* The information could be stored in an unstructured format in PmWiki. Gaining advantages from the stored information that exceeded reading by IT administrators was not possible, however.
  - *OTRS::ITSM:* Structured information about Incident and Problem Management, Service Level Management, Configuration Management, and Change Management can be stored [OTR13d, page 17]. Rich-media text can be stored alongside structured information.
  - *i-doit open:* Structured information with regard to Configuration Management is present in i-doit open. Furthermore, the difficulties experienced by users can be accessed by looking at the automatic association of tickets with configuration items [i-d10c]. The representation of information is limited mostly to structured information (with the exception of non-formatted text in description fields).
  - *ITSM Wiki:* In the ITSM Wiki, the information can be stored in a combination of structured and unstructured formats. This allows generating tables that represent the information based on Semantic MediaWiki properties, which are stored in the wiki pages of the individual CIs. With respect to the current state of consumption, the integration of sensors that provide that information (e.g., performance metrics of Web servers, database servers, or the overall CPU status of the server) would be required. An integration of these metrics into the ITSM Wiki is considered future work.
- Improvement **I-B01**
  - *Legacy tools:* PmWiki provided a number or information within a Web-based interface. With regard to the structure and the ability to find information that exceeded the limits of full-text search or browsing, it lacked functionality, however.
  - *OTRS::ITSM:* Information about Incident and Problem Management, Service Level Management, Configuration Management, and Change Management can be stored [OTR13d, page 17]. Retaining information is not as flexible as in a semantic wiki.
  - *i-doit open:* The structured information provided in the CMDB fulfills some of the information needs. Enterprise learning and development of ideas requires functionalities that also support collaboratively creating and retaining unstructured rich-media information, which is not possible in i-doit open.
  - *ITSM Wiki:* The ITSM Wiki, with its ability to retain structured and unstructured information, together with its ability to process queries, allows to find information better than when only relying on full-text search.

- Improvement **I-B02**
  - *Legacy tools:* Collaboration between customers and suppliers seems to be a promising approach. Setting access permissions in PmWiki in order to allow access to only a limited amount of information, on the one hand, and allowing true collaboration, on the other hand, is not feasible by the security model, however.
  - *OTRS::ITSM:* The ticketing system is the interface between customers and suppliers. The FAQ module [OTR13c] can be used for sharing information with customers.
  - *i-doit open:* Information sharing between customers and suppliers is not supported.
  - *ITSM Wiki:* The same as described for the legacy tools is basically true for the ITSM Wiki, with the exception that the results of queries can be displayed on dedicated pages for customers.
- Improvement **I-B03**
  - *Legacy tools:* PmWiki allowed the sharing of unstructured information between members of the IT department.
  - *OTRS::ITSM:* Lessons learned, and best practices can be shared with the organization by using the FAQ module [OTR13c].
  - *i-doit open:* Sharing and collectively annotating textual information is not supported.
  - *ITSM Wiki:* In the ITSM Wiki, the information can be stored in structured and unstructured formats. This allows to attach lessons learned or best practices to the relevant configuration items. With respect to access permissions, the ITSM Wiki at the current state of implementation provides a flat access model, which allows all members of the IT department access to the information. In this regard, potential for future work exists.
- Requirement **R-B01**
  - *Legacy tools:* PmWiki provided a wiki environment, which allowed the collaborative documentation of best practices by IT administrators. However, best practices could only be described in free text, without the possibility to store information in a structured format. This complicated finding best practices.
  - *OTRS::ITSM:* The FAQ module [OTR13c] can be used for documenting best practices.

  - *i-doit open:* The management of best practices benefits from a platform that supports the collaborative editing of information. This functionality is present in i-doit open.
  - *ITSM Wiki:* In the ITSM Wiki, best practices can be stored both, in free text, as well as in a structured format. This allows to build dynamic lists of best practices and to link best practices to configuration items.
- Requirement **R-B02**
  - *Legacy tools:* Lessons learned could be documented in the PmWiki in a textual format. While this was sufficient for basic needs, it did not allow more sophisticated uses of lessons learned.
  - *OTRS::ITSM:* The FAQ module [OTR13c] can be used for documenting lessons learned.
  - *i-doit open:* Lessons learned cannot be documented.
  - *ITSM Wiki:* The ITSM Wiki allows to store lessons learned in a combination of structured and unstructured format. The structured format is used to store information that can be used in queries in order to create tables. These tables list lessons learned that apply to a particular configuration item (e.g., list all lessons learned that are applicable for Windows Server hosts).
- Requirement **R-B03**
  - *Legacy tools and ITSM Wiki:* With regard to operating procedures and their representation in PmWiki and the ITSM Wiki, the same holds true as for the best practices and lessons learned, which were described in R-B01 and R-B02.
  - *OTRS::ITSM:* Operating procedures can be documented as work orders or in the FAQ module.
  - *i-doit open:* Operating procedures can be documented as workflows [i-d12]. Rich-media formatted text is not supported, however.
- Requirement **R-B04**
  - *Legacy tools and ITSM Wiki:* For the management of key persons and stakeholders, as well as their representations in PmWiki and the ITSM Wiki, the same basic observations hold true as for the best practices, lessons learned, and operating procedures, which were described in R-B01, R-B02, and R-B03. It can be seen, however that information about persons benefits from the representation of knowledge artifacts in a structured format (e.g., the name, e-mail address, as well as links to knowledge domains).
  - *OTRS::ITSM:* Information about persons can be stored in a structured format.

   - *i-doit open:* Persons can be associated with configuration items. Furthermore, structured information can be stored with contacts. Contacts can be grouped [i-d08c]. A textual rich-media description is not possible, however.

- Requirement **R-B05**
   - *Legacy tools:* Recommended literature and Web sites could be stored in PmWiki within wiki pages (e.g., as static tables). Because of the inherently highly structured format of the information, storing the information in a structured format within the wiki would provide benefits, however.
   - *OTRS::ITSM:* Information about literature can be stored as a special CI class. Furthermore, files can be attached.
   - *i-doit open:* Documentation can be attached as files to CIs [i-d08b].
   - *ITSM Wiki:* In the ITSM Wiki, the information is stored in a structured format, which allows to dynamically create tables by making use of Semantic MediaWiki queries.

Change Management The requirements for Change Management are described in detail in Section 4.2.3 (page 153). In Table 6.5, the scores of the validation of the Change Management criteria are listed for each of the evaluated tools, namely the legacy tools, OTRS::ITSM, i-doit open, and the ITSM Wiki.

ID	Criterion	Legacy	OTRS::ITSM	i-doit open	ITSM Wiki
R-C01	Management of changes in *structured* format.	0	4	0	4
R-C02	Management of changes in *unstructured* format.	4	3	0	4
R-C03	Management of changes in structured *and* unstructured format.	0	3	0	4
	Mean score	1.3	3.3	0.0	4.0
	Standard deviation	2.3	0.6	0.0	0.0

Table 6.5.: Validation of Change Management Criteria

The following list gives an explanation of the scores given in Table 6.5:

- Requirement **R-C01**
  - *Legacy tools:* It was not possible to store structured information about changes in PmWiki.
  - *OTRS::ITSM:* Structured information about changes can be stored.
  - *i-doit open:* Change Management is not supported at the current stage of implementation.
  - *ITSM Wiki:* In the ITSM Wiki, it is possible to store structured information in the form of semantic properties.
- Requirement **R-C02**
  - *Legacy tools and ITSM Wiki:* The representation of unstructured information is a strength of wikis. A combination of formatted text with embedded tables, lists, and images is supported.
  - *OTRS::ITSM:* Unstructured information can be stored in rich text. The embedded editor includes mechanisms for formatting text and adding lists and embedded images. Text is formatted as HTML, which means that additional elements (e.g., tables) can be added as HTML code. Links between changes or other elements of the CMS cannot be integrated as easily as in wikis.
  - *i-doit open:* Change Management is not supported at the current stage of implementation.
- Requirement **R-C03**
  - *Legacy tools:* PmWiki does not allow the combination of structured and unstructured information.
  - *OTRS::ITSM:* Changes are represented as a combination of structured and unstructured information. It is not possible to seamlessly integrate structured and unstructured information, however.
  - *i-doit open:* Change Management is not supported at the current stage of implementation.
  - *ITSM Wiki:* In the ITSM Wiki, the combination of the two types of information is possible. Furthermore, mechanisms such as queries allow to flexibly work on structured information and represent the results together with unstructured information.

ID	Criterion	Legacy	OTRS::ITSM	i-doit open	ITSM Wiki
R-D01	Storage of information about incidents and problems in *structured* format.	0	4	0	4
R-D02	Storage of information about incidents and problems in *unstructured* format.	4	3	0	4
R-D03	Combined storage of information about incidents and problems in structured *and* unstructured format.	0	3	0	4
	Mean score	1.3	3.3	0.0	4.0
	Standard deviation	2.3	0.6	0.0	0.0

Table 6.6.: Validation of Incident and Problem Management Criteria

Incident and Problem Management Section 4.2.4 (page 156) lists the requirements of Incident and Problem Management. In Table 6.6, the results of the Incident and Problem Management requirements validation are shown.

The following list gives an explanation of the scores given in Table 6.6:

- Requirement **R-D01**
  - *Legacy tools:* Structured information about incidents and problems could not be stored in PmWiki.
  - *OTRS::ITSM:* Incidents and problems are managed as tickets. The management of tickets is the core functionality of OTRS. Structured information, such as type, owner, and priority are stored in a structured format.
  - *i-doit open:* Incident and Problem Management is not supported at the current state of implementation.
  - *ITSM Wiki:* The ITSM Wiki, as a semantic wiki, allows storing and processing of structured information.
- Requirement **R-D02**
  - *Legacy tools:* PmWiki allows storing unstructured information. The wiki functionality allows to format that information and to link information between wiki pages.
  - *OTRS::ITSM:* Unstructured information can be edited and stored. Links between different incidents and problems from within the text is not supported.
  - *i-doit open:* Incident and Problem Management is not supported at the current state of implementation.

  - *ITSM Wiki:* The ITSM Wiki allows to store unstructured information. Furthermore, formatting of text, as well as links between wiki pages, is supported.

- Requirement **R-D03**
  - *Legacy tools:* Storing a combination of structured and unstructured information is not possible in PmWiki.
  - *OTRS::ITSM:* Incidents and problems are represented as a combination of structured and unstructured information. A seamless integration of structured and unstructured information, which exceeds the capabilities of HTML links, is not possible.
  - *i-doit open:* Incident and Problem Management is not supported at the current state of implementation.
  - *ITSM Wiki:* The ITSM Wiki allows to store and retrieve a combination of both, structured, as well as unstructured information.

Continual Service Improvement The validation of Continual Service Improvement, as described in Section 4.2.5 (page 158), is presented in Table 6.7.

ID	Criterion	Legacy	OTRS::ITSM	i-doit open	ITSM Wiki
G-E01	Provide mechanisms for service reporting and service measurement.	0	3	3	3
R-E01	Processing of queries for structured information.	0	4	4	4
R-E02	Presentation of results in tables.	0	4	4	4
R-E03	Access information from across all ITSM disciplines.	1	3	2	3
	Mean score	0.3	3.5	3.3	3.5
	Standard deviation	0.5	0.6	1.0	0.6

Table 6.7.: Validation of Continual Service Improvement Criteria

The following list gives an explanation of the scores given in Table 6.7:

- Goal **G-E01**
  - *Legacy tools:* Mechanisms for service reporting and service measurement were not present in the legacy tools (PmWiki and Excel).
  - *OTRS::ITSM:* Pre-defined reports can be generated. Furthermore, new reports can be defined by using a Web-based interface.

  - *i-doit open:* The report manager allows to create reports based on either a set of predefined queries, or based on SQL statements [i-d08d].
  - *ITSM Wiki:* In the ITSM Wiki, service reporting and service measurement can be implemented by using queries. In order to make use of queries, the user of the ITSM Wiki has to learn the query syntax, or re-use and modify existing queries.

- Requirement **R-E01**
  - *Legacy tools:* There were no mechanisms for query processing present in the legacy tools.
  - *OTRS::ITSM:* Statistics based on structured information can be accessed by using a Web-based interface.
  - *i-doit open:* IT administrators can access structured information by using SQL queries [i-d08d].
  - *ITSM Wiki:* In the ITSM Wiki, structured information can be processed by Semantic MediaWiki queries.

- Requirement **R-E02**
  - *Legacy tools:* While table views can be created in PmWiki, as well as Excel, these tables cannot be used as the basis for results generated by queries.
  - *OTRS::ITSM:* Results of searches and statistics are displayed as tables.
  - *i-doit open:* Results of SQL queries are presented as tables [i-d08d].
  - *ITSM Wiki:* In the ITSM Wiki, tables can be created from queries.

- Requirement **R-E03**
  - *Legacy tools:* PmWiki provided an environment, in which information about all ITSM disciplines could be stored. The information was not processable automatically in a satisfying way, however.
  - *OTRS::ITSM:* Information from the disciplines that are supported by OTRS-::ITSM can be accessed. The supported disciplines are Incident and Problem Management, Service Level Management, Configuration Management, and Change Management [OTR13d, page 17].
  - *i-doit open:* Access to information is limited to the disciplines that are represented in i-doit open (i.e., mostly Configuration Management).

- *ITSM Wiki:* As is the case with PmWiki, information about all ITSM disciplines can be stored in the ITSM Wiki. When compared to PmWiki, it can be seen that the Semantic MediaWiki extension adds value in the form of being able to store and process structured information. When compared to OTRS::ITSM, it shows that the integration of the service desk is better in OTRS::ITSM than in the ITSM Wiki. By providing a more flexible foundation than the other tools, the ITSM Wiki can be extended to support additional ITSM disciplines in an ad-hoc manner.

Usability Aspects Table 6.8 presents the results of the validation of the usability aspects. The requirements for the usability aspects are presented in Section 4.2.6 (page 159).

ID	Criterion	Legacy	OTRS::ITSM	i-doit open	ITSM Wiki
R-F01	Ability to easily edit structured data.	0	4	4	3
R-F02	Ability to easily edit unstructured data.	3	4	0	3
R-F03	Ability to selectively present relevant data.	0	2	2	3
	Mean score	1.0	3.3	2.0	3.0
	Standard deviation	1.7	1.2	2.0	0.0

Table 6.8.: Validation of Usability Criteria

The following list gives an explanation of the scores given in Table 6.8:

- Requirement **R-F01**
  - *Legacy tools:* PmWiki does not provide mechanisms for editing structured information.
  - *OTRS::ITSM:* Structured information can be easily edited.
  - *i-doit open:* Structured information about configuration items can be easily edited.
  - *ITSM Wiki:* In the ITSM Wiki, structured information can be edited. When using the Semantic Forms extension, editing structured information is easy. Generating forms and templates requires some work and expertise, however.

- Requirement **R-F02**
  - *Legacy tools:* PmWiki provides good editing capabilities with respect to unstructured information. Some learning is required, however, in order to be able to utilize more complex formatting, such as tables.
  - *OTRS::ITSM:* Unstructured information can be easily edited.
  - *i-doit open:* Editing unstructured information is limited to editing description fields, which are present in the representation of configuration items. No formatting is supported in the description fields.
  - *ITSM Wiki:* As is the case with PmWiki, the ITSM Wiki provides good editing capabilities with respect to unstructured information. Some learning is required, however, in order to be able to utilize more complex formatting, such as tables.
- Requirement **R-F03**
  - *Legacy tools:* In PmWiki, there are no mechanisms for representing relevant information in a dynamic and flexible way. While it is possible to manually generate tables that present relevant information, this is too work-intensive and error-prone for most use cases.
  - *OTRS::ITSM:* Reports are created from information stored in OTRS::ITSM via a Web-based assistant.
  - *i-doit open:* Relevant information is presented in reports. Reports are generated by using the Query Builder or SQL statements. The Query Builder offers a simple interface for selecting a limited set of criteria. By using SQL, more flexible statements can be created, with the disadvantage that SQL syntax has to be used [i-d08d].
  - *ITSM Wiki:* In the ITSM Wiki, relevant information is selectively presented by using Semantic MediaWiki queries. This needs some time spent on learning the syntax of the query statements, however.

Validation of the Components

In the following paragraphs, the requirements of the components that were described in Chapter 5 (page 185), are validated.

Because, in some cases, a direct reference is made to the ITSM Wiki in the definition of the criteria, the term *ITSM Wiki* is replaced by the more generic term *[tool]* in the following paragraphs. Furthermore, references to components presented in Chapter 5 (page 185) are replaced by a generic description of the component.

Information Gathering In Table 6.9, the validation of the requirements of the Information Gathering Component, as described in Section 5.1 (page 188), are presented.

Table 6.9.: Validation of Information Gathering Criteria

ID	Criterion	Legacy	OTRS::ITSM	i-doit open	ITSM Wiki
V-G01	To design and implement a tool that automatically reads data from the directory service, as well as from networked devices, and automatically writes the information into the [tool].	0	3	2	3
G-G01	Reduce the amount of work necessary for keeping up-to-date the information about configuration items in the [tool].	0	3	3	3
G-G02	Reduce the number of human errors by automating the process of maintaining information about configuration items.	0	4	4	4
G-G03	Store information about configuration items in the [tool], which can be used by system administrators as well as the other components presented in this thesis.	0	3	3	4
G-G04	Enable the ‘intelligent’ use of information stored in the [tool] by using an ontology as the data model.	0	0	0	4
R-G01	New information has to be integrated into the [tool] automatically and without user intervention.	0	4	4	4
R-G02	Changed information has to be detected and updated in the [tool].	0	4	4	4
R-G03	When upgrading changed information, a history of changes has to be kept and made available to the user of the [tool].	1	4	4	4
R-G04	Information should be gathered without the need for installing a dedicated agent on computers from which information is gathered.	0	1	1	4

(*table continues*)

Table 6.9.: Validation of Information Gathering Criteria (continued)

ID	Criterion	Legacy	OTRS::ITSM	i-doit open	ITSM Wiki
R-G05	Information relevant to users, computers, software, and hardware has to be gathered.	0	2	2	3
R-G06	Information about computers that are not available when gathering information has to be kept at the state of the last information gathering. The date of the last information gathering has to be shown to the user when accessing a page representing a configuration item.	1	4	4	4
R-G07	The mechanism for gathering information has to be smart (e.g., take into account the operating system installed on a computer when trying to gather information).	0	3	3	3
R-G08	Information gathered from components has to be retained in a structured format that is processable by [the tool] in order to be used in queries and dynamically created tables.	0	0	0	4
R-G09	A notification mechanism has to be present for changes to static information (e.g., users of the [tool] interested in a hardware component have to be notified when the mainboard is changed).	0	0	1	4
	Mean score	0.1	2.5	2.5	3.7
	Standard deviation	0.4	1.6	1.5	0.5

OTRS::ITSM and i-doit open have no included functionality for gathering information from hosts. In this paragraph, functionality that is provided by third-party tools for configuration gathering (e.g., OCS Inventory NG[2], and H-Inventory[3]) is included.

The following list gives an explanation of the scores given in Table 6.9:

[2] `http://www.ocsinventory-ng.org/`

[3] `http://sourceforge.net/projects/h-inventory/`

- Vision **V-G01**
  - *Legacy tools:* No mechanisms were available for automatically importing information from the directory service, as well as from networked hosts, into PmWiki or the Excel spreadsheet.
  - *OTRS::ITSM:* Information about hosts can be imported from external tools (e.g., from OCS Inventory NG). An LDAP directory service can be accessed in order to get information about persons.
  - *i-doit open:* The import of information about hosts (e.g., hardware and software configurations) is supported by i-doit open. Third-party tools (H-Inventory and OCS Inventory NG) are used to perform the actual reading of information from hosts [i-d11d, i-d10b]. The import of information from a directory (e.g., Microsoft Active Directory) is not supported.
  - *ITSM Wiki:* The Information Gathering Component provides the desired mechanisms for importing information from Active Directory and Windows hosts. With regard to non-Windows devices, future work is needed in order to create a solution that also supports the import of information from networked devices or Linux hosts.
- Goal **G-G01**
  - *Legacy tools:* There are no mechanisms for the automatic import of directory or host information into the legacy tools.
  - *OTRS::ITSM:* IT administrators do not have to manually input information about hosts and users. Information about hosts can be imported from external tools in a structured format. Information about users is read from an LDAP-based directory service.
  - *i-doit open:* IT administrators do not have to manually input information about hosts, if an external tool for information gathering is used.
  - *ITSM Wiki:* The Information Gathering Component reduces the amount of work with respect to importing information from the directory and Windows hosts. Further work is being necessary for non-Windows hosts.
- Goal **G-G02**
  - *Legacy tools:* Entering information has to be done manually for the legacy tools, which has the potential for human errors.
  - *OTRS::ITSM:* By importing information about hosts and users, human errors are reduced.
  - *i-doit open:* Human errors are reduced because the information is imported from tools that import the information from hosts.

  - *ITSM Wiki:* The Information Gathering Component prevents human errors with regard to information import, because information is imported automatically.

- Goal **G-G03**
  - *Legacy tools:* No mechanisms exist for automatically storing information in the legacy tools.
  - *OTRS::ITSM:* Information about hosts and users can be used by other subcomponents of OTRS.
  - *i-doit open:* Information about configuration items is stored in i-doit open. Components that can use the information with respect to Knowledge Management, or Incident and Problem Management, are not included.
  - *ITSM Wiki:* In the ITSM Wiki, the Information Gathering Component is used to automatically import information, which can be used by IT administrators, as well as the other components presented in this thesis.
- Goal **G-G04**
  - *Legacy tools*, *OTRS::ITSM*, and *i-doit open:* Neither the legacy tools, nor OTRS::ITSM, or i-doit open uses an ontology as its data model.
  - *ITSM Wiki:* Semantic MediaWiki, which is the technological basis for the ITSM Wiki, uses an ontology as the data model.
- Requirement **R-G01**
  - *Legacy tools:* Data had to be entered manually into the legacy tools.
  - *OTRS::ITSM:* Information from the directory and hosts can be imported regularly.
  - *i-doit open:* A recurring cron job can be used for regularly importing information from OCS [i-d10b].
  - *ITSM Wiki:* The Information Gathering Component automatically imports information from the directory and Windows hosts.
- Requirement **R-G02**
  - *Legacy tools:* Automatic detection of new or changed information and resulting updates are not possible within the legacy tools.
  - *OTRS::ITSM:* Information can be regularly updated.
  - *i-doit open:* A recurring cron job can be used for regularly importing (i.e., updating) information from OCS [i-d10b].

  - *ITSM Wiki:* The Information Gathering Component can detect and update new and changed information.

- Requirement **R-G03**
  - *Legacy tools:* Information in the legacy tools cannot be automatically updated. In PmWiki, a history of (manually performed) changes is kept, however.
  - *OTRS::ITSM:* Changes are retained in the history.
  - *i-doit open:* Changes are retained in the logbook.
  - *ITSM Wiki:* The ITSM Wiki retains a full history of changes by using the MediaWiki history.

- Requirement **R-G04**
  - *Legacy tools:* No mechanisms exist for information gathering in the legacy tools.
  - *OTRS::ITSM:* If using OCS, the installation of the OCS Inventory NG Agent is required on clients.
  - *i-doit open:* The installation of the OCS Inventory NG Agent is required in order to gather information from hosts via OCS [OCS13]. H-Inventory also requires the installation of an agent [Tri11].
  - *ITSM Wiki:* The Information Gathering Component does not require the installation of an agent on hosts, from which information is read.

- Requirement **R-G05**
  - *Legacy tools:* The legacy tools do not support information gathering.
  - *OTRS::ITSM:* Importing information about computers and users is supported. Computers have to be imported via CVS files, while information about users is automatically read from the directory via LDAP.
  - *i-doit open:* Reading information about computers, software, and hardware is supported. Reading information about users is not supported directly, but could be implemented as an add-on.
  - *ITSM Wiki:* In the ITSM Wiki, the Information Gathering Component supports reading information about users, computers, software, and hardware from Active Directory, and from Windows hosts. Non-Windows hosts are not supported at the current state of implementation, however.

- Requirement **R-G06**
  - *Legacy tools:* The legacy tools do not support the automatic gathering of information. Manually entered information is readable anytime, however.
  - *OTRS::ITSM:* Information about computers is stored in the OTRS::ITSM database.
  - *i-doit open:* Information is stored in the i-doit open database.
  - *ITSM Wiki:* The ITSM Wiki retains information in its database, which means that the information can be read even when the respective host is not available. The wiki furthermore stores the date of the last change to the page, as well as the date and time of the last successful gathering attempt.
- Requirement **R-G07**
  - *Legacy tools:* The legacy tools do not support automatic gathering of information.
  - *OTRS::ITSM* and *i-doit open:* The agent that is installed on the client transmits information about the operating system.
  - *ITSM Wiki:* The Information Gathering Component can make use of information stored in the ITSM Wiki in order to gather information selectively or in order to use the best available mechanism. At the current state of implementation, only gathering information from Active Directory and Windows hosts is supported, however.
- Requirement **R-G08**
  - *Legacy tools:* In the legacy tools, information cannot be automatically gathered, nor semantically annotated.
  - *OTRS::ITSM* and *i-doit open:* No semantic annotation is supported.
  - *ITSM Wiki:* The Information Gathering Component uses Semantic MediaWiki in order to store structured information. This information can be further processed by mechanisms provided by Semantic MediaWiki.
- Requirement **R-G09**
  - *Legacy tools:* No automatic gathering of information takes place in PmWiki or Microsoft Excel.
  - *OTRS::ITSM:* No notifications are sent when CIs are changed.
  - *i-doit open:* Notifications are not supported. The logbook can be searched for changes.

- *ITSM Wiki:* In the ITSM Wiki, MediaWiki mechanisms can be used in order to get a notification, when information is changed on pages that are of interest to the individual user of the ITSM Wiki.

Infrastructure Monitoring Table 6.10 shows the results of the validation of the Infrastructure Monitoring Component, as it is described in Section 5.2 (page 234).

Table 6.10.: Validation of Infrastructure Monitoring Criteria

ID	Criterion	Legacy	OTRS::ITSM	i-doit open	ITSM Wiki
V-H01	To design and implement a tool, which simplifies the management of infrastructure monitoring information by enabling the re-use of existing information.	0	1	4	4
G-H01	Reduce the need for keeping and maintaining duplicate information in the context of infrastructure monitoring.	0	1	4	4
G-H02	Lower the learning curve for users who are new to applying changes to infrastructure monitoring.	0	1	4	4
G-H03	Avoid the error-prone manual editing of infrastructure monitoring configuration files.	0	1	3	3
G-H04	Integrate infrastructure monitoring with Configuration Management, Change Management, and documentation into a unified user interface.	0	2	2	4
G-H05	Make use of existing information about hardware, software, and services, as well as their dependencies.	0	1	4	4
G-H06	Make 'intelligent' use of existing information for the purposes of infrastructure monitoring. Information which is implicitly known to the system should not have to be entered again if it can be derived from other information stored in the [tool].	0	1	1	2

(table continues)

Table 6.10.: Validation of Infrastructure Monitoring Criteria (continued)

ID	Criterion	Legacy	OTRS::ITSM	i-doit open	ITSM Wiki
R-H01	Add new hosts and services to infrastructure monitoring from within the [tool].	0	1	4	4
R-H02	Apply changes to existing host and service monitoring settings from within the [tool].	0	1	4	4
R-H03	Allow the specification of which services are run on which hosts.	0	3	4	4
R-H04	Define who is responsible for which hosts and services and how the responsible person can be contacted.	0	2	4	4
R-H05	Model the dependencies between various hosts and services (e.g., the mail service depends on a functioning mail server).	0	3	4	4
R-H06	Define which protocols and ports are used for which service (e.g., port 80 and protocol HTTP for a Web server).	0	0	3	3
R-H07	Specify how often a host or service has to be checked (e.g., once a minute, or once every 10 min).	0	0	2	4
R-H08	Define the time periods in which a service has to be checked (e.g., business hours, weekdays, or 24x7).	0	1	3	3
	Mean score	0.0	1.3	3.3	3.7
	Standard deviation	0.0	0.9	1.0	0.6

The following list gives an explanation of the scores given in Table 6.10:

- Vision **V-H01**
  - *Legacy tools:* Information stored in the legacy tools could not be re-used for infrastructure monitoring.
  - *OTRS::ITSM:* The system monitoring add-on for OTRS::ITSM allows the processing of mails sent by the Nagios infrastructure monitoring application. Mails are parsed and tickets are generated [OTR13e]. No mechanisms are implemented for automatically exporting relevant content of the CMDB into Nagios.

  - *i-doit open:* The Nagios module allows the re-use of structured information from i-doit open in order to configure a Nagios instance [i-d09b].
  - *ITSM Wiki:* The Infrastructure Monitoring Component allows the use of structured information that is stored in the ITSM Wiki.

- Goal **G-H01**
  - *Legacy tools:* Infrastructure monitoring configuration files had to be manually created and updated.
  - *OTRS::ITSM:* Information from the CMDB cannot be directly re-used for infrastructure monitoring. Due to the structured storage format, creating an application that exports and transforms data from OTRS::ITSM for the use in Nagios would be possible.
  - *i-doit open:* Information from the i-doit open CMDB can be used to generate Nagios configuration files [i-d09b], which helps in avoiding the maintenance of duplicate information.
  - *ITSM Wiki:* The Infrastructure Monitoring Component is able to export information from the ITSM Wiki to Nagios infrastructure monitoring configuration files.

- Goal **G-H02**
  - *Legacy tools:* The legacy tools did not provide mechanisms for easing the configuration of the infrastructure monitoring application. This resulted in the need to manually edit the text-based Nagios configuration files.
  - *OTRS::ITSM:* The learning curve is not reduced because the information from the CMDB cannot be directly used for configuring Nagios. An application could be created, which transforms the information from the CMDB into the Nagios configuration file format.
  - *i-doit open:* By generating Nagios configuration files from information that is maintained in the Web-based i-doit open, the learning of Nagios configuration file syntax can be avoided.
  - *ITSM Wiki:* By using the Infrastructure Monitoring Component, monitoring can be configured by editing form-based pages in the ITSM Wiki.

- Goal **G-H03**
  - *Legacy tools:* All configuration files of the infrastructure monitoring application had to be manually edited in the legacy environment.
  - *OTRS::ITSM:* Infrastructure monitoring configuration files cannot be directly created or modified by editing CI information. An application could be created, which transforms the information from the CMDB into the Nagios configuration file format.
  - *i-doit open:* Infrastructure monitoring configuration files do not have to be edited in order to perform the most often used types of configuration. Some less common settings have to be configured in Nagios configuration file syntax.
  - *ITSM Wiki:* By using the Infrastructure Monitoring Component, general settings (e.g., configuring, which hosts and services should be monitored) can be set from the ITSM Wiki. Some less common settings have to be configured by editing configuration files.
- Goal **G-H04**
  - *Legacy tools:* Infrastructure monitoring was not included in the legacy tools.
  - *OTRS::ITSM:* New tickets can be created from e-mails that are sent from the Nagios infrastructure monitoring application. Configuration Management, Change Management, and some aspects of documentation are integrated with tickets. Creating infrastructure monitoring configuration files would need an external tool, which parses CSV files that are exported from OTRS::ITSM.
  - *i-doit open:* Infrastructure monitoring is integrated with Configuration Management. Change Management and the ability for free-text documentation are not present in i-doit open, which means that infrastructure monitoring cannot be integrated with these aspects.
  - *ITSM Wiki:* The ITSM Wiki integrates infrastructure monitoring, Configuration Management, Change Management, and documentation.
- Goal **G-H05**
  - *Legacy tools:* The legacy tools did not make use of existing information.
  - *OTRS::ITSM:* Existing information cannot be used directly for infrastructure monitoring. An external application could be created, which transforms the information that is exported from the CMDB into the Nagios configuration file format.
  - *i-doit open:* Information about hardware, software, and services is re-used.

  - *ITSM Wiki:* The Infrastructure Monitoring Component re-uses information from the ITSM Wiki.

- Goal **G-H06**
  - *Legacy tools:* In the legacy tools, existing information cannot be re-used 'intelligently' for the configuration of infrastructure monitoring.
  - *OTRS::ITSM* and *i-doit open:* Because a database back-end is used in order to store the CMDB information, the 'intelligent' re-use of information is not possible without investing further work.
  - *ITSM Wiki:* In the ITSM Wiki, some information can be 'intelligently' re-used (e.g., the host type, which is derived from the operating system family that is installed on the host).

- Requirement **R-H01**
  - *Legacy tools:* The legacy tools did not provide mechanisms for adding hosts or services to the infrastructure monitoring configuration.
  - *OTRS::ITSM:* New hosts and services cannot be added to infrastructure monitoring from within OTRS::ITSM. Information that is stored in a structured format in the CMDB could be exported and converted into the Nagios configuration file format, however.
  - *i-doit open:* It is possible to add hosts and services to infrastructure monitoring from within the Web-based front-end.
  - *ITSM Wiki:* The Infrastructure Monitoring Component allows to add hosts and services to the monitoring configuration by creating or editing wiki pages.

- Requirement **R-H02**
  - *Legacy tools:* No mechanisms for changing monitoring configurations existed in the legacy tools.
  - *OTRS::ITSM:* Changes to hosts and services cannot be applied to infrastructure monitoring from within OTRS::ITSM. Information that is stored in a structured format in the CMDB could be exported and converted into the Nagios configuration file format, however.
  - *i-doit open:* Changes to configuration items are applied to Nagios when manually initiating an export in i-doit open.
  - *ITSM Wiki:* In the ITSM Wiki, monitoring settings can be modified by editing wiki pages. Changes are applied when saving the wiki page.

- Requirement **R-H03**
  - *Legacy tools:* Services could not be configured or associated to hosts in the legacy tools.
  - *OTRS::ITSM:* Services can be associated with hosts. Creating a Nagios configuration based on the relations between services and hosts would require the use of an external application, however.
  - *i-doit open:* Services can be associated with hosts.
  - *ITSM Wiki:* In the ITSM Wiki, services can be associated with hosts by editing form-based wiki pages. New services can be configured from within the wiki by editing service template pages.
- Requirement **R-H04**
  - *Legacy tools:* Persons could not be associated with hosts or services in the legacy tools.
  - *OTRS::ITSM:* Persons can be associated with hosts.
  - *i-doit open:* Contacts can be associated with hosts and services in order to be notified in case of host or service failures.
  - *ITSM Wiki:* In the ITSM Wiki, persons can be associated with hosts and services with regard to infrastructure monitoring. This means that information about persons, which is read from the directory by the Information Gathering Component, can be re-used.
- Requirement **R-H05**
  - *Legacy tools:* In the legacy tools, the dependencies between hosts and services could not be modeled in a structured format.
  - *OTRS::ITSM:* Dependencies can be modeled, but cannot be directly exported to Nagios.
  - *i-doit open:* Dependencies between hosts and services can be modeled in i-doit open and exported to Nagios.
  - *ITSM Wiki:* The Infrastructure Monitoring Component can use the information about dependencies, which is stored as Semantic MediaWiki properties, as input for monitoring configuration files.

- Requirement **R-H06**
  - *Legacy tools:* Services could not be configured from within the legacy tools.
  - *OTRS::ITSM:* The definition of concrete services for the use in Nagios is not possible.
  - *i-doit open:* Commands are configured in a Web-based interface, which requires some familiarity with Nagios with respect to the used commands.
  - *ITSM Wiki:* In the ITSM Wiki, service templates can be edited via form-based wiki pages. The definition of service templates needs some understanding of Nagios configuration file syntax, however.
- Requirement **R-H07**
  - *Legacy tools:* The legacy tools did not provide mechanisms for configuring how often hosts and services should be checked.
  - *OTRS::ITSM:* Mechanisms for configuring how often hosts and services should be checked are not present.
  - *i-doit open:* The time interval of host and service checks is configured centrally for all hosts and services in a Web-based interface.
  - *ITSM Wiki:* In the ITSM Wiki, the time intervals between checks can be configured by editing wiki pages.
- Requirement **R-H08**
  - *Legacy tools:* In the legacy tools, no mechanisms existed for configuring time periods, in which hosts or services should be checked.
  - *OTRS::ITSM:* No mechanisms for configuring time periods for the use in Nagios are present. SLAs can be defined, however.
  - *i-doit open:* Time periods can be edited in the i-doit open Web front-end.
  - *ITSM Wiki:* In the ITSM Wiki, time periods can be configured by editing form-based wiki pages. Some knowledge of Nagios configuration file syntax is required, however.

ID	Criterion	Legacy	OTRS::ITSM	i-doit open	ITSM Wiki
V-I01	To design and implement a tool that simplifies and extends the management of intrusion detection information by employing Semantic Web techniques, in combination with structured background knowledge stored in a semantic wiki.	0	0	0	4
G-I01	Provide a mechanism that enables the displaying of intrusion detection events within the [tool].	0	0	0	4
G-I02	Integrate intrusion detection with Configuration Management, Change Management, and documentation into a unified user interface.	0	0	0	4
G-I03	Make use of Semantic Web technologies in order to enable advanced query mechanisms.	0	0	0	4
G-I04	Use Semantic Web technologies in order to reduce the number of false positives.	0	0	0	3
R-I01	New intrusion detection data has to be integrated into the [tool] automatically and without user intervention.	0	0	0	3
R-I02	The reporting mechanisms with regard to intrusion detections have to be smart and avoid reporting false positives.	0	0	0	3
R-I03	Intrusion detection data has to be annotated semantically in order to be used in queries and dynamically created tables.	0	0	0	4
	Mean score	0.0	0.0	0.0	3.6
	Standard deviation	0.0	0.0	0.0	0.5

Table 6.11.: Validation of Intrusion Detection Criteria (Part 1)

ID	Criterion	Legacy	BASE	Snorby	ITSM Wiki
V-I01	To design and implement a tool that simplifies and extends the management of intrusion detection information by employing Semantic Web technology, in combination with structured background knowledge stored in a semantic wiki.	0	0	0	4
G-I01	Provide a mechanism that enables the displaying of intrusion detection events within the [tool].	0	4	4	4
G-I02	Integrate intrusion detection with Configuration Management, Change Management, and documentation into a unified user interface.	0	0	0	4
G-I03	Make use of Semantic Web technologies to enable advanced query mechanisms.	0	0	0	4
G-I04	Use Semantic Web technologies in order to reduce the number of false positives.	0	0	0	3
R-I01	New intrusion detection data has to be integrated into the [tool] automatically and without user intervention.	0	4	4	3
R-I02	The reporting mechanisms with regard to intrusion detection have to be smart and avoid reporting false positives.	0	1	1	3
R-I03	Intrusion detection data has to be annotated semantically in order to be used in queries and dynamically created tables.	0	0	0	4
	Mean score	0.0	1.1	1.1	3.6
	Standard deviation	0.0	1.8	1.8	0.5

Table 6.12.: Validation of Intrusion Detection Criteria (Part 2)

Intrusion Detection Table 6.11 and Table 6.12 show the results of the validation of the Intrusion Detection Component. The component is described in detail in Section 5.3 (page 261). Because OTRS::ITSM and i-doit open do not provide mechanisms for integrating data from the Snort intrusion detection system, specialized open source Web-based front-ends for Nagios intrusion detection data, namely BASE and Snorby, are used as additional reference tools in this paragraph.

The following list gives an explanation of the scores found in Table 6.11 and Table 6.12:

- Vision **V-I01**
  - *Legacy tools:* The legacy tools, namely PmWiki and Microsoft Excel, did not provide mechanisms for displaying intrusion detection information.
  - *OTRS::ITSM* and *i-doit open:* Intrusion detection events cannot be managed.
  - *BASE* and *Snorby:* Neither Semantic Web technology, nor a semantic wiki is used.
  - *ITSM Wiki:* The Intrusion Detection Component imports information provided by the external Snort IDS into the wiki. Information is stored as Semantic MediaWiki properties, which allow the processing of intrusion detection events by using query statements. Besides the properties that are generated by the Intrusion Detection Component, all other properties can also be used.
- Goal **G-I01**
  - *Legacy tools:* Intrusion detection events could not be displayed in the legacy tools.
  - *OTRS::ITSM* and *i-doit open:* Intrusion detection events cannot be displayed.
  - *BASE* and *Snorby:* Intrusion detection events are displayed in a Web-based user interface.
  - *ITSM Wiki:* In the ITSM Wiki, IDS data is stored as Semantic MediaWiki properties, which can be displayed by using MediaWiki or Semantic MediaWiki mechanisms.

- Goal **G-I02**
  - *Legacy tools:* Intrusion detection information could not be integrated with other information in the legacy tools.
  - *OTRS::ITSM* and *i-doit open:* No integration of intrusion detection events is implemented.
  - *BASE* and *Snorby:* A Web-based interface is provided, in which intrusion detection events can be viewed. Configuration Management, Change Management, and documentation cannot be integrated with the events.
  - *ITSM Wiki:* In the ITSM Wiki, intrusion detection information can be integrated with information from other ITIL disciplines, e.g., Configuration Management, Change Management, and documentation.
- Goal **G-I03**
  - *Legacy tools:* The legacy tools do not use Semantic Web technologies.
  - *OTRS::ITSM*, *i-doit open*, *BASE*, and *Snorby:* No Semantic Web technologies are used.
  - *ITSM Wiki:* The ITSM Wiki uses Semantic Wiki technologies in order to enable advanced queries.
- Goal **G-I04**
  - *Legacy tools:* In the legacy tools, false positives cannot be reduced.
  - *OTRS::ITSM*, *i-doit open*, *BASE*, and *Snorby:* No Semantic Web technologies are used.
  - *ITSM Wiki:* By using background knowledge, which is stored in a structured format as Semantic MediaWiki properties in the ITSM Wiki, the number of false positives can be reduced.
- Requirement **R-I01**
  - *Legacy tools:* Intrusion detection data cannot be integrated into the legacy tools.
  - *OTRS::ITSM* and *i-doit open:* Intrusion detection data is not integrated automatically.
  - *BASE* and *Snorby:* Events are imported automatically and retained in an SQL database.

  - *ITSM Wiki:* The Intrusion Detection Component automatically imports data from the Snort intrusion detection system. The import is not continuous, however, but accomplished by a cron job in defined time intervals (e.g., every 5 min).

- Requirement **R-I02**
  - *Legacy tools:* No intrusion detection was integrated into the legacy tools.
  - *OTRS::ITSM* and *i-doit open:* No reporting mechanisms about intrusion detection events are implemented.
  - *BASE* and *Snorby:* No smart mechanisms are implemented. Filters can be applied to events, however.
  - *ITSM Wiki:* The ITSM Wiki can take advantage of structured background information in order to lower the false positive rate. In some cases, manual classification of IDS rules is necessary, however.

- Requirement **R-I03**
  - *Legacy tools:* Intrusion detection information could not be semantically annotated in the legacy tools.
  - *OTRS::ITSM*, *i-doit open*, *BASE*, and *Snorby:* Intrusion detection data cannot be semantically annotated.
  - *ITSM Wiki:* Semantic MediaWiki, which is the basis of the ITSM Wiki, provides mechanisms for semantic annotations and the use of queries in order to generate dynamic tables.

Incident and Problem Analyzer The design and implementation of the Incident and Problem Analyzer Component is described in Section 5.4 (page 284). In Table 6.13, the results of the validation of the criteria of the Incident and Problem Analyzer Component are presented.

Table 6.13.: Validation of Incident and Problem Analyzer Criteria

ID	Criterion	Legacy	OTRS::ITSM	i-doit open	ITSM Wiki
V-J01	To design and implement a tool, which helps IT administrators to track down the cause of incidents and problems.	0	0	0	4
G-J01	Provide a mechanism for finding the cause of an incident or problem, given a number of affected configuration items.	1	1	1	3

(table continues)

Table 6.13.: Validation of Incident and Problem Analyzer Criteria (continued)

ID	Criterion	Legacy	OTRS::ITSM	i-doit open	ITSM Wiki
G-J02	Provide a mechanism for finding the cause of an incident or problem, given the history of the affected configuration item.	1	1	1	3
G-J03	Implement the capability to visualize the configuration items involved in causing the incident or problem.	0	0	0	3
R-J01	Ability to find the cause of class 2 incidents by comparing a given list of IT components for similarities, e.g., to identify a failing network switch from incidents reported by independent users indicating a problem.	1	1	1	3
R-J02	Ability to find the cause of class 3 incidents by comparing configurations in time. For example, to detect the cause of an incident report, which states that a program was running fine two days ago, was not used yesterday and does not start today.	1	1	1	3
R-J03	Ability to find class 4 incidents, which are a combination of class 2 and class 3 incidents. Class 4 incidents are most often caused by centrally applied configuration changes, e.g., the automatic distribution of a software package, or a setting to a set of computers. If there is an issue with the configuration change, a subset of the computers, or all computers of the set can be affected.	1	1	1	3

(*table continues*)

Table 6.13.: Validation of Incident and Problem Analyzer Criteria (continued)

ID	Criterion	Legacy	OTRS::ITSM	i-doit open	ITSM Wiki
R-J04	Ability to find problems, which were fixed on the same or other computers in the past, e.g., a browser update caused problems with a browser plugin, which happened again on another computer, with another browser version and another plugin.	1	1	1	3
	Mean score	0.8	0.8	0.8	3.1
	Standard deviation	0.5	0.5	0.5	0.4

The following list gives an explanation of the scores given in Table 6.13:

- Vision **V-J01**
  - *Legacy tools:* No support for tracking down the cause of incidents or problems was present in the legacy tools.
  - *OTRS::ITSM* and *i-doit open:* There is no support for helping IT administrators to automatically track down possible causes of incidents or problems.
  - *ITSM Wiki:* The Incident and Problem Analyzer Component, as part of the ITSM Wiki, provides mechanisms that help IT administrators in tracking down the causes of incidents and problems.
- Goal **G-J01**
  - *Legacy tools:* The legacy tools provided no support for tracking down the cause of incidents or problems given a number of CIs. A manual comparison of CIs represented in PmWiki would be possible, however.
  - *OTRS::ITSM* and *i-doit open:* No mechanisms for automatically finding the cause of incidents or problems are present at the current state of implementation. The structured form of retaining information makes possible the implementation of such a tool in the future, however. Furthermore, the manual comparison of CIs is possible.
  - *ITSM Wiki:* The Incident and Problem Analyzer Component implements a mechanism for finding possible causes of incidents and problems based on a given number of CIs. While the component helps the IT administrator by showing possible causes, the interpretation of the results is left to the IT administrator.

- Goal **G-J02**
  - *Legacy tools:* There is no support for finding the cause of incidents or problems based on the history of a CI in the legacy tools. In PmWiki, the history of a wiki page can be reviewed in order to find changes, however.
  - *OTRS::ITSM* and *i-doit open:* At the current state of implementation, OTRS::ITSM and i-doit open do not support the automatic finding of possible causes of incidents and problems based on the history of a CI. However, because OTRS::ITSM and i-doit open store a log of all changes, manually tracking down the cause is possible.
  - *ITSM Wiki:* The Incident and Problem Analyzer Component supports IT administrators in tracking down the cause of incidents or problems based on the history saved in the wiki page of a CI. The interpretation of the findings is left to the IT administrator, however.
- Goal **G-J03**
  - *Legacy tools:* Visualization was not implemented in the legacy tools.
  - *OTRS::ITSM* and *i-doit open:* No mechanisms for visualizing the possible causes of incidents or problems are implemented.
  - *ITSM Wiki:* The Incident and Problem Analyzer Component provides a mechanism for graphically showing the possible cause of an incident or problem.
- Requirement **R-J01**
  - *Legacy tools:* No mechanisms for supporting IT administrators in finding class 2 incidents or problems were implemented in the legacy tools. Manually comparing wiki pages that represent CIs would be possible in PmWiki, however.
  - *OTRS::ITSM* and *i-doit open:* No mechanisms for automatically detecting class 2 incidents or problems are present. Manually comparing configurations is possible, however.
  - *ITSM Wiki:* The Incident and Problem Analyzer Component provides mechanisms for helping IT administrators in tracking down possible causes of incidents and problems involving multiple CIs.

- Requirement **R-J02**
  - *Legacy tools:* No mechanisms for supporting IT administrators in finding class 3 incidents were implemented in the legacy tools. The history of wiki pages in PmWiki could be reviewed, however, in order to find differences between configurations.
  - *OTRS::ITSM* and *i-doit open:* No mechanisms for automatically detecting class 3 incidents or problems are implemented. Using the log of a configuration item in order to manually find the cause is possible.
  - *ITSM Wiki:* The ITSM Wiki's Incident and Problem Analyzer Component contains mechanisms for comparing versions of a CI in time, in order to help tracking down the cause of an incident or problem. The interpretation of the results is up to the IT administrator, however.
- Requirement **R-J03**
  - *Legacy tools:* No mechanisms for directly finding the cause of class 4 incidents or problems were present in the legacy tools. Manually comparing wiki pages that represent CIs, as well as their history, would be possible, but labor-intensive.
  - *OTRS::ITSM* and *i-doit open:* No mechanisms for tracking down class 4 issues are present. Manually using the CMDB in order to track down the cause of the incident or problem is possible.
  - *ITSM Wiki:* The Incident and Problem Analyzer Component treats class 4 issues as a combination of class 2 and class 3 issues. The interpretation of the results requires some expertise of the IT administrator.
- Requirement **R-J04**
  - *Legacy tools:* There were no mechanisms present in the legacy tool that helped in tracking down the described problems. Manually documenting known issues and searching PmWiki would be possible, however.
  - *OTRS::ITSM* and *i-doit open:* Changes and known errors can be stored in the CMDB. By searching for changes and known errors, administrators can track down the cause of an issue.
  - *ITSM Wiki:* In the ITSM Wiki, information about changes and known errors can be stored in a mixture of structured and unstructured formats. IT administrators can use this information together with the information from the Incident and Problem Analyzer Component in order to find previously fixed problems.

Virtualization and IaaS Connector Table 6.14 presents the results of the validation of the requirements of the Virtualization and IaaS Connector, which is described in detail in Section 5.5 (page 298).

The scores and descriptions in this paragraph are based on the requirements analysis, the description of the use cases, and the design of the Virtualization and IaaS Ontology.

Table 6.14.: Validation of Virtualization and IaaS Connector Criteria

ID	Criterion	Legacy	OTRS::ITSM	i-doit open	ITSM Wiki
V-K01	To implement a tool that simplifies the management of virtual machines, as well as of IaaS resources, by enabling the re-use of existing explicitly stored, and implicitly derived information.	0	0	0	4
G-K01	Integrate the management of virtual machines and IaaS resources into a unified interface for Configuration Management, Change Management, infrastructure monitoring, intrusion detection, Incident and Problem Management, as well as documentation.	0	0	0	4
G-K02	Reduce the need for keeping and maintaining duplicate information, e.g., as configuration in the virtualization management console, and as separate information in the Configuration Management System.	0	0	0	4
G-K03	Make possible the re-use of existing information about hardware, software, virtual machines, IaaS resources, services, as well as their dependencies.	0	1	1	4
G-K04	Allow structured linking between technical information and organizational information (e.g., between a virtual machine, the project in which the virtual machine is used, as well as the owner of the virtual machine).	1	2	2	4

(table continues)

Table 6.14.: Validation of Virtualization and IaaS Connector Criteria (continued)

ID	Criterion	Legacy	OTRS::ITSM	i-doit open	ITSM Wiki
G-K05	Allow the structured linking between service dependencies (e.g., between a Web server in a virtual machine, and a database server, which is run in another virtual machine).	0	4	4	4
G-K06	Make 'intelligent' use of existing information for the purposes of virtual machine management and IaaS resources management.	0	0	0	3
R-K01	The creation and maintenance of virtualized instances, as well as IaaS resources, has to be made possible from within the [tool].	0	0	0	4
R-K02	When creating and changing parameters of virtualized instances, and IaaS resources, consistency checks based on the information contained in the [tool] have to be performed in order to avoid misconfigurations.	0	0	0	3
R-K03	Virtualized instances and IaaS resources can be checked for availability by [an infrastructure monitoring application], based on information stored in the [tool].	0	3	3	4
R-K04	When encountering problems with virtualized instances and IaaS resources (e.g., due to failing hardware), the remaining resources have to be assigned according to information stored in the [tool]. This information can include dependencies between services and instances, as well as the priority of services and instances (e.g., depending on SLAs, projects, and people who make use of the services and instances).	0	1	1	2

(table continues)

Table 6.14.: Validation of Virtualization and IaaS Connector Criteria (continued)

ID	Criterion	Legacy	OTRS::ITSM	i-doit open	ITSM Wiki
R-K05	By providing information to [a component that can assist in finding the cause of incidents and problems], the diagnosis of the cause of incidents and problems should be simplified.	0	1	1	3
R-K06	[An intrusion detection tool] has to be able to use information about virtualized instances and IaaS resources stored in the [tool].	0	1	1	3
	Mean score	0.1	1.0	1.0	3.5
	Standard deviation	0.3	1.3	1.3	0.7

The following list provides an explanation of the scores given in Table 6.14:

- Vision **V-K01**
  - *Legacy tools:* It was not possible to re-use information stored in the legacy tools (Microsoft Excel and PmWiki) in order to support the management of virtual machines or IaaS resources.
  - *OTRS::ITSM* and *i-doit open:* Information that is stored in the CMDB cannot be re-used in order to directly manage virtual machines or IaaS resources.
  - *ITSM Wiki:* Information from the ITSM Wiki can be used by the Virtualization and IaaS Connector to apply changes to virtualization or IaaS environments (e.g., create, or modify virtual machines).
- Goal **G-K01**
  - *Legacy tools:* Mechanisms for managing information about virtual machines and IaaS instances was not included in the legacy tools.
  - *OTRS::ITSM:* Configuration Management, Change Management, and Incident and Problem Management are supported. The management of virtual machines and IaaS instances is not integrated, however.
  - *i-doit open:* While Configuration Management is fully supported, the management of virtual machines and IaaS instances together with Change Management, infrastructure monitoring, intrusion detection, Incident and Problem Management, and documentation are not supported.

  - *ITSM Wiki:* The Virtualization and IaaS Connector allows to control virtual machines from the ITSM Wiki. In the ITSM Wiki, information about Configuration Management, Change Management, infrastructure monitoring, intrusion detection, Incident and Problem Management, as well as documentation, are stored alongside structured information concerned with virtualization and IaaS.

- Goal **G-K02**

  - *Legacy tools:* Information was stored multiple times in the legacy tools. This was necessary, because the Xen-based virtualization environment was managed by the XenCenter software, while meta-data such as the owners of virtual machines were stored in an Excel spreadsheet. Furthermore, full-text information was stored in PmWiki.

  - *OTRS::ITSM* and *i-doit open:* Information about virtual machines has to be retained in at least two separate locations, namely the CMDB, and the virtualization management environment (e.g., XenCenter).

  - *ITSM Wiki:* In the ITSM Wiki, duplication of information is eliminated by combining structured and unstructured information about virtual machines in a single environment.

- Goal **G-K03**

  - *Legacy tools:* Information could not be re-used in the legacy tools. This was because information was, on the one hand, partly stored in an unstructured format, and on the other hand, distributed over multiple tools (e.g., PmWiki, Excel, and XenCenter).

  - *OTRS::ITSM* and *i-doit open:* In principle, the re-use of information that is stored in the CMDB about virtual machines is possible, due to the structured format. Mechanisms for taking advantage of the information are not available at the current state of implementation, however.

  - *ITSM Wiki:* In the ITSM Wiki, information about hardware, software, virtual machines, IaaS resources, services, as well as their dependencies, is retained. The Virtualization and IaaS Connector makes use of parts of that information in order to manage virtual machines.

- Goal **G-K04**

  - *Legacy tools:* Linking between technical information, which was stored in XenCenter, and organizational information was not possible. At most, the comment field of XenCenter could have been used to retain links to PmWiki pages that contain organizational information.

- *OTRS::ITSM:* The representation in the CMDB and the virtualization environment are separate from each other. Linking structured information with organizational information is possible for some types of information (e.g., virtual machines, and persons).
- *i-doit open:* Linking structured information with organizational information is possible for some types of information (e.g., virtual machines, persons, and non-hierarchical groups of persons) in the CMDB. The representation in the CMDB and the virtualization environment are separate, however.
- *ITSM Wiki:* The ITSM Wiki allows to retain both, technical information that is used to manage virtual machines, as well as organizational information, which in parts is read from the directory service by the Information Gathering Component.

- Goal **G-K05**
  - *Legacy tools:* Service dependencies could not be represented in a structured format in the legacy tools.
  - *OTRS::ITSM* and *i-doit open:* Dependencies between services and hosts can be expressed in a structured format.
  - *ITSM Wiki:* In the ITSM Wiki, dependencies between services can be represented as Semantic MediaWiki properties.
- Goal **G-K06**
  - *Legacy tools:* Information was not stored in a structured format in PmWiki, which prevented the 'intelligent' re-use of the information.
  - *OTRS::ITSM* and *i-doit open:* Information is retained in a structured form, namely in an SQL database. The information cannot be used 'intelligently' in the sense that information that is not explicitly stored, could be used.
  - *ITSM Wiki:* In the ITSM Wiki, the information is stored as Semantic MediaWiki properties, which can be used to make 'intelligent' use of information (e.g, for reporting purposes). With its focus on providing an extensible platform for collaborative IT management in SMEs, the ITSM Wiki does not provide capabilities for fully automated VM and IaaS management. However, the structured information can be used by external tools for this purpose.

- Requirement **R-K01**
  - *Legacy tools:* In the legacy environment, XenCenter was used to manage virtual machines. While this tool did not provide mechanisms for storing detailed organizational information or documentation, PmWiki did not have the functionality to create or maintain virtual machines.
  - *OTRS::ITSM* and *i-doit open:* Virtual machines and IaaS resources cannot be created or maintained from i-doit open at the current state of implementation.
  - *ITSM Wiki:* The Virtualization and IaaS Connector implements the mechanisms for creating and maintaining virtual machines from the ITSM Wiki.
- Requirement **R-K02**
  - *Legacy tools:* No structured information that could have been used for checks was available in PmWiki.
  - *OTRS::ITSM* and *i-doit open:* Creating and changing virtual machines is not possible.
  - *ITSM Wiki:* The structured information stored in the ITSM Wiki can be used to prevent misconfigurations. An example of a potential misconfiguration is shutting down the virtual machine, which provides a service that is needed by another service. In order to add more sophisticated checks, a rule-based system could be integrated as future work.
- Requirement **R-K03**
  - *Legacy tools:* Information stored in the legacy tools could not be re-used for infrastructure monitoring. This resulted in duplication of information and having to edit text-based configuration files.
  - *OTRS::ITSM:* A Nagios instance can generate events via e-mail, which are sent to OTRS::ITSM and are transformed into tickets.
  - *i-doit open:* Virtualized instances and IaaS resources can be checked from the i-doit open CMDB by making use of the Nagios module, which creates configurations for the Nagios infrastructure monitoring software. Furthermore, the status of servers is displayed in the CMDB. Direct interactions with the virtualization environment are not possible from the CMDB, however, which leaves the CMDB as an informational database.
  - *ITSM Wiki:* In the ITSM Wiki, information created for representing virtual machines can be re-used in the context of the Infrastructure Monitoring Component.

- Requirement **R-K04**
  - *Legacy tools:* The legacy tools did not provide mechanisms for reassigning resources.
  - *OTRS::ITSM* and *i-doit open:* Some of the structured information could be possibly used in order to support the reassignment of resources. However, an implementation of the feature is not available yet.
  - *ITSM Wiki:* Based on the structured information stored in the ITSM Wiki, reassigning of resources seems possible. A closer examination of the mechanisms and tools required for dynamic reassigning of resources is considered future work, however.
- Requirement **R-K05**
  - *Legacy tools:* No mechanisms for automatically detecting possible causes of incidents or problems with regard to virtualization or IaaS were implemented in the legacy tools.
  - *OTRS::ITSM* and *i-doit open:* An automatic mechanism for detecting the cause of an incident or problem is not implemented. Structured information provides the means for IT administrators to manually detect the cause of incidents and problems with respect to virtual machines or IaaS resources.
  - *ITSM Wiki:* The Incident and Problem Analyzer Component presents IT administrators with possible causes of incidents and problems with regard to virtualization or IaaS. The interpretation of the results is up to the IT administrator, however.
- Requirement **R-K06**
  - *Legacy tools:* In the legacy tools, no support for using information about virtualization or IaaS in the context of intrusion detection was present.
  - *OTRS::ITSM* and *i-doit open:* No mechanisms for making use of information about virtualized instances or IaaS resources in the context of intrusion detection are implemented. However, the structured information found in the CMDB could be used in order to implement a module that supports the displaying of intrusion detection data.
  - *ITSM Wiki:* In the ITSM Wiki, the Intrusion Detection Component can make use of structured information that describes virtual machines and IaaS resources. The integration of the tools is performed by formulating queries, which means that the IT administrators have to be familiar with the Semantic MediaWiki syntax in order to implement custom queries.

6.1.4. Interpretation of the Validation Results

In this subsection, the results of the validation are interpreted. First, a summary of the results is given. After that, a comparison of the relative strengths of the validated tools is presented. Following that, a comparison of the individual strengths of the validated tools is shown. Finally, the interpretation of the results of the validated tools is given.

Summary of Results

Table 6.15 shows a summary of the results of the validation, as presented in Section 6.1.3 (page 321). The bottom lines show the average scores per tool as the arithmetic mean of the blocks. In Table 6.16, a review of the results of the validation with regard to the intrusion detection front-ends, is shown.

Figure 6.1 shows a graphical representation of the results given in Table 6.15. The diagram lists the individual blocks, named from A to K on the radial lines. The scores are plotted on the radial lines, starting from zero in the center, and ending with four on the outer ending. Each tool is assigned a different symbol, which is plotted on the corresponding position on each of the radial lines. In summary, the further away each symbol is from the center, the better the tool performed in the corresponding block.

As can be seen in Figure 6.1, the legacy tools performed lowest in the evaluated criteria. The tool i-doit open performed better in almost all categories. OTRS::ITSM received even better scores in most of the criteria. Finally, the ITSM Wiki performed equal or better than the other tools in all criteria except in block F, where OTRS::ITSM performed better.

Comparison of the Relative Strengths of the Validated Tools

In this subsection, the results of a comparison between the validated tools is presented for each of the validated blocks. This metric measures how well the tools perform against each other in each block with regard to the validated requirements.

Table 6.17 shows the relative strengths of the validated tool compared to the arithmetic mean of each block. The values in the table are calculated as follows: First, the arithmetic mean of the scores of all tools in a single block is calculated. After that, for each block, the block's arithmetic mean is subtracted from the score of each tool. For example, in block A, the arithmetic mean of all validated tools is 2.1. The value for the legacy tools, is 0.4, as shown in Table 6.15. This means that 2.1 is subtracted from 0.4, in order to get the result that shows how the legacy tools performed against the other tools in block A. This leads to the result that the legacy tools were rated 1.7 points less than the average of all validated tools in block A. In contrast, the ITSM Wiki's result is 0.8 points higher than the arithmetic mean of block A.

Block	Topic	Leg.	OTRS::ITSM	i-doit o.	ITSM Wiki	Mean	SD
A	Validation of Configuration Management Criteria	0.4	2.7	2.3	2.9	2.1	1.1
B	Validation of Service Knowledge Management Criteria	1.3	2.5	1.5	3.4	2.2	1.0
C	Validation of Change Management Criteria	1.3	3.3	0.0	4.0	2.2	1.8
D	Validation of Incident and Problem Management Criteria	1.3	3.3	0.0	4.0	2.2	1.8
E	Validation of Continual Service Improvement Criteria	0.3	3.5	3.3	3.5	2.6	1.6
F	Validation of Usability Aspects	1.0	3.3	2.0	3.0	2.3	1.1
G	Validation of Information Gathering Criteria	0.1	2.5	2.5	3.7	2.2	1.5
H	Validation of Infrastructure Monitoring Criteria	0.0	1.3	3.3	3.7	2.1	1.7
I-1	Validation of Intrusion Detection Criteria	0.0	0.0	0.0	3.6	0.9	1.8
J	Validation of Incident and Problem Analyzer Criteria	0.8	0.8	0.8	3.1	1.3	1.2
K	Validation of Virtualization and IaaS Connector Criteria	0.1	1.0	1.0	3.5	1.4	1.5
	Mean score	0.6	2.2	1.5	3.5	2.0	1.2
	Standard deviation	0.6	1.2	1.3	0.4	0.5	

Table 6.15.: Summary of Validation Results (Part 1)

Block	Topic	Legacy	BASE	Snorby	ITSM Wiki	Mean	SD
I-2	Validation of Intrusion Detection Criteria	0.0	1.1	1.1	3.6	1.5	1.5

Table 6.16.: Summary of Validation Results (Part 2)

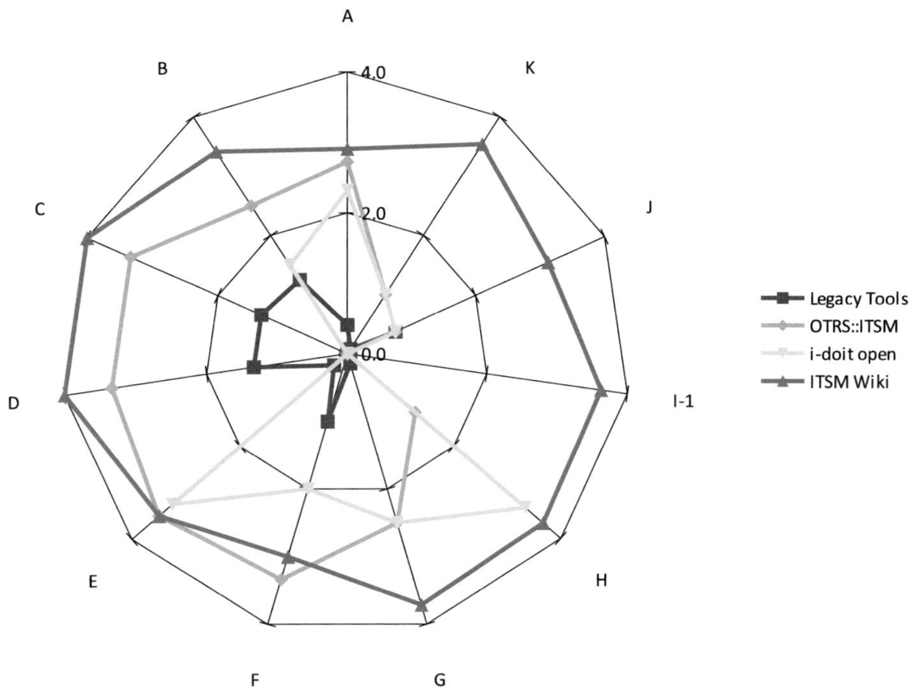

Figure 6.1.: Summary of Validation Results

Table 6.18 shows the relative strengths of the intrusion detection front-ends.

In Figure 6.2, a graphical representation of the relative strength of the validated tools, as presented in Table 6.17, is shown. The chart's purpose is to illustrate how the tools performed in each block. All values in the chart are relative to the arithmetic mean of the individual block. For example, in block A, the legacy tools performed 1.7 grade points worse than the average, while OTRS::ITSM performed 0.6 grade points better. As can be seen in Figure 6.2, the legacy tools performed lower than average in all blocks. In blocks B, C, D, F, I-1, J, and K, i-doit open performed lower than average. OTRS::ITSM performed lower than average in blocks H, I-1, J, and K. The ITSM Wiki performed better than average in all blocks.

Comparison of the Individual Strengths of the Validated Tools

In this subsection, it is shown for each tool, how it performs in the individual blocks compared to the mean of all blocks of the same tool. As such, the results show the individual strengths of the validated tools. It provides a metric on how well balanced the tools are with regard to implementing all validated blocks.

Block	Topic	Legacy	OTRS::ITSM	i-doit open	ITSM Wiki
A	Validation of Configuration Management Criteria	-1.7	$+0.6$	$+0.2$	$+0.8$
B	Validation of Service Knowledge Management Criteria	-0.9	$+0.3$	-0.7	$+1.3$
C	Validation of Change Management Criteria	-0.8	$+1.2$	-2.2	$+1.8$
D	Validation of Incident and Problem Management Criteria	-0.8	$+1.2$	-2.2	$+1.8$
E	Validation of Continual Service Improvement Criteria	-2.4	$+0.9$	$+0.6$	$+0.9$
F	Validation of Usability Aspects	-1.3	$+1.0$	-0.3	$+0.7$
G	Validation of Information Gathering Criteria	-2.1	$+0.3$	$+0.3$	$+1.5$
H	Validation of Infrastructure Monitoring Criteria	-2.1	-0.8	$+1.3$	$+1.6$
I-1	Validation of Intrusion Detection Criteria	-0.9	-0.9	-0.9	$+2.7$
J	Validation of Incident and Problem Analyzer Criteria	-0.6	-0.6	-0.6	$+1.8$
K	Validation of Virtualization and IaaS Connector Criteria	-1.3	-0.4	-0.4	$+2.1$
	Mean Relative Strength	-1.4	$+0.3$	-0.4	$+1.5$

Table 6.17.: Comparison of the Relative Strength of the Validated Tools (Part 1)

Block	Topic	Legacy	BASE	Snorby	ITSM Wiki
I-2	Validation of Intrusion Detection Criteria	-1.5	-0.3	-0.3	$+2.2$

Table 6.18.: Comparison of the Relative Strength of the Validated Tools (Part 2)

Table 6.19 shows a comparison of the individual strengths of the different tools. The values in the table are relative to the arithmetic mean of each tool's block scores. The results show how each tool was graded in each block relative to the other blocks.

The values in the table are calculated as follows: First, the arithmetic mean of the scores of all blocks for a single tool is calculated. After that, for each combination of block and tool, the tools' arithmetic mean is subtracted from the score of each table item. For example, for the legacy tools in block A, the arithmetic mean of all blocks is 0.6, and the value of the legacy tools in block A is 0.4, as shown in Table 6.15. This means that 0.6 is subtracted from 0.4, in order to get the result that shows how the legacy tools performed

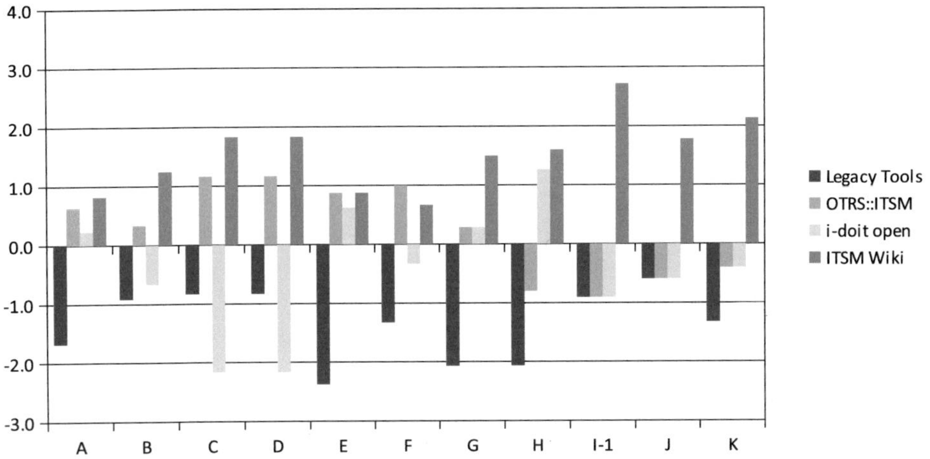

Figure 6.2.: Comparison of the Relative Strength of the Validated Tools

in block A compared to the mean of all blocks. This leads to the result that the legacy tools were rated 0.2 points less in block A compared to the legacy tool's average of all blocks.

Figure 6.3 shows how the different tools performed in each of the blocks relative to the other blocks. For example, it can be seen that the legacy tools performed worse in blocks A, E, G, H, I-1 and K, and performed better in blocks B, C, D, F, and J.

The results show, that the different tools differ in how the individual strengths and weaknesses are balanced. As can be seen in Figure 6.3, the legacy tools and the ITSM Wiki are more balanced than OTRS::ITSM and i-doit open. This can be interpreted as follows: Tools with more balanced strengths and weaknesses provide a comparable level of functionality in all the disciplines (i.e., the different blocks).

In contrast, tools that are less balanced provide different levels of functionality in the evaluated disciplines. For example, while the ITSM Wiki is about as good in block B (Service Knowledge Management) as in block H (Infrastructure Monitoring), OTRS::-ITSM is comparatively better in block B than it is in block H.

Please note that the results that are presented in Table 6.19 and Figure 6.3 only show the strengths within the individual tools, but do not allow a comparison of the strengths between the tools. This means that while the legacy tools and the ITSM Wiki are both balanced, the ITSM Wiki is balanced on a consistently higher level than the legacy tools.

Block	Topic	Legacy	OTRS::ITSM	i-doit open	ITSM Wiki
A	Validation of Configuration Management Criteria	−0.2	+0.5	+0.8	−0.6
B	Validation of Service Knowledge Management Criteria	+0.7	+0.3	−0.0	−0.1
C	Validation of Change Management Criteria	+0.7	+1.1	−1.5	+0.5
D	Validation of Incident and Problem Management Criteria	+0.7	+1.1	−1.5	+0.5
E	Validation of Continual Service Improvement Criteria	−0.3	+1.3	+1.7	+0.0
F	Validation of Usability Aspects	+0.4	+1.1	+0.5	−0.5
G	Validation of Information Gathering Criteria	−0.5	+0.3	+1.0	+0.2
H	Validation of Infrastructure Monitoring Criteria	−0.6	−0.9	+1.8	+0.2
I-1	Validation of Intrusion Detection Criteria	−0.6	−2.2	−1.5	+0.1
J	Validation of Incident and Problem Analyzer Criteria	+0.2	−1.5	−0.8	−0.4
K	Validation of Virtualization and IaaS Connector Criteria	−0.5	−1.2	−0.5	+0.0

Table 6.19.: Comparison of the Individual Strengths of the Validated Tools

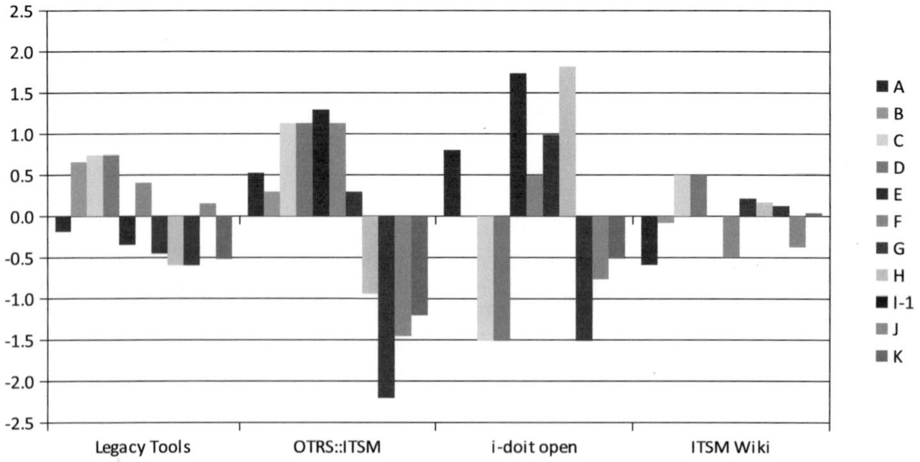

Figure 6.3.: Comparison of the Individual Strengths of the Validated Tools

Interpretation of the Results of the Validated Tools

The following paragraphs describe the individual strengths and weaknesses of the evaluated tools based on the results of the validation. Furthermore, explanations for the reasons of the scores are presented.

Legacy Tools As can be seen in Table 6.15 and Figure 6.1, the legacy tools (a combination of a non-semantic wiki, namely PmWiki, and a spreadsheet application, namely Microsoft Excel) were given the lowest scores. The reasons for this fact are grounded in the separation of structured and unstructured information. Structured information was stored in a number of two-dimensional spreadsheets, where the columns represented the attributes and the rows represented the individual configuration items. Unstructured information was stored in PmWiki, where rich-media hypertext (i.e., formatted text with embedded images and links between wiki pages) could be edited.

When looking at Microsoft Excel as a tool for storing structured information about configuration items, the following observations can be made:

- Each spreadsheet consists of a two-dimensional workspace, in which the information is stored.
- Additional attributes are added by extending the attribute dimension of the spreadsheet.
- Additional configuration items are added by extending the configuration item dimension.
- It is possible to sort the configuration items based on each attribute (e.g., by name).
- Performing calculations is easy (due to the fact that this is the core functionality of a spreadsheet).
- Storing larger amounts of rich-media text is not feasible.
- Dynamic functionalities require the use of a programming language (e.g., Visual Basic for Applications).

With regard to PmWiki, the following observations can be made:

- Information is organized in wiki pages.
- Wiki pages are edited by using a special syntax (wikitext). Wikitext allows to create rich-media text.
- Wiki pages can be linked to each other.
- Structured information cannot be represented satisfactorily because a non-semantic wiki does not provide the necessary technical functions.

When looking at the combination of the two platforms, it can be seen that the separation between structured and unstructured information in separate tools hampered the efficient use of the information.

OTRS::ITSM As shown in Table 6.15 and Figure 6.1, OTRS::ITSM received an average score of 2.2. The following observations can be made with regard to OTRS::-ITSM:

- OTRS::ITSM builds on the OTRS service desk software.
- With regard to the aspects of ITSM that were described in blocks A–F, OTRS::-ITSM scores high results.
- There are areas, namely blocks G–K, which are not supported by OTRS::ITSM.
- By providing means to store structured and unstructured information, OTRS::-ITSM is a good tool for retaining ITSM information.
- With respect to flexibility, the separation of structured and unstructured information is disadvantageous.
- New structured properties cannot be added ad-hoc when editing unstructured text.

In summary, OTRS::ITSM is a mature product, which excels in the areas in which it supports the corresponding ITIL processes. The integration of Incident and Problem Management is particularly strong, which stems from the fact that OTRS::ITSM is an add-on for the widely-used OTRS service desk software.

Areas that would benefit from the use of semantic wiki technologies lie in the processing of structured and unstructured information. Additional flexibility would be gained by removing the partition between the two types of information. Furthermore the query mechanism, as provided by Semantic MediaWiki, would exceed the capabilities provided by the search mechanisms that are currently present in OTRS::ITSM.

i-doit open As can be seen in Table 6.15 and Figure 6.1, i-doit open received an average score of 1.5. With regard to i-doit open, the following observations can be made:

- i-doit open is a CMDB tool, which enables IT administrators to primarily store structured information about IT infrastructures.
- While unstructured information can be added as comments to configuration items, the functionality is limited (for example, text cannot be formatted).
- While the aspects of IT Service Management that are described in blocks A and E–G are supported, the aspects described in blocks B–D, I-1, J, and K are not.

As is the case with OTRS::ITSM, i-doit open is a mature product that supports IT administrators in the areas for which it was designed.

By integrating features of semantic wikis, i-doit open would gain in flexibility and functionality. As is the case with OTRS::ITSM, an area that would benefit from a tighter integration of structured and unstructured information is the flexible displaying of aggregated structured information by using queries.

BASE and Snorby In Table 6.16, the results of the validation of the BASE and Snorby tools are presented. With respect to the criteria described in Section 5.3.2 (page 264), BASE and Snorby each received a score of 1.1. The following observations can be made about BASE and Snorby:

- BASE and Snorby are Web-based front-ends for displaying structured information about intrusion detection events.
- In contrast to OTRS::ITSM and i-doit open, which include various aspects of ITSM, BASE and Snorby only cover intrusion detection.
- No mechanisms for integrating additional structured and unstructured information are present.

While BASE and Snorby succeed in providing IT administrators with the functionality of displaying information about intrusion detection events, the lack of integration with other ITSM disciplines is disadvantageous. This is due to the fact that contextual information that could help in interpreting events is not present.

ITSM Wiki A summary of the results of the validation is presented in Table 6.15 and Figure 6.1. As can be seen, the ITSM Wiki reached an average score of 3.5. With regard to the ITSM Wiki, the following observations can be made:

- The ITSM Wiki makes use of Semantic MediaWiki in order to provide a tight integration of structured and unstructured information.
- On top of Semantic MediaWiki, an ontology was designed as the data model, which comprises the aspects of ITSM that are relevant for managing the IT infrastructure at FZI.
- The ontology is a flexible data model, which can be extended ad-hoc from within the wiki.
- In addition to functionality that is present in Semantic MediaWiki, specialized add-ons were created, which cover a number of ITSM-specific areas.
- The Semantic MediaWiki query mechanism can be used to generate dynamic tables of information based on data and object properties.

In contrast to the other validated tools, which are enterprise-ready products, the ITSM Wiki is much less mature. However, the strengths of the underlying semantic wiki platform came to light when validating the criteria defined in the requirements analysis phase. While the other tools separated structured and unstructured information, the integration of the two types of information shows its benefits in the ITSM Wiki. Areas in which the benefits are particularly significant lie in the extensible data model, as well as in the Semantic MediaWiki query mechanism, which provides a mighty basis for presenting aggregated structured information in combination with unstructured information.

6.2. User Study

The second part of the evaluation is the user study, in which the ITSM Wiki, as well as other ITSM platforms, were given to test persons for a hands-on comparison.

This section is organized as follows: In Section 6.2.1 (page 384), the theoretical foundation for user studies and the approach taken in this thesis is presented. After that, in Section 6.2.2 (page 386), the test plan is described. Following that, in Section 6.2.3 (page 386), the participants of the study, as well as the screening questionnaire are presented. In Section 6.2.4 (page 394), the test environment is described. Following that, the training phase of the user study is outlined in Section 6.2.5 (page 397). After that, in Section 6.2.6 (page 397) the tasks given to the participants, as well as the results of the user study are presented. In Section 6.2.7 (page 414), the System Usability Scale results are shown, followed by the results of the posttest questionnaire in Section 6.2.8 (page 419). Finally, Section 6.2.9 (page 420) provides a review of the free-text comments that the participants of the study were asked to give at the end of the study.

6.2.1. Foundation

The general approach of the user study follows the method described in [Rub94]. Moreover, additional references [Sau08, Bar10, AT13] were consulted.

Test Types

Reference [Rub94, pages 30–42] lists four different types of tests, which can be used to assess usability in different points of the development lifecycle. The test types are as follows:

- *Exploratory Test:* This test is used in early phases of product development. It is concerned with the high-level concepts of a design. Tests are performed on early prototypes, or mock-ups that cover only limited aspects of the product. About the level of formality, exploratory tests are informal, with interactions taking part between test monitor and participant [Rub94, pages 31–37].

- *Assessment Test:* Assessment tests are used in the early or midway phases of product development, "usually after the fundamental or high-level design or organization of the product has been established" [Rub94, page 37]. Users are required to perform tasks in the assessment test. There is a smaller number of interactions between the test monitor and the test participant. Furthermore, a collection of quantitative measures takes place [Rub94, pages 37–38].

- *Validation/Verification Test:* The validation, or verification test is conducted at a late stage in the product development cycle. It is used "to certify the product's usability" [Rub94, page 38]. The verification test's objective "is to evaluate how the product compares to some predetermined usability standard or benchmark, either a project-related performance standard, an internal company or historical standard, or even a competitor's standard of performance" [Rub94, page 38]. Typically, it is measured, how fast or accurate tasks can be performed. The focus of the verification test is on all components of the product (i.e., interactions between components of the product are tested). Compared to the assessment test, there is an even smaller amount of interactions between the test monitor and the participant, as well as a bigger focus on "experiment rigor and consistency" [Rub94, page 40].

- *Comparison Test:* The comparison test can be used at all stages of the development cycle. It can be used to compare the product to competitors' products and can be used together with any of the other test types [Rub94, pages 40–42].

The test type that was chosen for the user study of the components developed in the context of this thesis is the validation/verification test, together with the comparison test. In order to avoid confusion with the term validation, which was used in the context of the validation of the criteria, the term *verification test* is used to describe the validation/verification test.

The verification test has the following characteristics:

- "Prior to the test, benchmarks or standards for the task of the test are either developed or identified.

- "Participants are given tasks to perform with either very little or no interaction with the test monitor.

- "The collection of quantitative data is the central focus, although reasons for substandard performance are identified." [Rub94, pages 39–40]

Test Steps

Reference [Rub94, page 79] lists the following “six stages of conducting a test”:

1. “Developing the Test Plan”
2. “Selecting and Acquiring Participants”
3. “Preparing the Test Machines”
4. “Conducting the Test”
5. “Debriefing the Participant”
6. “Transforming Data Into Findings and Recommendations” [Rub94, page 79]

The user study that was performed in the context of this thesis roughly follows these six stages.

6.2.2. Test Plan

Figure 6.4 shows a graphical representation of the test plan. As can be seen in the figure, first, participants were selected, and a screening questionnaire was handed out to the participants. After that, the test was prepared. This step consisted of setting up the test environment, planning the tasks that were given to the participants, as well as the setup of the questionnaire.

After the test preparation was complete, a pilot test was conducted, which comprised the same steps as the actual test. The feedback given by the pilot testers was used in order to improve the test. After the pilot test, the actual test was performed. The test consisted of a training phase, the tasks, System Usability Score [Bro96] questionnaires, and a posttest questionnaire. Following the test, thc results of the test were analyzed.

6.2.3. Participants

The participants of the user study were members of FZI’s IT department. While, in most cases, it makes sense to use external participants in user research, in this case, the use of FZI employees was acceptable, because they exactly represented the targeted audience of the ITSM Wiki [Rub94, pages 129–130].

A total number of ten employees (n=10) were selected as participants for the user study.

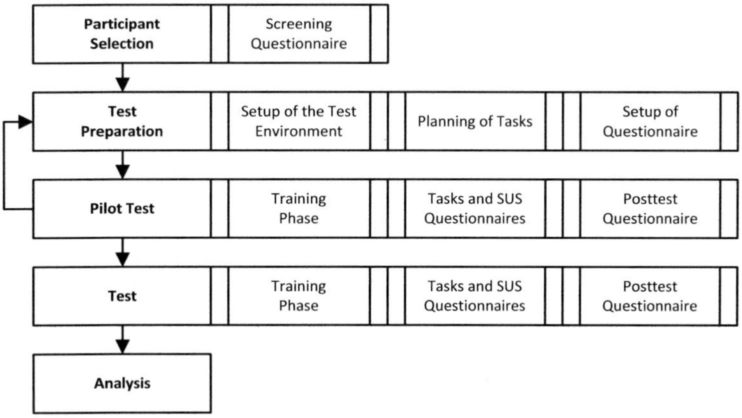

Figure 6.4.: Test Plan

Scale

Table 6.20 shows the scale that was used in questions in which participants were asked to rate aspects such as skills, or knowledge.

Textual	Numeric	Abbreviation
very good	4	V
good	3	G
fair	2	F
basic	1	B
none	0	N

Table 6.20.: Self-evaluation Scale

Screening Questionnaire

In order to get an initial assessment of the participants, a screening questionnaire was handed out to the intended participants several weeks before the test.

The following paragraphs show the questions that were asked, as well as the answers of the participants. The actual screening questionnaire was handed to the participants in German, because all participants were German natives. A copy of the original screening questionnaire can be found in Appendix C.1 (page 451).

Job Background Participants were asked for their job background.

Question 1: Do you work as an IT administrator?

Possible answers were:

- yes (full time)
- yes (part time)
- no

Table 6.21 shows the results of the first question.

Question	full time	part time	no
Do you work as an IT administrator?	5	5	0

Table 6.21.: Participants' Jobs (n=10)

IT Background Participants were asked to rank their IT skills on a five-point Likert scale.

Question 2: Please rate your skills in the following areas:

- General IT application
- Windows IT administration
- Linux IT administration
- IT Service Management

The results of question 2 are as shown in Table 6.22.

IT Skill	N	B	F	G	V	Mean	SD
General IT application	0	1	0	7	2	3.0	0.8
Windows IT administration	0	0	4	2	4	3.0	0.9
Linux IT administration	3	2	1	4	0	1.6	1.3
IT Service Management	2	1	5	1	1	1.8	1.2

Table 6.22.: Self-Assessment of Participants' IT Skills (n=10)

One of the participants did not give a rating for his or her IT Service Management skills. It is assumed that the participant did not give a rating because the term was unknown to him or her. Because of that, the missing answer was rated as the *none* option.

Wiki Type Experience Participants were asked with which wiki types they worked.

Question 3: With which of the following types of wikis did you work before?

Possible answers were:

- Classic (non-semantic) wikis
- Semantic wikis
- None

The participants' experiences with different wiki types are shown in Table 6.23.

Question	Classic Wikis	Semantic Wikis	None
With which of the following types of wikis did you work before?	6	8	1

Table 6.23.: Participants' Experiences with Wikis (n=10)

Wiki Platform Experience Participants were asked to rate their skills with respect to different wiki platforms and extensions.

Question 4: Rate your skills in the following wiki platforms and extensions:

- PmWiki
- MediaWiki
- Semantic MediaWiki
- Semantic Forms

In Table 6.24, the results of the participants' self-assessment with respect to wiki skills are listed. The results include information about the platforms PmWiki and MediaWiki and about the extensions Semantic MediaWiki and Semantic Forms.

Tool	N	B	F	G	V	Mean	SD
PmWiki	7	3	0	0	0	0.3	0.5
MediaWiki	2	2	3	3	0	1.7	1.1
Semantic MediaWiki	1	5	3	1	0	1.4	0.8
Semantic Forms	4	5	0	1	0	0.8	0.9

Table 6.24.: Self-Assessment of Participants' Wiki Skills (n=10)

Other Wiki Platforms Participants were asked for their experience with other wiki platforms.

Question 5: Name additional wikis, which you currently use or which you have used in the past.

The DokuWiki[4] platform was named by two participants.

Applications Participants were asked to rate their applications skills.

Question 6: Rate your skills in using the following applications:

- Microsoft Excel
- Active Directory Users and Computers

Table 6.25 lists the results of the participants' self-assessment about applications.

Tool	N	B	F	G	V	Mean	SD
Microsoft Excel	0	1	2	6	1	2.7	0.8
Active Directory Users and Computers	0	1	1	5	3	3.0	0.9

Table 6.25.: Self-Assessment of Participants' Applications Skills (n=10)

Infrastructure Monitoring Participants were asked to rate their IT infrastructure monitoring skills.

Question 7: Rate your skills with regard to the IT infrastructure monitoring software Nagios.

Table 6.26 lists the results of the participants' self-assessment about Nagios.

Tool	N	B	F	G	V	Mean	SD
Nagios application	6	0	0	4	0	1.2	1.5
Nagios configuration	6	0	0	4	0	1.2	1.5

Table 6.26.: Self-Assessment of Participants' Nagios Skills (n=10)

[4] `http://www.dokuwiki.org/`

Intrusion Detection Participants were asked to rate their skills with respect to intrusion detection front-ends.

Question 8: Rate your skills of the following Web-based platforms for displaying and analyzing intrusion attempts (intrusion detection front-ends):

- BASE
- Snorby

Table 6.27 lists the results of the participants' self-assessment about Web-based intrusion detection front-ends.

Tool	N	B	F	G	V	Mean	SD
BASE	8	1	0	1	0	0.4	0.9
Snorby	7	2	1	0	0	0.4	0.7

Table 6.27.: Self-Assessment of Participants' Intrusion Detection Front-end Skills (n=10)

IT Service Management Applications Participants were asked to rate their skills with respect to IT Service Management applications.

Question 9: Rate your skills with regard to the following IT Service Management applications:

- OTRS
- OTRS::ITSM
- i-doit open

Table 6.28 lists the results of the participants' self-assessment about IT Service Management applications.

Tool	N	B	F	G	V	Mean	SD
OTRS	1	2	2	5	0	2.1	1.0
OTRS::ITSM	8	2	0	0	0	0.2	0.4
i-doit open	9	0	1	0	0	0.2	0.6

Table 6.28.: Self-Assessment of Participants' ITSM Applications Skills (n=10)

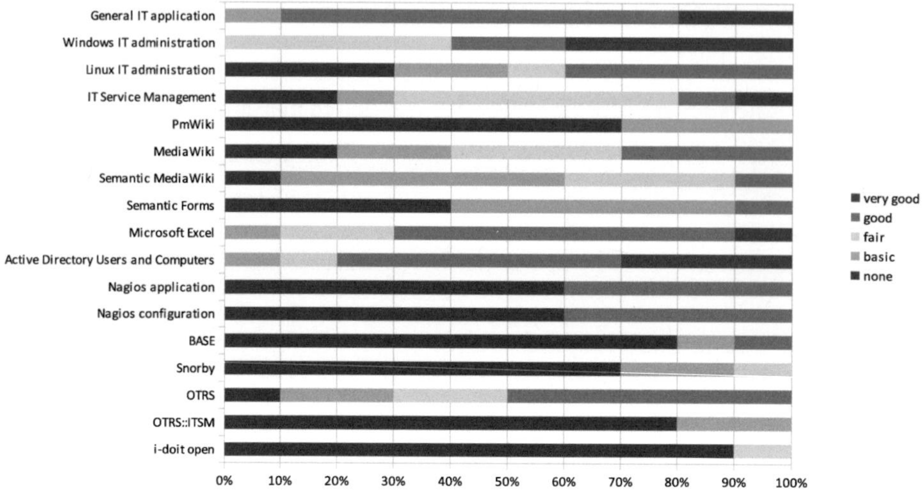

Figure 6.5.: Summary of the Results of the Screening Questionnaire

Interpretation of the Results of the Screening Questionnaire

Figure 6.5 shows a graphical summary of the results of the screening questionnaire.

As can be seen in the figure, almost all of the participants of the study showed good or very good general IT application skills. With regard to Windows IT administration, skills were equal or higher than the *fair* level. In contrast, Linux IT skills were lower, with almost a third of the participants indicating that they do not possess Linux skills. These results can be explained by the IT environment that is managed by the participants. In this environment, about 70 % of the computers are running Windows, while only about 30 % are running Linux.

IT Service Management skills were rated good or very good by only 20 % of the participants, while 30 % possessed none or basic skills. Half of the participants rated their skills as fair.

With respect to wikis, as shown in Table 6.23 (page 389), six participants said that they used non-semantic wikis before, while eight participants stated that they did use semantic wikis. Only one participant stated that he or she did not use wikis at all. The higher number of semantic wiki users in contrast to the lower number of non-semantic users might be explained by some participants only marking the semantic wiki option when, in fact, having used semantic and non-semantic wikis before.

While PmWiki was used as a tool for retaining textual information about the IT environment in the past, only 30 % of the participants rated their PmWiki skills as basic, while 70 % stated no PmWiki skills at all. This might be explained by the fact that PmWiki was replaced by MediaWiki about six years before performing the survey. Only two out of the ten participants of the study were working at FZI at that time.

With regard to MediaWiki, 60 % rated their skills fair or good, while 40 % rated their skills as none or basic. Semantic MediaWiki skills were present to a smaller amount, with 40 % having fair or good skills and 60 % having basic or no skills. Semantic Forms skills were present to an even lesser amount, with only one participant rating his or her skills as good, while five participants rated their skills as basic. Four participants did not possess Semantic Forms skills at all.

Microsoft Excel skills were rated as good or very good by seven of the ten participants. Only three participants rated their skills as basic or fair.

Eight of the participants of the study rated their skills of Active Directory Users and Computers, which is the computer and user management application provided by Microsoft Windows Server, as good or very good. Only two participants rated their skills as basic or fair.

With regard to the use and configuration of the Nagios infrastructure monitoring application, the skills were divided by a majority of six participants possessing no skills, and a minority of four participants that rated their skills as good. This result can be explained by the fact that the management of IT infrastructure components and services is performed only by a limited group of people within the IT department.

Skills in BASE and Snorby were even less common, with only one participant stating good skills in BASE, and only one participant stating fair skills in Snorby. The majority of nine out of ten participants stated no or basic skills with respect to the Web-based intrusion detection front-ends.

OTRS skills were rated as fair or higher by 70 % of the participants. One of the participants rated his or her OTRS skills as non-existent, which is a surprising finding because OTRS is used as the service desk system that is used by all IT administrators at FZI. An explanation might be that the participant is new at the IT department or does not know of the software behind the service desk system.

Skills in using the IT Service Management tools OTRS::ITSM and i-doit open were not widespread among the participants. Only two participants stated basic skills in OTRS::ITSM, while one participant stated fair skills in i-doit open.

In summary, the participants of the study are a representation of IT administrators that manage a heterogeneous Windows and Linux environment. The participants furthermore are familiar with wiki platforms, Microsoft Excel, OTRS, as well as IT administration tools (e.g., Windows user management tools), which are used in the user study. This qualifies the participants as a group that is able to compare the ITSM Wiki platform with legacy tools, as well as with OTRS::ITSM.

6.2.4. Preparation of the Test Environment

The user study took place in a testing setup with the properties that are described in this subsection. The test environment was set up to satisfy the following two goals: The first goal was to have an environment, which was as realistic as possible (i.e., include all the properties found in typical IT environments of small and medium-sized enterprises, such as at FZI). The second goal was to have an environment, which was as straightforward as possible, so participants of the user study could focus on the tasks at hand, without being disturbed by unnecessary details of real-world infrastructures.

The setup of the room, in which the testing took place, is an adapted version of the simple single-room setup that is described in [Rub94, pages 50–52]. As can be seen in Figure 6.6, the participant was seated before a computer, on which the tasks were performed. On the left side of the participant, the test monitor[5] was seated. To the participant's right, a video camera was mounted that was set up in order to capture the screen content. In addition, a screen capturing software was installed, which recorded the user's screen during the study. Behind the participant, five notebook computers were placed, which played a role in some of the tasks that the participant was asked to accomplish. The five notebooks were covered under boxes that were only removed after the participants of the study explicitly stated that they wanted to visit the notebook. This was done in order to simulate the physical visiting of a computer.

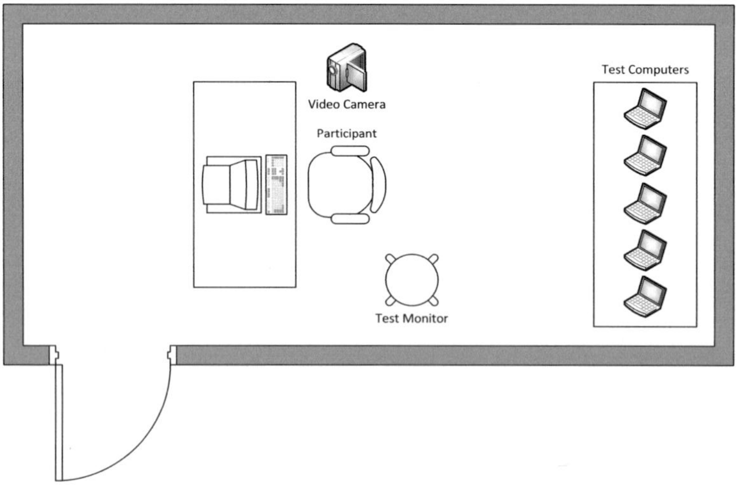

Figure 6.6.: User Study Setup

[5]For the role of the test monitor, an independent person was used. This person handed out the tasks and recorded the time, while keeping interactions with the participants to a minimum in order to avoid giving different information to different participants.

For each of the tools, a virtual machine was set up, which contained the tools required for the respective tasks. For the ITSM Wiki, an additional virtual machine was running on a server that provided the Web server and the Semantic MediaWiki instance. Each of the virtual machines, as well as the ITSM Wiki database, were reset after each of the participant completed his or her tasks.

Test Infrastructure

In order to satisfy the goal of having a realistic environment, the tests were conducted in FZI's IT environment, which at the time of the user study, consisted of the following components:

- Ethernet network with 27 switches
- Windows domain with approximately 500 computers and 650 user accounts

In order to satisfy the second goal, namely providing an easy to understand environment, the number of items were limited to a subset of the real world conditions.

Table 6.29 lists the computers that were physically present at the location of the user study and which were used in some of the tasks of the legacy tools.

Name	Model	Form	Specification	Operating System
Isidor	Lenovo ThinkPad T60p	Notebook	Intel Core 2 Duo CPU, 4 GB RAM, 120 GB SSD	Microsoft Windows 8.1 Professional 64 bit
Jesaja	Lenovo ThinkPad W500	Notebook	Intel Core 2 Duo CPU, 8 GB RAM, 120 GB SSD	Microsoft Windows 7 Professional 64 bit
Milka	Lenovo ThinkPad X200T	Notebook	Intel Core 2 Duo CPU, 4 GB RAM, 120 GB SSD	Microsoft Windows 7 Professional 64 bit
Ruben	Lenovo ThinkPad T60p	Notebook	Intel Core Duo CPU, 4 GB RAM, 100 GB HDD	Microsoft Windows 8.1 Professional 32 bit
Zippora	Lenovo ThinkPad T60p	Notebook	Intel Core 2 Duo CPU, 4 GB RAM, 300 GB HDD	Microsoft Windows 8.1 Professional 64 bit

Table 6.29.: Physically Present Computers Used in the User Study

ITSM Wiki Setup

With regard to the ITSM Wiki, the setup was as follows:

- ITSM Wiki as described in Chapter 4 (page 115)
- Components as described in Chapter 5 (page 185)
- Data about users and computers was gained from a gathering run before the user study

In order to be able to compare the results of the user study, all participants were working with the same information available in the ITSM Wiki. After each session, the wiki database was reset, in order to delete modifications performed by the participants of the study.

Legacy Tools Setup

The legacy tools included the following tools, which were used as parts of the production environment when beginning the conceptualization of the ITSM Wiki:

- Excel spreadsheet with computer names and information about computers
- PmWiki instance with textual documentation
- Windows administration tools

The information stored in the spreadsheet and the PmWiki instance was of the same quality as the one that was part of the production environment before starting work on the ITSM Wiki. This means that information was partly incomplete and obsolete. After each session, the virtual machine containing the legacy tools was reset, in order to delete modifications performed by the participants of the study.

OTRS::ITSM Setup

The OTRS::ITSM platform was used as an example of an integrated ITSM tool. OTRS-::ITSM used the same data as the legacy tools. OTRS and the OTRS::ITSM extension were installed locally in the virtual machine, in which the OTRS::ITSM tools were evaluated. After each session, the virtual machine was reset, in order to delete modifications performed by the participants of the study.

6.2.5. Training Phase

Before the tasks were given to the participants of the study, each participant was allowed to complete the training phase, in which a baseline of knowledge of each of the evaluated tools could be acquired.

The training phase was performed in order to bring participants to a common base level of familiarity with the used tools. Because the usage scope of the tools is in the business environment, basic training before using the tools is considered acceptable.

The documents that were handed out to the participants during the training phase can be found in Appendix C.1 (page 451).

More information about the training phase in general can be found in [Rub94, pages 185–198].

6.2.6. Tasks

In the main part of the study, participants were asked to perform a number of tasks. For each task, the task completion time [AT13, pages 74–82] was tracked. In addition, it was tracked whether the individual tasks were accomplished successfully [AT13, pages 65–74].

When comparing the task completion times of the individual tools, only the times of fully completed tasks are taken into account, while failed or partially completed tasks are not taken into account.

To minimize effects from the order, in which the participants used the tools, the order was varied. The order in which the three tools were presented to the participants were determined by drawing from a pool, in which each of the six combinations was included two times. Table 6.30 shows the order of the tools for each of the participants of the study.

In this subsection, the tasks that were given to the participants are presented, together with the results of the tasks. The results comprise two parts: First, the completion results are presented, which show for each tool, how many participants completed the task successfully or partially, or failed the task. The completion rate shows the percentage of participants who completed the task successfully.

The second part of the results are the completion times for each tool. Only successfully completed tasks are represented in the completion timetables. For each task and tool, the lower bound, mean, and upper bound were calculated. The mean was calculated by using the geometric mean, which, according to [Sau08, page 31] performs best for sample sizes less than 25. The confidence intervals were calculated based on a confidence of 95 %.

Participant	First Tool	Second Tool	Third Tool
P-01	ITSM Wiki	Legacy	OTRS::ITSM
P-02	ITSM Wiki	OTRS::ITSM	Legacy
P-03	OTRS::ITSM	Legacy	ITSM Wiki
P-04	OTRS::ITSM	ITSM Wiki	Legacy
P-05	Legacy	ITSM Wiki	OTRS::ITSM
P-06	Legacy	OTRS::ITSM	ITSM Wiki
P-07	OTRS::ITSM	Legacy	ITSM Wiki
P-08	OTRS::ITSM	ITSM Wiki	Legacy
P-09	Legacy	OTRS::ITSM	ITSM Wiki
P-10	ITSM Wiki	Legacy	OTRS::ITSM

Table 6.30.: Tool Order

Some tasks of the legacy tools included the possibility to simulate the physical visit to a computer in order to acquire relevant information. When choosing to physically visit a computer, a penalty time of 5 min was added in order to simulate the time it takes to walk to the computer.

The forms that were handed out to the participants of the user study can be found in Appendix C.1 (page 484).

Each of the following tasks was expected to be completed by using each of three tools, namely the legacy tools, OTRS::ITSM, and the ITSM Wiki. In the context of the user study, OTRS::ITSM was chosen over i-doit open, because of the following two reasons: First, OTRS::ITSM received higher scores in the validation, as described in Section 6.1 (page 318). Second, the results of the screening questionnaire, as presented in Section 6.2.3 (page 387) showed that the OTRS platform was already familiar to more participants of the study than i-doit open.

First Task Group: Accessing Information

The goal of the first task group was to find out, how the evaluated tools compare to each other with respect to accessing information. The following paragraphs present the tasks that were given to the participants, as well as the results of the tasks.

Task 1 The goal of the first task was to find out, how fast participants of the study were able to retrieve the model of a computer.

The first task contained two variations for the legacy tools: One, in which the relevant information was found in the Excel spreadsheet, and one which required to use the Windows administration tools.

Task: Name the model of the computers 'gowron' (legacy tools, using Excel), 'ruben' (legacy tools, using the Windows administration tools), 'paris' (OTRS::ITSM), and 'tabita' (ITSM Wiki).

Table 6.31 shows how many of the participants were able to solve the task, while Table 6.32 shows how much time was needed by the participants in order to successfully complete the task.

Tool	Fully	Partially	Failed	Completion Rate
Legacy (Excel)	10	0	0	100 %
Legacy (Windows tools)	10	0	0	100 %
OTRS::ITSM	10	0	0	100 %
ITSM Wiki	10	0	0	100 %

Table 6.31.: Completion Results of Task 1 (n=10)

Tool	Min [s]	LB [s]	Mean [s]	UB [s]	Max [s]
Legacy (Excel)	28	33	44	59	127
Legacy (Windows tools)	164	291	379	495	712
OTRS::ITSM	39	40	59	86	185
ITSM Wiki	18	22	24	28	30

Table 6.32.: Completion Time for Task 1

Task 2 The goal of the second task was to find out, how fast participants of the study were able to retrieve a list of computers with the same model type as a given computer.

Task: Name the computers that are of the same model as the computers 'kangaroo' (legacy tools), 'morn' (OTRS::ITSM), and 'borak' (ITSM Wiki).

Table 6.33 shows how many of the participants were able to solve the task, while Table 6.34 shows how much time was needed by the participants in order to successfully complete the task.

Tool	Fully	Partially	Failed	Completion Rate
Legacy	9	0	1	90 %
OTRS::ITSM	10	0	0	100 %
ITSM Wiki	10	0	0	100 %

Table 6.33.: Completion Results of Task 2 (n=10)

Tool	Min [s]	LB [s]	Mean [s]	UB [s]	Max [s]
Legacy	65	76	103	139	201
OTRS::ITSM	42	54	72	97	141
ITSM Wiki	31	38	54	78	122

Table 6.34.: Completion Time for Task 2

Task 3 The goal of the third task was to find out, how fast participants of the study were able to retrieve the names of local administrators of a given computer.

Task: Name the users that are local administrators on the computers 'zippora' (legacy tools), 'grima' (OTRS::ITSM), and 'kimara' (ITSM Wiki). Valid solutions are the given name and family name, the user name, or the group name.

Table 6.35 shows how many of the participants were able to solve the task, while Table 6.36 shows how much time was needed by the participants in order to successfully complete the task.

Tool	Fully	Partially	Failed	Completion Rate
Legacy	5	2	3	50 %
OTRS::ITSM	8	0	2	80 %
ITSM Wiki	9	0	1	90 %

Table 6.35.: Completion Results of Task 3 (n=10)

Tool	Min [s]	LB [s]	Mean [s]	UB [s]	Max [s]
Legacy	46	50	87	150	155
OTRS::ITSM	40	45	58	75	112
ITSM Wiki	54	52	85	140	376

Table 6.36.: Completion Time for Task 3

Task 4 The goal of the fourth task was to find out, how fast participants of the study were able to name all computers, on which a given person is an administrator.

Task: Name the computers, on which the users 'Lina Hartmann (hartmann@fzi.de)' (legacy tools), 'hschmidt' (OTRS::ITSM), and 'Max Jung (jung@fzi.de)' (ITSM Wiki) are administrators.

Table 6.37 shows how many of the participants were able to solve the task, while Table 6.38 shows how much time was needed by the participants in order to successfully complete the task.

Tool	Fully	Partially	Failed	Completion Rate
Legacy	0	1	9	0 %
OTRS::ITSM	8	2	0	80 %
ITSM Wiki	9	0	1	90 %

Table 6.37.: Completion Results of Task 4 (n=10)

Tool	Min [s]	LB [s]	Mean [s]	UB [s]	Max [s]
Legacy	–	–	–	–	–
OTRS::ITSM	28	31	39	49	65
ITSM Wiki	30	31	37	45	65

Table 6.38.: Completion Time for Task 4

Second Task Group: Adding Information

The goal of the second task group was to find out, how the tools compare to each other with regard to adding information.

Task 5 The goal of the fifth task was to find out, how much time it takes for the participants of the study to add a textual description to the representation of a computer.

Task: Add the text 'Hello world!' to the description of the computers 'mail1' (legacy tools), 'dns1' (OTRS::ITSM), and 'web1' (ITSM Wiki).

Table 6.39 shows how many of the participants were able to solve the task, while Table 6.40 shows how much time was needed by the participants in order to successfully complete the task.

Tool	Fully	Partially	Failed	Completion Rate
Legacy	10	0	0	100 %
OTRS::ITSM	10	0	0	100 %
ITSM Wiki	9	1	0	90 %

Table 6.39.: Completion Results of Task 5 (n=10)

Tool	Min [s]	LB [s]	Mean [s]	UB [s]	Max [s]
Legacy	18	22	35	57	185
OTRS::ITSM	23	30	47	73	188
ITSM Wiki	22	32	45	64	81

Table 6.40.: Completion Time for Task 5

Task 6 The goal of the sixth task was to find out, how much time is used by the participants in order to apply formatting to text in each tool.

Task: In the description, or notes of the computers 'mail1' (legacy tools), 'dns1' (OTRS-::ITSM), and 'web1' (ITSM Wiki), format the string 'World!' of the previously added text in boldface.

Table 6.41 shows how many of the participants were able to solve the task, while Table 6.42 shows how much time was needed by the participants in order to successfully complete the task.

The OTRS::ITSM installation did not support the formatting of text in the description field of computers, which led to the fact that the participants of the study were not able to complete this task in OTRS::ITSM.

Tool	Fully	Partially	Failed	Completion Rate
Legacy	10	0	0	100 %
OTRS::ITSM	0	0	10	0 %
ITSM Wiki	9	1	0	90 %

Table 6.41.: Completion Results of Task 6 (n=10)

Tool	Min [s]	LB [s]	Mean [s]	UB [s]	Max [s]
Legacy	10	11	21	42	239
OTRS::ITSM	–	–	–	–	–
ITSM Wiki	14	16	20	26	32

Table 6.42.: Completion Time for Task 6

Task 7 The goal of the seventh task was to find out, how much time is used by the participants in order to create links between representations of configuration items in each tool.

Task: Add the string 'This computer is replaced by the computer 'mail3' (legacy tools), 'dns3' (OTRS::ITSM), or 'web3' (ITSM Wiki)' to the computer 'mail1' (legacy tools), 'dns1' (OTRS::ITSM), and 'web1' (ITSM Wiki). Make the substrings 'mail3' (legacy tools), 'dns3' (OTRS::ITSM), and 'web3' (ITSM Wiki) links to the representations of the computers 'mail3' (legacy tools), 'dns3' (OTRS::ITSM), and 'web3' (ITSM Wiki).

Table 6.43 shows how many of the participants were able to solve the task, while Table 6.44 shows how much time was needed by the participants in order to successfully complete the task.

The OTRS::ITSM installation did not support links in the description field of computers, which led to the fact that the participants of the study were not able to fully complete this task in OTRS::ITSM.

Tool	Fully	Partially	Failed	Completion Rate
Legacy	10	0	0	100 %
OTRS::ITSM	0	1	9	0 %
ITSM Wiki	9	0	1	90 %

Table 6.43.: Completion Results of Task 7 (n=10)

Tool	Min [s]	LB [s]	Mean [s]	UB [s]	Max [s]
Legacy	32	45	74	121	240
OTRS::ITSM	–	–	–	–	–
ITSM Wiki	29	47	65	90	137

Table 6.44.: Completion Time for Task 7

Third Task Group: Querying Information

The goal of the third task group was to find out, how the tools compare to each other with respect to querying information.

Task 8 The goal of the eighth task was to find out, how much time is used by the participants in order to find all computers that are of a given model.

Task: Create a list of all computers that are of the model 'TestTech1000' (legacy tools), 'TestCom1000' (OTRS::ITSM), and 'TestGear1000' (ITSM Wiki).

Table 6.45 shows how many of the participants were able to solve the task, while Table 6.46 shows how much time was needed by the participants in order to successfully complete the task.

Tool	Fully	Partially	Failed	Completion Rate
Legacy	10	0	0	100 %
OTRS::ITSM	10	0	0	100 %
ITSM Wiki	10	0	0	100 %

Table 6.45.: Completion Results of Task 8 (n=10)

Tool	Min [s]	LB [s]	Mean [s]	UB [s]	Max [s]
Legacy	51	60	73	90	109
OTRS::ITSM	32	33	44	58	118
ITSM Wiki	36	52	87	145	264

Table 6.46.: Completion Time for Task 8

Task 9 The goal of the ninth task was to find out, how much time is used by the participants in order to find computers that match two given criteria.

Task: Create a list of all computers of the models 'OptiPlex 780' (legacy tools), 'ThinkPad T520' (OTRS::ITSM), and 'OptiPlex 790' (ITSM Wiki), which have 'Mark Berger' (legacy tools), 'Mark Schmidt' (OTRS::ITSM), or 'Mark Hahn (hahn@fzi.de)' (ITSM Wiki) as owner.

Table 6.47 shows how many of the participants were able to solve the task, while Table 6.48 shows how much time was needed by the participants in order to successfully complete the task.

Tool	Fully	Partially	Failed	Completion Rate
Legacy	9	1	0	90 %
OTRS::ITSM	9	0	1	90 %
ITSM Wiki	9	0	1	90 %

Table 6.47.: Completion Results of Task 9 (n=10)

Tool	Min [s]	LB [s]	Mean [s]	UB [s]	Max [s]
Legacy	61	73	112	171	346
OTRS::ITSM	42	49	85	149	443
ITSM Wiki	109	131	175	235	332

Table 6.48.: Completion Time for Task 9

Fourth Task Group: Finding Problem Causes

The goal of the fifth group of tasks was to test the ability of the evaluated tools in helping IT administrators to find the possible causes of incidents and problems.

Task 10 The goal of the tenth task was to find out, how much time is used by the participants in order to find similarities between two computers.

Task: The two computers 'isidor' and 'jesaja' (legacy tools), 'rom' and 'soran' (OTRS::-ITSM), and 'larissa' and 'zander' (ITSM Wiki) show the same symptoms that indicate a common problem cause. Find and name the properties that the two computers have in common. It is enough to give the results in note form (e.g., 'version of the office program').

Table 6.49 shows how many of the participants were able to solve the task, while Table 6.50 shows how much time was needed by the participants in order to successfully complete the task.

Tool	Fully	Partially	Failed	Completion Rate
Legacy	3	2	5	50 %
OTRS::ITSM	6	3	1	60 %
ITSM Wiki	9	1	0	90 %

Table 6.49.: Completion Results of Task 10 (n=10)

Tool	Min [s]	LB [s]	Mean [s]	UB [s]	Max [s]
Legacy	985	877	1072	1310	1157
OTRS::ITSM	97	105	161	245	328
ITSM Wiki	111	147	187	236	286

Table 6.50.: Completion Time for Task 10

Task 11 The goal of the eleventh task was to find out, how much time is used by the participants in order to find changes that were applied to a computer.

Task: The computers 'milka' (legacy tools), 'quark' (OTRS::ITSM), and 'orthos' (ITSM Wiki) currently show symptoms of a problem that were not evident before 2014-03-30, 23:30 (legacy tools), 2014-03-31, 00:15 (OTRS::ITSM), and 2014-06-01, 16:40 (ITSM Wiki). Find and name the properties of the host that changed since the given date. It is sufficient to give the results in note form (e.g., 'version of the office program').

Table 6.51 shows how many of the participants were able to solve the task, while Table 6.52 shows how much time was needed by the participants in order to successfully complete the task.

Tool	Fully	Partially	Failed	Completion Rate
Legacy	3	6	1	30 %
OTRS::ITSM	5	2	3	50 %
ITSM Wiki	10	0	0	100 %

Table 6.51.: Completion Results of Task 11 (n=10)

Tool	Min [s]	LB [s]	Mean [s]	UB [s]	Max [s]
Legacy	163	49	314	2007	708
OTRS::ITSM	87	88	110	138	138
ITSM Wiki	110	147	182	226	314

Table 6.52.: Completion Time for Task 11

Fifth Task Group: Infrastructure Monitoring

The fifth task group was concerned with finding out, which tool performs best with regard to enabling users to configure the Nagios infrastructure monitoring application.

Task 12 The goal of the twelfth task was to find out, how long it takes participants to activate infrastructure monitoring for a given computer.

In this task, the configuration of the infrastructure monitoring application was only performed in the legacy tools and ITSM Wiki parts of the user study. This is because OTRS::ITSM does not provide tools that support users in the configuration of Nagios. Because of that, configuring Nagios in the OTRS::ITSM part would have included the same steps as in the legacy part.

Task: Enable infrastructure monitoring (ping requests) for the computers 'marvin.fzi.de' (legacy tools and OTRS::ITSM), and 'eva.fzi.de' (ITSM Wiki).

Table 6.53 shows how many of the participants were able to solve the task, while Table 6.54 shows how much time was needed by the participants in order to successfully complete the task.

Tool	Fully	Partially	Failed	Completion Rate
Legacy and OTRS::ITSM	9	0	1	90 %
ITSM Wiki	9	0	1	90 %

Table 6.53.: Completion Results of Task 12 (n=10)

Tool	Min [s]	LB [s]	Mean [s]	UB [s]	Max [s]
Legacy and OTRS::ITSM	69	105	191	345	556
ITSM Wiki	21	33	46	63	78

Table 6.54.: Completion Time for Task 12

Task 13 The goal of the thirteenth task was to find out, how long it takes participants to enable the monitoring of a given service for a given computer.

As was the case in task 12, the configuration of the infrastructure monitoring application would have been the same for OTRS::ITSM and the legacy tools. Because of that, this task was omitted in the OTRS::ITSM part of the user study.

Task: Enable monitoring of the HTTP service (legacy tools and OTRS::ITSM), and the DHCP service (ITSM Wiki) for the computers 'marvin.fzi.de' (legacy tools and OTRS::ITSM), and 'eva.fzi.de' (ITSM Wiki).

Table 6.55 shows how many of the participants were able to solve the task, while Table 6.56 shows how much time was needed by the participants in order to successfully complete the task.

Tool	Fully	Partially	Failed	Completion Rate
Legacy and OTRS::ITSM	4	6	0	40 %
ITSM Wiki	9	0	1	90 %

Table 6.55.: Completion Results of Task 13 (n=10)

Tool	Min [s]	LB [s]	Mean [s]	UB [s]	Max [s]
Legacy and OTRS::ITSM	58	54	91	154	126
ITSM Wiki	19	23	30	39	57

Table 6.56.: Completion Time for Task 13

Interpretation of Task Completion Rates

Table 6.57 shows a comparison of the three tools with respect to task completion. As can be seen in the table, the ITSM Wiki accomplished a task completion rate of 93.1 %, while the legacy tools reached 72.9 %, and OTRS::ITSM reached 67.7 %. The higher total number of tasks in the legacy tools comes from the fact that the first task was given to the participants of the study in two different forms.

The first form was for solving the task with information found in the Excel spreadsheet, while the second form was for solving the task by using information that had to be gathered by the use of Windows administration tools.

Tool	Fully	Partially	Failed	Success Rate
Legacy Tools	102	12	26	72.9 %
OTRS::ITSM	88	6	36	67.7 %
ITSM Wiki	121	3	6	93.1 %

Table 6.57.: Task Completion Data

Figure 6.7 shows a graphical comparison of the completion rates. As can be seen, the completion rate of the ITSM Wiki is higher than the completion rates of the legacy tools and OTRS::ITSM.

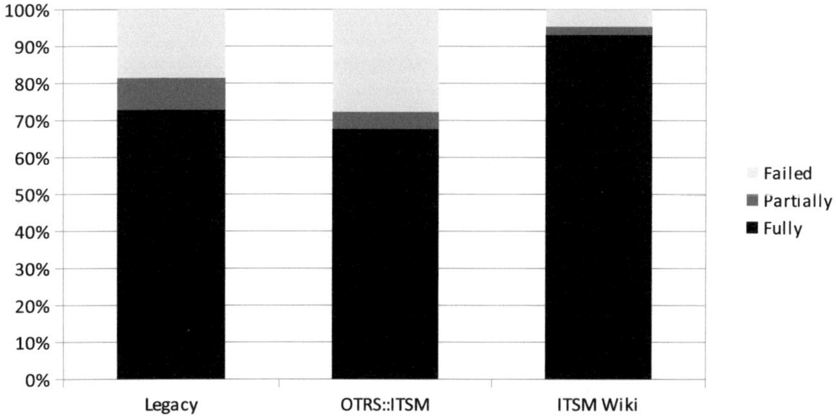

Figure 6.7.: Comparison of the Completion Rates

Interpretation of Task Times

Table 6.58 shows a comparison of the mean time it took the participants of the study to complete the tasks by using the legacy tools and the ITSM Wiki. In the table, only the tasks that were successfully completed, are included. The fourth column of the table shows the time differences between the tools. Positive values indicate the legacy tools being faster, negative values indicate the ITSM Wiki being faster. Furthermore, the mean and the standard deviation are included in the table, which are used later in this section in order to calculate the statistical significance and the confidence intervals. As can be seen in the table, the ITSM Wiki is, per task, on average about 70 s faster that the legacy tools. In the fifth column, the relation between the legacy tools and the ITSM Wiki can be seen. Values higher than 100 % indicate the legacy tools being faster, while values lower than 100 % indicate the ITSM Wiki being faster.

In Table 6.59, a comparison of the mean time it took the participants of the study to successfully complete a task by using OTRS::ITSM and the ITSM Wiki is shown. The fourth column of the table shows the time differences between OTRS::ITSM and the ITSM Wiki. Positive values indicate that OTRS::ITSM was faster, negative values indicate the ITSM Wiki being faster. As can be seen in the table, the ITSM Wiki is, per task, on average about 10 s faster that OTRS::ITSM. In the fifth column, the relation between OTRS::ITSM and the ITSM Wiki can be seen. Values higher than 100 % indicate OTRS::ITSM being faster, while values lower than 100 % indicate the ITSM Wiki being faster.

Figure 6.8 shows a graphical representation of the distribution of the mean completion times of the individual tools for all participants. Higher values in the boxplot indicate longer time, which means worse results.

Participant	Legacy [s]	ITSM Wiki [s]	Difference [s]	Percentage
P-01	69.5	98.3	28.8	141.4 %
P-02	132.6	109.3	−23.4	82.4 %
P-03	226.1	62.7	−163.4	27.7 %
P-04	205.0	64.8	−140.2	31.6 %
P-05	100.5	99.9	−0.6	99.4 %
P-06	276.2	99.9	−176.3	36.2 %
P-07	99.3	71.2	−28.2	71.6 %
P-08	112.7	83.7	−29.0	74.3 %
P-09	253.3	77.9	−175.4	30.8 %
P-10	119.3	124.9	5.6	104.7 %
Mean	159.5	89.2	−70.2	56.0 %
Standard deviation	73.5	20.5	83.0	

Table 6.58.: Task Time Difference (Legacy vs. ITSM Wiki)

Participant	OTRS::ITSM [s]	ITSM Wiki [s]	Difference [s]	Percentage
P-01	54.9	98.3	43.4	179.0 %
P-02	114.3	109.3	−5.0	95.6 %
P-03	111.6	62.7	−48.9	56.2 %
P-04	67.7	64.8	−2.9	95.7 %
P-05	75.0	99.9	24.9	133.2 %
P-06	212.0	99.9	−112.1	47.1 %
P-07	76.9	71.2	−5.7	92.6 %
P-08	99.9	83.7	−16.2	83.8 %
P-09	75.4	77.9	2.5	103.3 %
P-10	111.6	124.9	13.3	111.9 %
Mean	99.9	89.2	−10.7	89.3 %
Standard deviation	44.5	20.5	43.2	

Table 6.59.: Task Time Difference (OTRS::ITSM vs. ITSM Wiki)

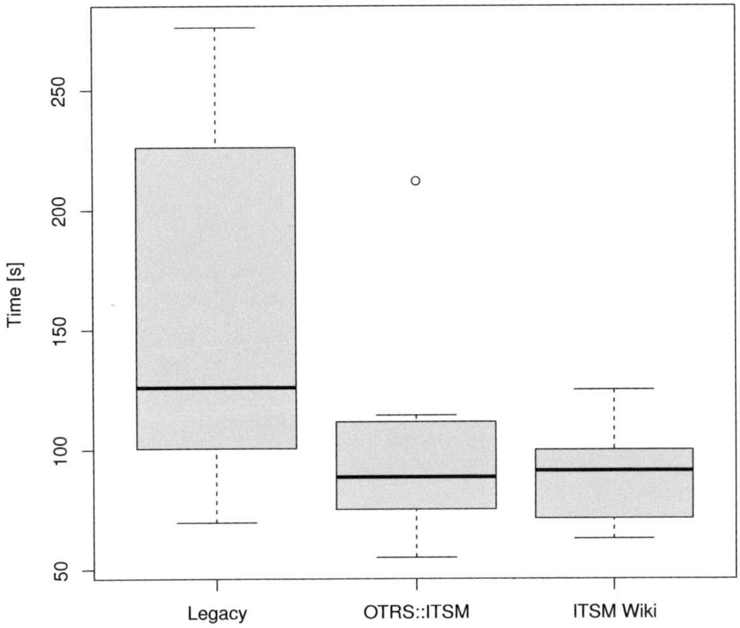

Figure 6.8.: Distribution of the Completion Times of the Individual Tools

Statistical Significance The statistical significance of the differences between the results of the task times of the individual tools is calculated as follows [Sau08, page 64]:

$$t = \frac{\hat{D}}{\frac{s_D}{\sqrt{n}}} \tag{6.1}$$

"where

$\hat{D}$ is the mean of the difference scores

s_D is the standard deviation of the difference scores

n is the sample size [...]

t is the test statistic" [Sau08, page 64]

Based on the mean and standard deviation shown in Table 6.58, the probability that the completion times of the legacy tools and the ITSM Wiki are the same can be calculated as follows:

$$t = \frac{-70.2}{\frac{83.0}{\sqrt{10}}} = -2.676 \tag{6.2}$$

From the t-value, the p-value of 0.025 is calculated[6]. This means that the probability of the completion times of the legacy tools and the ITSM Wiki being equal is about 2.5 %. This gives a probability of 97.5 % that the completion times of the legacy tools and the ITSM Wiki are different from each other.

The same calculation can be performed on the data found in Table 6.59, which contains the completion times of OTRS::ITSM and the ITSM Wiki. The equation is as follows:

$$t = \frac{-10.7}{\frac{43.2}{\sqrt{10}}} = -0.781 \tag{6.3}$$

The t-value -0.781 gives a p-value of 0.455. This means that the probability of the completion times of OTRS::ITSM and the ITSM Wiki being equal is about 45.5 %. This gives a probability of 54.5 % that the completion times of OTRS::ITSM and the ITSM Wiki are different from each other.

In summary, the results show that there is a high statistical significance with regard to the comparison of the legacy tools and the ITSM Wiki. In contrast, the statistical significance is low when comparing OTRS::ITSM and the ITSM Wiki.

Confidence Interval around the Difference As described in [Sau08, pages 65–66], the confidence interval around the difference of the task completion time results is calculated as follows:

$$\bar{D} \pm t_a \frac{s_D}{\sqrt{n}} \tag{6.4}$$

> "where
>
> $\bar{D}$ is the mean of the difference scores [...]
>
> n is the sample size (the total number of users)
>
> s_D is the standard deviation of the difference scores [...]
>
> t_a is the critical value from the t-distribution for $n-1$ degrees of freedom and the specified level of confidence" [Sau08, page 66]

[6] The calculation of the p-value was accomplished by using the TDIST() function in the LibreOffice Calc spreadsheet application.

Based on the data found in Table 6.58, the confidence interval for the difference of the task completion times between the legacy tools and the ITSM Wiki is calculated as follows[7]:

$$-70.2\,\text{s} \pm 2.26\frac{83.0}{\sqrt{10}}\,\text{s} \tag{6.5}$$

$$-70.2\,\text{s} \pm 59.4\,\text{s} \tag{6.6}$$

This means, that the task completion times of the ITSM Wiki are, with 95 % confidence, between 10.8 s and 129.6 s faster ($-70.2\,\text{s} \pm 59.4\,\text{s}$) than that of the legacy tools.

By using the data found in Table 6.59, the confidence interval for the difference of the task completion times between OTRS::ITSM and the ITSM Wiki is calculated as follows:

$$-10.7\,\text{s} \pm 2.26\frac{43.2}{\sqrt{10}}\,\text{s} \tag{6.7}$$

$$-10.7\,\text{s} \pm 30.9\,\text{s} \tag{6.8}$$

When compared to OTRS::ITSM, with 95 % confidence, the completion times of the ITSM Wiki are between 20.3 s slower and 41.6 s faster ($-10.7\,\text{s} \pm 30.9\,\text{s}$).

Table 6.60 shows the task completion times with a 95 % confidence.

Tool	Lower Bound [s]	Mean [s]	Upper Bound [s]
Legacy vs. ITSM Wiki	10.8	70.2	129.6
OTRS::ITSM vs. ITSM Wiki	−20.3	10.7	41.6

Table 6.60.: Differences between Task Completion Times

The interpretation of the results is as follows: Compared to the legacy tools, the ITSM Wiki is on average between approximately 11 s and approximately 130 s faster. When compared to OTRS::ITSM, the ITSM Wiki is between approximately 20 s slower and approximately 42 s faster. This means, that while users performed the tasks clearly faster when using the ITSM Wiki compared to the legacy tools, the results of the comparison between OTRS::ITSM and the ITSM Wiki are inconclusive (with a tendency of the ITSM Wiki performing faster).

[7]The t_a value was calculated using the TINV() function in the LibreOffice Calc spreadsheet application.

6.2.7. System Usability Scale

After the tasks of each tool were completed, a System Usability Scale (SUS) questionnaire was given to the participants. The SUS questionnaire was developed by Brooke in 1986 [Bro96].

As described in [AT13, page 137], the System Usability Scale is "[o]ne of the most widely used tools for assessing the perceived usability of a system or a product" [AT13, page 137].

The application of the questionnaire is as follows [Bro96]:

> "The SU scale is generally used after the respondent has had an opportunity to use the system being evaluated, but before any debriefing or discussion takes place. Respondents should be asked to record their immediate response to each item, rather than thinking about items for a long time.
>
> "All items should be checked. If a respondent feels that they cannot respond to a particular item, they should mark the centre point of the scale." [Bro96]

The questions are as follows [Bro96]:

1. "I think that I would like to use this system frequently."
2. "I found the system unnecessarily complex."
3. "I thought the system was easy to use."
4. "I think that I would need the support of a technical person to be able to use this system."
5. "I found the various functions in this system were well integrated."
6. "I thought there was too much inconsistency in this system."
7. "I would imagine that most people would learn to use this system very quickly."
8. "I found the system very cumbersome to use."
9. "I felt very confident using the system."
10. "I needed to learn a lot of things before I could get going with this system." [Bro96]

Each question can be answered on a five-point Likert scale, which ranges from 'strong disagree' to 'strong agree' [Bro96].

The answers to the questions are the basis for the calculation of the SUS score. The score is calculated as follows [Bro96]:

> "To calculate the SUS score, first sum the score contributions from each item. Each item's score contribution will range from 0 to 4. For items 1, 3, 5, 7, and 9 the score contribution is the scale position minus 1. For items 2, 4, 6, 8, and 10, the contribution is 5 minus the scale position. Multiply the sum of the scores by 2.5 to obtain the overall value of SU." [Bro96].

The reason for this form of calculation of the SUS score is that the questions alternate between an expected positive and an expected negative answer. This helps in mitigating the effect of participants with a bias to positive or negative answers.

More information about the System Usability Scale can be found in [AT13, pages 137–140].

As was the case with the other questionnaires, the System Usability Scale questionnaire was given to the participants in the German version. In order to avoid mistakes in translating the SUS questionnaire, a verified translation was used, which is available online [Rum13]. The forms that were handed out to the participants can be found in Appendix C.1 (page 451).

Results

Table 6.61 shows the System Usability Scale scores of the participants for each one of the evaluated tools.

Participant	Legacy Tools	OTRS::ITSM	ITSM Wiki
P-01	45.0	82.5	72.5
P-02	52.5	77.5	87.5
P-03	32.5	42.5	77.5
P-04	15.0	65.0	90.0
P-05	95.0	82.5	57.5
P-06	65.0	60.0	77.5
P-07	27.5	60.0	85.0
P-08	20.0	57.5	55.0
P-09	42.5	82.5	100.0
P-10	82.5	90.0	80.0

Table 6.61.: Results of the SUS Questionnaire (n=10)

Interpretation of the System Usability Scale Results

Table 6.62 shows a comparison of the results of the SUS questionnaire for the legacy tools and the ITSM Wiki. In addition, the difference between the tools is presented. Furthermore, the mean and the standard deviation are shown in the table.

Participant	Legacy	ITSM Wiki	Difference
P-01	45.0	72.5	27.5
P-02	52.5	87.5	35.0
P-03	32.5	75.5	45.0
P-04	15.0	90.0	75.0
P-05	95.0	57.5	−37.5
P-06	65.0	77.5	12.5
P-07	27.5	85.0	57.5
P-08	20.0	55.0	35.0
P-09	42.5	100.0	57.5
P-10	82.5	80.0	−2.5
Mean	47.75	78.25	30.50
Standard deviation	26.42	13.95	32.89

Table 6.62.: SUS Score Difference (Legacy vs. ITSM Wiki)

In Table 6.63, the results of the SUS questionnaire of OTRS::ITSM and the ITSM Wiki are shown. Furthermore, the difference between the tools as well as the mean and standard deviation are shown.

Figure 6.9 shows a graphical representation of the distribution of the SUS scores. In the boxplot, higher scores indicate better results.

Statistical Significance Based on the mean and standard deviation shown in Table 6.62, the probability that the SUS scores of the legacy tools and the ITSM Wiki are the same can be calculated as follows:

$$t = \frac{30.50}{\frac{32.89}{\sqrt{10}}} = 2.933 \qquad (6.9)$$

From the t-value, the p-value of 0.017 is calculated[8]. This means that the probability of the SUS scores of the legacy tools and the ITSM Wiki being equal is about 1.7 %.

[8]The calculation of the p-value was accomplished by using the TDIST() function in the LibreOffice Calc spreadsheet application.

Participant	OTRS::ITSM	ITSM Wiki	Difference
P-01	82.5	72.5	−10.0
P-02	77.5	87.5	10.0
P-03	42.5	75.5	35.0
P-04	65.0	90.0	25.0
P-05	82.5	57.5	−25.0
P-06	60.0	77.5	17.5
P-07	60.0	85.0	25.0
P-08	57.5	55.0	−2.5
P-09	82.5	100.0	17.5
P-10	90.0	80.0	−10.0
Mean	70.00	78.25	8.25
Standard deviation	15.14	13.95	19.26

Table 6.63.: SUS Score Difference (OTRS::ITSM vs. ITSM Wiki)

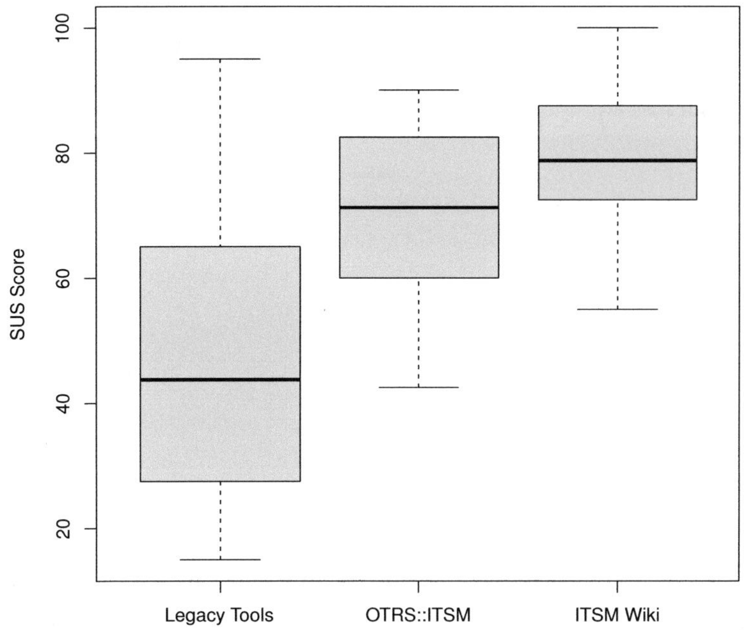

Figure 6.9.: Distribution of the SUS Scores

The same calculation can be performed on the data found in Table 6.63, which contains the SUS scores of OTRS::ITSM and the ITSM Wiki. The equation is as follows:

$$t = \frac{8.25}{\frac{19.26}{\sqrt{10}}} = 1.355 \tag{6.10}$$

The t-value 1.355 gives a p-value of 0.209. This means that the probability of the SUS scores of OTRS::ITSM and the ITSM Wiki being equal is about 20.9 %.

In summary, the results show that there is a high statistical significance (over 98 %) with regard to the comparison of the legacy tools and the ITSM Wiki. This means that it is very likely that the results of the legacy tools and the ITSM Wiki differ from each other. The statistical significance of the comparison of OTRS::ITSM and the ITSM Wiki is lower (about 79 %), which means that it is less likely that these two results differ from each other.

Confidence Interval around the Difference Based on the data found in Table 6.62, the confidence interval for the difference of the SUS scores between the legacy tools and the ITSM Wiki is calculated as follows[9]:

$$30.50 \pm 2.26\frac{32.89}{\sqrt{10}} \tag{6.11}$$

$$30.50 \pm 23.53 \tag{6.12}$$

By using the data found in Table 6.63, the confidence interval for the difference of the SUS scores between OTRS::ITSM and the ITSM Wiki is calculated as follows:

$$8.25 \pm 2.26\frac{19.26}{\sqrt{10}} \tag{6.13}$$

$$8.25 \pm 13.78 \tag{6.14}$$

As shown in Table 6.64, with a 95 % confidence, the SUS score of the ITSM Wiki is between 6.97 and 54.03 points (30.50 ± 23.53) higher than that of the legacy tools. When compared to OTRS::ITSM, the SUS scores of the ITSM Wiki are between 5.53 points lower and 22.03 points higher (8.25 ± 13.78).

The interpretation of the results is as follows: In the System Usability Scale questionnaire, with a confidence of 95 %, the participants of the study rated the ITSM Wiki higher than

[9] The t_a value was calculated using the TINV() function in the LibreOffice Calc spreadsheet application.

Tool	Lower Bound	Mean	Upper Bound
ITSM Wiki vs. Legacy	6.97	30.50	54.03
ITSM Wiki vs. OTRS::ITSM	−5.53	8.25	22.03

Table 6.64.: Differences between SUS Scores

the legacy tools (between approximately 7 points better and approximately 54 points better). With regard to the comparison of the ITSM Wiki and OTRS::ITSM, the results are inconclusive, as the ITSM Wiki is rated between approximately 6 points worse and approximately 22 points better than OTRS::ITSM (with a tendency of the ITSM Wiki being rated better).

6.2.8. Posttest Questionnaire

In addition to the generic statements of the System Usability Scale, as described in the previous paragraph, a number of additional statements were given to the participants. Participants were asked to indicate their agreement with the statements on a scale from one (strong disagree) to five (strong agree).

Table 6.65 shows the statements that were given to the participants, as well as the results.

Interpretation of the Posttest Questionnaire

Figure 6.10 shows a graphical representation of the mean score of each of the questions given to the participants in the posttest questionnaire. The questions and mean values can be found in Table 6.65.

As can be seen in the figure, the test participants agreed that they expect the ITSM Wiki to improve their work as an administrator (Statement 1: 4.4 out of 5.0 points). Furthermore, the participants agreed that finding information was easier for them with the ITSM Wiki, as compared to the legacy tools (Statement 2: 4.2 out of 5.0 points). Compared to OTRS::ITSM, finding information had about the same level of easiness with the ITSM Wiki (Statement 3: 3.3 out of 5.0 points).

About inserting information, the participants agreed that it is easier when using the ITSM Wiki than in the legacy tools (Statement 4: 3.9 out of 5.0 points). The level of easiness was rated to be about the same in OTRS::ITSM as compared to the ITSM Wiki (Statement 5: 3.0 out of 5.0 points). Having all information in a single, integrated tool was rated as beneficial (Statement 6: 4.4 out of 5.0 points).

Number	Statement	Mean	SD
1	'I think that using the ITSM Wiki can ease my work as an administrator.'	4.4	0.7
2	'Finding information was easier for me in the ITSM Wiki compared to the legacy tools.'	4.2	1.0
3	'Finding information was easier for me in the ITSM Wiki compared to OTRS::ITSM.'	3.3	1.5
4	'Inserting and editing information was easier for me in the ITSM Wiki compared to the legacy tools.'	3.9	1.2
5	'Inserting and editing information was easier for me in the ITSM Wiki compared to OTRS::ITSM.'	3.0	1.2
6	'I think it is an advantage that in the ITSM Wiki all information is integrated into a single tool.'	4.4	0.8
7	'A semantic wiki such as the ITSM Wiki provides advantages when accessing information compared to the tools I am currently using.'	4.1	0.7
8	'The ITSM Wiki makes easier the configuration of infrastructure monitoring.'	4.4	1.0
9	'The Problem Analyzer lessens the time and the effort when finding the causes of problems.'	3.7	0.8
10	'I can imagine that the integration of the mechanisms shown in the ITSM Wiki can improve other IT administration tools (e.g., by integrating wiki text and Semantic MediaWiki queries in the Windows user and computer management tool).'	4.1	0.6

Table 6.65.: Results of the Posttest Questionnaire (n=10)

When compared to the tools the participants were currently using, the ability of semantic wikis, such as the ITSM Wiki to access information was rated as advantageous (Statement 7: 4.1 out of 5.0 points). Using the ITSM Wiki to configure infrastructure management was also seen as being easier compared to manually editing configuration files (Statement 8: 4.4 out of 5.0 points). The statement that the Problem Analyzer helps in lessening the time and effort when finding the causes of problems was rated with a light agree (Statement 9: 3.7 out of 5.0 points). Finally, benefits provided by the integration of semantic wiki mechanisms into other tools were agreed upon by the participants (Statement 10: 4.1 out of 5.0 points).

6.2.9. Comments

At the end of the user study, participants were asked to answer a number of open-ended questions. This subsection lists a summary of the answers given by the participants

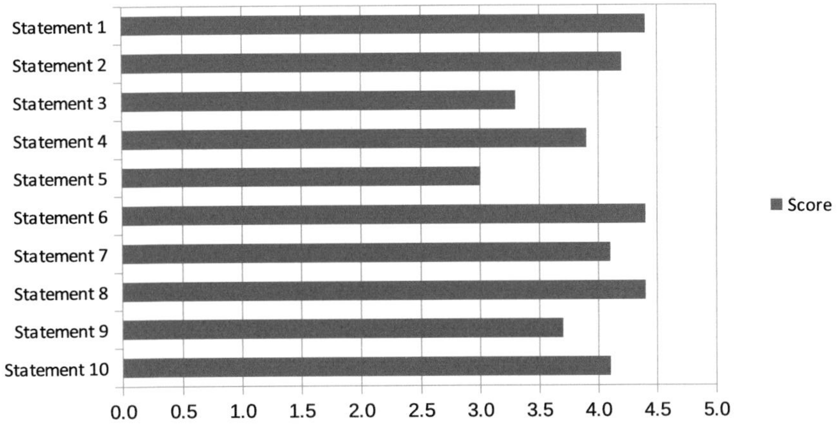

Figure 6.10.: Results of the Posttest Questionnaire

for each of the questions. If the same type of answer was given multiple times, this is indicated by the number it was given at the end of the answer.

'I especially liked the following about the ITSM Wiki:'

- Having all information in a single tool (4x)
- Easy to use and to learn (3x)
- Search (3x)
- Linking of functions like Nagios (2x)
- Problem Analyzer (2x)
- Web-based tool
- Easy orientation
- Easily extendable system
- Usable for heterogeneous environments
- Version history
- Ability to use custom queries
- Amount of provided information
- Use the wiki instead of manually having to configure external tools
- Design
- Use of Semantic MediaWiki, which is used by a large user base

'I did not like the following about the ITSM Wiki:'

- Active tab was not kept active when choosing to edit a page (2x)
- Problem Analyzer is slow (2x)
- Queries had to be formulated in text form (2x)
- Wiki syntax not intuitive (2x)
- Editing of page has to be selected explicitly
- Wiki navigation
- Color choice in Problem Analyzer confusing
- When comparing hosts, a tree of the differences is missing
- Too much information can be confusing
- Problem Analyzer lacks clarity with regard to displaying changes

'In my daily work, I would profit from the ITSM Wiki as follows:'

- Quick finding of information (5x)
- Central availability of information in a single tool avoids having to pick the right tool to complete a task (2x)
- Overview and configuration of Nagios
- Shorten the time of problem analysis
- Time saved by having information that would require to physically visit a computer
- Ability to access previously unavailable information
- Minimize inconsistencies because of single storage of information
- Use on mobile devices, because no local installation of administration tools is required

'I would improve the following aspects of the ITSM Wiki:'

- Stay in the current tab when changing to edit view (2x)
- Clarity of the graph layout of configuration items in Problem Analyzer (2x)
- Layout
- Navigation
- Add additional actions in addition to Nagios configuration
- Provide service view in addition to CI view

- Introduce ability to display filtered information
- Provide graphical tool which makes easier the formulation of queries
- Customizable themes (e.g., darker background color)
- Add a table view to the Problem Analyzer
- Add link to page that explains the wiki syntax
- Add description to infrastructure monitoring

'My additional comments are as follows:'

- Search and queries should be improved
- Non-obvious functionalities are included
- Nice tool
- Easy to use

Interpretation of the Comments

The results of the open-ended part of the posttest questionnaire can be summarized as follows: The participants liked about the ITSM Wiki that it provides all relevant information in a single tool, which is easy to learn and use. Moreover, the search functionality provided by MediaWiki was appreciated, as well as being able to quickly find information.

The integration of infrastructure monitoring was also seen positively. More positive aspects were based on using a semantic wiki as the underlying platform. In this respect, the tool being Web-based, the version history, the design, and the extensibility were mentioned.

Aspects of the ITSM Wiki which were negatively perceived were some usability and performance issues. Examples are that users explicitly had to choose to edit a page, as well as the selected tab being reset when switching to edit mode. Having to use Semantic MediaWiki syntax for formulating advanced queries was also regarded as cumbersome. With respect to performance, the Problem Analyzer was perceived as slow (the calculation of the results of a comparison takes about 10 s). Moreover, the Problem Analyzer was seen as containing too much information and because of that being confusing by some of the participants.

Being asked to imagine the potential impact of the ITSM Wiki on their daily work as an IT administrator, the participants wrote that they would benefit from being able to quickly find information. Further features that would save time were mentioned in the form of using the Infrastructure Monitoring Component, shorten the time required for finding the causes of problems, and saving time by not having to physically visit computers. In addition, it was mentioned that previously unavailable information would be accessible using the ITSM Wiki. Moreover, having a single, integrated tool for all aspects of information management, which minimizes inconsistencies in the information base, was seen as positive.

6.3. Summary of Evaluation Results

In this section, the evaluation of the ITSM Wiki was described. The evaluation consisted of two main parts: First, the validation, in which the ITSM Wiki, the legacy tools and two ITSM platforms were validated against the requirements. Second, the user study, in which the legacy tools, OTRS::ITSM, and the ITSM Wiki were evaluated by IT administrators.

As was shown in the validation, the ITSM Wiki, with its ability to flexibly retain structured and unstructured information, as well as being extensible, fulfills the requirements to a higher degree than the legacy tools, or the ITSM platforms that focus on retaining structured information. With regard to the maturity of the code base, however, the ITSM Wiki as a research project lacks the maturity of the established ITSM tools.

The user study showed that the ITSM Wiki performs better than the legacy tools and OTRS::ITSM with respect to the success rate. With regard to the time it took participants to successfully complete the tasks, the ITSM Wiki outperformed the legacy tools. Furthermore, the user study showed that the ITSM Wiki performs about as well as OTRS::ITSM in the combination of tasks given to the participants of the study.

Regarding the usability of the tools, the ITSM Wiki performed clearly better than the legacy tools and about as good as OTRS::ITSM. However, a number of usability issues have to be addressed in the ITSM Wiki in order to improve user satisfaction.

The posttest questionnaire and the comments revealed that the participants of the study see potential in the ITSM Wiki supporting their work as IT administrators. However, some issues were mentioned, which have to be improved, such as simplifying the editing of wikitext and queries.

7. Conclusion

This chapter lists the achievements of the thesis and gives an outlook on future work.

7.1. Achievements

Starting from practical observations gained from working in the field of IT administration in an SME environment, an analysis of the strengths and weaknesses of the existing tools which supported FZI's IT administrators in the areas of Configuration Management and documentation was performed. Based on the findings of the analysis, a semantic wiki was selected as a technical platform for the use as a unified Configuration Management and documentation tool.

The activities that were conducted in order to develop an improved and unified Configuration Management and documentation solution were the following:

- A semantic wiki-based solution for the integration of real world documentation and Configuration Management needs was established.
- Semantic MediaWiki mechanisms were used to implement tool support for various processes (e.g., account management), as well as the management of Configuration Management information (i.e., structured information) and free-text documentation (i.e., unstructured information) within a single platform.
- An ontology was engineered, which was done mostly implicitly during modeling processes and while using the semantic wiki to store structured information.
- The ITSM Wiki was populated with real world data and introduced as an essential information management tool for the use within FZI's IT department.
- ITSM-relevant extensions were designed and implemented, which further improved the usefulness of the semantic wiki-based platform.

The achievements of the thesis can be divided into two areas. The first area is the facilitation of a semantic wiki in the context of IT Service Management, as the central hub for the storage of structured, as well as unstructured information. This enables the management of ITSM-relevant information in a single information repository. The data model that was created as part of the thesis is an ontology, which contains all the concepts and properties relevant for conducting IT Service Management at FZI. Examples of information stored in the semantic wikis are as follows.

Structured information:

- Information about configuration items (e.g., computers, network equipment, and services)
- Accounting information (e.g., which contracts are booked by a department for a computer)
- Account management information (account creation, account changes, account removals)
- Documentation of changes to the IT infrastructure
- Documentation of incidents and problems

Unstructured information:

- Documentation of working procedures
- Plain-text documentation of configuration items, which extend the structured information

The second area of achievements of the thesis lies in the design and implementation of ITSM-specific extensions for the Semantic MediaWiki platform.

- Information Gathering: A component for the automatic gathering of configuration information from the directory service and networked clients for inclusion in the ITSM Wiki was designed and implemented.
- Infrastructure Monitoring: An interface to the infrastructure monitoring application Nagios was designed and implemented. This extension allows the management of what should be monitored from within the ITSM Wiki.
- Intrusion Detection: An extension for the integration of a network intrusion detection tool was designed and implemented.
- Incident and Problem Analyzer: This extension provides support for tracking down incidents and problems within IT infrastructures from within the ITSM Wiki.
- Virtualization and IaaS Connector: An interface for orchestrating virtualization and IaaS resources from within the ITSM Wiki was designed and implemented.

In summary, the result of the thesis is a Semantic MediaWiki-based tool, which allows to retain and manage structured and unstructured information in the context of IT Service Management. By using Semantic MediaWiki mechanisms, structured information can be accessed and presented alongside textual information. Information, that is generated and used in external applications and data stores can be imported and exported by components that were developed as part of the thesis.

7.2. Future Work

The work on the Semantic MediaWiki-based ITSM platform and the design and implementation of the extensions presented in the thesis led to a number of additional ideas for tools that have potential to further extend the usefulness of the ITSM Wiki. Due to the flexibility of the platform, additional extensions can be created with a limited amount of resources.

In general, the integration of external tools that are configured via structured text files or which provide a specialized API show the most potential for a successful implementation. In the area of using the ITSM Wiki as a front-end for creating configuration files, the wiki-based configuration of the Asterisk telephony software [Win10] seems promising. By re-using information about persons from the wiki, information duplication can be reduced. Another example of transferring information stored in the wiki into text-based configuration files is the configuration of firewalls from semantic relations. Firewall platforms, which are configured by text files, such as OpenBSD's PF [Han10] or Linux' iptables [Pur04], are candidates for this approach. Tools that provide API mechanisms for configuration and the change of run-time parameters are another area of potential extensibility. An example is the management and configuration of a storage device, e.g., NetApp hardware via its API [Net11].

By extending the SNMP part of the Information Gathering Component, which was only implemented as proof-of-concept in the thesis, information could also be read from additional devices, such as network switches. By reading information about the network topology that is kept partially on each network switch, a map of the network could be stored in a structured format in the ITSM Wiki. By further extending the component, the ability to write information by using the SNMP protocol could be implemented. This would make possible, for example, the configuration of network switches (e.g., modify the VLAN configuration) from within the ITSM Wiki.

Further extending the management of network hardware by using information stored in the ITSM Wiki seems a promising approach for reducing administration overhead. Structured information stored in the ITSM Wiki could be used as an input for the control layer of environments based on the software-defined networking (SDN) [Ope12a] approach. For example, the Virtualization and IaaS Connector could automatically configure the network to fit the specific requirements of the respective virtual machine, e.g., by using the OpenFlow [MAB+08] platform.

By using the information stored in the ITSM Wiki as the foundation for interactions with Windows via the PowerShell [Hol13] scripting language, routine tasks could be automated. Especially tasks in the user and computer management domain (e.g., creating or modifying users) seem promising. Analogously, the management of UNIX-based hosts such as Linux could be automated by running Bash [Rob10] scripts via the SSH [Luc12] secure shell based on information stored in the wiki. Furthermore, structured information from the ITSM Wiki could be used as input for IT automation software such as Puppet [Pup13], Chef [Ops13], or Microsoft System Center Orchestrator [Mic13b].

With regard to gathering data, sources other than the ones used in this thesis could be used to improve the data quality or simplify the gathering process. In environments, in which the commercially available Microsoft System Center Configuration Manager [Mic13a] is deployed, its database of device configurations could be used as a data source.

The work presented in the thesis is concerned mainly with using Semantic MediaWiki within a dedicated IT administration department. When looking at the social aspects provided by wiki platforms, an interesting perspective is making accessible the wiki to all employees of an organization. Potential examples of benefits gained from opening the ITSM Wiki for users outside the boundaries of the IT team are as follows: First, making use of the infrastructure monitoring component by all users in order to monitor their self-hosted services. Second, the use of the information found in the semantic wiki-integrated Configuration Management Database could help IT-savvy end users in tracking down problems or identifying potential problems with planned changes before actually performing the changes. Third, a mechanism for collaboratively documenting the IT infrastructure seems to provide potential benefits, especially in environments where IT-savvy non-IT department members manage various aspects of their IT environment on their own (e.g., install software or set up servers for internal use within their projects). While information that is maintained by the IT department can be used without concerns for the quality of the information due to the fact that only professional users are able to modify information, opening the ITSM Wiki for write access would create additional challenges with regard to maintaining the quality of the information.

Tightly coupled with opening the wiki to a larger group of employees is the integration of more sophisticated access control mechanisms, which is another area of future work. While access control plays a smaller role in small-sized IT administration teams, access control and privacy aspects become an issue with larger groups. For example, users should only be able to monitor the availability of their own services and servers, in contrast to other employees workstations, in order to prevent the generation of work profiles of other employees.

Selectively sharing structured information across the boundaries of organizations might result in benefits for all participating organizations. For example, sharing information about incompatibilities of hardware and software products might lower costs for troubleshooting compatibility-related problems. Approaches such as ontology mapping [Noy09] might have to be used in case the ontologies of involved organizations differ from each other. Furthermore, anonymization of information has to be considered in order to prevent giving away company secrets.

Further research should be invested in improving the usability of the wiki. By using additional extensions (e.g., Semantic Drilldown), interactively browsing information could be further simplified. Additionally, the structure of the wiki could be optimized based on feedback by users, which is possible due to the flexibility of the Semantic MediaWiki platform.

As an open platform, the ITSM Wiki can be extended to almost all areas of IT Service Management. While the data model and the layout can be modified even by non-programmers, the integration of additional external applications and data sources can be accomplished by creating additional MediaWiki extensions.

While the scope of this thesis was limited to the IT Service Management domain, the ITSM Wiki can be extended to be used in additional areas that require storing structured and unstructured information in a single system. Areas that could benefit from the wiki are, for example, facility management (e.g., using the wiki in order to document and control power connections, heating systems, water pipes, or fire alarm systems), or the construction, maintenance, and operation of complex technical systems (e.g., production plants in the context of the fourth industrial revolution).

Appendix

A. Installation Instructions

The following section describes which components are required in order to run the ITSM Wiki and how to install these requirements. Furthermore, it is described on a high level, how the components of the ITSM Wiki are installed and configured.

The ITSM Wiki depends on the requirements outlined in the following sections. Although it is possible to run the ITSM Wiki on configurations which differ from these requirements, it is recommended to use the software given in the following lists.

A.1. Operating System and Servers

- *CentOS Linux Operating System:* CentOS[1] is a Linux distribution which is freely available and which is based on the commercially distributed Red Hat Enterprise Linux (RHEL)[2] operating system. CentOS was selected as the platform for the ITSM Wiki because of its stability, its widespread use, and because it is freely available for download on the Internet. Information about the installation of CentOS Linux can be found in RHEL's official documentation [Red08b, Red08a], as well as in third-party guides [MVA09, SBM09, NB09].

- *Apache Web Server:* The Apache[3] Web server is used for running the MediaWiki software. More information about the Apache Web server in general can be found in [Ker08] and [Apa11]. More about configuring and running Apache on CentOS can be found in [SBM09, pages 289–312] and [MVA09, pages 79–111].

[1] `http://www.centos.org/`
[2] `http://www.redhat.com/`
[3] `http://httpd.apache.org/`

- *MySQL Database Server:* MySQL[4] is an open source SQL [Cha09] database server, which is used by the components of the ITSM Wiki for storing information. More information about using and configuring MySQL can be found in [Ora11] and [TW06]. Information about running MySQL on CentOS can be found in [SBM09, pages 261–271].

A.2. Libraries and Tools

- *PHP:* The PHP[5] scripting language is mostly used for Web development. MediaWiki, as well as the MediaWiki extensions and the ITSM Wiki extension are programmed in PHP. More information about PHP can be found in [LTM06].
- *Nagios:* Nagios[6] is an infrastructure monitoring application that is used by the Infrastructure Monitoring Component, which is described in detail in Section 5.2 (page 234). General information about Nagios can be found in [Bar05], while the use of Nagios on CentOS is described in [MVA09, pages 299–313].
- *WMI:* The wmi tool[7] is used for reading information from Windows hosts.

A.3. Wiki and Wiki Extensions

- MediaWiki: More information about MediaWiki in general can be found in [Bar08], while [Med11c] describes the installation of MediaWiki.
- Semantic MediaWiki
- Semantic Forms[8]
- Header Tabs[9]
- MagicNoCache[10]
- ParserFunctions

[4] `http://dev.mysql.com/downloads/mysql/`
[5] `http://www.php.net/`
[6] `http://www.nagios.org/`
[7] `http://dev.zenoss.org/svn/trunk/inst/externallibs/wmi-1.3.16.tar.bz2`
[8] `https://www.mediawiki.org/wiki/Extension:Semantic_Forms`
[9] `https://www.mediawiki.org/wiki/Extension:Header_Tabs`
[10] `https://www.mediawiki.org/wiki/Extension:MagicNoCache`

A.4. ITSM Wiki

The ITSM Wiki depends on a previously installed Semantic MediaWiki instance including the extensions named in the previous subsection.

The source code for the installation of the ITSM Wiki can be downloaded from the ITSM Wiki Website[11].

In order to install the ITSM Wiki, unpack the ITSM Wiki files into the MediaWiki extensions directory and add the following line to the file LocalSettings.php:

```
include_once( "$IP/extensions/ITSMWiki/ITSMWIKI.php" );
```

Please refer to the `INSTALL.txt` file for further setup instructions.

[11] `http://www.itsmwiki.de/`

B. Templates and Forms

In this chapter, a selection of templates and forms that are used in the ITSM Wiki is shown. The listings follow Semantic Forms syntax, which was described in Section 4.1.5 (page 132).

B.1. Person Template

Listing B.1: Person Template

```
<noinclude>This is the 'Person' template.<br>It is used to
    display persons and their attributes<br></noinclude><
    includeonly>

= General =
{| class="wikitable"
! Name
| [[Name::{{{Name|}}}]]
|-
! Description
| [[Description::{{{Description|}}}]]
|-
! FamilyName
| [[FamilyName::{{{FamilyName|}}}]]
|-
! GivenName
| [[GivenName::{{{GivenName|}}}]]
|-
! IsMemberOfOrganization
| {{#arraymap:{{{IsMemberOfOrganization|}}}|,|@@@|[[
    IsMemberOfOrganization::@@@]]}}
|-
! IsMemberOfOrganizationalUnit
| {{#arraymap:{{{IsMemberOfOrganizationalUnit|}}}|,|@@@|[[
    IsMemberOfOrganizationalUnit::OrganizationalUnit-@@@|@@@]]}}
|-
! PhoneNumber
| {{#arraymap:{{{PhoneNumber|}}}|,|@@@|[[PhoneNumber::@@@]]}}
```

```
|-
! FaxNumber
| {{#arraymap:{{{FaxNumber|}}}|,|@@@|[[FaxNumber::@@@]]}}
|-
! EmailAddress
| {{#arraymap:{{{EmailAddress|}}}|,|@@@|[[EmailAddress::@@@]]}}
|-
! HasOffice
| [[HasOffice::{{{HasOffice|}}}]]
|-
! HasRole
| {{#arraymap:{{{HasRole|}}}|,|@@@|[[HasRole::@@@]]}}
|-
! HasKnowledgeDomain
| {{#arraymap:{{{HasKnowledgeDomain|}}}|,|@@@|[[
   HasKnowledgeDomain::@@@]]}}
|-
! HasManager
| [[HasManager::{{{HasManager|}}}]]
|-
! JobTitle
| [[JobTitle::{{{JobTitle|}}}]]
|-
! IsMemberOfGroup
| {{#arraymap:{{{IsMemberOfGroup|}}}|,|@@@|[[IsMemberOfGroup::
   Group-@@@|@@@]]}}
|-
|}

= CI Information =
{| class="wikitable"
! Version
| [[Version::{{{Version|}}}]]
|-
! HasParent
| {{#arraymap:{{{HasParent|}}}|,|@@@|[[HasParent::@@@]]}}
|-
! IsConnectedTo
| {{#arraymap:{{{IsConnectedTo|}}}|,|@@@|[[IsConnectedTo::@@@
   ]]}}
|-
! IsRelatedTo
| {{#arraymap:{{{IsRelatedTo|}}}|,|@@@|[[IsRelatedTo::@@@]]}}
|-
|}
```

```
= AdditionalQueries =
You can add your own queries and information here.
{{{AdditionalQueries|}}}

= ProblemAnalyzer =
[http://itsmwiki.fzi.de/index.php/Special:ProblemAnalyzer?ci1={{
    PAGENAMEE}}&twpage={{PAGENAMEE}}&twbutton=Get+Revisions
    2FCompare Show Problem Analyzer]= SemanticGraph
    =GraphvizDotCode|= Notes =| class="wikitable"! Notes| Notes|
    #set:Notes=Notes| |-|<headertabs/>#set:Page has default
    form=Person[[Category:Person]]</includeonly>
```

B.2. Person Form

Listing B.2: Person Form

```
<noinclude>This is the 'Person' form.<br>To add a page with this
     form, enter the page name below;<br> If a page with that
    name already exists, you will be sent to a form to edit that
     page.<br> {{#forminput:Person}}</noinclude><includeonly>

{{{info|page name=Person-<Person[Name]><unique number>|create
    title=Create new person}}}
{{{for template|Person}}}

= General =
{| class="wikitable"
! Name:
| {{{field|Name|input type=text}}}
|-
! Description:
| {{{field|Description|input type=textarea}}}
|-
! FamilyName:
| {{{field|FamilyName|input type=text}}}
|-
! GivenName:
| {{{field|GivenName|input type=text}}}
|-
! IsMemberOfOrganization:
| {{{field|IsMemberOfOrganization|input type=text with
    autocomplete|values from category=Organization}}}
|-
! IsMemberOfOrganizationalUnit:
```

```
| {{{field|IsMemberOfOrganizationalUnit|input type=text with
    autocomplete|values from category=OrganizationalUnit}}}
|-
! PhoneNumber:
| {{{field|PhoneNumber|input type=text}}}
|-
! FaxNumber:
| {{{field|FaxNumber|input type=text}}}
|-
! EmailAddress:
| {{{field|EmailAddress|input type=text}}}
|-
! HasOffice:
| {{{field|HasOffice|input type=text with autocomplete|values
    from category=Room}}}
|-
! HasRole:
| {{{field|HasRole|input type=text with autocomplete|values from
    category=Role}}}
|-
! HasKnowledgeDomain:
| {{{field|HasKnowledgeDomain|input type=text with autocomplete|
    values from category=KnowledgeDomain}}}
|-
! HasManager:
| {{{field|HasManager|input type=text with autocomplete|values
    from category=Person}}}
|-
! JobTitle:
| {{{field|JobTitle|input type=text}}}
|-
! IsMemberOfGroup:
| {{{field|IsMemberOfGroup|input type=text with autocomplete|
    values from category=Group}}}
|-
|}

= CI Information =
{| class="wikitable"
! Version:
| {{{field|Version|input type=text}}}
|-
! HasParent:
| {{{field|HasParent|input type=text with autocomplete|values
    from namespace=Main}}}
|-
```

```
! IsConnectedTo:
| {{{field|IsConnectedTo|input type=text with autocomplete|
   values from namespace=Main}}}
|-
! IsRelatedTo:
| {{{field|IsRelatedTo|input type=text with autocomplete|values
   from namespace=Main}}}
|-
|}

= AdditionalQueries =
{| class="wikitable"
! AdditionalQueries:
| {{{field|AdditionalQueries|input type=textarea|editor=
   wikieditor}}}
|-
|}

= Notes =
{| class="wikitable"
! Notes:
| {{{field|Notes|input type=textarea|editor=wikieditor}}}
|-
|}

<headertabs/>
{{{end template}}}
{{{standard input|save|label=Save}}} {{{standard input|changes|
   label=Changes}}} {{{standard input|cancel|label=Cancel}}}</
   includeonly>
```

B.3. Physical Computer Form

Listing B.3: Physical Computer Form

```
<noinclude>This is the 'PhysicalComputer' form.<br>To add a page
    with this form, enter the page name below;<br> If a page
   with that name already exists, you will be sent to a form to
    edit that page.<br> {{#forminput:PhysicalComputer}}</
   noinclude><includeonly>

{{{info|page name=PhysicalComputer-<PhysicalComputer[Name]><
   unique number>|create title=Create new physical computer}}}
{{{for template|PhysicalComputer}}}
```

```
= General =
{| class="wikitable"
! Name:
| {{{field|Name|input type=text}}}
|-
! Description:
| {{{field|Description|input type=textarea}}}
|-
! CommisioningStatusType:
| {{{field|CommisioningStatusType|input type=text with
    autocomplete|values from category=CommissioningStatusType}}}
|-
! HasComputerUsageType:
| {{{field|HasComputerUsageType|input type=text with
    autocomplete|values from category=ComputerUsageType}}}
|-
! HasManufacturer
| {{{field|HasManufacturer|input type=text with autocomplete|
    values from category=Organization}}}
|-
! HasVendor:
| {{{field|HasVendor|input type=text with autocomplete|values
    from category=Organization}}}
|-
! HasModel:
| {{{field|HasModel|input type=text with autocomplete|values
    from category=Model}}}
|-
! ProductNumber:
| {{{field|ProductNumber|input type=text}}}
|-
! SerialNumber:
| {{{field|SerialNumber|input type=text}}}
|-
! HasOrganizationalUnit:
| {{{field|HasOrganizationalUnit|input type=text with
    autocomplete|values from category=OrganizationalUnit}}}
|-
! IsMemberOfGroup:
| {{{field|IsMemberOfGroup|input type=text with autocomplete|
    values from category=Group}}}
|-
! HasOwner:
| {{{field|HasOwner|input type=text with autocomplete|values
    from category=Person}}}
```

```
|-
! HasContactPerson:
| {{{field|HasContactPerson|input type=text with autocomplete|
    values from category=Person}}}
|-
! IsLocatedIn:
| {{{field|IsLocatedIn|input type=text with autocomplete|values
    from category=Location}}}
|-
! ComputerFormFactorType:
| {{{field|ComputerFormFactorType|input type=text with
    autocomplete|values from category=ComputerFormFactorType}}}
|-
|}

= CI Information =
{| class="wikitable"
! Version:
| {{{field|Version|input type=text}}}
|-
! HasParent:
| {{{field|HasParent|input type=text with autocomplete|values
    from namespace=Main}}}
|-
! IsConnectedTo:
| {{{field|IsConnectedTo|input type=text with autocomplete|
    values from namespace=Main}}}
|-
! IsRelatedTo:
| {{{field|IsRelatedTo|input type=text with autocomplete|values
    from namespace=Main}}}
|-
|}

= Domain =
{| class="wikitable"
! OperatingSystemInstallationDate:
| {{{field|OperatingSystemInstallationDate|input type=datepicker
    }}}
|-
! MemberOfWindowsDomain:
| {{{field|MemberOfWindowsDomain|input type=checkbox}}}
|-
! LastDomainConnectDate:
| {{{field|LastDomainConnectDate|input type=datepicker}}}
|-
```

```
! HasLocalAdministrator:
| {{{field|HasLocalAdministrator|input type=text}}}
|-
|}

= Monitoring =
{| class="wikitable"
! Monitored:
| {{{field|Monitored|input type=checkbox}}}
|-
! UsesHostTemplate:
| {{{field|UsesHostTemplate|input type=text with autocomplete|
   values from category=HostTemplate}}}
|-
! RunsService:
| {{{field|RunsService|input type=listbox|size=6|values from
   category=ConcreteService}}}
|-
|}

= Hardware =
{| class="wikitable"
! Mainboard:
| {{{field|HasInstalledHardware|input type=text with
   autocomplete|values from category=Mainboard}}}
|-
! Processor:
| {{{field|HasInstalledHardware|input type=text with
   autocomplete|values from category=Processor}}}
|-
! RAM:
| {{{field|HasInstalledHardware|input type=text with
   autocomplete|values from category=RAM}}}
|-
! NetworkAdapter:
| {{{field|HasInstalledHardware|input type=text with
   autocomplete|values from category=NetworkAdapter}}}
|-
! GraphicsAdapter:
| {{{field|HasInstalledHardware|input type=text with
   autocomplete|values from category=GraphicsAdapter}}}
|-
! SoundAdapter:
| {{{field|HasInstalledHardware|input type=text with
   autocomplete|values from category=SoundAdapter}}}
|-
```

```
! PersistentStorage:
| {{{field|HasInstalledHardware|input type=text with
    autocomplete|values from category=PersistentStorage}}}
|-
|}

= Software =
{| class="wikitable"
! HasInstalledSoftware:
| {{{field|HasInstalledSoftware|input type=textarea with
    autocomplete|values from category=Software}}}
|-
|}

= AdditionalQueries =
{| class="wikitable"
! AdditionalQueries:
| {{{field|AdditionalQueries|input type=textarea|editor=
    wikieditor}}}
|-
|}

= Notes =
{| class="wikitable"
! Notes:
| {{{field|Notes|input type=textarea|editor=wikieditor}}}
|-
|}

{{{end template}}}
<headertabs/>
{{{standard input|save|label=Save}}} {{{standard input|changes|
    label=Changes}}} {{{standard input|cancel|label=Cancel}}}</
    includeonly>
```

B.4. Physical Computer Template

Listing B.4: Physical Computer Template

```
<noinclude>This is the 'PhysicalComputer' template.<br>It is
    used to display physical computers and their attributes<br
    ></noinclude><includeonly>

= General =
```

```
{| class="wikitable"
! Name
| [[Name::{{{Name|}}}]]
|-
! Description
| [[Description::{{{Description|}}}]]
|-
! CommisioningStatusType
| [[HasCommisioningStatusType::{{{HasCommisioningStatusType
    |}}}]]
|-
! HasComputerUsageType
| [[HasComputerUsageType::{{{HasComputerUsageType|}}}]]
|-
! HasManufacturer
| [[HasManufacturer::{{{HasManufacturer|}}}]]
|-
! HasVendor
| [[HasVendor::{{{HasVendor|}}}]]
|-
! HasModel
| {{#if: {{{HasModel|}}} | [[HasModel::PhysicalComputerModel-{{{
    HasModel|}}}|{{{HasModel|}}}]] | }}
|-
! ProductNumber
| [[ProductNumber::{{{ProductNumber|}}}]]
|-
! SerialNumber
| [[SerialNumber::{{{SerialNumber|}}}]]
|-
! HasOrganizationalUnit
| {{#arraymap:{{{HasOrganizationalUnit|}}}|,|@@@|[[
    HasOrganizationalUnit::OrganizationalUnit-@@@]]}}
|-
! IsMemberOfGroup
| {{#arraymap:{{{IsMemberOfGroup|}}}|,|@@@|[[IsMemberOfGroup::
    Group-@@@|@@@]]}}
|-
! OrganizationalUnitOfOwner
| {{#if: {{{HasOwner|}}} | [[OrganizationalUnitOfOwner::{{#show:
     HasOwner | ?IsMemberOfOrganizationalUnit }}|]] | }}
|-
! HasOwner
| [[HasOwner::{{{HasOwner|}}}]]
|-
! HasContactPerson
```

```
| {{#arraymap:{{{HasContactPerson|}}}|,|@@@|[[HasContactPerson::
    @@@]]}}
|-
! IsLocatedIn
| [[IsLocatedIn::{{{IsLocatedIn|}}}]]
|-
! HasComputerFormFactorType
| {{#if: {{{HasComputerFormFactorType|}}} | [[
    ComputerFormFactorType::ComputerFormFactorType-{{{
    ComputerFormFactorType|}}}|{{{ComputerFormFactorType|}}}]] |
     }}
|-
|}

= CI Information =
{| class="wikitable"
! Version
| [[Version::{{{Version|}}}]]
|-
! HasParent
| {{#arraymap:{{{HasParent|}}}|,|@@@|[[HasParent::@@@]]}}
|-
! IsConnectedTo
| {{#arraymap:{{{IsConnectedTo|}}}|,|@@@|[[IsConnectedTo::@@@
    ]]}}
|-
! IsRelatedTo
| {{#arraymap:{{{IsRelatedTo|}}}|,|@@@|[[IsRelatedTo::@@@]]}}
|-
|}
{| class="wikitable"
! IsParentOf
| {{#arraymap:{{#ask: [[HasParent::{{PAGENAME}}]]|link=none|
    limit=1000}}|,|@@@|[[IsParentOf::@@@]]}}
|-
! HasConnectionTo
| {{#arraymap:{{#ask: [[IsConnectedTo::{{PAGENAME}}]]|link=none|
    limit=1000}}|,|@@@|[[HasConnectionTo::@@@]]}}
|-
! HasRelationTo
| {{#arraymap:{{#ask: [[IsRelatedTo::{{PAGENAME}}]]|link=none|
    limit=1000}}|,|@@@|[[HasRelationTo::@@@]]}}
|-
|}

= Domain =
```

```
{| class="wikitable"
! OperatingSystemInstallationDate
| [[OperatingSystemInstallationDate::{{{
    OperatingSystemInstallationDate|}}}]]
|-
! MemberOfWindowsDomain
| [[MemberOfWindowsDomain::{{{MemberOfWindowsDomain|}}}]]
|-
! LastDomainConnectDate
| [[LastDomainConnectDate::{{{LastDomainConnectDate|}}}]]
|-
! HasLocalAdministrator
| {{#arraymap:{{{HasLocalAdministrator|}}}|,|@@@|[[
    HasLocalAdministrator::@@@]]}}
|-
|}

= Monitoring =
{| class="wikitable"
! Monitored
| [[Monitored::{{{Monitored|}}}]]
|-
! UsesHostTemplate
| [[UsesHostTemplate::{{{UsesHostTemplate|}}}]]
|-
! RunsService
| {{#arraymap:{{{RunsService|}}}|,|@@@|[[RunsService::@@@]]}}
|-
! colspan="2" align="center"| [http://{{SERVERNAME}}/nagios/cgi-
    bin/statusmap.cgi?host=all NagiosStatusMap]
|-
|}

= ParentsAndDependencies =
{| class="wikitable"
! Has the same model as
| {{#if: {{{HasModel|}}} | {{#ask: [[Category:Host]] [[HasModel
    ::PhysicalComputerModel-{{{HasModel}}}]]|headers=plain|
    default=none|limit=1000}} | none }}
|-
! Has the same manufacturer as the host(s)
| {{#if: {{{HasManufacturer|}}} | {{#ask: [[Category:Host]] [[
    HasManufacturer::{{{HasManufacturer}}}]]|headers=plain|
    default=none|limit=1000}} | none }}
|-
! Has the same manufacturer as
```

```
| {{#if: {{{HasManufacturer|}}} | {{#ask: [[Category:Thing]] [[
    HasManufacturer::{{{HasManufacturer}}}]]|headers=plain|
    default=none|limit=1000}} | none }}
|-
! Has the same vendor as the host(s)
| {{#if: {{{HasVendor|}}} | {{#ask: [[Category:Host]] [[
    HasVendor::{{{HasVendor}}}]]|headers=plain|default=none|
    limit=1000}} | none }}
|-
! Has the same vendor as
| {{#if: {{{HasVendor|}}} | {{#ask: [[Category:Thing]] [[
    HasVendor::{{{HasVendor}}}]]|headers=plain|default=none|
    limit=1000}} | none }}
|-
|}

= AdditionalQueries =
You can add your own queries and information here.
{{{AdditionalQueries|}}}

= Hardware =
{| class="wikitable"
! Mainboard
| {{#arraymap:{{{Mainboard|}}}|,|@@@|[[HasInstalledHardware::
    Mainboard-{{PAGENAME}}-@@@|@@@]]}}
|-
! Processor
| {{#arraymap:{{{Processor|}}}|,|@@@|[[HasInstalledHardware::
    Processor-@@@|@@@]]}}
|-
! RAM
| {{#arraymap:{{{RAM|}}}|,|@@@|[[HasInstalledHardware::RAM-{{
    PAGENAME}}-@@@|@@@]]}}
|-
! NetworkAdapter
| {{#arraymap:{{{NetworkAdapter|}}}|,|@@@|[[HasInstalledHardware
    ::NetworkAdapter-{{PAGENAME}}-@@@|@@@]]{{#set:
    HasInstalledNetworkAdapter=NetworkAdapter-{{PAGENAME}}-@@@
    }}}}
|-
! GraphicsAdapter
| {{#arraymap:{{{GraphicsAdapter|}}}|,|@@@|[[
    HasInstalledHardware::GraphicsAdapter-{{PAGENAME}}-@@@|@@@
    ]]}}
|-
! SoundAdapter
```

```
| {{#arraymap:{{{SoundAdapter|}}}|,|@@@|[[HasInstalledHardware::
    SoundAdapter-{{PAGENAME}}-@@@|@@@]]}}
|-
! PersistentStorage
| {{#arraymap:{{{PersistentStorage|}}}|,|@@@|[[
    HasInstalledHardware::PersistentStorage-{{PAGENAME}}-@@@|@@@
    ]]}}
|-
|}

= Software =
{| class="wikitable"
! InstalledSoftware
| {{#arraymap:{{{HasInstalledSoftware|}}}|,|@@@|[[
    HasInstalledSoftware::Software-@@@|@@@]]}}
|-
|}

= ProblemAnalyzer =
[http://itsmwiki.fzi.de/index.php/Special:ProblemAnalyzer?ci1={{
    PAGENAMEE}}&twpage={{PAGENAMEE}}&twbutton=Get+Revisions/
    Compare Show Problem Analyzer]

= SemanticGraph =
{{{GraphvizDotCode|}}}

= Notes =
{| class="wikitable"
! Notes
| {{{Notes|}}} {{\#set:Notes={{{Notes|}}} }}
|-
|}

<headertabs/>
{{\#set:Page has default form=PhysicalComputer}}
[[Category:PhysicalComputer]]</includeonly>
```

C. User Study

This chapter presents the forms and data of the user study.

C.1. User Study Forms

The following pages show the forms that were used when performing the user study. The language of the forms is German, because all of the participants of the user study were native German speakers. An English translation of the questions and tasks is provided in Section 6.2 (page 384).

Vorab-Fragebogen

Vielen Dank im Voraus für die Teilnahme an der Benutzerstudie zum Thema "IT Service Management-Werkzeuge".

Dieser Fragebogen dient dazu, Informationen über Vorkenntnisse der Testpersonen festzustellen.

Um eine möglichst große Unvoreingenommenheit aller Testpersonen zu gewährleisten, bitte ich darum, bis zum endgültigen Abschluss der Studie nicht über deren Inhalte (Fragen, Antworten, Aufgaben, etc.) zu sprechen.

Bei Fragen können Sie sich gerne an den Testleiter wenden.

Name des Testleiters *(Wird vom Testleiter eingetragen)*:

....

Personennummer *(Wird vom Testleiter eingetragen)*:

....

Datum *(Wird vom Testleiter eingetragen)*:

....

---

1. Arbeiten Sie als IT-Administrator?

ja, in Vollzeit............................☐
ja, in Teilzeit............................☐
nein...................................☐

---

2. Bewerten Sie Ihre Kenntnisse der folgenden Themengebiete:

	keine	Grund-kenntnisse	mittel	gute	sehr gute
IT Anwendung allgemein	☐	☐	☐	☐	☐
Windows-Administration	☐	☐	☐	☐	☐
Linux-Administration	☐	☐	☐	☐	☐
IT Service Management	☐	☐	☐	☐	☐

1

3. Mit welchen der folgenden Wiki Typen haben Sie bereits gearbeitet?

Klassische (nicht-semantische) Wikis . . . . . . ☐
Semantische Wikis . . . . ☐
keine . . . . ☐

4. Bewerten Sie Ihre Kenntnisse der folgenden Wiki Plattformen bzw. Erweiterungen:

	keine	Grund-kenntnisse	mittel	gute	sehr gute
PmWiki	☐	☐	☐	☐	☐
MediaWiki	☐	☐	☐	☐	☐
Semantic MediaWiki	☐	☐	☐	☐	☐
Semantic Forms	☐	☐	☐	☐	☐

5. Nennen Sie weitere Wikis, welche Sie verwenden oder in der Vergangenheit verwendet haben:

. . . .
. . . .
. . . .
. . . .
. . . .
. . . .
. . . .
. . . .
. . . .

2

6. **Bewerten Sie Ihre Kenntnisse der folgenden Anwendungen:**

	keine	Grund-kenntnisse	mittel	gute	sehr gute
Microsoft Excel	☐	☐	☐	☐	☐
Active Directory-Benutzer und -Computer Verwaltung	☐	☐	☐	☐	☐

7. **Bewerten Sie Ihre Kenntnisse der IT Infrastruktur Monitoring Software Nagios:**

	keine	Grund-kenntnisse	mittel	gute	sehr gute
Nagios Anwendung	☐	☐	☐	☐	☐
Nagios Konfiguration	☐	☐	☐	☐	☐

8. **Bewerten Sie Ihre Kenntnisse der folgenden webbasierten Plattformen zur Anzeige und Auswertung von Einbruchsversuchen (Intrusion Detection Frontends):**

	keine	Grund-kenntnisse	mittel	gute	sehr gute
BASE	☐	☐	☐	☐	☐
Snorby	☐	☐	☐	☐	☐

9. **Bewerten Sie Ihre Kenntnisse der folgenden IT Service Management Anwendungen:**

	keine	Grund-kenntnisse	mittel	gute	sehr gute
OTRS	☐	☐	☐	☐	☐
OTRS::ITSM	☐	☐	☐	☐	☐
i-doit open	☐	☐	☐	☐	☐

3

10. Falls Sie Kommentare oder Verbesserungsvorschläge bzgl. des Fragebogens haben, möchte ich Sie bitten, diese hier zu nennen:

....

....

....

....

....

....

....

....

....

Vielen Dank für das Ausfüllen des Fragebogens!

4

Willkommen zur Benutzerstudie

Zu Beginn möchte ich mich für Ihre Teilnahme an der Benutzerstudie herzlich bedanken.

Die Studie ist folgendermaßen aufgebaut:

1. **Training:** Als erstes haben Sie in einer Trainingsphase die Gelegenheit, die in dieser Studie evaluierten Tools auszuprobieren. Hierfür erhalten Sie eine kleine Präsentation der relevanten Fähigkeiten der Tools und dürfen dazu passende Trainingsaufgaben lösen.
2. **Aufgaben:** Als nächstes erhalten Sie eine Anzahl von Aufgaben, welche Sie bitte mit den angegebenen Tools lösen. In dieser Phase wird vom Testleiter die Zeit gestoppt, die Sie für die einzelnen Aufgaben benötigen. Im Anschluss an die Aufgaben jedes Tools dürfen Sie das jeweilige Tool in einem standardisierten Fragebogen (System Usability Scale) bewerten.
3. **Fragebogen:** Im Nach-Test Fragebogen werden weitere Fragen gestellt, welche sich konkreter auf die untersuchten Tools beziehen.

Nach der Trainingsphase werden Sie darum gebeten, die Trainingsunterlagen dem Testleiter zu übergeben.

Während der Trainingsphase dürfen Sie sich jedoch gerne Notizen machen, welche Sie zur Lösung der Aufgaben verwenden dürfen.

Zur späteren Nachvollziehbarkeit der Ergebnisse würde ich gerne die Studie auf Video aufnehmen. Erfasst werden Bild und Ton. Das Videomaterial wird nur für Frank Kleiner sichtbar sein und dient dazu, ggf. einzelne Problemlösungsansätze nachzuvollziehen und damit das entwickelte Tool zu verbessern. Selbstverständlich erfolgt die Aufzeichnung nur mit Ihrem Einverständnis. Falls Sie dieses nicht geben, wird die Studie ohne Videoaufzeichnung fortgesetzt.

Sind Sie damit einverstanden, dass die Benutzerstudie aufgezeichnet wird?

ja .... □
nein .... □

Viel Erfolg bei der Bearbeitung der Aufgaben und
nochmals vielen Dank für Ihre Teilnahme!

1

Training

Name des Testleiters *(Wird vom Testleiter eingetragen)*:

. . . .

Personennummer *(Wird vom Testleiter eingetragen)*:

. . . .

Datum *(Wird vom Testleiter eingetragen)*:

. . . .

1

Hinweise:

- Die Trainingsphase dient dazu, dass die Teilnehmer mit den in der Studie verwendeten Programmen vertraut werden.
- Auf den folgenden Seiten werden die drei Tools vorgestellt und kurz beschrieben, welche in dieser Studie verwendet werden.
- Bearbeiten Sie die Trainingsaufgaben bitte in der Reihenfolge, in der Sie Ihnen gestellt werden.
- Sie können sich bei jedem der Tools so viel Zeit lassen, bis Sie den Eindruck haben, das Tool verstanden zu haben und gut bedienen zu können.
- Bei Fragen können Sie sich gerne an den Testleiter wenden.

2

Klassische Tools

Information:

- Die klassischen Tools sind eine Ansammlung der Programme Microsoft Excel, PmWiki, die in Windows 7 enthaltenen Administrations-Tools sowie die in den Microsoft Remoteserver-Verwaltungstools für Windows 7 enthaltenen Programme (z.B. Active Directory-Benutzer und -Computer). Der im Test verwendete Begriff "Windows-Tools" beinhaltet alle in Windows 7 mitgelieferten Tools sowie die in den Remoteserver-Verwaltungstools beinhalteten Tools.
- Auf dem Desktop der Umgebung der klassischen Tools finden Sie Shortcuts zu den folgenden Programmen, welche Sie zur Lösung der nachfolgenden Aufgaben benutzen können:
  - Link zur Excel-Tabelle Computerliste.xlsx, welche eine Liste der in der Testumgebung enthaltenen Computer enthält.
  - Links zu einer Auswahl der in Microsoft Windows enthaltenen Administrationswerkzeuge.
  - Link zu PmWiki, in dem textuelle Informationen über die IT-Umgebung enthalten sind.
  - Ordner mit Nagios-Konfigurationsdateien
- Abbildung 1 zeigt einen Screenshot des Desktops.

Abbildung 1: Screenshot des Legacy-Desktops mit markierten Shortcuts

3

Klassische Tools

Information:

- Die Umgebung für die Lösung der Aufgaben mit Hilfe der klassischen Tools befindet sich auf dem Computer "suzanna-eval-a.fzi.de" (blauer Desktophintergrund).
- Mit dem auf dem Computer "suzanna-eval-a.fzi.de" angemeldeten Benutzer "eval-a" haben Sie auf den in den Aufgaben genannten Computern Administrator-Rechte. Das Passwort des Benutzers befindet sich im vor Ihnen liegenden Briefumschlag. Falls notwendig, können Sie das Passwort nutzen, um sich an Computern anzumelden.

Anweisung:

- Öffnen Sie den Desktop der klassischen Tools auf Computer "suzanna-eval-a.fzi.de" durch Klicken auf das Symbol auf dem Computer vor Ihnen.

4

Klassische Tools

Information:

- In den klassischen Tools werden Informationen über Computer in einer Excel-Tabelle gespeichert.
- Diese Tabelle wird von den Administratoren manuell gepflegt und enthält teilweise Lücken.
- Abbildung 2 zeigt einen Screenshot der Excel-Tabelle.

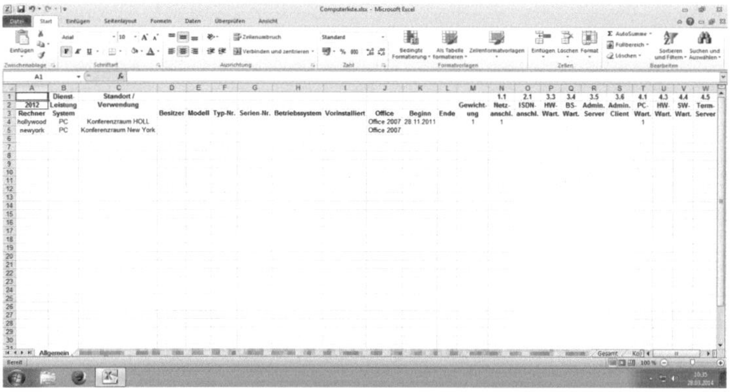

Abbildung 2: Screenshot der Excel-Tabelle

Anweisung:

- Öffnen Sie nun die Tabelle auf dem Desktop und machen Sie sich mit dem Aufbau der darin enthaltenen Informationen vertraut.
- Über die Tabs am unteren Rand der Tabelle können Sie zwischen den Computern verschiedener Organisationseinheiten wechseln.
- Sobald Sie sich sicher im Umgang mit der Tabelle fühlen, fahren Sie bitte mit der nachfolgenden Trainingsaufgabe fort.

Aufgabe 1. Wie lautet der Besitzer des Computers "morgul"?

Antwort:

....

5

Klassische Tools

Information:

- Textuelle Informationen werden in den klassischen Tools in PmWiki gespeichert.
- Abbildung 3 zeigt einen Screenshot der PmWiki-Umgebung.

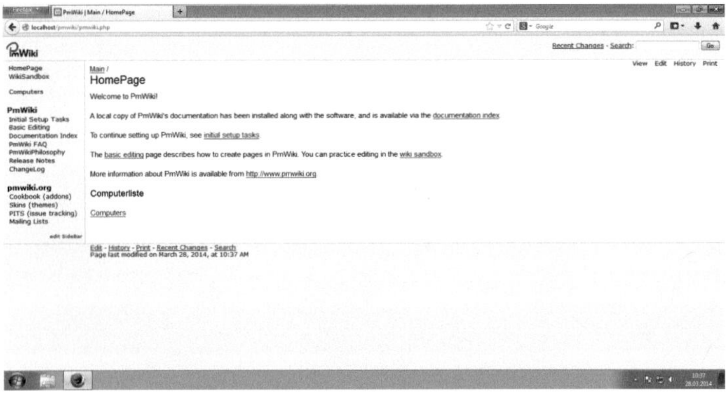

Abbildung 3: Screenshot der PmWiki-Umgebung

Anweisung:

- Öffnen Sie PmWiki durch Klicken auf das Icon auf dem Desktop und machen Sie sich mit dem Aufbau der darin enthaltenen Informationen vertraut.
- Durch Klicken auf den Link “Computers” auf der linken Seite navigieren Sie zu einer Seite, die die in PmWiki beschriebenen Computer enthält.
- Sobald Sie sich sicher im Umgang mit PmWiki fühlen, fahren Sie bitte mit der nachfolgenden Trainingsaufgabe fort.

Aufgabe 2. Navigieren Sie in PmWiki zur Seite “dc3”. Wie lautet das fett markierte Wort auf der Seite?

Antwort:

....

6

Klassische Tools

Information:

- Seiten lassen sich in PmWiki durch Klicken auf den Link "Edit" rechts oben editieren.
- Abbildung 4 zeigt einen Screenshot der Editier-Ansicht von PmWiki.

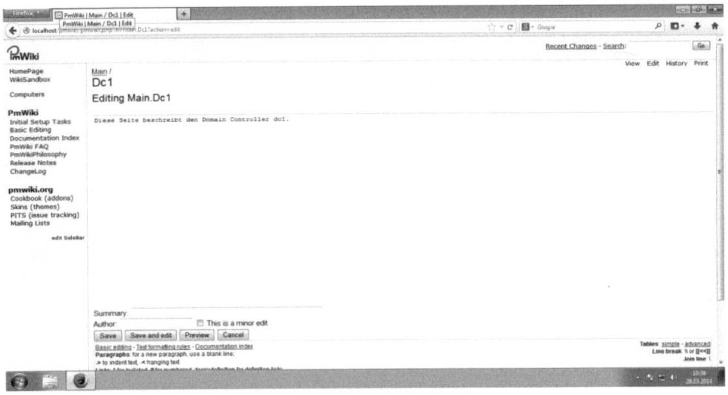

Abbildung 4: Screenshot der Editier-Ansicht von PmWiki

Aufgabe 3. Navigieren Sie in PmWiki zur Seite "dc2". Fügen Sie am Ende der Seite das Wort "Test" in kursiver Schrift hinzu und speichern Sie die Seite durch Klicken auf den "Save"-Button ab.

7

Klassische Tools

Information:

- Die Konfiguration des Infrastruktur-Monitoring-Programms Nagios erfolgt über das Editieren textbasierter Konfigurationsdateien.
- Die Konfigurationsdateien für das Training befinden sich auf dem Desktop im Verzeichnis "Nagios-Training", sowie in dessen Unterverzeichnis "objects". Neue Hosts (z.B. Computer) werden in der Datei "hosts.cfg" im Unterordner "objects" hinzugefügt. Hosts lassen sich in der Datei "hostgroups.cfg" zu Gruppen hinzufügen. Gruppen sind in der Datei "services.cfg" Diensten zugeordnet. Diese Dienste werden von Nagios überwacht.
- Abbildung 5 zeigt einen Screenshot des Ordners, der die Nagios-Konfigurationsdateien enthält.

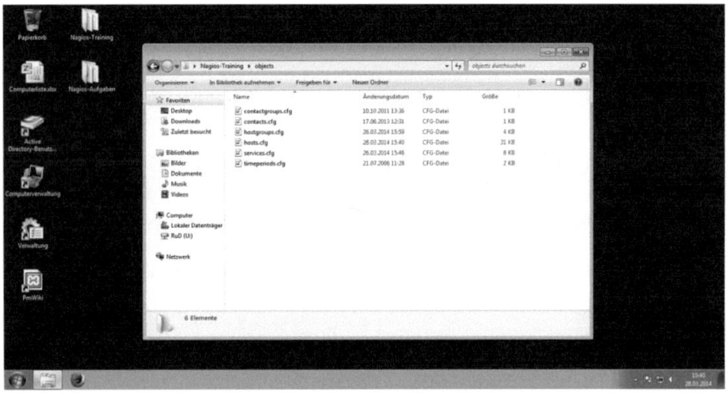

Abbildung 5: Screenshot der Nagios-Konfigurationsdateien

Anweisung:

- Öffnen Sie den Ordner "Nagios-Training" auf dem Desktop und danach den darin enthaltenen Unterordner "objects". Öffnen Sie nun die Datei "hosts.cfg" und machen Sie sich mit dem Aufbau der Datei vertraut.
- Sobald Sie sich sicher im Umgang mit den Nagios-Konfigurationsdateien fühlen, fahren Sie bitte mit der nachfolgenden Trainingsaufgabe fort.

Aufgabe 4. Öffnen Sie die Datei "hosts.cfg" und fügen Sie den Windows-Host "test1.fzi.de" am Ende der Datei hinzu. Der Host "test1.fzi.de" soll "test-switch.fzi.de" als Eltern-Host haben.

8

Klassische Tools

Information:

- Im Active Directory Verzeichnisdienst werden Informationen über Benutzer und Computer der Windows-Domäne gespeichert.
- Abbildung 6 zeigt einen Screenshot der Active Directory Benutzer- und Computerverwaltung.

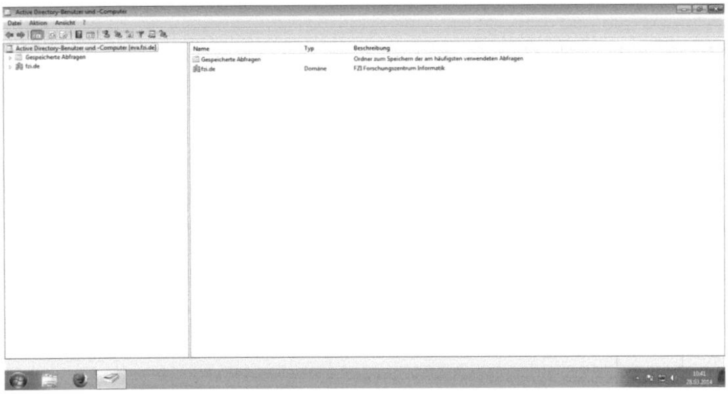

Abbildung 6: Screenshot der Active Directory Benutzer- und Computerverwaltung

Anweisung:

- Öffnen Sie das Programm “Active Directory-Benutzer und -Computer” durch Klicken auf das Icon auf dem Desktop.
- Navigieren Sie zum Computer “pfau” in der Organisationseinheit fzi.de → IPE → Computers.

Aufgabe 5. Wie lautet das auf “pfau” installierte Betriebssystem?

. . . .

9

Klassische Tools

Information:

- Über die Windows-Computerverwaltung können berechtigte Personen auf die Konfiguration von Computern zugreifen.
- Abbildung 7 zeigt einen Screenshot der Windows-Computerverwaltung.

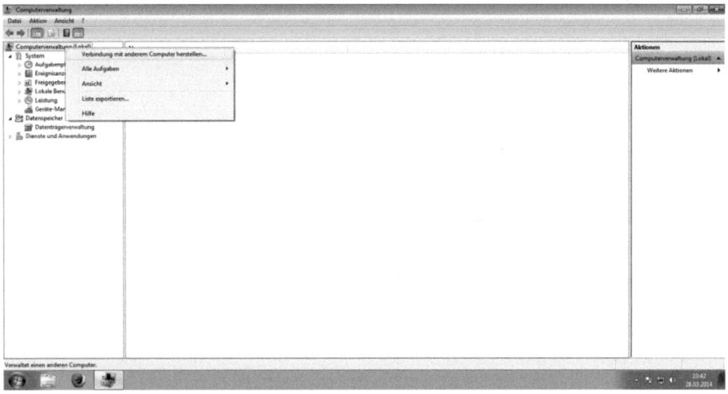

Abbildung 7: Screenshot der Windows-Computerverwaltung

Anweisung:

- Öffnen Sie das Programm "Computerverwaltung" durch Klicken auf das Icon auf dem Desktop.
- Verbinden Sie sich mit dem Computer "milka" durch Rechtsklick auf "Computerverwaltung (Lokal)" und auswählen der Option "Verbindung mit anderem Computer herstellen...".
- Navigieren Sie zu "Lokale Benutzer und Gruppen" $\rightarrow$ Benutzer.

Aufgabe 6. Welche lokalen Benutzer sind auf dem Computer "milka" vorhanden?

....

Bitte schließen Sie alle Fenster innerhalb der virtuellen Maschine und melden Sie sich ab.
Falls Sie möchten, können Sie an dieser Stelle eine kurze Pause einlegen.

10

OTRS::ITSM

Information:

- Das Tool OTRS::ITSM dient dazu, Informationen über für die Erbringung von IT-Diensten benötigte Einheiten (sogenannte Configuration Items) zu verwalten. Configuration Items sind z.B. Computer.
- Auf dem Desktop der Umgebung des Tools OTRS::ITSM finden Sie einen Shortcut zum Programm "OTRS Agent Interface", welche Sie zur Lösung der nachfolgenden Aufgaben benutzen können.
- Abbildung 8 zeigt einen Screenshot des Desktops.

Abbildung 8: Screenshot des OTRS::ITSM-Desktops mit markiertem Shortcut

Information:

- Bitte lösen Sie die nachfolgenden Aufgaben ausschließlich mit Hilfe von OTRS::ITSM.
- Die Umgebung für die Lösung der Aufgaben mit Hilfe von OTRS::ITSM befindet sich auf dem Computer "suzanna-eval-b.fzi.de" (grauer Desktophintergrund).

Anweisung:

- Öffnen Sie den Desktop von OTRS::ITSM auf Computer "suzanna-eval-b.fzi.de" durch Klicken auf das Symbol auf dem Computer vor Ihnen.

11

OTRS::ITSM

Information:

- Informationen über Configuration Items (z.B. Computer) werden in einer Configuration Management Database (CMDB) gespeichert. Auf diese Informationen kann über OTRS::ITSM webbasiert zugegriffen werden.
- Abbildung 9 zeigt einen Screenshot der CMDB-Übersicht von OTRS::ITSM.

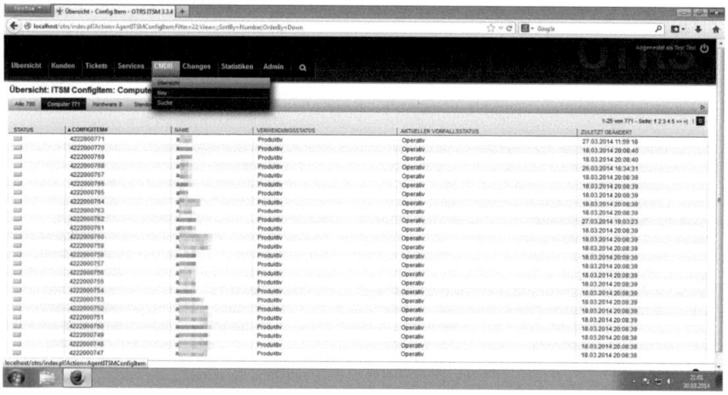

Abbildung 9: Screenshot der Computer-Übersicht in OTRS::ITSM

Anweisung:

- Öffnen Sie das Programm "OTRS::ITSM" durch Klicken auf das Icon "OTRS Agent Interface" auf dem Desktop.
- Melden Sie sich durch Klicken auf den Button "Anmeldung" mit den gespeicherten Logindaten an.
- Navigieren Sie durch Klicken auf "CMDB → Übersicht" zur Übersicht aller Configuration Items.
- Navigieren Sie durch Klicken auf verschiedene Computernamen um einen Gesamteindruck von OTRS::ITSM zu bekommen. Kehren Sie danach zur Übersicht der Configuration Items zurück.

Aufgabe 7. Wie lauten die ersten drei Computer in der nach Namen alphabetisch von A bis Z aufsteigend sortierten Liste?

....

12

OTRS::ITSM

Information:

- Je Configuration Item (z.B. ein Computer) existiert eine Seite in OTRS::ITSM, welche Informationen dazu enthält.
- Abbildung 10 zeigt einen Screenshot eines Computers in OTRS::ITSM.

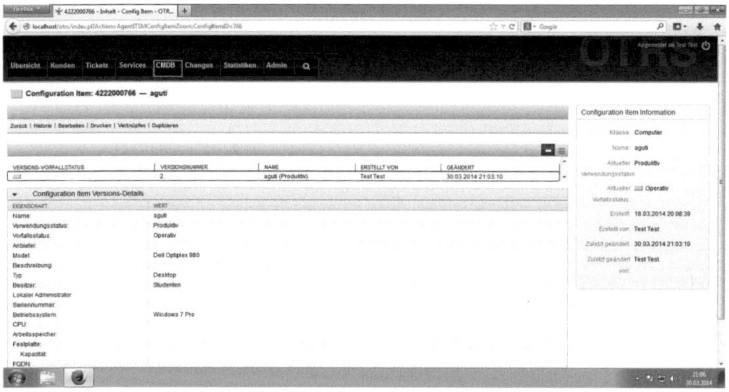

Abbildung 10: Screenshot eines Computers in OTRS::ITSM

Anweisung:

- Klicken Sie auf den Computer "akazie", um weitere Informationen zu diesem Computer zu erhalten.

Aufgabe 8. Welches Betriebssystem ist auf dem Computer "akazie" installiert?

....

13

OTRS::ITSM

Information:

- Informationen über Configuration Items (z.B. Computer) können webbasiert bearbeitet werden.
- Abbildung 11 zeigt einen Screenshot der Bearbeitungs-Ansicht eines Configuration Items in OTRS::ITSM.

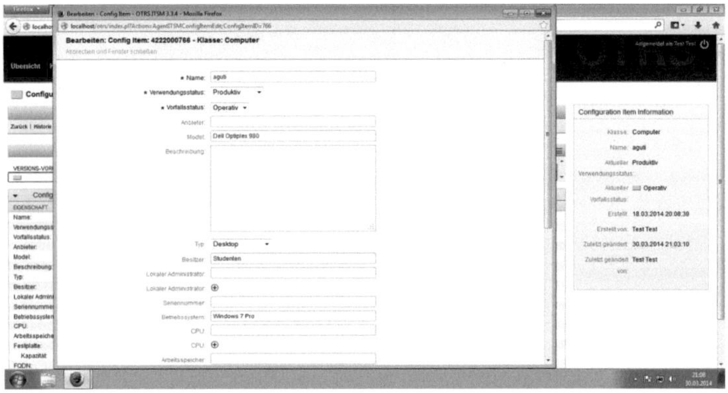

Abbildung 11: Screenshot der Bearbeitungsansicht eines Computers in OTRS::ITSM

Anweisung:

- Klicken Sie im Configuration Item "akazie" auf "Bearbeiten", um die Bearbeitungs-Ansicht zu öffnen.

Aufgabe 9. Ändern Sie den Besitzer des Computers "akazie" in "Chris Schwarz".

14

OTRS::ITSM

Information:

- OTRS::ITSM bietet die Möglichkeit, nach Configuration Items zu suchen.
- Die Suche ist über “CMDB → Suche” erreichbar.
- Abbildung 12 zeigt einen Screenshot der Suchfunktion in OTRS::ITSM, welche dazu dient, Configuration Items zu finden.

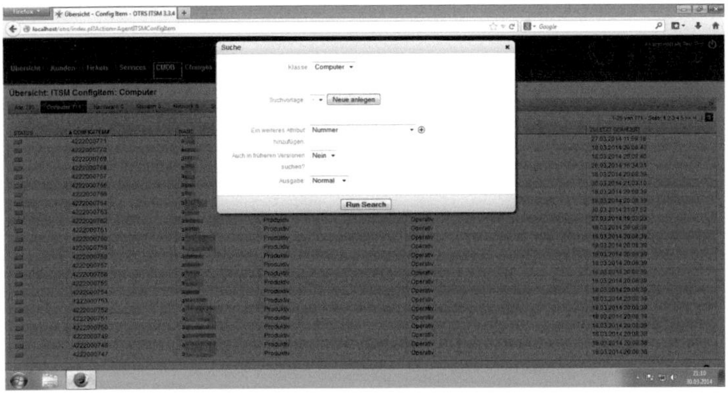

Abbildung 12: Screenshot der Suche nach Configuration Items in OTRS::ITSM

Anweisung:

- Klicken Sie auf “CMDB → Suche”.
- Wählen Sie als Klasse “Computer”
- Fügen Sie unter “Ein weiteres Attribut hinzufügen” durch Auswahl von “Name” und Klicken des Plus-Zeichens ein Namensfeld hinzu.
- Anschließend können Sie im Feld “Name” nach einem Computernamen suchen.

Aufgabe 10. Suchen Sie mit Hilfe der Suchfunktion nach dem Computer “colin”. Welches Betriebssystem ist auf diesem Computer installiert?

....

Bitte schließen Sie alle Fenster innerhalb der virtuellen Maschine und melden Sie sich ab.
Falls Sie möchten, können Sie an dieser Stelle eine kurze Pause einlegen.

15

ITSM Wiki

Information:

- Das ITSM Wiki ist eine auf einem semantischen Wiki basierende Plattform für die Verwaltung von IT Service Management Informationen.
- Informationen, die im ITSM Wiki verwaltet werden, sind unter anderem solche über Computer und Benutzer.
- Auf dem Desktop der Umgebung des Tools ITSM Wiki finden Sie einen Shortcut zum Programm “ITSM Wiki”, welches Sie zur Lösung der nachfolgenden Aufgaben benutzen können.
- Abbildung 13 zeigt einen Screenshot des Desktops.

Abbildung 13: Screenshot des ITSM Wiki-Desktops mit markiertem Shortcut

Information:

- Bitte lösen Sie die nachfolgenden Aufgaben ausschließlich mit Hilfe des ITSM Wikis.
- Die Umgebung für die Lösung der Aufgaben mit Hilfe des ITSM Wikis befindet sich auf dem Computer “suzanna-eval-c.fzi.de” (grüner Desktophintergrund).

Anweisung:

- Öffnen Sie den Desktop des ITSM Wikis auf Computer “suzanna-eval-c.fzi.de” durch Klicken auf das Symbol auf dem Computer vor Ihnen.

16

ITSM Wiki

Information:

- Im Wiki kann durch das Klicken auf Links navigiert werden.
- An der linken Bildschirmseite finden sich Links, welche zu Tabellen führen (z.B. "Show Computers" unterhalb von "ITSM show").
- Abbildung 14 zeigt einen Screenshot der Computerliste des ITSM Wikis.

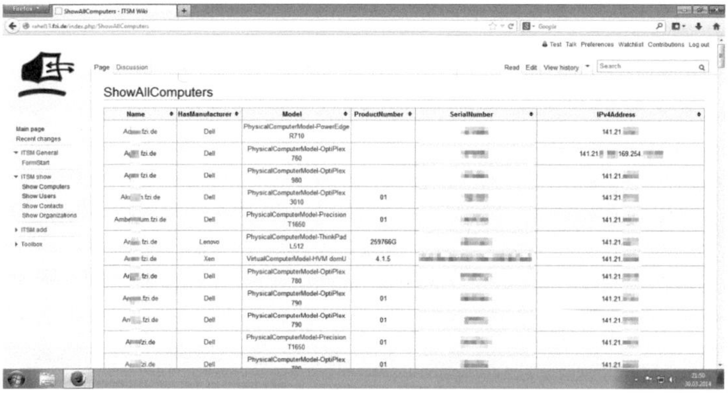

Abbildung 14: Screenshot der Computerliste des ITSM Wikis

Anweisung:

- Öffnen Sie das Programm "ITSM Wiki" durch Klicken auf das Icon "ITSM Wiki" auf dem Desktop.
- Navigieren Sie im ITSM Wiki durch Klicken auf "Show Computers" in der linken Leiste zur Übersicht aller Computer.
- Navigieren Sie durch Klicken auf verschiedene Computernamen und Eigenschaften der Computer, um einen Gesamteindruck des ITSM Wikis zu bekommen. Kehren Sie danach zur Übersicht der Computer zurück.

Aufgabe 11. Wie lauten die Namen der ersten drei Computer in der nach Namen alphabetisch von A bis Z aufsteigend sortierten Liste?

....

17

ITSM Wiki

Information:

- Die einzelnen Wiki-Seiten sind in Unterthemen unterteilt, welche über die Tabs unterhalb der Überschrift erreichbar sind (z.B. “General”, “Hardware”, “Software”).
- Abbildung 15 zeigt einen Screenshot des Computers “arve.fzi.de” im ITSM Wiki.

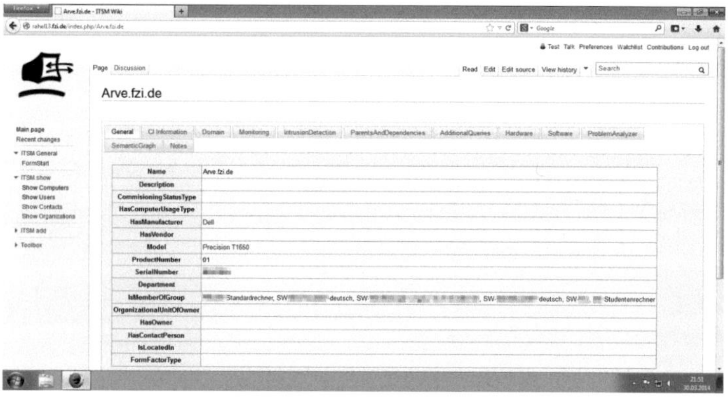

Abbildung 15: Screenshot des Computers “arve.fzi.de” im ITSM Wiki

Anweisung:

- Klicken Sie sich durch die einzelnen Tabs mehrerer Computer.
- Klicken Sie innerhalb der Tabs auf Links und navigieren Sie auf diese Weise durch das Wiki.

18

ITSM Wiki

Information:

- Der Tab "ParentsAndDependencies" beinhaltet u.a. Links zu Computern, welche vom selben Modell sind, sowie solche, die vom gleichen Hersteller sind.
- Über diese Links kann zwischen den Wiki-Seiten der einzelnen Computer navigiert werden.
- Abbildung 16 zeigt einen Screenshot des Tabs "ParentsAndDependencies" des Computers "arve.fzi.de".

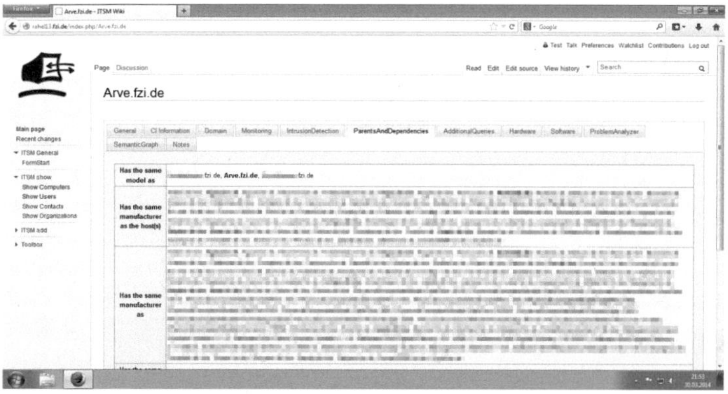

Abbildung 16: Screenshot des Tabs "ParentsAndDependencies"

Anweisung:

- Machen Sie sich mit der Navigation mit Hilfe des Tabs "ParentsAndDependencies" vertraut, indem Sie auf die Links innerhalb des Tabs klicken und damit zwischen verschiedenen Computern navigieren.

19

ITSM Wiki

Information:

- Der Tab "ParentsAndDependencies" bietet nützliche Informationen zu Benutzern.
- Ein Beispiel für Informationen zu Benutzern ist die, auf welchen Rechnern dieser Benutzer lokaler Administrator ist.
- Abbildung 17 zeigt einen Screenshot des Tabs "ParentsAndDependencies" eines Benutzers.

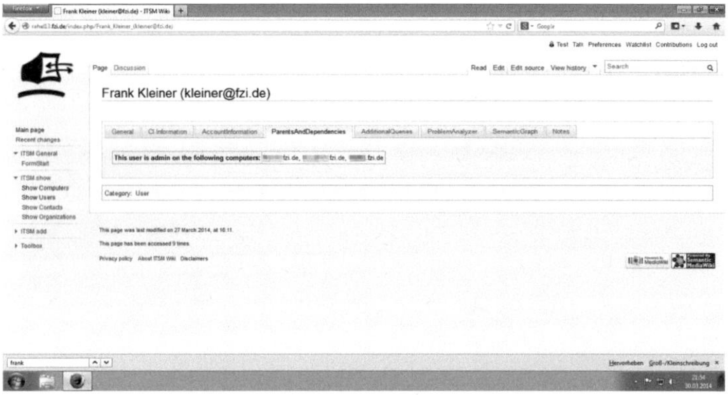

Abbildung 17: Screenshot des Tabs "ParentsAndDependencies" im Kontext eines Benutzers

Anweisung:

- Navigieren Sie über den Link "Show Users" am linken Rand zur Übersicht aller Benutzer.
- Klicken Sie dort auf den Link des Benutzers "Frank Kleiner (kleiner@fzi.de)".
- Klicken Sie innerhalb der Seite des Benutzers auf den Tab "ParentsAndDependencies", um zu sehen, auf welchen Computern dieser Benutzer lokaler Administrator ist.

20

ITSM Wiki

Information:

- Abbildung 15 zeigt einen Screenshot der auf dem Computer "arve.fzi.de" installierten Software.
- An erster Stelle ist das Betriebssystem zu sehen.

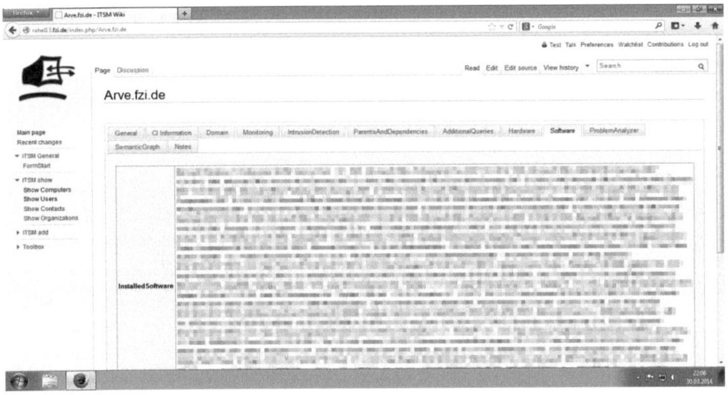

Abbildung 18: Screenshot der Softwareliste eines Computers im ITSM Wiki

Anweisung:

- Navigieren Sie zur Softwareliste des Computers "nerz.fzi.de".

Aufgabe 12. Welches Betriebssystem ist auf dem Computer "nerz.fzi.de" installiert?

....

ITSM Wiki

Information:

- Das ITSM Wiki bietet die Möglichkeit, Freitext-Notizen zu verfassen. Diese Notizen sind über den Tab "Notes" erreichbar.
- Freitext-Notizen können über die Iconleiste über dem Textfeld formatiert werden (z.B. fett oder kursiv).
- Außerdem können über das Kettensymbol (drittes Icon von links) Links erstellt werden (z.B. auf eine andere Wiki-Seite).
- Abbildung 19 zeigt einen Screenshot der Notizen-Ansicht des Computers "arve.fzi.de" im ITSM Wiki.

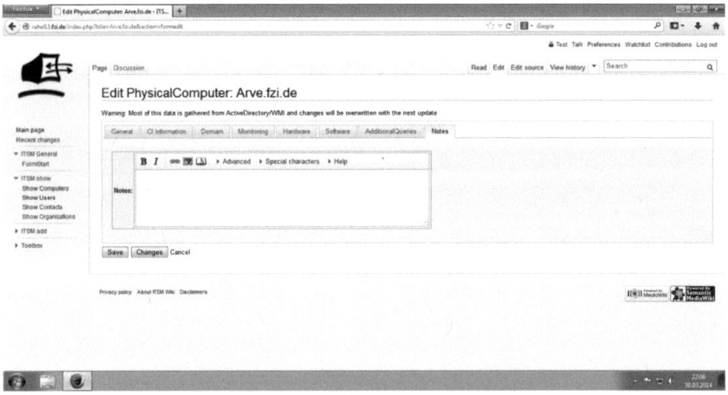

Abbildung 19: Screenshot der Notizen-Ansicht eines Computers im ITSM Wiki

Anweisung:

- Navigieren Sie zur Seite "nerz.fzi.de".
- Klicken Sie auf "Edit", um die Seite zu editieren und navigieren Sie zum "Notes"-Tab.
- Experimentieren Sie mit den in der Iconleiste gebotenen Möglichkeiten. Speichern Sie Änderungen mittels des "Save"-Buttons, um das Ergebnis Ihrer Änderungen zu sehen.

Aufgabe 13. Fügen Sie den Text "Test" in das Notes-Feld des Computers "nerz.fzi.de" ein und formatieren Sie den Text kursiv.

22

ITSM Wiki

Information:

- Das ITSM Wiki bietet die Möglichkeit, nach Configuration Items (z.B. Computern) zu suchen.
- Die Suche ist über das mit “Search” benannte Suchfeld rechts oben möglich.
- Es werden automatisch passende Vorschläge angezeigt, welche durch Klicken mit der Maus ausgewählt werden können.
- Abbildung 20 zeigt einen Screenshot der Suchfunktion des ITSM Wikis.

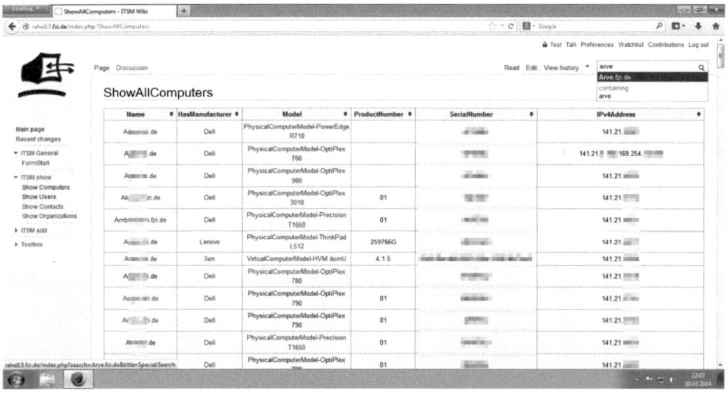

Abbildung 20: Screenshot der Suchfunktion des ITSM Wikis

Anweisung:

- Klicken Sie in das Suchfeld und machen Sie sich mit der Suchfunktion vertraut.

Aufgabe 14. Suchen Sie den Computer “argos.fzi.de”. Wie heisst dessen Hersteller (zu sehen unter “hasManufacturer”)?

....

23

ITSM Wiki

Information:

- Über Abfragen kann vom ITSM Wiki auf die darin gespeicherten Informationen zugegriffen werden. Abfragen ermöglichen es, mehrere Kriterien auszuwählen, die zu Und-Verknüpfungen zusammengefügt werden. Das Formulieren von Abfragen erfolgt im Wikitext einer beliebigen Wiki-Seite. Abbildung 21 zeigt die Trainingsseite, auf der Sie das Erstellen von Abfragen üben können.

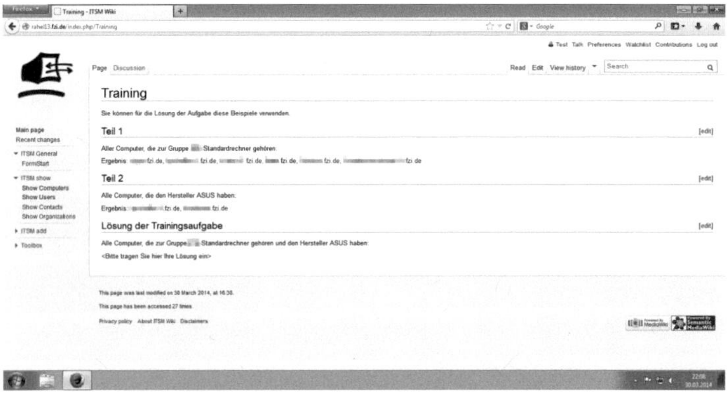

Abbildung 21: Screenshot der Ergebnisse von Abfragen

Anweisung:

- Navigieren Sie von der Wiki-Startseite aus zur Seite "Trainings-Beispiele" unterhalb der Überschrift "Trainings-Abfragen".
- Betrachten Sie die Ergebnisse der Beispielseite. Öffnen Sie danach mittels des Buttons "Edit" rechts oben den Wikitext der Seite "Trainings-Beispiele" und machen Sie sich mit der Syntax der Abfragen vertraut.
- Öffnen Sie nun auf der Wiki-Startseite die Seite "Training" unterhalb der Überschrift "Trainings-Abfragen". Formulieren Sie auf der Seite "Training" eine Abfrage, um die nachfolgende Aufgabe zu beantworten.

Aufgabe 15. Wie lautet der Name des Computers, der zur Gruppe IPE-Standardrechner gehört und den Hersteller ASUS hat?

....

24

ITSM Wiki

Information:

- Die Konfiguration des Infrastruktur Monitorings im ITSM Wiki erfolgt durch das formularbasierte Editieren der Wiki-Seite des jeweiligen Computers.
- Abbildung 22 zeigt einen Screenshot der Konfiguration des Infrastruktur Monitorings im ITSM Wiki.
- Im Tab "Monitoring" eines Computers können Sie durch das Setzen der Option "Monitored" die Verfügbarkeitsüberwachung aktivieren (Senden und Empfangen von Pings).
- Über das Auswählen eines Dienstes unter "RunsService" kann die Verfügbarkeit von Diensten überwacht werden.
- Durch Speichern der Wiki-Seite wird das Monitoring aktiviert.

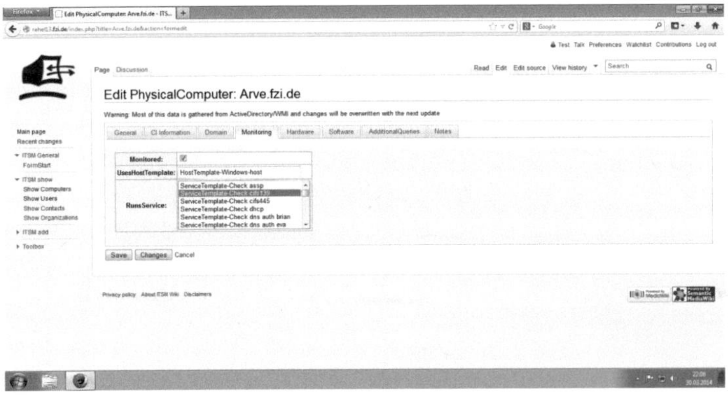

Abbildung 22: Screenshot der Infrastruktur Monitoring-Konfiguration im ITSM Wiki

Anweisung:

- Navigieren Sie zur Seite des Computers "arve.fzi.de" (z.B. durch Eingeben des Namens im Suchfeld rechts oben).
- Klicken Sie auf der Seite des Computers "arve.fzi.de" rechts oben auf "Edit".
- Wählen Sie den Tab "Monitoring" aus und machen Sie sich mit den möglichen Einstellungen vertraut.

Aufgabe 16. Aktivieren Sie das Monitoring für den Computer "agda.fzi.de". Aktivieren Sie außerdem für "agda.fzi.de" die Überwachung des Dienstes "https".

25

ITSM Wiki

Information:

- Das ITSM Wiki beinhaltet eine Komponente, welche das Finden von Fehlern erleichtert. Diese Komponente wird als Problem Analyzer bezeichnet.
- Der Problem Analyzer ist von Computer-Seiten aus über den Tab "ProblemAnalyzer" und anschließem Klicken auf "Show Problem Analyzer" zu erreichen.
- Abbildung 23 zeigt einen Screenshot des Problem Analyzers.
- Im oberen Teil des Problem Analyzers können zwei Configuration Items (z.B. Computer) miteinander verglichen werden. Dieser Teil des Assistenten wird dann eingesetzt, wenn ein Problem auf zwei unterschiedlichen Computern festgestellt wird. Der Assistent hebt beim Vergleich Gemeinsamkeiten hervor, da diese mögliche Ursachen für ein gemeinsames Problem sein können.
- Im unteren Teil des Problem Analyzers können zwei Konfigurationen eines Configuration Items (z.B. eines Computers) miteinander verglichen werden. Dieser Modus wird dann eingesetzt, wenn sich an einem Rechner ein Problem zeigt, welches vor einem bestimmten Zeitpunkt nicht existierte. Ein Beispiel ist ein durch die Installation einer bestimmten Software hervorgerufenes Problem.

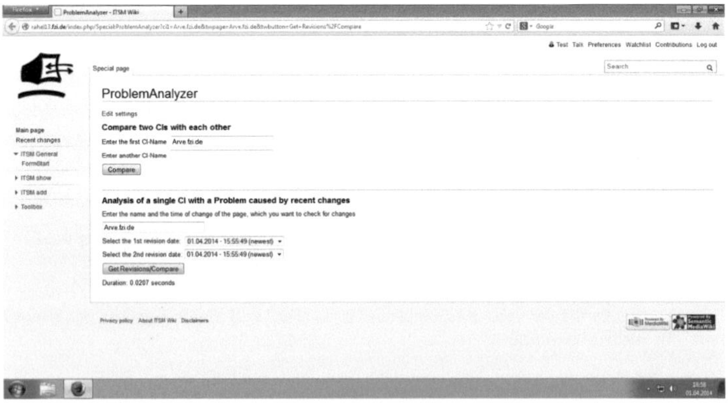

Abbildung 23: Screenshot des Problem Analyzers

26

ITSM Wiki

Anweisung:

- Machen Sie sich mit der Funktionsweise des Problem Analyzers vertraut, indem Sie die beiden Computer "argos.fzi.de" und "arve.fzi.de" miteinander vergleichen. Geben Sie hierfür die beiden Namen in die Felder "Enter the first CI name" und "Enter the second CI name" ein und klicken Sie auf "Compare". In der grafischen Visualisierung rot angezeigte Eigenschaften sind solche, die beide Computer gemeinsam haben (z.B. das Betriebssystem oder der Virenscanner).
- Vergleichen Sie für den Computer "argos.fzi.de" die aktuelle Revision mit der Version vom 01.04.2014, 15:08:12 Uhr. Belassen Sie hierfür unter "Select the 1st revision date" die aktuelle Version (newest) und ändern Sie diejenige der unter "Select the 2nd revision date" angezeigten in 01.04.2014, 15:08:12. Durch Klicken auf "Get Revisions/Compare" wird der Vergleich gestartet. Das Ergebnis sind die rot angezeigten Unterschiede zwischen den Versionen, also mögliche Problemursachen. Im Beispiel sind dies Änderungen an der Software "Notepad++" und "Java Auto Updater".

Bitte schließen Sie alle Fenster innerhalb der virtuellen Maschine und melden Sie sich ab.
Falls Sie möchten, können Sie an dieser Stelle eine kurze Pause einlegen.

27

Aufgaben

Name des Testleiters *(Wird vom Testleiter eingetragen)*:

. . . .

Personennummer *(Wird vom Testleiter eingetragen)*:

. . . .

Datum *(Wird vom Testleiter eingetragen)*:

. . . .

1

Hinweise:

- Dieser Teil der Benutzerstudie dient dazu, Informationen über die Benutzbarkeit der im vorangegangenen Training vorgestellten Tools zu gewinnen.
- Auf den folgenden Seiten werden Ihnen zu jedem der drei Tools Aufgaben präsentiert, die Sie bitte in der abgedruckten Reihenfolge beantworten.
- Für jede der Aufgaben wird vom Testleiter die Zeit gemessen, die Sie brauchen, um die Aufgabe zu bearbeiten.
- Jede Aufgabe ist auf einer separaten Seite abgedruckt. Eine Aufgabe gilt dann als angefangen, sobald Sie die Aufgabenstellung gelesen haben und dem Testleiter kommunizieren, dass Sie mit der Bearbeitung beginnen möchten.
  - Das Ende der Aufgabe ist dann erreicht, sobald Sie die Antwort vollständig niedergeschrieben haben und dies dem Testleiter kommunizieren.
  - Bitte warten Sie nach jeder Aufgabe, bis Sie der Testleiter bittet, mit der nächsten Aufgabe fortzufahren. Dies dient dazu, dass der Testleiter die Start- und Endzeit pro Aufgabe korrekt erfassen und dokumentieren kann.
- Manche Aufgaben überlassen Ihnen die Wahl des verwendeten Tools. Bitte kreuzen Sie bei diesen Aufgaben die von Ihnen verwendeten Tools an.
- Pro Aufgabe gibt es ein Zeitlimit von 10 Minuten. Sobald dieses erreicht ist, werden Sie vom Testleiter darauf hingewiesen und gebeten, mit der nächsten Aufgabe fortzufahren.
- Falls Sie der Meinung sind, dass eine Aufgabe nicht lösbar ist, sagen Sie dies bitte dem Testleiter und kreuzen Sie das Feld "Ich denke, dass diese Aufgabe mit den zur Verfügung gestellten Tools nicht lösbar ist" an. Fahren Sie dann mit der nächsten Aufgabe fort.
- Sobald die zu einem Tool gehörenden Aufgaben gelöst sind, können Sie vor dem Bearbeiten der Fragen des nächsten Tools gerne eine kurze Pause machen, falls dies erforderlich ist.
- Bei Fragen können Sie sich gerne an den Testleiter wenden.

2

Klassische Tools

Hinweise:

- Bitte lösen Sie die nachfolgenden Aufgaben mit Hilfe der klassischen Tools. Diese sind Microsoft Excel, PmWiki, die in Windows 7 enthaltenen Administrations-Tools, sowie die in den Microsoft Remoteserver-Verwaltungstools für Windows 7 enthaltenen Programme (z.B. Active Directory-Benutzer und -Computer). Der im Test verwendete Begriff "Windows-Tools" beinhaltet alle in Windows 7 mitgelieferten Tools, sowie die in den Remoteserver-Verwaltungstools beinhalteten Tools.
- Zusätzlich besteht bei den klassischen Tools die Möglichkeit, Computer physisch aufzusuchen. Je physischem Aufsuchen eines einzelnen Computers wird eine zusätzliche Wegezeit von fünf Minuten berechnet, welche die für den Weg zum Computer verbrauchte Zeit darstellt. Die in den nachfolgenden Aufgaben genannten Computer sind auf dem Tisch hinter Ihnen aufgebaut und abgedeckt. Sollten Sie sich für das physische Aufsuchen eines Computers entscheiden, kommunizieren Sie dies bitte vor dem Aufsuchen gegenüber dem Testleiter.
- Für jede Aufgabe ist angegeben, welche Tools zur Lösung verwendet werden dürfen. Sind mehrere Tools angegeben, dürfen Sie sich für eines oder mehrere der Tools entscheiden. Bitte markieren Sie nach Fertigstellung der Aufgabe, welche Tools Sie verwendet haben.
- Die Umgebung für die Lösung der Aufgaben mit Hilfe der klassischen Tools befindet sich auf dem Computer "suzanna-eval-a.fzi.de" (blauer Desktophintergrund).
- Mit dem auf dem Computer "suzanna-eval-a.fzi.de" angemeldeten Benutzer "eval-a" haben Sie auf den in den Aufgaben genannten Computern Administrator-Rechte. Das Passwort des Benutzers befindet sich im vor Ihnen liegenden Briefumschlag. Falls notwendig, können Sie das Passwort nutzen, um sich an Computern anzumelden.

Anweisung:

- Sobald Sie bereit sind, öffnen Sie bitte das Fenster für "suzanna-eval-a.fzi.de" und beginnen Sie mit dem Bearbeiten der Aufgaben.

3

Klassische Tools

Aufgabe 1. Nennen Sie das Modell des Computers "gowron".

Beispiel:

- ThinkPad 530

Verwenden Sie für das Lösen dieser Aufgabe die folgenden Hilfsmittel:

- Excel in Verbindung mit der auf dem Desktop abgelegten Datei "Computerliste.xlsx"

Geben Sie dem Testleiter Bescheid, sobald Sie bereit sind, mit der Aufgabe zu beginnen: ☐

Antwort:

....

....

Ich denke, dass diese Aufgabe mit den zur Verfügung gestellten Tools nicht lösbar ist: ☐

Geben Sie dem Testleiter Bescheid, sobald Sie die Aufgabe beendet haben: ☐

4

Klassische Tools

Aufgabe 2. Nennen Sie das Modell des Computers “ruben”.

Beispiel:

- ThinkPad 530

Verwenden Sie für das Lösen dieser Aufgabe eines oder mehrere der folgenden Hilfsmittel:

- Windows-Tools
- Begutachten des Computers vor Ort

Geben Sie dem Testleiter Bescheid, sobald Sie bereit sind, mit der Aufgabe zu beginnen: □

Antwort:

....

....

Ich denke, dass diese Aufgabe mit den zur Verfügung gestellten Tools nicht lösbar ist: □

Von mir zur Lösung der Aufgabe verwendete Tools:

□ Windows-Tools
□ Begutachten des Computers vor Ort

Geben Sie dem Testleiter Bescheid, sobald Sie die Aufgabe beendet haben: □

5

Klassische Tools

Aufgabe 3. Nennen Sie diejenigen Computer, die vom selben Modell sind wie der Computer "kangaroo".

Beispiel:

- seestern

Verwenden Sie für das Lösen dieser Aufgabe das folgende Hilfsmittel:

- Excel in Verbindung mit der auf dem Desktop abgelegten Datei "Computerliste.xlsx"

Geben Sie dem Testleiter Bescheid, sobald Sie bereit sind, mit der Aufgabe zu beginnen: □

Antwort:

....

....

....

....

....

....

....

....

....

....

Ich denke, dass diese Aufgabe mit den zur Verfügung gestellten Tools nicht lösbar ist: □

Geben Sie dem Testleiter Bescheid, sobald Sie die Aufgabe beendet haben: □

6

Klassische Tools

Aufgabe 4. Benennen Sie diejenigen Benutzer und Benutzergruppen, die lokale Administratoren auf dem Computer "zippora" sind. Als Lösungen werden Vor- und Nachname, der Benutzername oder der Gruppenname anerkannt.

Beispiel:

- Paul Krause
- krause

Verwenden Sie für das Lösen dieser Aufgabe eines oder mehrere der folgenden Hilfsmittel:

- Excel in Verbindung mit der auf dem Desktop abgelegten Datei "Computerliste.xlsx"
- Windows-Tools
- Begutachten der Computer vor Ort

Geben Sie dem Testleiter Bescheid, sobald Sie bereit sind, mit der Aufgabe zu beginnen: ☐

Antwort:

....

....

....

....

....

....

....

....

Ich denke, dass diese Aufgabe mit den zur Verfügung gestellten Tools nicht lösbar ist: ☐

Von mir zur Lösung der Aufgabe verwendete Tools:

☐ Excel-Liste
☐ Windows-Tools
☐ Begutachten der Computer vor Ort

Geben Sie dem Testleiter Bescheid, sobald Sie die Aufgabe beendet haben: ☐

7

Klassische Tools

Aufgabe 5. Benennen Sie diejenigen Computer, auf denen die Benutzerin "Lina Hartmann (hartmann@fzi.de)" Administrator ist.

Beispiel:

- seestern

Verwenden Sie für das Lösen dieser Aufgabe eines oder mehrere der folgenden Hilfsmittel:

- Excel in Verbindung mit der auf dem Desktop abgelegten Datei "Computerliste.xlsx"
- Windows-Tools
- Begutachten der Computer vor Ort

Geben Sie dem Testleiter Bescheid, sobald Sie bereit sind, mit der Aufgabe zu beginnen: □

Antwort:

....

....

....

....

....

....

....

....

....

....

Ich denke, dass diese Aufgabe mit den zur Verfügung gestellten Tools nicht lösbar ist: □

Von mir zur Lösung der Aufgabe verwendete Tools:

□ Excel-Liste
□ Windows-Tools
□ Begutachten der Computer vor Ort

Geben Sie dem Testleiter Bescheid, sobald Sie die Aufgabe beendet haben: □

8

Klassische Tools

Aufgabe 6. Fügen Sie den Text "Hallo Welt!" zur Beschreibung des Computers "mail1" hinzu.

Verwenden Sie für das Lösen dieser Aufgabe das folgende Hilfsmittel:

- PmWiki

Geben Sie dem Testleiter Bescheid, sobald Sie bereit sind, mit der Aufgabe zu beginnen: □

Ich denke, dass diese Aufgabe mit den zur Verfügung gestellten Tools nicht lösbar ist: □

Geben Sie dem Testleiter Bescheid, sobald Sie die Aufgabe beendet haben: □

9

Klassische Tools

Aufgabe 7. Formatieren Sie den in der vorigen Aufgabe eingefügten Text "Welt!" in der Beschreibung des Computers "mail1" in Fettschrift.

Verwenden Sie für das Lösen dieser Aufgabe das folgende Hilfsmittel:

- PmWiki

Geben Sie dem Testleiter Bescheid, sobald Sie bereit sind, mit der Aufgabe zu beginnen: ☐

Ich denke, dass diese Aufgabe mit den zur Verfügung gestellten Tools nicht lösbar ist: ☐

Geben Sie dem Testleiter Bescheid, sobald Sie die Aufgabe beendet haben: ☐

Klassische Tools

Aufgabe 8. Fügen Sie in der Beschreibung des Computers mail1 den Text "Dieser Computer wurde durch den Computer mail3 ersetzt." ein. Machen Sie die Zeichenfolge "mail3" zu einem Link zum Wiki-Artikel des Computers "mail3".

Verwenden Sie für das Lösen dieser Aufgabe das folgende Hilfsmittel:

- PmWiki

Geben Sie dem Testleiter Bescheid, sobald Sie bereit sind, mit der Aufgabe zu beginnen: □

Ich denke, dass diese Aufgabe mit den zur Verfügung gestellten Tools nicht lösbar ist: □

Geben Sie dem Testleiter Bescheid, sobald Sie die Aufgabe beendet haben: □

11

Klassische Tools

Aufgabe 9. Erstellen Sie eine Liste aller Computer, die vom Modell "TestTech1000" sind.

Beispiel:

- seestern

Verwenden Sie für das Lösen dieser Aufgabe das folgende Hilfsmittel:

- Excel in Verbindung mit der auf dem Desktop abgelegten Datei "Computerliste.xlsx"

Geben Sie dem Testleiter Bescheid, sobald Sie bereit sind, mit der Aufgabe zu beginnen: □

Antwort:

....

....

....

....

....

....

....

....

....

....

Ich denke, dass diese Aufgabe mit den zur Verfügung gestellten Tools nicht lösbar ist: □

Geben Sie dem Testleiter Bescheid, sobald Sie die Aufgabe beendet haben: □

12

Klassische Tools

Aufgabe 10. Erstellen Sie eine Liste aller Computer des Modells "Optiplex 780", die "Mark Berger" als Besitzer haben.

Beispiel:

- seestern

Verwenden Sie für das Lösen dieser Aufgabe das folgende Hilfsmittel:

- Excel in Verbindung mit der auf dem Desktop abgelegten Datei "Computerliste.xlsx"

Geben Sie dem Testleiter Bescheid, sobald Sie bereit sind, mit der Aufgabe zu beginnen: □

Antwort:

....

....

....

....

....

....

....

....

....

....

Ich denke, dass diese Aufgabe mit den zur Verfügung gestellten Tools nicht lösbar ist: □

Geben Sie dem Testleiter Bescheid, sobald Sie die Aufgabe beendet haben: □

13

Klassische Tools

Aufgabe 11. Die beiden Computer "isidor" und "jesaja" zeigen die selben Symptome, die auf eine gemeinsame Problemursache hindeuten. Finden und benennen Sie diejenigen Eigenschaften, die die beiden Computer gemeinsam haben. Es ist ausreichend, die Ergebnisse stichwortartig anzugeben (z.B. "Office-Version").

Beispiel:

- gleiches Modell
- gleicher Hersteller

Verwenden Sie für das Lösen dieser Aufgabe eines oder mehrere der folgenden Hilfsmittel:

- Excel in Verbindung mit der auf dem Desktop abgelegten Datei "Computerliste.xlsx"
- Windows-Tools
- Begutachten der Computer vor Ort

Geben Sie dem Testleiter Bescheid, sobald Sie bereit sind, mit der Aufgabe zu beginnen: ☐

Antwort:

....

....

....

....

....

....

....

....

Ich denke, dass diese Aufgabe mit den zur Verfügung gestellten Tools nicht lösbar ist: ☐

Von mir zur Lösung der Aufgabe verwendete Tools:

☐ Excel-Liste
☐ Windows-Tools
☐ Begutachten der Computer vor Ort

Geben Sie dem Testleiter Bescheid, sobald Sie die Aufgabe beendet haben: ☐

14

Klassische Tools

Aufgabe 12. Der Computer “milka” zeigt derzeit Symptome eines Problems, die sich vor dem 30.03.2014, 23:30 Uhr noch nicht gezeigt haben. Finden und benennen Sie diejenigen Eigenschaften des Computers, die sich seit diesem Zeitpunkt geändert haben. Es ist ausreichend, die Ergebnisse stichwortartig anzugeben (z.B. “Office-Version”).

Beispiel:

- Programm installiert

Verwenden Sie für das Lösen dieser Aufgabe eines oder mehrere der folgenden Hilfsmittel:

- Excel in Verbindung mit der auf dem Desktop abgelegten Datei “Computerliste.xlsx”
- Windows-Tools
- Begutachten der Computer vor Ort

Geben Sie dem Testleiter Bescheid, sobald Sie bereit sind, mit der Aufgabe zu beginnen: ☐

Antwort:

. . . .

. . . .

. . . .

. . . .

. . . .

. . . .

. . . .

. . . .

Ich denke, dass diese Aufgabe mit den zur Verfügung gestellten Tools nicht lösbar ist: ☐

Von mir zur Lösung der Aufgabe verwendete Tools:

☐ Excel-Liste
☐ Windows-Tools
☐ Begutachten der Computer vor Ort

Geben Sie dem Testleiter Bescheid, sobald Sie die Aufgabe beendet haben: ☐

15

Klassische Tools

Aufgabe 13. Aktivieren Sie das Infrastruktur Monitoring (Ping-Anfragen) für den (Windows-) Computer "marvin.fzi.de". Der Computer soll dabei den Host "test-switch.fzi.de" als Elternknoten haben.

Verwenden Sie für das Lösen dieser Aufgabe das folgende Hilfsmittel:

- Textbasierte Konfigurationsdateien im Ordner "Nagios-Aufgaben" auf dem Windows-Desktop

Geben Sie dem Testleiter Bescheid, sobald Sie bereit sind, mit der Aufgabe zu beginnen: ☐

Ich denke, dass diese Aufgabe mit den zur Verfügung gestellten Tools nicht lösbar ist: ☐

Geben Sie dem Testleiter Bescheid, sobald Sie die Aufgabe beendet haben: ☐

16

Klassische Tools

Aufgabe 14. Aktivieren Sie das Überwachen des HTTP-Dienstes für den Computer "marvin.fzi.de".

Verwenden Sie für das Lösen dieser Aufgabe das folgende Hilfsmittel:

- Textbasierte Konfigurationsdateien im Ordner "Nagios-Aufgaben" auf dem Windows-Desktop

Geben Sie dem Testleiter Bescheid, sobald Sie bereit sind, mit der Aufgabe zu beginnen: ☐

Ich denke, dass diese Aufgabe mit den zur Verfügung gestellten Tools nicht lösbar ist: ☐

Geben Sie dem Testleiter Bescheid, sobald Sie die Aufgabe beendet haben: ☐

17

Bewertung nach System Usability Scale

Hinweise:

- Dieser Fragebogen dient dazu, unmittelbar nach dem Ausführen der Aufgaben den Eindruck der Testpersonen von den getesteten Tools festzuhalten.
- Nachfolgend werden Ihnen zum gerade getesteten Tool zehn Aussagen präsentiert, zu der Sie bitte Ihren Grad der Zustimmung auf einer Skala von eins ("stimme überhaupt nicht zu") bis fünf ("stimme voll zu") ausdrücken.
- Bitte geben Sie Ihre Antworten spontan ab, d.h. kreuzen Sie diejenige Antwort an, welche Ihnen als erstes einfällt, ohne lange und intensiv nachzudenken.
- Es sollten alle Fragen angekreuzt werden. Falls Sie für eine Frage keine Antwort geben können, kreuzen Sie bitte die mittlere Position an.
- Bei Fragen können Sie sich gerne an den Testleiter wenden.

18

Klassische Tools

"Ich denke, dass ich das System gerne häufig benutzen würde."

stimme überhaupt nicht zu — stimme voll zu

□ □ □ □ □
1 2 3 4 5

"Ich fand das System unnötig komplex."

stimme überhaupt nicht zu — stimme voll zu

□ □ □ □ □
1 2 3 4 5

"Ich fand das System einfach zu benutzen."

stimme überhaupt nicht zu — stimme voll zu

□ □ □ □ □
1 2 3 4 5

"Ich glaube, ich würde die Hilfe einer technisch versierten Person benötigen, um das System benutzen zu können."

stimme überhaupt nicht zu — stimme voll zu

□ □ □ □ □
1 2 3 4 5

"Ich fand, die verschiedenen Funktionen in diesem System waren gut integriert."

stimme überhaupt nicht zu — stimme voll zu

□ □ □ □ □
1 2 3 4 5

19

Klassische Tools

"Ich denke, das System enthielt zu viele Inkonsistenzen."

stimme überhaupt nicht zu					stimme voll zu
	□	□	□	□	□
	1	2	3	4	5

"Ich kann mir vorstellen, dass die meisten Menschen den Umgang mit diesem System sehr schnell lernen."

stimme überhaupt nicht zu					stimme voll zu
	□	□	□	□	□
	1	2	3	4	5

"Ich fand das System sehr umständlich zu nutzen."

stimme überhaupt nicht zu					stimme voll zu
	□	□	□	□	□
	1	2	3	4	5

"Ich fühlte mich bei der Benutzung des Systems sehr sicher."

stimme überhaupt nicht zu					stimme voll zu
	□	□	□	□	□
	1	2	3	4	5

"Ich musste eine Menge lernen, bevor ich anfangen konnte das System zu verwenden."

stimme überhaupt nicht zu					stimme voll zu
	□	□	□	□	□
	1	2	3	4	5

20

Pause

Sie haben den Test der klassischen Tools beendet.

Bitte schließen Sie die Remoteverbindung zum Computer "suzanna-eval-a.fzi.de" und machen Sie eine kurze Pause, bevor Sie fortfahren.

21

OTRS::ITSM

Hinweise:

- Bitte lösen Sie die nachfolgenden Aufgaben ausschließlich mit Hilfe von OTRS::ITSM.
- Die Umgebung für die Lösung der Aufgaben mit Hilfe von OTRS::ITSM befindet sich auf dem Computer "suzanna-eval-b.fzi.de" (grauer Desktophintergrund).

Anweisung:

- Sobald Sie bereit sind, öffnen Sie bitte das Fenster für "suzanna-eval-b.fzi.de" und beginnen Sie mit dem Bearbeiten der Aufgaben.

22

OTRS::ITSM

Aufgabe 15. Nennen Sie das Modell des Computers “paris”.

Beispiel:

- ThinkPad 530

Geben Sie dem Testleiter Bescheid, sobald Sie bereit sind, mit der Aufgabe zu beginnen: ☐

Antwort:

. . . .

. . . .

Ich denke, dass diese Aufgabe mit den zur Verfügung gestellten Tools nicht lösbar ist: ☐

Geben Sie dem Testleiter Bescheid, sobald Sie die Aufgabe beendet haben: ☐

23

OTRS::ITSM

Aufgabe 16. Nennen Sie diejenigen Computer, die vom selben Modell sind wie der Computer "morn".

Beispiel:

- seestern

Geben Sie dem Testleiter Bescheid, sobald Sie bereit sind, mit der Aufgabe zu beginnen: □

Antwort:

....
....
....
....
....
....
....
....
....
....

Ich denke, dass diese Aufgabe mit den zur Verfügung gestellten Tools nicht lösbar ist: □

Geben Sie dem Testleiter Bescheid, sobald Sie die Aufgabe beendet haben: □

24

OTRS::ITSM

Aufgabe 17. Benennen Sie diejenigen Benutzer und Benutzergruppen, die lokale Administratoren auf dem Computer "grima" sind. Als Lösungen werden Vor- und Nachname, der Benutzername oder der Gruppenname anerkannt.

Beispiel:

- Paul Krause
- krause

Geben Sie dem Testleiter Bescheid, sobald Sie bereit sind, mit der Aufgabe zu beginnen: ☐

Antwort:

....

....

....

....

....

....

....

....

....

Ich denke, dass diese Aufgabe mit den zur Verfügung gestellten Tools nicht lösbar ist: ☐

Geben Sie dem Testleiter Bescheid, sobald Sie die Aufgabe beendet haben: ☐

25

OTRS::ITSM

Aufgabe 18. Benennen Sie diejenigen Computer, auf denen der Benutzer "hschmidt" Administrator ist.

Beispiel:

- seestern

Geben Sie dem Testleiter Bescheid, sobald Sie bereit sind, mit der Aufgabe zu beginnen: ☐

Antwort:

....

....

....

....

....

....

....

....

....

Ich denke, dass diese Aufgabe mit den zur Verfügung gestellten Tools nicht lösbar ist: ☐

Geben Sie dem Testleiter Bescheid, sobald Sie die Aufgabe beendet haben: ☐

26

OTRS::ITSM

Aufgabe 19. Fügen Sie den Text "Hallo Welt!" zur Beschreibung des Computers "dns1" hinzu.

Geben Sie dem Testleiter Bescheid, sobald Sie bereit sind, mit der Aufgabe zu beginnen: ☐

Ich denke, dass diese Aufgabe mit den zur Verfügung gestellten Tools nicht lösbar ist: ☐

Geben Sie dem Testleiter Bescheid, sobald Sie die Aufgabe beendet haben: ☐

27

OTRS::ITSM

Aufgabe 20. Formatieren Sie den in der vorigen Aufgabe eingefügten Text "Welt!" in der Beschreibung des Computers "dns1" in Fettschrift.

Geben Sie dem Testleiter Bescheid, sobald Sie bereit sind, mit der Aufgabe zu beginnen: □

Ich denke, dass diese Aufgabe mit den zur Verfügung gestellten Tools nicht lösbar ist: □

Geben Sie dem Testleiter Bescheid, sobald Sie die Aufgabe beendet haben: □

28

OTRS::ITSM

Aufgabe 21. Fügen Sie in der Beschreibung des Computers "dns1" den Text "Dieser Computer wurde durch den Computer dns3 ersetzt." ein. Machen Sie die Zeichenfolge "dns3" zu einem Link zum Computer "dns3".

Geben Sie dem Testleiter Bescheid, sobald Sie bereit sind, mit der Aufgabe zu beginnen: □

Ich denke, dass diese Aufgabe mit den zur Verfügung gestellten Tools nicht lösbar ist: □

Geben Sie dem Testleiter Bescheid, sobald Sie die Aufgabe beendet haben: □

29

OTRS::ITSM

Aufgabe 22. Erstellen Sie eine Liste aller Computer, die vom Modell "TestCom1000" sind.

Beispiel:

- seestern

Geben Sie dem Testleiter Bescheid, sobald Sie bereit sind, mit der Aufgabe zu beginnen: ☐

Antwort:

....

....

....

....

....

....

....

....

....

....

Ich denke, dass diese Aufgabe mit den zur Verfügung gestellten Tools nicht lösbar ist: ☐

Geben Sie dem Testleiter Bescheid, sobald Sie die Aufgabe beendet haben: ☐

30

OTRS::ITSM

Aufgabe 23. Erstellen Sie eine Liste aller Computer des Modells "ThinkPad T520", die "Mark Schmidt" als Besitzer haben.

Beispiel:

- seestern

Geben Sie dem Testleiter Bescheid, sobald Sie bereit sind, mit der Aufgabe zu beginnen: □

Antwort:

....

....

....

....

....

....

....

....

....

....

Ich denke, dass diese Aufgabe mit den zur Verfügung gestellten Tools nicht lösbar ist: □

Geben Sie dem Testleiter Bescheid, sobald Sie die Aufgabe beendet haben: □

31

OTRS::ITSM

Aufgabe 24. Die beiden Computer "rom" und "soran" zeigen die selben Symptome, die auf eine gemeinsame Problemursache hindeuten. Finden und benennen Sie diejenigen Eigenschaften, die die beiden Computer gemeinsam haben. Es ist ausreichend, die Ergebnisse stichwortartig anzugeben (z.B. "Office-Version").

Beispiel:

- gleiches Modell
- gleicher Hersteller

Geben Sie dem Testleiter Bescheid, sobald Sie bereit sind, mit der Aufgabe zu beginnen: □

Antwort:

....

....

....

....

....

....

....

....

....

....

Ich denke, dass diese Aufgabe mit den zur Verfügung gestellten Tools nicht lösbar ist: □

Geben Sie dem Testleiter Bescheid, sobald Sie die Aufgabe beendet haben: □

32

OTRS::ITSM

Aufgabe 25. Der Computer "quark" zeigt derzeit Symptome eines Problems, die sich vor dem 31.03.2014, 00:15 Uhr noch nicht gezeigt haben. Finden und benennen Sie diejenigen Eigenschaften des Computers, die sich seit diesem Zeitpunkt geändert haben. Es ist ausreichend, die Ergebnisse stichwortartig anzugeben (z.B. "Office-Version").

Beispiel:

- Programm installiert

Geben Sie dem Testleiter Bescheid, sobald Sie bereit sind, mit der Aufgabe zu beginnen: □

Antwort:

....

....

....

....

....

....

....

....

....

....

Ich denke, dass diese Aufgabe mit den zur Verfügung gestellten Tools nicht lösbar ist: □

Geben Sie dem Testleiter Bescheid, sobald Sie die Aufgabe beendet haben: □

33

Bewertung nach System Usability Scale

Hinweise:

- Dieser Fragebogen dient dazu, unmittelbar nach dem Ausführen der Aufgaben den Eindruck der Testpersonen von den getesteten Tools festzuhalten.
- Nachfolgend werden Ihnen zum gerade getesteten Tool zehn Aussagen präsentiert, zu der Sie bitte Ihren Grad der Zustimmung auf einer Skala von eins ("stimme überhaupt nicht zu") bis fünf ("stimme voll zu") ausdrücken.
- Bitte geben Sie Ihre Antworten spontan ab, d.h. kreuzen Sie diejenige Antwort an, welche Ihnen als erstes einfällt, ohne lange und intensiv nachzudenken.
- Es sollten alle Fragen angekreuzt werden. Falls Sie für eine Frage keine Antwort geben können, kreuzen Sie bitte die mittlere Position an.
- Bei Fragen können Sie sich gerne an den Testleiter wenden.

34

OTRS::ITSM

"Ich denke, dass ich das System gerne häufig benutzen würde."

stimme überhaupt nicht zu — stimme voll zu

☐ ☐ ☐ ☐ ☐
1 2 3 4 5

"Ich fand das System unnötig komplex."

stimme überhaupt nicht zu — stimme voll zu

☐ ☐ ☐ ☐ ☐
1 2 3 4 5

"Ich fand das System einfach zu benutzen."

stimme überhaupt nicht zu — stimme voll zu

☐ ☐ ☐ ☐ ☐
1 2 3 4 5

"Ich glaube, ich würde die Hilfe einer technisch versierten Person benötigen, um das System benutzen zu können."

stimme überhaupt nicht zu — stimme voll zu

☐ ☐ ☐ ☐ ☐
1 2 3 4 5

"Ich fand, die verschiedenen Funktionen in diesem System waren gut integriert."

stimme überhaupt nicht zu — stimme voll zu

☐ ☐ ☐ ☐ ☐
1 2 3 4 5

35

OTRS::ITSM

"Ich denke, das System enthielt zu viele Inkonsistenzen."

stimme überhaupt nicht zu				stimme voll zu
□	□	□	□	□
1	2	3	4	5

"Ich kann mir vorstellen, dass die meisten Menschen den Umgang mit diesem System sehr schnell lernen."

stimme überhaupt nicht zu				stimme voll zu
□	□	□	□	□
1	2	3	4	5

"Ich fand das System sehr umständlich zu nutzen."

stimme überhaupt nicht zu				stimme voll zu
□	□	□	□	□
1	2	3	4	5

"Ich fühlte mich bei der Benutzung des Systems sehr sicher."

stimme überhaupt nicht zu				stimme voll zu
□	□	□	□	□
1	2	3	4	5

"Ich musste eine Menge lernen, bevor ich anfangen konnte das System zu verwenden."

stimme überhaupt nicht zu				stimme voll zu
□	□	□	□	□
1	2	3	4	5

36

Pause

Sie haben den Test von OTRS::ITSM beendet.

Bitte schließen Sie die Remoteverbindung zum Computer "suzanna-eval-b.fzi.de" und machen Sie eine kurze Pause, bevor Sie fortfahren.

37

ITSM Wiki

Hinweise:

- Bitte lösen Sie die nachfolgenden Aufgaben ausschließlich mit Hilfe des ITSM Wikis.
- Die Umgebung für die Lösung der Aufgaben mit Hilfe des ITSM Wikis befindet sich auf dem Computer "suzanna-eval-c.fzi.de" (grüner Desktophintergrund).

Anweisung:

- Sobald Sie bereit sind, öffnen Sie bitte das Fenster für "suzanna-eval-c.fzi.de" und beginnen Sie mit dem Bearbeiten der Aufgaben.

38

ITSM Wiki

Aufgabe 26. Nennen Sie das Modell des Computers "tabita.fzi.de".

Beispiel:

- ThinkPad 530

Geben Sie dem Testleiter Bescheid, sobald Sie bereit sind, mit der Aufgabe zu beginnen: ☐

Antwort:

....

....

Ich denke, dass diese Aufgabe mit den zur Verfügung gestellten Tools nicht lösbar ist: ☐

Geben Sie dem Testleiter Bescheid, sobald Sie die Aufgabe beendet haben: ☐

39

ITSM Wiki

Aufgabe 27. Nennen Sie diejenigen Computer, die vom selben Modell sind wie der Computer "borak.fzi.de".

Beispiel:

- seestern.fzi.de

Geben Sie dem Testleiter Bescheid, sobald Sie bereit sind, mit der Aufgabe zu beginnen: ☐

Antwort:

....

....

....

....

....

....

....

....

....

....

Ich denke, dass diese Aufgabe mit den zur Verfügung gestellten Tools nicht lösbar ist: ☐

Geben Sie dem Testleiter Bescheid, sobald Sie die Aufgabe beendet haben: ☐

40

ITSM Wiki

Aufgabe 28. Benennen Sie diejenigen Benutzer und Benutzergruppen, die lokale Administratoren auf dem Computer "kimara.fzi.de" sind. Als Lösungen werden Vor- und Nachname, der Benutzername oder der Gruppenname anerkannt.

Beispiel:

- Paul Krause
- krause

Geben Sie dem Testleiter Bescheid, sobald Sie bereit sind, mit der Aufgabe zu beginnen: ☐

Antwort:

. . . .

. . . .

. . . .

. . . .

. . . .

. . . .

. . . .

. . . .

. . . .

. . . .

Ich denke, dass diese Aufgabe mit den zur Verfügung gestellten Tools nicht lösbar ist: ☐

Geben Sie dem Testleiter Bescheid, sobald Sie die Aufgabe beendet haben: ☐

41

ITSM Wiki

Aufgabe 29. Benennen Sie diejenigen Computer, auf denen der Benutzer "Max Jung (jung@fzi.de)" Administrator ist.

Beispiel:

- seestern.fzi.de

Geben Sie dem Testleiter Bescheid, sobald Sie bereit sind, mit der Aufgabe zu beginnen: ☐

Antwort:

....

....

....

....

....

....

....

....

....

....

Ich denke, dass diese Aufgabe mit den zur Verfügung gestellten Tools nicht lösbar ist: ☐

Geben Sie dem Testleiter Bescheid, sobald Sie die Aufgabe beendet haben: ☐

42

ITSM Wiki

Aufgabe 30. Fügen Sie den Text "Hallo Welt!" als Notiz im Tab "Notes" des Computers "web1.fzi.de" hinzu.

Geben Sie dem Testleiter Bescheid, sobald Sie bereit sind, mit der Aufgabe zu beginnen: □

Ich denke, dass diese Aufgabe mit den zur Verfügung gestellten Tools nicht lösbar ist: □

Geben Sie dem Testleiter Bescheid, sobald Sie die Aufgabe beendet haben: □

43

ITSM Wiki

Aufgabe 31. Formatieren Sie den in der vorigen Aufgabe eingefügten Text "Welt!" im Tab "Notes" des Computers "web1.fzi.de" in Fettschrift.

Geben Sie dem Testleiter Bescheid, sobald Sie bereit sind, mit der Aufgabe zu beginnen: ☐

Ich denke, dass diese Aufgabe mit den zur Verfügung gestellten Tools nicht lösbar ist: ☐

Geben Sie dem Testleiter Bescheid, sobald Sie die Aufgabe beendet haben: ☐

44

ITSM Wiki

Aufgabe 32. Fügen Sie im Tab "Notes" des Computers "web1.fzi.de" den Text "Dieser Computer wurde durch den Computer web3.fzi.de ersetzt." ein. Machen Sie die Zeichenfolge "web3.fzi.de" zu einem Link zum Computer "web3.fzi.de".

Geben Sie dem Testleiter Bescheid, sobald Sie bereit sind, mit der Aufgabe zu beginnen: □

Ich denke, dass diese Aufgabe mit den zur Verfügung gestellten Tools nicht lösbar ist: □

Geben Sie dem Testleiter Bescheid, sobald Sie die Aufgabe beendet haben: □

45

ITSM Wiki

Aufgabe 33. Erstellen Sie eine Liste aller Computer, die vom Modell "TestGear1000" sind.

Beispiel:

- seestern.fzi.de

Geben Sie dem Testleiter Bescheid, sobald Sie bereit sind, mit der Aufgabe zu beginnen: □

Antwort:

....

....

....

....

....

....

....

....

....

....

Ich denke, dass diese Aufgabe mit den zur Verfügung gestellten Tools nicht lösbar ist: □

Geben Sie dem Testleiter Bescheid, sobald Sie die Aufgabe beendet haben: □

46

ITSM Wiki

Aufgabe 34. Erstellen Sie eine Liste aller Computer des Modells "OptiPlex 790", die "Mark Hahn (hahn@fzi.de)" als Besitzer haben.

Beispiel:

- seestern.fzi.de

Verwenden Sie für das Lösen dieser Aufgabe die folgenden Hilfsmittel:

- Den aus dem Trainingsteil bekannten Semantic MediaWiki Abfrage-Mechanismus.
- Die aus dem Trainingsteil bekannten Beispiel-Abfragen befinden sich auf der Startseite unter dem Link "Aufgaben-Beispiele" unterhalb der Überschrift "Aufgaben-Abfragen".
- Bitte verwenden Sie für die Lösung der Aufgabe die Wiki-Seite "Aufgabe", welche von der Startseite aus unterhalb der Überschrift "Aufgaben-Abfragen" zu finden ist.

Geben Sie dem Testleiter Bescheid, sobald Sie bereit sind, mit der Aufgabe zu beginnen: ☐

Antwort:

....

....

....

....

....

....

....

....

....

....

Ich denke, dass diese Aufgabe mit den zur Verfügung gestellten Tools nicht lösbar ist: ☐

Geben Sie dem Testleiter Bescheid, sobald Sie die Aufgabe beendet haben: ☐

47

ITSM Wiki

Aufgabe 35. Die beiden Computer "larissa.fzi.de" und "zander.fzi.de" zeigen die selben Symptome, die auf eine gemeinsame Problemursache hindeuten. Finden und benennen Sie diejenigen Eigenschaften, die die beiden Computer gemeinsam haben. Es ist ausreichend, die Ergebnisse stichwortartig anzugeben (z.B. "Office-Version").

Beispiel:

- gleiches Modell
- gleicher Hersteller

Verwenden Sie für das Lösen dieser Aufgabe die folgenden Hilfsmittel:

- Den aus dem Trainingsteil bekannten Problem Analyzer.

Geben Sie dem Testleiter Bescheid, sobald Sie bereit sind, mit der Aufgabe zu beginnen: □

Antwort:

....

....

....

....

....

....

....

....

....

....

Ich denke, dass diese Aufgabe mit den zur Verfügung gestellten Tools nicht lösbar ist: □

Geben Sie dem Testleiter Bescheid, sobald Sie die Aufgabe beendet haben: □

48

ITSM Wiki

Aufgabe 36. Der Computer “orthos.fzi.de” zeigt derzeit Symptome eines Problems, die sich vor dem 01.04.2014, 16:40 Uhr noch nicht gezeigt haben. Finden und benennen Sie diejenigen Eigenschaften des Computers, die sich seit diesem Zeitpunkt geändert haben. Es ist ausreichend, die Ergebnisse stichwortartig anzugeben (z.B. “Office-Version”).

Beispiel:

- Programm installiert

Verwenden Sie für das Lösen dieser Aufgabe die folgenden Hilfsmittel:

- Den aus dem Trainingsteil bekannten Problem Analyzer.

Geben Sie dem Testleiter Bescheid, sobald Sie bereit sind, mit der Aufgabe zu beginnen: □

Antwort:

....

....

....

....

....

....

....

....

....

....

Ich denke, dass diese Aufgabe mit den zur Verfügung gestellten Tools nicht lösbar ist: □

Geben Sie dem Testleiter Bescheid, sobald Sie die Aufgabe beendet haben: □

49

ITSM Wiki

Aufgabe 37. Aktivieren Sie das Infrastruktur Monitoring (Ping-Anfragen) für den Computer "eva.fzi.de".

Geben Sie dem Testleiter Bescheid, sobald Sie bereit sind, mit der Aufgabe zu beginnen: ☐

Ich denke, dass diese Aufgabe mit den zur Verfügung gestellten Tools nicht lösbar ist: ☐

Geben Sie dem Testleiter Bescheid, sobald Sie die Aufgabe beendet haben: ☐

50

ITSM Wiki

Aufgabe 38. Aktivieren Sie das Überwachen des DHCP-Dienstes für den Computer "eva.fzi.de".

Geben Sie dem Testleiter Bescheid, sobald Sie bereit sind, mit der Aufgabe zu beginnen: □

Ich denke, dass diese Aufgabe mit den zur Verfügung gestellten Tools nicht lösbar ist: □

Geben Sie dem Testleiter Bescheid, sobald Sie die Aufgabe beendet haben: □

51

Bewertung nach System Usability Scale

Hinweise:

- Dieser Fragebogen dient dazu, unmittelbar nach dem Ausführen der Aufgaben den Eindruck der Testpersonen von den getesteten Tools festzuhalten.
- Nachfolgend werden Ihnen zum gerade getesteten Tool zehn Aussagen präsentiert, zu der Sie bitte Ihren Grad der Zustimmung auf einer Skala von eins ("stimme überhaupt nicht zu") bis fünf ("stimme voll zu") ausdrücken.
- Bitte geben Sie Ihre Antworten spontan ab, d.h. kreuzen Sie diejenige Antwort an, welche Ihnen als erstes einfällt, ohne lange und intensiv nachzudenken.
- Es sollten alle Fragen angekreuzt werden. Falls Sie für eine Frage keine Antwort geben können, kreuzen Sie bitte die mittlere Position an.
- Bei Fragen können Sie sich gerne an den Testleiter wenden.

52

ITSM Wiki

"Ich denke, dass ich das System gerne häufig benutzen würde."

stimme überhaupt nicht zu — stimme voll zu

☐ ☐ ☐ ☐ ☐
1 2 3 4 5

"Ich fand das System unnötig komplex."

stimme überhaupt nicht zu — stimme voll zu

☐ ☐ ☐ ☐ ☐
1 2 3 4 5

"Ich fand das System einfach zu benutzen."

stimme überhaupt nicht zu — stimme voll zu

☐ ☐ ☐ ☐ ☐
1 2 3 4 5

"Ich glaube, ich würde die Hilfe einer technisch versierten Person benötigen, um das System benutzen zu können."

stimme überhaupt nicht zu — stimme voll zu

☐ ☐ ☐ ☐ ☐
1 2 3 4 5

"Ich fand, die verschiedenen Funktionen in diesem System waren gut integriert."

stimme überhaupt nicht zu — stimme voll zu

☐ ☐ ☐ ☐ ☐
1 2 3 4 5

53

ITSM Wiki

"Ich denke, das System enthielt zu viele Inkonsistenzen."

stimme überhaupt nicht zu					stimme voll zu
	□	□	□	□	□
	1	2	3	4	5

"Ich kann mir vorstellen, dass die meisten Menschen den Umgang mit diesem System sehr schnell lernen."

stimme überhaupt nicht zu					stimme voll zu
	□	□	□	□	□
	1	2	3	4	5

"Ich fand das System sehr umständlich zu nutzen."

stimme überhaupt nicht zu					stimme voll zu
	□	□	□	□	□
	1	2	3	4	5

"Ich fühlte mich bei der Benutzung des Systems sehr sicher."

stimme überhaupt nicht zu					stimme voll zu
	□	□	□	□	□
	1	2	3	4	5

"Ich musste eine Menge lernen, bevor ich anfangen konnte das System zu verwenden."

stimme überhaupt nicht zu					stimme voll zu
	□	□	□	□	□
	1	2	3	4	5

54

Pause

Sie haben den Test des ITSM Wikis beendet.

Bitte schließen Sie die Remoteverbindung zum Computer "suzanna-eval-c.fzi.de" und machen Sie eine kurze Pause, bevor Sie fortfahren.

55

Nach-Test Fragebogen

Name des Testleiters *(Wird vom Testleiter eingetragen)*:

. . . .

Personennummer *(Wird vom Testleiter eingetragen)*:

. . . .

Datum *(Wird vom Testleiter eingetragen)*:

. . . .

1

Hinweise:

- Dieser Fragebogen dient dazu, nach dem Ausführen der Aufgaben einen Eindruck der Testpersonen von den getesteten Tools zu erhalten.
- Es sollten alle Fragen angekreuzt werden. Falls Sie für eine Frage keine Antwort geben können, kreuzen Sie bitte die mittlere Position an.
- Bei Fragen können Sie sich gerne an den Testleiter wenden.

2

"Ich denke, dass die Verwendung des ITSM Wikis meine Arbeit als Administrator vereinfachen kann."

stimme überhaupt nicht zu — stimme voll zu

☐ ☐ ☐ ☐ ☐
1 2 3 4 5

"Das Finden von Informationen fiel mir im ITSM Wiki leichter als mit den klassischen Tools."

stimme überhaupt nicht zu — stimme voll zu

☐ ☐ ☐ ☐ ☐
1 2 3 4 5

"Das Finden von Informationen fiel mir im ITSM Wiki leichter als mit OTRS::ITSM."

stimme überhaupt nicht zu — stimme voll zu

☐ ☐ ☐ ☐ ☐
1 2 3 4 5

"Das Einfügen und Editieren von Informationen fiel mir im ITSM Wiki leichter als mit den klassischen Tools."

stimme überhaupt nicht zu — stimme voll zu

☐ ☐ ☐ ☐ ☐
1 2 3 4 5

"Das Einfügen und Editieren von Informationen fiel mir im ITSM Wiki leichter als mit OTRS::ITSM."

stimme überhaupt nicht zu — stimme voll zu

☐ ☐ ☐ ☐ ☐
1 2 3 4 5

3

"Ich finde es vorteilhaft, dass im ITSM Wiki alle Informationen in einem Tool integriert sind"

stimme überhaupt nicht zu					stimme voll zu
	□	□	□	□	□
	1	2	3	4	5

"Ein semantisches Wiki wie das ITSM Wiki bietet mir Vorteile beim Abrufen von Informationen im Vergleich zu den von mir derzeit eingesetzten Tools."

stimme überhaupt nicht zu					stimme voll zu
	□	□	□	□	□
	1	2	3	4	5

"Das ITSM Wiki vereinfacht das Konfigurieren von Infrastruktur-Monitoring."

stimme überhaupt nicht zu					stimme voll zu
	□	□	□	□	□
	1	2	3	4	5

"Der Problem Analyzer verringert die Zeit und den Aufwand beim Finden von Problemursachen."

stimme überhaupt nicht zu					stimme voll zu
	□	□	□	□	□
	1	2	3	4	5

4

“Ich kann mir vorstellen, dass sich durch die Integration der im ITSM Wiki vorgestellten Mechanismen andere IT Administrations-Tools verbessern lassen (z.B. durch die Integration von Wiki-Freitext und Semantic MediaWiki Abfragen in die Windows Benutzer- und Computer-Verwaltung).”

stimme überhaupt nicht zu					stimme voll zu
	☐	☐	☐	☐	☐
	1	2	3	4	5

5

Am ITSM Wiki gefiel mir besonders:

....

....

....

....

....

....

....

....

....

....

Am ITSM Wiki gefiel mir nicht:

....

....

....

....

....

....

....

....

....

....

6

Bei meiner täglichen Arbeit würde ich vom ITSM Wiki folgendermaßen profitieren:

. . . .

. . . .

. . . .

. . . .

. . . .

. . . .

. . . .

. . . .

. . . .

. . . .

Am ITSM Wiki würde ich Folgendes verbessern:

. . . .

. . . .

. . . .

. . . .

. . . .

. . . .

. . . .

. . . .

. . . .

. . . .

7

Kommentare:

. . . .

. . . .

. . . .

. . . .

. . . .

. . . .

. . . .

. . . .

. . . .

. . . .

Um eine möglichst große Unvoreingenommenheit aller Testpersonen zu gewährleisten, bitte ich darum, bis zum endgültigen Abschluss der Studie nicht über deren Inhalte (Fragen, Antworten, Aufgaben, etc.) zu sprechen.

Vielen Dank für die Teilnahme an der Benutzerstudie!

8

C.2. User Study Data

The following tables show the raw data from the tasks of the user study:

- Table C.1 shows the raw task data of the legacy tools.
- Table C.2 shows the raw task data of OTRS::ITSM.
- Table C.3 shows the raw task data of the ITSM Wiki.

Numbers indicate the time in seconds that the participants needed to complete the tasks. The letters used in the tables have the following meanings:

- P: partial answer
- W: wrong answer
- C: canceled by participant

Raw data of the SUS and posttest questionnaires is shown in the following tables:

- Table C.4 shows the data of the legacy tools.
- Table C.5 shows the raw SUS scores of OTRS::ITSM.
- Table C.6 shows the raw SUS scores of the ITSM Wiki.
- Table C.7 shows the raw data of the posttest questionnaire.

Task	P01	P02	P03	P04	P05	P06	P07	P08	P09	P10
Task 1a	28	45	42	39	46	127	32	36	44	47
Task 1b	164	509	335	408	367	712	405	422	360	335
Task 2	76	94	65	155	97	149	76	80	201	W
Task 3	46	92	76	W	P	99	P	C	155	W
Task 4	C	C	C	P	C	C	C	C	C	C
Task 5	24	36	18	19	25	185	33	55	34	36
Task 6	17	22	12	10	11	239	14	12	24	42
Task 7	32	59	138	54	159	240	38	35	89	77
Task 8	53	69	51	62	69	109	61	80	101	105
Task 9	95	104	P	131	61	346	77	64	104	193
Task 10	P	W	985	1081	W	W	W	C	1157	P
Task 11	163	P	267	P	P	P	P	C	708	P
Task 12	78	303	498	91	69	556	158	230	222	C
Task 13	58	126	W	W	101	C	C	W	94	C

Table C.1.: Raw Task Data of the Legacy Tools

Task	P01	P02	P03	P04	P05	P06	P07	P08	P09	P10
Task 1	49	44	51	39	43	185	48	43	52	134
Task 2	59	110	61	42	141	96	73	54	62	C
Task 3	40	C	60	44	54	112	58	66	52	W
Task 4	28	C	45	33	41	65	32	34	47	C
Task 5	23	48	29	36	26	188	60	37	50	78
Task 6	C	C	C	C	C	C	C	C	C	C
Task 7	P	C	C	C	C	C	C	C	C	C
Task 8	32	48	38	32	39	51	36	48	34	118
Task 9	53	121	46	91	42	443	W	59	66	120
Task 10	97	P	163	131	169	W	150	328	P	P
Task 11	87	C	125	138	100	C	P	P	C	108

Table C.2.: Raw Task Data of OTRS::ITSM

Task	P01	P02	P03	P04	P05	P06	P07	P08	P09	P10
Task 1	21	30	27	24	21	29	18	26	22	30
Task 2	122	36	75	31	34	71	40	49	38	120
Task 3	58	C	54	57	64	133	63	62	109	376
Task 4	30	41	33	43	30	C	65	36	33	34
Task 5	22	56	75	25	P	81	41	58	41	42
Task 6	15	32	31	18	P	26	17	21	14	17
Task 7	74	85	56	55	C	137	29	54	68	76
Task 8	233	264	58	51	36	92	41	191	68	75
Task 9	207	332	109	156	152	C	218	112	137	261
Task 10	269	133	111	188	286	199	168	220	174	P
Task 11	123	191	110	154	314	196	169	200	224	218
Task 12	70	68	46	21	39	78	35	34	51	C
Task 13	34	43	30	19	23	57	21	25	34	C

Table C.3.: Raw Task Data of the ITSM Wiki

Statement	P01	P02	P03	P04	P05	P06	P07	P08	P09	P10
Statement 1	3	1	2	0	4	3	0	0	2	4
Statement 2	1	3	1	0	4	2	1	1	1	3
Statement 3	2	3	2	0	4	3	0	1	3	3
Statement 4	0	2	2	2	4	3	3	1	2	4
Statement 5	1	1	1	1	3	3	0	1	2	4
Statement 6	0	2	1	0	4	3	3	1	1	3
Statement 7	2	1	1	1	4	3	0	0	1	3
Statement 8	2	1	0	0	4	3	1	1	1	3
Statement 9	4	3	2	1	3	1	1	1	1	3
Statement 10	3	4	1	1	4	2	2	1	3	3
Sum	18	21	13	6	38	26	11	8	17	33
Result (Sum*2.5)	**45**	**52.5**	**32.5**	**15**	**95**	**65**	**27.5**	**20**	**42.5**	**82.5**

Table C.4.: Raw SUS Scores of the Legacy Tools

Statement	P01	P02	P03	P04	P05	P06	P07	P08	P09	P10
Statement 1	4	2	0	2	3	3	2	1	4	4
Statement 2	3	2	2	3	3	1	1	3	3	4
Statement 3	4	3	2	3	4	3	1	3	4	3
Statement 4	3	4	4	4	3	3	4	4	4	4
Statement 5	1	2	0	1	3	3	1	1	3	3
Statement 6	4	4	1	2	3	2	4	2	4	4
Statement 7	4	3	2	3	3	1	3	1	4	4
Statement 8	3	4	0	2	4	3	2	1	1	3
Statement 9	4	3	2	2	3	2	2	3	2	3
Statement 10	3	4	4	4	4	3	4	4	4	4
Sum	33	31	17	26	33	24	24	23	33	36
Result (Sum*2.5)	**82.5**	**77.5**	**42.5**	**65**	**82.5**	**60**	**60**	**57.5**	**82.5**	**90**

Table C.5.: Raw SUS Scores of OTRS::ITSM

Statement	P01	P02	P03	P04	P05	P06	P07	P08	P09	P10
Statement 1	3	3	4	4	1	3	3	3	4	3
Statement 2	2	4	3	3	3	3	3	1	4	4
Statement 3	2	3	4	3	2	4	2	3	4	3
Statement 4	4	4	4	4	3	3	4	3	4	4
Statement 5	4	3	2	4	2	3	4	1	4	3
Statement 6	4	4	3	3	2	4	4	1	4	4
Statement 7	3	3	1	4	2	2	3	1	4	4
Statement 8	2	4	3	4	3	3	4	3	4	3
Statement 9	3	3	3	3	1	3	3	2	4	3
Statement 10	2	4	4	4	4	3	4	4	4	1
Sum	29	35	31	36	23	31	34	22	40	32
Result (Sum*2.5)	**72.5**	**87.5**	**77.5**	**90**	**57.5**	**77.5**	**85**	**55**	**100**	**80**

Table C.6.: Raw SUS Scores of the ITSM Wiki

Statement	P01	P02	P03	P04	P05	P06	P07	P08	P09	P10
Statement 1	5	4	5	5	3	4	4	5	5	4
Statement 2	3	4	5	4	2	4	5	5	5	5
Statement 3	2	5	5	3	2	5	4	4	2	1
Statement 4	2	5	3	5	2	4	5	4	5	4
Statement 5	2	5	3	4	2	4	3	3	3	1
Statement 6	5	5	5	3	3	5	5	4	5	4
Statement 7	4	4	5	5	3	3	5	4	4	4
Statement 8	5	4	5	5	2	5	5	4	4	5
Statement 9	3	4	4	4	4	4	4	3	5	2
Statement 10	3	4	5	4	4	4	5	4	4	4

Table C.7.: Raw Posttest Questionnaire Scores

List of Abbreviations and Acronyms

ADDS	Active Directory Domain Services
AMIS	Availability Management Information System
API	Application Programming Interface
ARP	Address Resolution Protocol
ATA	Advanced Technology Attachment with Packet Interface
BCP	Business Continuity Plan
BIA	Business Impact Analysis
BIOS	Basic Input/Output System
CAB	Change Advisory Board
CI	Configuration Item
CIM	Common Information Model
CIO	Chief Information Officer
CMDB	Configuration Management Database
CMIP	Common Management Information Protocol
DML	Definitive Media Library
CMS	Configuration Management System
CPU	Central Processing Unit
CSI	Continual Service Improvement
CSV	Comma-separated values
DHCP	Dynamic Host Configuration Protocol
DL	Description Logics
DNS	Domain Name System
DSL	Domain-Specific Language
ECAB	Emergency Change Advisory Board
FCMDB	Federated Configuration Management Database
FOAF	Friend of a Friend
FTA	Fault Tree Analysis
FZI	Forschungszentrum Informatik
GPL	GNU General Public License
HDD	Hard Disk Drive
HTML	Hypertext Markup Language
IaaS	Infrastructure-as-a-Service

IDE	Integrated Drive Electronics
IDS	Intrusion Detection System
IEC	International Electrotechnical Commission
IP	Internet Protocol
ISO	International Organization for Standardization
ISM	Information Security Management
IP	Internet Protocol
IT	Information Technology
ITIL	IT Infrastructure Library
ITSCM	IT Service Continuity Management
ITSM	IT Service Management
KBS	Knowledge-Based Systems
KIT	Karlsruhe Institute of Technology
KM	Knowledge Management
LAMP	Linux, Apache, MySQL, PHP
LB	Lower Bound
LDAP	Lightweight Directory Access Protocol
MAC	Media Access Control
MIB	Management Information Base
MW	MediaWiki
N3	Notation 3
OCL	Object Constraint Language
OLA	Operational Level Agreement
OSI	Open Systems Interconnection
OTRS	Open-source Ticket Request System
OWL	Web Ontology Language
PDCA	Plan-Do-Check-Act
PDF	Portable Document Format
PHP	PHP Hypertext Preprocessor
RA	Risk Analysis
RAM	Random Access Memory
RDF	Resource Description Framework
RDFS	Resource Description Framework Schema
RfC	Request for Comment
RFC	Request for Change
RuD	Rechner- und Datenkommunikationsdienste
SACM	Service Asset and Configuration Management
SAS	Serial Attached SCSI
SATA	Serial ATA
SCD	Supplier and Contract Database
SCM	Service Capacity Management
SCSI	Small Computer System Interface
SD	Standard Deviation

SDN	Software-defined Networking
SIP	Service Improvement Plan
SKMS	Service Knowledge Management System
SLA	Service Level Agreement
SLM	Service Level Management
SLR	Service Level Requirement
S.M.A.R.T.	Self-Monitoring, Analysis and Reporting Technology
SME	Small and Medium-sized Enterprise
SMIv2	Structure of Management Information Version 2
SMW	Semantic MediaWiki
SMW+	Semantic MediaWiki+
SNMP	Simple Network Management Protocol
SPARQL	SPARQL Protocol and RDF Query Language
SPM	Service Portfolio Management
SPoF	Single Point of Failure
SQL	Structured Query Language
SSD	Solid-state Drive
SSH	Secure Shell
SUS	System Usability Scale
SWRL	Semantic Web Rule Language
TCP	Transmission Control Protocol
TMG	Microsoft Forefront Threat Management Gateway
UB	Upper Bound
UDP	User Datagram Protocol
UML	Unified Modeling Language
UPS	Uninterruptible Power Supply
URI	Uniform Resource Identifier
URL	Uniform Resource Locator
URN	Uniform Resource Name
USB	Universal Serial Bus
VM	Virtual Machine
VoIP	Voice over Internet Protocol
W3C	World Wide Web Consortium
WAP	Wireless Access Point
WBEM	Web-Based Enterprise Management
WebDAV	Web-based Distributed Authoring and Versioning
WMI	Windows Management Instrumentation
WSUS	Windows Server Update Services
WYSIWYG	What You See Is What You Get
XHTML	eXtensible HyperText Markup Language
XML	Extensible Markup Language
XSD	XML Schema (Definition)

List of Figures

List of Tables

List of Algorithms

Listings

Bibliography

[ACC+10] Yatresh K Agarwal, Bill Cary, Sandy Cash, Leandro Cassa, Brian Demartini, Chris Duplantis, Alisson Negrisolo de Godoi, Douglas Barranqueiros Gomes, Vasfi Gucer, Murat Kipel, Antonio Orlando Neto, Caio Saad, Ghufran Shah, Peterson Domingos Tamarindo, and Krishnan Venkitasubramanian. *IBM Tivoli Change and Configuration Management Database (CCMDB) V7.2.1 Implementation Guide*. IBM Redbooks. IBM Corporation, International Technical Support Organization, Poughkeepsie, first edition, December 2010. `http://www.redbooks.ibm.com/redbooks/pdfs/sg247879.pdf`. (accessed 2011-03-07). ISBN: 978-0-7384-3494-0. 109

[Add07] Rob Addy. *Effective IT Service Management: To ITIL and Beyond!* Springer, Berlin, first edition, September 2007. ISBN: 978-3-540-73197-9. 12, 19, 32, 42, 52, 59, 98, 100, 101, 102, 190, 191, 192, 199

[ADR06] Sören Auer, Sebastian Dietzold, and Thomas Riechert. OntoWiki – A Tool for Social, Semantic Collaboration. In Isabel F. Cruz, Stefan Decker, Dean Allemang, Chris Preist, Daniel Schwabe, Peter Mika, Michael Uschold, and Lora Aroyo, editors, *The Semantic Web – ISWC 2006: 5th International Semantic Web Conference, ISWC 2006*, volume 4273 of *Lecture Notes in Computer Science (LNCS)*, pages 736–749, Athens, GA, USA, November 2006. Springer, Berlin. ISBN: 978-3-540-49029-6. 118, 119

[AGJP09] Ofer Arazy, Ian Gellatly, Soobaek Jang, and Raymond Patterson. Wiki Deployment in Corporate Settings. *Technology and Society Magazine, IEEE*, 28(2):57–64, Summer 2009. 77

[AH06] Robbie Allen and Laura E. Hunter. *Active Directory Cookbook*. O'Reilly Media, Sebastopol, second edition, June 2006. ISBN: 978-0-596-10202-9. 213

[AH08] Dean Allemang and James A. Hendler. *Semantic Web for the Working Ontologist: Effective Modeling in RDFS and OWL*. Morgan Kaufmann, Burlington, second edition, June 2008. ISBN: 978-0-12-373556-0. 62, 63, 64, 65, 66, 67, 69

[AK09] F. Abdoli and M. Kahani. Ontology-based Distributed Intrusion Detection System. In *Computer Conference, 2009. CSICC 2009. 14th International CSI*, pages 65–70, 2009. 283

[Ama12] Amazon Web Services LLC. AWS Management Console. `http://aws.amazon.com/console/`, 2012. (accessed 2012-12-07). 314

[AMJ09] Laurent Alquier, Keith McCormick, and Ed Jaeger. knowIT, a Semantic Informatics Knowledge Management System. In Riehle and Bruckman [RB09], pages 20:1–20:5. ISBN: 978-1-60558-730-1. 160

[Apa11] Apache Software Foundation. Apache HTTP Server Version 2.2 Documentation. `http://httpd.apache.org/docs/2.2/`, 2011. (accessed 2011-02-02). 433

[Apa12] Apache CloudStack Project. CloudStack User Interface Customization Guide. `http://docs.cloudstack.org/@api/deki/files/191/CloudStack3.0UserInterfaceCustomization.pdf`, June 2012. (accessed 2012-12-07). 314

[Arr13] Valerie Arraj. ITIL: The Basics. `http://www.best-management-practice.com/gempdf/ITIL_The_Basics.pdf`, July 2013. (accessed 2014-10-01). 1

[AT13] Bill Albert and Tom Tullis. *Measuring the User Experience (Interactive Technologies): Collecting, Analyzing, and Presenting Usability Metrics*. Morgan Kaufmann, Burlington, second edition, August 2013. ISBN: 978-0-12-415781-1. 384, 397, 414, 415

[AvH04] Grigoris Antoniou and Frank van Harmelen. *A Semantic Web Primer*. Cooperative Information Systems. MIT Press, Massachusetts, first edition, July 2004. ISBN: 978-0-262-01210-2. 62

[Axe99] Stefan Axelsson. The Base-Rate Fallacy and its Implications for the Difficulty of Intrusion Detection. In Juzar Motiwalla and Gene Tsudik, editors, *CCS '99: Proceedings of the 6th ACM Conference on Computer and Communications Security*, pages 1–7, New York, USA, 1999. ACM. ISBN: 1-58113-148-8. 263

[Axe00] Stefan Axelsson. The Base-Rate Fallacy and the Difficulty of Intrusion Detection. *ACM Trans. Inf. Syst. Secur.*, 3(3):186–205, 2000. 263

[Bal09] Helmut Balzert. *Lehrbuch der Softwaretechnik: Basiskonzepte und Requirements Engineering*. Spektrum Akademischer Verlag, Heidelberg, third edition, September 2009. ISBN: 978-3-8274-1705-3. 192, 193, 194, 196, 237, 240, 264, 266, 267, 285, 287, 301, 302, 318

[Bar05] Wolfgang Barth. *Nagios: System and Network Monitoring*. No Starch, San Francisco, first edition, December 2005. ISBN: 978-1-59327-070-4. 187, 236, 243, 247, 434

[Bar08] Daniel J. Barrett. *MediaWiki (Wikipedia and Beyond)*. O'Reilly Media, Sebastopol, first edition, October 2008. ISBN: 978-0-596-51979-7. 77, 121, 122, 123, 124, 434

[Bar10] Carol M. Barnum. *Usability Testing Essentials: Ready, Set...Test*. Morgan Kaufmann, Burlington, October 2010. ISBN: 978-0-12-375092-1. 384

[BC08] Rory Bray and Daniel Cid. *OSSEC Host-Based Intrusion Detection Guide*. Syngress, Burlington, March 2008. 271

[BCC06] Graciela Brusa, Ma. Laura Caliusco, and Omar Chiotti. A Process for Building a Domain Ontology: An Experience in Developing a Government Budgetary Ontology. In Mehmet A. Orgun and Thomas Meyer, editors, *Proceedings of the Second Australasian Workshop on Advances in Ontologies – Volume 72*, AOW '06, pages 7–15, Darlinghurst, Australia, 2006. Australian Computer Society, Inc. ISBN: 1-920682-53-8. 163

[BCCG09] G. Baioco, A.C.M. Costa, C.Z. Calvi, and A.S. Garcia. IT Service Management and Governance Modeling an ITSM Configuration Process: A Foundational Ontology Approach. In *International Symposium on Integrated Network Management, Workshops, 2009. IM '09. IFIP/IEEE*, pages 24–33, June 2009. 182, 183

[BDF+03] Paul Barham, Boris Dragovic, Keir Fraser, Steven Hand, Tim Harris, Alex Ho, Rolf Neugebauer, Ian Pratt, and Andrew Warfield. Xen and the Art of Virtualization. *SIGOPS Oper. Syst. Rev.*, 37:164–177, October 2003. 299, 306

[Bec04] Dave Beckett. RDF/XML Syntax Specification (Revised): W3C Recommendation 10 February 2004. `http://www.w3.org/TR/2004/REC-rdf-syntax-grammar-20040210/`, February 2004. (accessed 2010-10-10). 65, 66

[BG10] Dan Brickley and R.V. Guha. RDF Vocabulary Description Language 1.0: RDF Schema: W3C Recommendation 10 February 2004. `http://www.w3.org/TR/2004/REC-rdf-schema-20040210/`, February 2010. (accessed 2010-10-11). 66, 67

[BGE+08] Michel Buffa, Fabien Gandon, Guillaume Ereteo, Peter Sander, and Catherine Faron. SweetWiki: A Semantic Wiki. *Web Semantics: Science,*

Services and Agents on the World Wide Web, 6(1):84–97, 2008. 118, 119

[BHL01] Tim Berners-Lee, James Hendler, and Ora Lassila. The Semantic Web. *Scientific American*, May 2001. 61

[Bis04] Matt Bishop. *Introduction to Computer Security*. Addison-Wesley Longman, Amsterdam, December 2004. ISBN: 978-0-321-24744-5. 31

[BKNT09] Christian Baun, Marcel Kunze, Jens Nimis, and Stefan Tai. *Cloud Computing: Web-basierte dynamische IT-Services*. Informatik im Fokus. Springer, Berlin, first edition, November 2009. ISBN: 978-3-642-01593-9. 16, 299

[BKvH02] Jeen Broekstra, Arjohn Kampman, and Frank van Harmelen. Sesame: A Generic Architecture for Storing and Querying RDF and RDF Schema. In Ian Horrocks and James Hendler, editors, *The Semantic Web – ISWC 2002: First International Semantic Web Conference*, volume 2342 of *Lecture Notes in Computer Science (LNCS)*, pages 54–68, Sardinia, Italy, June 2002. Springer, Berlin. ISBN: 978-3-540-43760-4. 65

[BMC06] BMC Software. BMC Atrium CMDB – Das Herzstück Ihrer IT-Infrastruktur. `http://documents.bmc.com/products/documents/32/11/63211/63211.pdf`, 2006. (accessed 2010-09-14). 109

[BnLC96] Amaia Bernaras, Iñaki Laresgoiti, and Jose Manuel Corera. Building and Reusing Ontologies for Electrical Network Applications. In Wolfgang Wahlster, editor, *Proceedings of the 12th European Conference on Artificial Intelligence (ECAI 96)*, pages 298–302, Budapest, Hungary, August 1996. Wiley. 163

[Bro96] John Brooke. SUS – A Quick and Dirty Usability Scale. In P. W. Jordan, B. Thomas, B. A. Weerdmeester, and A. L. McClelland, editors, *Usability Evaluation in Industry*. Taylor and Francis, 1996. 386, 414, 415

[BRP10] Joachim Baumeister, Jochen Reutelshoefer, and Frank Puppe. KnowWE: A Semantic Wiki for Knowledge Engineering. *Applied Intelligence*, pages 1–22, 2010. 119

[Bru06] Jochen Brunnstein. *ITIL Security Management realisieren: IT-Service Security Management nach ITIL – So gehen Sie vor*. Vieweg+Teubner, Wiesbaden, first edition, September 2006. ISBN: 978-3-8348-0165-4. 32

[BSVW12] François Bry, Sebastian Schaffert, Denny Vrandečić, and Klara Weiand. Semantic Wikis: Approaches, Applications, and Perspectives. In Thomas Eiter and Thomas Krennwallner, editors, *Reasoning Web. Semantic Technologies for Advanced Query Answering*, volume 7487 of *Lecture Notes in Computer Science (LNCS)*, pages 329–369, Berlin, 2012. Springer. ISBN: 978-3-642-33157-2. 2, 118

[BT05] Ulrike Buhl and Jürgen Töns. *ITIL Praxisbuch. Beispiele und Tipps für die erfolgreiche Prozessoptimierung*. mitp, Frechen, first edition, 2005. ISBN: 978-3-8266-1583-2. 19, 24, 98

[BVGM08] Ralf Buchsein, Frank Victor, Holger Günther, and Volker Machmeier. *IT-Management mit ITIL(R) V3: Strategien, Kennzahlen, Umsetzung*. Vieweg+Teubner, Wiesbaden, second edition, 2008. ISBN: 978-3-8348-0526-3. 17

[CA07a] CA. CA CMDB r11.1. `http://www.ca.com/files/ProductBriefs/ca_cmdb_pb_de.pdf`, 2007. (accessed 2010-09-14). 109

[CA07b] CA. Technologie im Überblick: Implementierungsansätze für die CA CMDB: Implementierungsstrategien für die CMDB. `http://www.ca.com/files/TechnicalDocuments/cmdb_impl_tech_brief_de.pdf`, 2007. (accessed 2010-09-14). 109

[Car08] Nicholas G. Carr. *The Big Switch: Our New Digital Destiny*. Norton, New York, January 2008. ISBN: 978-0-393-06228-1. 16

[CEL+08] Denny Carl, Horst Eidenberger, Maik Ludewig, Stefan Mintert, Carlo Schulz, Bastian Spanneberg, and Gerhard Völkl. Mit heißer Feder – Fünf freie Wiki-Systeme im Vergleich. *iX – Magazin für professionelle Informationstechnik*, 12:50, December 2008. 117

[CFLGP06] Óscar Corcho, Mariano Fernández-López, and Asunción Gómez-Pérez. Ontological Engineering: Principles, Methods, Tools and Languages. In Coral Calero, Francisco Ruiz, and Mario Piattini, editors, *Ontologies for Software Engineering and Software Technology*, pages 1–48. Springer, Berlin, December 2006. ISBN: 978-3-540-34518-3. 163

[CFLGPLC03] Óscar Corcho, Mariano Fernández-López, Asunción Gómez-Pérez, and Angel López-Cima. Building Legal Ontologies with METHONTOLOGY and WebODE. In V. Richard Benjamins, Pompeu Casanovas, Joost Breuker, and Aldo Gangemi, editors, *Law and the Semantic Web*, volume 3369, pages 142–157, 2003. ISBN: 3-540-25063-8. 163

[CFSD90] Jeffrey D. Case, M. Fedor, Martin L. Schoffstall, and J. Davin. Simple Network Management Protocol (SNMP). RFC 1157 (Historic). http://www.ietf.org/rfc/rfc1157.txt, May 1990. (accessed 2011-03-01). 187

[Cha09] Don Chamberlin. SQL. In Liu and Özsu [LO09], pages 2753–2760. ISBN: 978-0-387-35544-3. 434

[Cho08] Mark S. Choate. *Professional Wikis: Collaboration on the Web*. Programmer to Programmer. Wiley & Sons, Hoboken, first edition, January 2008. ISBN: 978-0-470-12690-5. 77

[CHR+08] Alison Cartlidge, Ashley Hanna, Colin Rudd, Ivor Macfarlane, John Windebank, and Stuart Rance. An Introductory Overview of ITIL V3. http://www.itsmfi.org/content/introductory-overview-itil-v3-pdf, June 2008. (accessed 2009-10-15). 19

[Chr09] Vassilis Christophides. Resource Description Framework (RDF) Schema (RDFS). In Liu and Özsu [LO09], pages 2425–2428. ISBN: 978-0-387-35544-3. 67

[Cit10a] Citrix Systems Inc. XenServer 5.6 Feature Pack 1 Software Development Kit. http://support.citrix.com/servlet/KbServlet/download/25593-102-648887/sdk.pdf, December 2010. (accessed 2011-02-28). 306

[Cit10b] Citrix Systems Inc. XenServer Management API Revision 1.8. http://support.citrix.com/servlet/KbServlet/download/25589-102-648883/xenenterpriseapi.pdf, December 2010. (accessed 2011-02-28). 306

[Cit12] Citrix Systems, Inc. XenCenter. http://community.citrix.com/xencenter, 2012. (accessed 2012-12-07). 314

[CJ07] Ben Clacy and Brian Jennings. Service Management: Driving the Future of IT. *Computer*, 40(5):98–100, 2007. 12, 13

[Com00] Douglas E. Comer. *Internetworking with TCP/IP, Vol.1: Principles, Protocols, and Architectures*. Prentice Hall, Upper Saddle River, fourth edition, March 2000. ISBN: 978-0-13-018380-4. 217

[Con00] Dan Connolly. A Little History of the World Wide Web. http://www.w3.org/History.html, 2000. (accessed 2010-10-07). 61

[Cos09a] CosmoCode. WikiMatrix. http://www.wikimatrix.org/, 2009. (accessed 2009-11-09). 117

[Cos09b] CosmoCode. WikiMatrix Wiki Statistics – Open Source vs. Commercial. http://www.wikimatrix.org/statistic/Open+Source+vs.+Commercial, November 2009. (accessed 2009-11-09). 117

[Cos09c] CosmoCode. WikiMatrix Wiki Statistics – Programming Languages. http://www.wikimatrix.org/statistic/Programming+Languages, November 2009. (accessed 2009-11-09). 117

[CS07] Gary Case and George Spalding. *Continual Service Improvement*. ITIL Version 3. Stationery Office Books, Norwich, May 2007. ISBN: 978-0-11-331049-4. 13, 19, 53, 54, 55, 56, 57, 58, 59, 142, 143, 148, 158, 333, 334

[Cun02] Ward Cunningham. What Is Wiki. http://www.wiki.org/wiki.cgi?WhatIsWiki, June 2002. (accessed 2009-11-11). 70, 77

[Cun09a] Cunningham & Cunningham, Inc. Top Ten Wiki Engines. http://c2.com/cgi/wiki?TopTenWikiEngines, September 2009. (accessed 2009-11-09). 117

[Cun09b] Cunningham & Cunningham, Inc. Why Wiki Works. http://c2.com/cgi/wiki?WhyWikiWorks, October 2009. (accessed 2009-11-11). 71

[CW07] David Cannon and David Wheeldon. *Service Operation*. ITIL Version 3. Stationery Office Books, Norwich, May 2007. ISBN: 978-0-11-331046-3. 12, 19, 43, 44, 45, 46, 47, 48, 49, 50, 51, 52, 156, 181, 263, 293, 294

[Dar99] Keith Darlington. *The Essence of Expert Systems*. The Essence of Computing Series. Prentice Hall, Upper Saddle River, September 1999. ISBN: 978-0-13-022774-4. 297

[Dav00] Thomas H. Davenport. *Working Knowledge: How Organizations Manage What They Know*. McGraw-Hill Professional, New York, June 2000. ISBN: 978-1-57851-301-7. 145

[Dav05] Thomas H. Davenport. *Thinking for a Living: How to Get Better Performance and Results from Knowledge Workers*. McGraw-Hill Professional, New York, October 2005. ISBN: 978-1-59139-423-5. 145

[DDS10] Yuri Diogenes, Harrison Diogenes, and Mohit Saxena. *Microsoft Forefront Threat Management Gateway (TMG) Administrator's Companion*. Microsoft Press, Redmond, pap/cdr edition, February 2010. ISBN: 978-0-7356-2638-6. 94

[Dis09] Georg Disterer. Zertifizierung der IT nach ISO 20000. *Wirtschaftsinformatik*, 51:530–534, 2009. 16

[DMT03] DMTF. CIM Overview Document. `http://dmtf.org/sites/default/files/Why%20CIM%20Overview%20Document_2010.pdf`, June 2003. (accessed 2013-09-03). 214

[DMT12a] DMTF. Common Information Model (CIM) Infrastructure. `http://dmtf.org/sites/default/files/standards/documents/DSP0004_2.7.0.pdf`, April 2012. (accessed 2013-09-03). 214

[DMT12b] DMTF. Common Information Model (CIM) Metamodel. `http://dmtf.org/sites/default/files/standards/documents/DSP0004_3.0.0.pdf`, December 2012. (accessed 2013-09-03). 214

[DMT12c] DMTF. Managed Object Format (MOF). `http://dmtf.org/sites/default/files/standards/documents/DSP0221_3.0.0.pdf`, December 2012. (accessed 2013-09-03). 214

[DMT13a] DMTF. CIM FAQ. `http://dmtf.org/about/faq/cim_faq`, 2013. (accessed 2013-09-04). 214

[DMT13b] DMTF. Common Information Model (CIM) Standards. `http://dmtf.org/standards/cim`, 2013. (accessed 2013-09-03). 213

[DNMN09] Antonio De Nicola, Michele Missikoff, and Roberto Navigli. A Software Engineering Approach to Ontology Building. *Inf. Syst.*, 34:258–275, April 2009. 163

[DOS03] Michael C. Daconta, Leo J. Oberst, and Kevin T. Smith. *The Semantic Web: A Guide to the Future of XML, Web Services, and Knowledge Management*. Wiley & Sons, Hoboken, first edition, July 2003. ISBN: 978-0-471-43257-9. 66

[Dou01] Dale Dougherty. LAMP: The Open Source Web Platform. `http://onlamp.com/lpt/a/566`, January 2001. (accessed 2011-02-23). 194

[DS04] Mike Dean and Guus Schreiber. OWL Web Ontology Language Reference: W3C Recommendation 10 February 2004. `http://www.w3.org/TR/2004/REC-owl-ref-20040210/`, February 2004. (accessed 2010-10-12). 69

[Due08] Gunter Dueck. Bluepedia. *Informatik-Spektrum*, 31:262–269, 2008. 77

[dVVAB03] Jorge E. López de Vergara, Víctor A. Villagrá, Juan I. Asensio, and Julio Berrocal. Ontologies: Giving Semantics to Network Management Models. *Network, IEEE*, 17(3):15–21, May-June 2003. 232

[dVVB04] Jorge E. López de Vergara, Víctor A. Villagrá, and Julio Berrocal. Applying the Web Ontology Language to Management Information Definitions. *Communications Magazine, IEEE*, 42(7):68–74, July 2004. 232, 233

[dVVB05] Jorge E. López de Vergara, Víctor A. Villagrá, and Julio Berrocal. On the Formalization of the Common Information Model Metaschema. In Jürgen Schönwälder and Joan Serrat, editors, *Ambient Networks*, volume 3775 of *Lecture Notes in Computer Science (LNCS)*, pages 1–11. Springer, Berlin, 2005. 233

[EGHW07] Anja Ebersbach, Markus Glaser, Richard Heigl, and Alexander Warta. *Wiki: Web Collaboration*. Springer, Berlin, second edition, November 2007. ISBN: 978-3-540-35150-4. 1, 74, 77

[Fag11] Enrico Fagnoni. ITSMO User's Guide. `http://ontology.it/itsmo/v1/userguide/`, 2011. (accessed 2013-03-06). 182

[Fag12] Enrico Fagnoni. ITSMO IT Service Management Ontology. `http://ontology.it/itsmo/v1/itsmo.html`, 2012. (accessed 2013-03-06). 182

[FB05] Andrea Forte and Amy Bruckman. Why Do People Write for Wikipedia? Incentives to Contribute to Open-Content Publishing. In *GROUP 05 Workshop: Sustaining Community: The Role and Design of Incentive Mechanisms in Online Systems*, pages 6–9, Sanibel Island, USA, 2005. 76

[FCeA08] Jorge Manuel Freitas, Anacleto Correia, and Fernando Brito e Abreu. An Ontology for IT Services. In Ana Moreira, María José Suárez Cabal, Claudio de la Riva, and Javier Tuya, editors, *Proceedings of the XIII Jornadas de Ingeniería del Software y Bases de Datos (JISBD)*, pages 367–372, Gijón, Spain, October 2008. 182

[FE10] Borko Furht and Armando Escalante, editors. *Handbook of Cloud Computing*. Springer, New York Dordrecht Heidelberg London, first edition, September 2010. ISBN:978-1-4419-6523-3. 306, 307, 308

[FG05] Jörg Fritsch and Steffen Gundel. *Firewalls im Unternehmenseinsatz: Grundlagen, Betrieb und Produkte*. dpunkt.verlag, Heidelberg, second edition, August 2005. ISBN: 978-3-89864-322-1. 94

[FGM+99] R. Fielding, J. Gettys, Jeffrey C. Mogul, H. Frystyk, Larry Masinter, P. Leach, and Tim Berners-Lee. Hypertext Transfer Protocol – HTTP/1.1. RFC 2616 (Draft Standard). http://www.ietf.org/rfc/rfc2616.txt, June 1999. (accessed 2011-02-01). 244, 245

[FL99] Mariano Fernández-López. Overview Of Methodologies For Building Ontologies. In V.R. Benjamins, B. Chandrasekaran, Asunción Gómez-Pérez, Nicola Guarino, and M. Uschold, editors, *Proceedings of the IJCAI-99 Workshop on Ontologies and Problem-Solving Methods (KRR5)*, Stockholm, Sweden, August 1999. 163

[FLGPJ97] Mariano Fernández-López, Asunción Gómez-Pérez, and Natalia Juristo. METHONTOLOGY: From Ontological Art Towards Ontological Engineering. In *AAAI'97 Spring Symposium on Ontological Engineering*, pages 33–40, Stanford, USA, March 1997. 163

[FLGPSS99] Mariano Fernández-López, Asunción Gómez-Pérez, Juan Pazos Sierra, and Alejandro Pazos Sierra. Building a Chemical Ontology Using Methontology and the Ontology Design Environment. *IEEE Intelligent Systems*, 14(1):37–46, January/February 1999. 163

[FT02] Roy T. Fielding and Richard N. Taylor. Principled Design of the Modern Web Architecture. *ACM Transactions on Internet Technology*, 2:115–150, 2002. 308

[FZI14] FZI Forschungszentrum Informatik. Jahresbericht 2013/2014, May 2014. 82

[GA07] Peter H. Ganten and Wulf Alex. *Debian GNU/Linux Grundlagen, Einrichtung und Betrieb. Version Etch.* X.systems.press. Springer, Berlin, third edition, June 2007. ISBN: 978-3-540-73338-6. 210

[Gal08] Ethan Galstad. Nagios Version 3.x Documentation. http://nagios.sourceforge.net/docs/3_0/, November 2008. (accessed 2009-03-20). 247

[Gal09] Avigdor Gal. Ontology Engineering. In Liu and Özsu [LO09], pages 1972–1973. ISBN: 978-0-387-35544-3. 163

[GBS09] S. Graupner, S. Basu, and S. Singhal. Collaboration Environment for ITIL. In *International Symposium on Integrated Network Management, Workshops. IM '09. IFIP/IEEE*, pages 44–47, June 2009. 161

[GF95] Michael Grüninger and Mark S. Fox. Methodology for the Design and Evaluation of Ontologies. In Doug Skuce, editor, *Workshop on Basic Ontological Issues in Knowledge Sharing, held in conduction with IJCAI-95*, Montréal, Canada, 1995. 163

[Gil05] Jim Giles. Internet Encyclopaedias Go Head to Head. *Nature*, 438(7070):900–901, December 2005. 76

[GOS09] Nicola Guarino, Daniel Oberle, and Steffen Staab. What Is an Ontology? In Staab and Studer [SS09], pages 1–17. ISBN: 978-3-540-70999-2. 61

[Gra12] Graphviz. Graphviz – Graph Visualization Software: About. `http://www.graphviz.org/About.php`, December 2012. (accessed 2013-01-08). 288, 295

[Gre07] Lynn Greiner. ITIL: The International Repository of IT Wisdom. *netWorker*, 11(4):9–11, December 2007. 19

[Gru93] Thomas R. Gruber. A Translation Approach to Portable Ontology Specifications. *Knowl. Acquis.*, 5(2):199–220, 1993. 59

[Gru95] Thomas R. Gruber. Toward Principles for the Design of Ontologies Used for Knowledge Sharing. *International Journal of Human-Computer Studies*, 43(5–6):907–928, November 1995. Special Issue on the Role of Formal Ontology in the Information Technology. 59, 163

[Gru09] Thomas R. Gruber. Ontology. In Liu and Özsu [LO09], pages 1963–1965. ISBN: 978-0-387-35544-3. 59, 60

[Gua98] Nicola Guarino. Formal Ontology and Information Systems. In Nicola Guarino, editor, *Proceedings of FOIS'98, Trento, Italy*, pages 3–15, Amsterdam, The Netherlands, June 1998. IOS Press. 59

[GW05] Giancarlo Guizzardi and Gerd Wagner. Towards Ontological Foundations for Agent Modelling Concepts Using the Unified Fundational Ontology (UFO). In Paolo Bresciani, Paolo Giorgini, Brian Henderson-Sellers, Graham Low, and Michael Winikoff, editors, *Agent-Oriented Information Systems II*, volume 3508 of *Lecture Notes in Computer Science (LNCS)*, pages 110–124. Springer, Berlin, 2005. ISBN: 978-3-540-25911-4. 182

[GWS06] Andreas Gruber, Rupert Westenthaler, and Sebastian Schaffert. IkeWiki: A User-Friendly Semantic Wiki. In *Demos and Posters of the 3rd European Semantic Web Conference (ESWC 2006)*, Budva, Montenegro, June 2006. 119

[Han10] Peter N. M. Hansteen. *The Book of PF: A No-Nonsense Guide to the OpenBSD Firewall.* No Starch, San Francisco, second edition, November 2010. ISBN: 978-1-59327-274-6. 427

[Hay04] Patrick Hayes. RDF Semantics: W3C Recommendation 10 February 2004. `http://www.w3.org/TR/2004/REC-rdf-mt-20040210/`, February 2004. (accessed 2010-10-10). 66

[HBEV04] Peter Haase, Jeen Broekstra, Andreas Eberhart, and Raphael Volz. A Comparison of RDF Query Languages. In Sheila A. McIlraith, Dimitris Plexousakis, and Frank van Harmelen, editors, *The Semantic Web – ISWC 2004: Third International Semantic Web Conference*, volume 3298 of *Lecture Notes in Computer Science (LNCS)*, pages 502–517, Hiroshima, Japan, November 2004. Springer, Berlin. ISBN: 978-3-540-23798-3. 65

[HBS09] Alice Hertel, Jeen Broekstra, and Heiner Stuckenschmidt. RDF Storage and Retrieval Systems. In Staab and Studer [SS09], pages 489–508. ISBN: 978-3-540-70999-2. 65

[Hef04] Jeff Heflin. OWL Web Ontology Language Use Cases and Requirements. `http://www.w3.org/TR/2004/REC-webont-req-20040210/`, February 2004. (accessed 2010-10-12). 69

[Hew11] Hewlett-Packard Development Company, L.P. HP Universal CMDB. `https://h10078.www1.hp.com/cda/hpdc/display/main/download_pdf_unprotected.jsp?zn=bto&cp=54_4000_5`, February 2011. (accessed 2011-07-04). 109

[HG03] Stephen Harris and Nicholas Gibbins. 3store: Efficient Bulk RDF Storage. In Raphael Volz, Stefan Decker, and Isabel F. Cruz, editors, *Proceedings of the 1st International Workshop on Practical and Scalable Semantic Systems (PSSS-1)*, volume 89 of *CEUR Workshop Proceedings*, Sanibel Island, USA, October 2003. CEUR-WS.org. 65

[HH05] Simon Hansman and Ray Hunt. A Taxonomy of Network and Computer Attacks. *Computers & Security*, 24(1):31–43, 2005. 283

[HKRS08] Pascal Hitzler, Markus Krötzsch, Sebastian Rudolph, and York Sure. *Semantic Web – Grundlagen*. eXamen.press. Springer, Berlin, first edition, October 2008. ISBN: 978-3-540-33993-9. 62, 69

[HLS+08] Peter Haase, Holger Lewen, Rudi Studer, Duc Thanh Tran, Michael Erdmann, Mathieu d'Aquin, and Enrico Motta. The NeOn Ontology Engineering Toolkit. In *WWW 2008 Developers Track*, Beijing, China, April 2008. 69

[HMS+10] Peter Haase, Tobias Mathäß, Michael Schmidt, Andreas Eberhart, and Ulrich Walther. Semantic Technologies for Enterprise Cloud Management. In Peter F. Patel-Schneider, Yue Pan, Pascal Hitzler, Peter Mika, Lei Zhang, Jeff Z. Pan, Ian Horrocks, and Birte Glimm, editors, *The Semantic Web – ISWC 2010: 9th International Semantic Web Conference, ISWC 2010*, volume 6497 of *Lecture Notes in Computer Science (LNCS)*, pages 98–113, Shanghai, China, November 2010. Springer, Berlin. ISBN: 978-3-642-17748-4. 314, 315

[Hol13] Lee Holmes. *Windows PowerShell Cookbook: The Complete Guide to Scripting Microsoft's Command Shell*. O'Reilly Media, Sebastopol, third edition, January 2013. ISBN: 978-1-4493-2068-3. 428

[Hor11] Matthew Horridge. A Practical Guide To Building OWL Ontologies Using Protégé 4 and CO-ODE Tools Edition 1.3. `http://owl.cs.manchester.ac.uk/tutorials/protegeowltutorial/resources/ProtegeOWLTutorialP4_v1_3.pdf`, March 2011. (accessed 2012-11-07). 61

[HPGA02] John L. Hennessy, David A. Patterson, David Goldberg, and Krste Asanovic. *Computer Architecture: A Quantitative Approach*. Morgan Kaufmann, Burlington, third edition, May 2002. ISBN: 978-1-55860-724-8. 206

[HPPSH05] Ian Horrocks, Bijan Parsia, Peter Patel-Schneider, and James Hendler. Semantic Web Architecture: Stack or Two Towers? *Principles and Practice of Semantic Web Reasoning*, pages 37–41, 2005. 62

[HR10] Marianne Hickey and Maher Rahmouni. Modelling Cloud Computing Infrastructure. In Burkhard Stiller and Filip De Turck, editors, *Mechanisms for Autonomous Management of Networks and Services*, volume 6155 of *Lecture Notes in Computer Science (LNCS)*, pages 106–109. Springer, Berlin, 2010. 10.1007/978-3-642-13986-4_15. 314

[HSP09] Daniel Hansch, Hans-Peter Schnurr, and Peter Pissierssens. Semantic MediaWiki+ als Wissensplattform für Unternehmen. In Knut Hinkelmann and Holger Wache, editors, *Wissensmanagement*, volume 145 of *LNI*, pages 211–221. GI, 2009. 80, 119, 120

[i-d08a] i-doit. FAQ. `http://doc.i-doit.org/index.php?title=FAQ&oldid=2164`, August 2008. (accessed 2011-07-04). 111

[i-d08b] i-doit. i-doit Benutzerhandbuch 0.9.x – DE:Dateien. `http://doc.i-doit.org/index.php?title=DE:Dateien&oldid=2022`, March 2008. (accessed 2014-01-11). 339

[i-d08c] i-doit. i-doit Benutzerhandbuch 0.9.x – DE:Kontakte. `http://doc.i-doit.org/index.php?title=DE:Kontakte&oldid=2089`, April 2008. (accessed 2014-01-11). 339

[i-d08d] i-doit. i-doit Benutzerhandbuch 0.9.x – DE:Report Manager. `http://doc.i-doit.org/index.php?title=DE:Report_Manager&oldid=2278`, October 2008. (accessed 2014-01-11). 343, 345

[i-d08e] i-doit. i-doit Benutzerhandbuch 0.9.x – DE:Verbindungen. http://doc.i-doit.org/index.php?title=DE:Verbindungen&oldid=2018, January 2008. (accessed 2014-01-11). 328

[i-d09a] i-doit. i-doit Benutzerhandbuch 0.9.x – DE:Grundlagen. http://doc.i-doit.org/index.php?title=DE:Grundlagen&oldid=2469, October 2009. (accessed 2014-01-11). 327

[i-d09b] i-doit. i-doit Benutzerhandbuch 0.9.x – DE:Nagios. http://doc.i-doit.org/index.php?title=DE:Nagios&oldid=2394, March 2009. (accessed 2014-01-11). 354

[i-d10a] i-doit. i-doit Benutzerhandbuch 0.9.x. http://doc.i-doit.org/index.php?title=DE:Handbuch&oldid=2515, April 2010. (accessed 2011-07-04). 112

[i-d10b] i-doit. i-doit Benutzerhandbuch 0.9.x – DE:OCS. http://doc.i-doit.org/index.php?title=DE:OCS&oldid=2579, April 2010. (accessed 2014-01-11). 348, 349

[i-d10c] i-doit. i-doit Benutzerhandbuch 0.9.x – DE:Request Tracker. http://doc.i-doit.org/index.php?title=DE:Request_Tracker&oldid=2513, April 2010. (accessed 2014-01-11). 336

[i-d11a] i-doit. Features im Vergleich. http://www.i-doit.com/i-doit/featureliste/, July 2011. (accessed 2011-07-29). 111

[i-d11b] i-doit. i-doit Benutzerhandbuch 0.9.x – DE:Allgemeine Kategorien. http://doc.i-doit.org/index.php?title=DE:Allgemeine_Kategorien&oldid=2592, January 2011. (accessed 2014-01-11). 328

[i-d11c] i-doit. i-doit Benutzerhandbuch 0.9.x – DE:Handbuch. http://doc.i-doit.org/index.php?title=DE:Handbuch&oldid=2622, July 2011. (accessed 2014-01-11). 320

[i-d11d] i-doit. i-doit Benutzerhandbuch 0.9.x – DE:Inventory & Import. http://doc.i-doit.org/index.php?title=DE:Inventory_%26_Import&oldid=2604, March 2011. (accessed 2014-01-11). 348

[i-d11e] i-doit Open Source CMDB. About i-doit. http://www.i-doit.org/en/about-i-doit/, 2011. (accessed 2011-07-04). 112

[i-d12] i-doit. i-doit Benutzerhandbuch 0.9.x – DE:Workflows. http://doc.i-doit.org/index.php?title=DE:Workflows&oldid=2684, April 2012. (accessed 2013-01-11). 338

[i-d14] i-doit. Features. http://www.i-doit.org/cmdb-it-documentation/83-2/, January 2014. (accessed 2014-01-13). 320, 321

[IBM10] IBM Corporation. IBM Tivoli Change and Configuration Management Database. http://public.dhe.ibm.com/common/ssi/ecm/en/tid10375usen/TID10375USEN.PDF, January 2010. (accessed 2011-07-04). 109

[IN07] Majid Iqbal and Michael Nieves. *Service Strategy*. ITIL Version 3. Stationery Office Books, Norwich, May 2007. ISBN: 978-0-11-331045-6. 12, 16, 17, 18, 19, 20, 21, 22, 23, 24, 27

[JBD+08a] Bart Jacob, Michael Brokmann, Scott Dickerson, Douglas Barranqueiros Gomes, Rainer Hoppen, Arsalan Lodhi, Kapil Madaan, Annelie Meels-Kurz, Rosemeire Oikawa, and Tadeu Stellet Teixeira. *Deployment Guide Series: IBM Tivoli CCMDB Overview and Deployment Planning*. IBM Redbooks. IBM Corporation, International Technical Support Organization, Poughkeepsie, first edition, May 2008. http://www.redbooks.ibm.com/redbooks/pdfs/sg247565.pdf. (accessed 2011-03-07). ISBN: 978-0-7384-8526-3. 109

[JBD+08b] Bart Jacob, Michael Brokmann, Scott Dickerson, Douglas Barranqueiros Gomes, Rainer Hoppen, Arsalan Lodhi, Kapil Madaan, Annelie Meels-Kurz, Rosemeire Oikawa, and Tadeu Stellet Teixeira. *IBM Tivoli CCMDB Implementation Recommendations*. IBM Redbooks. IBM Corporation, International Technical Support Organization, Poughkeepsie, first edition, May 2008. http://www.redbooks.ibm.com/redbooks/pdfs/sg247567.pdf. (accessed 2011-03-07). ISBN: 978-0-7384-8527-0. 109

[JDBN+10] Holger von Jouanne-Diedrich, Juliane Blechinger, Christoph P. Neumann, Stefan Schwarz, and Richard Lenz. Integration verteilter und heterogener Configuration-Management-Datenbanken. *Informatik-Spektrum*, 33:351–362, 2010. 103

[Jon07] Don Jones. *VBScript, WMI, and ADSI Unleashed: Using VBScript, WMI, and ADSI to Automate Windows Administration*. Unleashed. Addison-Wesley Longman, Amsterdam, second edition, June 2007. ISBN: 978-0-321-50171-4. 215

[Kö7] Peter T. Köhler. *ITIL: Das IT-Servicemanagement Framework*. Xpert.Press. Springer, Berlin, second edition, 2007. ISBN: 978-3-540-37950-8. 19

[KA09] Frank Kleiner and Andreas Abecker. Towards a Collaborative Semantic Wiki-based Approach to IT Service Management. In Adrian Paschke,

Hans Weigand, Wernher Behrendt, Klaus Tochtermann, and Tassilo Pellegrini, editors, *Proceedings of I-SEMANTICS '09, 5th International Conference on Semantic Systems*, pages 424–434, Graz, Austria, September 2009. 115, 186

[KA10] Frank Kleiner and Andreas Abecker. Semantic MediaWiki as an Integration Platform for IT Service Management. In Klaus-Peter Fähnrich and Bogdan Franczyk, editors, *Informatik 2010 – Service Science – Neue Perspektiven für die Informatik*, volume P-176 of *Lecture Notes in Informatics (LNI)*, pages 73–78, Leipzig, Germany, September 2010. Köllen, Bonn. 5th International Workshop on Applications of Semantic Technologies (AST 2010). 115, 186

[KAB09a] Frank Kleiner, Andreas Abecker, and Sven F. Brinkmann. WiSyMon – Managing Systems Monitoring Information in Semantic Wikis. In *Proceedings of the Third International Conference on Advances in Semantic Processing 2009 (SEMAPRO '09)*, pages 77–85, Sliema, Malta, October 2009. IEEE Computer Society. 234, 251

[KAB09b] Frank Kleiner, Andreas Abecker, and Sven F. Brinkmann. WiSyMon: Managing Systems Monitoring Information in Semantic Wikis. In Riehle and Bruckman [RB09]. Poster Session. 234, 251

[KAL09] Frank Kleiner, Andreas Abecker, and Ning Liu. Automatic Population and Updating of a Semantic Wiki-based Configuration Management Database. In Stefan Fischer, Erik Maehle, and Rüdiger Reischuk, editors, *Informatik 2009 – Im Focus das Leben*, volume P-154 of *Lecture Notes in Informatics (LNI)*, pages 3076–3090, Lübeck, Germany, October 2009. Köllen, Bonn. 4th International Workshop on Applications of Semantic Technologies (AST 2009). 188

[KAM12] Frank Kleiner, Andreas Abecker, and Marco Mauritczat. Incident and Problem Management Using a Semantic Wiki-enabled ITSM Platform. In Joaquim Filipe and Ana Fred, editors, *4th International Conference on Agents and Artificial Intelligence (ICAART 2012)*, pages 363–372, Vilamoura, Portugal, February 2012. SciTePress, Setubal. ISBN: 978-989-8425-95-9. 284, 297

[KBNT11] Marcel Kunze, Christian Baun, Jens Nimis, and Stefan Tai. *Cloud Computing: Web-Based Dynamic IT Services*. Springer, Berlin, July 2011. ISBN: 978-3-642-20916-1. 306, 307, 308, 314

[KC04] Graham Klyne and Jeremy J. Carroll. Resource Description Framework (RDF): Concepts and Abstract Syntax: W3C Recommendation 10 February 2004. `http://www.w3.org/TR/2004/REC-rdf-concepts-20040210/`, February 2004. (accessed 2010-10-10). 66

[KC12] Abhishek Kaushik and Inderveer Chana. Ontology based Cloud Framework. *IJCA Special Issue on Advanced Computing and Communication Technologies for HPC Applications*, ACCTHPCA(1):37–41, July 2012. Published by Foundation of Computer Science, New York, USA. 314

[Ker08] Sascha Kersken. *Apache 2: Das umfassende Handbuch*. Galileo Computing, Bonn, third edition, December 2008. ISBN: 978-3-8362-1325-7. 433

[Kie06] Malte Kiesel. Kaukolu: Hub of the Semantic Corporate Intranet. In Max Völkel and Sebastian Schaffert, editors, *Proceedings of the First Workshop on Semantic Wikis – From Wiki to Semantics co-located with the ESWC2006*, volume 206 of *CEUR Workshop Proceedings*, Budva, Montenegro, June 2006. CEUR-WS.org. 119

[Kni10] Silvia Knittl. Unterstützung der IT-Service-Management-Prozesse an der Technischen Universität München durch eine Configuration-Management-Database. In Arndt Bode and Rolf Borgeest, editors, *Informationsmanagement in Hochschulen*, pages 97–106. Springer, Berlin, first edition, March 2010. ISBN: 978-3-642-04719-0. 111

[Kor10] Yaron Koren. Semantic MediaWiki Quick Reference. `http://postable.net/smwqr/smw-quick-reference.pdf`, August 2010. (accessed 2010-10-19). 129, 130

[Kor12] Yaron Koren. *Working with MediaWiki*. WikiWorks Press, New York, November 2012. ISBN: 978-0-615-72030-2. 133

[KRS07] Heinrich Kersten, Jürgen Reuter, and Klaus-Werner Schröder. *IT-Sicherheitsmanagement nach ISO 27001 und Grundschutz: Der Weg zur Zertifizierung*. Vieweg+Teubner, Wiesbaden, first edition, October 2007. ISBN: 978-3-8348-0178-4. 32

[KT06] Ramisa Kashanchi and Janet Toland. Can ITIL Contribute to IT/business Alignment? An Initial Investigation. *Wirtschaftsinformatik*, 48(5):340–348, 2006. 19

[KV04] Vassiliki Koutsonikola and Athena Vakali. LDAP: Framework, Practices, and Trends. *IEEE Internet Computing*, 8(5):66–72, September–October 2004. 212

[KVV+07] Markus Krötzsch, Denny Vrandečić, Max Völkel, Heiko Haller, and Rudi Studer. Semantic Wikipedia. *Web Semantics: Science, Services and Agents on the World Wide Web*, 5(4):251–261, 2007. World Wide Web Conference 2006, Semantic Web Track. 2, 80, 120, 162

[KZKB09] Yong-Bin Kang, A. Zaslavsky, S. Krishnaswamy, and C. Bartolini. A Computer-facilitated Method for Matching Incident Cases Using Semantic Similarity Measurement. In *Integrated Network Management-Workshops, 2009. IM '09. IFIP/IEEE International Symposium on*, pages 10–19, June 2009. 298

[Lan06] Christoph Lange, editor. *Wikis und Blogs: Planen. Einrichten. Verwalten.* C&L Computer- und Literaturverlag, Böblingen, first edition, September 2006. ISBN: 978-3-936546-44-6. 83

[Lan10a] Ryan Lane. Creating a Simple Ticketing System with Semantic MediaWiki. `http://ryandlane.com/blog/2010/04/01/creating-a-simple-ticketing-system-with-semantic-mediawiki`, April 2010. (accessed 2010-04-21). 161

[Lan10b] Ryan Lane. Helpdesk System and Datacenter Inventory Semantic MediaWiki Prototypes Added to My Prototype Wiki. `http://ryandlane.com/blog/2010/03/29/helpdesk-system-and-datacenter-inventory-semantic-mediawiki-prototypes-added-to-my-prototype-wiki`, March 2010. (accessed 2010-04-21). 161

[LDR03] Emmanuel Lavinal, Thierry Desprats, and Yves Raynaud. A Conceptual Framework for Building CIM-based Ontologies. In Germán S. Goldszmidt and Jürgen Schönwälder, editors, *Integrated Network Management*, volume 246 of *IFIP Conference Proceedings*, pages 135–138. Kluwer, 2003. 233

[LM07] Shirley Lacy and Ivor Macfarlane. *Service Transition.* ITIL Version 3. Stationery Office Books, Norwich, May 2007. ISBN: 978-0-11-331048-7. 19, 33, 34, 35, 36, 37, 38, 39, 40, 41, 42, 99, 100, 101, 102, 103, 104, 105, 106, 107, 108, 137, 138, 139, 140, 141, 142, 143, 144, 145, 146, 147, 148, 153, 155, 173, 174, 175, 176, 178, 179, 190, 322, 323, 324, 325, 333

[LO09] Ling Liu and M. Tamer Özsu, editors. *Encyclopedia of Database Systems.* Springer, Berlin, first edition, August 2009. ISBN: 978-0-387-35544-3. 573, 574, 578, 579, 595, 603

[LR07] Vernon Lloyd and Colin Rudd. *Service Design.* ITIL Version 3. Stationery Office Books, Norwich, May 2007. ISBN: 978-0-11-331047-0. 16, 19, 25, 26, 27, 28, 29, 30, 31, 32, 263

[LTM06] Rasmus Lerdorf, Kevin Tatroe, and Peter MacIntyre. *Programming PHP.* O'Reilly Media, Sebastopol, second edition, May 2006. ISBN: 978-0-596-00681-5. 434

[Luc12] Michael W Lucas. *SSH Mastery: OpenSSH, PuTTY, Tunnels and Keys*. CreateSpace Independent Publishing Platform, North Charleston, February 2012. ISBN: 978-1-4700-6971-1. 428

[MAB+08] Nick McKeown, Tom Anderson, Hari Balakrishnan, Guru Parulkar, Larry Peterson, Jennifer Rexford, Scott Shenker, and Jonathan Turner. OpenFlow: Enabling Innovation in Campus Networks. *SIGCOMM Comput. Commun. Rev.*, 38(2):69–74, March 2008. 428

[Mad07] Stewart Mader. *Wikipatterns*. Wiley & Sons, Hoboken, first edition, December 2007. ISBN: 978-0-470-22362-8. 77

[MADM+11] F. Moscato, R. Aversa, B. Di Martino, T. Fortis, and V. Munteanu. An Analysis of mOSAIC Ontology for Cloud Resources Annotation. In *Computer Science and Information Systems (FedCSIS), 2011 Federated Conference on*, pages 973–980, September 2011. 314

[Maj10] Frederic Majer. *Semantisches Informationsmodell für die Betriebsunterstützung dienstorientierter Systeme*. PhD thesis, Karlsruher Institut für Technologie, February 2010. 233

[Mas06] Dieter Masak. *IT-Alignment: IT-Architektur und Organisation*. Xpert.Press. Springer, Berlin, first edition, July 2006. ISBN: 978-3-540-31153-9. 13, 14, 15

[Med09a] MediaWiki. Category:All extensions. `http://www.mediawiki.org/wiki/Category:All_extensions`, November 2009. (accessed 2009-11-18). 122

[Med09b] MediaWiki. Extension:Semantic Drilldown. `http://www.mediawiki.org/w/index.php?title=Extension:Semantic_Drilldown&oldid=284553`, 2009. (accessed 2009-11-09). 121, 136

[Med09c] MediaWiki. Extension:Semantic Forms. `http://www.mediawiki.org/w/index.php?title=Extension:Semantic_Forms&oldid=284794`, November 2009. (accessed 2009-11-09). 121, 132, 133

[Med09d] MediaWiki. Extension:Semantic Maps. `http://www.mediawiki.org/w/index.php?title=Extension:Semantic_Maps&oldid=284783`, November 2009. (accessed 2009-11-09). 121

[Med09e] MediaWiki. Manual:Hooks. `http://www.mediawiki.org/w/index.php?title=Manual:Hooks&oldid=285571`, November 2009. (accessed 2009-11-18). 122

[Med09f] MediaWiki. MediaWiki API. http://en.wikipedia.org/w/api.php, November 2009. (accessed 2009-11-20). 124

[Med10a] MediaWiki. Help:Formatting. http://www.mediawiki.org/w/index.php?title=Help:Formatting&oldid=354702, October 2010. (accessed 2010-10-15). 73

[Med10b] MediaWiki. Help:Links. http://www.mediawiki.org/w/index.php?title=Help:Images&oldid=355205, October 2010. (accessed 2010-10-15). 73

[Med10c] MediaWiki. Help:Links. http://www.mediawiki.org/w/index.php?title=Help:Links&oldid=354897, October 2010. (accessed 2010-10-15). 73

[Med10d] MediaWiki. Help:Tables. http://www.mediawiki.org/w/index.php?title=Help:Tables&oldid=352104, September 2010. (accessed 2010-10-15). 73

[Med10e] MediaWiki. Wikitext. http://www.mediawiki.org/w/index.php?title=Wikitext&oldid=335540, July 2010. (accessed 2011-07-26). 72

[Med11a] MediaWiki. Developer hub. http://www.mediawiki.org/w/index.php?title=Developer_hub&oldid=381379, February 2011. (accessed 2011-02-23). 194, 239, 265, 287, 301

[Med11b] MediaWiki. Extension:Header Tabs. http://www.mediawiki.org/w/index.php?title=Extension:Header_Tabs&oldid=416844, July 2011. (accessed 2011-07-26). 159

[Med11c] MediaWiki. Manual:Installing MediaWiki. http://www.mediawiki.org/w/index.php?title=Manual:Installing_MediaWiki&oldid=373713, January 2011. (accessed 2011-02-08). 434

[Med11d] MediaWiki. WYSIWYG editor. http://www.mediawiki.org/w/index.php?title=WYSIWYG_editor&oldid=417612, July 2011. (accessed 2011-07-26). 159

[Med12a] MediaWiki. API:Edit. http://www.mediawiki.org/w/index.php?title=API:Edit&oldid=560537, July 2012. (accessed 2012-08-07). 257

[Med12b] MediaWiki. Extension:GraphViz. http://www.mediawiki.org/w/index.php?title=Extension:GraphViz&oldid=610131, November 2012. (accessed 2013-01-08). 288

[Med13] MediaWiki. Manual:Special pages — MediaWiki, The Free Wiki Engine. http://www.mediawiki.org/w/index.php?title=Manual:Special_pages&oldid=645468, February 2013. (accessed 2013-03-08). 124

[Mic00] Microsoft MSDN Library. Windows Management Instrumentation: Background and Overview. http://msdn.microsoft.com/en-us/library/ms811553.aspx, November 2000. (accessed 2009-04-16). 215

[Mic09] Microsoft MSDN Library. Windows Management Instrumentation. http://msdn.microsoft.com/en-us/library/aa394582(VS.85).aspx, April 2009. (accessed 2009-04-16). 187, 215

[Mic10] Microsoft. Windows 7: Compare Windows 7 Home Premium, Professional, and Ultimate. http://www.microsoft.com/windows/windows-7/compare/default.aspx, 2010. (accessed 2010-02-23). 207

[Mic11a] Microsoft. About WMI. http://msdn.microsoft.com/en-us/library/windows/desktop/aa384642%28v=VS.85%29.aspx, September 2011. (accessed 2011-09-20). 215

[Mic11b] Microsoft. SAM Tools. http://www.microsoft.com/sam/en/us/toolsoverview.aspx, 2011. (accessed 2011-08-02). 232

[Mic11c] Microsoft. WMI Architecture. http://msdn.microsoft.com/en-us/library/windows/desktop/aa394553%28v=VS.85%29.aspx, September 2011. (accessed 2011-09-20). 216

[Mic12a] Microsoft. Dev Center – Desktop: Active Directory Schema: All Classes. http://msdn.microsoft.com/en-us/library/windows/desktop/ms680938(v=vs.85).aspx, February 2012. (accessed 2012-04-18). 212

[Mic12b] Microsoft. Dev Center – Desktop: Active Directory Schema: Computer Class. http://msdn.microsoft.com/en-us/library/windows/desktop/ms680987(v=vs.85).aspx, February 2012. (accessed 2012-04-18). 212

[Mic13a] Microsoft. System Center 2012 Configuration Manager Overview. http://www.microsoft.com/en-us/server-cloud/system-center/configuration-manager-2012-overview.aspx, 2013. (accessed 2013-09-26). 428

[Mic13b] Microsoft. System Center 2012 Orchestrator Productive Infrastructure. http://download.microsoft.com/download/5/B/C/5BC5EBD5-129C-43D8-8769-AC5BBFE665DB/SC%202012%20Orchestrator%20Datasheet.pdf, 2013. (accessed 2013-09-25). 428

[MJL11] Yong Ma, Sung Jang, and Jong Lee. Ontology-Based Resource Management for Cloud Computing. In Ngoc Nguyen, Chong-Gun Kim, and Adam Janiak, editors, *Intelligent Information and Database Systems*, volume 6592 of *Lecture Notes in Computer Science (LNCS)*, pages 343–352. Springer, Berlin, 2011. 10.1007/978-3-642-20042-7_35. 314

[MK09] Riichiro Mizoguchi and Kouji Kozaki. Ontology Engineering Environments. In Staab and Studer [SS09], pages 315–336. ISBN: 978-3-540-70999-2. 69

[MKK07] Marta Majewska, Bartosz Kryza, and Jacek Kitowski. Translation of Common Information Model to Web Ontology Language. In Yong Shi, Geert van Albada, Jack Dongarra, and Peter Sloot, editors, *Computational Science – ICCS 2007*, volume 4487 of *Lecture Notes in Computer Science (LNCS)*, pages 414–417. Springer, Berlin, 2007. 233

[MM04] Frank Manola and Eric Miller. RDF Primer: W3C Recommendation 10 February 2004. http://www.w3.org/TR/rdf-primer/, February 2004. (accessed 2008-07-30). 66, 67

[Mur08] James Murty. *Programming Amazon Web Services – S3, EC2, SQS, FPS and Simple DB*. O'Reilly Media, Sebastopol, first edition, April 2008. ISBN: 978-0-596-51581-2. 307

[MVA09] Peter Membrey, Tim Verhoeven, and Ralph Angenendt. *The Definitive Guide to CentOS*. Books for Professionals by Professionals. Apress, Berkeley, first edition, July 2009. ISBN: 978-1-4302-1930-9. 433, 434

[MvHe04] Deborah L. McGuinness and Frank van Harmelen (ed.). OWL Web Ontology Language Overview. http://www.w3.org/TR/2004/REC-owl-features-20040210/, February 2004. (accessed 2009-11-14). 67, 68, 69

[MY06] Carl Mattocks and Peter Yim. ONION Project Home Page. http://ontolog.cim3.net/cgi-bin/wiki.pl?ONION, December 2006. (accessed 2010-11-30). 181

[Nag10] Nagios. Nagios Configuration Files. http://nagios.sourceforge.net/download/contrib/documentation/misc/config_diagrams/nagios-config.png, 2010. (accessed 2010-05-15). 248

[Nag11a] Nagios Enterprises, LLC. About Nagios. http://www.nagios.org/about/, 2011. (accessed 2011-02-01). 236

[Nag11b] Nagios Exchange. Category: Configuration. http://exchange.nagios.org/directory/Addons/Configuration, 2011. (accessed 2011-07-11). 261

[NB09] Christopher Negus and Timothy Boronczyk. *CentOS Bible*. Wiley & Sons, Hoboken, first edition, August 2009. ISBN: 978-0-470-48165-3. 433

[NCo09] NConf. Introduction. http://www.nconf.org/dokuwiki/doku.php?id=nconf:about:introduction, November 2009. (accessed 2011-07-11). 261

[Net11] NetApp. NetApp Manageability (NM) SDK Introduction and Download Information. http://communities.netapp.com/docs/DOC-1152, April 2011. (accessed 2011-05-18). 427

[Nis08] Christian F. Nissen. *Passing your ITIL Foundation Exam: Study Aid from the Official Publisher of ITIL*. Stationery Office Books, Norwich, second edition, 2008. ISBN: 978-0-11-331079-1. 19, 59

[NM01] Natalya F. Noy and Deborah L. McGuinness. Ontology Development 101: A Guide to Creating Your First Ontology. http://protege.stanford.edu/publications/ontology_development/ontology101.pdf, 2001. (accessed 2010-10-15). 163, 164

[Nor02] Klaus North. *Wissensorientierte Unternehmensführung. Wertschöpfung durch Wissen*. Gabler, Wiesbaden, third edition, October 2002. ISBN: 978-3-409-33029-9. 42, 145

[Noy09] Natalya F. Noy. Ontology Mapping. In Staab and Studer [SS09], pages 573–590. ISBN: 978-3-540-70999-2. 429

[NT95] Ikujiro Nonaka and Hirotaka Takeuchi. *The Knowledge-Creating Company: How Japanese Companies Create the Dynamics of Innovation*. Oxford University Press, Oxford, September 1995. ISBN: 978-0-19-509269-1. 42, 145

[NWG+09] Daniel Nurmi, Rich Wolski, Chris Grzegorczyk, Graziano Obertelli, Sunil Soman, Lamia Youseff, and Dmitrii Zagorodnov. The Eucalyptus Open-Source Cloud-Computing System. In *Proceedings of the 2009*

9th IEEE/ACM International Symposium on Cluster Computing and the Grid (CCGRID '09), pages 124–131, Washington, DC, USA, 2009. IEEE Computer Society. 308

[OCS11a] OCS Inventory NG. Inventory feature. http://www.ocsinventory-ng.org/en/about/features/inventory.html, 2011. (accessed 2011-08-02). 232

[OCS11b] OCS Inventory NG. OCS Inventory NG Agent 2.0 on Windows Operating Systems. http://wiki.ocsinventory-ng.org/index.php/Documentation:WindowsAgent, April 2011. (accessed 2011-08-02). 232

[OCS13] OCS Inventory NG. Documentation:WindowsAgent. http://wiki.ocsinventory-ng.org/index.php?title=Documentation:WindowsAgent&oldid=11028, may 2013. (accessed 2014-01-14). 350

[O'L08] Daniel E. O'Leary. Wikis: 'From Each According to His Knowledge'. *Computer*, 41(2):34–41, 2008. 77

[One09] OneCMDB. Main Page. http://www.onecmdb.org/wiki/index.php?title=Main_Page, December 2009. (accessed 2011-07-26). 112, 113, 261

[ONI06] ONION Project. ONION Ontology. http://ontolog.cim3.net/file/work/ONION/reference/onionCPLv1.owl, December 2006. (accessed 2010-12-21). 182

[Ont09] Ontoprise GmbH. SMW+ Semantic Enterprise Wiki – Product tour/overview. http://wiki.ontoprise.de/wiki/index.php/Product_tour/overview, 2009. (accessed 2009-11-17). 128, 131

[Ope11] Open-AudIT. About Open-AudIT. http://www.open-audit.org/index.php, 2011. (accessed 2011-08-02). 232

[Ope12a] Open Networking Foundation. Software-Defined Networking: The New Norm for Networks. https://www.opennetworking.org/images/stories/downloads/sdn-resources/white-papers/wp-sdn-newnorm.pdf, April 2012. (accessed 2013-09-25). 427

[Ope12b] OpenStack LLC. OpenStack Compute: Administration Manual. http://docs.openstack.org/folsom/openstack-compute/admin/bk-compute-adminguide-folsom.pdf, November 2012. (accessed 2012-12-07). 314

[Ops13] Opscode. Why Chef? http://docs.opscode.com/chef_why.html, 2013. (accessed 2013-09-25). 428

[Ora11] Oracle. MySQL 5.0 Reference Manual. http://downloads.mysql.com/docs/refman-5.0-en.a4.pdf, February 2011. (accessed 2011-02-02). 434

[OTR09] OTRS AG. OTRS::ITSM 2.0 – Basic. http://ftp.otrs.org/pub/otrs/doc/doc-itsm/2.0/en/pdf/otrs_itsm_book.pdf, 2009. (accessed 2011-07-04). 111

[OTR10] OTRS AG. OTRS 3.0 – Developer Manual. http://ftp.otrs.org/pub/otrs/doc/doc-developer/3.0/en/pdf/otrs_developer_book.pdf, 2010. (accessed 2011-07-04). 111

[OTR11a] OTRS AG. OTRS 3.0 – Admin Manual. http://ftp.otrs.org/pub/otrs/doc/doc-admin/3.0/en/pdf/otrs_admin_book.pdf, 2011. (accessed 2011-07-04). 111

[OTR11b] OTRS AG. OTRS ITSM 3.0 IT Service Management. http://www.otrs.com/fileadmin/mediafiles/New_Website/Products/017-ENG-Productbrochure_OTRS_ITSM30.pdf, 2011. (accessed 2011-07-04). 110

[OTR11c] OTRS AG. What is OTRS ITSM? http://otrs.org/products/otrs-itsm, 2011. (accessed 2011-07-04). 110

[OTR13a] OTRS AG. OTRS 3.3 – Admin Manual. http://ftp.otrs.org/pub/otrs/doc/doc-admin/3.3/en/pdf/otrs_admin_book.pdf, April 2013. (accessed 2014-01-16). 320

[OTR13b] OTRS AG. OTRS 3.3 – Developer Manual. http://ftp.otrs.org/pub/otrs/doc/doc-developer/3.3/en/pdf/otrs_developer_book.pdf, August 2013. (accessed 2014-01-16). 320

[OTR13c] OTRS AG. OTRS FAQ Documentation. included in http://ftp.otrs.org/pub/otrs/packages/FAQ-2.3.1.opm, November 2013. (accessed 2014-01-22). 320, 337, 338

[OTR13d] OTRS AG. OTRS ITSM 3.3 Documentation. http://ftp.otrs.org/pub/otrs/doc/doc-itsm/3.3/en/pdf/otrs_itsm_book.pdf, October 2013. (accessed 2014-01-07). 320, 326, 328, 335, 336, 343

[OTR13e] OTRS AG. OTRS SystemMonitoring Documentation. included in http://ftp.otrs.org/pub/otrs/packages/SystemMonitoring-2.5.2.opm, September 2013. (accessed 2014-01-16). 320, 353

[OTR14a] OTRS AG. OTRS 3.3.3 Appliance Software. http://ftp.otrs.org/pub/otrs/otrs-3.3.3-appliance-1.0.3.iso, January 2014. (accessed 2014-01-22). 320

[OTR14b] OTRS AG. OTRS 3.3.3 Software. http://ftp.otrs.org/pub/otrs/otrs-3.3.3.zip, January 2014. (accessed 2014-01-22). 320

[OTR14c] OTRS AG. OTRS FAQ Module 2.3.1 Software. http://ftp.otrs.org/pub/otrs/packages/FAQ-2.3.1.opm, January 2014. (accessed 2014-01-22). 320

[OTR14d] OTRS AG. OTRS IT Service Management Software Features. https://www.otrs.com/software/otrsitsm-features/, 2014. (accessed 2014-01-07). 320

[OTR14e] OTRS AG. OTRS SystemMonitoring Module 2.5.2 Software. http://ftp.otrs.org/pub/otrs/packages/SystemMonitoring-2.5.2.opm, January 2014. (accessed 2014-01-22). 320

[OTR14f] OTRS AG. OTRS::ITSM Bundle 3.3.3 Software. http://ftp.otrs.org/pub/otrs/itsm/bundle33/ITSM-3.3.3.opm, January 2014. (accessed 2014-01-22). 320

[PBD+06] Lydia Parziale, David T. Britt, Chuck Davis, Jason Forrester, Wei Liu, Carolyn Matthews, and Nicolas Rosselot. *TCP/IP Tutorial and Technical Overview*. IBM Redbooks. IBM Corporation, International Technical Support Organization, Poughkeepsie, eight edition, December 2006. http://www.redbooks.ibm.com/redbooks/pdfs/gg243376.pdf. (accessed 2012-04-19). ISBN: 978-0-7384-9468-5. 213, 215, 216, 217

[Pin12] Maurizio Pinotti. CMon :: CMDB-2-Nagios Interface. http://www.8p8web.it/cmon/, 2012. (accessed 2012-06-20). 261

[PNJB08] Frederik Pfisterer, Markus Nitsche, Anthony Jameson, and Catalin Barbu. User-Centered Design and Evaluation of Interface Enhancements to the Semantic MediaWiki. In *Semantic Web User Interaction: Exploring HCI Challenges (SWUI2008CHI) at CHI2008*, 2008. 131, 132

[Pos81] Jon Postel. Internet Control Message Protocol. RFC 792 (Standard). http://www.ietf.org/rfc/rfc792.txt, September 1981. (accessed 2011-02-01). 244

[PRR03] Gilbert J. B. Probst, Steffen Raub, and Kai Romhardt. *Wissen managen. Wie Unternehmen ihre wertvollste Ressource optimal nutzen*. Gabler, Wiesbaden, fourth edition, March 2003. ISBN: 978-3-409-49317-8. 42, 145

[PS08] Eric Prud'hommeaux and Andy Seaborne. SPARQL Query Language for RDF: W3C Recommendation 15 January 2008. http://www.w3.org/TR/2008/REC-rdf-sparql-query-20080115/, January 2008. (accessed 2008-07-30). 65

[PSHH04] Peter F. Patel-Schneider, Patrick Hayes, and Ian Horrocks. OWL Web Ontology Language Semantics and Abstract Syntax. http://www.w3.org/TR/2004/REC-owl-semantics-20040210/, February 2004. (accessed 2010-10-12). 69

[Pup13] Puppet Labs. What is Puppet? http://puppetlabs.com/puppet/what-is-puppet, 2013. (accessed 2013-09-25). 428

[Pur04] Gregor N. Purdy. *Linux iptables Pocket Reference*. O'Reilly Media, Sebastopol, first edition, September 2004. ISBN: 978-0-596-00569-6. 427

[QAW+04] Stephen Quirolgico, Pedro Assis, Andrea Westerinen, Michael Baskey, and Ellen Stokes. Toward a Formal Common Information Model Ontology. In C. Bussler, S.-k. Hong, W. Jun, R. Kaschek, Kinshuk, S. Krishnaswamy, S.W. Loke, D. Oberle, D. Richards, A. Sharma, Y. Sure, and B. Thalheim, editors, *Web Information Systems – WISE 2004 Workshops*, volume 3307 of *Lecture Notes in Computer Science (LNCS)*, pages 11–21, Brisbane, Australia, 2004. Springer, Berlin. 233

[RA08] Sheizaf Rafaeli and Yaron Ariel. Online Motivational Factors: Incentives for Participation and Contribution in Wikipedia. In A. Barak, editor, *Psychological Aspects of Cyberspace: Theory, Research, Applications*. Cambridge University Press, Cambridge, first edition, April 2008. ISBN: 978-0-521-69464-3. 76

[RB09] Dirk Riehle and Amy Bruckman, editors. *WikiSym '09: Proceedings of the 5th International Symposium on Wikis and Open Collaboration, Orlando, Florida*. ACM, New York, NY, USA, 2009. ISBN: 978-1-60558-730-1. 570, 584

[Red08a] Red Hat, Inc. Red Hat Enterprise Linux 5.2: Red Hat Enterprise Linux Installation Guide 5.2. `http://www.centos.org/docs/5/html/5.2/pdf/Installation_Guide.pdf`, 2008. (accessed 2011-02-02). 433

[Red08b] Red Hat, Inc. Red Hat Enterprise Linux: Deployment Guide 5.2. `http://www.centos.org/docs/5/html/5.2/pdf/Deployment_Guide.pdf`, January 2008. (accessed 2011-02-02). 227, 433

[Rei04] Chris Reid. Snort Database Schema v1.06. `http://projects.cs.luc.edu/comp412/dredd/docs/software/snort_schema_v106.pdf`, September 2004. (accessed 2009-11-22). 274

[RHTN01] Victor Raskin, Christian F. Hempelmann, Katrina E. Triezenberg, and Sergei Nirenburg. Ontology in Information Security: A Useful Theoretical Foundation and Methodological Tool. In *Proceedings of the 2001 Workshop on New Security Paradigms*, pages 53–59. ACM, 2001. 283

[Ris09] Tore Risch. Distributed Architecture. In Liu and Özsu [LO09], pages 875–879. ISBN: 978-0-387-35544-3. 103

[RKM+08] Stan Reimer, Conan Kezema, Mike Mulcare, Byron Wright, and Microsoft Active Directory Team. *Windows Server 2008 Active Directory Resource Kit*. Microsoft Press, Redmond, March 2008. ISBN: 978-0-7356-2515-0. 201

[RNM07] Daniel L. Rubin, Natalya F. Noy, and Mark A. Musen. Protégé: A Tool for Managing and Using Terminology in Radiology Applications. *Journal of Digital Imaging*, 2007. 69, 163

[Rob10] Arnold Robbins. *Bash Pocket Reference*. O'Reilly Media, Sebastopol, first edition, June 2010. ISBN: 978-1-4493-8788-4. 428

[Roe99] Martin Roesch. Snort – Lightweight Intrusion Detection for Networks. In *LISA '99: Proceedings of the 13th USENIX Conference on System Administration*, pages 229–238, Berkeley, CA, USA, 1999. USENIX Association. 188, 271

[RR07] Leonard Richardson and Sam Ruby. *RESTful Web Services*. O'Reilly Media, Sebastopol, first edition, May 2007. ISBN: 978-0-596-52926-0. 308

[Rub94] Jeffrey Rubin. *Handbook of Usability Testing: How to Plan, Design, and Conduct Effective Tests*. Wiley Technical Communication Library. Wiley & Sons, New York, April 1994. ISBN: 0-471-59403-2. 384, 385, 386, 394, 397

[Rum13] Bernard Rummel. System Usability Scale (Translated into German). http://www.sapdesignguild.org/resources/sus.asp, April 2013. (accessed 2014-03-11). 415

[Sau08] Jeff Sauro. *Quantifying the User Experience: Practical Statistics for User Research*. Morgan Kaufmann, Burlington, first edition, March 2008. ISBN: 978-0-12-384968-7. 384, 397, 411, 412

[SBBK08] Sebastian Schaffert, François Bry, Joachim Baumeister, and Malte Kiesel. Semantic Wikis. *IEEE Software*, 25(4):8–11, 2008. 77, 80, 117

[SBBK09] Sebastian Schaffert, François Bry, Joachim Baumeister, and Malte Kiesel. Semantische Wikis. In Andreas Blumauer and Tassilo Pellegrini, editors, *Social Semantic Web*, X.media.press, pages 245–258. Springer, Berlin, first edition, 2009. ISBN: 978-3-540-72215-1. 77, 78, 79

[SBF98] Rudi Studer, V. Richard Benjamins, and Dieter Fensel. Knowledge Engineering: Principles and Methods. *Data Knowl. Eng.*, 25(1–2):161–197, 1998. 59, 60, 162, 163

[SBH06] Nigel Shadbolt, Tim Berners-Lee, and Wendy Hall. The Semantic Web Revisited. *IEEE Intelligent Systems*, 21(3):96–101, 2006. 61

[SBM09] Chivas Sicam, Ryan Baclit, and Peter Membrey. *Foundations of CentOS Linux: Enterprise Linux on the Cheap*. Books for Professionals by Professionals. Apress, Berkeley, first edition, November 2009. ISBN: 978-1-4302-1964-4. 433, 434

[Sch05] Thomas Schwenkler. *Sicheres Netzwerkmanagement: Konzepte, Protokolle, Tools*. X.systems.press. Springer, Berlin, first edition, December 2005. ISBN: 978-3-540-23612-2. 217

[Sch06] Sebastian Schaffert. IkeWiki: A Semantic Wiki for Collaborative Knowledge Management. In *WETICE '06: Proceedings of the 15th IEEE International Workshops on Enabling Technologies: Infrastructure for Collaborative Enterprises*, pages 388–396, Washington, DC, USA, 2006. IEEE Computer Society. 119

[SEG+09] Sebastian Schaffert, Julia Eder, Szaby Grünwald, Thomas Kurz, and Mihai Radulescu. KiWi – A Platform for Semantic Social Software (Demonstration). In Lora Aroyo, Paolo Traverso, Fabio Ciravegna, Philipp Cimiano, Tom Heath, Eero Hyvönen, Riichiro Mizoguchi, Eyal Oren, Marta Sabou, and Elena Paslaru Bontas Simperl, editors, *The Semantic Web: Research and Applications: 6th European Semantic Web Conference, ESWC 2009*, volume 5554 of *Lecture Notes in Computer*

Science (LNCS), pages 888–892, Heraklion, Crete, Greece, June 2009. Springer, Berlin. ISBN: 978-3-642-02120-6. 71, 72, 119

[Sem09] SemanticWeb.org. Semantic Wiki Projects. `http://semanticweb.org/wiki/Semantic_wiki_projects`, September 2009. (accessed 2009-11-08). 80, 118, 119

[Sem12] Semafora Systems GmbH. SemanticGuide: Finding Solutions for Your Technical Customer Service. `http://www.semafora-systems.com/fileadmin/user_upload/Flyer_EN/Flyer_SRM-SemanticGuide_en_s.pdf`, 2012. (accessed 2013-01-10). 297

[Sem13] Semantic MediaWiki. Help:Properties and Types. `http://semantic-mediawiki.org/w/index.php?title=Help:Properties_and_types&oldid=26454`, February 2013. (accessed: 2013-03-10). 128

[Ser06] J. Sermersheim. Lightweight Directory Access Protocol (LDAP): The Protocol. RFC 4511. `http://tools.ietf.org/html/rfc4511`, June 2006. (accessed 2012-04-16). 213

[SFGPFL12] Mari Carmen Suárez-Figueroa, Asunción Gómez-Pérez, and Mariano Fernández-López. The NeOn Methodology for Ontology Engineering. In Mari Carmen Suárez-Figueroa, Asunción Gómez-Pérez, Enrico Motta, and Aldo Gangemi, editors, *Ontology Engineering in a Networked World*, pages 9–34. Springer, Berlin, 2012. 163

[Shi08] Clay Shirky. *Here Comes Everybody: The Power of Organizing Without Organizations*. Penguin, New York, March 2008. ISBN: 978-1-59420-153-0. 76

[SK06] Michael Sintek and Malte Kiesel. RDFBroker: A Signature-Based High-Performance RDF Store. In York Sure and John Domingue, editors, *The Semantic Web: Research and Applications: 3rd European Semantic Web Conference, ESWC 2006*, volume 4011 of *Lecture Notes in Computer Science (LNCS)*, pages 363–377, Budva, Montenegro, June 2006. Springer, Berlin. ISBN: 978-3-540-34544-2. 65

[Sno11] Snort.org Blog. GUIs for Snort. `http://blog.snort.org/2011/01/guis-for-snort.html`, January 2011. (accessed 2011-08-02). 282

[Sno14a] Snorby. Snorby 2.6.2 Software. `https://snorby.org/redirect?version=2.6.2`, January 2014. (accessed 2014-01-22). 321

[Sno14b] Snorby. Snorby E Book. `https://github.com/Snorby/snorby/wiki/Snorby-E-Book`, January 2014. (accessed 2014-01-13). 321

[Som07] Wolfgang Sommergut. Enterprise-Wikis erlauben zwanglose Teamarbeit. http://www.computerwoche.de/592752, May 2007. (accessed 2009-11-07). 76

[Sou10] Sourcefire, Inc. Snort FAQ. http://www.snort.org/snort/faq, 2010. (accessed 2013-01-18). 271

[Sou14a] SourceForge. Download BASE from SourceForge.net. http://sourceforge.net/projects/secureideas/files/BASE/base-1.4.5/base-1.4.5.tar.gz/download, January 2014. (accessed 2014-01-22). 319

[Sou14b] SourceForge. Download i-doit - CMDB and IT documentation from SourceForge.net. http://sourceforge.net/projects/i-doit/files/i-doit/0.9.9-7/idoit-0.9.9-7.zip/download, January 2014. (accessed 2014-01-22). 320

[Sou14c] SourceForge. Download Semantic MediaWiki from SourceForge.net. http://sourceforge.net/projects/semediawiki/files/semediawiki/Semantic%20MediaWiki%201.9.0.1/Semantic%20MediaWiki%201.9.0.1.zip/download, January 2014. (accessed 2014-01-22). 320

[SP04] Ben Shneiderman and Catherine Plaisant. *Designing the User Interface: Strategies for Effective Human-Computer Interaction*. Addison-Wesley, Amsterdam, fourth edition, April 2004. ISBN: 978-0-321-19786-3. 159

[Spi11] Spiceworks. Spiceworks IT Desktop. http://www.spiceworks.com/product/, 2011. (accessed 2011-08-02). 231

[SPKR97] Bill Swartout, Ramesh Patil, Kevin Knight, and Tom Russ. Toward Distributed Use of Large-Scale Ontologies. In A. Farquhar, M. Gruninger, A. Gómez-Pérez, M. Uschold, and P. van der Vet, editors, *AAAI'97 Spring Symposium on Ontological Engineering*, pages 138–148, Stanford, USA, March 1997. 163

[SS02] York Sure and Rudi Studer. On-To-Knowledge Methodology – Final Version. On-To-Knowledge EU IST-1999-10132 Project Deliverable D18, Institute AIFB, University of Karlsruhe, September 2002. 163, 164

[SS03] Steffen Staab and Rudi Studer. *Handbook on Ontologies*. International Handbooks on Information Systems. Springer, Berlin, first edition, 2003. ISBN: 978-3-540-40834-5. 61

[SS09] Steffen Staab and Rudi Studer. *Handbook on Ontologies*. International Handbooks on Information Systems. Springer, Berlin, second edition, July 2009. ISBN: 978-3-540-70999-2. 61, 578, 579, 589, 591

[SSB07] Christoph Sauer, Chuck Smith, and Tomas Benz. WikiCreole: A Common Wiki Markup. In *Proceedings of the 2007 International Symposium on Wikis (WikiSym '07)*, pages 131–142, Montréal, Canada, 2007. ACM. 72, 73

[SSFH08] Steffen Staab, Hans-Peter Schnurr, Thomas Franz, and Daniel Hansch. Semantische Technologien und Auswirkung auf Informations- und Wissensmanagementsysteme. *IM – die Fachzeitschrift für Information Management & Consulting*, 2, May 2008. 80

[SSSS01] Steffen Staab, Rudi Studer, Hans-Peter Schnurr, and York Sure. Knowledge Processes and Ontologies. *IEEE Intelligent Systems*, 16(1):26–34, January/February 2001. 163, 164, 165

[SSZ11] Alexander Sellner, Christopher Schwarz, and Erwin Zinser. Semantic-ontological Combination of Business Rules and Business Processes in IT Service Management. In Carlos Viegas Damásio, Alun Preece, and Umberto Straccia, editors, *The 5th International Symposium on Rules: Research Based and Industry Focused*, July 2011. Poster Paper. 183

[Sta98] W. Stallings. SNMP and SNMPv2: The Infrastructure for Network Management. *Communications Magazine, IEEE*, 36(3):37–43, March 1998. 217

[Ste93] W. Richard Stevens. *TCP/IP Illustrated Volume 1: The Protocols*. Addison-Wesley Longman, Amsterdam, December 1993. ISBN: 978-0-201-63346-7. 217, 244

[Str09] Rolf Strathewerd. Struktur fürs Wiki – Die Wiki-Erweiterungen Semantic Mediawiki und Semantic Forms. *Linux-Magazin*, 07:60–65, 2009. 80

[SWM04] Michael K. Smith, Chris Welty, and Deborah L. McGuinness. OWL Web Ontology Language Guide. `http://www.w3.org/TR/2004/REC-owl-guide-20040210/`, February 2004. (accessed 2010-10-12). 69

[TC09] David Trastour and Athena Christodoulou. Towards Robust IT Service Portfolio Management. In Claudio Bartolini and Luciano Gaspary, editors, *Integrated Management of Systems, Services, Processes and People in IT: 20th IFIP/IEEE International Workshop on Distributed Systems: Operations and Management, DSOM 2009*, volume 5841 of *Lecture Notes in Computer Science (LNCS)*, pages 152–163, Venice, Italy, October 2009. Springer, Berlin. ISBN: 978-3-642-04988-0. 24

[TCC04] Roberto Tazzoli, Paolo Castagna, and Stefano Emilio Campanini. Towards a Semantic Wiki Wiki Web (Extended Version). http://platypuswiki.sourceforge.net/whatis/documents/platypuswiki.pdf, 2004. (accessed 2012-04-19). extended version of a poster summary, presented at the Third International Semantic Web Conference (ISWC 2004), Hiroshima, Japan. 119

[TEG+04] Steven Tuttle, Ami Ehlenberger, Ramakrishna Gorthi, Jay Leiserson, Richard Macbeth, Nathan Owen, Sunil Ranahandola, Michael Storrs, and Chunhui Yang. *Understanding LDAP – Design and Implementation*. IBM Redbooks. IBM Corporation, International Technical Support Organization, Poughkeepsie, second edition, June 2004. http://www.redbooks.ibm.com/redbooks/pdfs/sg244986.pdf. (accessed 2012-04-24). ISBN: 978-0-7384-9786-0. 187, 211, 212, 213

[The12a] The PHP Group. PHP Manual – Lightweight Directory Access Protocol. http://www.php.net/manual/en/book.ldap.php, April 2012. (accessed 2012-04-18). 213

[The12b] The PHP Group. PHP Manual – SNMP. http://www.php.net/manual/en/book.snmp.php, April 2012. (accessed 2012-04-18). 217

[The12c] The Snort Project. SNORT Users Manual – 2.9.4. http://s3.amazonaws.com/snort-org/www/assets/166/snort_manual.pdf, November 2012. (accessed 2013-01-18). 271

[TNNM13] Tania Tudorache, Csongor Nyulas, Natalya F. Noy, and Mark A. Musen. WebProtégé: A Collaborative Ontology Editor and Knowledge Acquisition Tool for the Web. *Semantic Web*, 4(1):89–99, January 2013. 163

[TNTM08] Tania Tudorache, Natalya F. Noy, Samson Tu, and Mark A. Musen. Supporting Collaborative Ontology Development in Protégé. In Amit Sheth, Steffen Staab, Mike Dean, Massimo Paolucci, Diana Maynard, Timothy Finin, and Krishnaprasad Thirunarayan, editors, *The Semantic Web – ISWC 2008: 7th International Semantic Web Conference*, volume 5318 of *Lecture Notes in Computer Science (LNCS)*, pages 17–32, Karlsruhe, Germany, October 2008. Springer, Berlin. ISBN: 978-3-540-88563-4. 163

[Tre09a] Trend Micro, Inc. Getting started with OSSEC. http://www.ossec.net/main/getting-started-with-ossec/, 2009. (accessed 2009-12-15). 271

[Tre09b] Trend Micro, Inc. OSSEC Architecture. http://www.ossec.net/main/ossec-architecture/, 2009. (accessed 2009-12-15). 271

[Tri11] TrileX Labs. H-Inventory – About H-Inventory. `http://www.trilexnet.com/labs/hinventory/`, 2011. (accessed 2014-01-14). 350

[TSK10] Andreas Textor, Jeanne Stynes, and Reinhold Kroeger. Transformation of the Common Information Model to OWL. In Florian Daniel and Federico Facca, editors, *Current Trends in Web Engineering*, volume 6385 of *Lecture Notes in Computer Science (LNCS)*, pages 163–174. Springer, Berlin, 2010. 233

[TSK11] Andreas Textor, Jeanne Stynes, and Reinhold Kröger. IT Management Using a Heavyweight CIM Ontology. In Norbert Luttenberger and Hagen Peters, editors, *KiVS*, volume 17 of *OASICS*, pages 73–84. Schloss Dagstuhl – Leibniz-Zentrum fuer Informatik, Germany, 2011. 233

[TW06] Seyed Tahaghoghi and Hugh E. Williams. *Learning MySQL*. O'Reilly Media, Sebastopol, first edition, November 2006. ISBN: 978-0-596-00864-2. 434

[TW07] Don Tapscott and Anthony D. Williams. *Wikinomics*. Portfolio, New York, January 2007. ISBN: 978-1-59184-138-8. 76

[UJP03] Jeffrey Undercoffer, Anupam Joshi, and John Pinkston. Modeling Computer Attacks: An Ontology for Intrusion Detection. In Giovanni Vigna, Christopher Kruegel, and Erland Jonsson, editors, *Recent Advances in Intrusion Detection*, volume 2820 of *Lecture Notes in Computer Science (LNCS)*, pages 113–135. Springer, Berlin, September 2003. ISBN: 978-3-540-40878-9. 283

[UK95] Mike Uschold and Martin King. Towards a Methodology for Building Ontologies. In Doug Skuce, editor, *Workshop on Basic Ontological Issues in Knowledge Sharing, held in conduction with IJCAI-95*, Montréal, Canada, 1995. 163

[UPJF04] Jeffrey Undercoffer, John Pinkston, Anupam Joshi, and Timothy Finin. A Target-Centric Ontology for Intrusion Detection. In *Proceeding of the IJCAI-03 Workshop on Ontologies and Distributed Systems. Acapulco, August 9th, 2004*, pages 47–58. Morgan Kaufmann, 2004. 283

[VB11] María Cruz Valiente Blázquez. *Improving IT Service Management using an Ontology-Based and Model-Driven Approach*. PhD thesis, Universidad de Alcalá, 2011. In Spanish. 183, 184

[VGBS12] María-Cruz Valiente, Elena García-Barriocanal, and Miguel-Ángel Sicilia. Applying Ontology-Based Models for Supporting Integrated

Software Development and IT Service Management Processes. *Systems, Man, and Cybernetics, Part C: Applications and Reviews, IEEE Transactions on*, 42(1):61–74, January 2012. 182

[VKV+06] Max Völkel, Markus Krötzsch, Denny Vrandečić, Heiko Haller, and Rudi Studer. Semantic Wikipedia. In Les Carr, David De Roure, Arun Iyengar, Carole A. Goble, and Michael Dahlin, editors, *WWW '06: Proceedings of the 15th International Conference on World Wide Web*, pages 585–594, Edinburgh, Scotland, May 2006. ACM. 119, 120, 124, 125, 126, 127, 128

[VRVC10] María-Cruz Valiente, Daniel Rodríguez, and Cristina Vicente-Chicote. Defining the Semantics of IT Service Management Models Using OWL and SWRL. In Joaquim Filipe and Jan L. G. Dietz, editors, *KEOD 2010 – International Conference on Knowledge Engineering and Ontology Development*, Valencia, Spain, October 2010. SciTePress, Setubal. ISBN: 978-989-8425-29-4. 183

[VVCR11] María-Cruz Valiente, Cristina Vicente-Chicote, and Daniel Rodríguez. An Ontology-Based and Model-Driven Approach for Designing IT Service Management Systems. *International Journal of Service Science, Management, Engineering, and Technology (IJSSMET)*, 2(2):65–81, 2011. 183

[W3C05] W3C Process Document. W3C Technical Report Development Process. `http://www.w3.org/2005/10/Process-20051014/tr`, October 2005. (accessed 2010-10-26). 63

[W3C07] W3C. Semantic Web Layer Cake. `http://www.w3.org/2007/03/layerCake.png`, March 2007. (accessed 2010-10-12). 62

[W3C09] W3C OWL Working Group. OWL 2 Web Ontology Language Document Overview: W3C Recommendation 27 October 2009. `http://www.w3.org/TR/2009/REC-owl2-overview-20091027/`, October 2009. (accessed 2009-11-14). 69

[W3C10a] W3C. OWL Web Ontology Language Current Status. `http://www.w3.org/standards/techs/owl`, 2010. (accessed 2011-04-05). 69

[W3C10b] W3C. W3C Semantic Web Activity. `http://www.w3.org/2001/sw/`, February 2010. (accessed 2010-10-10). 62

[Wei09] Michael Weiss. Resource Description Framework. In Liu and Özsu [LO09], pages 2423–2425. ISBN: 978-0-387-35544-3. 66

[Wik09a] Wikimedia. Help:Special page. http://meta.wikimedia.org/wiki/Help:Special_page, October 2009. (accessed 2009-11-19). 123, 124

[Wik09b] Wikimedia. Wikimedia Report Card September 2009. http://stats.wikimedia.org/reportcard/, September 2009. (accessed 2009-11-22). 121

[Wik10a] Wikimedia. Help:Template. http://meta.wikimedia.org/w/index.php?title=Help:Template&oldid=1802618, January 2010. (accessed 2010-01-22). 133

[Wik10b] Wikipedia. History of Wikipedia. http://en.wikipedia.org/w/index.php?title=History_of_Wikipedia&oldid=389465615, October 2010. (accessed 2010-10-14). 74

[Wik10c] Wikipedia. Karlsruhe. http://en.wikipedia.org/w/index.php?title=Karlsruhe&oldid=384574672, October 2010. (accessed 2010-10-15). 75

[Wik11] Wikipedia. Comparison of Network Monitoring Systems. http://en.wikipedia.org/w/index.php?title=Comparison_of_network_monitoring_systems&oldid=415597350, February 2011. (accessed 2011-02-24). 243

[Wik14a] Wikimedia. MediaWiki 1.22.0 Software. http://download.wikimedia.org/mediawiki/1.22/mediawiki-1.22.0.tar.gz, January 2014. (accessed 2014-01-22). 320

[Wik14b] Wikimedia. Semantic Forms Software. https://git.wikimedia.org/zip/?r=mediawiki/extensions/SemanticForms.git&h=c1b52276c2492a51bc4153a96072da0ea487c5b7&format=zip, January 2014. (accessed 2014-01-13). 320

[Wik14c] Wikimedia. Wikipedia Statistics: Article count (official). https://stats.wikimedia.org/EN/TablesArticlesTotal.htm, August 2014. (accessed 2014-10-01). 74

[Win10] Stefan Wintermeyer. *Asterisk 1.4 + 1.6 – Studentenausgabe: Installation, Programmierung und Betrieb*. Addison-Wesley, München, first edition, September 2010. ISBN: 978-3-8273-3033-8. 427

[WL02] Brent Ware and James B. Lee. *Open Source Development with LAMP: Using Linux, Apache, MySQL, Perl, and PHP*. Addison-Wesley Longman, Amsterdam, December 2002. ISBN: 978-0-201-77061-2. 194

[WSKR03] Kevin Wilkinson, Craig Sayers, Harumi A. Kuno, and Dave Reynolds. Efficient RDF Storage and Retrieval in Jena2. In Isabel F. Cruz, Vipul Kashyap, Stefan Decker, and Rainer Eckstein, editors, *Proceedings of the First International Workshop on Semantic Web and Databases (SWDB '03), co-located with VLDB 2003*, pages 131–150, Berlin, Germany, September 2003. 65

[WVV+01] Holger Wache, Thomas Vögele, Ubbo Visser, Heiner Stuckenschmidt, Gerhard Schuster, Holger Neumann, and Sebastian Hübner. Ontology-Based Integration of Information – A Survey of Existing Approaches. In A. Gómez Pérez, M. Gruninger, H. Stuckenschmidt, and M. Uschold, editors, *Proceedings of the IJCAI-01 Workshop on Ontologies and Information Sharing*, International Joint Conference on Artificial Intelligence, pages 108–117, Seattle, WA, USA, August 2001. 163

[XX06] Hui Xu and Debao Xiao. A Common Ontology-Based Intelligent Configuration Management Model for IP Network Devices. In *Innovative Computing, Information and Control, 2006. ICICIC '06. First International Conference on*, volume 1, pages 385–388, September 2006. 182

[zAg09] zAgile, Inc. Wikidsmart for Atlassian Confluence. `http://www.zagile.com/products/wikidsmart.html`, 2009. (accessed 2009-11-09). 120

[ZCGZ10] Xin Zhang, Xingyu Chen, Shaoyong Guo, and Zhiqiang Zhan. Ontology-based ITSM Knowledge Representation Research. In *Advanced Intelligence and Awareness Internet (AIAI 2010)*, pages 230–235, October 2010. 183

[Zei06a] K. Zeilenga. Lightweight Directory Access Protocol (LDAP): Directory Information Models. RFC 4512. `http://tools.ietf.org/html/rfc4512`, June 2006. (accessed 2012-04-18). 213

[Zei06b] K. Zeilenga. Lightweight Directory Access Protocol (LDAP): Technical Specification Road Map. RFC 4510. `http://tools.ietf.org/html/rfc4510`, June 2006. (accessed 2012-04-18). 213

[ZHB05] Rüdiger Zarnekow, Axel Hochstein, and Walter Brenner, editors. *Service-orientiertes IT-Management: ITIL-Best-Practices und Fallstudien (Business Engineering)*. Springer, Berlin, first edition, January 2005. ISBN: 978-3-540-20532-6. 24, 32, 52

Index